GARY SOUCIE

Collins Encyclopedia of FISHING in Britain and Ireland

Published by William Collins Sons and Company Limited
Glasgow and London

First published in 1977
Eighth reprint 1981
This revised edition 1982

Created and designed for Collins by Berkeley Publishers Ltd.
Composition in Photina by Filmtype Services Limited, Scarborough,
North Yorkshire
Printed in Spain

ISBN 0 00 411694 1

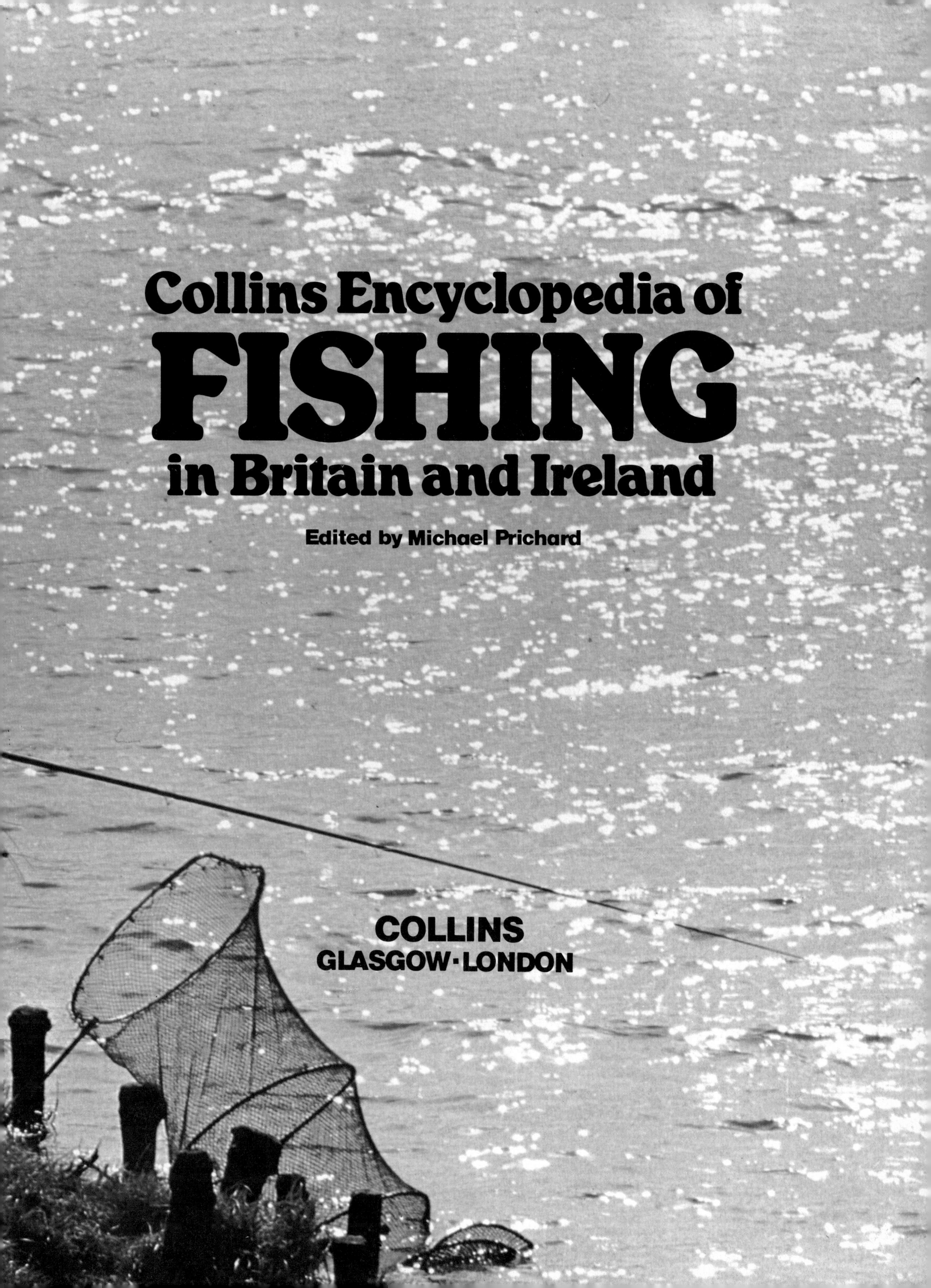

Collins Encyclopedia of FISHING in Britain and Ireland

Edited by Michael Prichard

COLLINS
GLASGOW · LONDON

THE CONTRIBUTORS

Introduction by Ken Sutton

Allen Edwards/Coarse fishing as a pleasure angler

Allen Edwards is a born fisherman – indeed, he was born on the opening day of the coarse fishing season in 1930. Educated at King Edward's Grammar School, Birmingham, he took his first roach under the tuition of "Ginger" Brain from Cannon Hill Park pool and has been fishing for them ever since.

Edwards contributes to the angling Press and has written for the Fishing Gazette, Angling Times, The Field, The Fisherman *and his voice is well-known to Nottinghamshire radio listeners as the BBC's Angling Correspondent.*

He is a council member of the Nottingham Trust for Nature Conservation Ltd and is worried about the apathy shown by many anglers towards the problem of water pollution. He founded the Mid-Trent branch of The Anglers' Co-operative Association in 1967 and is now a full-time officer of the Association. He has become angling's anti-pollution fighter.

Allen Edwards describes himself as "a family man angler". He dedicates his contribution to this book to his wife Helen.

Edwards has fished in Norway, Ireland, Denmark and Scotland. Today he has two ambitions – "To stay happily married and to spend time trying for a 30 lb pike" – ambitions which, he adds with a grin, may prove to be incompatible.

Ivan Marks/ Coarse fishing-the match fisherman

Ivan Marks has been far and away the most successful match angler in Britain in recent years. He has won many senior competitions, including three Great Ouse Championships, topping big contests on all the major rivers used on the match fishing circuit.

Ivan's successes are legion. In the 1978 season he won over £7,000, a total no one has equalled, and also took the Embassy Trophy, the NFA contest fished that year in Denmark. To carry off that win Ivan weighed in 110 lb 7 oz and came close to a second win in the same competition the following year when he came second to Fenland angler Bryan Lakey with a weight of 74 lb 3 oz.

Marks was instrumental in creating the successful Leicester AS team, but then moved on to join the Barnsley Blacks, itself one of the best match fishing teams ever. Ivan has been a regular member of the England World Championship squad and is dedicated to developing the best of the Continental methods for use in Britain. At the same time he is convinced that our own methods are superior, on waters where large fish make up the match weights.

He is noted for his affable disposition and partners Roy Marlow in a Leicester-based fishing tackle shop. Since he has been Britain's foremost float angler, it follows that the quality and design of his floats have become standards that others strive to equal.

Marks is an instinctive angler who also has great technical knowledge and ability that has attracted the attentions of overseas tackle manufacturers seeking to enter the British tackle market.

Michael Prichard/ Sea angling from inshore and deepsea boats

Michael Prichard – the editor of this book – is an Associate of the Royal Photographic Society and is well known as a photographer journalist. Prichard regularly writes and broadcasts on all aspects of angling. Among his many books are his Pocket Guides *to* Freshwater Fishing *and* Saltwater Fishing, *and* Fishing for Beginners, *all published by Collins.*

Prichard will fish for almost anything but has a preference for porbeagle shark and reef pollack fishing. His sport has taken him to many parts of the world – halibut fishing in Japan, sea trout fishing in Norway, swordfishing in Portugal – but he believes that some of the finest sport is to be had in home waters.

His local sea fishing is from the Essex mud creeks and sandbanks but he makes annual pilgrimages to Scotland, Ireland and the West Country for the species and action that East Anglia cannot provide.

Prichard is keenly interested in all aspects of natural history. He worked as a scientific field officer with the Universities Federation for Animal Welfare and is particularly interested in aquatic mammals and "those creatures that are allowed to remain wild".

He expects the true angler and sportsman to understand both conservation and species preservation.

John Holden/ Sea angling from shingle, strand and off the rocks

John Holden is involved in the fishing tackle industry as a designer and has gained a nationwide reputation for his ability to teach modern casting techniques. Holden describes himself as a "saltwater fisherman who is content to fish for anything" although he is happiest angling for porbeagle sharks.

He won the British Amateur Surfcasting Championship – a 6-oz multiplier event – in 1969 and 1970. These triumphs consolidated his growing reputation as a saltwater fisherman. He turned professional and won the professional silver medal in the 4-oz fixed-spool event of the 1973 World Casting Championships.

With Terry Carroll he was one of the first two British anglers to cast more than 200 yards using standard fishing tackle.

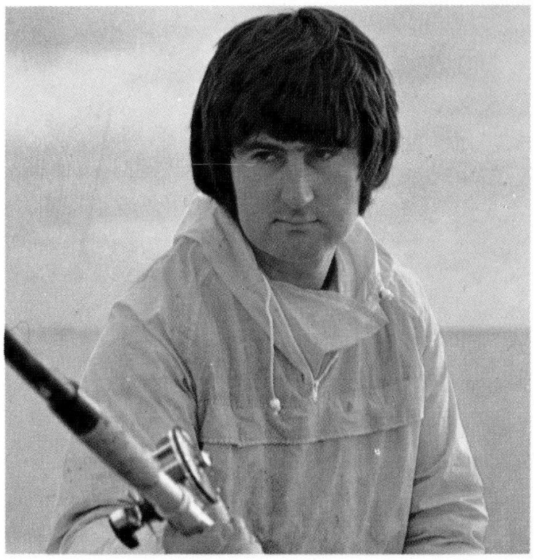

Holden is well known to readers of the angling Press both as a photographer and as a writer. He is especially interested in the illustration of marine and freshwater biology.

Reg Righyni/ Game fishing for salmon, trout and grayling

Although R. V. Righyni is one of Britain's leading game fishermen – a specialist in the art of salmon and trout angling – he comes from a non-angling family. A Yorkshireman who now lives in Lunesdale, Righyni says the strongest memory of his childhood is "the obsessive desire to fish".

He attributes this infant ambition to one greatly prized picture book.

He struggled alone – but happily

with his fishing problems until he reached his early teens when he was lucky enough to fall in with Jesse Mitchell, the famous Bradford all-rounder angler and tackle dealer.

"Mitchell", says Righyni, "gave me all the help a lad could wish for."

Some time later – and by then considerably more expert – he received several years of instruction from J. H. Hirst, of Cleckheaton, and a great deal of encouragement and advice from that great angler, J. H. R. Bagley, of Leeds.

Righyni is an established and authoritative fishing writer and is known throughout the sport as something of an angling philosopher. He is a quietly-spoken man whose views on the sport carry real authority.

Among his many other interests, he acts as a tackle consultant.

After his early training and experience he was left, as he puts it, "to follow my nose and have a thorough enjoyment of fishing throughout my life".

Picture Credits

All photographs by Michael Prichard, except those by Dietrich Burkel: page 28, 168, 169, 174; Dennis Burgess: 16, 17 (Nos 3, 4, 5), 20, 45 (top); Allen Edwards: 17 (top), 18; John Goddard: 217, 227; John Holden: 102, 176 (bottom), 179, 187 (top), 189, 195 (top), 200, 201, 202, 203, 206, 207, 209; William Howes: 236; Arthur Oglesby: 239.

Line diagrams by Stobart and Sutterby.

Index to the fish illustrations

Identification of the various species found in the waters of the British Isles.

The artist Dr. Dietrich Burkel

Dr Dietrich L. Burkel was born in Wildau – now part of East Germany – an industrial town south of Berlin, in 1936. The town has a river, a canal and some old clay pits and as a boy Dr Burkel developed an early interest in natural history – especially fish. Angling soon became part of his life.

His family left Germany for Glasgow in 1948 where he lived until 1980. He studied at Glasgow University and gained a Ph.D. degree in palaeontology, specializing in fossil corals.

With a group of friends, Burkel formed the Glasgow and West of Scotland Coarse Fishing Association. After pike fishing in Loch Lomond he began fishing for tope in Luce Bay. He spent his free time, in the early seventies, trying to hook the first rod-caught porbeagle shark to be taken in Scottish waters. He boated a 173 lb fish from a 15 foot dinghy in August 1970, at the Mull of Galloway 50 yds offshore below the Mull Lighthouse.

He became fish recorder for the Scottish Federation of Sea Anglers and this task enabled him to draw original illustrations for fish identification lectures and also to collect specimens for the Natural History department of the Glasgow Museum and Art Gallery, where he worked as Assistant Keeper.

Dr Burkel has represented Scotland in the field of international sea angling, once as a member of the team that won the International Team Event at Milford Haven in 1974.

He was invited to accompany a group of German ichthyologists on research trips to the deep waters off the west coast of Britain and this enabled him to establish a representative collection of deepwater fish at the Glasgow Museum.

Dr Burkel took up diving a few years ago so that he could make definitive studies of fish within their particular habitats. He plans to continue to explore the Scottish waters for new angling grounds, seeking the larger, more exotic species such as tunny and swordfish, although he has moved back to Germany for a time. Dr Burkel is now working at the Zoological Institute and Museum of Hamburg University where he continues to study Europe's fishes, both freshwater and marine.

Dr Burkel is a gifted artist as the original illustrations in this book, both in line and in colour, demonstrate.

Coarse fish

Sea fish

Game fish

CONTENTS

Introduction by Ken Sutton

Executive Vice-Chairman of the Anglers' Cooperative Association

The mainstream of angling books flows into three broad channels: how to fish, where to fish, and reminiscences. In the marginal waters there are the few publications on such subjects as fly-tying, tackle repairs, and the rest, but these are outside the mainstream. This book is basically in the "How to fish" channel, although in some chapters there is a natural – indeed, necessary – infusion from the other channels.

Michael Prichard, for instance, reminisces about his catches in the coastal waters around the British Isles, but he does so to explain more vividly his tactics in given circumstances. Ivan Marks, too, has to relate his strategy and tactics to a variety of match-angling waters. And what better way of doing so than by recalling what happened to him in such and such a match on such and such a river?

To a lesser extent locations are referred to in chapters by Allen Edwards, John Holden and Reg Righyni, but the Editor has succeeded in his intention of providing a practical "How to fish" guide for the catching of all the anglers' fishes to be found in the coastal, deep-sea and inland waters of the British Isles.

All the contributors have been known to me for many years and I have fished with three of them on many occasions. That, perhaps, is why Michael Prichard asked me to write the introduction. Let me, then, introduce the five contributors.

Allen Edwards, who writes the first section, has shared bank and boat with me on countless occasions, from which you may rightly infer that he is as good a companion as he is an angler. More often than not his aptitude and skill win him better and bigger catches than mine. He is the epitome of the pleasure angler: as pleased with the joint catch as he is with his own, more than competent in all forms of angling, wise in the ways of the fish, and successful because of his wide experience on both flowing and still water. His final chapter on small fish reveals his abiding interest in conservation.

My long-standing acquaintance with Ivan Marks has been more that of match-organizer to winner rather than learner to master. I expect him to win any

Ken Sutton in action. "This book will add immeasurably to the enjoyment of angling", he says.

match I organize and in past years he has lived up to my expectations. His astonishing record of success in match angling is due to a number of factors that will become apparent in the reading of his section in this book but, having watched him in scores of matches, I believe he has the inborn gift that few – very, very few – of his fellow match anglers possess: he can read the water. On any river or lake quite unknown to him he can select the best swim with uncanny accuracy. If he draws it he will win, and if he draws a less-productive swim he still might win! In addition, his skill and accuracy in casting with float or leger tackle are proverbial. Finally, he has no secrets: what he learns he readily teaches. That, perhaps, is why Leicester's 'Likely Lads' group led by Marks were such successful competitors.

Sea-fishing, and especially deep-sea boat fishing, is Michael Prichard's first preference, although he is a more-than-adequate coarse angler and fly-fisherman. Few sea-anglers have had wider experience of deep-sea fishing: his work has taken him to all parts of the British coastline and to many foreign waters. On the

occasions when we have fished together his knowledge of tackle and methods and his wide interest in ecology have been remembered features of an always enjoyable day. Add to this his outstanding skill as a photographer and his never-failing good humour and it will be appreciated that a day's fishing with him is an occasion I anticipate with more than usual relish. His chapters impart not merely a deep knowledge of tackle and tactics but an understanding of the fishes' movements and environment. No comment of mine is needed about the quality of his photography: the reader of this book holds the evidence in his hands.

John Holden, who writes the section on beach and estuary fishing, is best known as a competition caster of phenomenal ability, a world-class competitor to whom a 200-yard-plus cast is no more than an occasion for satisfaction rather than elation. Yet this does less than justice to John Holden because, as the reader will guess, long-distance casting is no more to him than a means to an end. All his long-distance casting is a form of competition against the fish that are out of reach of most beach anglers. In short, he developed his skill, as all of us should but few can, the better to catch fish, and his section on beach and estuary fishing reveals an all-round knowledge of sea-fishing as deep as his knowledge about the ballistics involved in casting.

I meet Reg Righyni – we are fellow-Yorkshiremen, and we have close mutual friends – but I have never fished with him. That is entirely my loss. I first heard about him some 25 years ago: stories of a prodigiously successful salmon, trout and grayling angler on North Yorkshire and north-west waters; a Yorkshireman with a most unlikely-sounding Yorkshire name who had a partiality for fast Bristol cars, and a fervour for fly-fishing that captivated all who met him. His section on game fishing makes it easy to see why. His approach is deeply thoughtful, his choice and use of tackle exacting and precise. His success as an angler, a designer of tackle, an author and teacher was established years ago, but his enthusiasm is as fresh as ever.

Here, then, are five diverse forms of angling presented by five writers, each expert in his particular subject. There is good reason for including all five in one volume. It is because in recent years more and more anglers are extending their fishing activities into wider spheres. There are now scores of active sea-fishing clubs in traditional match-fishing centres in the Midlands; there are thousands of erstwhile coarse-fishermen who have embraced reservoir fly-fishing with enthusiasm: there is, in short, an ever-increasing number of anglers who are not content, as once they were, to store their tackle away during one of the two traditional, statutory close seasons. They have become all-round anglers. This book will widen their knowledge and skills and will add immeasurably to their enjoyment.

Allen Edwards/Coarse fishing as a pleasure angler

Traditionally, winter is the time to fish for pike, mainly because old-time anglers did not have the proper equipment; nor did they wish to cope with summer and autumn weed growths. The modern pike angler can cope with most water conditions, but the tradition lingers on and the pike is seen as a prime target for winter fishing. To the angler looking for big pike, the late winter does present the best opportunity of connecting with a monster for the following reasons: pike which have come together in loose packs to follow the movement of their fodder fish begin to feel the urge to reproduce. The pike spawns, if water conditions are satisfactory, from late February until May and even later at the northern edge of their distribution.

They tend to return to the same spot to spawn year after year and these recognized gathering points become the angler's "hot spots" – the areas from which big pike are taken. The pleasure angler's biggest problem is not the taking of the pike but that of locating these hot spots. The pike can be taken in dozens of different ways but pike anglers, in common with all others, proliferate. The recognized gathering points for the pike take a hammering and the big pike become difficult to tempt except at the top of their feeding cycle. At this time, therefore, it pays to look for good spawning facilities for the female pike, allied to a reasonable larder of bait fish.

PIKE SPAWNING POINTS

The greatest prerequisite for big pike holding-points is the closeness of cover. This may be in the form of relatively deep water or, in late spawning situations, in weed beds. Some of these factors are easily visible. For instance, the pike spawns on flooded and marshy meadow land or in shallow drains and ditches. Such spots are readily recognized. Not so easily recognizable are the spawning points on still waters with acres of withered sedges around the rims or, indeed, spawning areas such as low lying meadow land.

The pike *will* spawn, however, and if the other factors are borne in mind an intelligent assessment can be made as to where they are likely to be. It is not necessary, however, to carry out the prospecting process with the eye alone. It makes far more sense to use a sporting method of taking pike of all sizes from various places in the search for the ideal, but possibly unrecognizable, spawning points. These areas, when found, will hold the bigger fish. Time enough then to set about capturing them.

Spinning in all its forms must, I suppose, rank as the most attractive method of taking pike, and as a tool for pinpointing concentrations of *Esox* it has no rivals. A good combination on most waters is an 8 ft long medium spinning rod of fibre glass, used in conjunction with a fixed spool reel loaded with 8 lb breaking strain line.

The pleasure of angling lies in out-thinking, hooking and landing the fish, says

Allen Edwards, seen here practising his belief.

Coarse fishing

In this book the general classification of freshwater fish is based on EIFAC, the European Fisheries Advisory Commission's publication. The freshwater zoological classification follows that of P. H. Greenwood, D. E. Rosen, S. H. Weitzman and G. S. Myers in Bull. Am. Mus. Nat. Hist. 131(4) 339–457.

Pike larvae – growth and development

At all stages, pike larvae become increasingly brown. This is unusual in fish larvae.

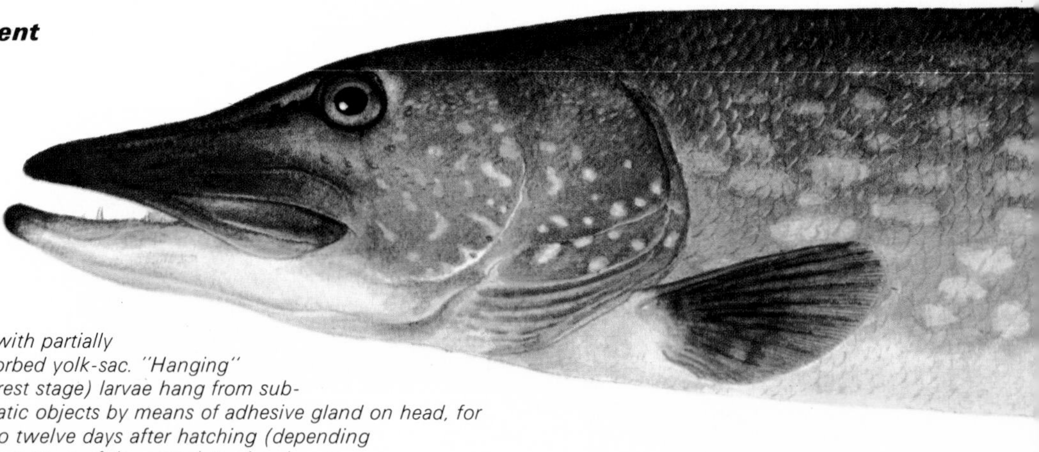

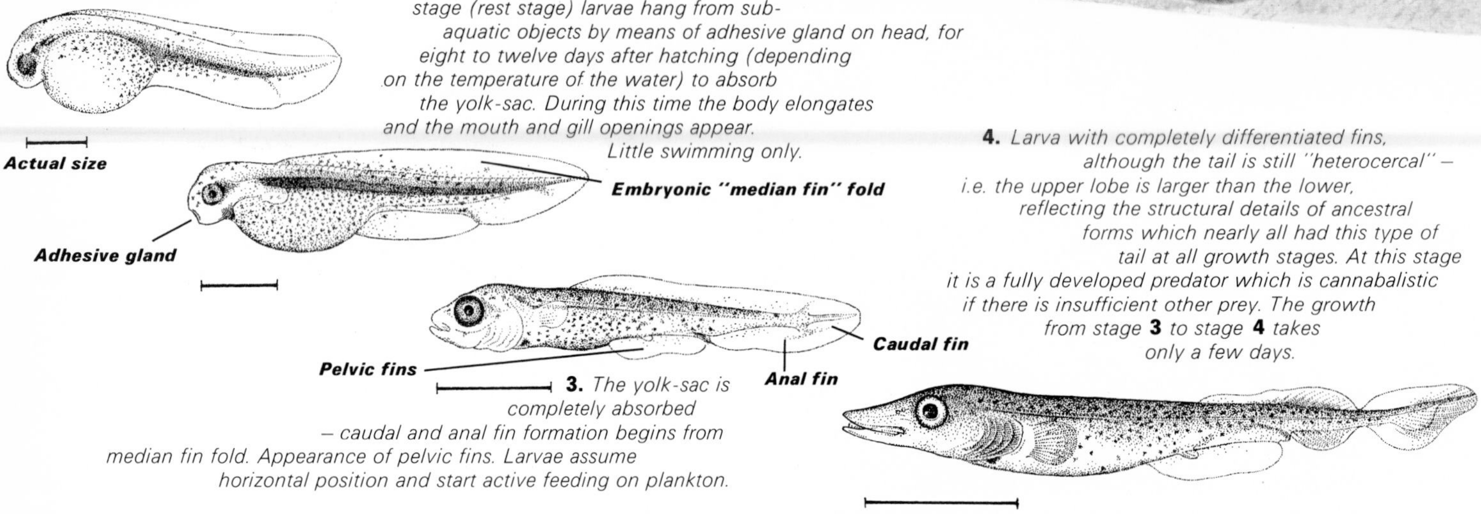

1. *Newly hatched larva with yolk-sac (no mouth or gill openings)*

2. *Larva with partially absorbed yolk-sac. "Hanging" stage (rest stage) larvae hang from sub-aquatic objects by means of adhesive gland on head, for eight to twelve days after hatching (depending on the temperature of the water) to absorb the yolk-sac. During this time the body elongates and the mouth and gill openings appear. Little swimming only.*

3. *The yolk-sac is completely absorbed – caudal and anal fin formation begins from median fin fold. Appearance of pelvic fins. Larvae assume horizontal position and start active feeding on plankton.*

4. *Larva with completely differentiated fins, although the tail is still "heterocercal" – i.e. the upper lobe is larger than the lower, reflecting the structural details of ancestral forms which nearly all had this type of tail at all growth stages. At this stage it is a fully developed predator which is cannabalistic if there is insufficient other prey. The growth from stage* **3** *to stage* **4** *takes only a few days.*

At the business end of the tackle a swivel, a 12 ins wire trace and a link swivel are required. To this a spinner, or even better, a wobbling lure, is attached and this should weigh around the $\frac{3}{4}$ oz mark. Some lures are prone to cause kinking of the line unless an anti-kink lead is used. This should be placed just above the top swivel on the wire trace.

Most lures have a more attractive action if the lead can be dispensed with. A lure of $\frac{3}{4}$ to 1 oz weight will, in all but the strongest of waters, give a really positive fall through the water once a cast has been made and it is possible to search out the deeper, holding waters by casting, engaging the pick-up and counting the seconds that it takes the bait to reach the bottom. As soon as the lure touches bottom, the rod top should be lifted and the bait retrieved in as slow and erratic a manner as possible. The prospecting value of this method is best realized by keeping on the move. Three casts into each area are enough, including one to get the depth and to wake the pike up.

The lure should not be allowed to hit the bottom on casts two or three. Engage the pick-up and start the retrieve just a second or so before the spoon is due to touch. It is not always necessary to take a pike to realize that a holding area has been discovered. A close watch should be kept behind the bait at the moment it is being lifted from the water. Quite often pike will follow a spoon or wobbling bait in an interested but suspicious, curious but careful manner. This does not matter since the aim is to find the gathering area. Providing the pike has not been pricked or really turned away by a carelessly cast shadow it may fall victim to another form of attack.

Once a gathering point has been located, the angler's problems become much more simple. Now it is a matter of choice. Which method will be the most effective in the prevailing conditions? Which method gives the angler the most pleasure? There are those who will prefer to carry on using spinning gear; others will decide that dead baiting will lure their fish more

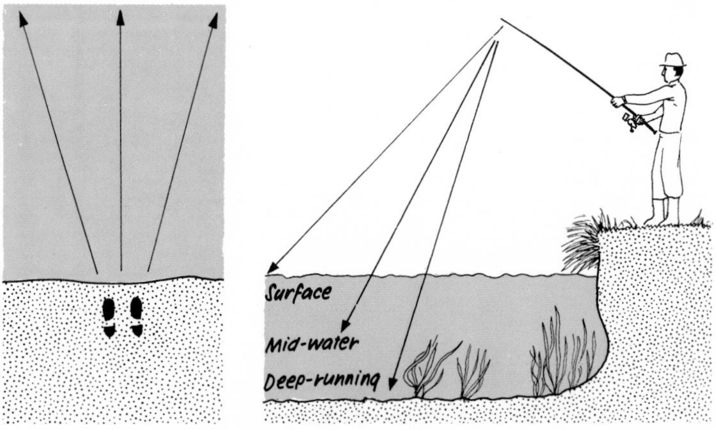

Fan casting: Three casts are the rule, to the left, right and centre of the angler's position, each direction receiving three separate casts timed to allow the bait to sink to differing depths in the swim. The first cast is to wake the pike, the second to set it on the fin and the last cast to induce a strike.

PIKE
Esox lucius

The pike is widely distributed throughout the British Isles and is equally at home in rivers, lakes, canals, gravel pits and the smallest of farm ponds. Principal requirement in a water is a good supply of fodder fish, which might be perch in a Scottish Loch, bream in a Midland reservoir or trout on a neglected stretch of Southern chalkstream. In British waters the maximum weight attained by the species is between 40 and 50 lbs but a double figure fish is considered to be a good pike on most waters.

Bait: *Most fish as livebaits, herring, sprat and mackerel as deadbaits and all forms of artificial spinning lures.*

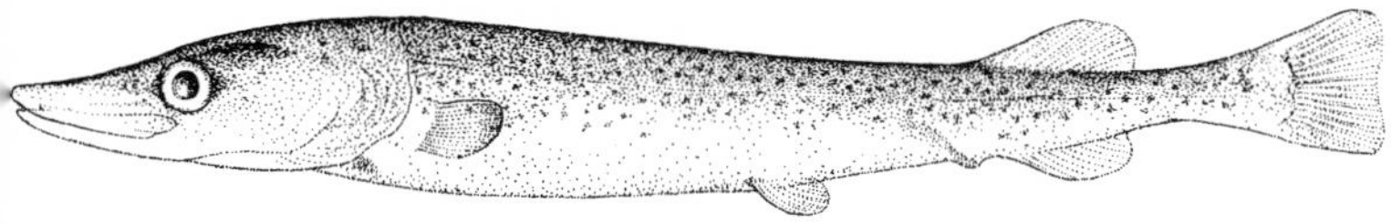

5. *The fully formed pike, still brown in colour and rather long. Growth depends very much on the food supply, which includes plankton and other fish larvae, including its own kind.*

effectively. This may be in a static or moving method. Others will use their spinning gear allied with plug baits. It is simply a matter of choice and what pleases the angler best.

Spinning will take big pike and it is a pleasant way to fish. But it has one disadvantage which is not always apparent. It is repetitive and seems to reduce many anglers to the level of an automaton.

The bait is cast, the pick-up engaged and the reel handle turned. The movement becomes automatic and the angler stops thinking. Sheer boredom drives the angler to move – often away from where the pike are concentrated. Apart from this danger, spinning will take pike of all sizes, although many anglers believe that it accounts for mainly smaller fish. Spinning works because it induces a feeding response in the pike. It triggers off an attack which is unpremeditated and a reflex action on the part of the pike. When the angler understands this, his appreciation of the art of spinning increases – and, just as important, he does not get bored.

Once a suspected concentration has been located, spinning should begin in earnest. The heavy spoon used to locate the pike may not be the ideal one with which to continue the attack. A lighter bait will enable the angler to spin more slowly and to create the attack-inducing conditions more times in the space of a cast. Standard practice for the spin fisherman is to cast in a fan-shaped series of throws, for much better results.

A good method is to allow the first cast to sink to the bottom so that the number of seconds sinking time may be counted for the new, lighter, spoon. Subsequent casts should allow the lure to settle almost to the bottom and to retrieve as close to the bottom as conditions will allow.

The pike requires a reasonably steady target at which to aim. Ideal retrieves often prove to be those that pull the bait through 3 ft long, level, or slightly rising movements.

This produces an escaping prey effect on the lure and will tempt all but the most replete pike to strike. Accurate casting is called for, since, as we have said, three casts into each spot is a good rule – one to wake the pike up, two to set him on the fin and three to induce the strike. Constant spinning across a known pike-holding area will sometimes take a sleepy fish and I believe this to be due to irritation or something very like anger on the part of the pike.

The correct method for any angler is that which produces results. It follows that it is illogical to have one method only in your armoury but a pleasure angler may have his favourite. For me, that favourite is spinning in all its forms but with particular emphasis on the use of dead baits to simulate the actions of sickly fish or to impart the escaping prey movement.

Rod and reel may be the same as for ordinary spinning but the business end of the tackle changes. For light work any small fish will do for bait. Sprats, gudgeon, dace, roach, perch, trout and grayling have all produced pike for me fished on the simplest of rigs. This involves the use of two size 8 treble hooks fished in tandem.

The first treble is used to hook the bait through the lips. The second is hooked into the wrist of the tail of the bait fish, both hooks being fixed on single strand Alasticum wire trace of between 8 and 14 lbs breaking strain. The baits are fished as straight as possible and are intended to wobble but not to spin.

The technique is exactly the same as for ordinary spinning but with the emphasis on imparting movement to the bait in such a way that a pike is fooled into thinking that the bait is an escaping fish and that it must grab it. The beauty of this rig is that the pike may be struck as soon as it attacks the bait. There is no need to wait for runs to develop or for the bait to be turned.

If larger baits are used it is important to take into account the pike's method of attack. This usually involves a short, savage, lunge or sweep from ambush. The prey is seized crosswise and held in a vice-like grip while the pike returns to its holt. There, if the fish is on the feed in earnest, the bait fish will be turned and swallowed head first. This "attack and swallow" pattern can appear to be continuous movement and in clear water I have watched a pike strike and settle to the bottom to digest its meal and the only visible sign of any action on the part of the fish has been a water-borne settling of scales dislodged in the first moments of the pike's attack and a hovering cloud of mud which has been caused by the first drive of its tail to the attack. The holding and pressure work from the pike's powerful jaws is often longer for a large bait fish or, indeed, a small fish if the pike is not really on the feed.

By using a simple tandem rig, as illustrated, it is possible to strike and hook the pike sooner rather than later in the attack stage. This results in fewer pike being badly hooked or hooked anywhere other than in the corner of the jaw. If baits larger than 3 to 4 ozs are being used, it is as well to step up the scale of the tackle. For this work a 10 ft long, powerful fibre glass rod becomes necessary, together with a stepping up of line strength to around the 14 lb breaking strain range.

I have two rods in this category, one of which has been made up from blanks usually used for making bass fishing rods. I find that this particular weapon will throw baits of around 8 ozs with the minimum of effort providing a steady swing is employed in the casting. Not that the weight of the bait to be used is the only consideration. It is not. The biggest problem in pike fishing is the vexed question of striking or setting the hooks. Since this usually involves pulling the hooks out from the dead bait and into the pike's jaw, the tackle has to be capable of transmitting the power to carry out this operation. This also applies to live and static dead-baiting rigs and must always be borne in mind by the pike angler.

The simple two-hook rig will work well in clear, slow moving water up to 6 ft deep. For water which is deeper, or which has a strong flow, it is necessary to load the bait with a lead weight so that it is, in fact, presented to the ambush or holding point of the pike. Once again this is a case of "you pays your money and you takes your choice." Some anglers will opt to place a weight just up the line away from the bait. The weight might be a bullet or a wye lead. Others will thread the trace through the dead bait and slide the weight down the trace and into the mouth of the bait. On balance, I prefer the latter method since a weight up the line sometimes produces a

1

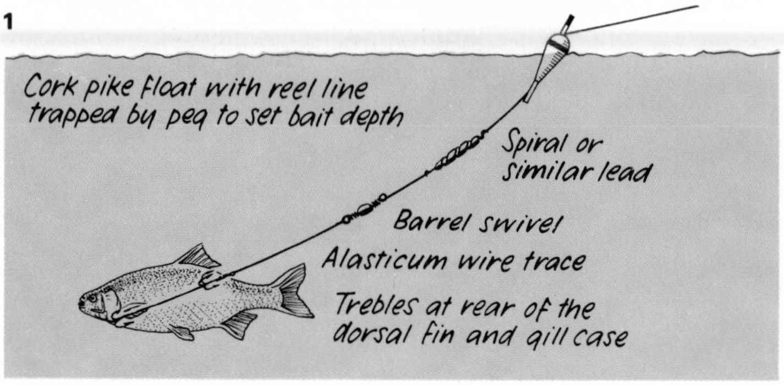

1 *A conventional shallow water live-baiting rig formed from Alasticum wire and two treble hooks. The depth of the bait is set by trapping the line inside the bored-out float with a wooden or plastic peg.*

2 *Even the smallest of jack pike should be treated with respect. Keep fingers away from the sharp teeth and use artery forceps when you are removing the hooks from the fish's jaw.*

2

rolling effect on the dead bait which, while it will not actually prevent the pike from striking when they are on the feed, will not allow the angler to present the long, steady, draw that will induce a pike to attack.

Incidentally, it is surprising how little lead is required to sink and keep a bait near to the bottom in all but heavy water flows. A single swan shot is often all that is required. The less weight that is used, the better the action that can be imparted to the bait by the angler and it does mean that the prime consideration in dead bait spinning may be observed. And this can be simply stated: fish slowly and deeply, giving the pike the ideal target at which to aim in such a manner that it can be expected to hit it.

Now for the question of striking and hooking the fish. When small baits – anything up to 6 ins in length – are being used, the pike should be struck at once, just as when spinning with spoon baits. A method which works well is to put a bend into the rod by winding on the reel handle, at the same time lowering the rod tip sideways until it is some 2 ft from the surface of the water. At this point a firm sweep to either side – and parallel with the surface – should result in the hooking of the pike. The rod tip should then be raised and the fish played out in the usual way. In the case of a small pike this is usually a short affair.

If a bigger specimen has been encountered this may involve allowing the fish to run against the combined pull of the slipping clutch of the fixed spool reel and the pressure on the rim of the reel drum from finger or thumb. It follows that the clutch setting should be fairly light. The fish is then brought nearer to the gaff or landing net by clamping the finger on the rim of the drum and pumping the fish in with alternate dipping of the rod and leaning back and raising so that the fish is brought steadily nearer. The two points to watch in this operation are that the tension must always be maintained on the fish by ensuring that no slack line is given, and that a lively fish must be allowed to run against the slipping clutch if it gets a sudden burst of energy.

At no time should the handle of the reel be cranked while a fish is taking line.

If a bait larger than 2 or 3 ozs is being used, a different method of hooking may be required. This is because the take of the pike on larger baits often appears to be that much more deliberate, and sometimes downright stealthy. While it is possible to go into the tighten-and-strike routine as used for smaller fish, this may result in lightly hooked or pricked fish. A better technique is to take into account the *seize, squeeze, turn and swallow* characteristics of the pike's attack. With a larger bait there is usually a time lag between the seize and squeeze stages while the pike returns to its ambush point.

A method which has worked for me with fish of more than 20 lbs is to slacken off as soon as the first attack is felt. Allow the fish to return to its holt without let or hindrance and then gently wind in until the line is

A pike will grab a live fish across the body, squeeze it and then turn the fish to swallow it head first.

tight but not under real pressure. Ideally, this takes the sequence up to the pike's squeeze and kill point. The line should now be watched carefully and held lightly between finger and thumb just forward of the reel.

Any movement on the line signifies the turning of the bait by the pike and after a second or two the strike should be made in the usual way. Some anglers advocate waiting until a second run develops but this too often results in a deeply hooked fish and, while the pike may survive the subsequent surgical operation to remove the hooks, I prefer to avoid the need. As a broad principle the working of a dead bait is the deadliest and most enjoyable method of taking pike but it is not the only way in which this type of bait can be used.

The popularity of deliberate static deadbait fishing for pike increases season by season, no doubt because it works. It is effective on most waters and seems to produce a better class of fish than other methods.

The pike is associated in the minds of most anglers with a ruthless, systematic and actively predatory life style and it seems strange at first meeting that the fish will skulk along the bottom quietly shovelling up corpses. And yet this is no more than a logical extension of their usual hunting pattern. There can be few anglers who have not watched quite small pike slamming into shoals of roach fry. The attack is usually short and swift, characterized by a swirl as the pike slams its tail over and heads back to its starting point. It may or may not have scooped up small fish on the way through. One thing that is certain is that the rush and slamming action of the pike's drive and sweeping tail will have stunned a quantity of small fry. These flutter slowly to the bottom and fall a much easier victim to the forager. Incidentally, I believe that this particular method is used by most predators, especially trout. The pike, then, is accustomed from an early age to scooping up the results of its own depredations, and the modern pike angler turns this fact to advantage by using baits that are long dead and may not even be freshwater fish at all.

Herrings and sprats are ideal baits for this particular series of methods. They are readily available, are relatively inexpensive and can be kept frozen for long periods if need be. If the static method has a disadvantage it is that its use is responsible for the death of many fine pike unless care is exercised by the angler.

This must be so since the pike is accustomed to mooching along picking up its stunned or dead victims. There is no sudden attack by the pike, no run back to the holt, just a stealthy and imperceptible scoop, turn and swallow sequence.

If an angler uses bite detection methods which are less than good, he is, in fact, stepping back into the dark ages of pike-fishing techniques and using gorge-fishing tactics. For this reason I find that a float is essential when laying on with a deadbait. This should be used in conjunction with an instant striking rig and a sweeping strike should be made, away from the direction in which the pike appears to be moving, as soon as any movement is registered on the float.

These tactics minimize the dangers of deeply hooked and possibly doomed pike but even the most careful of anglers will have his casualties. These may be lessened and given greater prospects of surviving deep hooking if single hooks are used wherever possible in the rigs, although I believe that the use of small No 8 or 6 sized treble hooks gives the best prospect of connecting with the fish.

Simplicity is the key word when dealing with deadbaiting techniques. The business end should consist of a trace of new single strand alasticum wire approximately 18 ins long. A No 8 treble hook is whipped on at the end and one point of the hook is inserted into the deadbait just behind the head. A No 2 single carp hook

1

2

Many anglers abhor the use of a gaff. For the mobile angler a gaff is less cumbersome than a landing net but a badly gaffed pike becomes a dead pike. Clive Loveland shows how to use a gaff on his 39 lb Knipton monster. The fish was then weighed and released unharmed.

is then slipped down the wire trace until it is in position to act as holding hook through the tail wrist of the bait. The hook should be fixed there by an extra turn of the alasticum through the eye of the hook and the point firmly fixed into the wrist of the tail.

The whole bait should be as straight as possible, with the wire from treble to single hook lying close to the side of the bait. The trace is connected to the reel line at a swivel. The rig is completed by adding a float, which should be a slider set a little over depth by a stop knot.

This tackle arrangement is ideal for hard-bottomed waters with gravel or clay ledges. It is not effective in waters which have a fine silty bed since the action of wind and wave pulls the float through an arc and this usually means that the bait is buried to a greater or lesser degree in silt and is invisible to the pike.

In these conditions the baits may be doctored by

3

4

5

1 *The jetty at Little Ormesby Broad, Norfolk, in early autumn.*

2 *A pike on and diving under the boat takes the rod to its test curve.*

3 *The first of the Broadland pike comes to the surface.*

4 *In the late evening pike can be seen chasing fry in the margins.*

5 *With the hooks carefully removed, the jack goes back into the Broad.*

1 *Allen Edwards cuddles his winter chub from the Upper Witham at Long Bennington, a river made famous in the writings of "Trent Otter", J. W. Martin.*

2 *A chub river in the winter. The Upper Great Ouse near Beachampton. With the dying down of vegetation, chub are more easily located.*

pushing a small piece of polystyrene tile down the throat of the bait or, if a head-down feeding impersonation of a bait is required, a small slit should be cut behind the vent of the bait, the flesh scooped out and a small piece of polystyrene substituted. Baits which are to be prepared in this manner are best operated on at home since a finishing touch is required in the shape of a sewing up with ordinary white cotton. A variation on this theme is to remove the stomach of the bait and insert the polystyrene, completing the job with needle and thread.

Too much buoyancy inbuilding on the part of the angler is a mistake, since the baits then require to be tethered by the use of an Arlesey bomb and the simplicity of the rig begins to get out of hand. A legitimate and killing method of angling with the deadbait is to lay it out in position and then to spin with spoon or dead bait over the same area. Pike which follow the spinning lure will often pick up the static bait.

There comes a time when the pike angler has to admit that all of the plugs, spoons, deadbaits, static or moved, allied to skilful presentation, will not tempt all of the pike. In known big fish holding waters the smaller fish will fall victim but the crafty old female pike, with her surfeit of cunning, lies stoney-eyed and immune. In such circumstances the pleasure angler will introduce the ultimate in methods and, if he is to take his fish, is compelled to stoop to livebaiting tactics.

In many ways the method holds more attraction for an angler than simply laying on with deadbaits. There is a hypnotic fascination in watching the movements of the float. The mind transforms each little movement of the tell-tale into a sub-surface drama. The pike is imagined sidling up to and engulfing the luckless bait and each run of the float as a pike strikes is an event. It is a method that can be used when fishing for other species, such as roach. Indeed, it is a good idea to try to work up a roach swim with groundbait and loose offerings. This is to attract a good shoal of roach. The pike will surely follow if there is enough activity to attract her attention. Once she is there the chances are that she will take a tethered livebait.

Conventional livebaiting gear consists of a 10 ft long fibre-glass rod capable of casting heavy baits and of driving home the hooks into the pike's bony jaw. To this is allied line of around 12–20 lbs breaking strain, used in conjunction with a fixed spool reel. For water up to 6 ft in depth a fixed float is satisfactory and many anglers will use the well established "Fishing Gazette" type bung. This is held in position by a peg through the centre which traps the line. Water of any greater depth requires the use of a slider float and those with a fine tube through the centre are the best. These should be stopped at the correct setting by the use of a stop knot made from nylon line. Weights to get the bait down to the correct depth should be of the drilled bullet, barrel

1

or barley corn lead type. These are stopped from sliding down the line by a swivel. The tackle is completed by the addition of a trace, once again of new alasticum single strand wire and the armoury of hooks.

On the question of hooks and live baiting, I believe that most anglers overload their rigs with too many hooks – most of which are too large, anyway. For shallow water the old fashioned Jardine snap tackle works well and permits an instant strike; in water which is 10 ft or over I use a single treble hook. One point only is inserted under the dorsal of the bait and this ensures that a live bait will stay as a live bait for a longer period of time. The pike, it seems to me, strike with much more confidence at these depths and are usually cleanly hooked in the scissors.

For livebaiting in moving waters I prefer to use Captain Parker's rig. This involves the use of a couple of hooks. One of these, a single No 2 carp hook, is placed through the top lip of the bait. The other, a treble, is attached to the trace and one point of the hook is lightly snicked into the underside of the fish. This acts as a keel. In fishing the live bait, the critical point to watch is that of the depth at which the bait is set. The pike, unless on the rampage, is usually very low in the water. The live bait should be set to swim 2 ft above the bottom although it never bothers me if my float is set over depth and the bait is hard on the bottom for a considerable period of the time. This is because, providing not too much lead has been used, the bait fish will rise up from time to time and flutter in a half circle emitting attractive vibrations for the pike to home in on. Too much lead and the bait will not move.

2

Leaded nymph – fished across shallows with a sinking fly line.

Bushy floating fly – fished on a floating fly line or alternated with a live insect for dapping in overgrown river stretches.

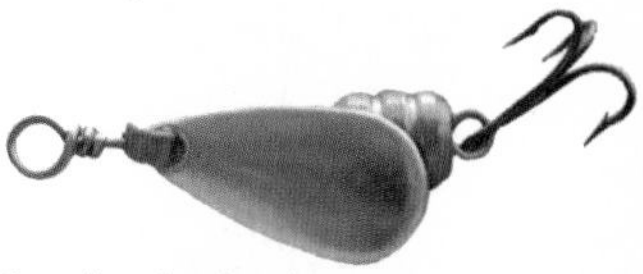

Small spinning lures – a small fly spoon fished in conjunction with a fly rod or light spinning rod.

Freshly killed natural minnow or quill minnow – fished in conjunction with a light spinning outfit.

There are times when the use of lead becomes taboo. This applies when, in very deep water, it is felt that live bait must be used. In such cases I prefer to dispense with float and leads and to *freeline fish* the bait. This involves the use of a very short trace, a single treble hook through the root of the dorsal, as in deep water conventional fishing, and the patience to await the arrival of the fish in the depths. It also demands the use of concentration on rod tip for bite detection to avoid the danger of gorge-fishing results, if not gorge-fishing intentions. In known pike-holding spots the simple static legering of the live bait will often produce results but the float has its fascinations and in this case the good old fashioned paternoster allied to a sliding float comes into its own.

To sum up, then, the late winter is a time of opportunity for the pleasure angler. It is the time when sensible fishing and reasonable deductions are most likely to put him in contact with a large pike. It is a time when weather conditions allow him to use varied methods to find and take his fish. It is a time of maximum pleasure to the angler who delights in using sporting methods but then one would expect it to be, since it is a clear case of "find the lady"!

LATE WINTER – THE CHUB

The chub, more than any other, is a convenient fish. He swarms almost nationally, the exceptions being parts of the West Country and Scotland. He is greedy, aggressive, bold, not too bright but with just enough awareness of danger to make his capture far from a foregone conclusion. His distribution, density of population and challenge are not the only features that classify him as convenient for the pleasure angler, especially in the late winter. The fish will feed throughout wide variations in temperature and water conditions; but more important to the jaded end-of-season angler, he can be taken from the same spot by many different methods. It is the choice of methods open to the angler which, perhaps, most qualifies the chub for the title "convenient". To the angler who has spent some time in a concentrated effort to catch a fair sized pike, the thought of a few hours float fishing or legering for the chub and the prospect of a full keep net can be a real pleasure.

Not that catching chub needs to be restricted by time or method since there is no period of the angler's season when the *chevin* or old *loggerhead*, to give him earlier titles, may not be taken. One of my favourite methods is to take him from the shallows of the River Trent in the summer, on fly fishing tackle. It has to be admitted that this early season fishing spotlights the main reason for considering the chub as a quarry for the late winter period. The chub which swarm in the shallows in late June and early July have completed their spawning. They revel in the highly oxygenated water and they take the fly, nymph, fly spoon, live minnow, worm, cheese or whatever with a bang. That, however, is about all the bang that there is in the whole encounter.

Too often the fish comes to the net like a piece of old sacking. Flabby, ill-conditioned and exhausted, after a few short plunges the chub soon gives in. The same fish taken in the last few weeks of the season is a very different proposition. The chub does not deserve the evil reputation which the trout angler, who takes him in early season, has bestowed upon him. In the right place at the right time *Leuciscus cephalus* is a great contender. The right place is a streamy run on the Trent, Severn, Wye, Stour, Avon or Thames. The right time is the late winter.

The right method, of course, is always a matter of individual choice but since the chub is not usually

Much the easiest and safest way in which to remove the hook from a fish. Allen Edwards removing his tackle from a Fenland chub with artery forceps.

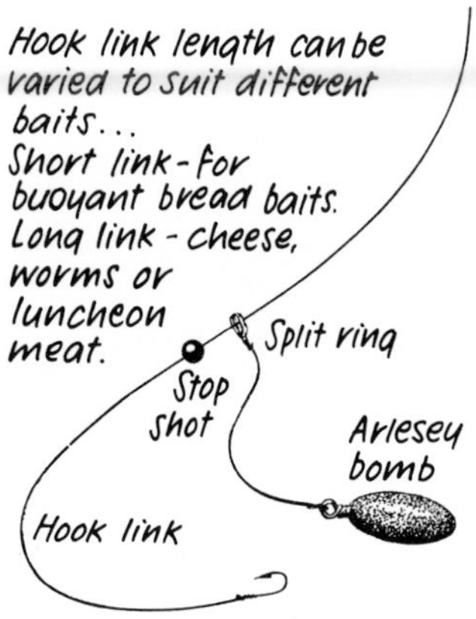
Hook link length can be varied to suit different baits...
Short link - for buoyant bread baits.
Long link - cheese, worms or luncheon meat.
Split ring
Stop shot
Arlesey bomb
Hook link

fussy about the bait, the angler's preference for style becomes the deciding factor. The main question to be answered is: Will my method put the bait in front of the fish? The choice then becomes that of float fishing or some style of legering. All will work but some give more pleasure than others.

There is no denying the satisfaction of watching and controlling a float to present a bait to the chub at a distance. The float has its own particular attraction and the time spent in casting, trotting and retrieving soon speeds by and is therapeutic in itself. Pleasurable and healing it may be, on balance it will not produce the fish that legering will. This applies particularly to the latter part of the season when the fish are much more likely to be hugging the bottom than swimming at mid-water.

Basic tackle for legering for chub consists of an Avon-style rod. My preference is for an Avon Perfection which is 12 ft long and weighs 10 ozs. To this is allied a fixed-spool reel loaded with monofilament line which may range between 4 and 6 lbs breaking strain. This choice is governed by the conditions, snags or hazards in a particular swim. The rig is completed with split ring, weights and eyed hooks. The latter may be as small as a No 12 or as large as a No 2.

There was a time when legering was considered the last resort on an unsuccessful day, and in unpractised hands the method, or series of methods, still qualifies for that denigration. The factor that lifts the method from the "chuck and chance it" category into the skilled area is itself split into two facets. These concern the correct choice of weight and the recognition of a bite. On the question of the choice of weights the rule should be to choose just the amount of lead that will hold the bait where you want it to be. This might, at its simplest, involve having no lead at all. It could involve choosing a drilled bullet to enable the angler to roll the bait into the fish-holding swim. It might mean the choice of a large coffin lead to drop the bait straight into position and to hold it there against the push of the current on both bait and line.

If the second facet of the whole problem, namely the recognition of a bite, is not to be jeopardized the choice of weight should be governed by one simple rule. Choose just enough lead to put the bait in front of the fish. A surplus grain may not react against the presentation of the bait but it will certainly affect the bite detection problem. That bite detection *is* a problem is proved by the number of aids on the market. These include quiver tips, spring tips, swing tips and a host of butt indicators. These have their places in the angler's armoury but not, I suggest, when fishing for chub. This is because the chub is a shoal fish in competition with the rest of the group for its food. If the presentation is right the chub will usually take the bait with a thump. Touch legering, coupled with the watching of the rod tip, will usually give the angler all the indication that he requires to strike and connect with the fish.

To list the baits on which the chub may be taken would be tedious, in fact it would be more simple to list the baits which the fish will not take, if I could think of any! A range including worms, cheese, bread, luncheon meat, sausage and live and dead fish baits, not forgetting the ubiquitous maggot, will all take chub. For long-range legering I prefer lob worms, cheese and sausage meat; bread-based baits I reserve for closer work.

Style is considered, by some, to be everything. In angling terms the aim and object of any method must be to catch fish but that is not all for the pleasure angler. There has to be the basic enjoyment provided by the actual fishing. The fish themselves may be an added bonus but the fishing is the thing. The main pleasure for the angler when legering comes from the practised control, the placing of the bait just where it should be. Late winter fishing for chub provides the perfect opportunity for indulging in the use of the rolling leger, perhaps the most enjoyable method of presenting a bait to bottom-feeding chub.

Autumn and winter floods have cleared much of the weed growth and scoured the bottom of early autumn leaf deposits. The way is clear to roll or shoot the leger and attendant bait across the front of feeding fish. The

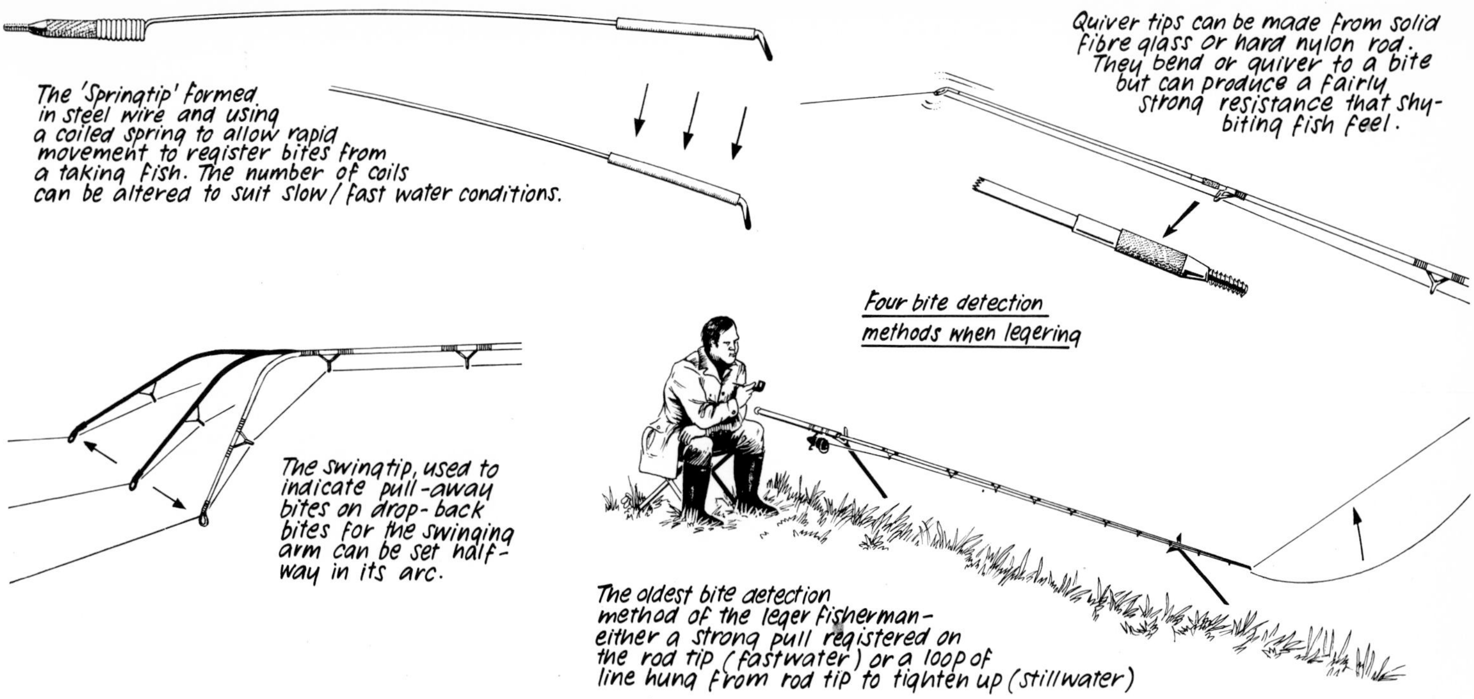
The 'Springtip' formed in steel wire and using a coiled spring to allow rapid movement to register bites from a taking fish. The number of coils can be altered to suit slow/fast water conditions.
Quiver tips can be made from solid fibre glass or hard nylon rod. They bend or quiver to a bite but can produce a fairly strong resistance that shy-biting fish feel.
Four bite detection methods when legering
The swingtip, used to indicate pull-away bites on drop-back bites for the swinging arm can be set half-way in its arc.
The oldest bite detection method of the leger fisherman – either a strong pull registered on the rod tip (fastwater) or a loop of line hung from rod tip to tighten up (stillwater)

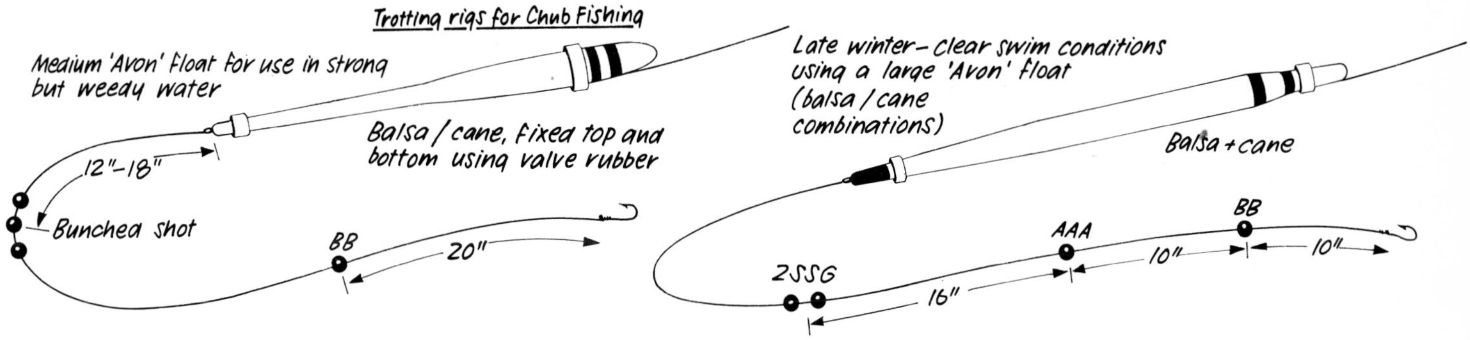
Trotting rigs for Chub Fishing
Medium 'Avon' float for use in strong but weedy water
Balsa/cane, fixed top and bottom using valve rubber
12"–18"
Bunched shot
BB
20"
Late winter – clear swim conditions using a large 'Avon' float (balsa/cane combinations)
Balsa + cane
BB
AAA
10"
10"
2SSG
16"

terminal tackle is made up of an eyed hook which is tied direct to the reel line. A break is made in the line some 18 ins above the hook and a split ring is tied in. To the split ring a piece of line, which is of finer gauge than the reel line, is tied. To this finer nylon, which should be about 10 ins long, an Arlesey bomb is attached and this may be of any weight from $\frac{1}{8}$ oz to 2 ozs depending upon the strength of the current.

The cast is made across and slightly downstream but the pick-up of the reel is not engaged at once. This is because the leger is required to fall into the fishing area. An immediate engagement means that the bait will be swept round and away too quickly from the shoal-holding area.

The rod is held, in the first instance, at an angle of about 45 to 50 degrees. The bait is persuaded to move through the swim by gently lifting the rod tip; the pressure of the water on the line then sweeps the leger downstream. The bait is thus alternately static and rolling and bites may be expected at any time. The bite may come as a slight pull or as an *honest-to-goodness downright thump* in which the rod tip is slammed over.

Variations on the legering technique include upstream legering where a bait is cast up and across and the straightforward static leger. The upstream method is especially useful in the summer for placing baits in the fish-holding areas at the tail end of long strands of water crowsfoot and ranunculus weed. Bites are usually indicated by a slight slackening in the line.

The static leger comes into its own in snaggy waters and, of course, the rolling leger may be converted into a static one by the maintenance of a fixed angle of the rod by the angler. The rolling leger, of course, becomes static at the end of a controlled rolling sequence and bites are often registered at this point.

A pleasure angler may get his fun from using float fishing tackle – and why not? The trotted bait will at times take more fish and there is the sheer pleasure inherent in the use of float fishing gear. The rod for float fishing for chub should be of the same type as that used for legering. A 12 ft long Avon is ideal since the requirements are that a long sweeping strike must be made and the rod must be capable of absorbing the heavy initial plunges of a chub determined to go home.

The reel, however, may differ. Some anglers maintain that it is not possible to trot successfully while using a fixed spool reel and prefer to use a free running centre-pin reel. For the pleasure of the thing, a good centre pin takes some beating. The line strength should be the same, never below $3\frac{1}{2}$ lbs breaking strain and up to 6 lbs in especially overgrown conditions.

Floats are the key to successful trotting and many anglers make the mistake of using floats that are too small. It should be remembered that the float has to be seen for a very long way and that it has to support a lot of shot so that the bait will get down to the fish. It follows, therefore, that a trotting float should be a big one and cane and balsa combinations are ideal in this context. A refinement in this type of float is to have the balsa constituent fluted with concave faces. This aids the mending of the line when trotting mid-stream across varying degrees of current speed.

A typical float fishing session for the club entails the use of groundbait into which liberal quantities of the hookbait have been blended. For sheer convenience, therefore, breadbaits, maggots, worms, wasp grubs come into their own as choices for the angler. These should be fished on hooks that will hold the bait in a secure fashion. For instance, a bunch of maggots on a size 10 hook will take chub. A hook to hold bread flake or crust to be trotted through the same swim might be a size 6 through to size 2 depending upon the size of the bait. For me, two kernels of wheat on a size 12 hook have often accounted for chub on the upper Witham. The chub is blessed with a large mouth. The criterion, therefore, becomes the size of bait to be fished. No hook is too big to use for the chub. Much more important than hook size is the question of getting the bait down to the fish. Too much actual trotting time can be wasted if the bait is set too shallow and is wafted gaily through the swim, feet above the heads of the feeding chub. For this reason I much prefer to fish over depth when trotting and to ensure correct presentation by holding the float back slightly. The exception to this rule comes in those rare instances when a long clear swim of even depth has been located. In this ideal situation the classic trotting method of setting the float at the exact depth of the swim may be employed – and great fun it is, too!

The chub, then, is a fish for all seasons. He presents the angler with more legitimate methods of angling than any other fish that swims. The use of those methods when the chub has been at less than his best has resulted in his patchy reputation – loved here, loathed there. For the pleasure angler, though, the chub – big, brassy and beautiful – is very good value, especially in the late winter.

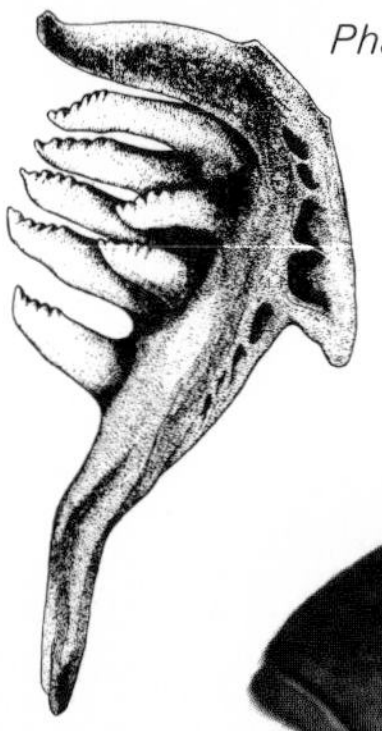

Pharyngeal teeth of the chub.

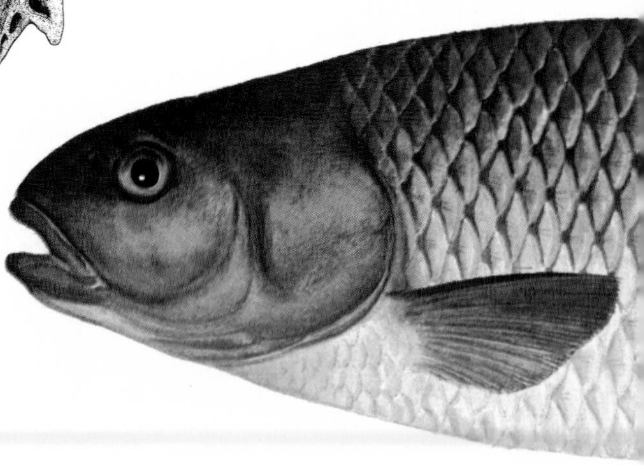

Pharyngeal teeth of the dace.

DACE

Leuciscus (leuciscus) leuciscus

A delicate fish of the fast water, fond of shallows and rapids with aerated water. The dace is a shoal fish so often mistaken for an immature chub. A quick method of identification is to spread the dorsal and anal fins. In the dace these are concave in form, whereas the chub has rounded, convex fins. Dace average 8 to 12 oz.

Bait: *Bread and the smaller grub baits. Dace can*

LATE WINTER – THE ROACH

For many pleasure anglers the word fishing means, quite simply, roach fishing. The fish has a grip on the interest of most anglers which ensures that it is fished for throughout the season but the late winter is a favourite period since the banks and river bed are clean and the roach shoals are localized.

The obsession with roach is hard to rationalize unless the fish's broad distribution is taken into account. There is hardly a water from the South Coast to the approaches to the Scottish Highlands that does not contain its population of roach. Perhaps, after all, this is the key to the fascination which the fish holds for the angler. The fish is tolerant of pollution, it will stand over-crowding and, while it will grow large in a favourable environment, it appears to thrive as a stunted dwarf in the smallest of farm ponds. The fish presents a challenge, then, to the angler. A 6 in specimen from a polluted canal may rank as a prize catch with a 2 lbs plus fish from the Hampshire Avon. From both venues the fish will be finicky and shy but the fishing will be fine.

The fish has a mixed diet which includes fly larvae, freshwater shrimps, snails and vegetable matter including algae. Converted to angling terms this means that the fish may be tempted by a whole range of baits. In practice, most roach fishers are content to operate with variations on three. These are bread in diverse forms, seeds such as wheat and hemp and – most importantly to many anglers – the larvae of the bluebottle or the maggot. Take the maggot away from most

CHUB

Leuciscus (squalius) cephalus

Widely distributed in England but absent from Ireland and most of Scotland, the extreme western parts of Wales and south-west Cornwall, the chub prefers to live in rivers but will adapt to stillwater, such as those left by flooding in oxbow lakes and backwaters. Chub grow to 9 or 10 lbs but generally a fish of 3 lbs is regarded as a good specimen. It is at its fighting best at the back end of the angling season.

Bait: *Will take most cereal and grub baits. Fly fishing and livebaiting will also lure the species.*

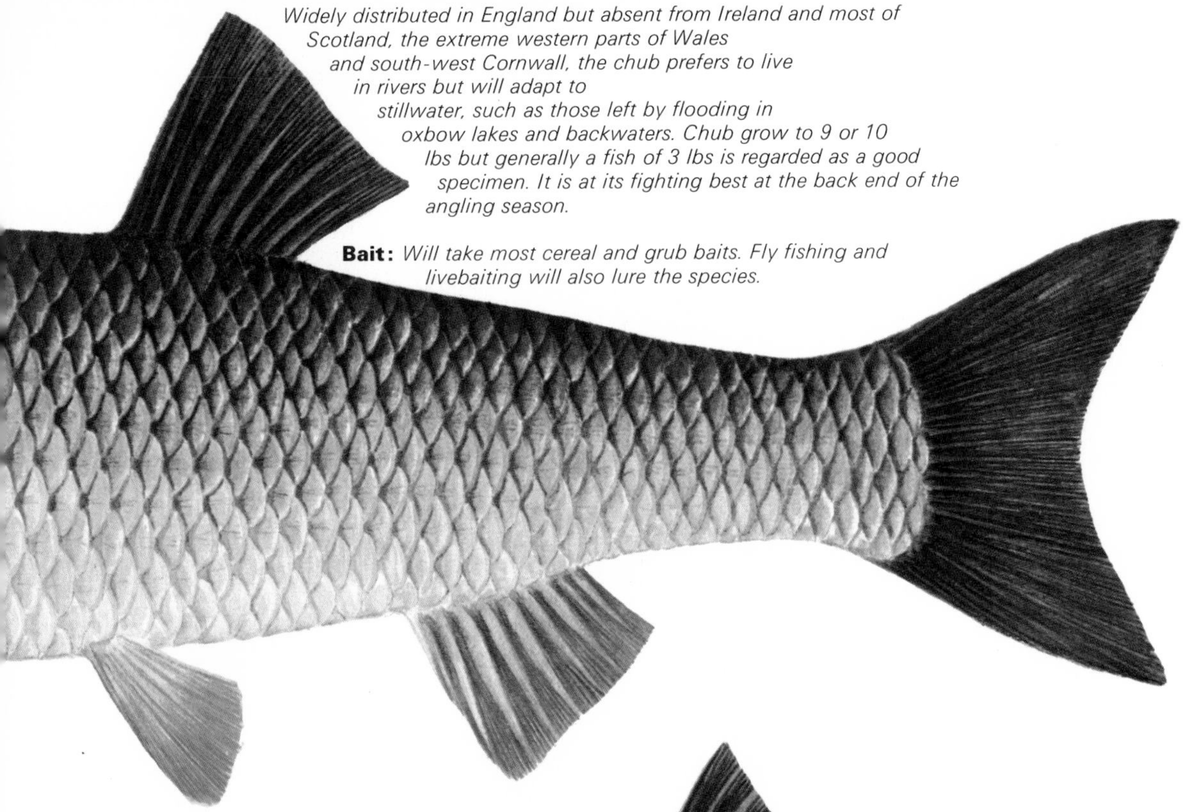

be fished for with either dry or wet flies in the smaller sizes.

anglers and they are likely to feel it is pointless to go on fishing. That statement can be extended further, for if the maggot at the chrysalis stage (the caster) is taken from many anglers' armoury, they feel that they have no chance of taking fish. Different baits require varied techniques, just as different waters and river conditions need a different approach, so let us look first at general roach fishing in moving waters using maggots and casters for bait.

The rod should be of fibre-glass and may be between 11 and 14 ft in length with a tippy action. The reel could be a fixed spool or a centre pin loaded with line from 4 lbs breaking strain down to 1 lb. The principal factors in this choice are the strength of current, the length of swim and the size of fish likely to be encountered. I prefer to go up in line strength and to add a cast of lower breaking strain if the fish prove to be line shy and if bait presentation is causing problems. Float choice will vary with wind and current conditions but a combination of cane and balsa or cane and wire stem will be used for swimming the stream, with a swing to peacock quill if downstream winds are making the fishing difficult. Hook size will vary from size 20 for fishing the caster, through to a size 12 for a bunch of maggots.

Groundbaiting is important to get the fish feeding but this should be done sparingly – even, perhaps, just using small quantities of ground breadcrumbs as a vehicle to transport maggots and casters into a concentrated area of water. If this is done with care the roach can be persuaded to feed with confidence, the shoal becomes concentrated and fish will take the bait on the drop. For many this is the most exciting form of roach fishing, although it is unselective. The ideal combination, then, in this situation, is the stick float with an evenly shotted line below it to a size 20 hook baited with a single caster. The bait is run through the swim with an occasional holding back of the float by the angler, especially over the part of the swim that has been baited.

This has the effect of lifting the bait in the water in a tantalizing manner. It is fascinating fishing but sometimes the fish will have none of it. They want a bait laid on or dragging the bottom.

Sometimes a downstream wind will prevent the proper control of a trotted float-fishing rig. Fortunately the roach will follow and take a dragging bait and in clear Scottish trout streams I have watched them do just that, rather like a flock of sheep. The leading fish has picked up the bait and been hooked while the rest of the shoal has milled about for a few moments in an uncertain manner. The uncertainty does not appear to last long, providing the angler remains unseen or does not scare the shoal in any other way. Judicious groundbaiting soon gets the shoal heads down and feeding again.

The best method of beating both the downstream wind situation and of presenting a dragging bait is to use the peacock quill waggler-type float, fixed by a shot at either side of the float stem. In extreme conditions it might be necessary to back shot by another 18 ins to overcast the swim and to plunge the rod tip below the water surface so that the line from tip to float is completely submerged.

Roach may be fished for at long range and with similar tackle, as described for the chub. In this case the choice of float is just as important. The standard cane and balsa stick or quill and cork, Avon-type, float will do the job but I prefer to use a balsa and wire stem float which appears to ride better in streamy or roily water with the consequent advantage of better bait presentation to the roach.

There comes a time when the roach, although in the swim, are not responding to the trotted, trailed or held-back bait and a variation in tackle is called for. The fish will fall to the use of ordinary leger tactics with maggots or casters hard on the bottom with quiver or spring tips making fair bite indicators in most conditions. The roach, however, is a shy biter on most hard fished rivers and bite detection can be a big problem on such waters.

For the pleasure angler much of the fun of angling comes from the use of the tackle. It is the fishing that matters, not necessarily the fish. For this reason, therefore, it is always a pleasure to fish for the roach by laying on, fishing the bait over depth, but switching the tackle from an 11 to 14 ft running line rod combination to a 21 ft, fixed line fibre-glass roach pole rig. This tackle gives the maximum control over bait presentation. It permits the use of absolutely accurate plumbing so that the shot may be placed close to the hook. This improves the registering of a bite from the shyest of fish, enabling an instant strike to be made. The rig also scores from the fact that it enables pin-point accuracy in groundbaiting if a maggot dropper is lowered directly below the rod tip to release casters or maggots along the floor of the swim. The pole can be used with ordinary *swimming-through* terminal tackle, but I prefer to use it as specialist laying-on or stret-pegging material.

The baited hook is swung out and gently lowered into position over the groundbaited spot and is then held back until a bite is registered. It helps if the line between rod tip and float is kept as short as possible but in any event the combined length of line from tip to float and from float to hook should never be longer than the length of the pole.

All these methods will work when used to fish bread baits or seeds such as wheat and hemp, but variations in shotting techniques are called for.

The whole point of being a pleasure angler is that the fisherman can please himself. He can get hooked on catching a single species. He may, if he chooses, become one-eyed over a particular method or a particular bait and if that is his pleasure – well, why not? I knew just such a man who fished the Trent year in and year out with nothing but stewed wheat. He caught a lot of roach and had a lot of fun fishing with a clean and wholesome bait. He dispelled the notion that wheat is an autumn-only bait.

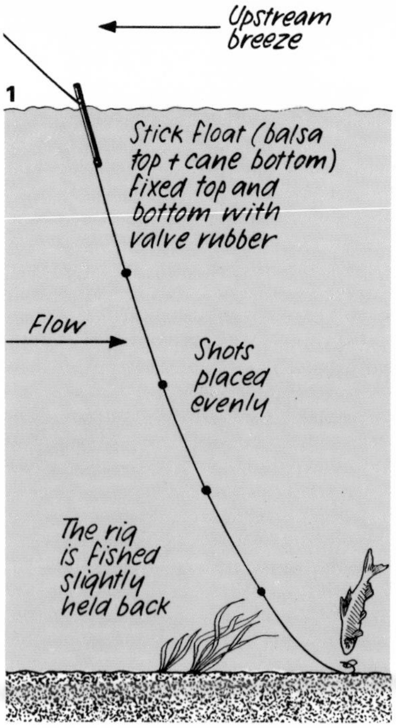

1 *Fishing an upstream breeze: A stick float used on a river flowing at an even pace, ideally against an upstream breeze. Fix the float top and bottom, space the shot evenly down the line. This rig is often fished over depth with the float held back to flutter the pinkie or caster bait in front of the fish. Exceptions to this method are when the fish are boiling and taking on-the-drop or when the river bed is unsatisfactory due to pollution.*

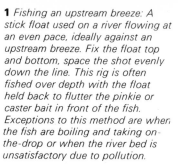

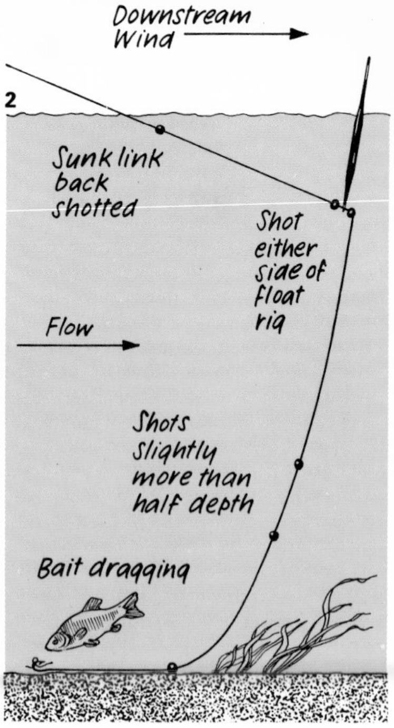

2 *Fishing the downstream wind: A waggler float in use in difficult conditions of strong current flow and downstream wind. The float is fixed at its base by a shot either side; a further shot is pinched on up the line to sink it. Cast over the swim, draw the rig back into the swim whilst sinking the rod tip into the water. The bait should then be allowed to trundle down through the swim.*

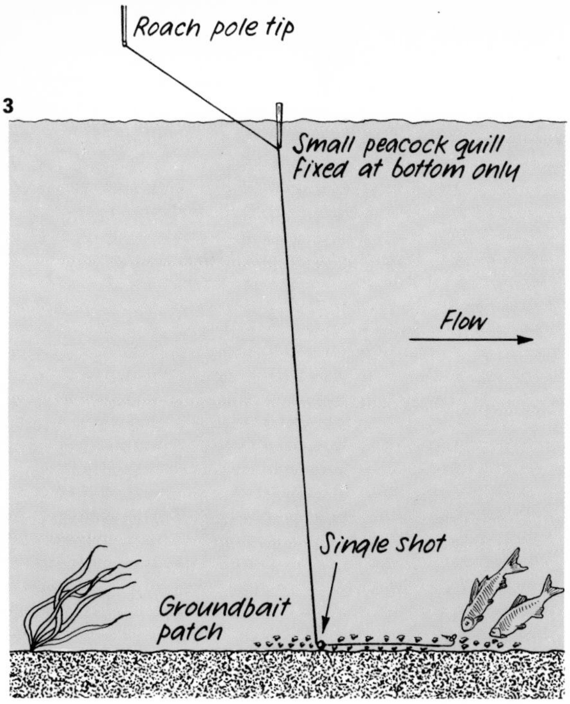

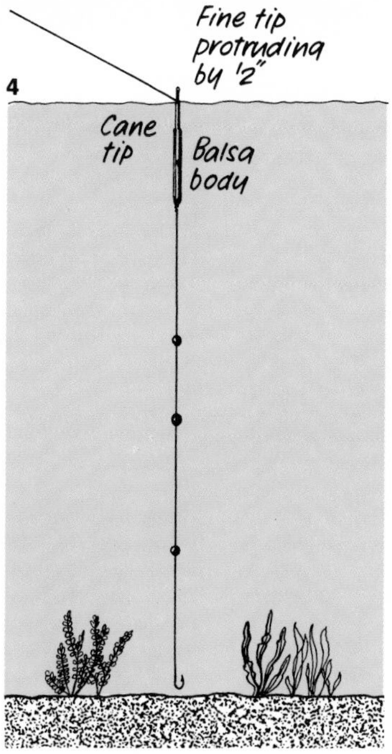

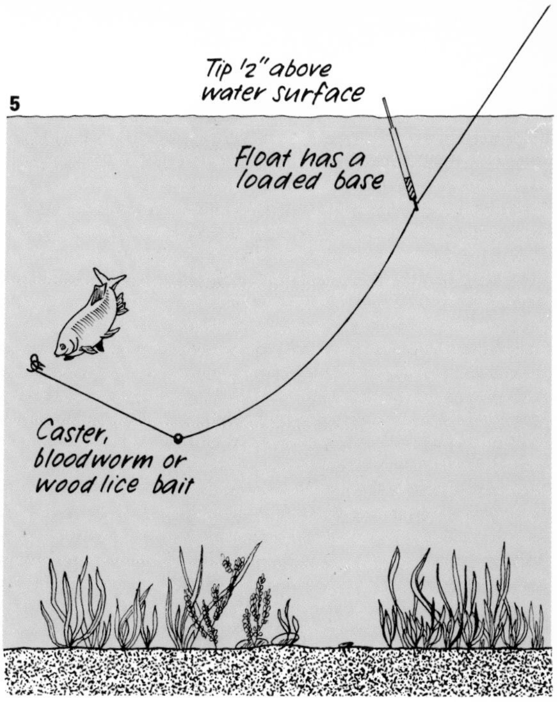

3 Fishing the roach pole: A small peacock quill float used in conjunction with a single shot terminal rig and a roach pole rod is fished at right angles to the flow, the depth is plumbed and a short link between hook and shot is fixed. The bait can then be held in this position or fished in a series of arcs by lifting the rod tip slightly downstream, thus altering the fishing angle. Bites are often registered as a straight lift.

4 Fishing ideal conditions on a still-water: Use a balsa-bodied float, with a fine cane tip, shotted down to within ½ inch of the tip. This method should be used to fish a pinkie maggot or a tiny piece of bread with effect.

5 Fishing on-the-drop: A loaded balsa and cane tipped float fished with caster pinkie or bloodworm baits designed to take roach feeding sub-surface. Fix the float at the bottom only to counter surface drift or breezy conditions.

The bait, to be effective, requires care in preparation. Buy the largest kernels you can find. These may be red or white. Wash them in a sieve and soak them overnight. The next step is to bring the pan to the boil then simmer until the kernels swell and split, showing the white fluffy interior. Surplus water should be drained away and the wheat transferred into a cloth bag. I prefer to use all seedbaits as fresh as possible and take great care to shield them from the sun when fishing since they will quickly sour if exposed for too long. A cloth bag is used for the same reason since, in my experience, seed-baits kept in plastic bags are susceptible to rapid souring.

This preparation is basic for all seedbaits, including hemp seed and tares, but care must be taken with the latter to soak overnight and to carry out the final washing with hot water. A dousing of cold water will split the bait, which is wrong for the tares. Not that ruined hookbait batches should be thrown away, for they make excellent groundbaits. An addition to the boiling process for both hemp and tares is a pinch of bicarbonate of soda. This helps the final appearance of the bait, producing a dark, shining, clean and killing bait.

Wheat may be used on the rigs already described for maggot fishing but the deadliest combination in most circumstances is the pole, peacock quill float and fine laying-on set-up. If there is a problem associated with the use of seed baits, especially hemp and tares, it is that of false bites caused when the feeding roach mistake the shot for the bait. This is best overcome by using either a tiny half moon fold-over lead to cock the float or making a spiral of lead wire. The beauty of the second method is that when laying-on it becomes, in effect, a mini running leger. The spirals may be made by rolling the wire around a pin or needle and may be carried safely on a safety pin.

Baits go in and out of fashion almost as quickly as clothes, usually as the direct result of the publicity accorded some notable catch. This might reflect the intelligent use of a change bait by a matchman trying to stay ahead of the game, or it may be the result of a pleasure fisherman carrying out a long period of pre-baiting a swim.

The bait, whatever it is, will only take fish when it acts upon the sight, taste, scent and sometimes touch senses of the fish. Bread, in all its forms, has been doing this for roach fishermen since time immemorial and it is a prime bait in the pleasure angler's armoury. Once again great care is required in the preparation of some of its variants; paste, for instance, falls into this category.

One way of producing a good soft paste is to take the inside of a stale loaf, saving the crust for adding to the groundbait. Place the bread onto a large piece of clean white cloth and, by picking up the four corners of the cloth, put the whole lot into a large bowl, cloth underneath and draped over the sides of the bowl.

Now add a few drops of water to the bread and, keeping the cloth between your hands and the bread, knead it. Keep adding water until the right consistency is obtained – the rule on this is that it should be soft.

Handling the paste in this manner ensures that at no times does the angler's hand come into contact with the paste. Additives such as sugar, honey and aniseed are simply added by folding back the cloth, but there is no need for the angler to transmit his hand scent to the bait if the cloth method is used.

Other killing bread baits are best taken from new bread. Two firm favourites are the crust, cut into ½-in squares, and flake from the inside of the loaf. They both have the advantage of being slow-sinking baits which present the angler with the opportunity of inducing a take from the roach by holding back the float and generating a fluttering effect upon the bread.

A long trail on leger tackle will also have the same effect as the current varies and lifts the bread in a tantalizing fashion.

The best methods for presenting the bread baits to the roach are trotting, using the small Avon-type float, or laying-on; once again the pole comes into its own in this respect. Paste may also be used for legering and is useful because it is heavy in its own right, thus decreasing the amount of lead required to hold bottom. As an aid to casting flake or crust, the bait should be dunked into the water. This increases the weight and ensures a quicker fall through the water to the fishing area if this is required. I rarely fish any of the bread baits on hooks smaller than size 12 and often find that an 8 or 10 is required to fish the bait adequately. The exception to this is when fishing fine tackle in gin-clear waters such as the disused canals, at which time a bread punch is used to bait the smaller hooks. The roach shoals of these waters do present a special challenge to the pleasure angler but they also present another dimension in the pleasurable use of fine tackle.

At one time fine quill floats such as the crow were considered the best medicine for presenting a bait to, and registering a bite from, educated stillwater roach. They have a drawback, however, in that the tip is fairly robust and does represent resistance to a taking fish.

Man-made floats of balsa bodies with fine cane tips have supplanted them in the baskets of many anglers since their finer tips have solved this problem. In ideal conditions, which do apply at times on sheltered canals, the floats are fixed top and bottom. If there is a surface drift the best results are obtained by fixing at the bottom only. In any event, this rig enables the pleasure angler to fish any bait so that it falls through the water in a fish-provoking manner. All of the baits described so far may be used on this gear plus others, such as woodlice or bloodworms. In these cases the hook size must be reduced to a fine wire size 20. A variation on the rig for a falling bait is to use a loaded float, such as a Dart, which requires little extra shot so that the bait gets a very slow fall-through.

A tench in the morning, from a lake in Lincolnshire. This species responds to careful and selective pre-baiting of the swim.

No self-respecting pleasure angler would dream of tackling a long session at the roach without worms in his bait box. This applies particularly in coloured water conditions when the tail of a lob worm or a couple of small red worms will often take a fish. They will encourage bites from fish when trotted through, but they are most effective when laid on.

The roach, then, is *the* fish for many pleasure anglers. Like the chub he is a fish for all seasons and all methods. To take him consistently requires patience and skill but the enjoyment comes from practising that skill. If one thing is certain about roach fishing it is that it is *always a pleasure*.

SUMMER FISHING – THE TENCH

If any fish is the symbol of summer for the angler it is the tench. It conjures up visions of typical British countryside with a tench fisher's dawn breaking like an animated Constable painting. For many anglers who

One of the strongest fighters in freshwater, the tench hooked and fought in the half-light of an early dawn will severely test both angler and his tackle.

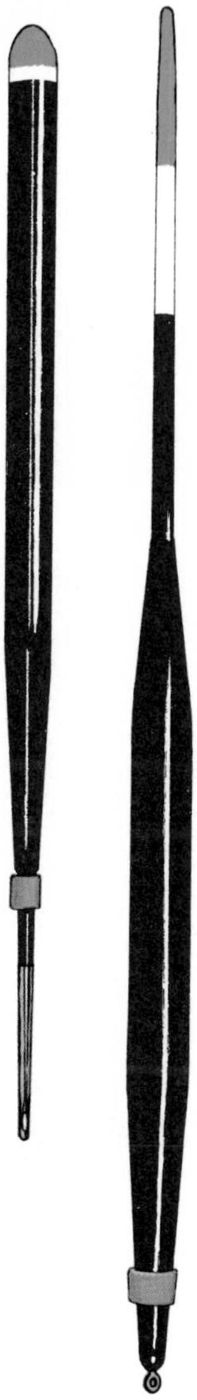

Right: A balsa bodied roach float with cane tip. Left: A loaded balsa float that self cocks with just half an inch of tip showing. The addition of a No 4 shot will sink the body down to the white sight ring. Both of these roach floats give maximum sensitivity in detecting the shy bites.

Allen Edwards preparing the groundbait for a tench fishing session: made up of breadcrumbs and whole lobworms to be laid as a carpet in a position best suited to hooking and playing a fish in the dawn.

The correct method for hooking a lobworm.

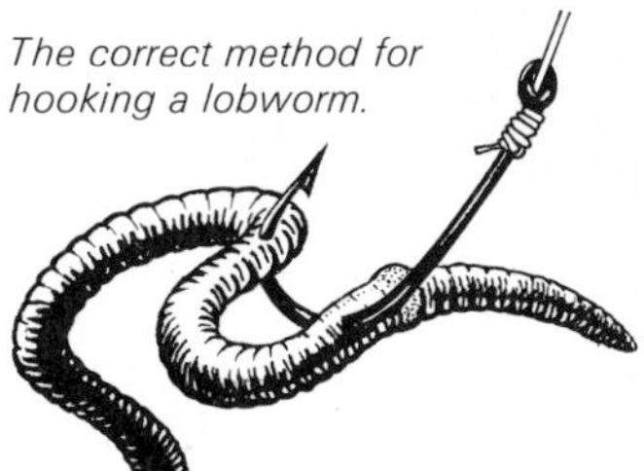

fish in the summertime it represents the prime quarry since it is a relatively common fish and can be found in most stillwaters and slow rivers, except in the north of Scotland.

The fish is strong, handsome and not too difficult to catch if adequate preparation has been carried out, but therein lies the rub. Too many anglers are prepared to fish for the tench without giving thought to a plan of campaign. No preparation is carried out, the fish fail to respond to casual angling and the tench is then labelled as capricious or inconsistent. All of which is strange when you consider that the tench will stand more in the shape of water disturbance by the angler than any other fish. The fish will respond to ritual pre-baiting programmes like the carp but it is not by any means necessary to go to such lengths on most waters. What is required is a double-edged rake of heavy gauge metal, something that will bite deep into the weed beds and stay down long enough for a good strip of weed and muddy bottom to be cleared.

Providing the water is shallow enough there is no better way than to don chest waders and to get in to the water and work the bottom over with an ordinary garden rake on a long handle. The resulting disturbance frees myriads of midge larvae, water hog louse and the like into the water, quickly attracting the tench. It is not unusual to take tench within minutes of clearing a swim in this manner. This attraction may be increased by the provision of groundbaits which should be of the usual bread and cereal base to which has been added chopped worms and dried ox blood.

If maggots are going to be used as hookbait it is a good idea to add blanched maggots to the basic ground bait. These are made by dropping maggots into boiling water for a short time. They stretch and become white and, of course, very dead but this is an advantage on a freshly-raked silty bed where live maggots quickly work through the detritus to disappear.

The choice of baits for tench fishing is large since they will take most of the seed and animal baits but, in practice, it usually comes down to a choice between bread, worms and maggots. My own preference goes, without hesitation, to bread flake since its use answers most of the traditional problems associated with tench fishing. These are caused, in the main, by the fish's feeding method. When well and truly "on", their

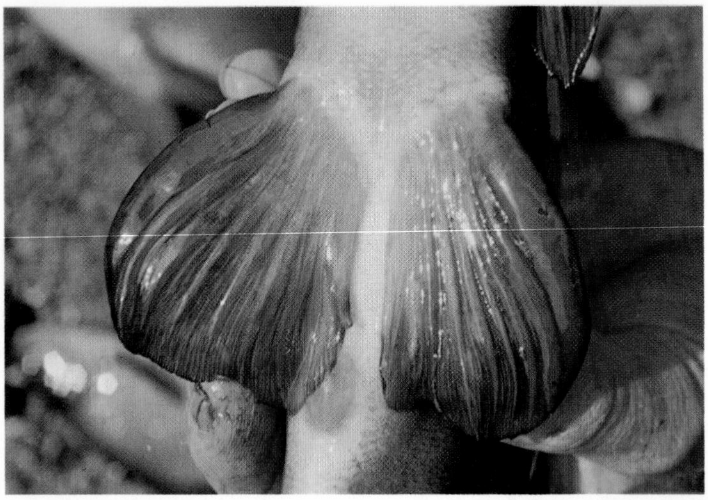

♂

♀

Coarse fishing

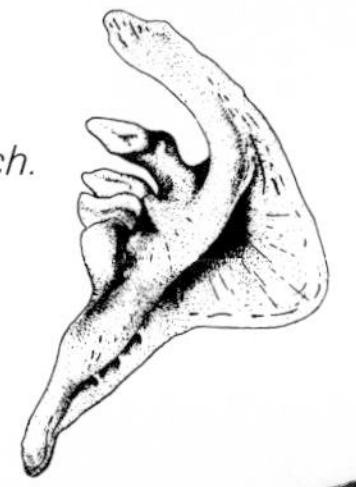

Pharyngeal teeth of the tench.

The tench is the only British freshwater fish which, outside of the breeding season, shows sexual dimorphism. * *This is not obvious at first, the differences being confined to the shape of the pelvic fins. Those of the male fish being heavier, more solidly constructed, than those of the female. When spread out sideways, the males have a distinct hump just in front of the fins. This hump is the external reflection of differences in skeletal structure between the sexes.*

** Sexual dimorphism between sexes of other species – the kype (salmon) and tubercles of males of many cyprinids during breeding season.*

heads go down, their tails go up and they appear to be doing a slow pirouette in reverse. Often their tails are moving, no doubt to aid their balance, but they give every indication of pleasure – like Labrador puppies round a bowl. While all of this is happening, their pectoral fins are fanning, streams of minute bubbles are moving up their sides from the gills and the net result is a lot of water and silt disturbance. On clay or gravel this does not matter too much but on silty bottoms worm and bunches of maggots have a tendency to become buried. Bread flake, on the other hand, tends to be wafted up by the movement and tempts the fish which are moving in towards the baited area.

Single maggots, small red worm, pieces of crust when presented on fine tackle all react in the same way and, once a shoal is feeding well, it often pays to fish for them on the drop but this is not the basic technique. The tench grows satisfyingly large and fights strongly, often in overgrown conditions, so the tackle must be capable of subduing, or at least turning, a fish before it reaches sanctuary. It is better, therefore, to over tackle when tench fishing and, while a minimum requirement would be the use of an Avon-style rod with 4 lb breaking strain line, a mark 4 carp rod and 6 lb line would not come amiss if fishing in real water-jungle conditions.

The reel is a matter of individual choice but since long casting is sometimes required I prefer to use a fixed-spool. Hook size is governed by the type of bait to be used. For bread flake a size 8 is all right, although this might be scaled down to a size 12 if the fish are taking on-the-drop and a smaller, waftable, bait is required.

Apart from the attractiveness of the fish itself, and there can be no denying the beauty of the rounded fins, little red-eye and distinctive green colouring, the fun in tench fishing comes from the use of the float. After all, even a 2 lb tench will give a positive reaction on a butt or rod tip indicator, but a lot of the pleasure comes from the surroundings, which are missed when the angler's glance is down to the rod butt! Since as far as I am concerned pleasure is the name of the game, I invariably use the float and hope that the morning, between dawn and breakfast, will be a fine one. If this is the case, and there is no surface ripple or drift, I use laying-on tactics with a quill float much as in fishing for crucians. If longer casting is required I use similar tactics but tackle with a loaded, zoomer, type float as an aid to casting.

Fate is rarely kind enough to allow this and a float legering set-up, rigged to take account of the pitfalls to legering caused by silt or silk weed, is more usual. This involves using the lightest Arlesey bomb which will hold bottom in the prevailing conditions but this

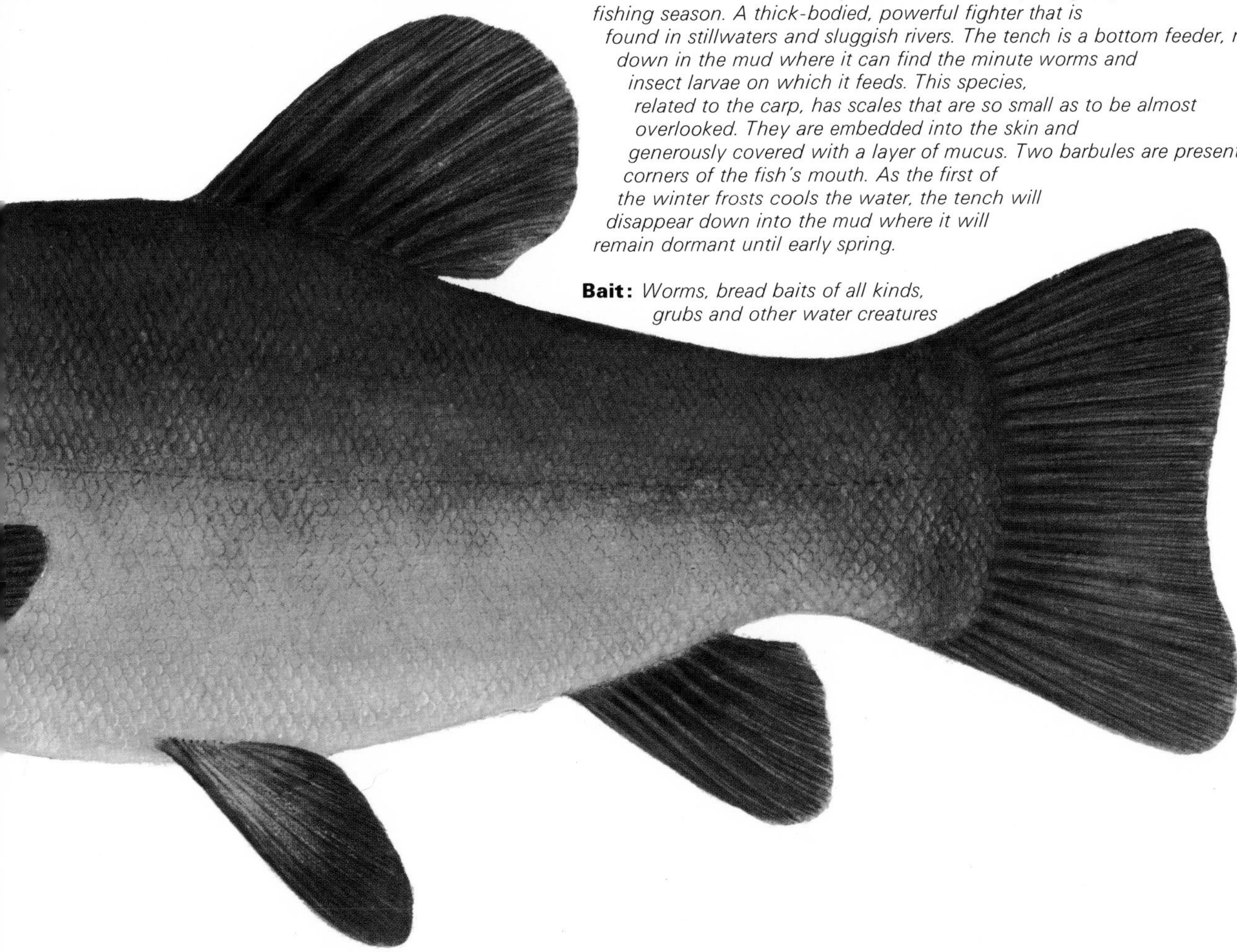

TENCH
Tinca tinca

The fish of summer, traditionally fished for on the opening day of the coarse fishing season. A thick-bodied, powerful fighter that is found in stillwaters and sluggish rivers. The tench is a bottom feeder, right down in the mud where it can find the minute worms and insect larvae on which it feeds. This species, related to the carp, has scales that are so small as to be almost overlooked. They are embedded into the skin and generously covered with a layer of mucus. Two barbules are present at the corners of the fish's mouth. As the first of the winter frosts cools the water, the tench will disappear down into the mud where it will remain dormant until early spring.

Bait: *Worms, bread baits of all kinds, grubs and other water creatures*

is linked to the line by a short length of nylon and a swivel. The bomb may sink into silt or weed but the bait is still presented well. The float in these circumstances is an antenna fixed at the bottom only.

In each case the swim is over-cast and the tackle drawn back so that the bait settles as near as possible over the centre of the baited pitch. The position of the nearest shot to the hook is rarely nearer than $2\frac{1}{2}$ ft, and I find that this obviates a lot of the nail biting frustration caused to the angler who is watching a float being wafted around the swim by the tails of the tench but imagines that this is caused by a fish playing with the bait. The tench fisher's dawn then is a joy in itself and, providing there have been no rapid temperature changes which do seem to throw the fish off the feed, that is the time when most fish are taken. But it is by no means the only time. Quite often the fish will feed in the early evening at midwater or nearer the surface over deep water. This seems to be a prelude to moving into shallower water as dusk approaches but once again the migration appears to be dependent upon a fairly constant temperature being maintained.

It is always worthwhile trying for the tench on a slowly sinking bait in the early evening, although interruptions from rudd, roach or bream may have to be borne philosophically. For the pleasure angler the tench has just about everything. It fights well and feeding times can be predicted so that fishing may be fitted into the routine of earning a living. It takes the angler into beautiful places so perhaps it is no wonder that the tench is a favourite for the all-round fisherman.

SUMMER – THE CARP

If the roach is the fish for all seasons for many pleasure anglers, the carp most definitely is not. In common with the tench, it is seen as the fish of the summer. It has its devotees, the specialists who have invested the catching of the carp with a mixture of mysticism and an old-time religion, and these men are prepared to go on worshipping throughout the winter months.

For ordinary mortals the period from 16th June through to October's end will see the main angling activity. For most that is quite long enough, for the game is rarely one to be undertaken lightly. It calls for planning, dedication, skill and more than a modicum of luck.

Not that there are not plenty of carp about. Thanks to the popularity of carp fishing and to the efforts of club secretaries to cater for their members' interests, the numbers swell year by year. Except in carp-only waters – and these are few – the problem is to sort the carp from the tench, bream, roach and eels with which many waters abound.

This increase in the availability of carp and carp fishing is an accelerating process the start of which took place when the fish were first introduced into Britain. As the fish became naturalized they spread into waters across the countryside, although their main concentration is in the southern half of the island. The common carp is a strong, hard-fighting fish and the angler's conquest of the species was never really a viable proposition until comparatively recent times when tackle capable of handling the fish became available to the ordinary angler.

The range, designed mainly by Richard Walker, who caught the 44 lb carp which holds the record at the time of writing, is based on two rods. The first of these is the Richard Walker Mark IV carp-rod which has a test curve of $1\frac{1}{2}$ lbs and takes line strengths of between 7 and 11 lbs. The second is the Mark IV Avon rod for use with lines of between 3 and 7 lbs. Since the advent of fibre-glass there has been an increase in the types of rod and actions available but, unless the angler has a special problem to resolve on a given water, the rods described are adequate for general carp fishing. My own Mark IV has seen service as a medium spinning rod for pike and as a weapon for thumping out bream and tench at long range. It has been good in all circumstances!

These rods, then, in conjunction with quality monofilament line and specially chosen hooks, became the standard equipment for use against the carp. They were highly successful and the carp began to lose its label of "uncatchable". At the same time a national newspaper devoted only to angling appeared on the scene, publicity was given to a constant stream of fish-catching exploits and the carp-catching boom was set in motion with a vengeance. The bonanza has been a mixed blessing since, to cope with the demand for carp fishing, unwise stockings have taken place. Fully mature carp have been placed into waters that are already overcrowded and the angler knows not whether the carp he gets on the bank is a wild fish or an over-hungry, Continental fish-farm-introduced newcomer. The dangers inherent in this situation have now been recognized and it is now illegal to import fish into the country except under the most stringent officially controlled situations.

Meanwhile, many waters have populations of wild carp, whose forefathers may have been introduced in medieval times. They are currently interbreeding with much later introductions of the so-called king carp from the Continent. The angler may connect with one of these. He may tangle with a partly-scaled mirror carp or a no-scaled leather carp. On the other hand he might be lucky and connect with the smaller but harder fighting wildie. The fishing methods have varied little over the years. Only the ancillaries have become more sophisticated.

The pleasure angler who is prepared to put in his homework and preparation at the bankside can have a lot of fun fooling the wily carp.

If the basic tackle for taking the carp has changed little in 25 years, the range of baits most certainly has. The angler's most likely preparation is, in fact, the formulation of a baiting policy and the weaning of the carp from other baits and natural foods to the acceptance of the angler's bait. Carp learn quite quickly and the bait that works for one week of a season on a given

A coloured and weeded carp pool in Nottinghamshire. Allen Edwards, fishing floating crust, has hooked a fish which runs hard for the bottom.

Coming to the net but not yet beaten, this fish lashes the water in a fierce flurry as it nears the bank and gets a first glimpse of the angler and net.

water may be less effective as the season progresses. Simple baits, like bread, are always worth a try but here the problem of unwanted species nipping in and pinching the bait has to be faced. The same can be said of worm baits and there can be nothing more frustrating to the carp hunter than to answer the signal of the running line with a hefty strike and to feel the sinuous backing away of the unwanted eel.

This, then, is the second reason for seeking out and then pre-conditioning the carp to take a specially concocted bait by judicious groundbaiting.

The list of baits that will tempt the carp is limitless, a feature which the fish shares with the apparently less bright chub. Bread, worms, maggots, wheat, hemp, sweet corn have all been instrumental in tempting countless carp.

Cheese-flavoured pastes, sausage, honey, banana, Marmite, tinned cat and dog food, dried blood, minced worms all have brought about the downfall of their share of carp. Having worked for a time, however, the highly developed scent and taste senses of the carp convert the once attractive flavours of the one-time magic bait into an out-and-out danger signal and they silently steal away.

Current favourites in the armoury of dedicated carp anglers are combination baits which have a high protein content. They have advantages for the angler in as much as they can be changed, quite radically, by switching the proportions of the ingredients, thus obviating the problems of danger identification by the carp. They also give a plus in that they make good casting baits if frozen and taken to the water in a thermos flask.

A No 2 hook can be slipped into the bait with the aid of a baiting needle. A long cast is made and after a few minutes in the water the bait will have thawed to present a highly tasty, correctly textured, bait to attract the carp.

One does not need to fall into the trap of fanaticism to get the best out of carp fishing. On many carp waters the optimum feeding time is around dawn and a sensible evening time pre-baiting session, coupled with the careful approach and tackling-up sequence of an experienced angler, is all that is required to take a fish or two before breakfast.

The bug, however, does bite many anglers and when that happens the addiction inevitably shows itself in the compulsion to be at the water's edge for 24 hours or more at a stretch. The variations which this produces in fishing techniques are minimal in the case of the angler who intends to fish the night through.

Groundbaiting with samples of the hookbait will be carried out, one or two rods will be set up and it is important to use two rod rests for each rod to ensure that a running carp will feel no resistance and take the bait. Bite detection is likely to be more of a problem and electric bite indicators are advisable for the night fishers.

An exciting variation of fishing for the night angler is crust or bread fishing at the margins. On many waters which receive attention from humans, anglers or just feeders of the ducks, there is a constant supply of half-soaked bread, much of which finds its way by wind drift to the edges. The carp are well aware of this additional food supply and, when all is quiet, they will patrol the margins, slobbering the bread away in a

Up with the net and it is a plump, full-bodied mirror carp going nearly 5 lbs. The pool has a massive head of carp but very few of them over 10 lbs.

A sample of the mirrors that abound in this pool. Although taken on crust, these fish have developed a taste for grains of boiled maize.

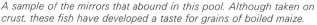

methodical manner. A good hunk of bread or crust lowered gently into the path of one of these wanderers will often be taken with confidence – and very exciting it is, too!

Comes the day and the realization that, although the carp are feeding, they are not taking advantage of the groundbaited pitch nor of the generously placed hook bait. This often generates a panic response from the angler who sets out to stalk individual carp which are signalling their presence by stirring up clouds of mud and bubbles. Good baits for this type of operation are small bunches of red worm or maggots. The excitement comes when the carp does suck in the morsel which has often been presented on scaled-down tackle. A middleweight carp, on a 4 or 5 lb line to a size 12 hook, has the advantage. Add to that the fact that by this time the angler is tired and frustrated and it is not difficult to appreciate why this type of battle is often lost by the angler.

There is no denying the fascination which the carp holds for the pleasure angler. Not the least of these attractions is the fact that carp are often visible or give clear indications of their whereabouts by lifting lily pads as they move about their business below. They can, at times, be easy to catch, conforming to all of the rules and making the whole sport appear simple. At other times they mooch about like inviolate, blue-black submarines, appearing to be well aware of the angler's presence and treating his baits with disdain.

On reflection, perhaps this is the greatest fascination of carp fishing. The water positively reeks of carp, the angler knows that the fish feeds readily in the summer but he also knows that he will have earned every fish that he catches.

SUMMER – THE CRUCIAN CARP

Even Mr Average, the pleasure angler, tends to get intense about the capture of the larger carps. The crucian carp, however, pulls the balance back the other way and is seen by many as presenting the opportunity for a little light relief. The fish has a similar distribution to the larger carps but will exist in conditions which the barbuled carp and many other coarse fish cannot tolerate.

It will live in overgrown, shallow farm ponds and appears to thrive in waters which have a thick, silty bottom. The crucian rarely grows large and a 2 lb fish is a good one so it can be fished for with the lightest of tackle. This sometimes poses problems for the angler since the crucian can share a water with tench which, even in the worst of conditions, tend to grow much larger. The angler is tempted to step up tackle to cope with the occasional tench and this reacts against correct bait presentation to entice the browsing crucian. On balance it is better to scale the tackle to

Rigs and tackles for the pleasure angler

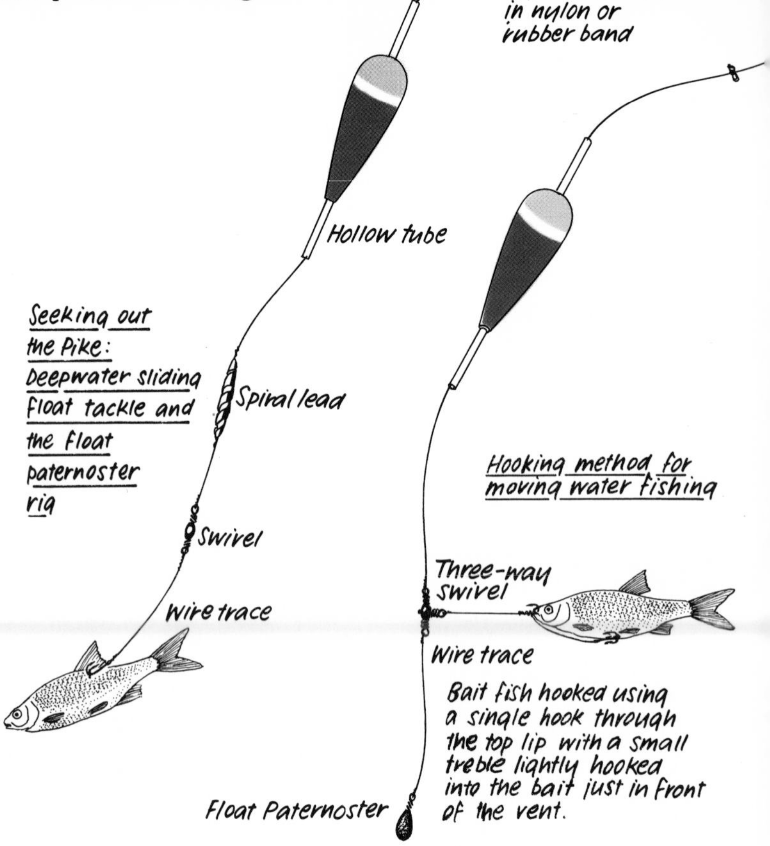

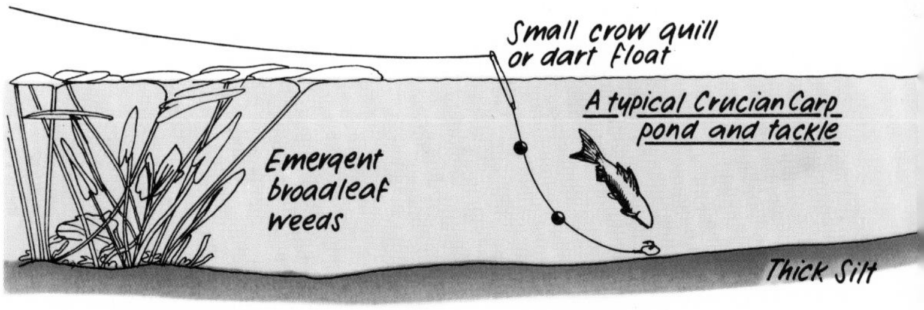

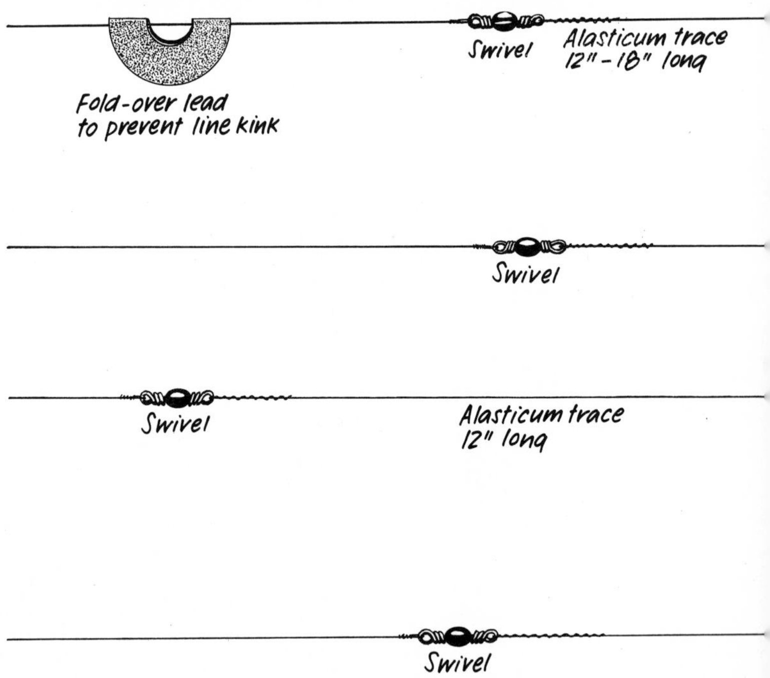

Rigs and tackle for the Pleasure Angler

Tench fishing rigs

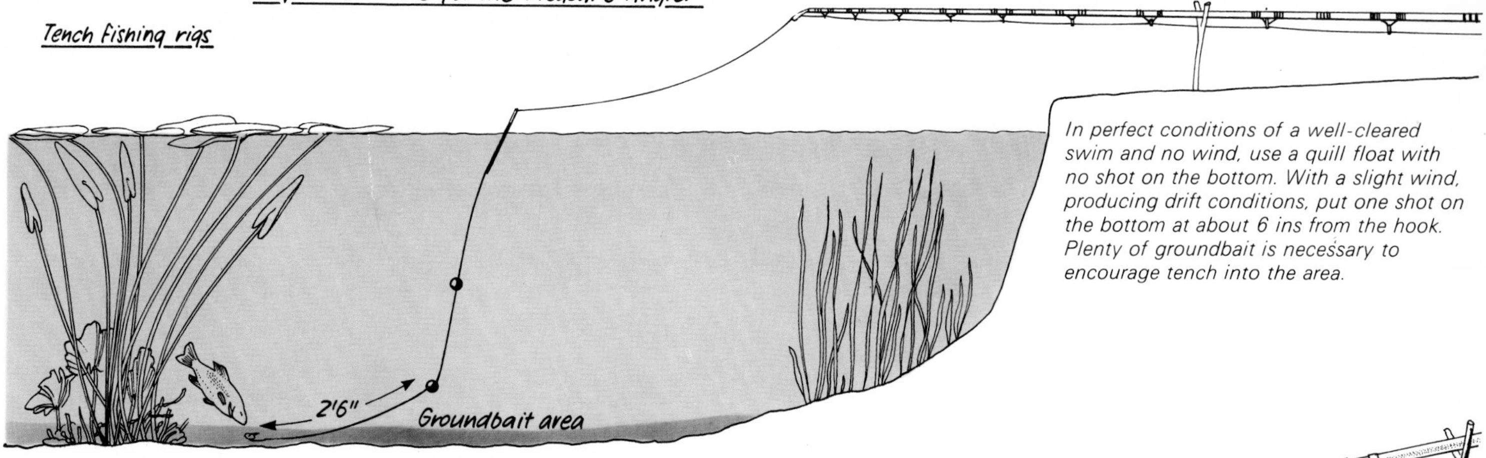

In perfect conditions of a well-cleared swim and no wind, use a quill float with no shot on the bottom. With a slight wind, producing drift conditions, put one shot on the bottom at about 6 ins from the hook. Plenty of groundbait is necessary to encourage tench into the area.

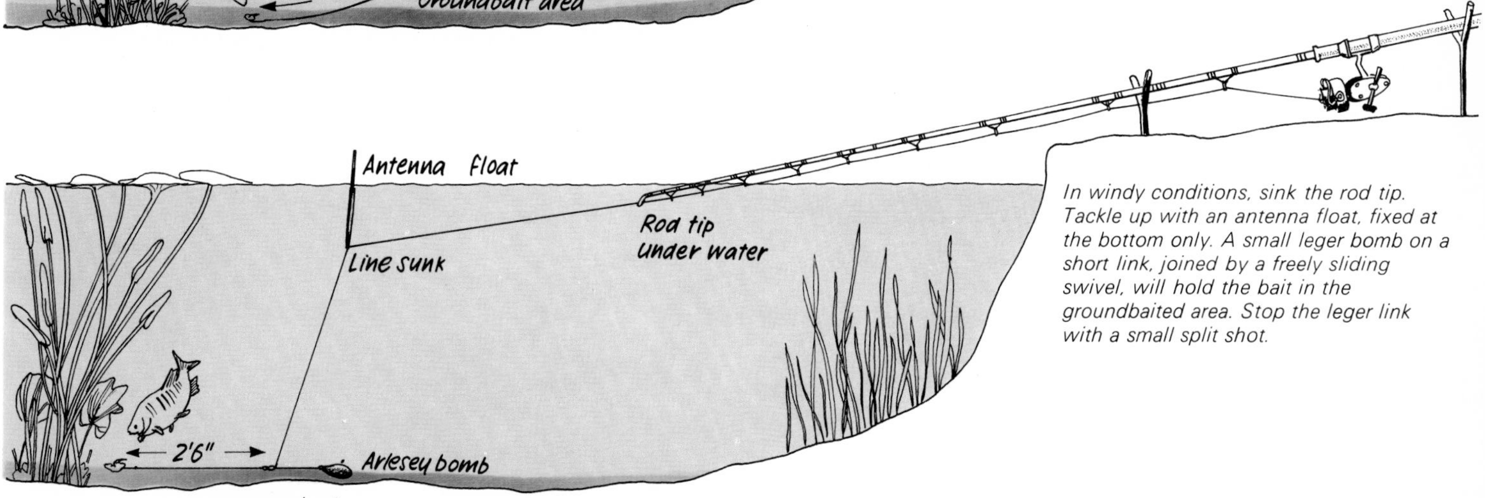

In windy conditions, sink the rod tip. Tackle up with an antenna float, fixed at the bottom only. A small leger bomb on a short link, joined by a freely sliding swivel, will hold the bait in the groundbaited area. Stop the leger link with a small split shot.

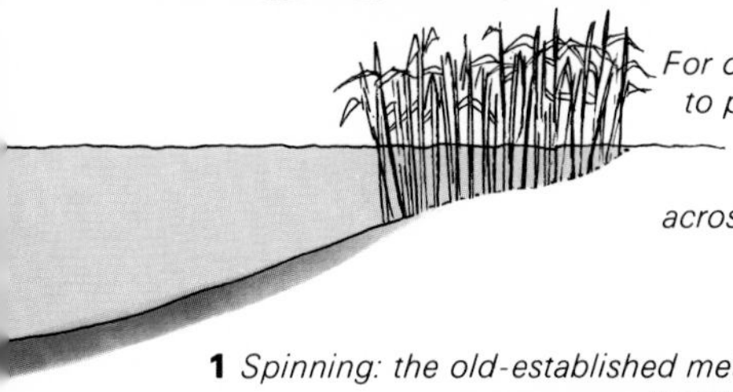

For crucian carp use fine tackle to present small baits, worms, maggots, casters or breadflake. The reel is laid across the edge of the weed to prevent float drift.

Seeking out the Pike: mobility is the key to success.

1 *Spinning: the old-established method using large spoon baits that do in fact wobble rather than spin.*

2 *Plug fishing is a modern but very popular method of taking pike. It can be especially productive when using floating plugs that can be fished over thick weedbeds that would seriously hamper spinning with a metal lure.*

3 *Sink and draw with a small deadbait: use sprat, gudgeon or a small roach.*

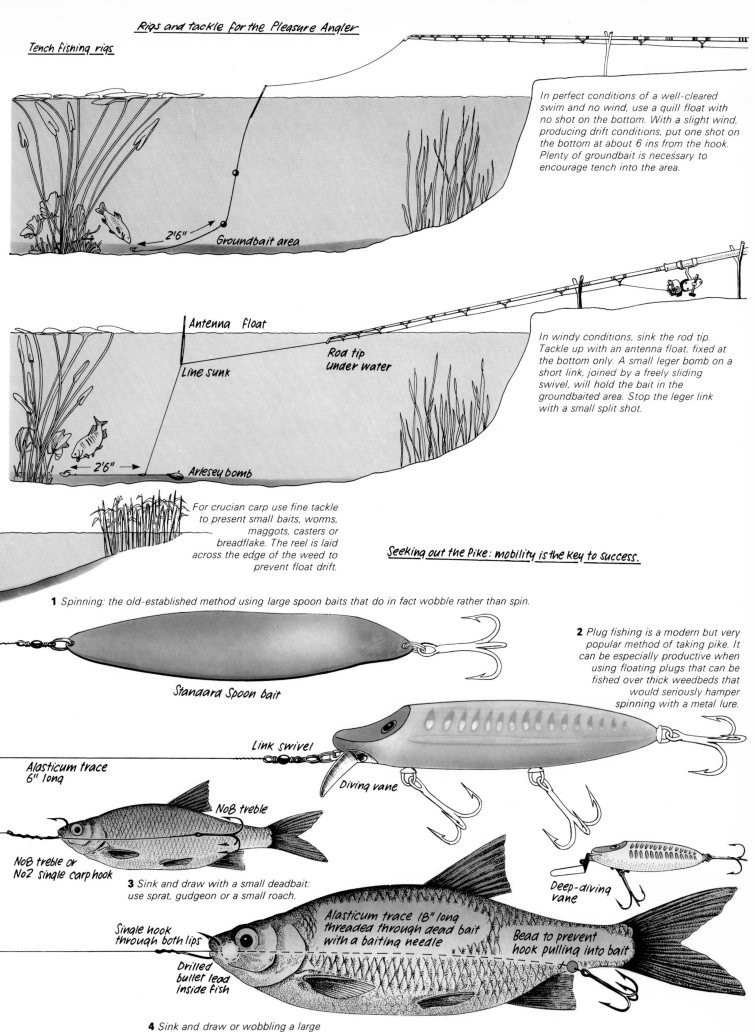

4 *Sink and draw or wobbling a large deadbait: use a large roach, dace or herring.*

suit the crucian and to fight a marauding tench with care when it does show up.

The careful angler will not often break on the strike since the key to successful crucian fishing is in delicacy. This applies right through the process from scaled-down tackle to the gentlest of strikes to set the hook. The tackle then may be a typical 12 ft long roach rod with tippy action or, if conditions are less than ideal, a roach pole.

The line should be around 2 lbs breaking strain but in gin-clear conditions this may be scaled down even further. The float should be small, a crow quill or a loaded canal-style float is ideal. The hook may be a 16 through to a 12 if bread flake is used as bait. The fishing is delightful, often fishing in miniature with one or two anglers operating fairly closely together on a tiny farm pond.

The crucian is, in my experience, susceptible to careful groundbaiting and the groundbait is the better for the inclusion of sugar. Bread crumb is all right but biscuit crumb is better and even this is improved if samples of the hookbait are included. This may be maggot or caster, tiny red worm or small pieces of bread flake.

It should be remembered that the typical crucian water will have a soft, oozy bottom and worms and maggots often bury themselves very quickly so it is better to feed these in at fairly frequent intervals than to rely upon one heavy bombardment of groundbait.

Care should be taken in the plumbing of the depth before fishing for the crucian, taking a special note of the likely depth of the ooze. The float tackle should be rigged so that no shot rests upon the bottom, the only variation to this rule being in those instances where the fish has been found in waters having a clay or gravel bed. In circumstances like these, the *lift method* of fishing will be effective.

At first sight a plump rudd but something says "hybrid" about this fine fish.

The crucian is peculiar in that it often manages to take a bait so gently that no movement is registered upon the float. For this reason I prefer to bait up a pitch which is close to broadleaved pond weed, if possible. With a breeze and consequent drift it is possible to lay the line across the top of a strand of weed and to hold the bait in position in this manner. The roach pole is also of use in this circumstance since it is possible to hold back against the drift.

Fishing for crucians, then, is the essence of pleasure fishing. It is a phlegmatic and soothing pastime for the summertime angler. The chubby little carp take the bait freely, rest easily in the keep net and scamper back to their swim when released.

No one has a coronary when crucian fishing, just a lot of fun.

SUMMER – THE RUDD

The rudd, with the perch, shares the distinction of being the most handsome fish in the British list, and this applies particularly to the larger fish. Short and deep bodied, with vermillion-coloured fins, bronze or brassy flanks and backs topping off with dark green to black shading, they make a pretty picture. For the pleasure angler they are very much a *sometime* fish, chiefly because of their indifferent distribution in England and Wales, although they are widespread in Ireland.

This is not the only reason why they may be regarded as an optional extra by anglers who have access to rudd fishing, a sort of light entertainment choice. The fact is that they are relatively easy to catch in some conditions and their fight is a lot less than dramatic.

They do, however, have the saving grace of being a fish which it is possible to avoid catching unless being specifically sought, so that the angler is less likely to have his carp bait pinched by a rudd than he is by a roach or bream. This is because most of the rudd's feeding is carried out at the surface and in and around reedy margins. But not to decry the rudd. There is pleasure for the angler in tracking down and extracting good rudd from a shoal, especially in the weather conditions in which the fish is most active. The rudd will feed on the hottest of July or August "dog days" and, in this respect, is very much a bonus fish. Specimens of 2 lbs are common and 3–4 pounders are always on the cards but this is *not* the reason for recommending an Avon-style rod and 3 lb breaking strain line on fixed spool reel as ideal tackle with which to fish.

The fact is that the rudd is very shy and, if approached clumsily, will soon move away to new reed

1 *Rudd are surface feeding fish during the warmer months. They can be brought on to feed by floating a crust. Allen Edwards uses crusts on a small raft.*

2 *The raft has a perforated zinc bottom, which allows minute pieces of crumb to wash through. The whole contraption is contained within an old hairnet.*

A superb rudd water in East Anglia. Formerly a gravel working, it has become totally naturalized. The long, narrow fingers of deepish water are almost grown over with reedmace and over-hanging vegetation. Great sport can be had fishing from a punt whilst drifting small pieces of crust to attract fish.

beds. Long casting is sometimes necessary and this tackle will do that job and set the hook in answer to a sweeping strike.

The most efficient method of angling for rudd on most waters is to fish from a boat – the broader and more stable the better. The old fashioned two-man punt is ideal for this game, providing the rowing is not left entirely to one angler!

A boat and long casting are just part of the equation in rudd fishing. The third, and probably most important, need is to entice the fish into a situation in which they can be angled for. The rudd, and this applies particularly to good fish, spend a lot of time deep in the reed beds. There they browse away on the stems taking aquatic insects and the odd terrestrial casualty that becomes trapped in the surface film.

Groundbaiting is the answer to the problem – first to get the fish feeding on the intended hookbait and second to draw the fish to the front of the reed bed and into the open water where the angler may present the baited hook.

Maggots, casters and bread are all good hookbaits for the rudd and serve equally well as groundbaits. The maggots and casters are best placed into the front of the reed bed with the aid of a throwing stick or a catapult. The same weapons may be used to put small pieces of cloudbait and maggots just off the front of the reeds where the fish can be held away from their cover with the aid of tethered groundbait, which is made to float at the surface. This is done very simply but effectively by placing a piece of white polystyrene ceiling tile into a hairnet together with dry bread crumbs, maggots and casters. The whole lot is tethered to the bottom of the swim by a length of cord or line. This is best lowered into position before starting to fish and is fixed, to depth, with the aid of a stone. Quite large slices of bread may be included in the net at which the shoal will work until they have cleared it all away. The white tile continues to act as a marker. It goes without saying that these groundbaiting aids should be removed when the fishing is finished as they are indestructible and soon constitute an eyesore, to say nothing of the danger the cord constitutes to water fowl.

The rudd will take a bunch of maggots on a size 12 gilt crystal hook. A size 8 or 10 will not be too large if bread flake is being used. Small red worm will also take rudd but, whatever the bait, it should be presented so that it falls through the water *as slowly as possible*. This means that the shot must be bunched beneath the float or that a loaded float should be used. Rudd make a considerable disturbance at the surface when feeding, which, I suppose, is the reason that they do not seem to mind when a large float is used and comes plonking down among them.

An ideal way of presenting a slow-falling bait is to deliver it with the aid of fly-fishing tackle. Maggots are best for this operation since a bunch will stand being false cast, which bread flake will not. Not that it is necessary to use any bait other than an artificial fly, for the rudd will take both dry or wet fished patterns, as used in trout fishing. Bait or fly, the rule is to fish shallow. If the wet fly is used it pays to allow the flies to sink and then to impart movement with a steady pull on the line between the rod handle and the first rod ring, at the same time lifting the rod tip. Flies that glitter are most effective: silver or gold-bodied offerings such as Butcher, Wickham's Fancy, Cinnamon and Gold are favourites. For dry-fly work tiny Black Gnats work well with the leader tapered and silicone-sprayed to ensure that line and fly float well.

The rise to the fly varies from a nudging, scrambling, affair if the shoal is milling about to a deliberate gulp from a solitary fish which knows that it has all the time in the world. Whatever the method used to take the rudd it should be led away from the shoal as soon as possible and with the minimum of fuss. A fish that is allowed to thrash around on the surface will soon put the others down.

A rudd of any size is not to be despised. A big rudd is a thing of beauty. This, coupled with the fact that the fish comes from beautiful surroundings, is the reason why, for me, rudd fishing is a pleasure.

SUMMER – THE DACE

Many fish draw unto themselves armies of specialist followers. Some fish attract by virtue of size, some by ferocity, some by the fact that they present a challenge to the angler. Not many pleasure anglers chase the dace with dedication and this is probably because the fish is not large, fierce or difficult to catch. The discerning pleasure angler can, however, put two large plus signs against the fish's place in the list. The dace, especially in the summer, will always be found in attractive surroundings and presents the pleasure angler with the opportunity to practise his skill with fly-fishing gear.

There can be few streamy runs on any unpolluted river in England and Wales which has not got a population of dace, for the fish is very common. Often it rivals in numbers and, in the winter, competes for habitats with, the roach. Nor is the fish restricted to the runs of the larger rivers. Many small tributaries harbour specimen dace although their capture requires techniques differing from those that would be used on the main stream.

The dace is fished for by all of the usual river methods, as used for roach in streamy conditions, and it will take the same range of baits. In practice, maggots and casters are the most widely used with worms and wasp grub also taking their share of fish. Cereal baits are effective and the fish can be as daft as roach on hemp seed.

The dace will live in pockets on runs of white water in which the angler may be excused for imagining that no fish could survive. Typical examples of this occur

on the upper Severn or on the Teme, which rises in Wales and meets the Severn in Worcestershire. These waters push, with white-fronted energy, from side to side of their channels. The result of each succeeding run is a hollowed-out pool where the river regains its breath and the chub reign supreme. On many of the rapids there are pockets of dace-holding water looking like old stains on a freshly laundered baby's bib and the dace in these can be superb – fine sporting fish of half a pound or so.

One method of taking these fish is to use an ordinary roach action rod with fixed spool reel and $2\frac{1}{2}$ or 3 lb breaking strain line. No float is used, as such, but a 3 ins length of cigar-shaped balsa wood controller which is painted to make it waterproof. The controller is fitted with an eyelet at each end and the reel line is passed through each one and stopped from running to the hook by a stop shot. The angler fishes the holding pools by wading into the edge of the current, holding the rod tip high and allowing the controller to run down stream until the dark water is reached when the cigar is manoeuvred and held, for as long as possible, in the slightly slacker water.

Ideal terminal tackle is a No 12 hook baited with wasp grub. A steady trickle of bait is fed into the swim and each likely spot should be tested out. It has to be admitted, perhaps slightly tongue in cheek, that trout

ROACH
Rutilus rutilus

Probably the most important coarse fish from an angling point of view, the roach is found throughout the British Isles although it is not widely distributed in Ireland, where it is found in only two major river systems. It is a shoal fish in both still and running water where it feeds on minute water creatures, worms and some plant life. There is confusion between this species and the rudd, a close relative within the Cyprinidae. *The roach has a dorsal fin positioned directly above the pelvics. Both jaws are of equal length. A 2 lbs fish is considered a specimen and the record in British waters is 4 lbs 1 oz.*

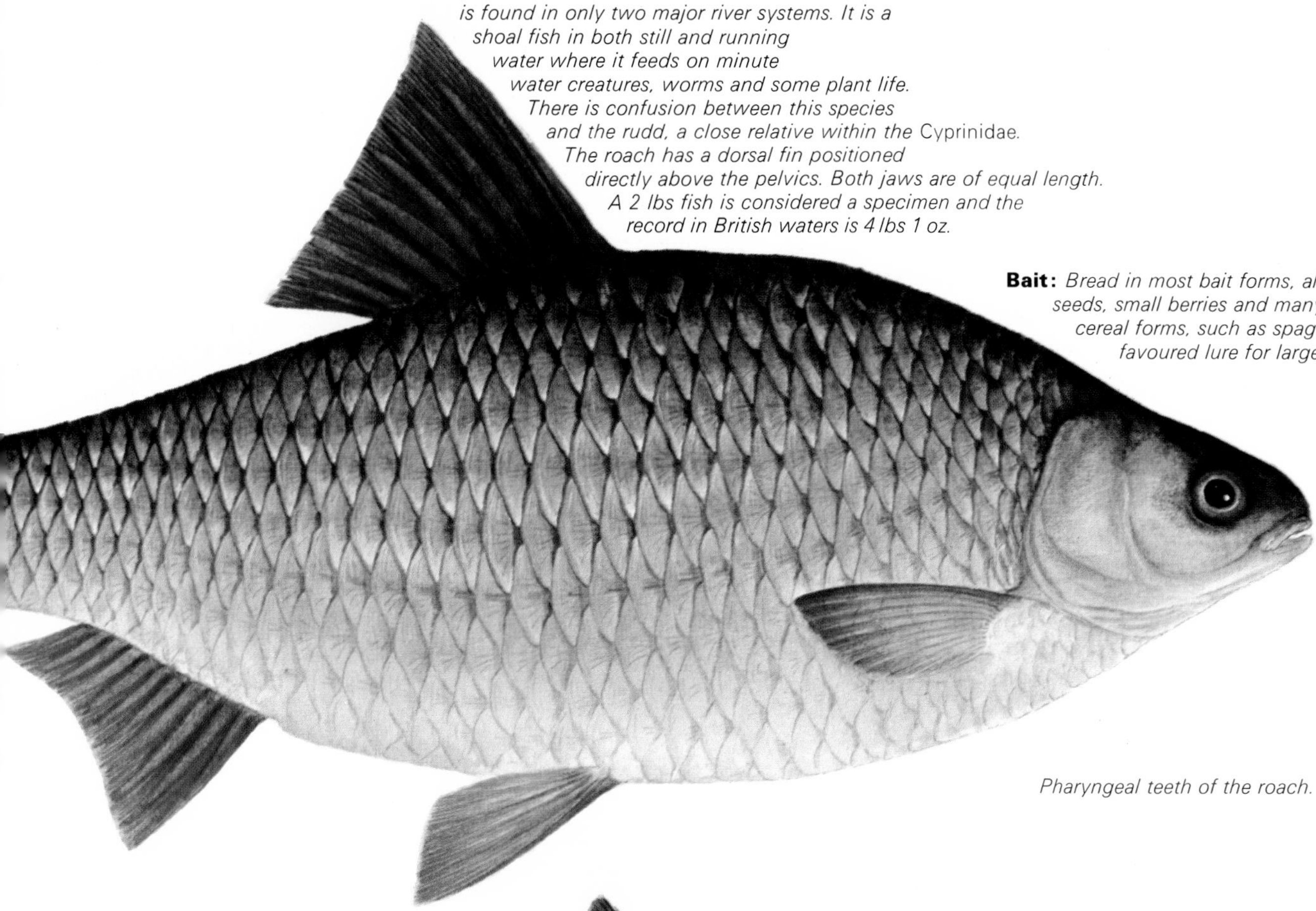

Bait: *Bread in most bait forms, all manner of grubs, seeds, small berries and many household cereal forms, such as spaghetti. Worms are a favoured lure for large roach.*

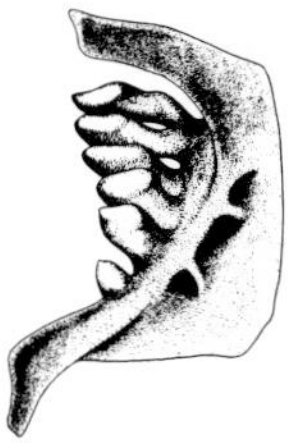

Pharyngeal teeth of the roach.

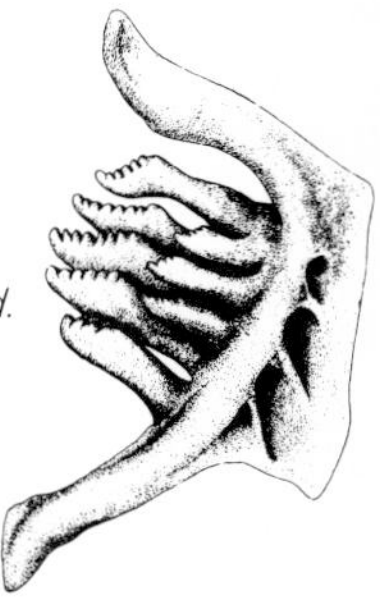

Pharyngeal teeth of the rudd.

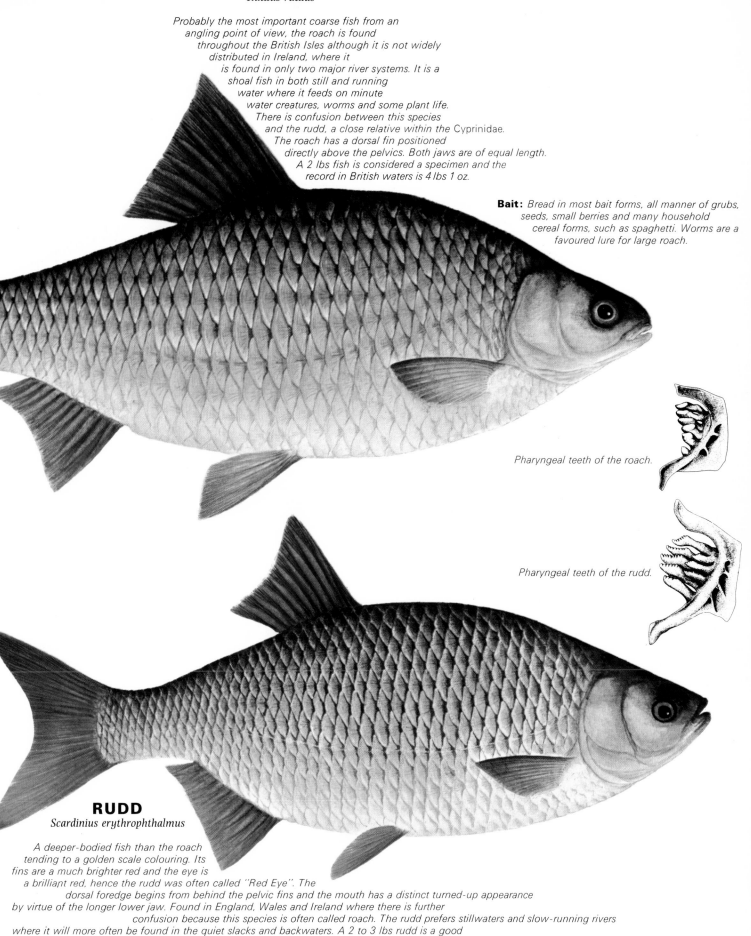

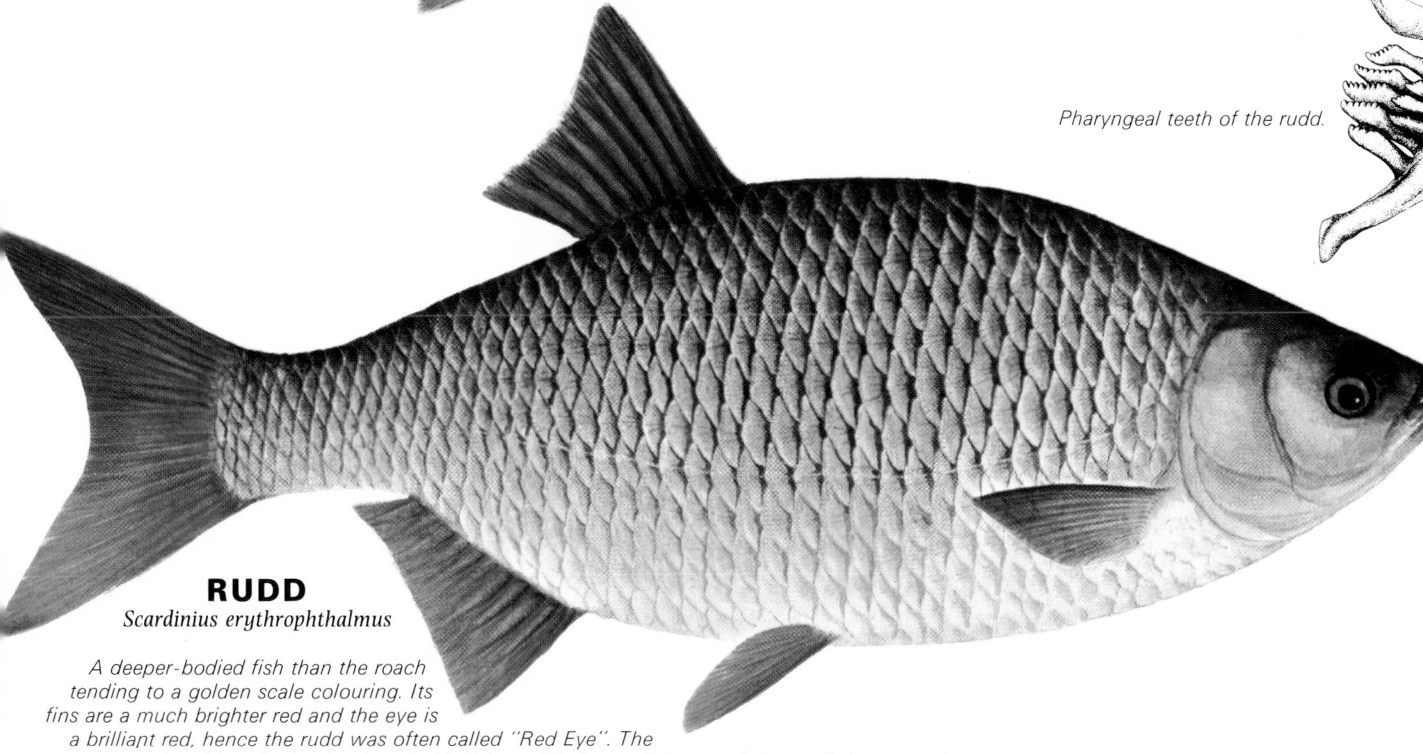

RUDD
Scardinius erythrophthalmus

A deeper-bodied fish than the roach tending to a golden scale colouring. Its fins are a much brighter red and the eye is a brilliant red, hence the rudd was often called "Red Eye". The dorsal foredge begins from behind the pelvic fins and the mouth has a distinct turned-up appearance by virtue of the longer lower jaw. Found in England, Wales and Ireland where there is further confusion because this species is often called roach. The rudd prefers stillwaters and slow-running rivers where it will more often be found in the quiet slacks and backwaters. A 2 to 3 lbs rudd is a good specimen in any water.

Bait: *The rudd will accept all baits suitable for the roach but will also rise freely, in the warm summer evenings, to a small dry fly.*

1

2

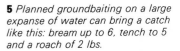

3

1 Having observed the feeding path of a bream shoal, Allen Edwards rows out in the late evening with two large buckets of prepared groundbait.

2 Small amounts are put around a central carpet of feed in an attempt to draw bream into a concentrated feeding area.

3 Every little helps!

4 The groundbaiting and all-night vigil pay off with a bream of $6\frac{1}{2}$ lbs in the early morning. Allen's fishing started with a number of line bites as the huge fish swept into the feed.

5 Planned groundbaiting on a large expanse of water can bring a catch like this: bream up to 6, tench to 5 and a roach of 2 lbs.

are sometimes taken in addition to the dace. Bite detection is no problem since the line is held between finger and thumb and the pluck is felt.

On broader shallows of larger rivers, like the Trent, the dace provides much more fun on fly-fishing tackle. I use a 6 ft wand, a split cane rod that throws a No 5 floating line very well. The trick with this is to cast a fixed length of line while wading gently up the shallows. Runs between islands are often very productive. Floating patterns which I tie on No 16 hooks are Black Gnat and Red Tag. The cast is made up and across and is allowed to float only a short distance before the fly is lifted off and recast.

For downstream work I use weighted nymphs which I tie on size 12 hooks. The cast is made across and slightly downstream. Movement is imparted to the nymph by a slight lifting of the rod tip. This, I feel, imparts the escaping prey movement to the lure and the takes from both dace and chub require no strike as the fish hooks itself. The dace gives a good account of itself when caught in these circumstances but it has to be admitted that the chief pleasure comes from the methods employed rather than from the landing of the fish which, once hooked, is seldom in doubt.

Paradoxically, while the dace is rising freely in the summer it is seldom fished for but, once the move to winter quarters in slacker water has been made, he is sought by the pike anglers as live bait.

The best winter tactics for the dace are laying-on or light legering. An effective method on small waters is to work quietly upstream flicking a maggot-baited hook, weighted with a single swan shot, into the run of the current but holding the rod high so that the bait is carried back under the angler's bank. This is particularly effective under hollow banks and tree roots. The dace then is great fun to fish for, especially if the tackle is scaled down to suit the fish.

LATE SUMMER – THE BREAM

There was a time when the breams, common or bronze and the smaller silver, were regarded as fish of the summer. For many casual pleasure anglers this is still the case but these fish, too, have their fans who will angle for them throughout the year. They have a wide distribution, being absent only from parts of Wales, the far West Country and northern Scotland.

They abound in the flatter regions and great concentrations of them are within easy reach of the major centres of population, so the fish is a popular quarry. This is especially so since fish in the 3 to 4 lb class are common and will turn up in the catch of the most casual of summertime anglers. The fish will fall to a tiny bait which has been presented for roach. It will whittle away and finally engulf the large piece of paste aimed at the carp. There are times when it can be the easiest of fish to take. The temptation, therefore, is to dismiss bream fishing as simple but this does the fish and the sport less than justice. This applies, in particular, to the fishing for bronze bream which falls into two categories covering fishing in still and running water. Both sections have, besides the fish itself, a common denominator.

In both instances the basic problem when fishing for the larger fish is that of locating the shoals. The fish is a wanderer and I know of still waters where great shoals of dark-backed fish, which run up to 6 lbs in weight, can be seen patrolling set beats. They remind one, irresistibly, of great herds of American buffalo munching their way across a prairie, slow moving, numberless but tightly packed.

The still waters, perhaps, present the angler with the best opportunity of tangling with a good bream since, with study, it becomes possible to predict the movements of the shoal. On the rivers, on the other hand, the problems are compounded by fluctuating levels and possibly by the unwelcome attentions of the boating fraternity. In any event the key to the problem is the understanding of the shoal movements since this does introduce a note of regularity into the proceedings. Each year, if spawning has been successful,

4

5

vast shoals of tiny fry gather and begin to move in a glittering mass around the perimeter of the lake. Predation is great and large numbers of the tiny fish are killed off. The search for food, perhaps aided by the herding action of predators, initiates a wandering style of life on the shoal which, except in winter when the shoal may become static, will never cease.

They roll around a set beat and their movements become predictable. On each water there will be shoals of bream perambulating their chosen way, feeding as they go and acting as fodder for the predators. It follows that the shoals shrink in size year by year as the fish grow larger and each water that holds bream has shoals of varying sizes and numbers rolling around the lake crossing each others' paths.

The location of a meeting place can be a hot spot for the casual angler with the possibility of a good fish always on the cards. To be selective, however, the angler needs to pinpoint the feeding path of the small shoal of big fish. This, of course, is specialist's work. On large expanses of water where the clarity of the water is not always impaired by the bream's feeding, this may be done by observation. On smaller waters where the bream have coloured the water with their constant rooting for food, the job becomes more difficult. Incidentally, for general fishing on narrow drains many anglers look for these coloured patches of water as indication of a shoal at work. As a general guide it pays to prospect on the north or north-eastern shore of a water since this is where the prevailing winds sweep the surface water of the lake, uncovering food by wave action, or simply delivering insects trapped in the surface film.

Once the fish have been located the fishing becomes something of a ritual in which the sacrificing of large quantities of groundbait becomes an important part. This may be on the once-and-for-all principle of the casual angler but is probably much more effective on a smaller amount but constantly fed technique. The difference is that in the second case the angler prebaits on the bream run at regular times. The aim is not to attempt to hold the bream in swim but to accustom the fish to finding the angler's bait in a set place at a set time. In both cases the groundbait may be the same – bread and bran type mixture, soaked to ensure that it stays down on the bed of the swim. Chopped worms, blanched maggots, sweet corn and crushed hemp seed all make very acceptable additives to the bread and bran basic mix.

On the question of hookbaits, the choice is wide but,

in practice, can be covered with four. These are breadbaits, flake and paste, worms and maggots. In the summer months the baits may be fished large but, as the waters cool, smaller baits – even down to single maggots – will become more effective.

No angler will claim that bream fight very strongly but, by virtue of their large flank, the bream will test out weak tackle. Many big bream are lost by the casual angler by breaking on the strike since gossamer tackle and tiny hooks are unable to stand the initial impact of the contact with a slab-sided 4- or 5-pounder.

Add to the fish's bulk the fact that it may be necessary to cast a long way to lay the bait before the bream and it makes no sense to use very fine tackle for this fishing. In still water a line with a minimum 4 lbs breaking strain should be used. In running water where large bream are expected this may even be too light. Hook size will vary with the baits but for bread flake and paste a size 8 is not too large. A bunch of maggots may be fished on a size 12. All of this, by the way, presupposes that the bronze bream is the quarry. Ordinary roach fishing tackle will suffice for tackling the silver bream. A 9 to 10 ft leger rod and fixed spool reel completes the tackle and the rod incorporates a tip ring that will take a swing tip attachment.

On hard-fished waters bite detection may be a problem so swing and quiver tips come into their own in these circumstances. In general, however, the bream is not a shy biter and butt indicators and dough bobbins are adequate as warnings to the angler. If the action is slow and the bream have not yet reached the swim it is an advantage to have the rod at right angles to the bank, resting on two rod rests, with the rod tip buried beneath the surface. The reel pick-up should be off so that, if the angler's attention should wander, a taking fish will feel less resistance.

When the fish do come on, a switch to swing tip or quiver tip indication may be an advantage, especially on waters which receive a lot of attention from fishermen. On still waters the bait should be fished hard on the bottom and conventional leger or laying-on float tackle may be used.

For many anglers part of the attraction of fishing for bream is the leisurely way in which the fish appears to take the bait. The fact that the fish is standing on his head and lifting the bait causes the float to lie flat upon the surface before moving off below the surface. There is a fascination in it but it can be avoided by using a longer trail between the bottom shot and the hook. On moving waters a bottom-fished bait may take fish but there are times when the bream is taking on-the-drop and careful plumbing of the depth is required to ensure that the bait runs through just tripping the bottom, or is just away from it when the float is held back, in order to attract the fish.

The bream, then, is an important fish to the pleasure angler. It is not the greatest fighter in the world but it is plentiful and accommodating. To catch large specimens consistently requires skill and dedication. What more should we ask of a fish?

LATE SUMMER – THE EEL

There can be few fish so reviled by the majority of anglers as the common eel. No one will deny the fascination which it exercises but for many it is the fascination of the "horrible". Certainly the small specimens, bootlace eels, get nothing but curses heaped upon their heads.

This, of course, is not surprising when one considers the awful mess that the contorting little fish will generate in slime, knots and tangles. They mean lost fishing time, rising blood pressure and general harrassment for the average pleasure angler. Bigger eels, anything over 2 lbs in weight, are an altogether different proposition. Many anglers accord them a wholesome respect.

There are few waters in the British Isles which do not have a population of eels and since the fish may stay in a given water for 12 or more years it follows that most waters have a head of large specimens. This is especially so when one considers that the eel will often take a bait when other, perhaps first choice, fish are refusing to co-operate.

A successful method for bream fishing that relies on the fact that bream pick up a bait by "standing on their heads", which lifts the lead shot.

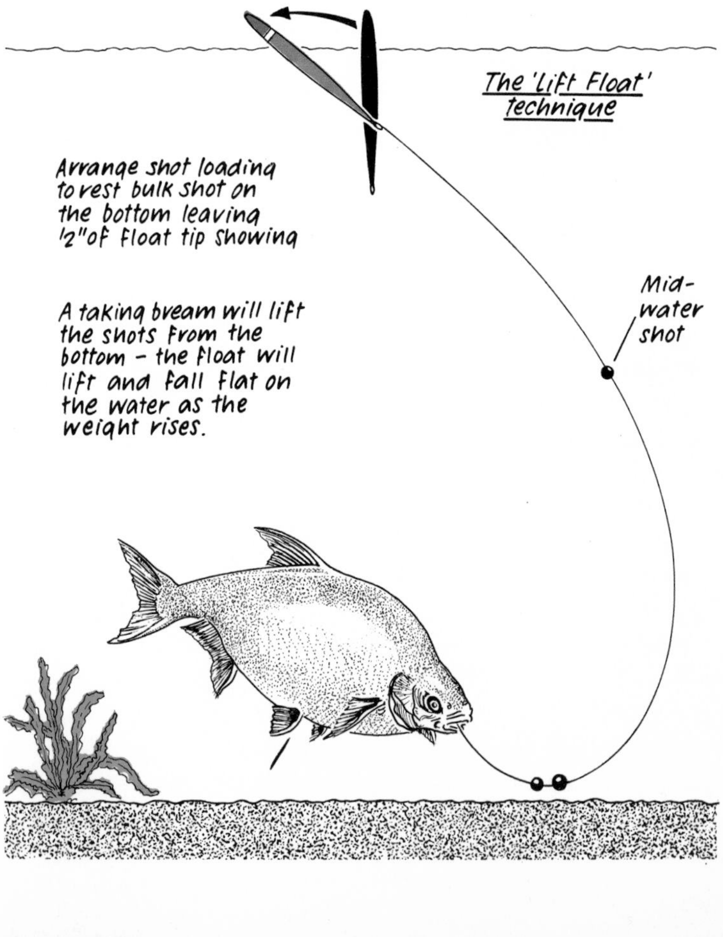

The 'Lift Float' technique
Arrange shot loading to rest bulk shot on the bottom leaving ½" of float tip showing
A taking bream will lift the shots from the bottom - the float will lift and fall flat on the water as the weight rises.
Mid-water shot

Not that the fish is seen in this light by all anglers, for there are those who specialize in their capture to the exclusion of other species.

Fishing tackle for these larger eels should be strong, with a capital S. The fish must be hauled up and away from snags with as much speed as possible. The fish that is allowed to back away from the angler in its characteristically sinuous, almost corkscrew-like, motion will be lost. This is because the eel lodges itself under rocks or roots or simply wraps its tail around a snag. When this happens the angler might just as well pull for a break. In these circumstances there is simply no point in being under-rodded, under-lined or at any other kind of disadvantage.

A stepped-up carp rod is not too heavy, 10 to 12 lb breaking strain line is adequate, flat-forged hooks are right. A fixed-spool reel with the slipping clutch screwed down tight completes the rig.

The most commonly used bait is the lob worm but it is unselective and is as likely to take a small eel as a big one. Small fish are good baits, freshly killed, with the swim bladder pierced so that the fish rests on the bottom. This last step also helps the eels to find the bait since they hunt by scent and will pick up minute traces of blood from long distances. The eels are not fussy concerning the species of bait fish but a 4 ins roach or bleak is about the ideal. The reel line should be threaded through the bait fish from the tail and out

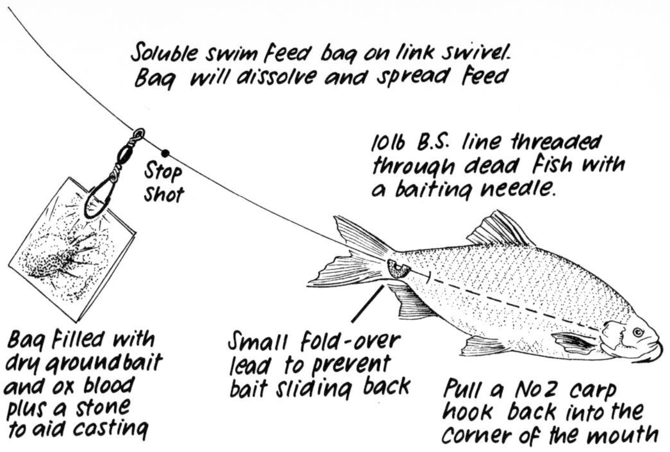
Soluble swim feed bag on link swivel. Bag will dissolve and spread feed
Stop Shot
10lb B.S. line threaded through dead fish with a baiting needle.
Bag filled with dry groundbait and ox blood plus a stone to aid casting
Small fold-over lead to prevent bait sliding back
Pull a No 2 carp hook back into the corner of the mouth

A deadbait leger rig for eel fishing.

of the mouth. A size 2 carp hook is then tied onto the line and is pulled back into the bait fish's mouth so that the barbed, business, end is curved outside the corner of the mouth.

A tiny half-moon lead is folded over the line and crimped into position at the point where the line enters the fish's tail. This prevents the bait from slipping up the line should the eel attempt to eject it. The bait is cast out and the waiting game begins. In daylight hours it is as well to cast as far as possible and this rig can be improved by placing a link swivel 12 ins above the bait. This swivel is used to attach a soluble swim-feeder bag which is loaded with a stone, to aid the casting, holding a mixture of dried groundbait and dried blood. The bag dissolves in a few seconds and explodes a mini scent bomb to attract the eels. This also obviates the need for any lead on the line since the ▶44

An eel from a Fenland drain. Allen Edwards fishing the Great Ouse Relief Channel at Downham Market, Norfolk. Tremendous catches of good eels, fish to 3 lbs and more, can be taken from the many waters that drain the eastern counties and agricultural lands of the south Midlands.

LEATHER CARP
Cyprinus carpio

MIRROR CARP
Cyprinus carpio

WILD CARP
Cyprinus carpio

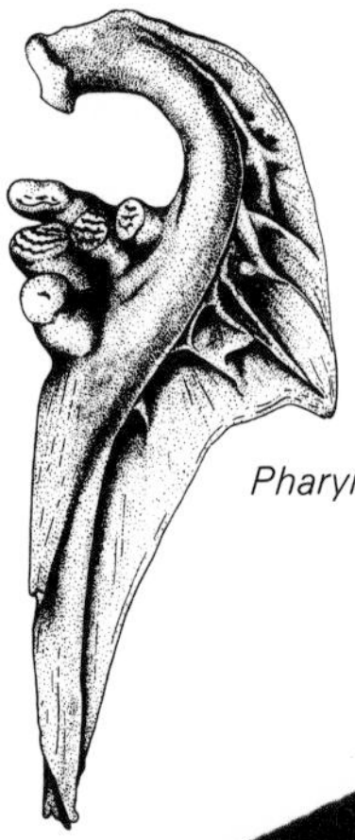

Pharyngeal teeth of the carp.

COMMON CARP
Cyprinus carpio

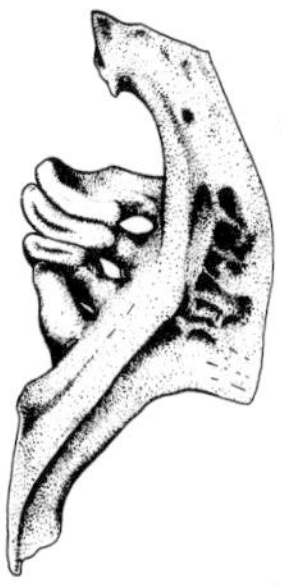

Pharyngeal teeth of the crucian carp.

Pharyngeal teeth of the goldfish.

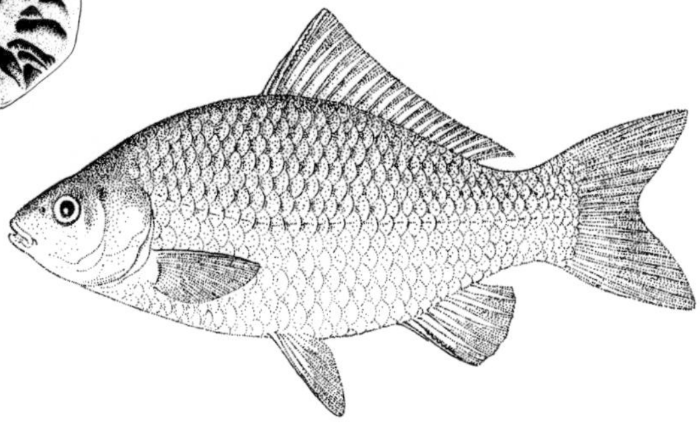

CRUCIAN CARP
Carassius carassius

A small, deep-bodied fish found in a wide variety of waters, although the species is generally associated with the small pond. It resembles the larger carp but has no barbules on the snout. The mouth is small and blunt with the upper jaw slightly longer than the lower. Crucian carp are all fully scaled fish resembling a near relative, the goldfish.

Bait: *Small pellets of bread, tiny worms and a single grub bait are among the best offerings.*

GOLDFISH
Carassius auratus

A carp that exhibits a fantastic variety of both colour and fin arrangement as a result of selective breeding by man. Not really regarded as an angler's fish although there are a number of lakes, particularly in the grounds of Stately Homes, where this species and another, the golden orfe, have grown to considerable sizes. There is some evidence to suggest that goldfish will spawn with crucian carp, the resultant fry reverting to the crucian pelage.

CARP
Cyprinus carpio

A species that dwells in stillwaters of all kinds, ponds, lakes and many man-made situations. The carp will also be found in a number of slow-running rivers and drains. There are three varieties of the carp: the common, a fully scaled fish; the mirror, a fish that has a number of large scales generally found along the lateral line; and the leather variety which has a total absence of scaling. There are also two distinct types of common carp. The huge deep-bodied type that has been introduced to many stillwaters from stock bred on the Continent and a slimmer, more slightly built fish, known as the "Wildie" which is thought to be derived from the original fish brought to Britain by ecclesiastics in the Middle Ages. Carp can grow to 50 lbs or more. The carp has four barbules, two protuberances from above the upper jaw and one at each corner of the mouth. There are no teeth in the jaws but teeth are present on the pharyngeal bones. Carp prefer a soft, muddy bottom in which they find much of their food and into which they can sink to lie during the cold winter months. As the year warms, carp begin to rise in the water seeking their diet of minute invertebrates. During the summer they can be said to be surface feeders.

Bait: *Anglers have taught carp to accept most baits. Worms, maggots and other grubs, bread in all its forms, luncheon meat, tinned animal foods and even boiled potatoes will be taken at some period during the carp season.*

41◀ larger and craftier eels will eject a bait if they feel any drag at all when they first take a bite.

The take, when it comes, is usually in the form of a few marked tugs at the bait, followed by a run. This run should not be impeded in any way. The fish will stop for a few moments and will begin a second run. The strike and instant pressure should be made at this point. The fish should be kept on the move by maintaining even pressure and if the fish can be slithered up the bank, so much the better. Some anglers use an alasticum trace as the link between the link swivel and the bait but I do not advocate this since, especially with the peculiar nature of the eel's struggle, it is apt to kink and break. On the other hand there have been odd times when a pike has picked up the legered bait and the wire cast has saved the day.

The eel is nocturnal but I have had very exciting daylight sessions with them particularly when thunderstorms have been in the offing and I recall one real red letter day when dozens of fish were caught and appeared to be queueing up to take the bait.

For many anglers the biggest problem in eel fishing is how to cope with the fish once it is on the bank. Certainly a blunt instrument should be part of the standard equipment but this should not be aimed at the fish's head. A good, hefty, whack across the vent will stun it, if you can connect. This procedure has the disadvantage of transmitting noisy thumps and vibrations to fish within a large area of the fishing spot. If the eel has taken a bait intended for a nobler species, better, by far, to drop it alive into a sack. It can then be taken along the bank and dealt with where the noise doesn't matter quite so much.

A quicker and cleaner way of despatching the eel is to use a very sharp knife and to cut through the backbone just behind the head. Big eels are formidable opponents and I believe the present British record does not represent anything like the potential. However, this is one record which I am not too anxious to break when I am all on my own at the side of a carp pool, threatened with such a confrontation.

AUTUMN – THE PERCH

A perch of any size looks exactly what he is, bold, boisterous and out-and-out trouble for the small fry which get in his way. There are large shoals of small and medium-sized fish in most waters in the British Isles and these roister their way around, feeding as they go on anything small that moves. Cyclops, mayfly larvae, elvers, small roach, gudgeon and their own kith and kin all come alike as food to the perch.

The shoals are themselves part of the food chain and provide a larder for the pike, zander, big eel and heron. This constant predation whittles away at the numbers forming the shoals so that by the time the perch has reached a size at which it begins to interest the pleasure angler the fools, or just plain unlucky fish, have left the scene.

The perch has only his looks to commend him. His strength is not of the kind that promotes great struggles but the fun is in the chase and no one will deny the bristling good looks of an old stager that has been hooked at last.

The fish may be taken in many ways but the better specimens usually fall to a fish, or simulated fish, bait. Worms, too, have their place in the perch fisher's armoury and many fish fall victim to the humble maggot. These, however, are the accidental catches, the demonstration of the constant readiness of the perch to dart in and mix, or possibly feed upon, the shoal of roach or other bait fish working over the angler's groundbait. It also illustrates perhaps the most effective way of setting about taking the perch when a known holding spot is being fished. Cloud baiting techniques are used to attract and set the small fry feeding in a concentrated area. Sooner or later the perch will swagger in to begin to beat up the smaller fish which, of course, presents the angler with the

There are many ways in which to weigh a specimen fish using a spring balance. Probably the best is to contain fish in a bag or the landing net, weighing everything and then subtracting the weight of the container. Never hang a fish from the hook of the balance by mouth or gill case.

opportunity of presenting his bait to the marauding bully and catch him unawares.

Scaled-down live baiting tackle is used. A minnow or small gudgeon is lip-hooked on a single size 8 or 10 hook which is tied to 3 or 4 lb breaking strain nylon monofilament line. At its simplest this will be fished on straightforward float-fishing tackle with the float taking the form of a mini Fishing Gazette or similar swollen-bodied bung.

The bait will be held down in the swim by shots or fold-over leads on the line about 12 ins above the hook. The disadvantage in using this method is that the bait can be swept, by wind or current action, away from the groundbaited area.

The alternative is to use a paternoster rig in which the lead is placed at the end of the line and the hook link is fished, at right angles to the main line, by means of a three-way swivel. This method can be particularly effective when used in conjunction with a long rod. Small openings in dense patches of lilies may be searched. Resist the temptation to step up line strength in these circumstances since the big, solitary, old stager is wary and will not be fooled by coarse gear!

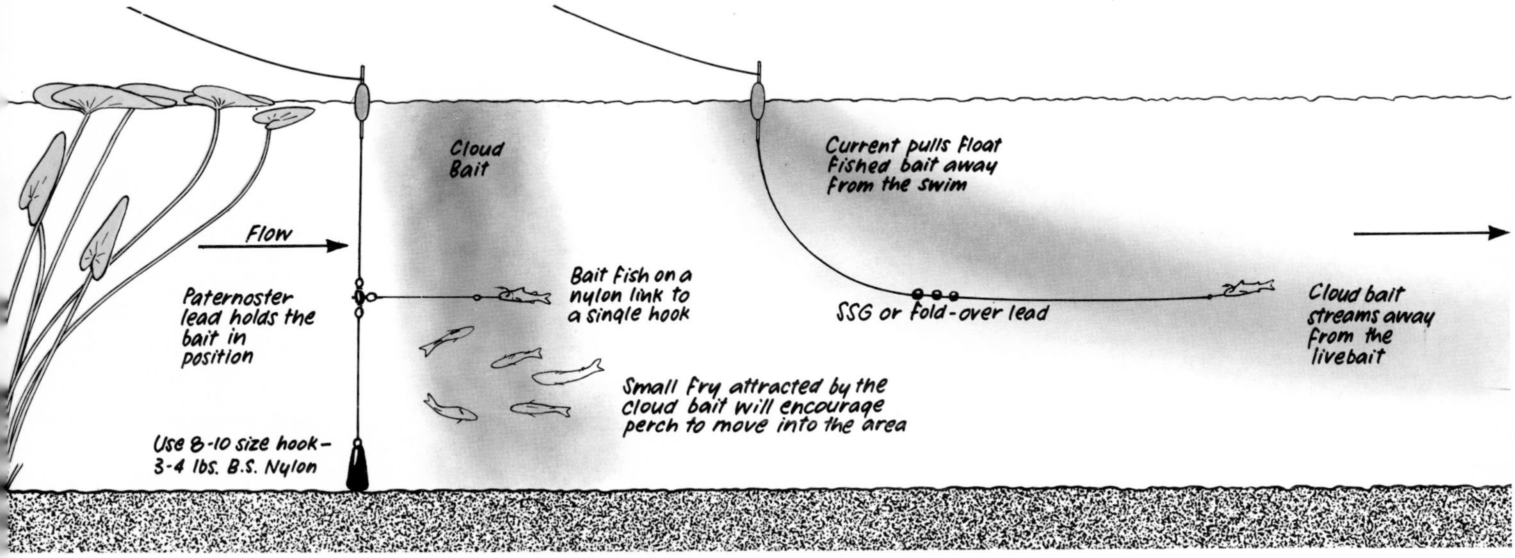
Cloud Bait
Flow
Paternoster lead holds the bait in position
Bait fish on a nylon link to a single hook
Small fry attracted by the cloud bait will encourage perch to move into the area
Use 8-10 size hook - 3-4 lbs. B.S. Nylon
Current pulls float fished bait away from the swim
SSG or fold-over lead
Cloud bait streams away from the livebait

Allen Edwards with a pike from an East Anglian naturalized sandpit. This type of environment has the facility to produce quality still-water fish with a remarkable growth rate, easily maintained by man. There is, however, a delicate balance between fodder fish and predators that must never be disregarded.

Prime predatory species of the British Isles, the pike and perch are in any water for a reason, if only to preserve the balance that nature has set.

It is an education to watch a perch muscling his way into an attack. The fins are erect and the fish appears to be driving in on an out-and-out attack, but often this is not the case.

The fish will dart in but, with outspread pectorals, stop just short of the bait. The eyes will roll, the fins will quiver and the fish will slowly back away for a few inches. This station will be maintained for a few seconds when another false attack may be made, but if the perch has not been made too suspicious it will take the little fish. Fine tackle may not, necessarily, allay all of the perch's suspicions but coarse tackle will, most certainly, fuel them.

The perch is not a strong fighter and heavy lines are not required on this account. For the same reasons the rod need not pack too much power, although I often use a light Avon-style rod when perch fishing since it does give more power to deal with the inevitable marauding jack pike.

A variation on this style of angling may be provided by the use of tiny deadbaits, especially during the months of September or October when large concentrations of fry of that year are being harassed by the perch. The trick is to use a child's fishing net to scoop out a supply of bait. These are often concentrated in the margins, under landing stages or boats. The baits are fished single and dead, hard on the bottom. The perch will pick them up, especially when they are fished in an area where the perch have been seen to be attacking the fry.

On large waters the biggest problem for the angler may well be that of locating good perch. Mature gravel pits, for instance, are perfect waters for the perch. But a lot of fishing time may be wasted in an area which, for reasons which may not be obvious, is devoid of perch. The answer, in these circumstances, is to roam until a dependable holding area is located. Ideal tackle for this operation is a 6 ft light spinning rod with a fixed-spool reel loaded with 5 lb breaking strain line. Small swivels and blade spinners complete the rig. The technique is to wander along casting into each likely looking area, throwing, whenever possible, across known sand and gravel bars.

The perch will respond to a steadier retrieve than the pike and an even pace may be a decided advantage. The angler should stand well back from the water and care should be taken as the lure approaches the bank. The perch will often be seen darting at the rear of the lure, making abortive little attacks.

They often mill about for a few moments when the lure is taken from the water as if asking each other, "Where did the little beast go?" A quick underhand flick to one side of the little shoal will sometimes tempt a wholehearted grab from one of the outsiders. There is no doubt that many anglers see this section of the sport as supreme in perch fishing and it is a lot of fun.

A barbel swim on the River Severn at Arley Ferry.

Fly fishing for perch comes into the same category with the emphasis coming rather on the pleasure provided by the method than on the effectiveness. A 10 ft fibre-glass rod used in conjunction with a No 7 sinking line and a 10 ft leader to 5 lbs point is adequate for this method.

The perch will take nymphs, fished in a slow sink and draw manner, or hair-winged streamer flies worked to simulate a small fish. The method suffers, as does the use of worm, from the fact that it is as likely to take tiny perch as it is good ones. On balance, therefore, it is probably better to use the spinning rod and fly

rod to locate the shoal of perch and to attempt to lure the big fish by using lob worms or small fish in that area.

One final word of warning on the perch. The dorsal spines and the sharp edge of the gill cover can inflict a nasty wound if the fish is not handled with care. It is a lot less than sensible to spend time plotting the downfall of a crafty old perch if, in the end, it is allowed to draw blood. Especially if it is yours.

AUTUMN – THE BARBEL

If one word could be used to sum up the characteristics of the barbel it would be "strength". One word will not, of course, do because the fish has a lot more going for it than strength alone. It has a certain tenacity which will not allow it to give up the struggle without the ultimate in angler-versus-fish contests. It will, if allowed to, exhaust itself almost to death before being towed over the rim of a landing net.

The barbel will bore, head down and tail thrumming, against the line in sheer pig-headed determination not to give in. It is small wonder, then, that the fish is popular with pleasure anglers and, since its distribution is increasing, this popularity will build.

The fish is found in the Yorkshire Derwent, Nidd, Wharfe and Swale, and it is making a comeback in the Trent. It is present in the Nene, Bristol Avon, Hampshire Avon, Dorset Stour and the Thames, as well as being found in many of their tributary streams.

The population is on the increase in the Severn and the prospects for anglers anxious to tangle with the barbel are good. The fish thrives in waters that are attractive to most pleasure anglers. Strong flows, glides and ripples suit it as well as the stronger conditions of weir pools. Since it is using its strength constantly to hold position in the flow, it is small wonder that it should give such good account of itself when hooked. The fish are adapted to feed principally on the bed of the river and they hug this tightly for much of the time, allowing their taste and scent organs, the barbules, to advise them of items of food which are theirs for the sucking up. Barbel feed in fairly compact shoals and they resemble a good, head-down scrum of Irish rugby forwards with the outside forward occasionally dropping back to add his weight to the back of the scrum.

It is this basic, scrum down, feeding pattern that sets the pattern for most anglers' attack on the barbel. This has varied little over the years for even in the old days the need was recognized to concentrate the fish in one spot and to set them feeding on one type of bait so that the angler's job would become that much more simple. Old-timers used to accomplish this by lavish pre-baiting schedules, feeding many hundreds of lobworms into Thames weirpools before fishing them seriously. There are more anglers pounding in more

In a channel between slabs of jagged rock a barbel is hooked and swimming powerfully up and downstream. Gradual pressure and side strain bring this fish to the net. Luncheon meat is the bait; the grass stalk keeps it on the hook in a strong current.

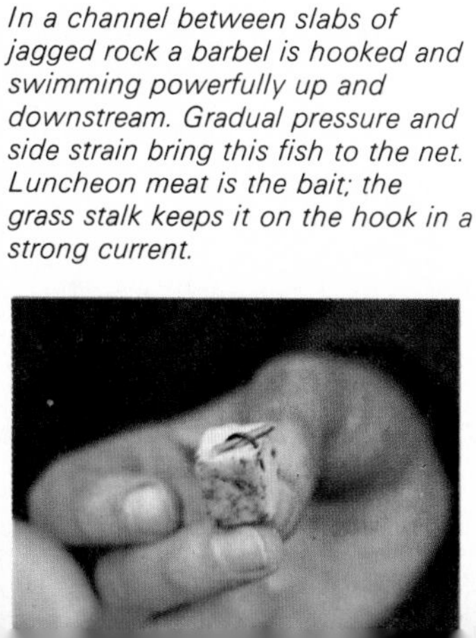

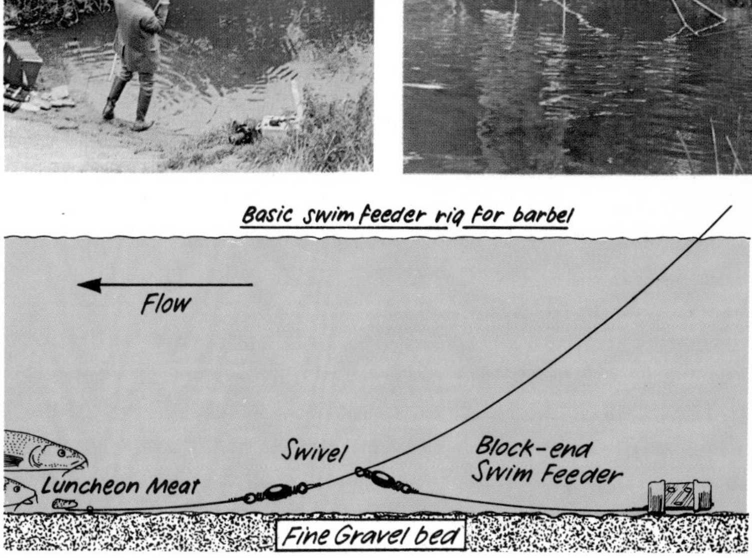

groundbait now so that such rituals are rarely called for, although a spot which is not often fished might pay well for such specialist attention.

Worms used to be the bait for barbel fishing. They are still good today but the less expensive and more readily available maggots and cereal baits, like hemp seed, are more in the modern angler's line. It matters not since the barbel's taste is catholic, but groundbaiting while fishing is very important. If there is one thing that emphasizes the importance of this technique it is the dependence placed by many anglers upon the use of the swim feeder when barbel fishing. There is no doubt that the "feeder" meets all of the requirements of successful groundbaiting for the barbel. Filled with a sample of the hookbait they allow a steady trickle of tempting morsels to float straight down current to where the barbel shoal is foraging. The fish move up the stream to meet this obliging food supply and, sooner or later, come across the angler's bait. The advantages over normal groundbaiting methods are that there is no guesswork concerning the strength of the current or, indeed, concerning the consistency of the groundbait. The swim feeder, however, poses its own problems, mainly on the strength of line to be used and on the type of rod. Many anglers tend to step up their line strength and to fish with rods sold as leger rods at between 10 and 11 ft in length. I prefer to stick to the Avon Perfection or Winfield Long-trotter style of rod, finding that the length at 12 ft and the softer type of action makes a better cushion for the strike against the swim feeder and the fish. It also enables me to use line of around 5 to 6 lbs breaking strain – and even lighter where the fish run small.

The other benefit when using these types of rods is the ease with which a change can be made to float fishing. These rods are ideal for trotting on long swims of streamy water. Swim feeders, like everything else in this modern world, become more sophisticated but they all do the same job.

At their simplest there are two types, the block-ended and the open-ended. The block-ended is ideal for use with maggots since they allow the bait to come out in a steady stream. Open-ended feeders are better for use with groundbait of stiff consistency containing samples of the hookbait. Examples of this are chopped worms and bread bait or ordinary groundbait and hemp seed or tares. Yet another example is a mixture of groundbait containing cat or dog food. This would be used in conjunction with a hookbait of paste containing the animal food. All of which leads us to the question of hooks and hookbaits. My own preference for hooks, for barbel fishing, is for flat-forged "in line" straight-eyed hooks. These can be bought with eyes that are no larger than a spade end hook, size for size, and will not let the angler down. They can be tied direct to the reel line. On the question of hookbaits a list would be endless but there are clear favourites. Bread baits, flake and paste, luncheon meat, sausages, worms, cheese, maggots and casters all have their adherents. On a hard-fished water, like much of the Severn, it pays to find out what most of the other anglers are using at a given period. The same could, I suppose, be said of the Thames. What is as important is tailoring the size of the hook to the size of the bait. A good bait of sausage needs a hook of around the number 2 size, whereas a single caster might be fished on a size 16. Bread flake and chunks of cheese will probably call for an 8 or 10 but, in each instance, it is as well to sharpen the hook before fishing.

The only item of tackle so far not discussed is the reel and for legering I use only the fixed spool. This is because the slipping clutch is set against the first carthorse run of the barbel and this adjustment can be finely tuned after the first fish. For long-trotting, the centre pin comes into its own. The basic requirements for float fishing for the barbel are much the same as those for chub fishing. A good Avon-style float capable of carrying some sizeable leads is required but it is important to ensure that the bait is well and truly down

Barbel from the River Severn below Arley. The rapidly growing barbel population in the river is a result of a stocking by Angling Times.

in the swim. Worm and maggot baits are comparatively easy to get down but bread flake requires to be fished well over-depth and held back just slightly to ensure correct presentation to the barbel.

The barbel gives very good value to the pleasure angler but, too often, it receives scant consideration from the captor. Large catches of small- and medium-sized fish are crammed, willy nilly, into keepnets which are too small or which are made of material which is too rank. The third ray of the barbel's dorsal becomes entangled in the mesh of the net and the fish suffers damage. The barbel deserves better treatment than this and the largest possible net, preferably knotless, should be used to retain the catch. A fish which bites, in most conditions, boldly and which always fights to the limit of its endurance cannot stand the additional hazard of being cooped up for long periods so it is as well to empty the keep net frequently once the fish are on an even keel. It is, perhaps, the least that can be done for the fish whose capture is such a pleasure.

EARLY WINTER – THE ZANDER

To have written about the zander a decade ago would have been regarded as novel, perhaps even fanciful. It is true that the fish was established in a few land-locked waters but its presence was very much a fringe benefit for the local angler who was in the know. This situation has turned around to the extent that many pleasure anglers now make regular pilgrimages to the Fenlands not only for the superb pike fishing but to get to grips with the zander.

The fish were introduced to the Great Ouse Relief Channel in 1963, since when they have spread into the Great Ouse itself, the Old Bedford river, the Delph and the cut-off Channel. There is no doubt that the zander is still colonizing waters and there seems every likelihood that it will eventually become established across much of the southern part of the country. To say that this is regarded by many as a mixed blessing is to understate the case. The fish is an out-and-out predator and in the first full flush of a population explosion it will decimate the fry and immature second and third year stages of a fishery's stocks of fodder fish. This causes grief to perhaps the most vociferous section of the angling scene, the competition angler, since one of his techniques has been to build up a big weight by concentrating on catching many small fish. It is safe to say, then, that the matchmen are not happy about the introduction. Many pleasure anglers, too, have reservations on the subject but their main concern is centred on the long-term effect on the stocks of native pike and the shoals of middle-weight bream. It is, perhaps, too early to make judgments on these questions but it does look as though the pike are holding their own and mature fodder fish still appear to be abundant. The talk matters not, for the zander are here to stay and the wise pleasure angler will treat their presence as an opportunity rather than as a penalty to be endured.

The fish feeds best in dull light conditions and will take well in coloured water, which gives the pointer to

The zander feeds best in dull coloured water conditions. It will take live and deadbaits fished at all depths but is wary of line drag and will drop a bait if it feels any resistance to its attack. Small hooks are a necessity. Zander are present in Norfolk waters, into which they were introduced, and are rapidly spreading to other East Anglian rivers and land drains.

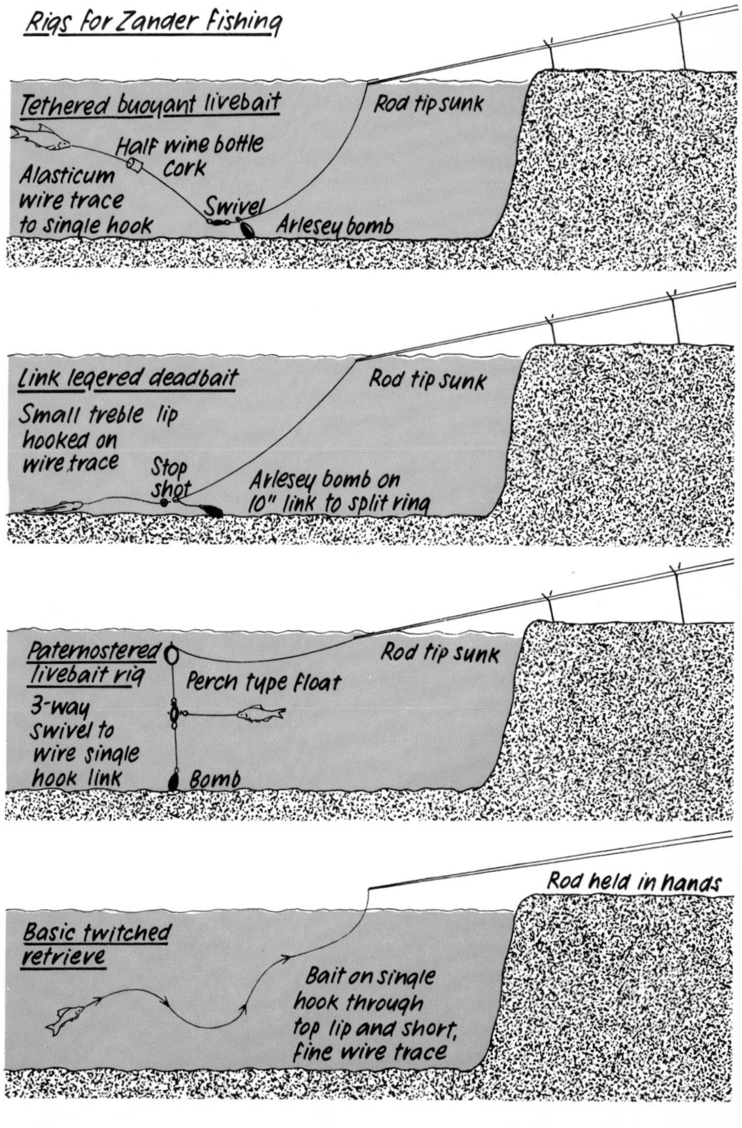

the angler as to whether or not to concentrate on the zander. If the water is clear, and light conditions are on the bright side, the choice could be to go for the pike. Choice there should be, for the zander do not run to the same heavy weights as the pike and a scaling down of tackle may be made with both safety and advantage. This is because the zander is quick to drop a bait if it feels tension, and lighter-running line and terminal rigs will produce more fruitful runs. A good combination is a carp rod, a fixed-spool reel loaded with 6 lb breaking strain line and the terminal tackle should be based upon an alasticum trace to combat the needle-sharp teeth of the fish. The bait must, of course, be a fish of some sort. Fish, live or dead, is a matter of individual preference for the angler but deadbaits appear to be as good as live ones in attracting the feeding zander.

The fish will feed at all levels in the water so it pays not to become too hooked upon one method of angling. Nevertheless, deadbaits legered just slightly off the bottom appear to be as effective as any in producing strikes and it often pays to use a razor blade to slit the bait so that it exudes a scent.

A favourite rig of mine is the 6 lb strain running line taken through the eye of an Arlesey bomb and stopped with a swivel. The bomb is chosen to suit conditions of water flow but it should always be as light as possible so that when the rod tip is lifted the bomb will be moved downstream for a few feet. A 12 ins long trace of monofilament is then joined to the swivel and threaded through a section of an ordinary wine bottle cork to another swivel. To this is joined the single strand alasticum trace onto which two size 12 or 8 treble hooks are placed, around 3 ins apart. The deadbait is hooked through the lips and on the flank towards the tail with the bait being kept straight. Some anglers maintain that this is incorrect and that the bait should be hooked through the wrist of the tail first. I believe that it matters little anyway since the zander is usually moving pretty fast, often in competition with fellow members of a pack, and the take is very much a smash-and-grab affair. The fish just doesn't have the time to carry out an inspection of the rig. This is not to say that the moment of attack is not important, for the fish will drop the bait instantly if it becomes aware of drag. For this reason I prefer to sink the rod tip well into the water and to use a butt indicator, striking at the first sign of a bite.

Variations in rig are numerous. Straightforward float live baiting will take a share of fish. Link legering with live or freshly killed baits hard on the bottom will work. Very slow twitch-retrieving along the bottom produces fish. Baits in the 2 to 4 ozs category are ideal, with roach and dace figuring high in the list of favourites. Even this I believe to be simply a matter of the greater availability of these fish and that the zander

Pharyngeal teeth of the bream.

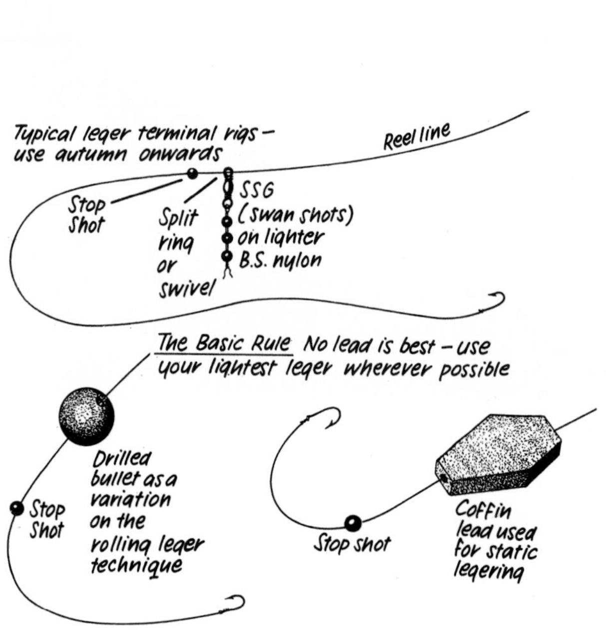

BRONZE OR COMMON BREAM

Abramis brama

A deep, slab-sided fish of sluggish rivers and most stillwaters. The species predominates in the Midlands and South of England and throughout Ireland. The bronze bream has a small mouth but a voracious appetite. Living and moving in shoals, these fish can rapidly denude an underwater area of feed. Consequently the fish can be hard to find in a water. Anglers have to rely on heavy ground-baiting intended to draw the bream toward the angling pitch. The bronze bream is an awkward fish, its body lacks a smooth, rounded, shape to the curves. They are angular and this feature becomes more pronounced as the bream gets older and larger. The body is keeled between the pelvic and anal fin. Fish of 5 lbs are common, especially in Ireland, and the species certainly attains weights of 15 lbs or more.

Bait: *Bread baits, worms and most grubs.*

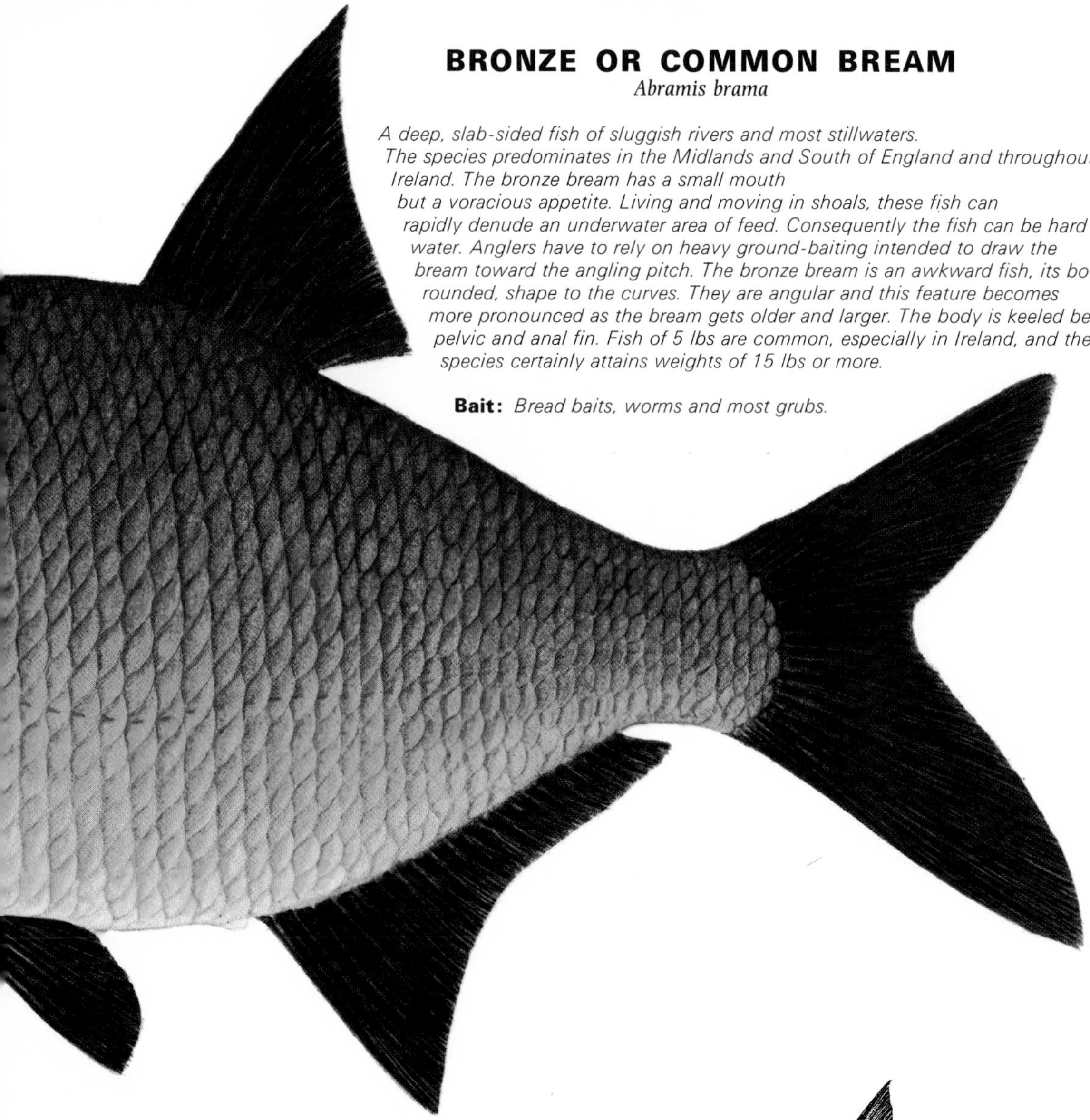

Pharyngeal teeth of the silver bream.

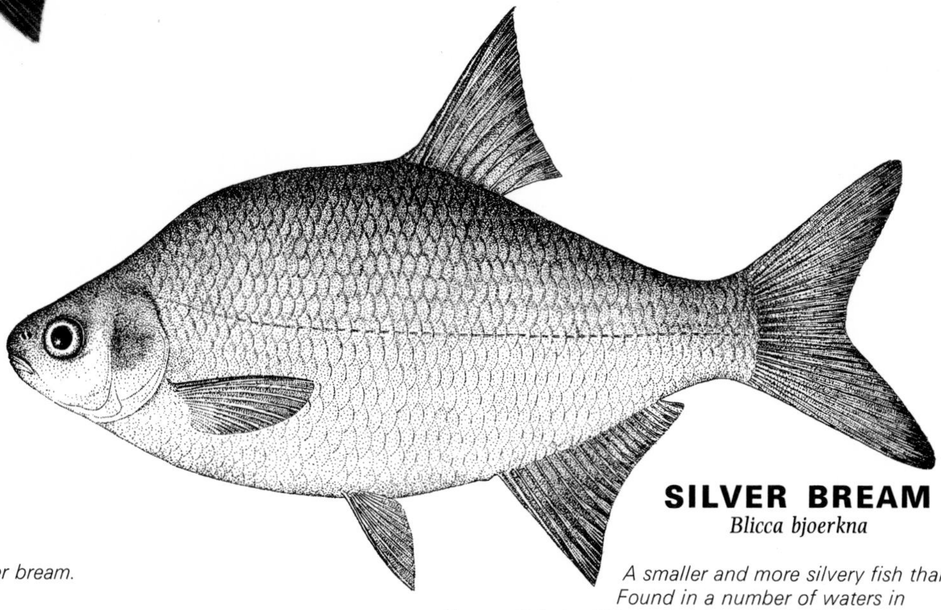

SILVER BREAM

Blicca bjoerkna

A smaller and more silvery fish than its relative. Found in a number of waters in Eastern Britain. Although slab-sided, its body curves are more rounded and gentle than the bronze variety. Not a fish that groups into big shoals, although the feeding pattern is similar. A silver bream of 1 lb is regarded as a specimen.

Bait: *As for the bronze bream.*

will take any small fish whenever it is on the hunt.

The zander, then, is with us for good. It will, inevitably, attract its adherents who will raise its capture into a great cult scene. It will also produce human enemies and probably become the fish that many anglers love to hate. Taken as a simple addition to the pleasure angler's list of predatory species it will, I believe, prove to be of benefit.

AUTUMN – THE GUDGEON, RUFFE AND BLEAK

Ask any non-angler for his impressions of an angler and you will get one of two responses. Some will trot out the old "a worm at one end and a fool at the other" routine. Most will deliver the semi-obligatory "I don't know where you get the patience" bit or the "I don't know how you can sit there for hours in the rain catching nothing" speech. In almost all cases the reply will end on a note of kindly condescension along the lines that, after all, it is the contemplative man's recreation.

The angler has painted a picture of a world-weary individual being anaesthetized by his surroundings and his angling activities. The non-angler has bought it and hung it on permanent exhibition in the galleries of his mind. They are wrong, of course, since the picture is a fake in many respects. The pleasure angler is rarely rendered insensible by his sport. Indeed, many anglers turn more brain power on to their fishing than towards the earning of their daily bread. The hours flash by as the angler poses himself innumerable questions concerning bait presentation, water flow, weather conditions, tackle strengths, anything that affects his prospects for sport. Some anglers ask and answer these questions by instinct and are called lucky by their fellows. Others build up a computer bank of experience and take their share of fish.

Fishing for the pleasure angler is a constant effort involving thought and action but there is a little group of fish whose capture has always been recognized as providing the opportunity for the angler's mind to wander. The gudgeon, for instance, was once the published reason for family outings on the River Thames. The picnic basket was probably an equal attraction, together with the sheer pleasure of fishing from a punt moored across the current. Judicious groundbaiting and the raking of the bottom by the boatman assured a steadily feeding shoal and the fishing was a pleasure.

Times have changed, but the shoals of gudgeon still abound and can be taken by tripping small worms or maggots along the bottom of a gravel-bedded swim. The tackle should be scaled right down with the float so shotted that just the tip is above the water line. The raking of the bottom is still a good ploy and a simple

1

2

method of creating this effect is to wade the shallows, stirring up the gravel and silt by shuffling the feet from time to time. The soporific aspect of the fun is there. It really does not matter if a fish is missed. There is no doubt that the mind of the thinking angler will wander. He might, for instance, have difficulty in finding a clear patch of gravel from which to operate. He might have to clear for himself a patch of blanket weed which has been multiplying as the result of the over-enrichment of the water by sewage effluents and the washing of too liberal applications of fertilizers on the neighbouring farm lands. He might, if he is fishing the Severn or Trent, consider the report of the Water Quality Advisory Panel of the Severn-Trent Water Authority on the state of sewage disposal arrangements when they began operations on 1st April 1974.

Fishing for chub on the River Trent with a silver-bodied minnow fly. The fast water below the weir creates an ideal habitat for small fry that fall to the marauding chub and occasional pike.

Allen's chub minnow fly, dressed on a long-shanked hook. Tie on the peacock hurl with black tying silk then thread on the mylar tubing. Make fast with a whip finish. Tie down the mylar at the front of the hook and dub on a collar of red fluorescent wool. Complete dressing with a head of black chenille.

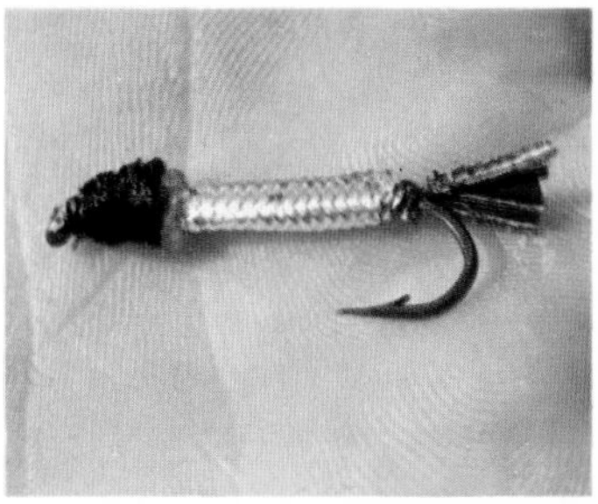

3

4

1 *Allen Edwards trotting down the near bank on the Trent. Clumps of streamer weed provide ideal habitat for the small chub.*

2 *It can be awkward to land your fish and turn to the keep net with such steep and undercut banks. But success with the chub so often depends on being down low to the water and off the skyline.*

3 *The long stretch to a chub hooked on fly. Fish take well on the artificial in the streamy water below the shingle bank.*

4 *A typical-sized chub from the middle reaches of the River Trent. The larger fish seem to be moving away as the barbel gain a hold in cleaner stretches of the water.*

He might miss the odd gudgeon or two while he thinks on the fact that the panel reported that nearly 300 of the 700 sewage works in the area produced unsatisfactory effluents based upon the conditions of consent given by the former river authorities.

He might miss the odd tremble of the float when he recalls that a number of river authority consents for major discharges contained quality conditions geared to the capability of the sewage works and not to the requirements of the receiving stream.

The fishing is an easy-going concern and he might stop altogether for a few moments to consider that, on that basis, 43 per cent of the sewage works discharging 66 per cent of a daily volume of sewage effluent, 291 million gallons would be classed as unsatisfactory. The gudgeon, of course, do not care. They do live in a river like the Trent which the Water Authority, using Department of the Environment classification standards, calls doubtful. They will continue to feed while the angler shuffles his feet to keep the tasty morsels floating downstream to the feeding fish. The detergent-like odour which comes from the river as the result of his shufflings will be recognized as the legacy of pollutions some 20 or 30 miles upstream where the classification is poor or bad. The catch may be built up whilst the angler ponders the fact that an authority which has called for £100 million per year for 10 years to enable it to act upon these problems has had the 1975/76 capital expenditure cut from £92·6 million to £83·7 million . . .!

Another little fish which turns up in the catches of the pleasure angler, from time to time, is the ruffe. ▶56

MOUNTAIN LAKE : *very deep, vegetation poor and only marginal water clear. Cold except in uppermost layer near surface.*

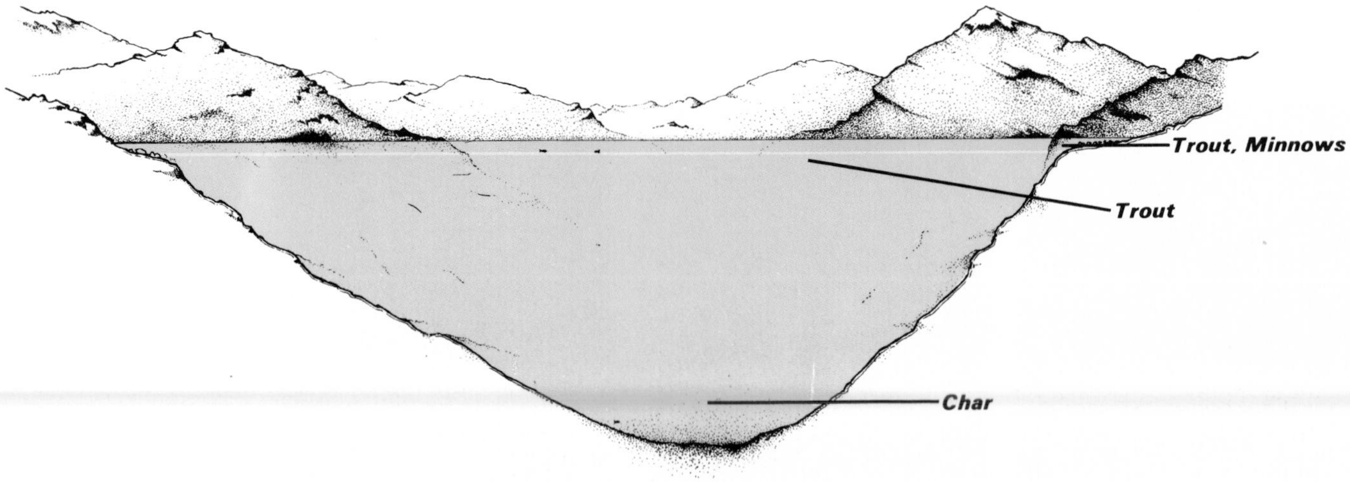
Trout, Minnows
Trout
Char

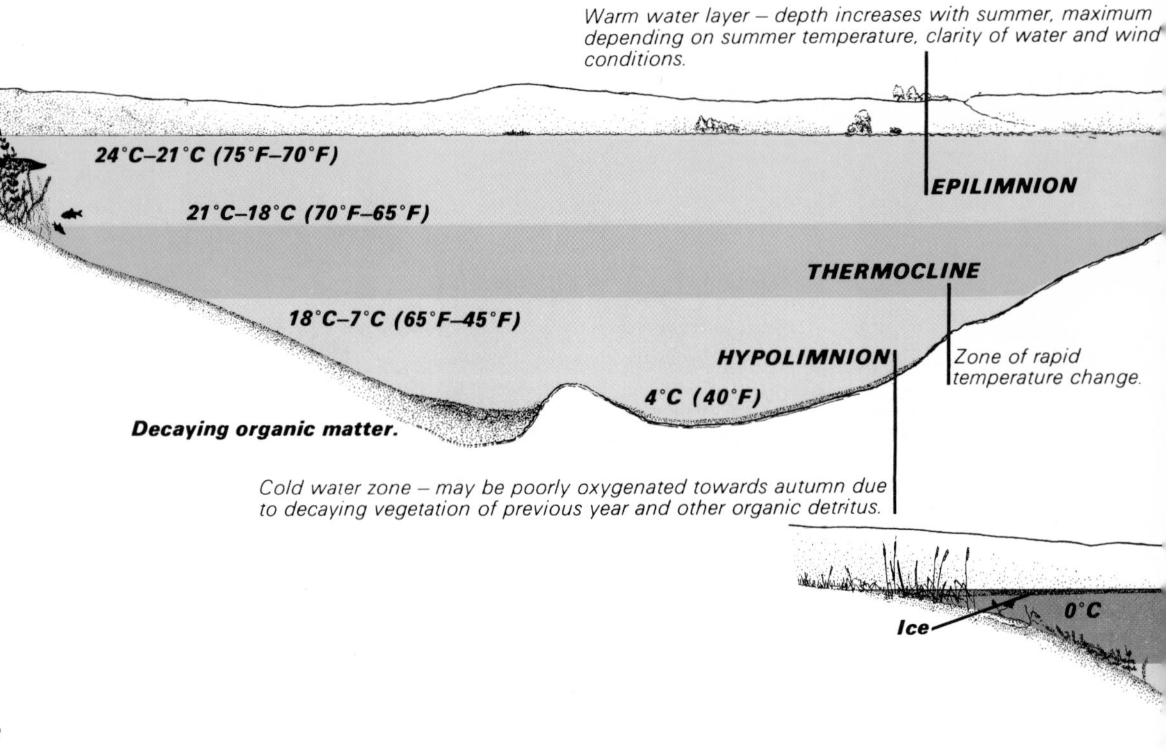
Warm water layer – depth increases with summer, maximum depending on summer temperature, clarity of water and wind conditions.
24°C–21°C (75°F–70°F)
EPILIMNION
21°C–18°C (70°F–65°F)
THERMOCLINE
18°C–7°C (65°F–45°F)
HYPOLIMNION
Zone of rapid temperature change.
4°C (40°F)
Decaying organic matter.
Cold water zone – may be poorly oxygenated towards autumn due to decaying vegetation of previous year and other organic detritus.
0°C
Ice

This chart deals with the natural stillwater areas in Britain. These consist of mountain tarns or corries, mountain lakes (in both late summer and mid-winter conditions) and lowland ponds. Where the bands on the pools and lakes shown are of the same colour, then the same temperatures apply. For example, the area of warm water in mountain lakes, lowland lakes in late summer and lowland ponds in late summer are coloured the same. Of course, the warm water depth varies considerably. In the high mountain tarns there is no warm water level.

By reading the chart in this way you will get a quick idea of the life and ecology of these waters.

Lowland pond : *shallow, water warm in late summer when there may be an oxygen deficiency throughout. Water turbid.*

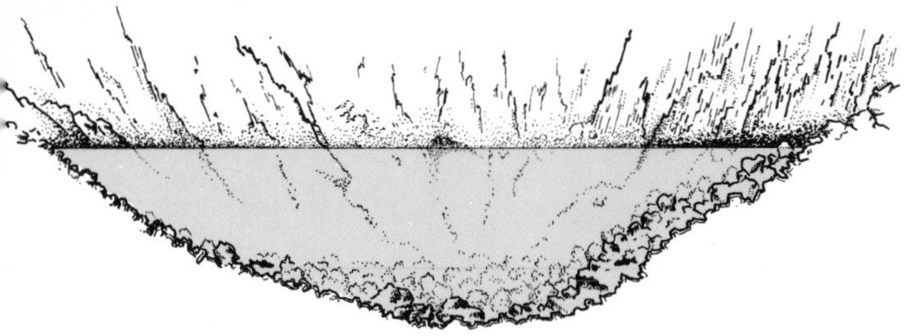

MOUNTAIN TARN OR CORRIE LAKE: *always cold, vegetation and other life is very poor. There may be small trout and char if the water is deep enough to withstand freezing to base.*

1

2

3

Some of the creatures that contribute to the fish life-support system.

1. *The water louse,* Asellus aquaticus, *found in most slow-running and stillwaters. Feeds on decaying material related to marine crustaceans on the bottom of streams and ponds.*

2. *A water beetle larva, one of the many species of carnivorous beetles found during the warmer months in freshwater.*

3. *Snails and their eggs are a source of food for many fish species. The Great Pond snail,* Limnaea stagnalis, *and ramshorn snail,* Planorbis planorbis, *with their spawn.*

LOWLAND LAKE: *vegetation marginal and rich.*

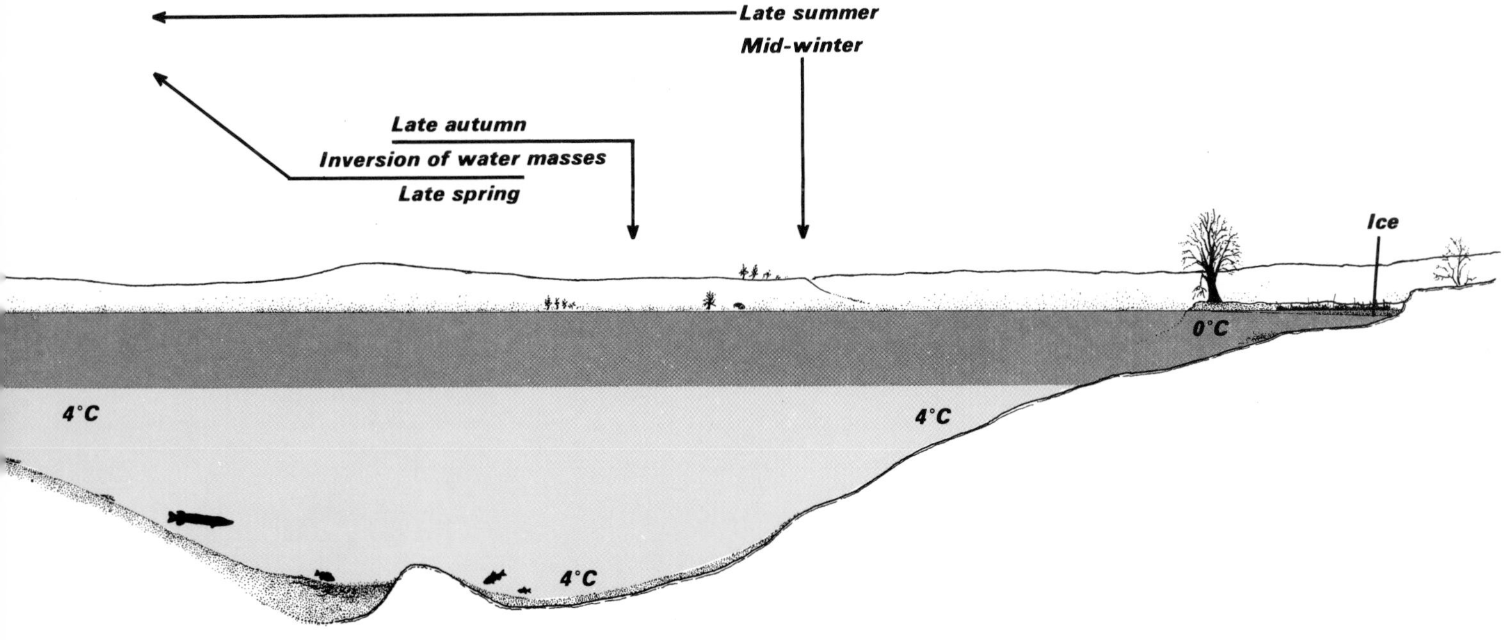

53◀ He is like the fragile ghost of a perch who demonstrates his worldliness by pinching the worm or maggot bait intended for other fish. He rewards the captor with a view of his violet eyes and, to the unwary, a good gash or two on the hand from the spines on the opercular bones. The fish is greedy and does not seem to be affected by the disappearance of its fellows from the shoal.

Ruffe fishing is a trauma-free affair with the bites bold and clear, impossible to miss. There is no pressure and the thinking angler has time enough to consider the national situation of over-abstraction of water from the land, of the shrinking streams and of the sizeable rivers which have been lost to angling in the last 20 years. The odd fish will be missed as the significance of the whole problem sinks in.

More anglers are appearing on the scene with each successive season while the available fishing shrinks. Fish or no fish, the contemplative angler cannot afford to be complacent about his sport.

No discussion of the pleasure angler's small fish quarry would be complete without a mention of the bleak. This common fish is regarded by many as an out-and-out nuisance, swarming to attack the caster or maggot, flake or paste intended for the roach, dace or rudd. There are times, however, when the pleasure angler needs to take a bleak or two for live or deadbait and there can hardly be a better one for most predators.

Once again the tackle should be scaled right down to the finest of lines, the most sensitive of floats and the smallest of hooks. The fish is easily gathered into a surface feeding shoal by the use of cloud groundbait and maggots or casters. There can be a sort of repetitive pleasure in building up a catch of these little fish.

The bleak, in a way, symbolize the ever-growing body of British pleasure anglers. They are a swarming, restless gathering. They are mobile and constantly trying to get into what they believe is the action. Taken singly they have a distinction and attractiveness of their own. They emanate life.

The angler, unlike the bleak, can affect his own environment. He is doing this at the moment with a massive display of indifference but time is running out. For how much longer will we be able to say that fishing has been a pleasure?

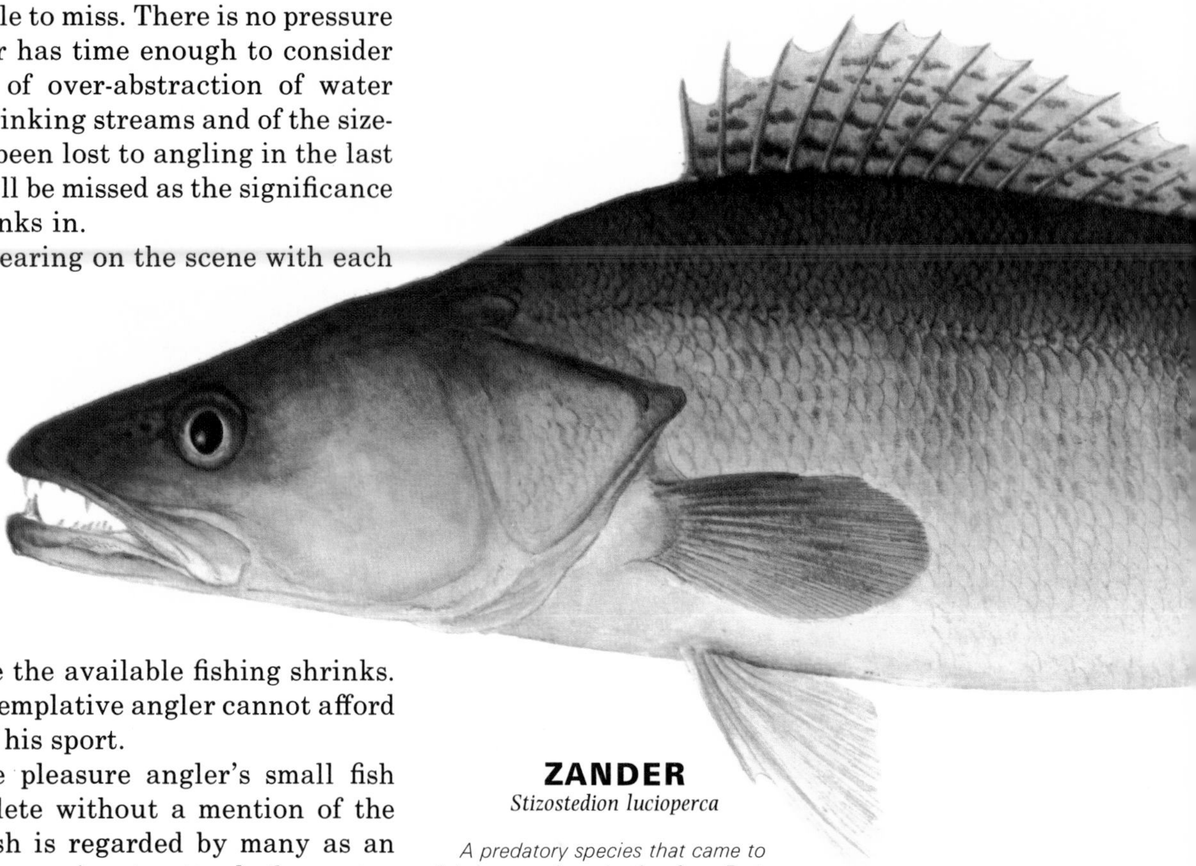

ZANDER
Stizostedion lucioperca

A predatory species that came to Britain as an introduction from Eastern Europe. The zander has some of the appearance of both the pike and perch, indeed some anglers refer to it by the species couplet pike-perch, but it is not a relative of either. The first dorsal fin is composed of sharp spikes with the second formed of soft rays. Some fish exhibit broad, dark, vertical bars along the flanks. The species grows to huge weights in Europe but a fish of 10 lbs is good for the East Anglian waters throughout which it is quickly spreading.

Bait: *Live fish or deadbaits that are worked to attract the fish. Small artificial spinning lures are fished by Continental anglers with great success.*

RUFFE OR POPE
Gymnocephalus cernua

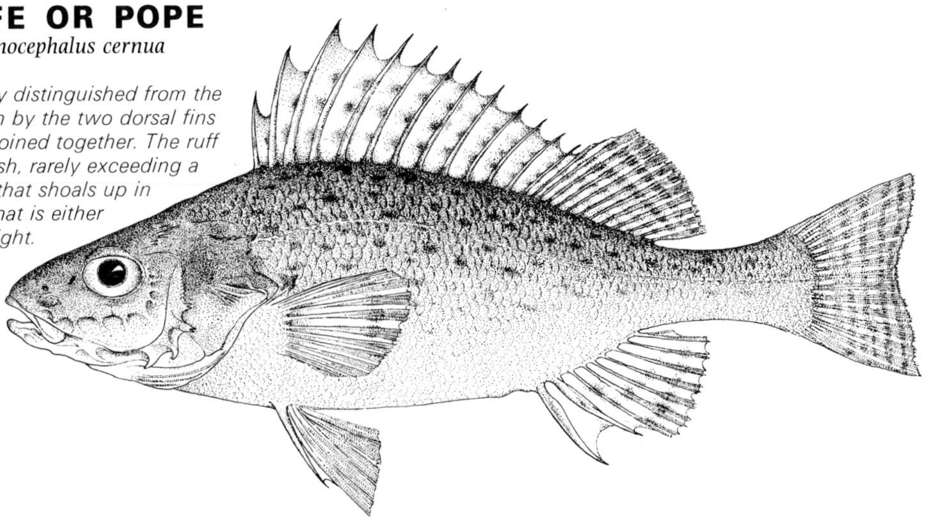

Can be easily distinguished from the perch by the two dorsal fins that are virtually joined together. The ruff is a small fish, rarely exceeding a few ounces in weight, that shoals up in deepish water that is either coloured or shaded from direct light.

Bait: *Small worms, fry and insect larvae.*

PERCH
Perca fluviatilis

A striking predatory species, possessing two dorsal fins that are separated. The first with 14 stiff spines and the second with one or two short spines followed by 14 soft rays. Often there are one or two black spots on the base of the first dorsal fin. Perch are found in practically every water in the British Isles. They have a preference for the slow-running stretches on rivers and streams, preferably where there is cover from over-hanging trees and banks. The species adopts a more brilliant coloration at the spawning season. Perch do not grow to massive weights. A fish of 4 lbs is regarded as a superb specimen.

Bait: *Almost anything, insects, freshwater shellfish, worms, grub baits and bread. Perch will take an artificial fly and many forms of spinning lure.*

Ivan Marks/Coarse fishing – the match fisherman

Coarse fishing has two distinct attractions for the fisherman across the broad spectrum of water types and species. Most freshwater anglers take up the sport as pleasure anglers, getting out into the open for a variety of reasons. Many claim there is a therapeutic value in what they do; others would say that anglers are fulfilling the latent hunting instinct that is said to lie in all of us.

Some fishermen, having enjoyed the success of catching coarse fish in a number of different situations, look for something else – an extension, in a sense, of their skills in a competitive way. Whereas the pleasure angler pits his skills and wits against fish on a personal basis, the match angler seeks to expend additional efforts against the skills of his fellow anglers. Let us dispose of one misconception immediately. Matchmen do not fish for money. It is handy to have and there is undoubted pride in winning, but any angler who expects to earn a large part of his living as a match angler is doomed to worse than breadline poverty. This aspect of the sport is both expensive and hard work. A tremendous amount of unseen preparation goes into the build-up to any match. Whole seasons of fishing on many waters and in all kinds of weather conditions are needed before one's standard of fishing ability rises to the pitch where an angler can expect to be among the winners – and much will also depend on the luck attached to drawing the right peg on the water.

What is the motivation that drives the matchman on? Simply, it is the urge to excel, to be a good competitor and even to be the top competitor. There is not one matchman worth his salt who does not long to be the best on the river, or the man who can *read the conditions* of the day. Match angling brings such hard personal disciplines of time, practice and preparation only to find that the draw, on a swim that would be ignored by the pleasure angler, is not capable of producing the weight of fish that will bring a chance of getting among the top catches.

The more relaxed pleasure angler has the choice of pitches, friends to fish with, and a choice of the conditions that he will fish in. The matchman cannot choose his fishing situation. The draw, from the hat, will decide his pitch and he will have to make the best of it. This, I believe, makes him a better angler, an all-rounder who has to rely on his own ability to bring success, rather than on a known concentration of fish available in the swim.

The mental picture of a cash-oriented angler, driving himself in an all-out bid to win by sheer speed of hooking and re-baiting for a never-ending sequence of tiny fish is far from the truth. Where practical, match fishing is a quest for big fish. Each river, each variable in wind, water and weather condition will pose its own problems: either because the conditions make fish

Ivan Marks fishing the Lawden Masters' Championship at Evesham, on the Avo

difficult to catch, when it is impossible to present a bait as the fish expect to find it, or when fish, in the swim, are not feeding and have to be tempted into grabbing something they do not really want. The fishing style must match the mood of the fish, so skill in presentation is the first essential. The skill of angling judgment must then be applied. This is the ability to decipher conditions and to know exactly what is right to do.

No matchman wins consistently without his share of luck, but so many expert anglers make their own "luck". Where one man misses two bites out of ten and never quite gets into the winning numbers, another will miss only one bite in ten because he followed an instinct, rather than a positive indication of a bite. And he wins the match. This may be luck or an awareness of what ought to be happening in the swim.

Top quality bait and its preparation is of paramount importance. So is a good memory, for fishing is ever changing. Last year's winning style may be of little assistance unless it can be related to this year's conditions. Continually successful anglers are those who can accurately recall the previous years' cycle of events, and can anticipate that today is the day for fishing tight under the rod top because the conditions determine that big fish will not feed, whereas 8 lbs weight of small fish will win a place in the frame.

FITNESS AND THE ANGLER

In angling, physical fitness is essential and impeccable eyesight a primary requirement. Most match anglers will be at their peak performance around 30 to 40 years of age. By that time they have amassed the knowledge to sum up conditions quickly. Later in life, as the eyesight starts to lose its efficiency, opportunities begin to slip away. Extra knowledge and experience may help to remedy this sight deficiency, but the older the angler the more difficult it becomes for him to win. Match angling is a hard, unyielding business calling for strength of character and the will to win. Its challenge is enormous; its popularity grows.

Each matchman chooses his own type of sport and angling endeavour. Some will specialize, others will

BARBEL
Barbus barbus

A fish of running water with a long, slender, but powerful body. It possesses four barbules, two protruding from the tip of its long snout and one from each corner of the leathery mouth. The snout has a drooping shape indicating that the barbel spends much of its time rooting around on the river bed among weeds and stones for the aquatic animals, weed and worms that form its diet. The presence of barbel in any water is an indication of the degree of purity of the water. Barbel rarely thrive in polluted surroundings. They have been introduced to a number of rivers in England, although the species is concentrated in the Thames Valley, southern chalkstreams, Yorkshire rivers and the Severn.

Bait: *Bread baits, cheese, worms, grub baits and tinned meat. The latter is now producing massive catches on the Severn where the species has really taken hold.*

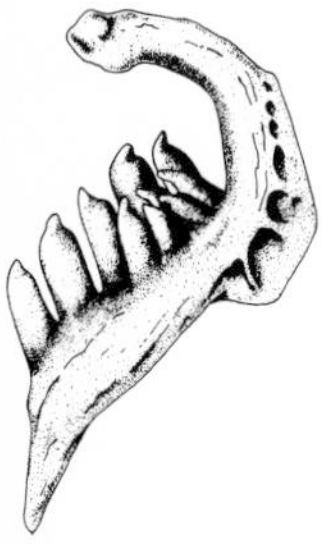

Pharyngeal teeth of the barbel.

SPINY LOACH
Cobitis tania

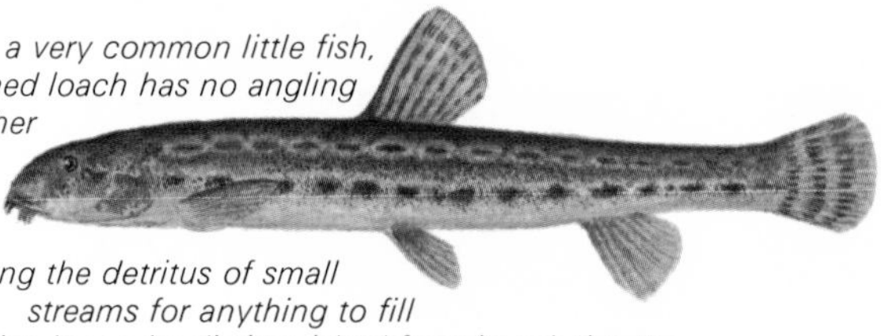

Not a very common little fish, the spined loach has no angling value other than to small boys who search among the detritus of small streams for anything to fill the jam jar. It can be distinguished from its relative the stone loach by the double-pointed spine below the hind nostril. Both species have six barbules.

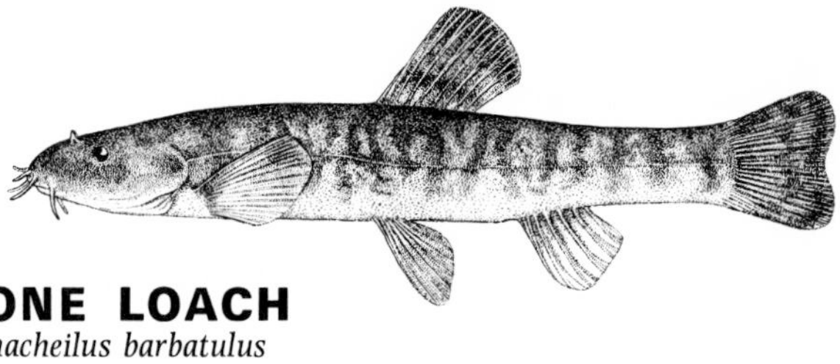

STONE LOACH
Nemacheilus barbatulus

More widespread than the spined species and preferring cleaner water. Found under stones and gravel in small streams and ponds. Look for the pronounced barbel-like snout that overhangs the fish's mouth.

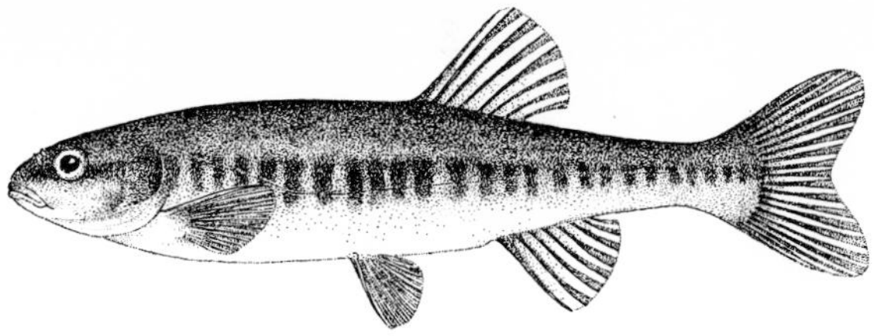

MINNOW
Phoxinus phoxinus

One of the small species used by anglers as a bait fish. Silvery in colour with occasional dots or black stripes. The minnow has an incomplete lateral line and averages about 3 ins in length. It is found in shoals feeding in shallow, running water.

BLEAK
Alburnus alburnus

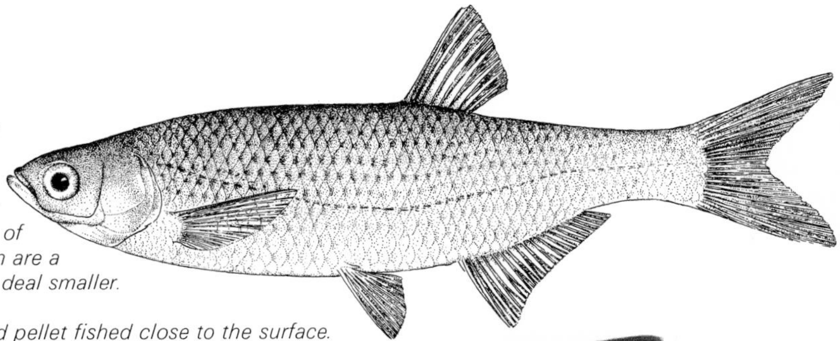

Recognized by its projecting, up-turned mouth, the bleak is used as a bait fish and appears among the catches of match anglers on many of our major river systems. Bleak can grow to a length of 8 ins, although most specimens taken are a good deal smaller.

Bait: *A single maggot or tiny bread pellet fished close to the surface.*

Pharyngeal teeth of the gudgeon.

GUDGEON
Gobio gobio

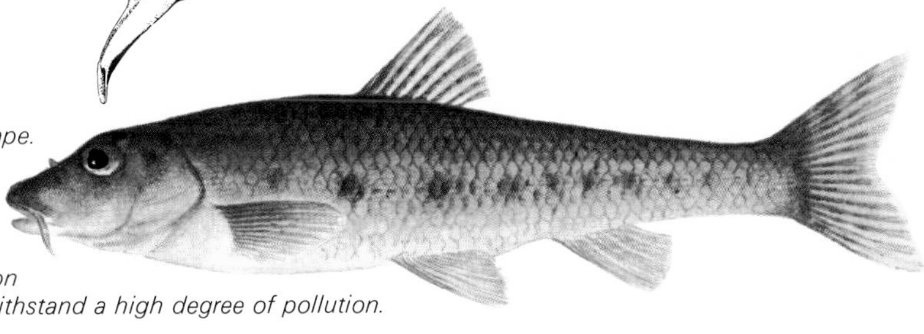

A small fish showing certain similarities to the barbel in body shape. It has just two barbules, one at each top corner of the mouth. The body of the gudgeon is almost straight from the mouth to the anal fin. The species prefers running water over gravel or sandy bottoms and feeds on minute organisms. The gudgeon would seem to be one species that is able to withstand a high degree of pollution.

Bait: *Maggots and small worms.*

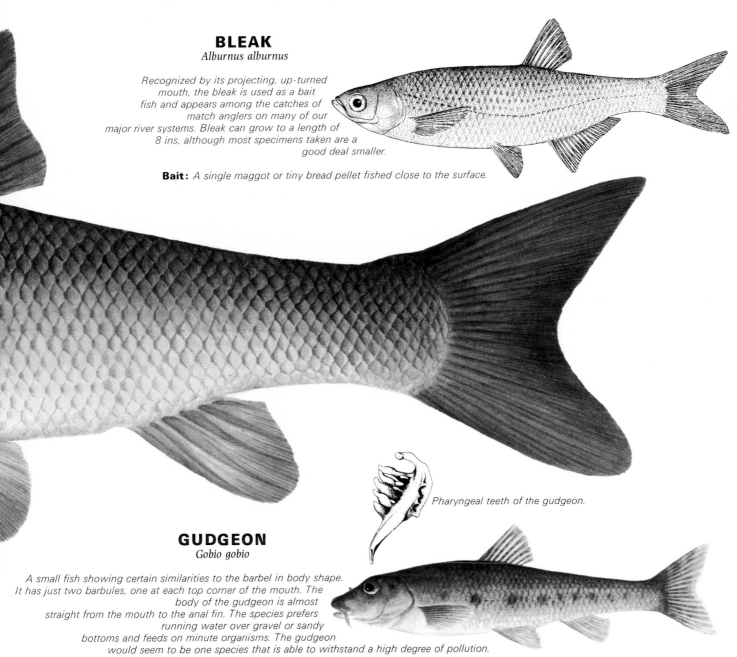

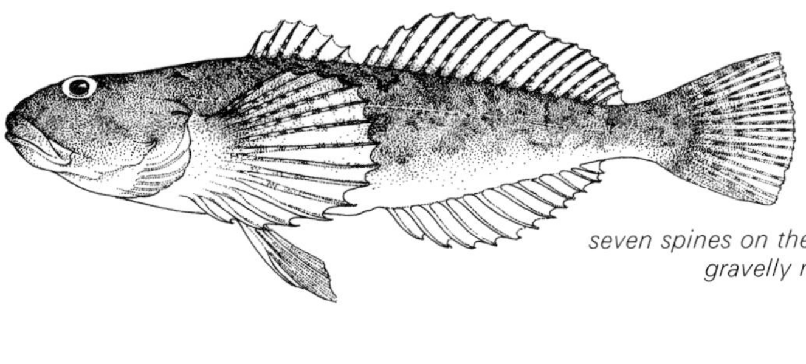

MILLER'S THUMB
Cottus gobio

This tiny fish possesses two dorsal fins, the first six to eight spines and the anterior dorsal of soft rays are almost joined. The miller's thumb has a broad, flat head with fewer than seven spines on the gill cover. Search for this little fellow in the gravelly runs of clear water in small streams.

try to succeed at all forms of their fishing, tackling a wide variety of both still and running water. In my view there are times to fish rivers and times to leave them well alone. I have my own way of arriving at the necessary decision about where to fish and on what kind of water. If the river is on form, with catches likely to be high and prize money good, I will be there fishing. I prefer the big-weight matches where lots of fish are likely to be caught on each succeeding match, simply because the men in good form are likely to win.

If a river is fishing only moderately well, but the prize money is good, I might still consider fishing the match, providing there was nothing better somewhere else. With poor prize money but good fishing, a venue will often attract me. Only when the prize money is poor and the fishing is of the same calibre will I consistently stay away from a match. This is the main reason why I rarely travel up into Yorkshire although the Huntspill, in far-away Somerset, will call me when it is in peak summer fishing form.

The seasons of the year affect my choice of angling venue. Throughout the summer months I find that I tend to fish the Welland and Nene with visits in between to the Great Ouse Relief Channel. With the coming of autumn and the first of the frost, I switch some of my fishing time to the River Trent, where the constant flow of the river, combined with the relatively high water temperature, keeps the fish in a feeding mood. I do fish the Severn when it is in top condition. Whether I travel to the River Witham rather depends on the current form of the water. The river is fished so hard that the different species go off the feed for weeks on end. No doubt they do take feed in the night hours, when the anglers have returned home. They then seem to lie dormant throughout the next angling day before repeating their nightly feeding on the groundbait that has been thrown in by the new batch of fishless anglers.

It is one of match angling's biggest problems that popular sections – particularly accessible sections – of the river take more than their share of the fishing load. Some fishermen will never walk far from the parked car, which ensures that some parts of the river are always more heavily fished than others. The fish are hooked and landed so often that they become extra cautious, at times impossible to hook. Only the very best bait presentation will stand a chance of taking the fish when they are in that sort of mood. This problem is likely to intensify as the years pass and angling activity increases.

Who knows? We may find in years to come that we are the proud possessors of match rivers full of fine, healthy fish that have become so bait-and-hook educated that they are impossible to catch. But that, perhaps is too gloomy an outlook. As the fish learn so we must learn to extend our tactics. As a bait becomes slow to work we must look for others to tempt the fish.

1

2

3

In the last ten years a clear picture has emerged on the heavily fished bream waters. We had the squatt and the annato maggot years, followed by times when the white, milky gozzer was the supreme fish-taking bait. Then came the caster which took over as the top hookbait, but it soon had to be fished in a combination with worm. Bread had an excellent year on the Welland in 1974. The future combinations are likely to include the bloodworm and the pinkie. Once one of the old favourites has been out of angling use for a period of time it will then return to take fish once more. Fish will not associate the bait with danger or whatever it is that makes them wary.

The continually successful match fishermen are those who are aware of the ever-changing scene and who react accordingly by tempting the fish with the right methods. Other anglers may have a couple of seasons in which they hit the headlines of the angling weeklies before lapsing into insignificance. Their failure is simply that they continue to use last year's methods for this year's fish. This is why match practice is so important. When I pleasure fish on any water I am not setting out my stall for a mammoth catch to fill the keep net. I know that I ought to be able to catch my share of fish by the successful method of the moment. What I seek to do is to stay one jump ahead of the rest of the field. Practice means constant experiment with new ideas or variations on proven methods. These

1 *Float selection and the way in which a matchman's floats are stored is of vital importance. Familiarity with each float's characteristics and shot loading are second nature.*

2 *A fine bream is netted from the Grand Canal at Prosperous, in Co. Kildare, by Gordon Dickison, an English angler who is having a lot of success in Ireland, as is well shown by this catch.*

3 *Gordon Dickison, fishing the Grand Canal with John Woods, took this mixed catch of rudd, bream and rudd/bream hybrids from the Tichnevin stretch – another good day's catch.*

4 *Like a Roman road, the Grand Canal reaches out from Dublin across the Midland Plain towards the west of Ireland. Although a relatively slow-flowing water, there are huge catches to be had.*

4

variations of bait, line strength, distance fished, the method of bait presentation and permutations with groundbait are endless. Only by paying heed to these factors can I remain among the consistent winners. I cannot tell any of you what will be the winning method on the River Nene in 1990. I can only reveal some of the things I do and the way in which I do them. Each of you has to make your own decision as to what is right or wrong, for any one fishing venue or day.

BREAM IN THE SUMMER

As my own fishing is most often done on the bream rivers, where roach will be a secondary target fish, let us look at the bream as a species together with their pattern of living and fishing behaviour. No one can hope to succeed as a matchman if he cannot build up a clear mental picture of what happens under the water. Because we fishers cannot see below the surface we sometimes ignore vital factors which could make the difference between a full and a dry net.

I look at it this way: if you throw half a dozen stones into a field it is almost certain that you will frighten every bird in sight! They will be on the wing and away fast. Bream behave in the same way when bombarded with angler's groundbait. The fish will pack tight and run. Bream will dash headlong through the swims, giving false bites to everyone as they run into the fishermen's lines. The foolish throw in even more groundbait, which hits the already disturbed water with a great clomp and the fish continue on their way.

So, first and foremost, remember that fish are live creatures with strong instincts of self-preservation. On no account must they be frightened. Bream must be encouraged to move slowly and undisturbed on to your groundbait – and to stay there. Also, the fish must be hooked cleanly and drawn clear of the shoal without the other members of that shoal taking fright. A bream that is hooked and allowed to dash freely around the swim will scatter the feeding fish, driving them off to another matchman's swim.

How can you hold fish in the swim? A good question that is best answered by pattern-feeding at the right time with balls of groundbait of the right consistency that hit the water surface softly to shower their contents into a confined area on the bed of the river or stillwater. No matter which bream river I fish, you will never find me indulging in the too-often seen opening bombardment. I let other anglers do that. My first objective is to see *where* everyone else is feeding and *where* they plan to fish. This system is of equal importance in both summer and winter fishing. On most of the rivers I have a plan in my mind of where I want to fish. It has taken a long time to store up this knowledge but before using it I must first see what the opposition is going to do.

Once the matchmen alongside me have made their decisions and the splashes from their groundbait have told me what they intend doing, I start to search my swim *before groundbaiting*.

It is vital to know the type of river bed that you are groundbaiting. Ideally, I want a clear patch of clean bottom, free from growing weed or accumulated rubbish. So first I cast around, feeling for tension on the line where there should be none if the bottom is clean. The hook is examined on each retrieve for signs of rubbish and leaves. If the fishing area in front of me proved likely to hold fish I feed it, making sure that my groundbait takes a different flow line from the stuff put in by the anglers pegged on both sides of me.

Bream roam around during a contest, so the feed must be on a line in the water that is not blocked at either end by other groundbaited patches where the bream are likely to linger before they reach my swim. Ideally, I feed close to a ledge. Bream rove around but their movements are to some extent dictated by the contours of the bottom. There are, of course, greater variations in the bed of a stillwater lake or pond. But the bed of rivers can vary tremendously. I prefer to place my groundbait on the deep edge of the shelf, knowing that the bream will wander along the bottom edge of the underwater cliff until they come upon something interesting enough to hold their attention.

Matches are not often won from the middle ground in the river but on the flat bed between the ledges. Even today, with anglers far more capable than they were, say, fifteen years ago, there are many anglers who do not feed the far side well – who do not, in fact, make a conscious choice. They just heave the groundbait in and sit hoping for the best.

Bream almost always roam around a river regardless of the depth of that river. They will run on the shallow South Holland Drain, on the deeper Welland, the deepish Witham and on the very deep Lower Great Ouse. This means that sufficient feed must be placed on the bottom to hold what could be a shoal several hundred fish strong long enough for them all to get their heads down to feed. While the fish are settling down they must not be groundbaited. That is a rule that should never be broken for feeding will frighten them and scatter your shoal over the river. Anglers must assess the correct time to re-commence groundbaiting. Too soon and the fish will take fright, too late and the fish will already have begun to move off since all the feed will have been eaten.

My usual style of feeding is to put in 2 or 3 balls of groundbait, laced with whatever hookbait is in favour at the time. The lacing could be squatts, casters, pinkies or worms. Then I leave the offering to get to work. Nothing else goes into the water for an hour, or until the first 4 or 5 fish have been caught. Then I will feed 2 more balls, usually smaller, repeating the dose every 20 minutes or so while the fish are around in the swim.

Most of my bream fishing is done with either swingtip or quivertip bite indicators, the swingtip for still- to slow-running waters, while the quivertip is best in faster-flowing water. Float fishing is reserved for the smaller bream, the 2 to 12 ozs fish, since these can be brought to the net faster with float tackle than when using a leger set-up. But, since the bigger bream – fish weighing 1 to 5 lbs and more – usually show a marked preference for a still bait, where the bait lies absolutely static on the riverbed, legering is most often the winning style of fishing.

I set myself a target in every match I fish. The target must relate, in a realistic manner, to the swim that I have drawn and not necessarily to the weight that I feel will be needed to win the match. Sometimes the swim will be such that it would be impossible to aim for a higher than section win, but I try to translate a potential winning weight into a set number of bream. If, for instance, I am fishing the Great Ouse Relief Channel in summer, when big catches are on the cards, I set myself a 15 bream target. Relief Channel bream average around 3 lbs each, which says that I expect to catch 45 lbs of fish. There are times when that weight will not be enough to get a place. I won one Great Ouse Championship with 65 lbs. That was 22 fish, which at

Using a bait table, carrying the various hook and loose feed baits, ensures that time is saved in the match and particularly when the angler spends the entire match fishing from a standing position.

least proves that the 3 lbs average size for the bream is about right!

It is impossible to lay down a hard and fast groundbait content for the match rivers. What was right last year is likely to be way off the mark for the future. One thing is certain: it is far more important when and how to feed rather than what the groundbait is made from.

Now to tackle. The rod for most breaming is a specialist, 9 ft 6 ins swingtipping rod that is not so stiff that fish cannot put a bend into it. Stiff rods will lose you lightly hooked specimens. My line strength is 2 lbs 8 ozs. Plenty of strength there for bream. I fish the same weight of Arlesey bomb lead on every water – $\frac{3}{8}$ oz is just right. Stay with a lead of that weight as much as possible and your casting distance and accuracy will become constant. There are times when I must add weight to the dropper, either to combat the flow of strong water or to give me the casting distance and accuracy needed to combat a troublesome wind. Then I add 1, 2, 3 or even 4 swan shots if necessary, nipping them on to the dropper close to, but above, the bomb.

The terminal rig and its component parts are vitally important to the match angler. First, let us take the hook. I believe that fishermen are at last beginning to agree with me on this point. When I first said that it is feasible to use a size 20 hook for big bream, anglers were sceptical. But a 20 hook will successfully hold 3 gozzers, or even 2 casters, so the hookbait can be large enough to attract a big fish. But *it is the weight of the hook* that is the critical factor. The smaller a hook is the less it will weigh – and the less it weighs the more naturally it will sink through the water before settling to the bottom. A 20 hook is far less likely to put a bream off feeding than a size 14. Any wary fish must feel the weight of a hook. This may not put the fish off all the time but if by scaling the hook size down I can lure just one or two more fish it may mean the difference between winning and remaining a constant "also ran".

My choice for the hook is a size 20 flat-forged, reversed hook. The hook is strong and for its size gets as good a hold as some brands of 18s. Try not to put too much stress on the hook hold when playing your fish.

Loose feeding a particular line, especially if under the far bank, calls for accuracy in placing the feed. Ray Mumford, a matchman from Thameside, uses a catapult to feed his maggots into a concentrated area during the Lawden Masters' match.

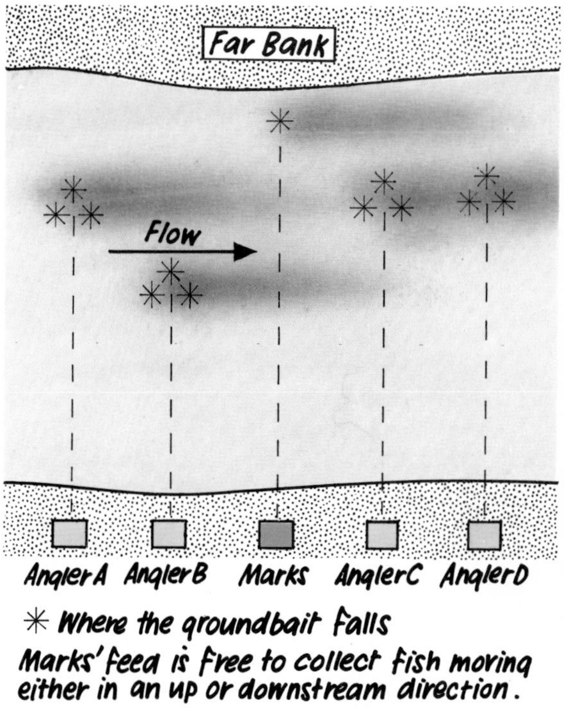

Ivan's groundbaiting plan is initially to feed the far side along a different line to other competitors.

Coarse fishing

Let the fish swim towards you of its own accord by leading it rather than dragging it. There is more than one advantage in leading a fish quietly, fairly quickly and naturally away from its companions in the shoal. If you allow a hooked bream to dive and flash around among the other fish they will soon take fright. Get your fish away and let it scrap, if necessary, under the rod tip. It will not do much harm, neither will it create a great disturbance there. Eventually the bream will lie flat and can be netted with ease.

The breaking strain of the hook length is another vital factor. It is an incontestable fact that the finer the nylon to the hook the more bites will be had. If I could always use a breaking strain of $\frac{1}{2}$ lb nylon I could guarantee that I would always get more offers than when using a 1 lb bottom. But the fish have to be played as well as hooked so I feel that 1 lb nylon is the lower safety limit. It is a combination of the fine nylon and small hook that lets the bait sink slowly to the bottom. The slower the bait sinks, the greater the chance of a bream taking on-the-drop. In every summer contest I hope to get at least one, sometimes more, bream taking a dropping bait. Another most important requirement is for anglers to be able to distinguish between *line* bites and *real* bites. It is vital to be able to sort the positive bite out from the indication given as a bream swims into or against the line. Line bites usually come when fish are moving around the swim, before they have settled onto the feed. If you scare them at this time it is almost certain they will be off. Every time an angler strikes at a line bite he is likely to hit fish with the lead weight and disturb others with the nylon as it is lifted or sharply retrieved.

There is a clearly visible difference between line (false) and true bites. The false bite moves the swingtip up only for it to fall back again soon afterwards as the bream's body moves off from the line. With a true bite the swingtip lifts and stays lifted. There is ample time to give oneself the opportunity to distinguish between the two distinct types of bite for it isn't often necessary to react too quickly to a bream bite – that is if your tackle is delicate and unlikely to frighten the fish.

Bream bites usually come in sequences. In the first spate of action, on the Relief Channel for instance, you may land 5 or 6 bream fairly quickly. Then the fish will lose interest for a time and maybe even wander out of your swim. Then, if you are lucky, back they come when you may take another 3 or 4. Next we may experience a total lull in the fishing activity before more bream bites are obtained. A further lull, broken by an occasional bream bite or a landed fish before the swim becomes dour and you may be struggling for a bite. It is when the struggling stage is reached that many matches are won or lost. There is often no more than a two-fish difference between winner's and runner's-up catches. So it is quite usual to finish the

1

1 *A bonus in any match – this roach turned the scales at just over the 2 lbs mark.*

2 *Intense concentration on the face of Tony Knight as he fishes to build a weight on the River Avon at Evesham. Strong summer sunshine can mask the subtle movements of the float, hence the eyeshade.*

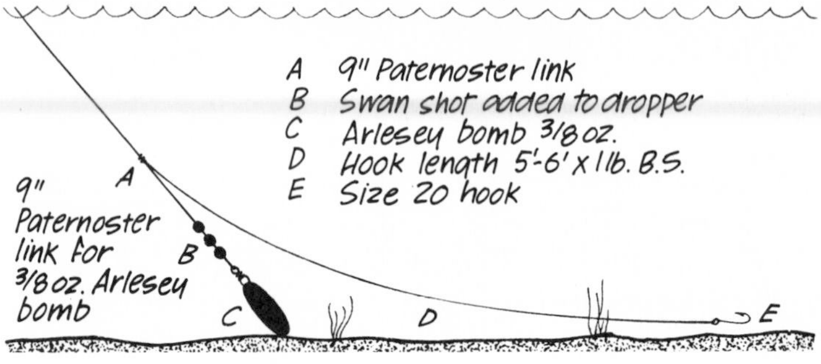

Basic leger rig.

end period of a match by striving to take that one extra fish. Whether it is by multiple changes of the bait, by casting a little wide of the groundbait, fishing a longer "tail" or twitching the bomb to produce the reaction, one must constantly try to lure that extra bonus bream.

When all else has failed and I have been biteless for a long period I will sometimes resort to shock tactics. Out go three big balls of groundbait in rapid succession hoping that this will stir up the swim, producing a reaction among the remaining fish in my section of the river. Occasionally this will work when the "gently-does-it" approach has failed, but be warned that doing this is a make or break measure. On one occasion, fishing the Welland when I was desperate for another fish, I killed the swim in this way and a large shoal of bream, that had been lying peacefully below my rod tip, took fright and gave anglers around me a short but sharp session of line bites as they fled. Needless to say, I didn't get another fish!

Shallow rivers, like the Welland, carry rather more mid-summer weed growth than their east of England neighbours the Witham, Great Ouse and Relief Channel. Whereas on the deeper rivers the fish can be brought to your net through clear, weed-free space, the Welland can prove more difficult. Winning weights on the Welland are rarely as high as on the Relief Channel but I think you need 26 lbs of bream (12 fish) to win there. Twenty pounds is a certainty to win a place in the list, but many of the swims can be heavily weeded that will produce this amount of bream. Take the permanent pegs in the early 800s or around the 540s. Both

2

have extensive weedbeds through which hooked fish have to be landed. Bear in mind that the fish know the lie of the land in their home areas in much the same way as you know your dining room. They realize the security value in a weedbed. Draw a hooked fish gently toward the weeds, so that the fish is swimming and you are simply retrieving line. The fish will usually find its own way through the weed because it knows where the gaps are! If you haul hard you will divert the fish from its chosen path so it and you are likely to run into trouble and be stuck fast.

SUMMER ROACH FISHING

As a general rule roach fishing is not very successful on our bream rivers during the summer period. With the usual clear, slow moving or even stillwater conditions there is always a chance that the occasional roach will be taken. But anglers who think they can match bream catches with roach are wrong. Roach can be caught in summer but only when conditions are absolutely right. I know "pleasure fishing" can sometimes produce good weights of roach under still conditions but there is a world of difference between a match and pleasure fishing.

It is likely that roach would make a better showing through the summer if the permanent match pegs on the major rivers, Witham, Welland and Nene, were spaced farther apart. The 17 yds that exist between Nene and Welland pegs makes roach fishing very difficult. The 12 yds of space on the Witham make it all but impossible. Sooner or later, angling administrators will learn that 20 yds is the *minimum* acceptable distance between pegs – acceptable to the fish that is!

The summer of 1974 was unusual. We had a lot of rain with the result that the river carried a much stronger flow and water colour than usual. After a period during which the bream had been rather heavily fished for, I concluded that it might be worthwhile having a go at winning with roach. It was a calculated gamble, although the decision was not made until mid-week practice had helped to convince me that I had a chance with the species. Together with my friends, who became known as the Leicester quartet, I set out to muster a winning team bag float fishing for roach. We succeeded in taking this top place by a substantial margin. I might have had the individual winning bag had I not lost a number of 1 lb fish due to the density of the nearbank weed and the associated problems of bringing fish through it to the waiting net.

The prime essential for summer roach fishing is to have good colour in the water. Secondly, there must be a flow – not a fast-flowing river but enough movement to allow an angler to trot his float and bait downstream at a modest pace. A good swim needs bankside cover if the fish are to stay in close to the margins. Some swims on the Welland lack this growth but are perfect by midsummer when the water weed is at peak height. A combination of hemp seed and caster feed will bring the big roach around and, although you are likely to get the small 2–6 ozs fish early in the match, their size can improve as time goes on. It is always ▶70

Perch Pike Perch

TROUT, SALMON PARR, Minnow, Stoneloach, Miller's Thumb

GRAYLING

BARBEL, CHUB, Dace, Gudgeon, Bleak

Roach Roach

Broadly speaking, British rivers can be divided into five main zones – trout, grayling, barbel, bream and a final or tidal zone in which flounders, smelt, shads, grey mullet and bass may be found. These are not, of course, sharply defined areas. There are blurred areas where the various environmental conditions merge.

TROUT ZONE

GRAYLING ZONE (Minnow Zone)

BARBEL ZONE (Chub Zone)

Increase in bank and river-bed vegetation

BOTTOM SPAWNING FISH

OXYGEN CONTENT OF WATER

Extremely high to very high.	Very high.	High in surface waters, decreasing with depth – especially during warm weather.

AVERAGE TEMPERATURE DURING SUMMER

Rarely above 10°C (50°F).	Rarely above 15°C (59°F).	Frequently above 15°C (59°F).

ike Perch Pike Perch Pike

Salmon, Sea Trout, Eels migrate to headwaters of river

Roach Roach Roach

BREAM

Tench, Carp, Rudd, Silver Bream

Zander, Ruffe

Flounder, Smelt, Shads, Grey Mullet, Bass

Fish are responsive to basic, life-sustaining conditions appropriate to the individual species. The oxygen content of the water, the variety and type of vegetation, the depth of the water and the speed of the water – all these are vital factors for the fish.

This chart of the average river tells the story in quick, outline terms. To discover where you are likely to find the fish referred to on the colour bands at the top of the chart drop a "mind's eye" line down to the bottom of the chart from the two pointed ends of the band you have selected. You will then have a reading on the colour bands at the bottom of the chart – ie, those below the river line – of the conditions the particular fish can tolerate. As we said, there is always a degree of overlap but this knowledge of the broad rules of fish survival in the various conditions a river undergoes in its journey is vital to the angler.

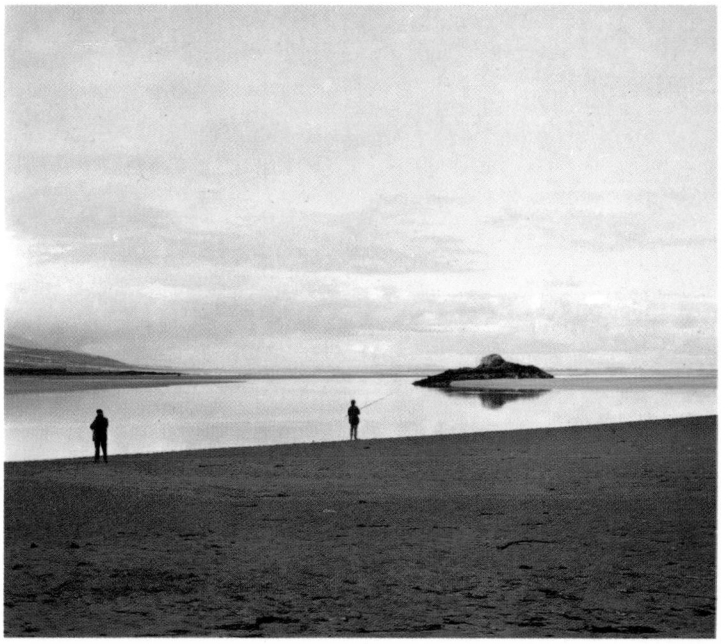

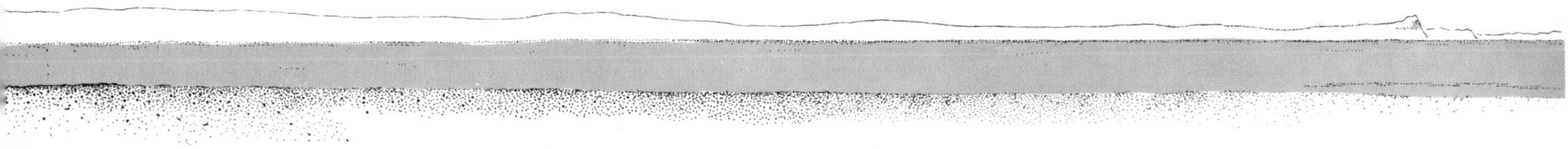

BREAM ZONE

TIDAL ZONE and ESTUARY

FISH SPAWNING ON VEGETATION

Sufficient oxygen in surface waters, frequently insufficient to support fish life in bottom layers of deepest parts.

Frequently up to 20°C (68°F) and higher.

Frequently above 20°C (68°F).

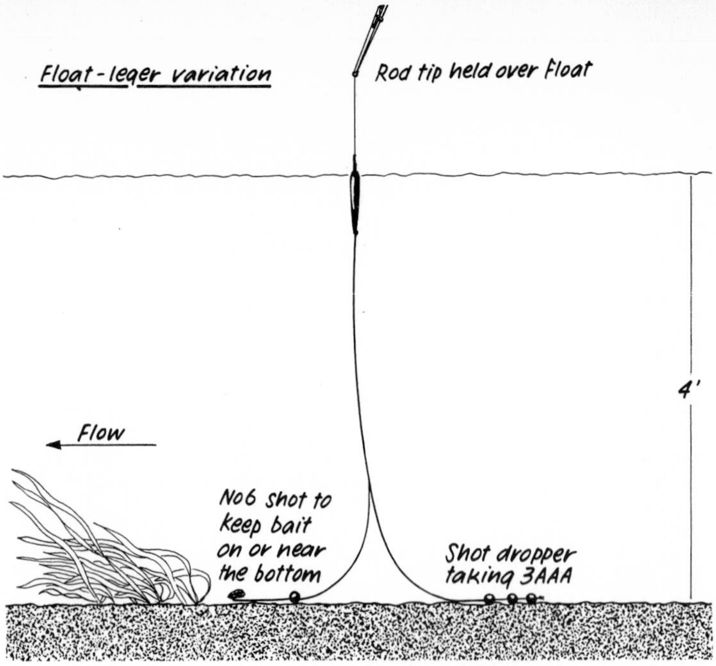

See this page.

67◀ possible that a short encounter with a number of 12 ozs to 1 lb fish will boost the weight of your catch.

One thing can kill a roach swim fast – that is a bombardment of unnecessary groundbait. You will be able to catch the roach that are in your swim if you proceed about the fishing quietly. Your up and downstream neighbour's activities will not interfere with your swim, but if they start bombing groundbait along the near edge, the roach will certainly depart to the other parts of the river. There are occasions when roach on the River Nene can be caught, in substantial numbers, on the shelf which shows along the north bank, in the areas of pegs 260 to 300. Again, to be successful on the pitch, a degree of colour in the water is the first requirement with the help given by nearby weedbeds. The weed provides the cover to keep roach in position on this 4 ft deep shelf. Without the weed cover fish will swim out and down into the deeper 8 to 11 ft areas. To achieve match winning weights of 18 to 20 lbs, caster and hemp feeding is vital. It will keep the roach constantly interested in the hookbait and bring weights that the bream anglers will find hard to beat on this moody river!

The River Witham has a fine stock of healthy roach. There are big specimens but they are becoming increasingly hard to catch. As I pointed out, the too-close pegging is the prime reason for this difficulty of getting to the large fish. Given a good water colour and no interference from anglers pegged close by, there is every chance of a section win with 4 to 7 lbs of roach in areas where the bream are either not feeding or are absent from the swim. I fish for the roach with tackle as fine as I use for bream fishing. My reel line would be 1½ lbs breaking strain with the hook length at 1 lb B.S. The hook is usually a size 20. I seek to apply the on-the-drop technique wherever possible but I recognize that when there is an excess of flow and colour in the water this method will not work. Shotting must be finely tapered from the base of the float to within 15 to 18 ins of the hook. This will ensure the finest presentation of the bait and it is customary for me to fish anything from 6 to as much as 18 ins overdepth. Doing this will help to fish the bait through the swim at a speed that the quality fish will accept.

I have been experimenting with a method for fishing a river that has an excess of current flow and water colour. The method has already won for me a number of section prizes. It is a variation on float legering and is mainly used on waters like the Nene which have a shallow near-bank shelf. The method demands the use of the roach pole for it is crucial that the float is controlled from immediately above it. Normal 13 ft casting rods are just not long enough but an 18 ft pole is right. I use up to 4 AAA shots and a float to match. The shot is carried on a paternoster dropper in the same way as a legered Arlesey bomb. The float is cast slightly upstream and is held in position by all the shot resting on the bottom. When fish bite they move the shot and the float registers lift bites.

See page 71.

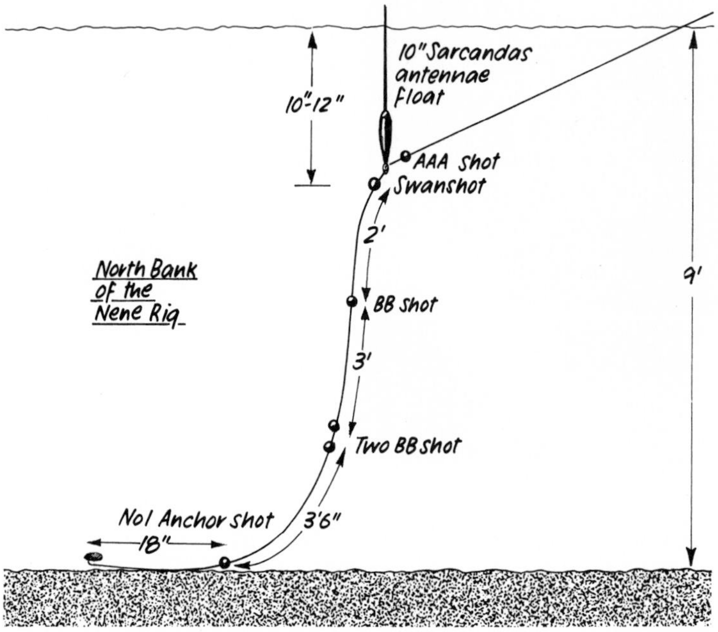

Although the bulk of the catch made using this technique will be roach, there is always the chance of a big bream or two.

It will be argued that quivertipping is as good a method in the same situation but that cannot be valid. When any river is running fast with high colour it follows that a lot of displaced rubbish is being carried downstream. If your legered line is across the flow it could pick up masses of rubbish that will constantly register false bites. Also, you will spend much of the available fishing time clearing the line of twigs and leaves instead of effectively fishing the swim. On the other hand, the float leger rig has little line in the water. Your line goes from the float direct to the shot on the bed of the river which means that you are putting your line through a very small width of water indeed. The rubbish factor ceases to be a major problem so that you can leave your tackle in the water long enough for a fish to get at the bait. Knowing that the hook is not fouled with displaced and decaying vegetation allows fishing with confidence.

WINTER ON THE BREAM RIVERS

Once autumn arrives, bream on many rivers become hard to catch. I remember the 1974 Division One National Championship fished on the River Welland during September. The water temperature had dropped and the water was gin clear. There were only three shoals of bream prepared to show any interest in the angler's baits whereas in August bream would have been feeding along most of the match length. With the first frosts the small bream are quick to stop feeding. Bigger bream also become inactive but after a time they will show a renewed interest, but rarely do they feed again with the same appetites as they displayed in the summer months!

If there are substantial amounts of autumn rain the water will be coloured and it will have to run off, at least from time to time, to clear the surplus from the watercourse. When that happens, the bream are made to swim and to use up energy. They will then try to replace that energy by feeding. Therefore, there are times in winter when the big bream of the Welland, Witham, Nene, Relief Channel and other popular summer fisheries can be caught. Of course we cannot be *absolutely* certain that this feeding behaviour will happen.

Let us look at two typical rivers, the Witham and the Nene. In both it is possible to catch both roach and bream in winter. The Witham, though, can fish poorly at times and my inclination is to go for the bream as the prime objective. I fish with the swing-tip, legering about two-thirds to three-quarters of the width of the river. No groundbait is used for the first 20 minutes of the match as it is best to see whether there are already feeding fish in the swim. Hookbait is alternated between casters and worm. After 15 minutes, 3 cricket ball sized handfuls of groundbait are fed in, each containing worms and casters. The river is likely to be flowing in winter so the feeding must be repeated every 20 minutes or so because my feed will tend to be swept out from the swim. The worm is my main hookbait. I never use a single worm on the hook, preferring a cocktail of worm and caster or worm and maggot. Sometimes the bait is best offered as a bunch of 2 or 3 worms but even though the hook-bait is quite large I still keep to my small hook. A size 18 is usual but if necessary I will reduce to a 20!

On the winter Nene there are more swims that will produce roach than bream. Of the 380 permanent pegs only 60 are bream-or-nothing swims. On the remaining sections of both rivers I settle for a float-fishing style that will cope with both species. The style will also take the chub that are around in small numbers. These fish justify a series of brief casts to the area over the river to the far bank.

Because roach will form more than 50 per cent of a match weight I do not bother with worm hookbaits when float fishing. Instead casters are the mainstay on the hook. The idea is to develop the main swim two thirds out from my bank although I am sure to feed the far side of the river with large handfuls of feed, groundbait containing caster, as soon as the whistle starts the contest. I do not fish over the feed. It is there to create a potential for later in the match! The main swim is loose-fed with two batches of casters and is then fed regularly with 6 more casters with every third cast. All are delivered loose. The float used is a 10 ins balsa on peacock quill with a cherry stick insert to form the tip. It will carry a $2\frac{1}{2}$ swan shot load. I also have two other rods made up – one with a similar but heavier float taking 3 swan shots, and the other a swingtip rod. The lighter outfit is used to fish the near line into my bank with the float set not less than 6 ins overdepth. The bait is a single caster on a size 20 to a 1 lb hook length. Bites come in an irregular fashion. There would be no pattern about them and the fish would be roach of 2–8 ozs. After 45 minutes it would be time to take a look at the swim that was baited over on the far side of the river. The bottom feed will have got to work and I fish over it using the heavier float rod baited with a single caster for possible chub.

If lucky there will be a chub on the first cast that could go to 3 lbs, but is more likely to be a fish of around 1 lb. The longer one fishes the far swim, the less chance there is of the chub staying. So after 15 minutes I would come back to the near swim for more roach. If that move proves unsuccessful I would return again to the far swim for chub on float tackle. Should this in turn fail me, it is time to take up the swingtip rod and attack the far swim for chub or the possibility of a bream that may have moved in on the bait. The last tactic likely to have an effect on a dour river is to switch the hookbait from caster to yellow-stained pinkies fished on the float along the near side swim on a 20 hook. The fish caught wouldn't be big but they could keep the catch building.

THE RIVER TRENT AT THE BACK END OF THE YEAR

For me the Trent is an autumn and winter river. It replaces the slow-moving east of England bream fisheries that are so affected by the first frosts. The Trent can, of course, be successfully fished in summertime although it does not have the huge catches of rivers further east. The River Trent is not a big match water simply because it is impossible to get more than 300 anglers pegged out in an unbroken line. The best and longest match length is Winford to Holme Marsh. Trent fishing is in the process of change as the pollution that has marred its progress through the 20th century becomes less damaging. The river is beginning to show its capacity to hold large heads of both roach and gudgeon.

Bream stocks and the chub are building in numbers while the barbel may burst on the scene as the Trent fish of the 1980s. All the indications are that these 3 species will produce the match angler's winning weights of the future. The roach disease of the mid-1960s sadly depleted this species and this space in the ecology allowed the chub to multiply. The river below Holme Weir now has many fine chub averaging 1 lb. Bream shoals are growing particularly in the tidal areas and anglers would catch more of them if they would only adapt themselves to the Fenland style of angling.

To date, many Trent anglers remain obsessed with the traditional Trent style–feeding loose caster and trotting through the swims with a stick or waggler float. Nottingham anglers are the best in the country at fishing this method, but if they are not careful they could be left behind the times. It has already been proved, particularly in the bays and slack-paced water where bream have comfortable conditions, that fishermen prepared to fish overdepth, working their baits through the swim, can really catch and win with bream. Another facet of Trent fishing coming into prominence is quivertipping. During 1974 at least 30 per cent of the competitors in lower Trent contests were legering, mainly for chub. This style has now become even more widespread, especially when the chub stocks have grown in size and maturity.

I spent a lot of fishing time using bloodworm during the 1974 season. There is a phenomenal head of small fish in the lower Trent and it is possible to take 200 or more tiny fish in 4 hours' angling. These little fish, gudgeon, bleak and small roach, can be taken at the shortest range imaginable. In fact, to prove a point, I one day fished with what amounted to a handline for a short spell. I maintained a regular bite sequence with the float a mere 2 ft from the bank of the river. I will acknowledge that bloodworming is unlikely to prove a match-winning style on the river, though. The chub are now too numerous and they are forcing match weights up every season. Catches of around 18 lbs will become more widespread making it pointless to fish with bloodworm. Probably the greatest use of this bait will be in team fishing as the bait prevents a *water-licking*. Bloodworm vastly increases the number of bites gained in fishing poor pegs and is therefore a useful bait to back up with in a team contest. Bloodworming means pole fishing with no reel. I trot a very short swim of no more than 2 yds using a light, bristle-antenna float requiring no more than three No 4 shots to cock it. Plumbing for depth is vital as the hook needs to be just ½ in from the river bed for the greatest bait effectiveness! The shots are bunched and much closer to the hook than for most other types of fishing – 6 to 15 ins is about correct. My bristle-topped float is made of balsa and, when it is properly set, all the balsa is submerged with only the ½ in of bristle above the surface. The bristle is easy to see and it helps to locate the upper white tip of the balsa body which is just under the water. I watch this submerged white ring for bites, striking at any movement.

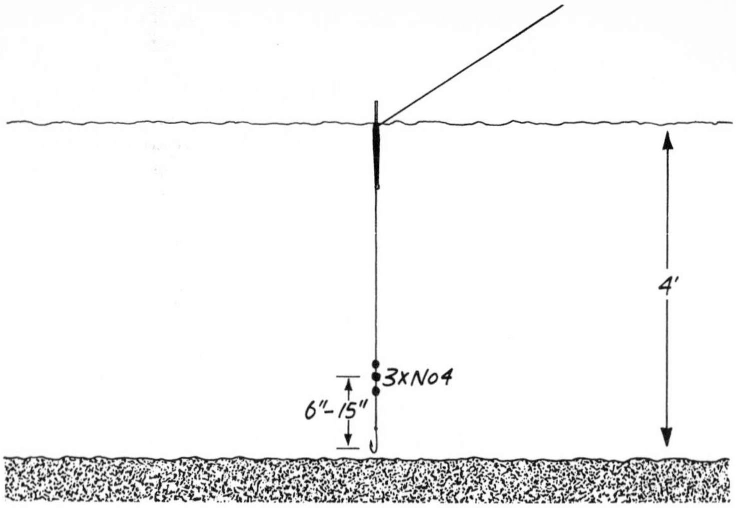

Bloodworm rig – see this page.

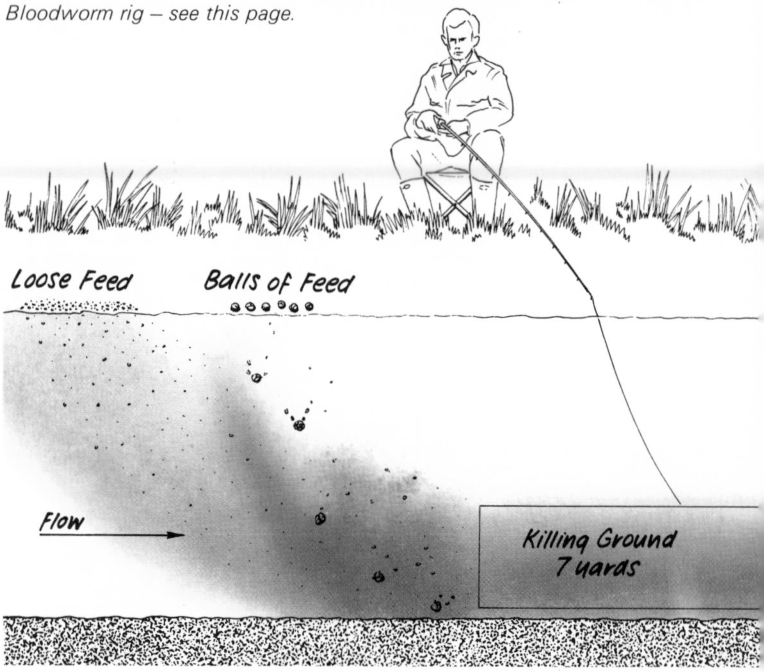

Ivan's method for groundbaiting and loose-feeding within a defined killing area – see this page.

Cane and balsa stick floats are favourites for inside fishing on the Trent and other relatively shallow rivers that have a fair speed of flow. An ideal shotting technique is to string the shot out evenly between the float and hook so that the bait is presented to the best advantage. Casters have been the successful Trent bait for the last 10 years, but I would emphasize that the river is changing daily and this bait may not see us successfully through the next decade. By the close of the 1974 season, yellow maggots were bringing success

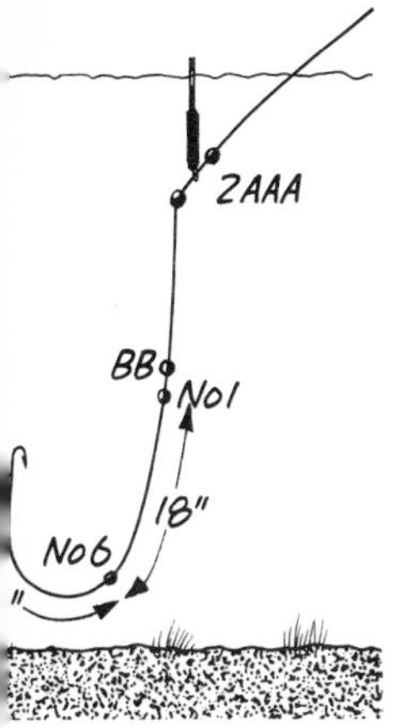

Witham on-the-drop style rig – details on this page.

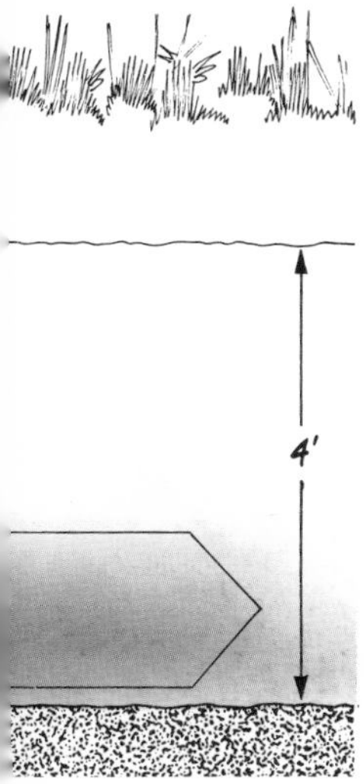

The Hampshire Avon near Durrington, not a matchman's water but ideal pleasure-fishing country.

and I know that Sheffield anglers took their best weights on wasp grub.

I feed the Trent with cereal groundbait loaded with casters, using small balls only at the beginning of the contest, gradually reducing the amount of cereal and increasing the loose-feeding. I start with 3 walnut-sized balls of feed together with some loose casters, approximately 7 or 8 casters every other swim down and a little nut of feed every 10 minutes. Sometimes the fish, mainly roach and gudgeon, can be brought right up the swim where they are easiest to hook. But on occasion it is necessary to trot the float as far as the pegging distance permitted to reach fish that are hanging well downstream.

SUMMER BREAM ON FLOAT TACKLE

Small bream are better fished for on float tackle. It is much faster in operation than leger gear. It is also easier to catch fish that are swimming off the bottom and produces less water disturbance with each cast. An excess of either wind or water flow can make float fishing difficult or nearly impossible but during spells of light-wind and slow-flowing conditions the float can bring heavy catches of small bream. During the 1973 Division One National, fished on the Witham, I was drawn at Langrick where I took around 11 lbs of small fish, mostly bream, weighing from 1 to 6 ozs. Most of the catch was taken on-the-drop. The same method will cope with the skimmer bream that have recently shown on the Welland.

Ideally, you will want to catch these small bream at close range but this will be a distance that also allows you to keep the fish feeding for the entire duration of the match. You will need to take advantage of any cover, such as inshore weedbeds, to mask your outline and movement. On the Witham, the on-the-drop style can be most successful fished 3 or 4 rod lengths out from the bank. I use a $5\frac{1}{2}$ ins reed on balsa float carrying 3 AAA shots. The water is normally about $5\frac{1}{2}$ ft deep during the summer so I set the float at 5 ft to fish 6 ins over depth. Two of the AAA shot are required to be set either side of the float as lock shot, one at each side of the base ring, the float being fished *bottom* only. The remaining AAA shot is divided into 3, one BB with perhaps a No 3 and a No 6. The two bigger shot are nipped onto the 2 lb breaking strain reel line 3 ft 3 ins from the hook, with the smallest No 6 shot placed 18 ins from the size 20 hook.

My groundbait is likely to be fairly sloppy and liberally laced with casters. The sloppy groundbait keeps the bleak occupied while the casters drop through to the bream that swim lower in the water. I will feed quite heavily with loose casters at the start, sometimes throwing in as many as 150 as soon as the whistle goes. This is another measure intended to beat the bleak for the casters settle quickly with little interference, whereas later in the match feeding will almost certainly bring bleak in hordes.

Most bites will come as the caster hookbait is actually settling down to the bottom. The No 6 shot will not come into register as the fish takes the bait and the weight of the shot . . . that is a bite! If there is no bite forthcoming from the on-the-drop process, I would be happy to let the hookbait lie on the river bed for a couple of minutes: it could bring a larger fish but the bait is never left there too long. As the range to be cast and the depth to be fished increase one is obliged to use a heavier float. This makes casting easier and more accurate while giving greater control over the tackle. If, for instance, I was on-the-drop fishing beside the shelf in the Coronation Channel, I would use a balsa-on-reed antenna float taking around 3 swan shots. Two and a quarter swan shots, of that load, is placed around the base ring of the float. Three-quarters of a swan shot (an AA and a BB) go on the line at 4 ft 6 ins from the hook. The rig is completed by either a No 1 or No 4 shot 18 ins from the bait.

There are some flowing rivers where float fishing beats legering for bream. Typical of these are the Norfolk Ant and the Cam. On the Ant, an overdepth style of float fishing, involving holding back the tackle against the flow, produces good results. On the Cam, float fishing ensures a match weight with a sprinkling of roach among the bream. For each river $3\frac{1}{2}$ AAA–4 AAA balsa-on-reed float is my choice. Both rivers are about $4\frac{1}{2}$ ft deep and both flow quite hard at times. On both rivers it is necessary to ensure that the bait moves downstream at slower than the speed of flow. The Ant is now a weedless river but the far bank is frequently covered by extensive reedbeds, while the cover on the far bank of the Cam comes from a heavy growth of water lilies. On both rivers the tackle is fished close to this cover of reeds or lilies. The float is set to fish 6 ins deeper than the river and is likely to be moved another 6 ins up, during the contest, once the feeding pattern of the fish becomes apparent.

A catching method on these rivers, and others like them, is reverse trotting. This means, in effect, that the float precedes the bait downstream with the bait and bottom shot trailing along over the bed of the stream.

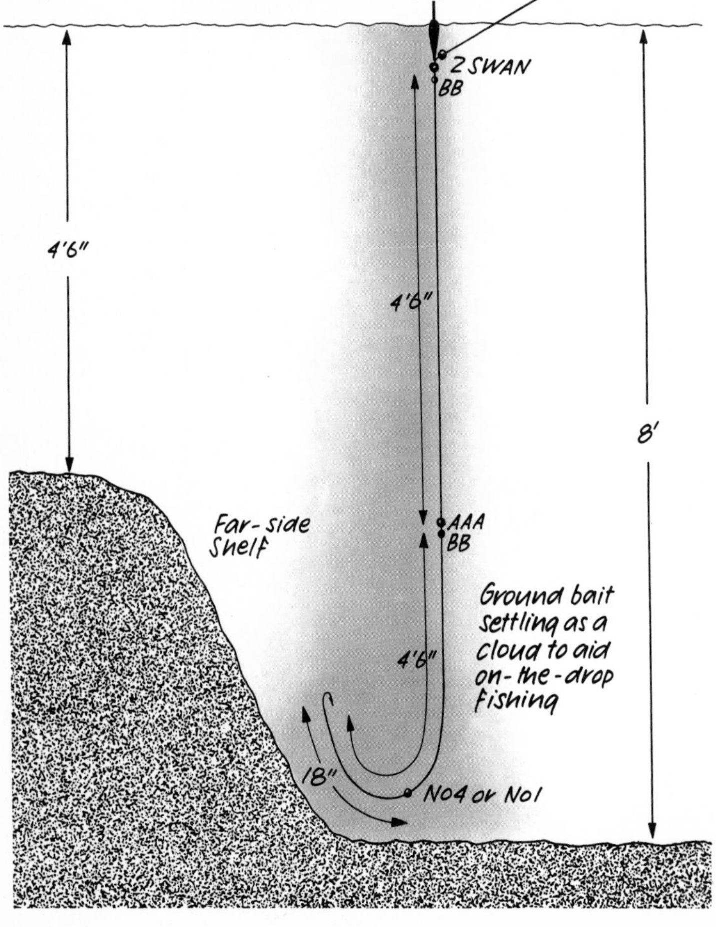

A rig for the Coronation Channel – see this page.

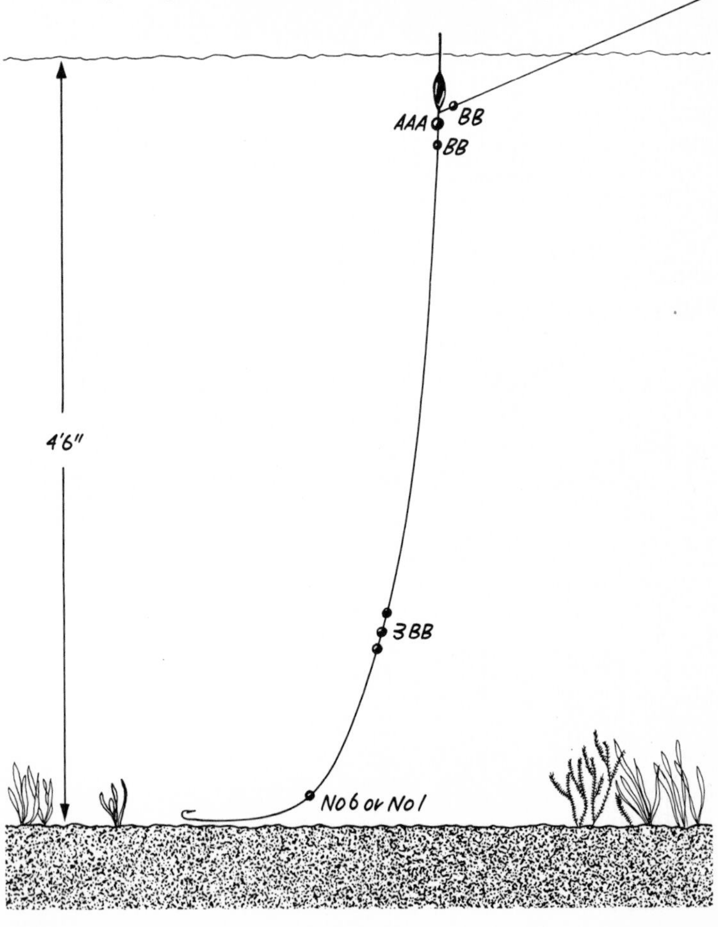

An "overdepth" rig for the Rivers Ant and Cam – see this page.

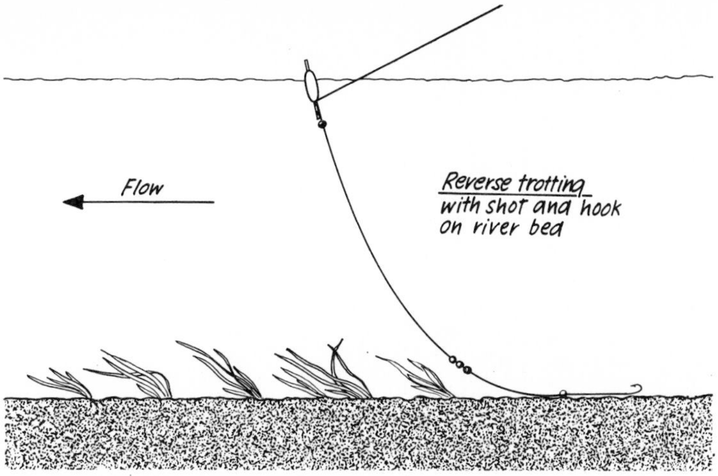

Reverse trotting rig – see page 74.

The Hampshire Avon, at Downton, is one of the best coarse-fishing rivers in the British Isles but match fishing is virtually impossible because of the lack of a continuous length of open bankside.

This trailing shot slows the drift down substantially. A bait is virtually trailed into the fish's mouth and the bites show as lifts rather than sinking of the float.

CHUB RIVERS

Matches based on catching chub are rarely big affairs. The banks of the chub rivers tend to be controlled by a variety of organizations, each with its own different objectives. This means that it is rare for such contests to have big entries simply because the bank space is not available. This does not mean that I do not fish the Severn, Wye or Hampshire and Warwickshire Avons – I do, but in match-fishing terms I rate the River Trent and the bream rivers as better prospects. I fish the

2

1 *Although thickly wooded, this section of the middle Severn is often included within the match lengths. There are fine dace in the shallows and the inevitable barbel will show in the deeper holes between the rock strata.*

2 *Both pleasure angler and matchman have to share the river with the canoeists. The presence of these fast, shallow draught boats appears to have little effect on the fish but the anglers tend to take offence.*

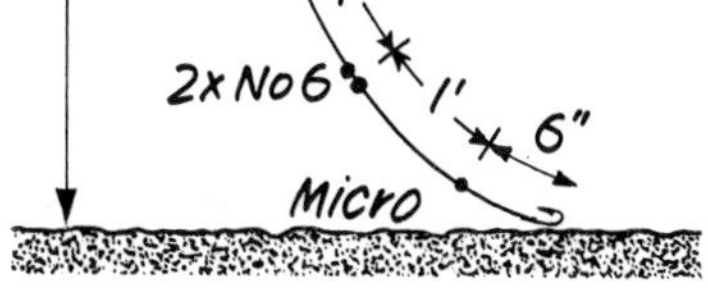

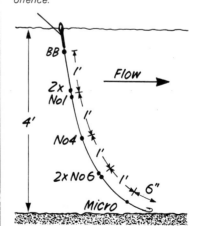

A shotting rig for the Severn at Stourport – see page 76.

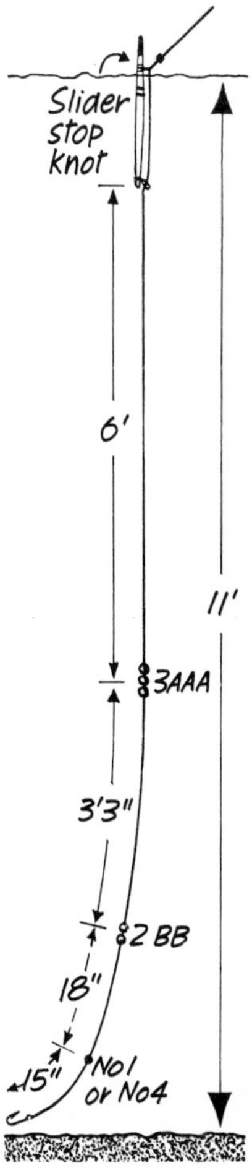

A deepwater sliding float rig for chub on the Severn – see page 78.

always take 20 lbs of groundbait, 6 pints of casters and 3 of pinkies to this stretch. Hemp has so far not produced good catches on this water for the flow is fast and the river generally dirty. It would be foolish to ignore the presence of the bream, so feed a swim 30 yds out with 5 big balls of groundbait loaded with pinkies . . . just in case. I wouldn't attempt to try that swim for at least 90 minutes and only then if the chub are slow to arrive and other anglers begin to catch a bream or two. The bream are slow to settle down onto the feed. They are small fish with the possibility of a 3-pounder. My hookbait for them would be white gozzers fished using a swingtip and not float tackle.

For the chub, I fish a 2-ring all-balsa sliding float taking a $4\frac{1}{2}$ AAA shot load. The inside chub swim is 11 ft deep at 2 rod lengths out from the bank and requires a trot of 20 yards. Fishing 12 ins over-depth, the bulk shot are positioned 6 ft 6 ins below the nylon stop knot that sets the float depth. A further 3 ft 3 ins down the line, I place 2 BB shot. That leaves only the lowest shot, a No 1 or No 4 to be positioned 15 ins from the hook. The speed of flow and depth of water together dictate that the trot down must not be longer than in most other situations but I do not attempt to shorten it. The groundbait should be light, almost sloppy, and loaded with nothing but casters. I feed a golf-ball-sized helping every trot down, for bear in mind that it will take 2 minutes to trot the float through a 20 yd long run. Eventually, when the feeding sequence begins to take effect, the chub will move into the swim. They feed rather like bream on the Welland, with 3 or 4 fish being hooked fairly quickly. Then there is a lull as the chub shoal regroups, but with continuous feeding you can draw the shoal again and again.

For the hookbait, use a single caster on a size 20 hook. As the action quickens, I would change to an 18 and vary the number of casters on the hook. When the fishing is slow use a single caster. When you begin to hook fish give them 2 or 3 casters in an attempt to speed the rate of take and the possible size of fish being caught.

The Warwickshire Avon is a far less powerful river than the Severn but it has a similar stock of fish, although barbel are missing as far as I know. Avon bream are best taken on swing or quivertip methods, but my float fishing shot pattern is sufficiently varied from the usual to be worth explanation. If I float fish the river, at Evesham for instance, I set up 2 float rods. One is fitted with a 3 BB stick float and the other with a $7\frac{1}{2}$ ins balsa-on-reed waggler taking 4 AAA shots. The shotting for the stick float is much as for the Trent style, with BB shot tight under the float while the remaining shot load is split No 1 and No 4 shots that are positioned equidistant through the $5\frac{1}{2}$ ft setting needed for the 5 ft deep swim. The bottom shot is a No 8.

The waggler float is shotted in much the same fashion except that $2\frac{1}{2}$ AAA shot is used as lock shot. The system of tapered shotting is then maintained with the remaining shot being equally spaced out. Of course, I use the waggler float fastened at the base only when I need to present the bait to chub or dace at the speed of current flow. Sometimes they will take the bait better than when it is held back, so the stick float is fished, fastened top and bottom, for a slow-through trot with the waggler used for faster movement.

I always find that in this river the chub and dace lie along the shadow line cast by the trees that grow on the bankside. Dace will make an appearance first, followed by the chub as the feed gets to work drawing fish into the swim. This takes sustained feeding using more casters than hemp. My feeding plan is to feed 12 grains each fourth swim down with casters introduced at the rate of 24 every trot. Use casters on the Avon as hookbait, with white or yellow gozzers as a change bait if bites are slow in coming. If the loose-feeding tactics fail, and they may, it is worthwhile trying casters and hemp introduced via sloppy groundbait. But always loose feed first, never the other way round!

The Wye and Hampshire Avon are both strong, powerful rivers containing bumper stocks of big fish. Unfortunately, match fishing on anything like a grand scale is virtually impossible on either river. The Hampshire Avon Championship hasn't been staged for several years now. There is no shortage of anglers to fish the match; it is only that the bank is not available in a continuous length. The Wye Championship is a regular October feature on the match calendar.

1 *Ivan Marks places great importance on accurate depth setting of his float. Measurement can be made of any setting against the fixed position of fittings on the rod. Speed in making a depth adjustment is all important to the matchman.*

2 *Ivan Marks contacts a fish at distance. Fishing a small mid-week competition on the River Trent, Ivan fished almost on the centre-line of the river to take roach, skimmer bream and gudgeon.*

1

The main species on the Wye are chub and dace, with frequent dace nets being mustered of 40 to 50 lbs taken trotting through with either caster or maggot. Maggots, casters and grub are banned from the opening of the coarse-fishing season until October 26th; they can then be used up to the end of the season. Chub are best taken on wasp grub, but to fish it effectively one would need 4 complete nests – as well as 6 pints of casters!

A stick float rig for the Warwickshire Avon – see page 78.

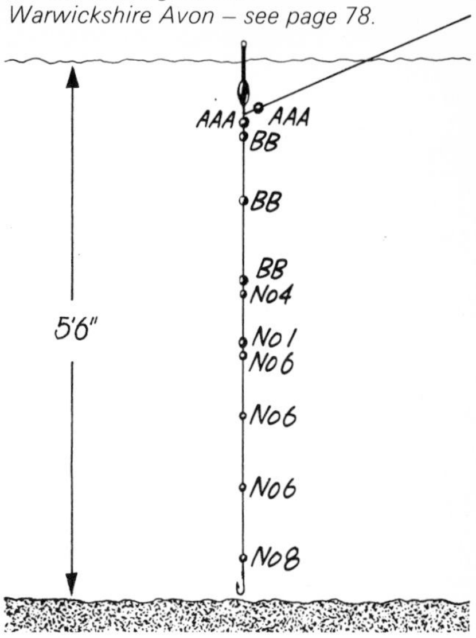

A waggler rig to present the bait at the speed of current – see page 79.

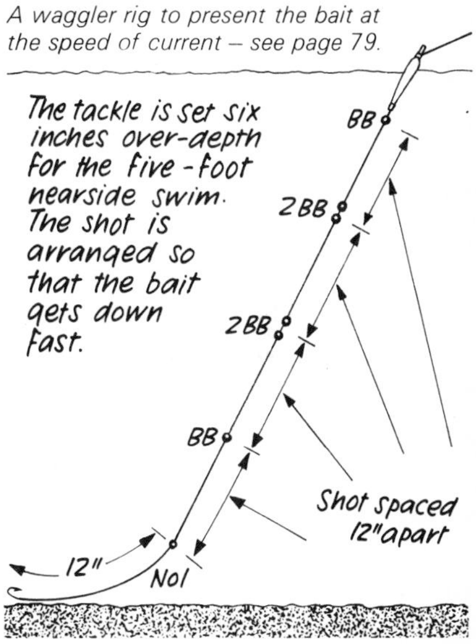

A shotting rig for the near-side swim – see page 78.

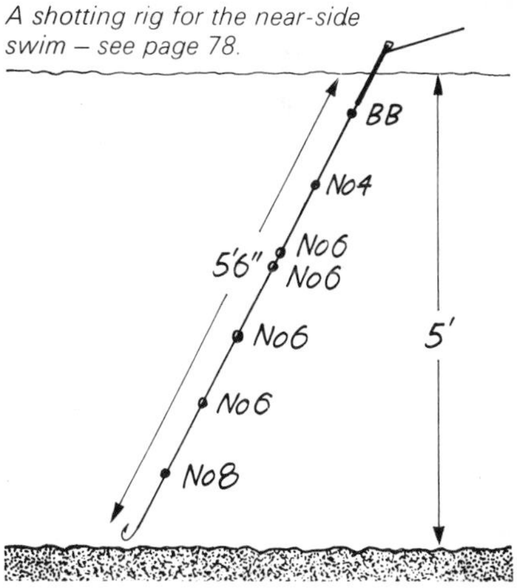

2

This is a mammoth amount of bait that can be further increased by the addition of 2 pints of commercial maggots and a loaf of bread. But, the Wye can produce heavyweight bags for everyone.

I prefer, where possible, to fish the edge of the current flow rather than the full force of the stream. I use an all-balsa or waggler trotting float. Shot-carrying capacity will be determined by the distance that has to be cast and trotted. It could be as little as 3 AAA for a shallow swim and as much as 4½ swan for a deep one. The chub average 2 lbs in weight but there could be larger fish brought in as the feed begins to pull. Start with the dace first, while the feed gets to work. They are big on the river and can average 3 to the pound. As the chub arrive you may switch to a bigger hook and bait, size 8 or 10 baited with 4 wasp grubs, if the chub decline to accept your casters. My wasp nests are broken up to be mixed in with the groundbait. I don't scald wasp nests, although most Midland anglers do. It is a matter of personal choice but I prefer particles of my nests to float. Pieces break away from the groundbait and must be particularly attractive to the chub! Sometimes big

1 *A stillwater match on the Winfield Lagoon at the National Watersport Centre, Holme Pierrepont, Nottingham. This type of situation fishes better in the summer and autumn months, for the lowered temperatures of winter soon put the fish down, making them difficult to lure.*

2 *There are not many people who would consider holding a match on this small Kentish stream but the fish in the water would surprise many an angler. They are not easy to catch and would call for the acquired skills of the match angler to hook them.*

3 *Canals are virtually stillwater fisheries. They are better in the warmer months for there is little if any pull in the current against which fish have constantly to move. The canals are subject to rapidly falling temperatures in the cold months.*

1

chub will crash up to the surface to take these morsels but I prefer to take chub on casters if possible, for I can stay with a smaller hook. A size 16 is correct, for if the chub become inactive I will still be able to hook the dace to add to the net.

The Hampshire Avon holds just about every coarse fishing species. There are hordes of dace, many chub, lots of barbel, some roach and even hefty bream and perch in favoured swims. You should go for a match-weight of dace and chub, regarding everything else as a bonus. I have always found that I have to search the Hampshire Avon for fish, gradually lengthening the cast throughout the day. In the early stages of a match, I am happy to catch dace on maggot for they are so numerous that they can be taken at all depths but I will feed with casters, for this bait will attract the chub and bring them to my peg.

It is most unlikely that any big Avon contest can ever be won without chub being included in the catch so one must really concentrate on fishing for them. I have found myself casting farther and farther out across the river to locate the chub and eventually may be fishing within a couple of yards of the far bank. The River Avon is almost always gin-clear, unlike other English match rivers, which is the main reason why we have to cast to fish instead of expecting them to come to us. The near side of the river can be almost fishless after an hour, so as you cast progressively across the river you will have to feed over there. I do this by introducing casters, a dozen at a time, using my catapult. The feed will not be very compact but that doesn't matter. If it disperses, at least it will be doing a fine searching job and the bulk of the chub will congregate where the feed lies thickest.

It is worth remembering that the flowing rivers mentioned in this chapter tend to fish much the same throughout the season. Since the water flow is often substantial, the fish remain much more active in both summer and winter than fish in slow or stillwaters. Chub and dace will feed in cold weather, in fact the chub has a reputation in conditions too cold for most species. Barbel fishing is brought to a halt by the frosts, but they are the only fish to discount in mid-winter. On the other hand, these fast rivers are susceptible to a rapid rise and fall of water level, running as they do through hilly, even mountainous terrain. So they, too, have their off periods. The rivers should be avoided immediately after heavy rain in their catchment areas but unless flooding is severe they quickly come back into condition, for the run-off of surplus-water to the estuary is very fast indeed.

STILLWATERS – LAKES AND PONDS

As pressure on river space increases, anglers are making more use of enclosed lakes and ponds, places which at one time were never match-fished. Waters which have sprung into prominence in recent years, as match venues, include Coombe Abbey Lake, near Coventry, and the lakes in the Leisure Sport angling scheme network.

Bloodworms may yet prove themselves to be a superior bait in many of these stillwaters, but until they do I believe that long-range fishing for quality specimens is the best technique. Learn to feed and fish at distance if you want to extend your angling ability. Remember that stillwaters are often quite clear and that they are match-fished mostly in the summertime when the sun is likely to shine brightly overhead. Fish will enjoy almost perfect vision and are unlikely to spend time in the margins during a match.

I spend time continually casting and searching with

2

3

4

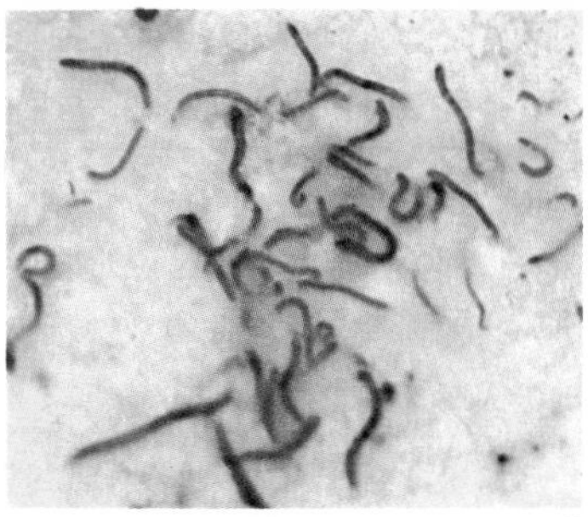

5

4 *The baits for the match – squatts, gozzers and annatto maggots to tempt all but the shyest biting fish in a stillwater competition.*

5 *Bloodworm, spread across the surface of a matchman's groundbait. He will use the mixture to pull fish into his swim. The Continental matchman regularly uses bloodworm as a hookbait but it is not used by most British anglers as it is difficult to obtain.*

a leger bomb to find the location of deepwater channels that are sure to exist in these lakes and certainly can be found in man-made gravel pits. I fish close to the edges of the rising contours in the knowledge that bream roam around to follow the shelf lines. Because of the clarity of the water, it is unlikely that many bream will settle down to feed for any length of time. There will rarely be huge weights built up in these conditions, although Coombe Abbey, which has a better water colour, seems to be an exception to the rule. The fishing is a waiting game, where eventually a shoal of bream may move into the swim giving an angler time to catch two or three in quite rapid succession before they take fright and depart. It is particularly important not to strike at line bites in a stillwater. Bream will usually give an impressive indication on the swingtip so there will be time to decide whether or not the bite is valid before responding!

Most of the swim-feeding should be given at the start of the contest. I put mine in by catapult. This can be topped up at hourly intervals, but as a general rule it is better to underfeed rather than overfeed after the initial baiting. Fish do not usually hang around long enough to clean up all the feed so there will be a reasonable amount to hold the interest of new fish that move into your bait. On stillwater lakes that hold bream, it is my policy to rely on squatt feed rather than casters in the groundbait, and I choose to fish either yellow or white gozzers on the hook. It is unlikely that many of these waters will have been heavily fished with casters, and since one ought to fish at maximum range it is a reasonable assumption that the fish will not have seen much rod and line activity before. It is a tragedy that still waters are so easily upset by frosts, and the consequent loss of water temperature makes them poor winter venues for the matchman.

Michael Prichard / Sea angling from inshore anc

Anyone who seeks to fish the seas must first of all find out something about the sea itself. You can begin by noting the encouraging fact that two thirds of the earth is covered with water, both salt and fresh. Admittedly this water is unevenly distributed – there is more water than land in the southern hemisphere and less in the northern – but the amount of sheer water available is a stimulating fact for a fisherman to dwell upon. Not, of course, that it can all be fished. For although the seas of the earth are teeming with fish in an almost infinite variety of shapes and sizes, there are limits to the depths at which a fisherman can present his baits. The sea angler must be satisfied – and heaven knows there is a plenitude in these areas – with that narrow band of waters that wash around the Continent stretching out from the shoreline to around the hundred fathom mark. Known as the Continental Shelf, this relatively shallow ground has been formed by the constant flow of silt and debris from the rivers, together with soil, containing, of course, minerals, washed into the rivers from the land or eroded from the coastline by the constant movement of tide, current and wind.

All this has fed into the seas a never-ending supply of enriching material, which has formed a fertile underwater plateau perfectly suited to the support of varied marine flora and fauna.

In Britain, the fisherman is particularly fortunate since he has a larger area of fishable water than most other countries in Europe can offer. But although commercial fishermen from these countries are inclined to seek their living in our waters, and our popular species are therefore under great pressure, we have many things apart from the natural fertility of our seas working in our favour. And the most important of these are the warm water currents that bring a vast variety of spawning species into our waters every year.

These currents are important and a knowledge of them is essential to the sea angler. Our main warm water current is the North Atlantic Drift which is a spur of the Gulf Stream. The Drift starts far down in the equatorial region of the Atlantic Ocean bringing rich, plankton-laden water to the western coasts of Britain. Many species of fish – shark, sea bream, mackerel and other members of the tunny family – tend to travel within the sharply defined path of the Drift, foraging annually from the warmer regions and sometimes reaching into sub-Arctic seas.

Our sea angler must also know something about tides. The twice-daily influence of the tide not only cleanses the inshore zones, and in so doing brings new food supplies to the native fish population. It also stimulates the pattern of life in the littoral waters.

Fish react to the state of the tide as it ebbs and flows. Just as we are regulated by clock and calendar, so a flowing tide will encourage fish to move out from their hiding and resting places to feed and to re-establish

Michael Prichard fighting a porbeagle shark of 147 lbs, on 50 lbs class gear,

deepsea boats

under the Cliffs of Moher, Co. Clare. The fish was taken trolling over a reef at the cliff base.

their territorial rights. Slack water produces a lethargy among sea-dwelling animals which in turn is conveyed, by lack of bites, to the angler. But immediately there is a freshening in the tidal strength life comes to the sea and angling activity begins.

There are two high and two low tides in each 24-hour day, although a few British coastal areas experience a peculiar tidal phenomenon resulting in more than one high tide for each tidal phase. High tide does not always achieve the same height; nor does it arrive at the same time every day. The height and time of arrival are dictated by the gravitational pull of the moon. Exceptionally high tides, or springs, are brought about when the moon and sun produce a combined pulling effect. Neap tides occur when the sun and moon are pulling in opposing directions and this tends to cancel out the effect of both.

Fortunately sea anglers need not worry too much about the state of the tide on any particular day since tidal predictions are published yearly by the Admiralty and extracts from these are available at most coastal towns for the surrounding sea areas. Anglers owning their own boats will need to know a little more about both time and height of tide when plans to leave and return to harbour are being made. Obviously it is essential to know the amount of water required to float the boat and whether the tide will produce enough.

WIND AND SALINITY

Two other important matters must be considered by sea anglers when deciding where to fish and for what. These are wind and salinity. Wind is important because it will affect the strength and height of the tide especially when is blowing in the same direction as the flow of the tide. For example, a gale blowing up the English Channel from the west will create a bigger tidal rise at Dover than the tables predict and will also delay the ebb by holding up the water at the high water period. The long stand of tide is probably more noticeable to the shore fisherman when out on shallow beaches or estuaries. The temperature of a wind can also make or break a fishing day. Should the wind be cold, or from the east, it will have a cooling effect on the sea which can put fish down and off the feed.

Salinity, or the amount of mineral salts dissolved in the water, will establish the range of species to be found in the sea area. Some of our sea species are more tolerant of the inflow of freshwater than others. Bass, flounders and mullet will live contentedly in estuaries and bays into which large rivers and streams discharge their flow. But very few fish will stay and feed in polluted water, and those that do so tend to be sickly, indifferent feeders unfit for the angler's kitchen.

If we take an underwater look at the ground around the whole of the British Isles we find that a soft bottom predominates. More than two thirds of the ground out to the Continental Shelf and down the steep slope into the deeps will be composed of sand, mud, shingle, shell, clay, chalk and small rock. In general the bottom ground will consist of a mixture of them all. The composition of the sea bed material will dictate what plant life can grow on it and what form of food chain will be present to provide a life support system for fish species. The turbidity, or amount of solid matter in suspension in the water, will also affect the plant life. If the water is highly coloured this will severely cut down the penetration of light to the sea bed, which in turn will control the growth of plant life.

A heavy outflow of silt from rivers and streams will tend to overlay the ground, preventing plants from establishing root growth, and it will also cut down available light to levels that will not encourage strong plant production. Fortunately, fish do not depend entirely on plant life, or its associated small animal life, for their food. Their animal food requirements can be obtained from what lives and reproduces in the mud and sand forming the sea bed, or from zoo (animal) and phyto (plant) plankton which drift on tidal currents.

As a result of the continual movement of the currents, which over long periods cut channels in the sea bed, small patches of slacker water are formed. These areas allow plant and animal life, such as mussels and scallops, to settle and establish colonies. As the colonies grow they help to slow down the action of current

1

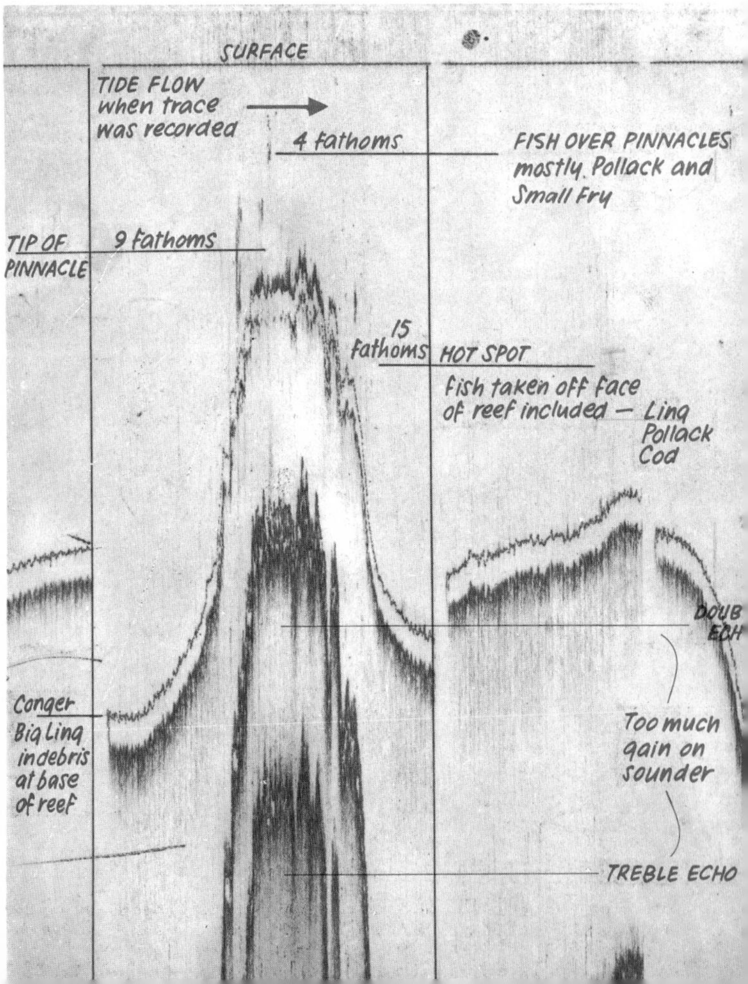

A sharking boat en route for the grounds north-west of the Blasket Islands, Co. Kerry. Blue shark move into Irish waters in early June each year.

by forming a natural barrier to the flow. This in turn helps to create suitable conditions for even lusher growth and, possibly, for the establishment of other species of both plants and animals. Fish then move in to take up permanent residence and a virtually self-supporting ecological system results. When we, as anglers, find this "underwater larder" it soon becomes a popular place to fish and is called a *mark*.

You may say, this is all very well, but why should a sea angler need to know about the conditions on the bed of the sea? After all, it is normally the skipper of the boat who decides just where the boat will be anchored for the day's sport. I think the answer is that to become a good angler, in any environment, it helps to know something of the needs and behaviour of the species you are seeking to land. Given that a skipper is able to tell his anglers that the boat is positioned above a mussel bed, it then helps them to know that some species – plaice, for example – are habitually found on a mussel bed and that they will be conditioned to feeding on mussels. This knowledge will establish the bait to be offered on the hook, and lead to tackling up with a rig suitable for the flatfish.

If we seek larger fish that not only need food from a particular ground but cover in which to seek security from predators, then we must turn our attention to broken ground. This can be found quite close inshore, where cliffs have either fallen into the sea or have become eroded by wind and water. These areas are easily recognized but there are other cliffs which produce the same ground and can be far out in deeper water. These are not so easy to find without advice from the commercial fishermen who trawl the offshore waters but you can spot them in the Admiralty Charts and, of course, you can also use an echo sounder. Basically, the difference between the two varieties of broken ground is the species that will be found on them. The shallow water ground will support masses of small invertebrates and members of the crab and lobster families which in turn will provide food for the smaller fish. Pollack, wrasse, codling and young conger will lurk there until they grow too large to hide or until the feed runs out. Then they will move to the deeper water and broken ground to join other species and the larger members of their own kind.

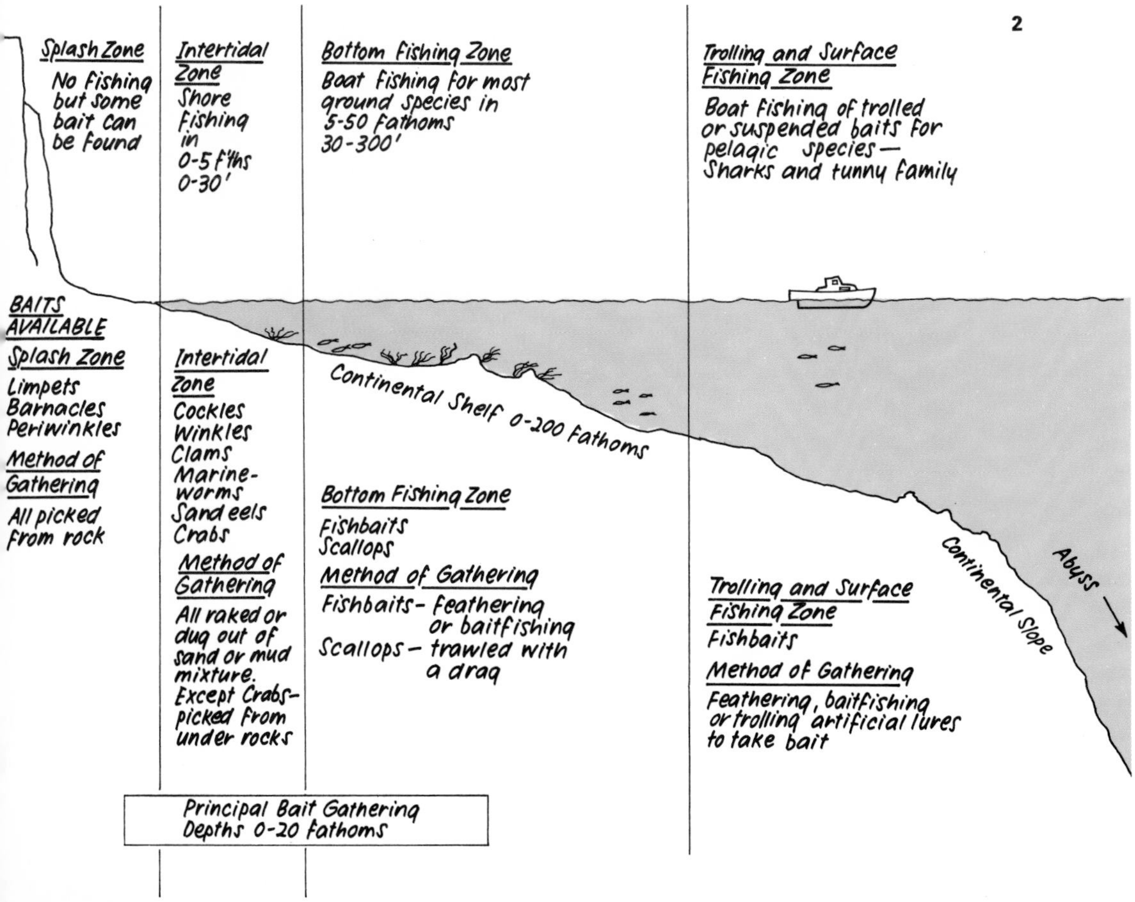

1 *A section of echo-sounder trace that shows clearly the undersea picture. Towering pinnacle rocks rise sheer from the sea bed to within fathoms of the surface. Many species will be found on such a rock mass but each will choose different depths and habitat according to its life style.*

2 *The sea is available to all sea anglers around the British Isles, but not all of it is accessible to the rod and line angler. It is impracticable to fish the bottom in depths of over 50 fathoms although shark fishing can be undertaken out beyond the Continental Shelf.*

There are several offshore locations in British waters where the tidal flow has brought vast quantities of soft material down from the areas of maximum flow to form deposits as the strength of the flow decreases. In this way both sand and mudbanks have been formed which lie in the currents and are established as fish holding grounds. The currents remain too strong for a vigorous plant growth to populate the banks so life has to exist down in the mass of the bank.

Sand eels and marine worms favour these conditions. They rest within the bank when the currents are strong and come out of the sand to feed when the water is slack. To remain on a sandbank throughout the tidal phase requires great strength, but some species balance the energy needed to combat the power of water flow with the quality and quantity of the feed they can expect from the area. Cod and powerful predators such as the tope and the turbot are frequently fished for on these offshore marks. The cod in its greed seems to forget the buffeting in the tide stream as its lust for sand eels overcomes it. Tope are such strong swimming fish that they are able to combat the strong water while turbot (flatfish) are able to flatten their bodies down in the sand to escape from the pressure of water.

Although sandbanks and similar tidal obstructions are excellent fishing marks they do pose considerable problems to the boat fisherman. For one thing, they rarely have a fish population spread evenly across the banks. This is because at various stages of the tidal phase the fish must move their position in relation to the flow of natural food that is being swept along to them. Then, of course, there is a measure of danger to the boat in these often precarious anchorages.

The pinnacle rock or reef is another form of fishing mark in which the fish congregate because of the nature of the habitat and the food availability. There are not very many of these in southern or eastern British waters. They are more common in the rest of England and Ireland and, of course, in Scotland. Often such fishing locations are the undersea continuation of the land mass – huge bulks of rock rising in solid buttresses from the sea bed with often just a few fathoms of water over the peaks. Because these rocks form such vast obstructions to the tides and deflect the flow from its normal path, many types of holding ground conditions are created. Small fish can live near the surface in the many crevices while feeding on plankton and fry brought in by the tides. In turn, they form a splendid diet for the larger species living slightly deeper down the rock faces. The largest fish, living off the reef or the pinnacle, tend to dwell in the deep, darker regions from which they can ambush their lesser brethren. Scavengers such as the skate, conger and the slow-moving fish that depend more on the animal debris sinking into the depths tend to live at the base of the rock.

All this proves the importance of a golden rule for all anglers – to find fish one must learn to "read" the water, giving consideration to the basic needs of the fish and to where they can live, grow and breed, before we attempt to drop a bait. Fish are not spread evenly over the bed of the sea or down through the depths. They inhabit particular sites that provide security, food and the general conditions necessary to their species. Any natural or unnatural obstruction to the free passage of the water flow will create some form of home for some form of marine life – a wreck, a conglomeration of rocks, channels and gullies in the sea bed; almost anything where fish can hide from enemies, find food without too great an effort or even escape from the noise and disturbance of man will be a haven.

THE BOAT FISHERMAN'S SPECIES

At least 400 species of fish inhabit or visit the shores of the British Isles, although not all of them are of interest to the sea angler. Of the 40 or so species that receive regular attention from anglers about 10 per cent can be regarded as seasonal visitors. Sometimes the appearance of migratory species is not a regular year by year event, for the warm or cold currents that lead the fish to us are themselves sporadic. Pressures by commercial fishing may be such that species are virtually removed from the angling scene and it is often a long wait before they are again caught in sufficient numbers to be talked about or written about. The red bream virtually disappeared from the West Country marks for a period and they have only recently reappeared in the bream marks of Devon and Cornwall. Hake, a deep-water member of the cod family, were caught regularly on rod and line in the Irish Sea and up into The Minch but they suffered the attentions of trawlermen and long-liners and are now rarely to be seen among the angler's catch. When mackerel and herring species fail to shoal annually in areas famed for catches, it is safe to assume that most predatory fish will also fail to show.

Almost anything can cause a change in the path of a sea current. This obstruction is a favourite bait for anglers – the queen scallop, which has its own mini-ecology in the shape of acorn barnacles and serpulid worms.

A smile from Dennis Burgess as he brings another prime cod from the Dysaghy Rocks mark in the prolific cod ground of Achill Island, Co. Mayo.

The species illustrated in this book are those with a priority for anglers. You may notice colour variations from fish that you have caught. This is understandable when we consider that marine animals, like so many of their freshwater counterparts, often adapt body coloration to blend into the surroundings. Not only are fish in many cases subject to annual sexual colour variation, but immature specimens often display a diluted pattern of adult dress. Ideally an illustrator would choose faithfully to reproduce the colour and shape seen as a fish is lifted from the water before it has become dulled and shapeless by drying out. This we have tried to do.

THE SEA ANGLER'S TACKLE

Sea angling with rod and line is a comparatively new sport in Britain. The fishing rod, as we know it, came into use during the latter part of the 19th century. It is doubtful if anglers of that era concerned themselves with the sporting aspect of what they were engaged in, more likely that the rod was easier on the hands than the rough cord of the traditional handline. Used in conjunction with a large, wooden, centre-pin reel they were able to winch fish up for the pot in a more gentlemanly fashion than their pals using the handline.

Leslie Moncrieff successfully boats a fine halibut for Michael Shepley. The fish was taken in Scapa Flow, Orkney Islands, on a mackerel bait.

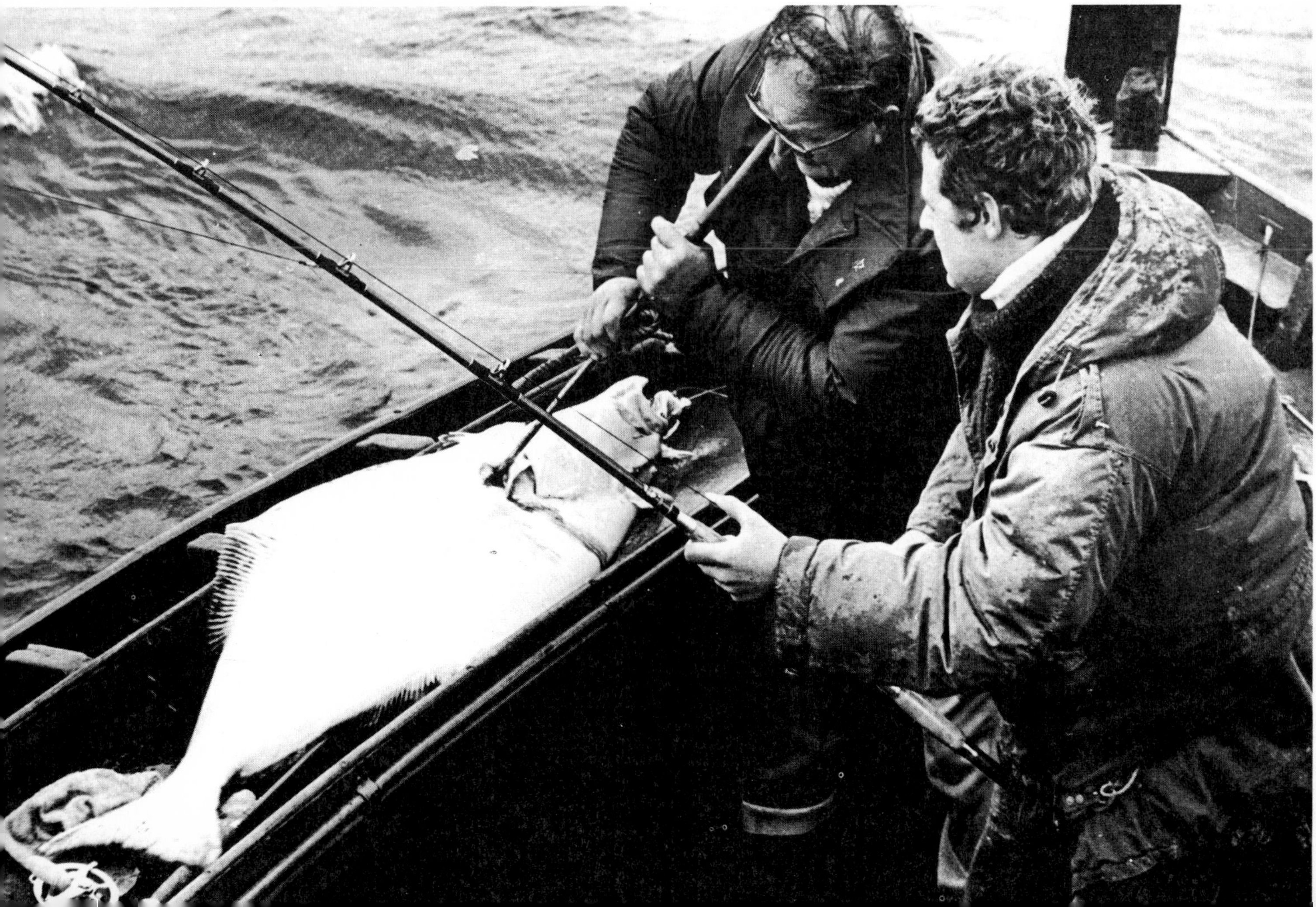

Some powerful rods and most of the declared IGFA-class rods will have a gimbal fitting. This prevents the rod twisting by having grooves or a slot in the end of the handle. The idea is that this groove will locate within a similar fitting on a heavy-duty butt pad or fighting chair. Ensure that you have a shroud to put on the fitting when you are not using the non-twist facility.

Handles are important on any rod but a handle on a boat rod that slips is a menace! A cork top grip to which both hands can be put is a good feature. Beware of a grip that is too thick as a hand that cannot close around the grip loses much of its power.

Not all boat rods require roller guides but there is a need at times for a substantial low-set cradle-type ring that is braced and hard-chromed for the heavy work that general-purpose boat rods are subjected to.

A 30 lb fast taper light tackle boat rod, 6 ft 9 in long with rings and roller tip.

The boat angler's rods

An IGFA 50 lb class rod. Compound taper, 7 ft long with roller guides.

A modern grip formed from a modern material – cork-rubber composite. It does not go slimy and, with a subtle resilience in the material, gives a positive handhold. Unfortunately for the angler it is fairly expensive.

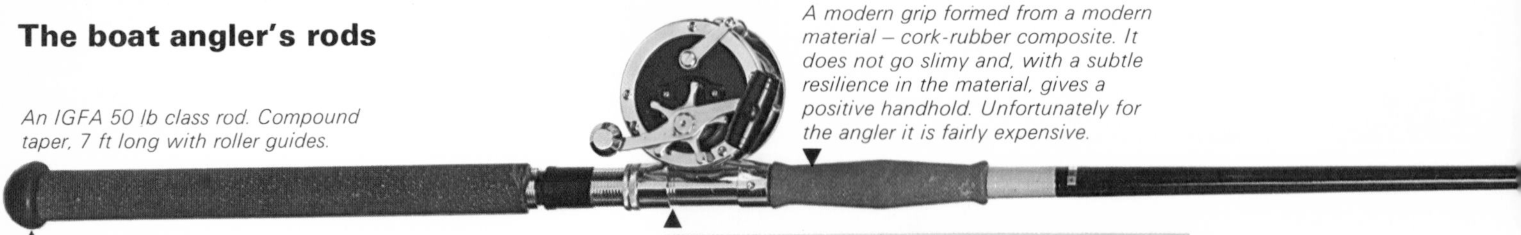

On a light boat rod a rubber butt cap or button will suffice to finish the handle neatly. Ensure that the button is reasonably large to spread the load of a hard-fighting fish on your midriff; alternatively, use a belly pad.

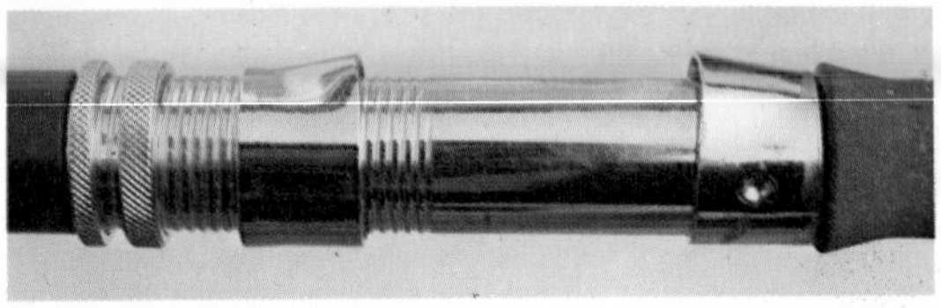

A most important feature on any rod – the winch fitting. It should have good quality parts and a positive locking action to make certain that the rod rings are always in perfect alignment with the line running from the reel. The threads should be deepcut and not rolled. Obviously there will be some play in the reel seat collars so that the fitting will accommodate a wide variety of reels. Much of this play can be taken up by locking the reel on with the supplied saddle and nuts.

Sea angling

The forerunner of the modern fibreglass rod was a thick, unwieldy and sometimes unbendable extension of the angler's arm, usually constructed from built cane. But although such a rod had many drawbacks in use, it did bring to sea fishing one thing – vibration, the feel of the fish moving urgently in an attempt to break free from restraint. This feeling, expressed as a series of tremors transmitted through rod and arm, is what angling is all about. Once people realized that there was more to fishing than the plain winching in of the fish, the sport of sea angling was born. Almost immediately the rod makers began to lighten their products in an effort to increase the sensitivity of the tackle. Other rod building materials were tried – steel tubes and lighter cane rods reinforced with a steel core – but they all had some form of problem in use, either the formation of rust, resulting in fracture, or breakdown due to the infiltration of salt water.

With the appearance of glass fibre many of the former troubles were overcome. Here was a material unaffected by salt, rust or engine oil, that could be extruded as a solid rod or wrapped around a forming, tapered mandrel to produce a light but strong stick that would bend in a satisfactory curve with a good recovery when not under stress. Solid glass fibre came first and soon became the standard material for building boat-fishing rods. However, they still lacked a certain sensitivity. But as the solid glass rod was lightened (and accepted), so the

The modern sea angling multiplier is a fairly complicated piece of machinery. With minimal maintenance, cleaning after use in freshwater and regular oiling of moving parts, most reels will give years of service. Saltwater will corrode any reel in time, eating away chromium plating, pitting bearing surfaces and alloy parts. The modern water-repelling aerosols, like WD40, help to prevent the problem but only care from the angler will keep any reel fit to tackle the big fish.

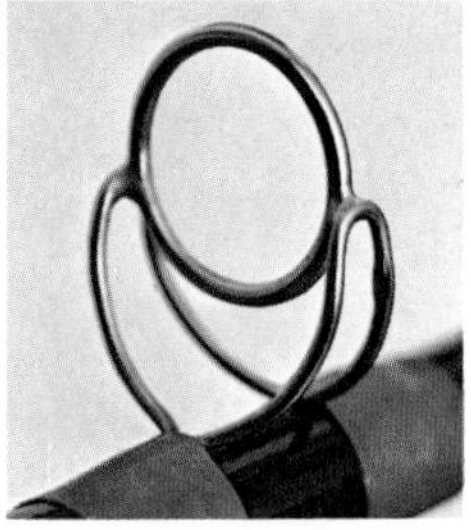

High-set stainless steel bridge guides that are ideal for light tackle boat rods, although a braced, reinforcing strut may be thought necessary. Providing a rod has enough rings to spread and support the line stress imposed, these rings are able to withstand the strains of playing quite big fish. They are also suitable for all beachcasting rods and sea spinning rods.

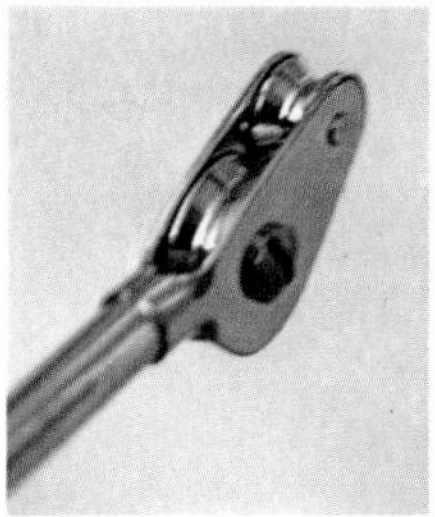

A form of non-strutted double roller tip ring found on 30–50 lb class rods. It withstands the use of wire, is neat and made to close tolerances.

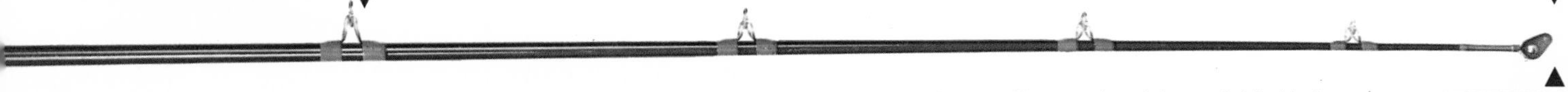

Stand-off strutted end rings of this kind are completely suitable for use with both braided and monofilament lines. Rub a piece of silk stocking within the seamless centre ring to ensure that there are no high spots or rough edges left after manufacture. Make sure that any alternative type of strutted end ring is also free from rough spots.

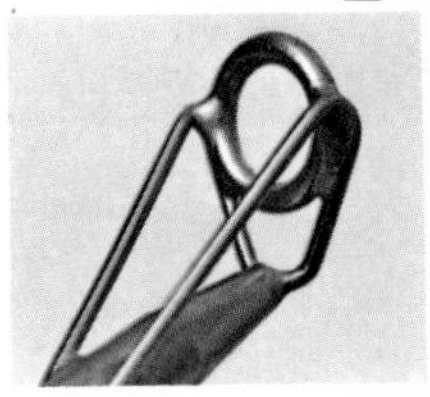

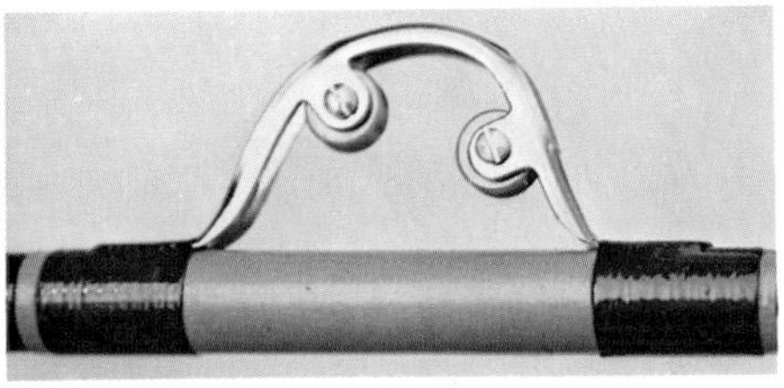

An AFTCO-type double roller ring for use on big-game rods and other heavy duty tackle. The rollers are of hardened steel within a cage of stainless steel that has been chromium-plated to withstand the corrosion of saltwater. This guide is best placed as the first guide out from the reel.

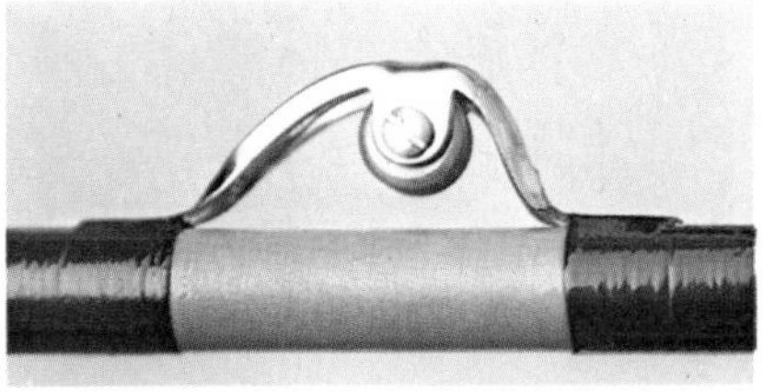

AFTCO roller guides are available as single roller units ideal for using as intermediate guides between a double roller butt guide and the tip roller.

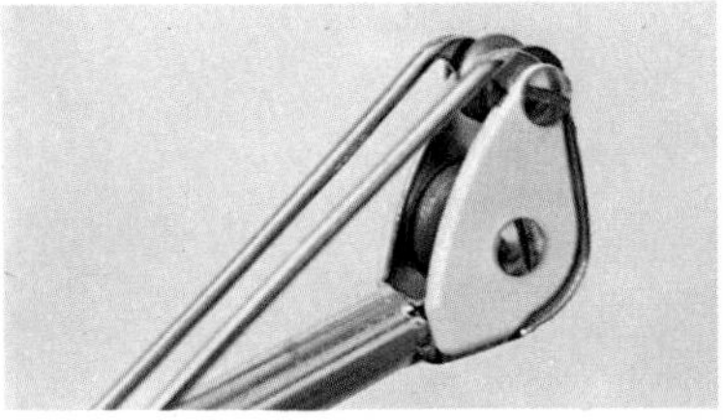

A double roller tip ring suitable for use with both braided and monofilament lines. If the rod is to be used with wire line, care must be taken to ensure that the rollers are of a sufficiently hard material to withstand the wearing properties of wire.

techniques of wrapping a hollow glass rod also hit the market. The two materials now run side by side in angling favour. Both are capable of doing the job, of playing and landing a fish successfully, but I find the hollow glass rod gives a definite improvement in striking and playing species of fish that move fast in the water.

Let us take a look at various types of boat rod, bearing in mind our basic requirements. A rod should obviously be of sound construction and design. The glass must be evenly wrapped and, if it is made in two pieces, the ferrule or junction should be strong enough to overcome any tendency to "break away" under the angler's left hand in a "dog's leg". Ensure that a rod has enough rings to support the line, keeping it clear of the blank when the rod is under stress. This will enable the rod blank to adopt the curve corresponding to its taper while spreading the load evenly throughout the power section. Although this is important in all sea rods, it is particularly important in a rod used with a reel hung below the blank, where the stress is not down onto the rod but hung from it. The rings are then taking all the strain of a heavy pull from the rod tip.

The modern glass rod often has a wooden handle. This handle is perfectly adequate providing the wood is straight in the grain and not cut away too much where it insets into winch fittings. There is a move toward extending the handle, in the form of a spigot, into the rod blank, which ensures a stronger union between sections and gives increased power beyond the handle when the rod is under extreme compression.

Nothing is gained by fitting a rod with cheap rings. Remember, that all the stresses and strains of an angling day are transmitted by the line to the rings. Choose or fit hard chrome bridge or roller rings especially when contemplating the use of wire line. Even braided Dacron and Terylene lines have an abrasive effect, made more so if the water has any amount of silt and sand suspended in it. Finally the length of a rod can be a problem when the choice is being made to cover all angling eventualities. Remember that your fishing may take place from a crowded charter boat or from an inshore dinghy, so a long rod could be awkward to use. About 6 to 7 ft is a comfortable length for the angler and a convenient length for the designer to work to when incorporating various working tapers for a definite action.

Most sea anglers choose a multiplying reel for boat fishing. Simple in use, they drive through a gear train giving a number of turns of the spool to one turn of the reel handle. All but a few have a slipping clutch mechanism (often called the drag), which allows a strong fish to take line when the pull on the line is greater than the amount of drag that has been set. Their only shortcoming is that they are fairly complicated pieces of machinery, made almost entirely of metal, so that regular cleaning and maintenance is vital after ▶98

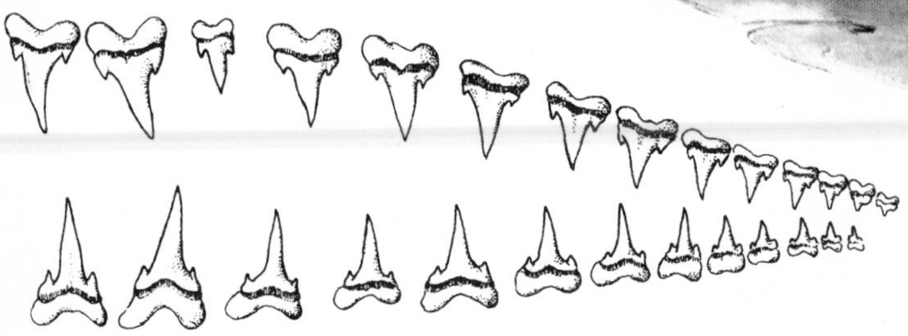

Teeth, shapes and patterns are an identifying feature between similar fish. The porbeagle shark has basal cusps, small pointed ridges, on each tooth. The mako below has teeth that are without cusps but are not as neat and regular

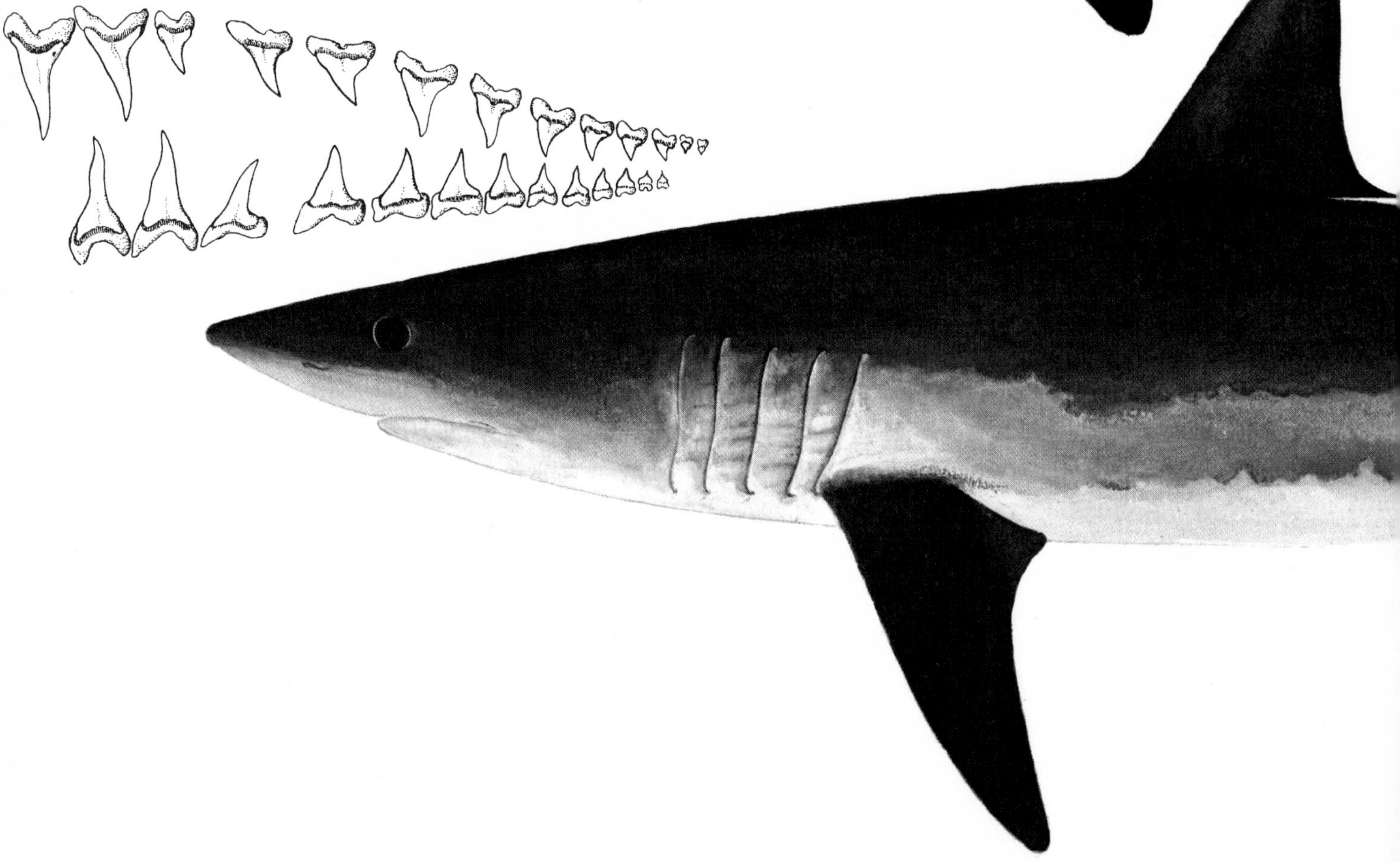

The marine fish classifications are as defined in CLOFNAM. Check list of the fish of the North-Eastern Atlantic and Mediterranean, a publication produced for Unesco (1973) under the editorship of J. C. Hureau and Th. Monod.

PORBEAGLE SHARK

Lamna nasus

A stout-bodied fish with the bulk of the body above the pectoral fins. The dorsal fin begins just above the posterior edges of the pectorals. There is a keel on both sides of the body beginning below the second dorsal with a small secondary keel, on the caudal surface, below the primary keel. This fish can be said to be, in British Isles terms, a true big-game species. It fights well and is present around our shores for most of the year, as witness the catches made by commercial trawlers during the cold winter months. The porbeagle shark is fairly common, although fished on rod and line in few areas, throughout the waters of the Northern Hemisphere. There is confusion between the species and the mako shark but the secondary keel and basal cusps to the porbeagle teeth should separate these two fish. The porbeagle shark is generally found to weigh between 100 and 200 lbs on the established marks but fish of 400 lbs swim in British waters.

Bait: *Live mackerel, presented on a suitable rig, or dead baits of most species of fodder fish. The porbeagle is a cautious feeder so lashes of mackerel or similar offerings may tempt the slow-taking shark.*

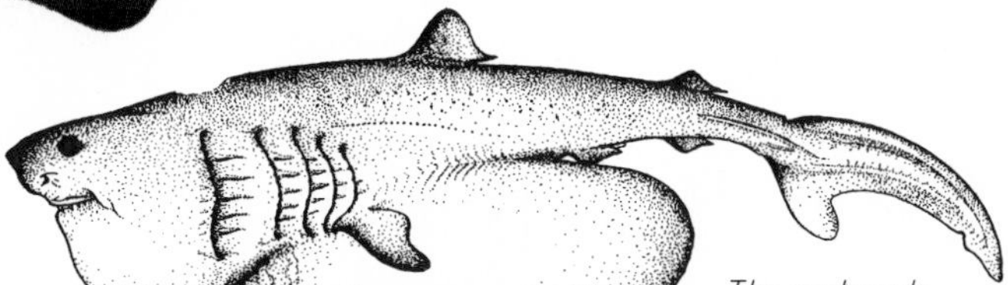

The porbeagle, like the other sharks, is a live bearer. The young develop from the fertilized egg into a fully-formed fish within the female's body cavity. The pups are expelled after the yolk sac is fully absorbed.

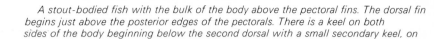

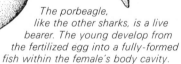

MAKO SHARK

Isurus oxyrinchus

A more slender fish that does have certain of the porbeagle identification points. There is only one fin, placed horizontally on the fish's body, and the mako teeth are without basal cusps and thinner in section. The mako shark is known for its habit of jumping clear of the water when hooked, sometimes repeatedly, though this behaviour alone will not identify the species. Many porbeagle sharks will also jump out of the water after hooking but generally they only jump once. There is similarity in colouring but the mako has a definite blue-ish tone on its back and flanks. Very few mako shark are boated in Britain, and most of them have been big sharks. The species has a world-wide distribution with fish of over 1000 lbs a distinct angling possibility.

Bait: *As for the porbeagle shark.*

BLUE SHARK
Prionace glauca

This is a streamlined, slender fish possessing large pectoral fins and a sloping caudal fin. The colour is a brilliant blue as the fish leaves the water but the vivid coloration soon dulls to a drab black. Blue shark have tearing teeth, extremely sharp and with a saw edge with which they strip long gouges in a bait that is attacked but not taken. In British waters, the species has shown a marked decline in average weight, with small fish of 30 lbs caught off Cornwall and 50 lbs off the southern shores of Ireland. There is world-wide distribution and the blue shark is reported to grow to over 20 ft long. There would appear to be a shoaling by sex factor as the species hunts in packs.

Bait: *Fresh deadbaits, mackerel, herring and other fodder fish.*

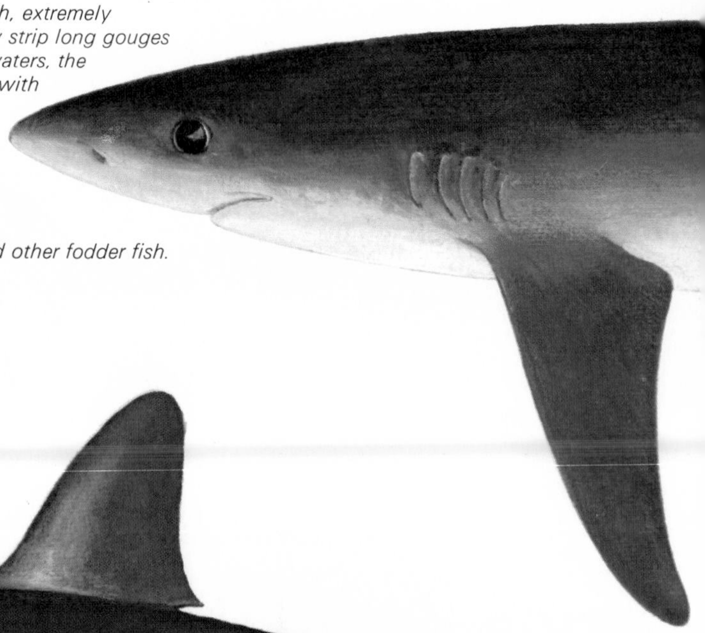

♀

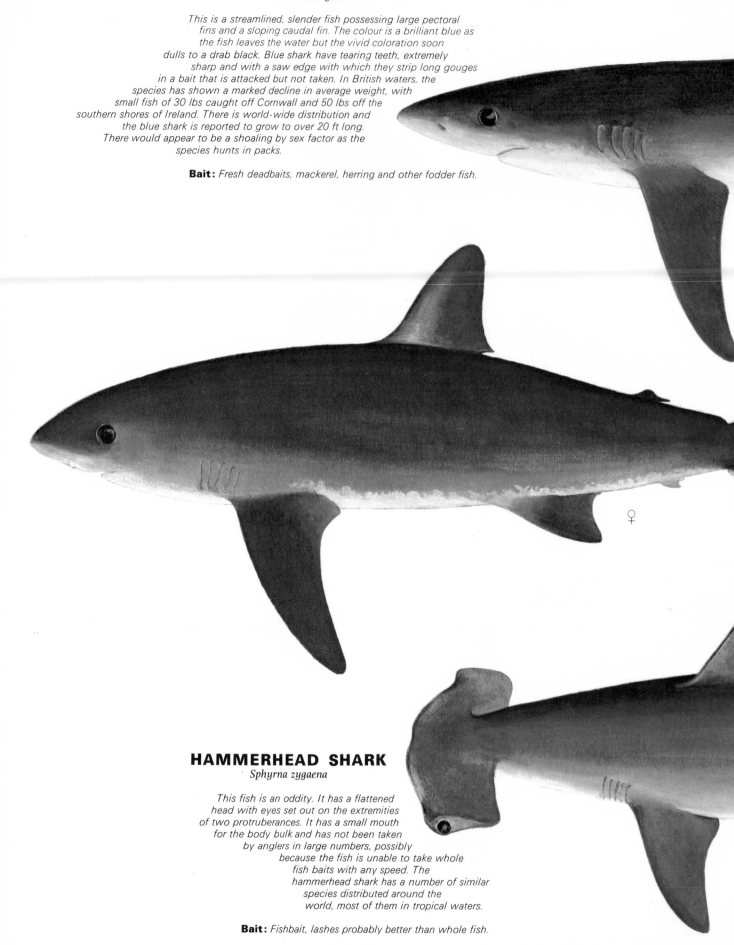

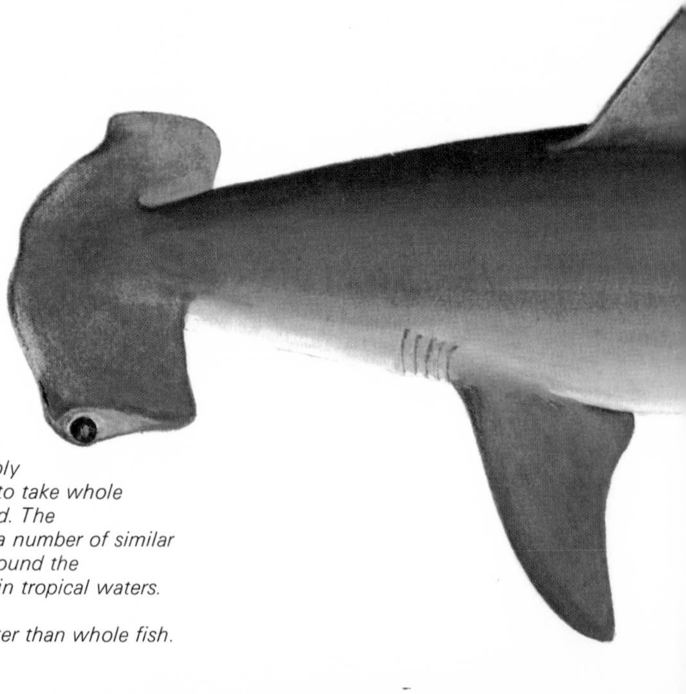

HAMMERHEAD SHARK
Sphyrna zygaena

This fish is an oddity. It has a flattened head with eyes set out on the extremities of two protruberances. It has a small mouth for the body bulk and has not been taken by anglers in large numbers, possibly because the fish is unable to take whole fish baits with any speed. The hammerhead shark has a number of similar species distributed around the world, most of them in tropical waters.

Bait: *Fishbait, lashes probably better than whole fish.*

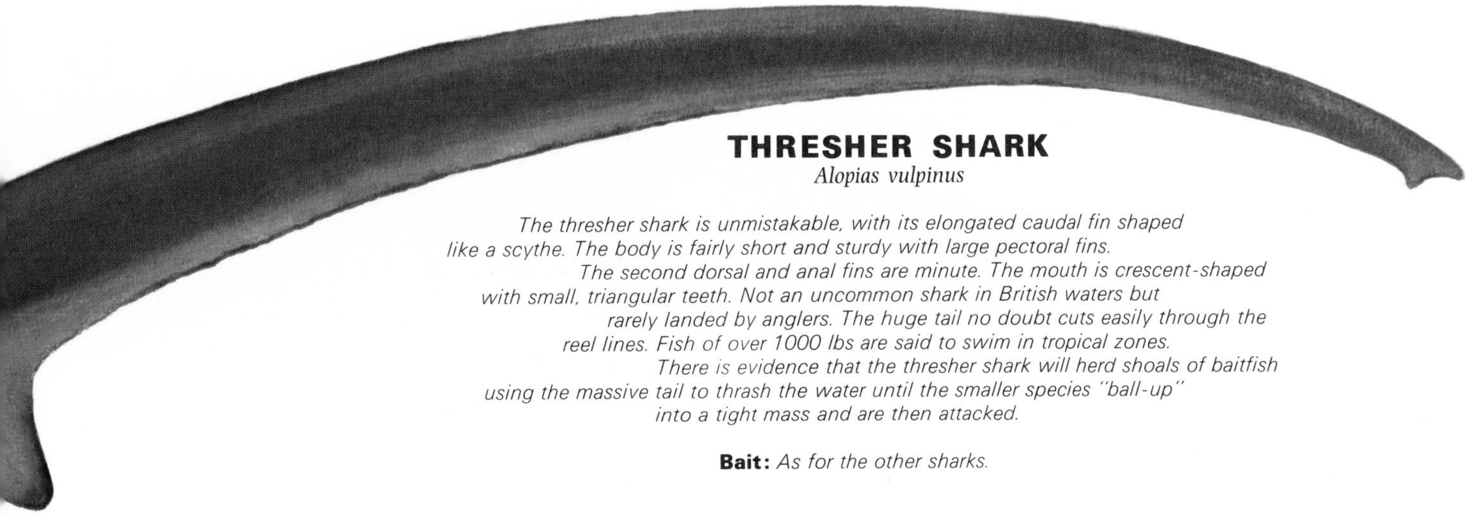

THRESHER SHARK

Alopias vulpinus

The thresher shark is unmistakable, with its elongated caudal fin shaped like a scythe. The body is fairly short and sturdy with large pectoral fins. The second dorsal and anal fins are minute. The mouth is crescent-shaped with small, triangular teeth. Not an uncommon shark in British waters but rarely landed by anglers. The huge tail no doubt cuts easily through the reel lines. Fish of over 1000 lbs are said to swim in tropical zones. There is evidence that the thresher shark will herd shoals of baitfish using the massive tail to thrash the water until the smaller species "ball-up" into a tight mass and are then attacked.

Bait: *As for the other sharks.*

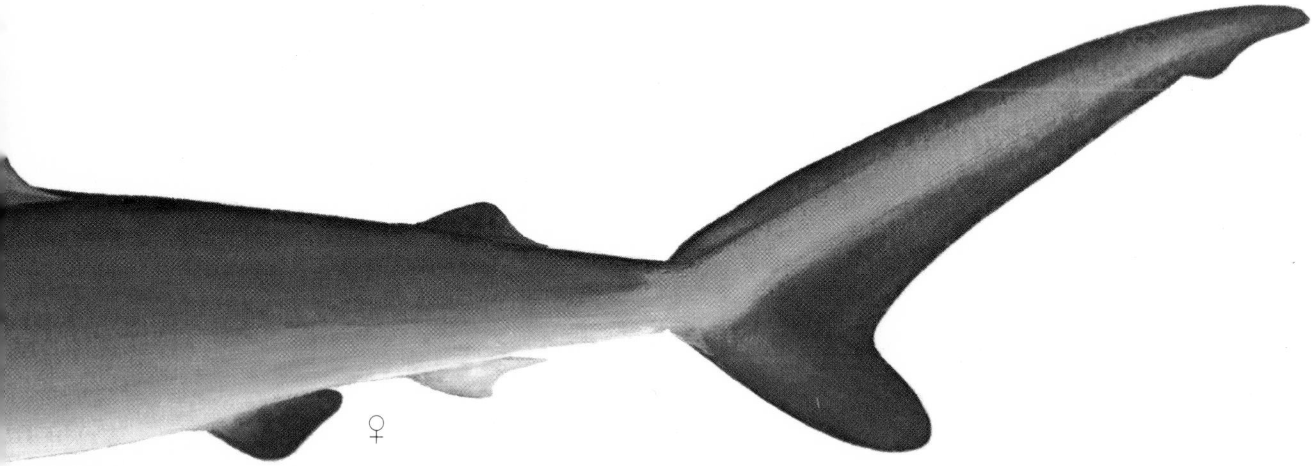

SPURDOG

Squalus acanthias

The most prolific member of the shark family found in the waters of the British Isles, its name comes from the two spurs or pikes that are present at the leading edge of the dorsal fins. There is no anal fin. This shark moves in huge shoals, cropping the sea as sheep do on the land. They are found down on the bottom during the colder months but will follow baits and hooked fish to the surface in warmer times of the year. A voracious fish can provide good sport on light tackle. Spurdog can reach 4 ft in length.

Bait: *Fish strips or small whole fish, such as "joey" mackerel and pouts.*

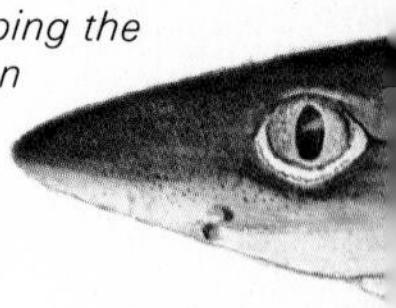

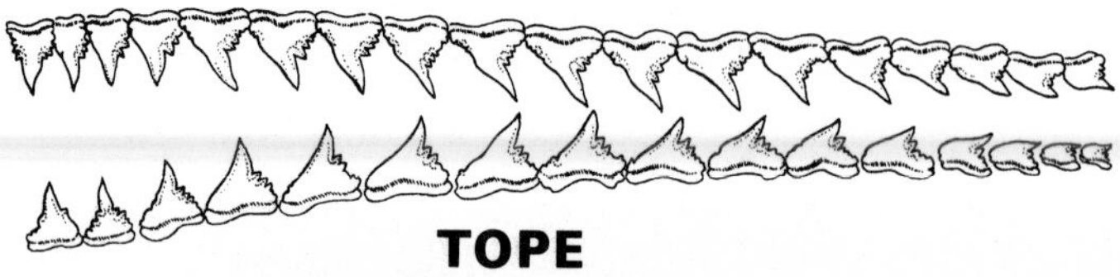

TOPE

Galeorhinus galeus

The most sporting fighter of the smaller sharks, the tope can put up a tremendous struggle in shallow water or when fished on suitable tackle that allows the fish to show its speed. The dorsal fins are spaced far apart with the pelvics exactly midway between them. The lower lobe of the caudal fin is deeply notched in an unmistakable pattern. A tope's teeth are large, sharp and with a slight serration to the inner edges. Tope have a wide distribution and are present throughout the year in British waters, although the winter months will see them out in the deeps. Fish of 30 to 40 lbs are the average with the possibility of a 70-pounder.

Bait: *Fish, as whole baits or lashes. It is a good idea to tie the lash on with elasticated thread as tope will tear at a bait, leaving a clean hook.*

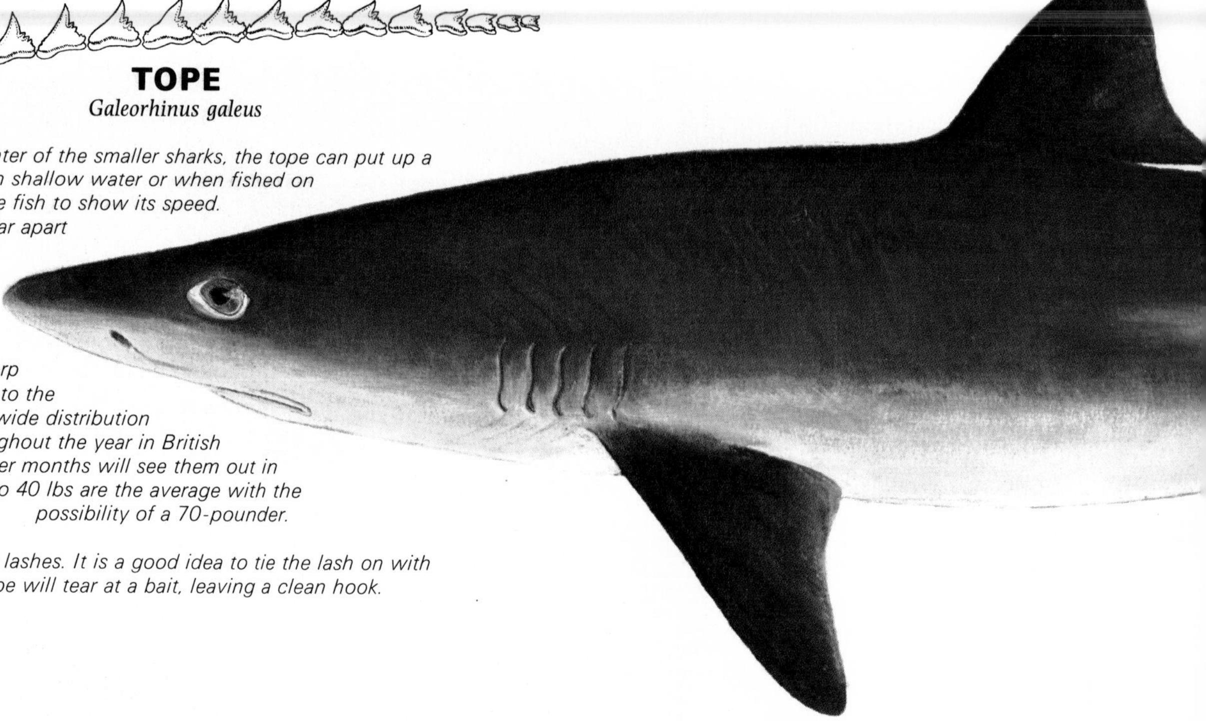

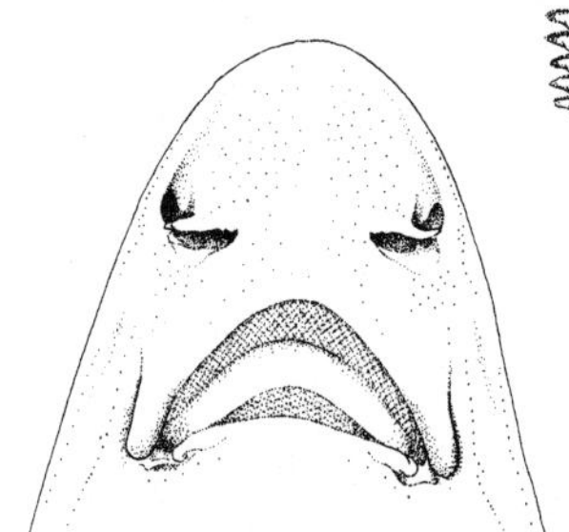

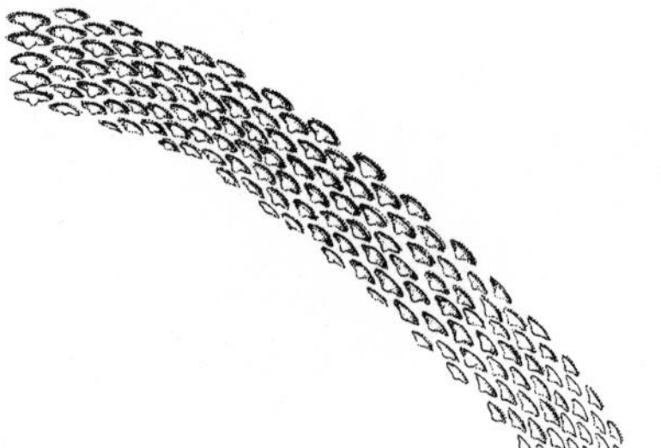

The underside of the smooth hound jaw showing the teeth rows and pattern.

So often, when caught and brought into the angling boat, female spurdogs will eject the young that they are carrying. Some will not have absorbed the yolk-sac but are perfect replicas of the parent fish.

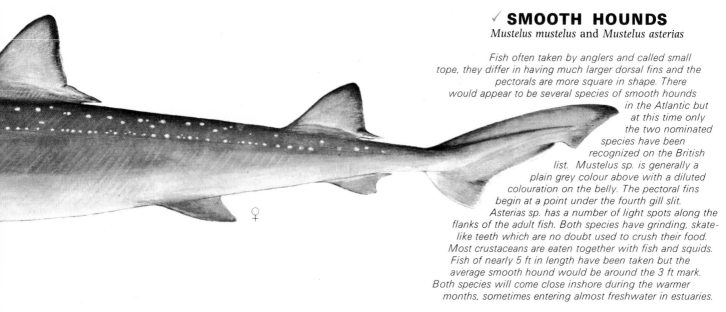

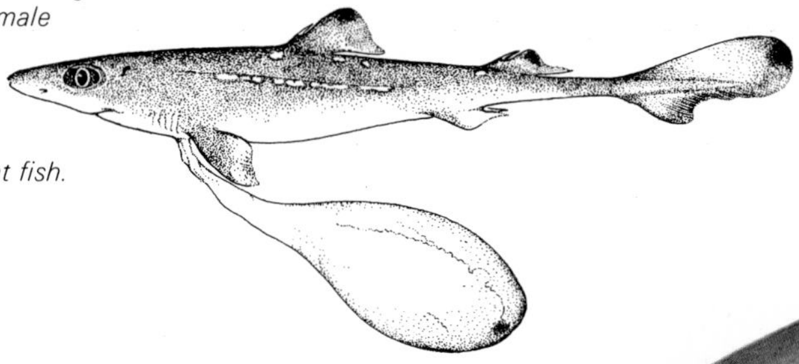

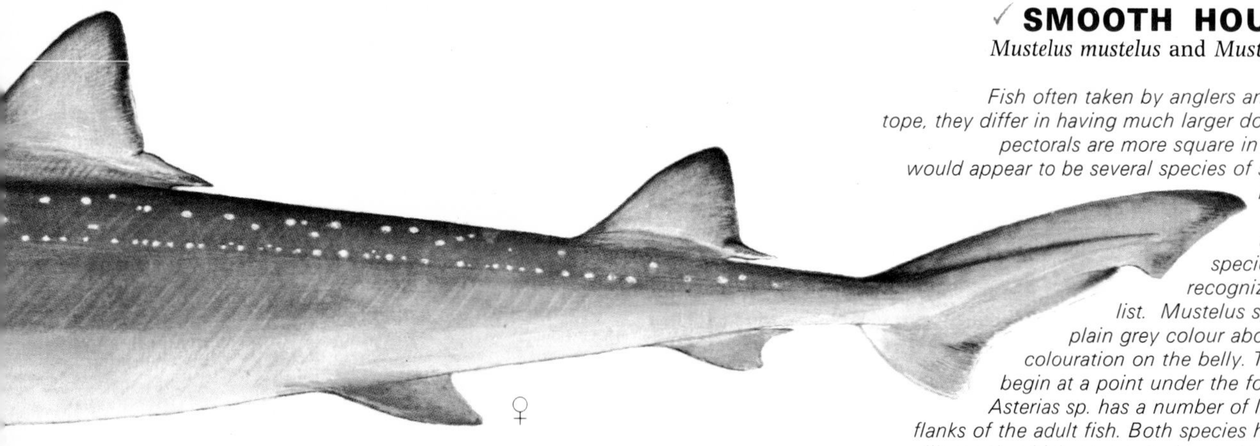

SMOOTH HOUNDS

Mustelus mustelus and *Mustelus asterias*

Fish often taken by anglers and called small tope, they differ in having much larger dorsal fins and the pectorals are more square in shape. There would appear to be several species of smooth hounds in the Atlantic but at this time only the two nominated species have been recognized on the British list. Mustelus sp. is generally a plain grey colour above with a diluted colouration on the belly. The pectoral fins begin at a point under the fourth gill slit. Asterias sp. has a number of light spots along the flanks of the adult fish. Both species have grinding, skate-like teeth which are no doubt used to crush their food. Most crustaceans are eaten together with fish and squids. Fish of nearly 5 ft in length have been taken but the average smooth hound would be around the 3 ft mark. Both species will come close inshore during the warmer months, sometimes entering almost freshwater in estuaries.

Bait: *Fish strips, squids and crab baits.*

MONKFISH

Squatina squatina

An ugly fish, half skate and half shark with a wide flattened body and large paired fins. The dorsal fins are the same size and far to the rear of the body. There is no anal fin present. The mouth is large and placed on the extreme fore-edge of the head unlike sharks to which it is related. The monkfish can grow to huge weights and seems to feed over known flatfish habitats. It cannot be said to be a very sporting fish and is often confused, in name, with the angler fish.

Bait: *Fish baits, although most worm-squid cocktails and some shellfish will tempt this species.*

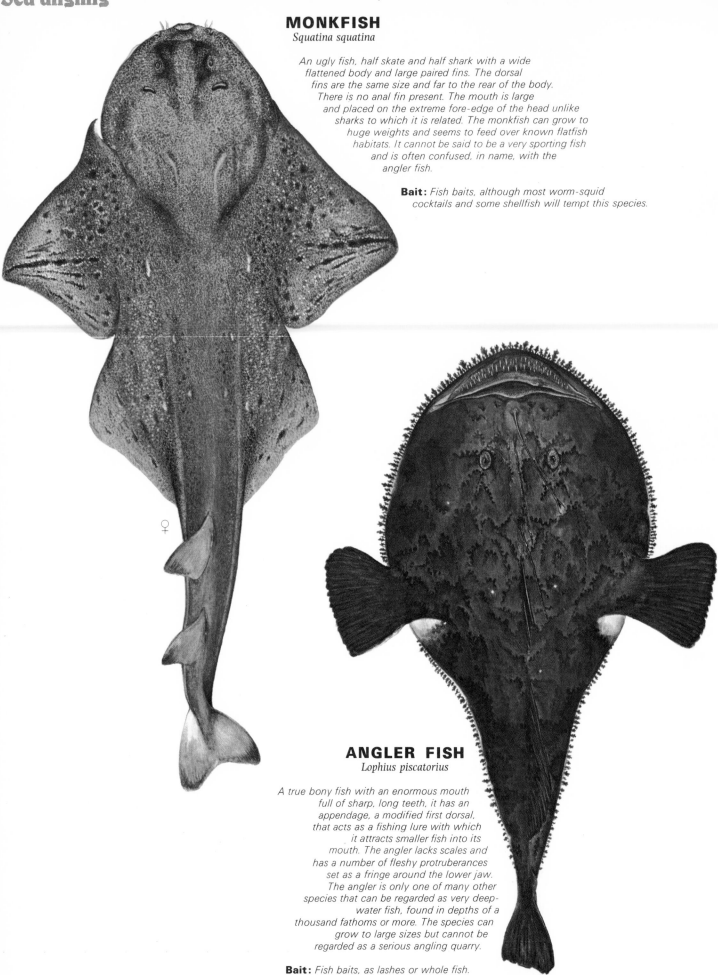

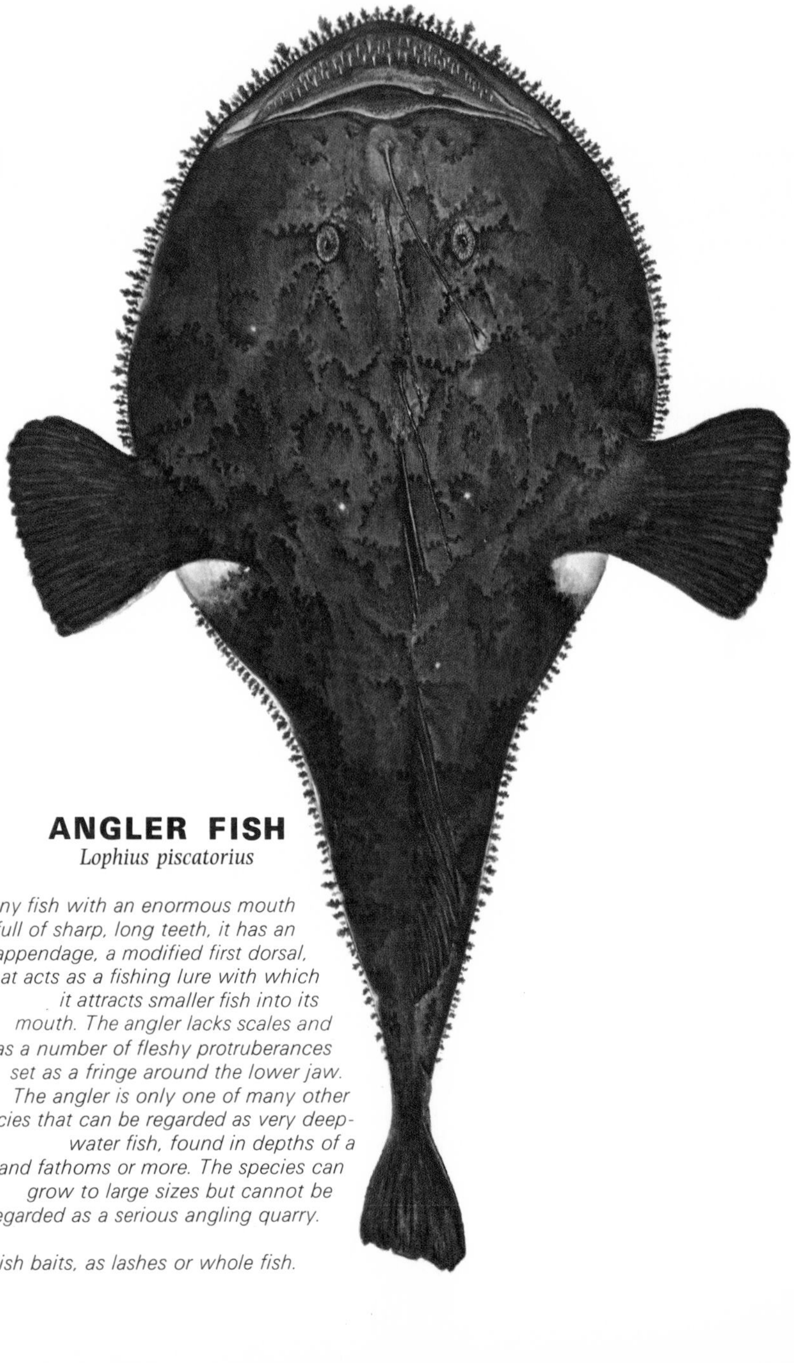

ANGLER FISH

Lophius piscatorius

A true bony fish with an enormous mouth full of sharp, long teeth, it has an appendage, a modified first dorsal, that acts as a fishing lure with which it attracts smaller fish into its mouth. The angler lacks scales and has a number of fleshy protruberances set as a fringe around the lower jaw. The angler is only one of many other species that can be regarded as very deep-water fish, found in depths of a thousand fathoms or more. The species can grow to large sizes but cannot be regarded as a serious angling quarry.

Bait: *Fish baits, as lashes or whole fish.*

Typical pattern of *Lophius piscatorius* and *L. budegassa*

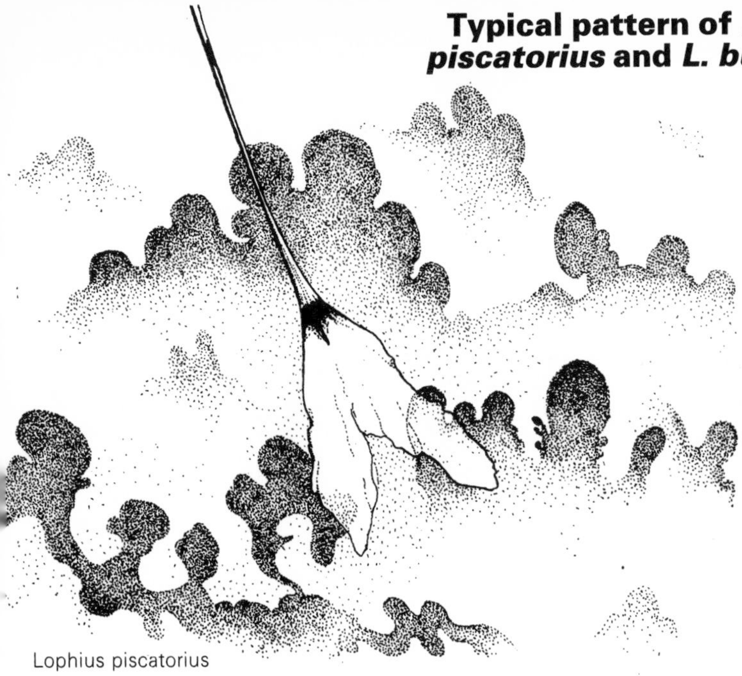

Lophius piscatorius

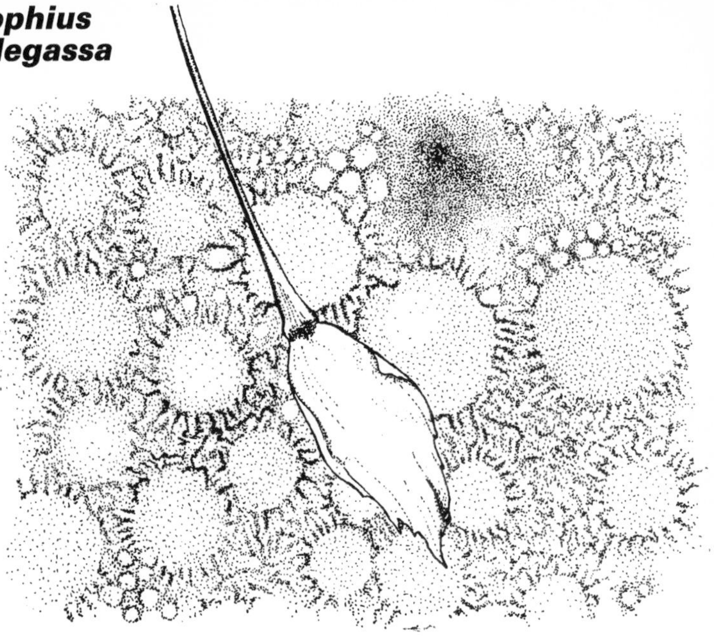

Lophius budegassa

Many species of angler fish have been reported by scientific expeditions since the turn of the century. Taken in trawls at great depth, the fish have little colour. Those from the deepest water are a drab dark brown or black. All of these fish rely on a frilled, broken outline shape to break-up their body contours and aid camouflage. A lesser species, *Budegassa*, is beginning to appear among the fish taken by British trawlers and there is no doubt that this fish will appear as a table species of the future, providing some disguise is attempted by the fishmonger.

All angler fish have hinged, curved teeth that act as a one-way trap to the unwary. Easily entered by small fish that have been attracted by the waving lure, the mouth of the angler is enormous but is extremely difficult to escape from. Anglers should be wary of retrieving a hook from this fish for a nasty gash can result should there be any life left in the creature. The angler's body appears disproportionate in size to its head. This is because the mouth has to open like a gintrap, using a hinged jawbone. Quite large fish could be lured into – and impaled on – the ferocious and needle-sharp teeth.

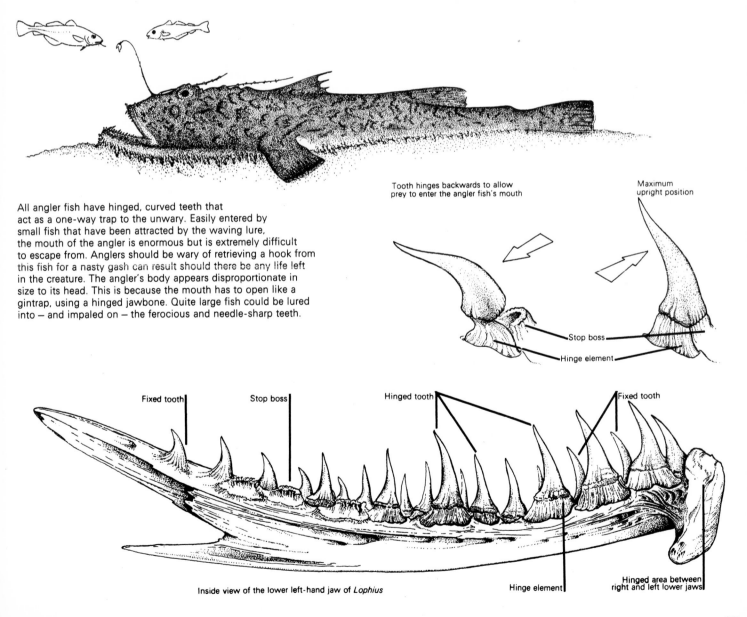

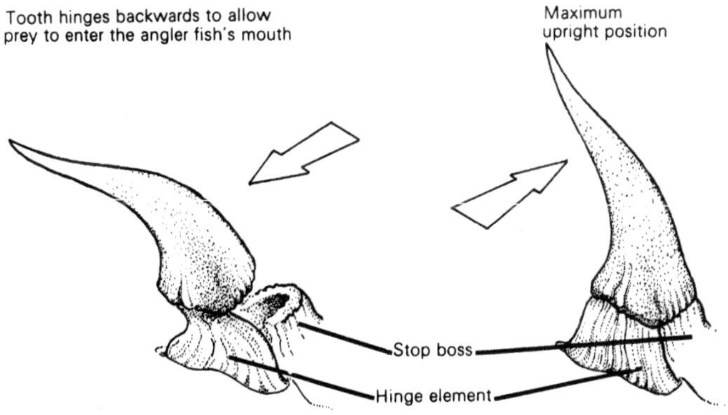

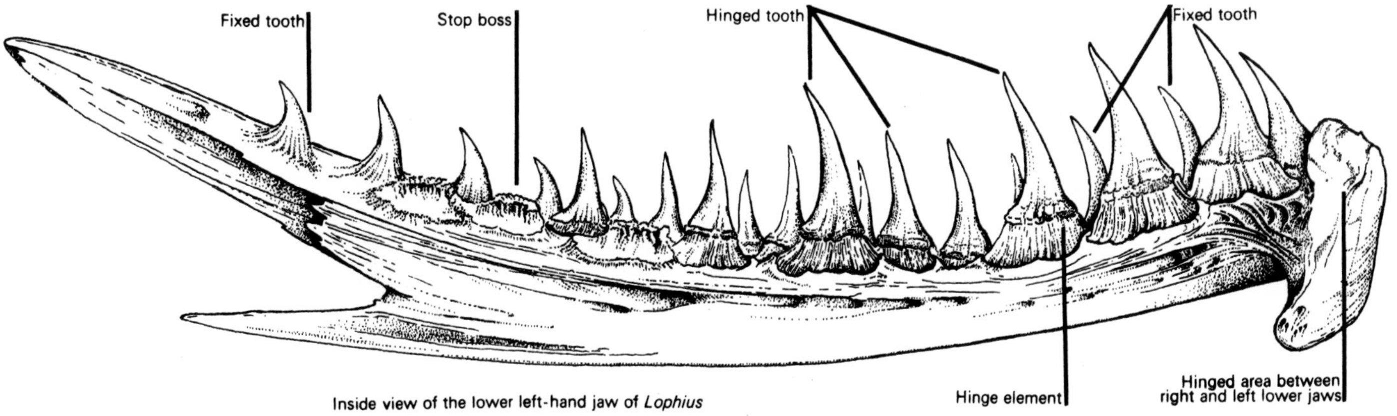

Inside view of the lower left-hand jaw of *Lophius*

LESSER-SPOTTED DOGFISH

Scyliorhinus canicula

Known by many anglers as the rough hound, the fish is sleek, with a rough skin that can easily strip the skin from your arm when the fish attempts to wrap its body around the angler that is attempting to remove a hook. Easily distinguished from its larger relative by the single nasal flap and the anal fin with end at a point between the dorsal fins, this small member of the shark family is a bottom feeder, mainly on crustaceans and small fish. Its egg cases are narrow, with thin arms and spiral filaments.

Bait: *Practically anything, but worms and fish-strip work best as the species is fond of open, shady ground.*

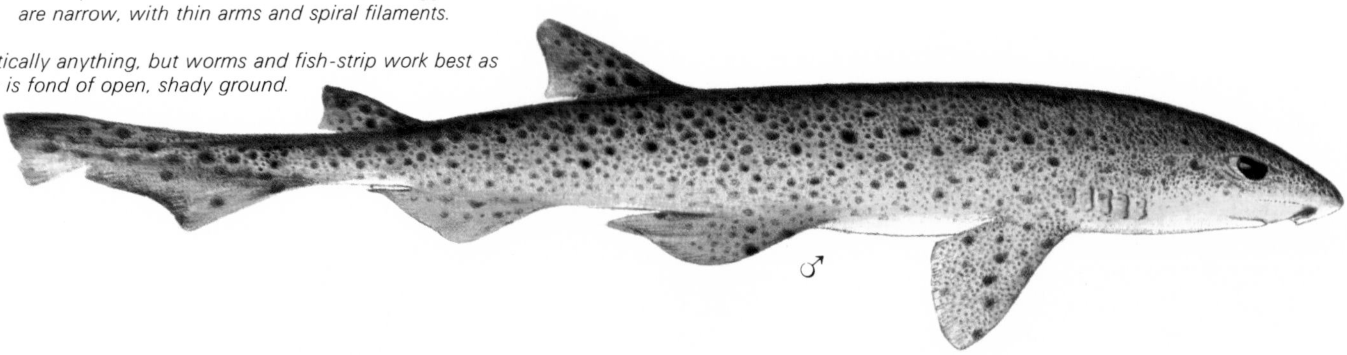

GREATER-SPOTTED DOGFISH

Scyliorhinus stellaris

A thick-bodied fish of the rocky, deepwater marks, it is often named bull huss or nurse hound. There are two separate nasal flaps which are clear of the fish's mouth and the anal fin extends to the middle of the second dorsal fin. The greater-spotted dogfish can grow to over 5 ft in length and is credited with displaying better fighting qualities than the smaller dogfish. The egg cases are similar but rather stouter in build with stronger spiral filaments.

Bait: *Fish baits are probably best, though the species will accept shellfish and marine worms.*

89◀ use in saltwater. On the other hand, the centre-pin reel – which is a simple drum revolving on a spindle, set at right angles to the rod axis – is relatively simple both in manufacture and in use.

This can be made of metal, plastic or wood and needs considerably less attention after fishing. Working in direct drive through line to fish gives an impression of complete contact when playing but on some reels this can be a danger. If, on a centre-pin without a slipping drag feature, a fish runs powerfully and needs line, the handles of the reel will revolve at a great rate. If your fingers get in the way of the handle they will be badly bruised or worse. One scoring point over the multiplier is that the centre-pin is fairly big in drum diameter, giving a large line capacity and a rapid rate of retrieve.

The fixed-spool reel does not have a place in deep-sea boat fishing. It is an ideal spinning and casting reel but is of little use when attempting to lift heavy fish from the depths. American anglers do use the fixed spool but only to fight fish that are hooked near to the surface and which continue the fight on or near the top of the water. The British Isles have only a few species who fight in that fashion, although there must be places where tope could be sought in shallow water.

There are four main types of line available to the boat angler and all have different characteristics and drawbacks. Nylon is by far the most popular and important. Terylene, formed as a braid, rates second, while lead-cored braided Terylene and wire line are the least important but are gaining favour each year for specific angling situations. All sea fishing is very much an up-and-down affair, lowering a bait and lead to the bottom and retrieving the end tackle with or without hooking a fish. This means that the strain on any form of line lies necessarily in lifting the combined weight of fish and lead, or so it would at first seem. However, a further force has a part to play in exerting stress on the line and this force is tide. When at anchor, a line leaves a fixed point (the rod tip) and forms a resistance to the passage of the tidal current, thereby adopting a curved

The egg cases of the dogfish are characterized by the long, sinewy tendrils at each corner of the purse.

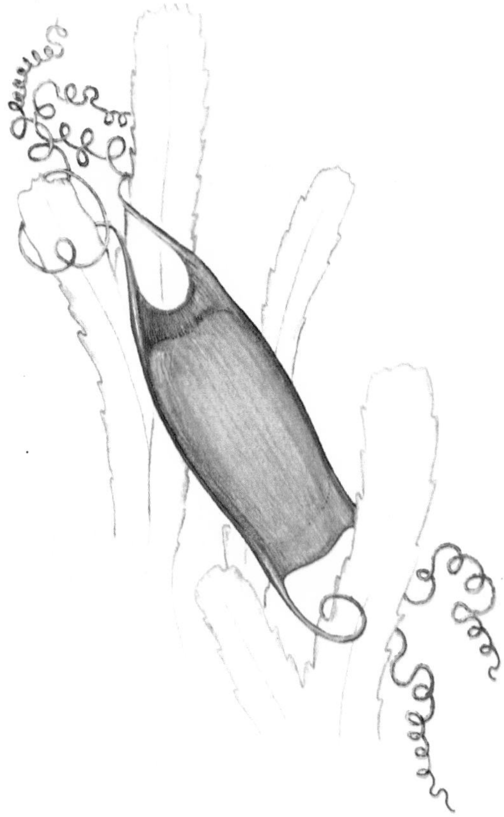

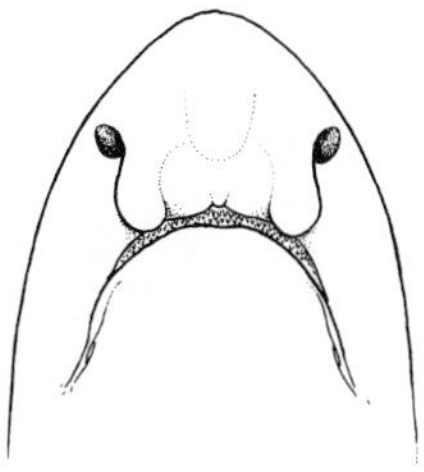

Underside of the head of the lesser-spotted dogfish. The nasal flaps are joined in this species but distinctly separate in the larger bull huss.

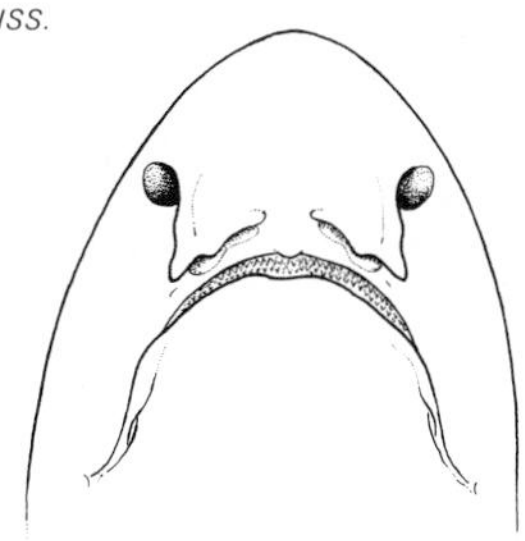

path down to another fixed point – the lead. Now it is this pressure of water against the line that is so often overlooked when calculating the breaking strain of line to be fished with, so bear this in mind when using nylon or braided material. If conditions are such that an excessively heavy line is called for, consider the use of a wire or lead-cored line, for these have an in-built weight which tends to overcome some of the tidal pressure.

Ideally your line should be balanced to the rod in use and to the weight of lead necessary to hold the ground. In reality it is often a question of compromise between a rod, line and lead combination light enough for sensitive fishing but powerful enough to boat a heavy fish. If a light rod is overloaded with a very heavy lead and line out of balance with the test curve of the rod, the rod will be unable to break out the lead should it become snagged. Worse still, with a large fish which pulls the rod past its test curve, the rod will not return to the straight section and will therefore be unable to exert any further pressure on the fish. Beating a fish demands a combination of pumping action by the angler and power in the rod as it attempts to return from an arc to its former straight shape. One could, of course, resort to a more powerful rod and line pairing but this would mean a certain loss in pleasure from feeling the progression of the fight.

Nylon monofilament is cheaper and finer in diameter than all forms of line, with the exception of wire. It stretches possibly up to 10 per cent of its length and this can be a cause of failure to detect a shy biting fish or to hook a fish, because the natural elasticity absorbs the power imparted to the strike. Furthermore, when wound back onto the reel spool, under strong pressure, it can exert tremendous outward strain on the side flanges and this often bursts the drum. This strain can be alleviated to some degree by winding on a bed of braided line before loading the reel with nylon. The softer braided line will absorb some of the crushing effect. Pumping a fish, which entails lifting the rod to ▶106

Anatomy of the Skates and Rays

THE THORNBACK RAY

Raja (Raja) clavata

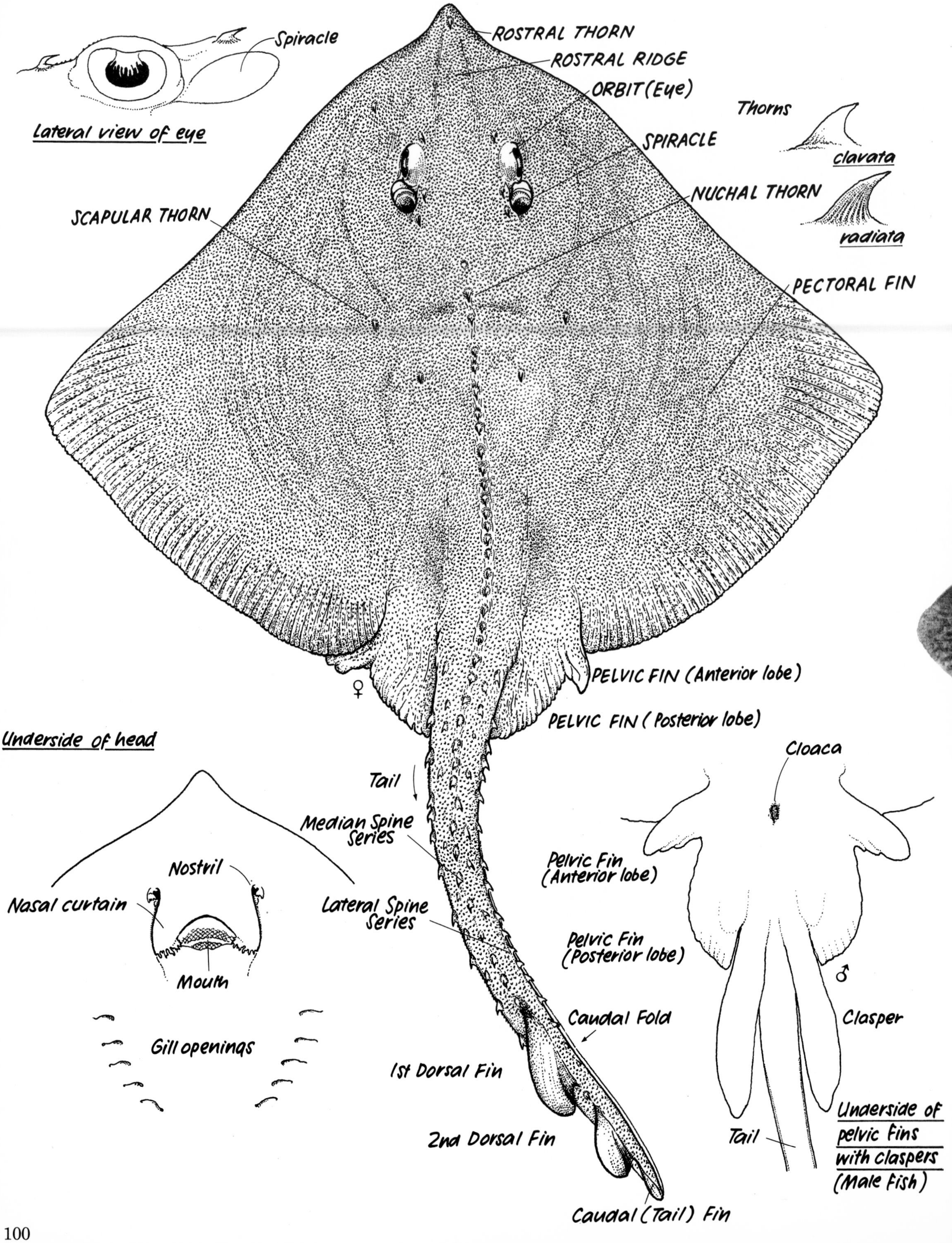

There are many variations in both coloration and thorn position in the species. The snout is short with a pronounced wave in the anterior edge of the wings. The fish is more sharp-angled than the other rays. There are two dorsal fins, the hindmost running into the minute caudal fin. Most fish caught will have spines along the back and tail, either in two rows curved on the upper surface of the wings with a further row along the top of the spine and tail, or spaced out as an irregular pattern on the wings but clearly defined on the tail. Sometimes there are spines on the under-surface of the wings. Colour is a brown-grey mixture with either dark or light irregular blotches on the upper surface. The belly is white.

Thornbacks frequent the shallow, inshore waters where they can reach over 20 lbs in weight. They feed on almost any marine creature.

Bait: *Marine worms and fish baits.*

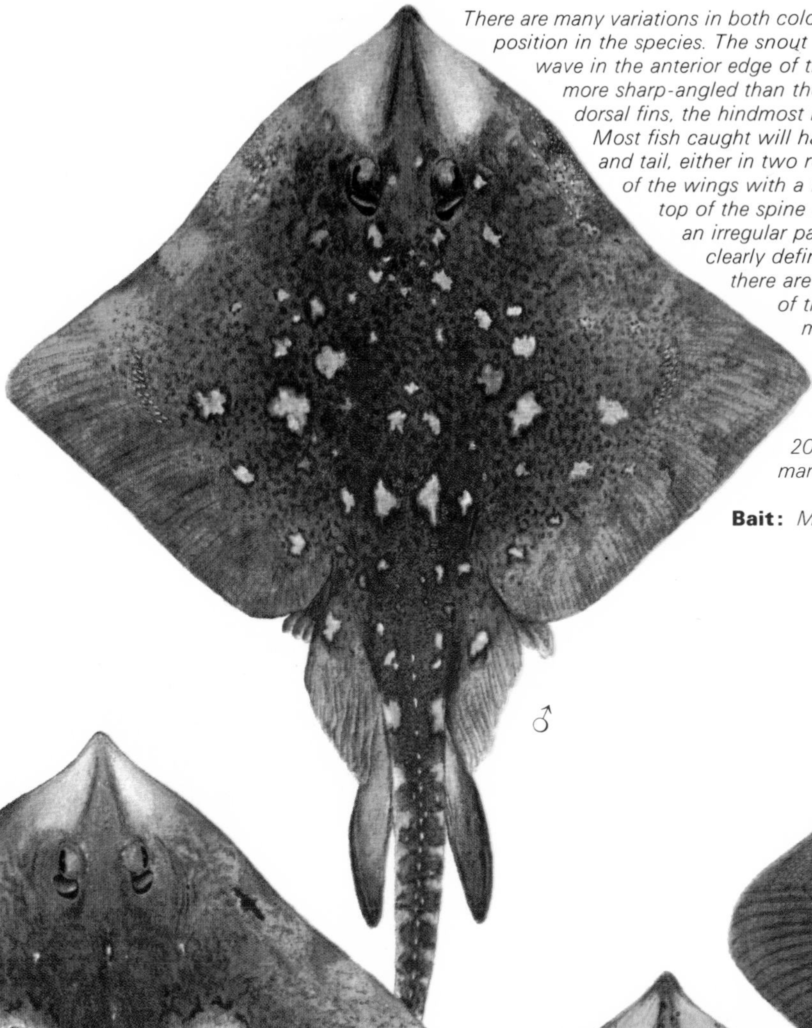

Some colour/spine variations found in the thornback ray

THORNBACK RAY
Raja (Raja) clavata

A shallow water ray that grows to 30 lbs or more, the species has 36–44 teeth rows in the upper jaw.

The mouth of a thornback ray. As with all rays, there are many rows of grinding teeth.

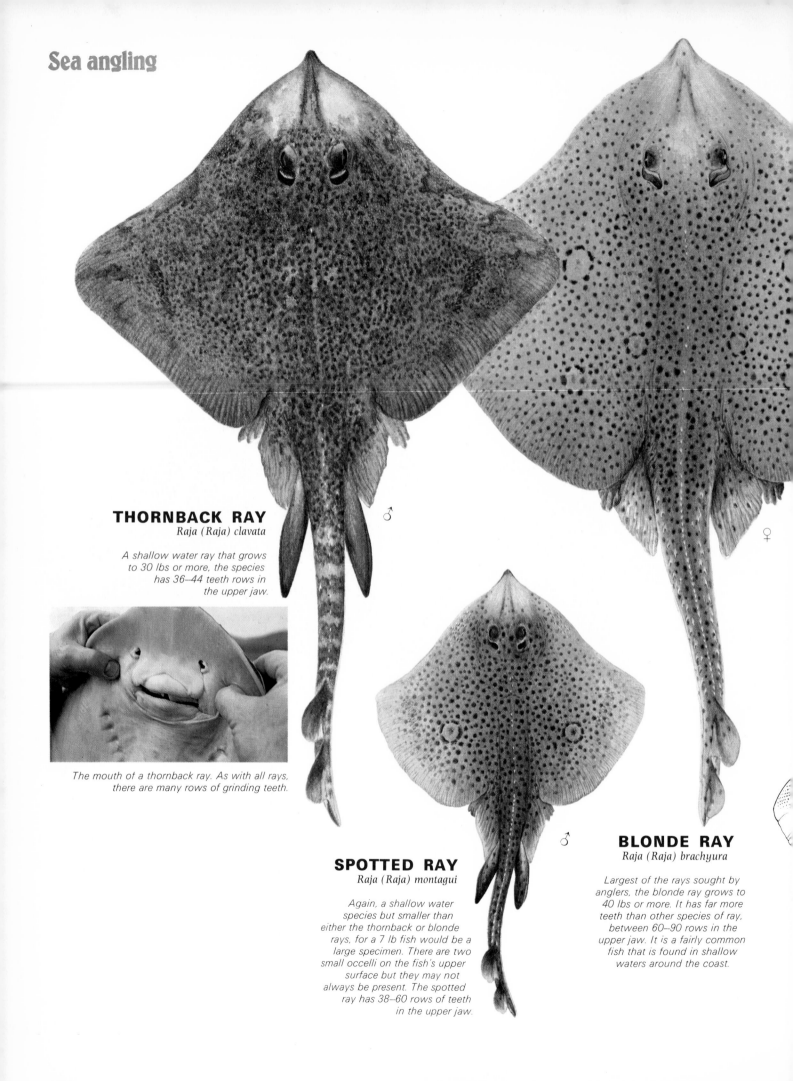

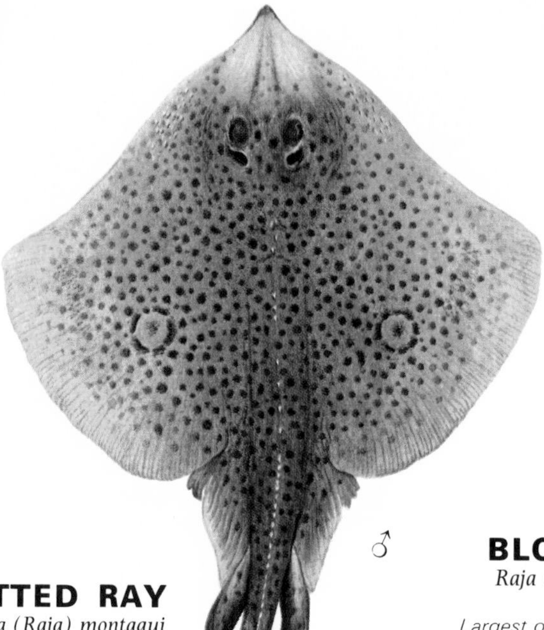

BLONDE RAY
Raja (Raja) brachyura

Largest of the rays sought by anglers, the blonde ray grows to 40 lbs or more. It has far more teeth than other species of ray, between 60–90 rows in the upper jaw. It is a fairly common fish that is found in shallow waters around the coast.

SPOTTED RAY
Raja (Raja) montagui

Again, a shallow water species but smaller than either the thornback or blonde rays, for a 7 lb fish would be a large specimen. There are two small occelli on the fish's upper surface but they may not always be present. The spotted ray has 38–60 rows of teeth in the upper jaw.

GENERAL NOTE ON RAYS

All skates and rays are internally fertilized. The males possess claspers by which both coupling and transfer of sperm is accomplished. The females produce a number of eggs that are enclosed within a pouch or " Mermaid's purse". The young fish develop within the pouch and then break out as a complete, although miniature, version of the parent stock.

Bait: *Most fish baits will take rays. Both marine worms and shellfish are readily accepted. Crabs and other crustaceans will also take most of the species.*

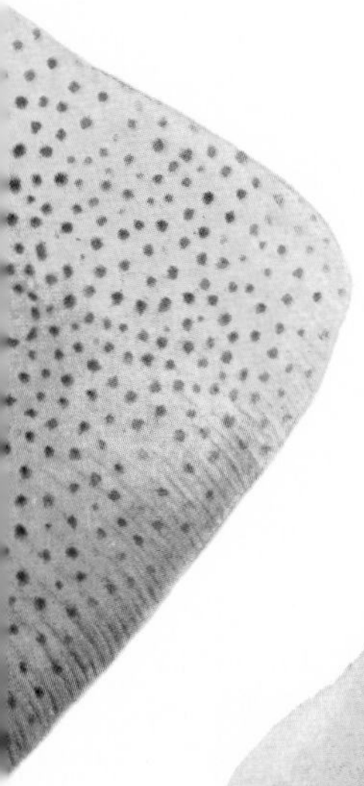

CUCKOO RAY
Raja (Leucoraja) naevus

A distinctive, small, deepwater ray that possesses two dark spots, one on each wing, that are broken up by a variety of wavy, yellowish markings. It is not a large fish, rarely exceeding 5 lbs in weight.

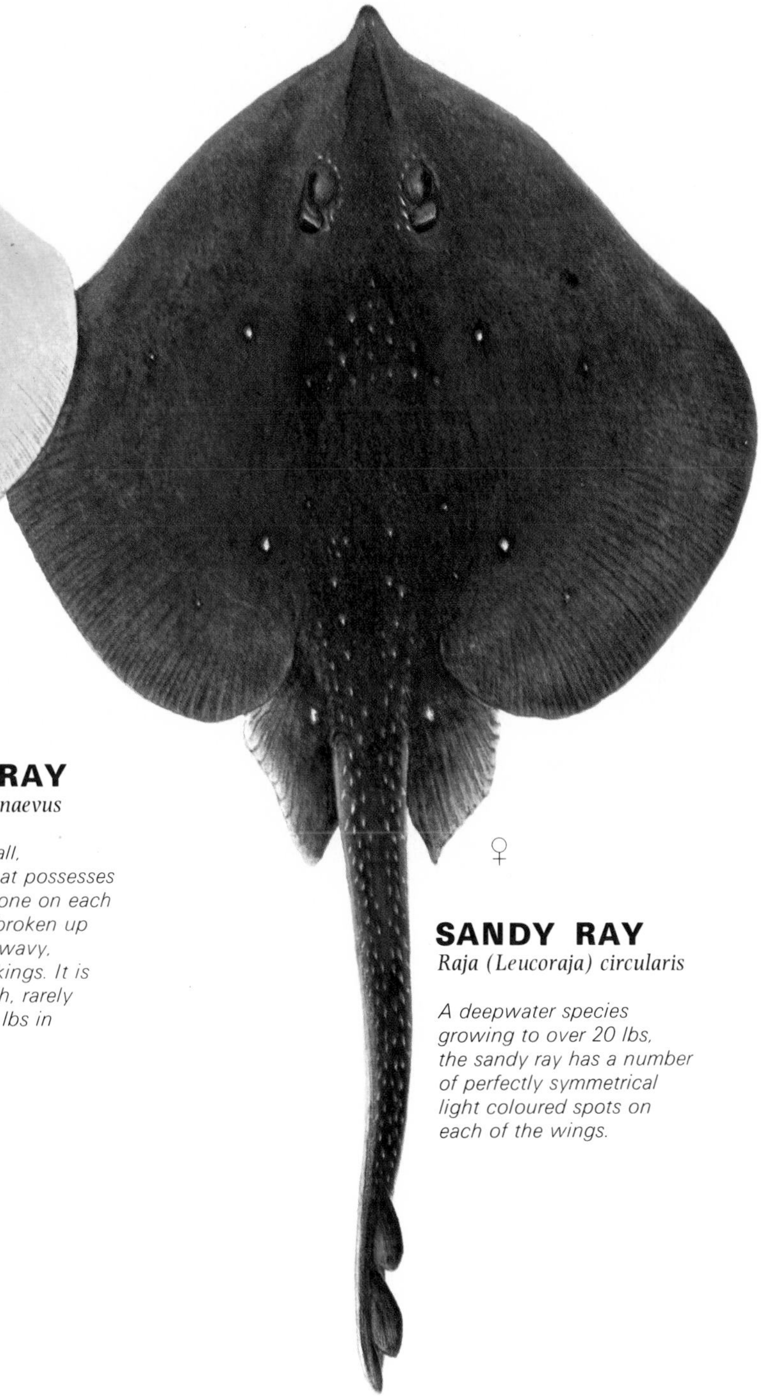

SANDY RAY
Raja (Leucoraja) circularis

A deepwater species growing to over 20 lbs, the sandy ray has a number of perfectly symmetrical light coloured spots on each of the wings.

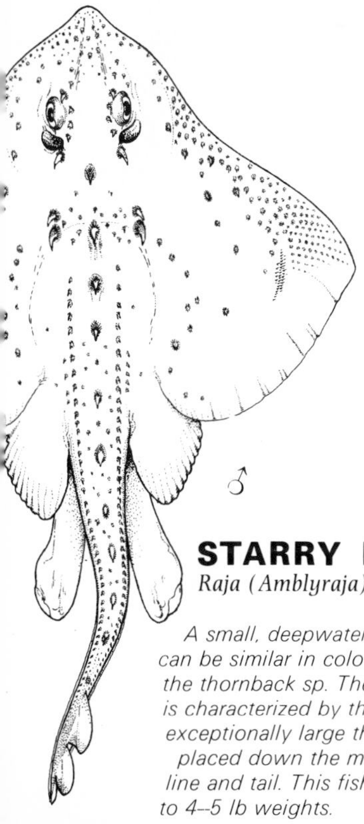

STARRY RAY
Raja (Amblyraja) radiata

A small, deepwater ray that can be similar in colouring to the thornback sp. The species is characterized by the exceptionally large thorns placed down the median line and tail. This fish grows to 4–5 lb weights.

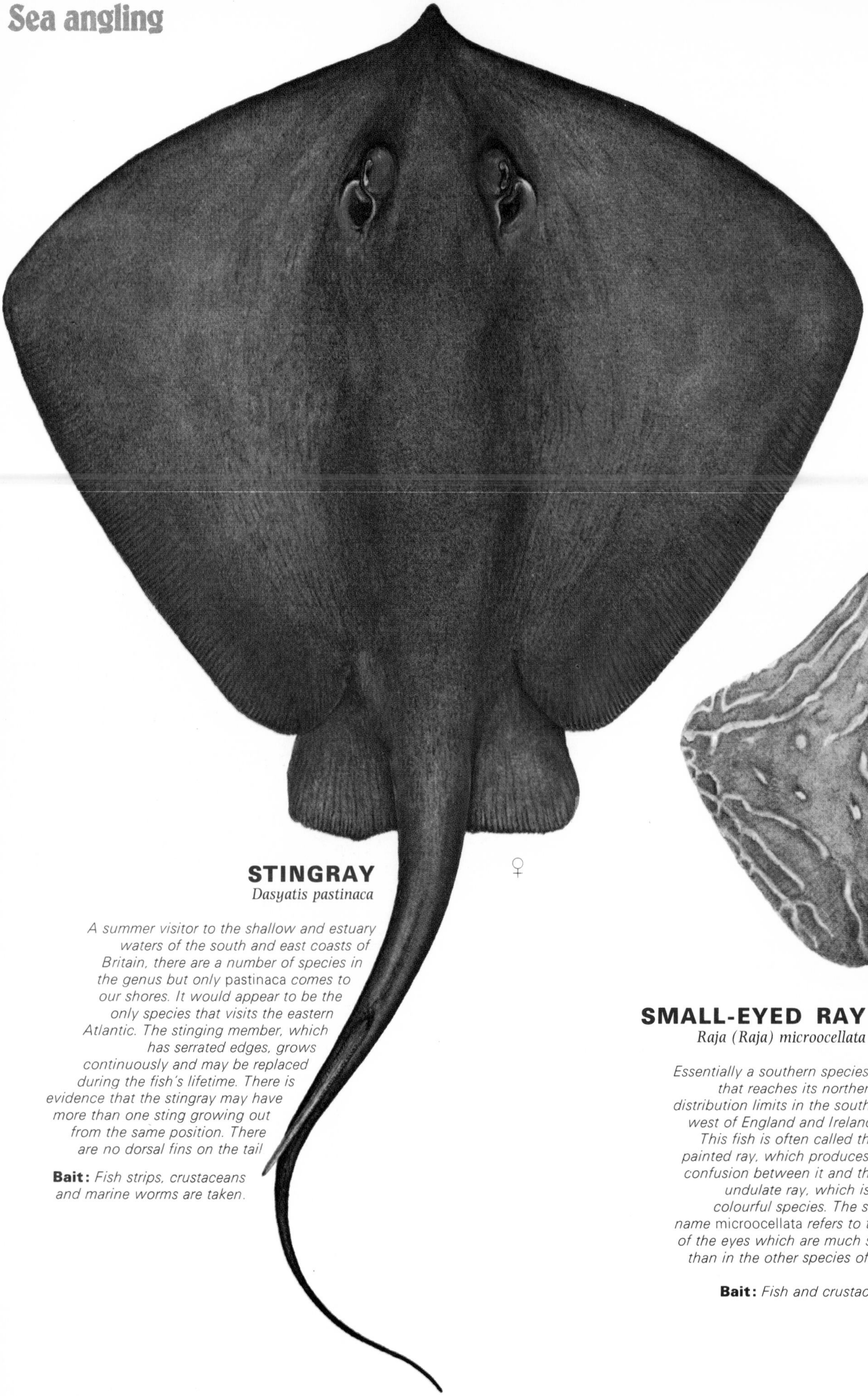

STINGRAY
Dasyatis pastinaca

A summer visitor to the shallow and estuary waters of the south and east coasts of Britain, there are a number of species in the genus but only pastinaca *comes to our shores. It would appear to be the only species that visits the eastern Atlantic. The stinging member, which has serrated edges, grows continuously and may be replaced during the fish's lifetime. There is evidence that the stingray may have more than one sting growing out from the same position. There are no dorsal fins on the tail*

Bait: *Fish strips, crustaceans and marine worms are taken.*

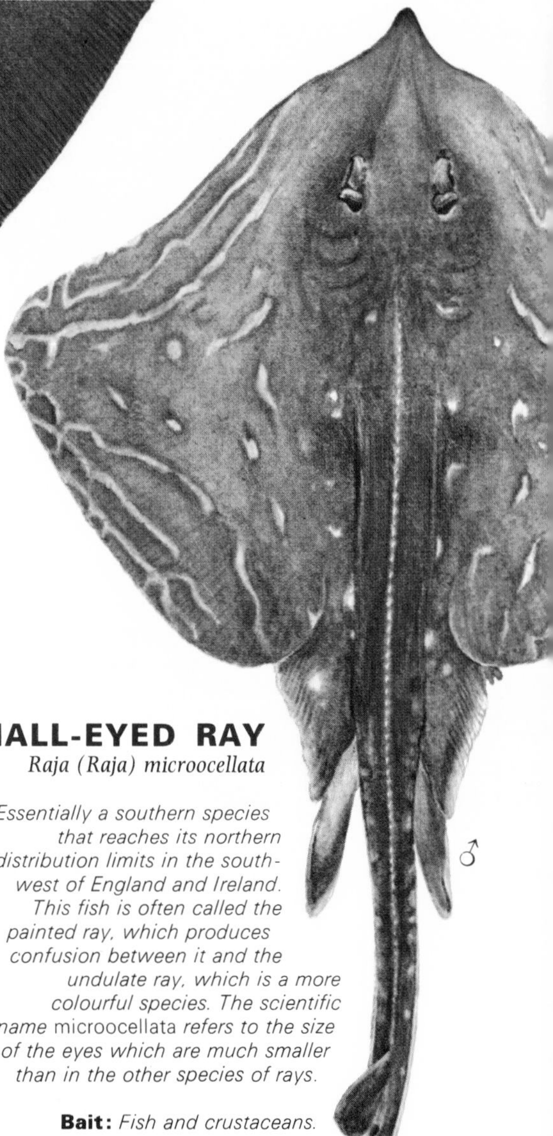

SMALL-EYED RAY
Raja (Raja) microocellata

Essentially a southern species that reaches its northern distribution limits in the south-west of England and Ireland. This fish is often called the painted ray, which produces confusion between it and the undulate ray, which is a more colourful species. The scientific name microocellata *refers to the size of the eyes which are much smaller than in the other species of rays.*

Bait: *Fish and crustaceans.*

UNDULATE RAY

Raja undulata

Has a similar distribution to microocellata. *The fish is more rounded in outline shape and the markings are dark on a lighter ground.*

Bait: *As for the other small rays.*

TORPEDO OR ELECTRIC RAY

Torpedo (Tetronatee) nobiliana

A summer visitor to the British Isles, this species is most common although there are at least two others in the North Atlantic. It is a flaccid fish lacking firmness in handling. The body is relatively thick in section for the pectorals contain specialized muscular cells with which the fish can generate electricity said to be in the order of 200–250 volts. The species is not specifically fished for.

Bait: *Most fish and invertebrate offerings.*

LIGHT TACKLE RIGS FOR THE BOAT FISHERMAN

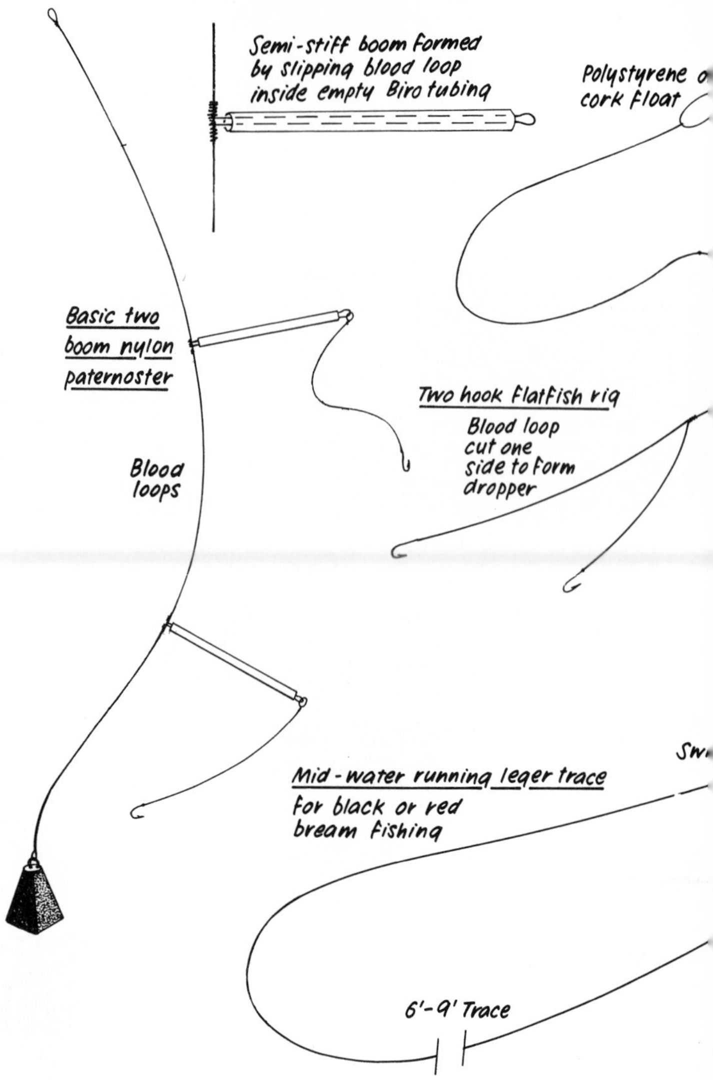

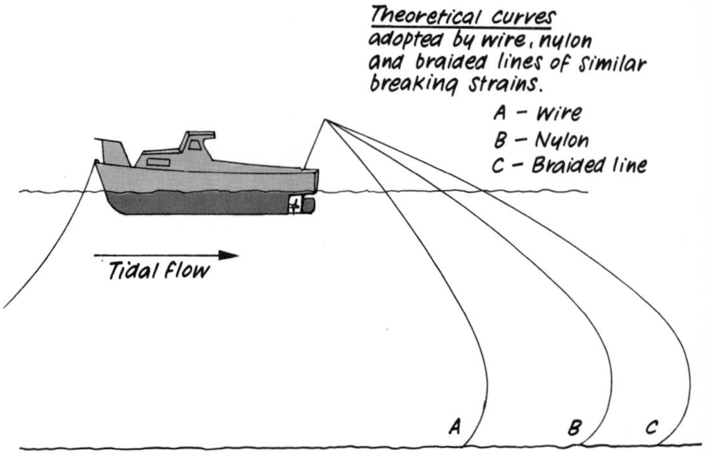

Two methods of baiting with either soft or peeled crab.

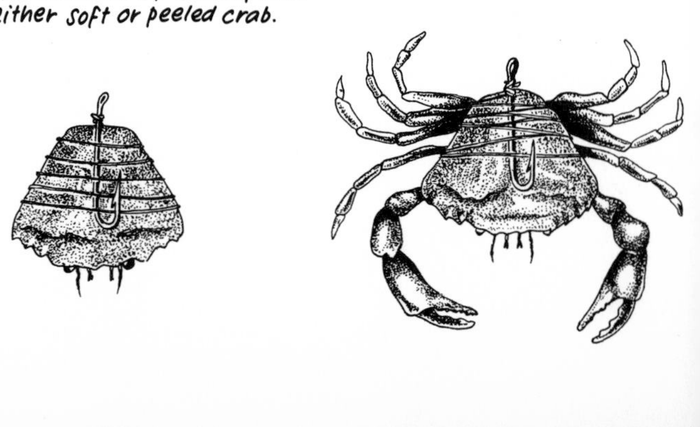

99◀ an angle of 160 degrees, then winding in the line as the rod is lowered to a 90 degrees position, thus taking up the line without carrying the whole weight of your catch, will also help to prevent an explosion of the spool.

All braided lines, whether Terylene or nylon, have a larger diameter than monofilament nylon. This calls for a slightly larger lead to hold the bottom. Braids are also more likely to suffer from breakage brought about by rubbing on rocks, or line contact with the hull of the angling boat. Where this line scores is in its non-stretch properties. The contact with hooked fish is more definite and the satisfaction in knowing what is happening below the keel is more pronounced. Lead-cored braid is a compromise line, having no stretch and a certain amount of in-built weight intended to counteract the increased diameter of the braid. It was never intended for bottom fishing and is used in American waters in trolling for surface-feeding game species. The core, which is of soft lead, can break up under stress, forcing a passage through the outer braid which then weakens the line. If conditions demand a self-weighted line, plain single-strand or braided wire is far slimmer in section and heavier along its length. But take care when using it because, since it is both metal and thin, it can slice through human flesh very easily, especially when under tension.

If you are seeking record fish then, under the rules of the International Game Fishing Association, do make sure your line conforms to their specification. Most braided Dacron and Terylene and some nylon monofilament lines will conform, but it pays to check.

So much, in sea angling, depends on the hook. It is the only connection between angler and fish and must never be suspect. To use cheap, rusted or unsharp hooks is a false economy. A newcomer to the sport may find himself bewildered by the varieties of hook patterns available. There are certain guidelines to observe when choosing any particular hook. How big is the fish and will it put up a short, sharp, fight or a sustained battle? How large a bait has to be placed on the hook and are there any peculiarities concerning the mounting of the bait? Has the species fished for an awkward shaped mouth requiring a long or short shanked hook? Will any dressing have to be applied to the hook, such as feathers or rubber tube when making a sand eel?

Let us deal with these points one by one. Members of the shark and skate families, with the conger eel and the halibut, are our largest species. It is general practice to fish large baits, such as a large lash or whole mackerel, which cannot be securely placed on a small hook. The fighting qualities of these fish call for a strong, preferably forged, hook fairly thick in the wire. This is vitally necessary when one considers the weight/strength combination of these species allied to ▶110

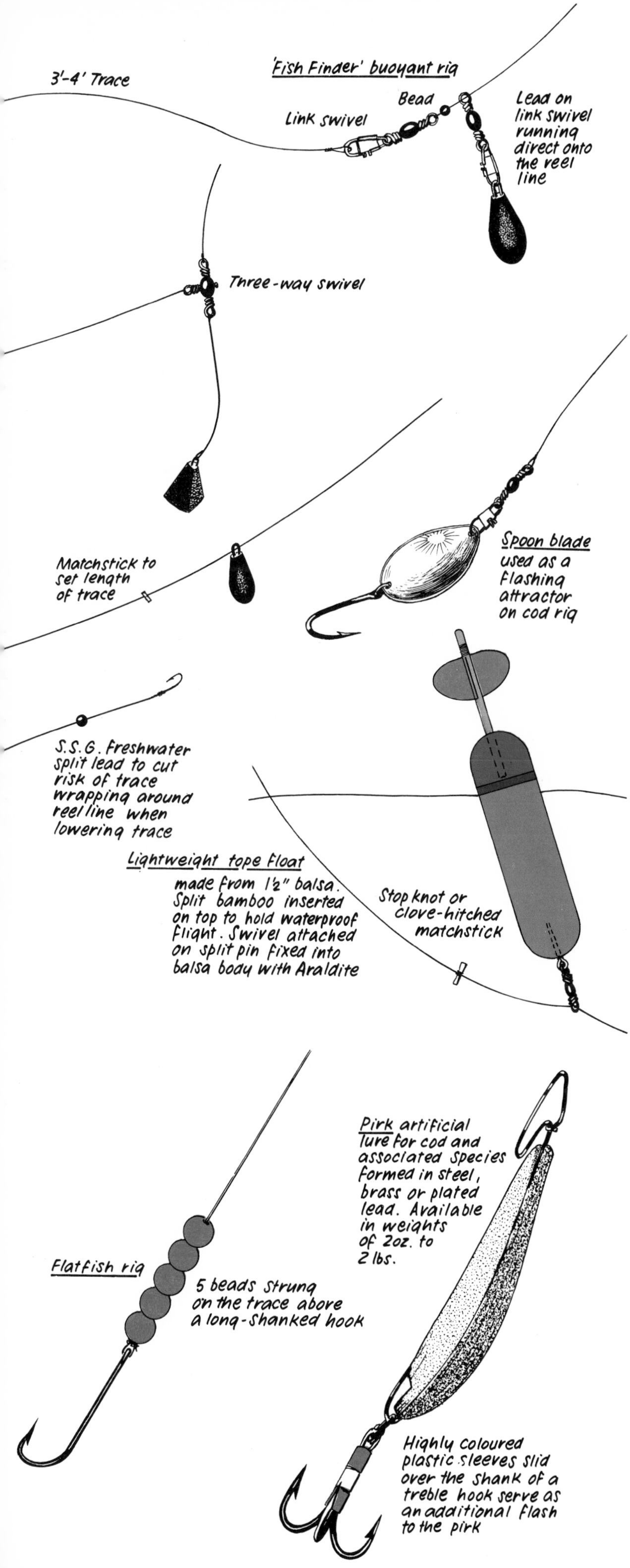
3'-4' Trace
'Fish Finder' buoyant rig
Bead
Link swivel
Lead on link swivel running direct onto the reel line
Three-way swivel
Matchstick to set length of trace
Spoon blade used as a flashing attractor on cod rig
S.S.G. freshwater split lead to cut risk of trace wrapping around reel line when lowering trace
Lightweight tope float made from 1½" balsa. Split bamboo inserted on top to hold waterproof flight. Swivel attached on split pin fixed into balsa body with Araldite
Stop knot or clove-hitched matchstick
Pirk artificial lure for cod and associated species formed in steel, brass or plated lead. Available in weights of 2oz. to 2 lbs.
Flatfish rig
5 beads strung on the trace above a long-shanked hook
Highly coloured plastic sleeves slid over the shank of a treble hook serve as an additional flash to the pirk

Mustad split link
Barrel swivel
Link swivel
Lead links for running leger rigs
Snap link
Three-way swivel
Drilled bullet lead
Barrel lead
Plastic bead used to set length of trace

Tying a cod feather

In order to show the whipping method clearly, feathers have not been used in the initial illustrations.

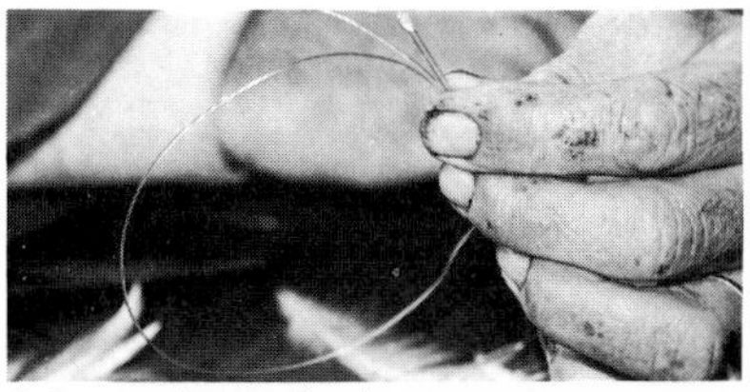

1 *Form a loop of nylon.*

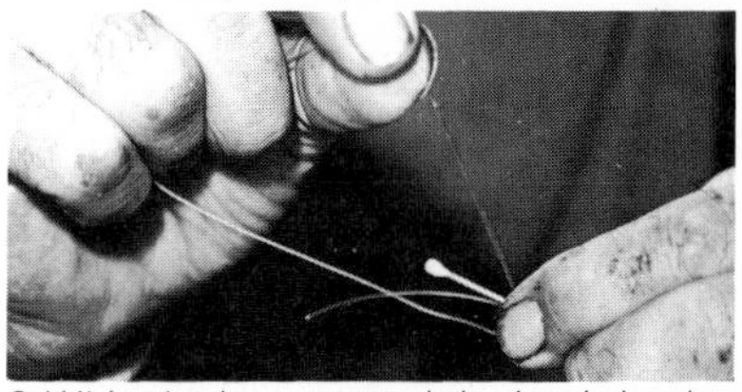

2 *Whip the loop around the hookshank, starting at the hook bend (feathers are tied in at this stage).*

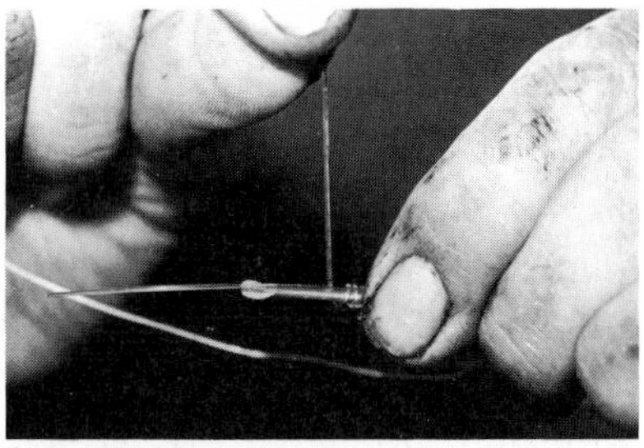

3 *Continue to whip around the hook for about six turns.*

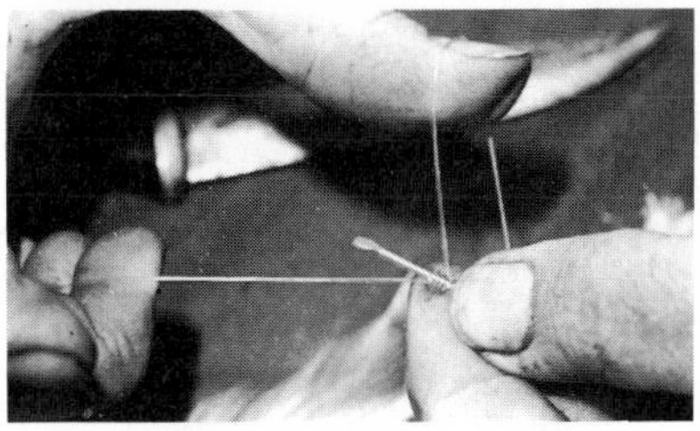

4 *Form the last turn of nylon, hold it open and pass the free end through the loop.*

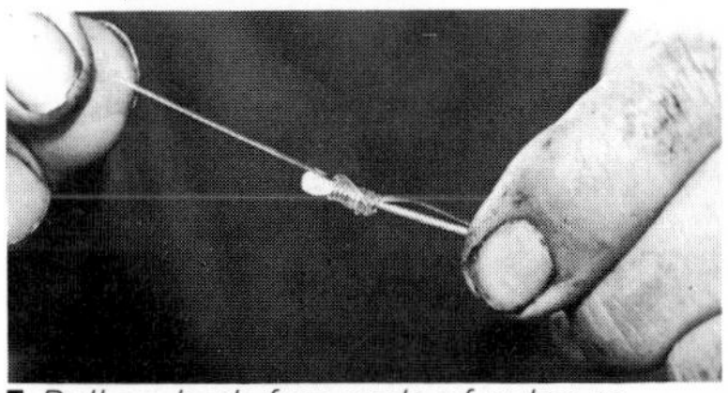

5 *Pull on both free ends of nylon to draw the whipping tight.*

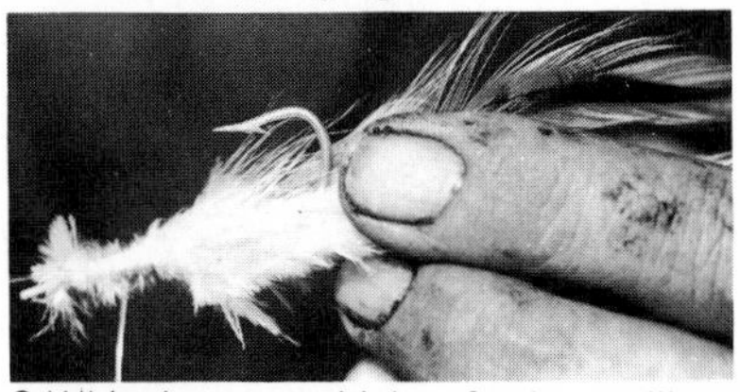

6 *Whipping over chicken feathers will produce an untidy concoction like this.*

7 *With a pair of sharp scissors trim off the loose ends of nylon and shape the feathers to simulate a small fish.*

♀

WHITE SKATE

Raja (Rostroaja) alba

Has a pronounced snout projecting from a convex fore-edge to the wings. The underside is a definite white, complete with the pores found on all skates. These are not fringe-marked with brown or black as in the common skate. The white skate is often taken by anglers in Ireland, where it is admitted that a number of commons may well have been white skate. Possibly the same mistake has been made in Scotland. The species is thought to grow to a larger weight than either the common or long-nosed species.

Bait: *Most fish baits, presented as lashes or whole fish.*

♀

COMMON SKATE

Raja (Dipturus) batis

As with all skates, rays and sharks, there are anatomical differences between the sexes. The female fish have pelvic fins divided by the tail whereas in the males there are two elongated, fleshy appendages known as claspers. These are the sexual organs and in the common skate are almost two thirds of the length of the tail. All skates lack anal fins though they possess two dorsal fins set far back on the tail and a caudal fin which shows great variance in size between species. The common skate has a fairly smooth skin with a single row of spines along the centre of the tail and at the sides. In the males there is usually a patch of spines out toward the edges of each wing. The species favours broken ground, composed of a mixture of sand, mud and rocky outcrops. Skate prey on live fish, crustaceans and other slow-moving fodder species. They can grow up to weights of over 200 lbs in waters of the northern hemisphere.

Bait: *Fish, as lashes or whole.*

LONG-NOSED SKATE

Raja (Dipturus) oxyrinchus

This species has a marked concave shape to the fore-edge of the wings, with an almost straight trailing edge. Its snout is long and comes to a sharp point. There is a row of spines at each side of the tail but none on the upper surface. Like the common skate, it has dark openings to the pores. The fish is associated with deeper water and can grow to large weights.

Bait: *As for the other skate species.*

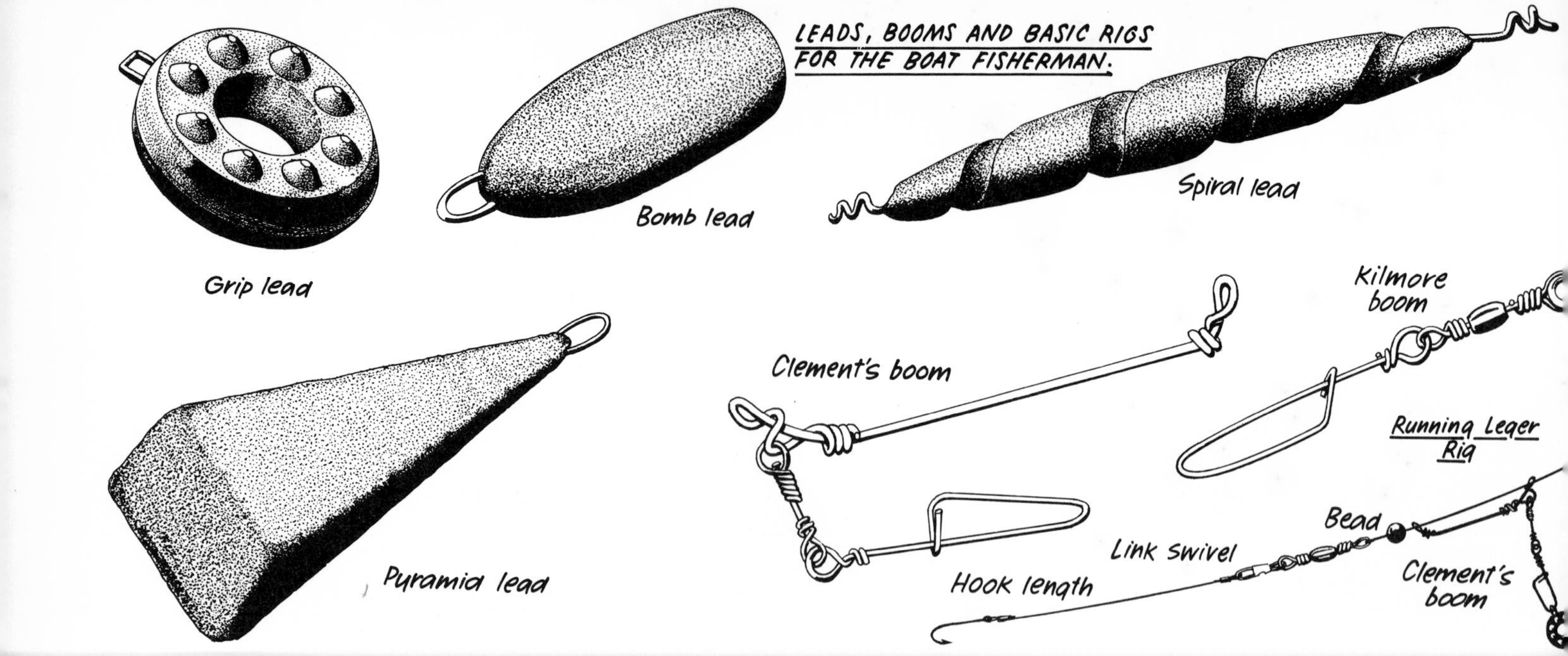

106◀ their extremely sharp or powerful grinding teeth. Providing a forged hook has been correctly tempered, a long drawn out fight should not weaken the hook unduly, whereas an untempered hook would tend to pull, weaken and then straighten out. The only problem likely to be encountered when using a heavy wire forged hook is that it tends to be rank in the barb and not too sharp in the point when purchased. Small attention with an oil stone will correct the failing.

Large baits will demand a reasonably large hook to present them in an attractive fashion. One may have to sew the hook within the bait for a trolled presentation. On the other hand, the flatfish will require slender baits of a suitable size that they can take. They may be big in body size but their mouths are relatively small.

The sea breams, flatfish and shy-biting fish such as the mullets have either small mouths or are very hook shy. Attention must be paid to both the size and the pattern of the hook, baiting in such a way that the fish can take the offering without feeling the metal. With the flats, a long shank to the hook will ease the removal of the hook by the captor.

Whether one prefers spade end or ringed hooks when dressing mackerel, cod or pollack feathers, the fact remains that the shank of the hook must allow both the dressing of the feather and the necessary whipping of nylon to be accommodated. Similarly, a hook used to form a rubber eel should be long enough to carry a swivel attached to the eye, yet it should reach down the body of the eel to a sensible position for the hook bend and barb. Too short a hook will result in the fish "taking short", grabbing the tail of the lure without getting a firm grip on the hook area.

There are two basic types of lead weight used in the sport of boat fishing. First, and most important, those leads intended to take a bait down to the sea bed and to tether it there securely. Shape is of some importance because a lead is constantly subjected to the pressure of currents that seek to move it with that current. Some streamlining is helpful in preventing interference from the tide while a smooth, rounded, shape will often pass freely through rough ground where a squared-off lead will often become trapped. Another form of lead is used to take a bait out to fish when spinning – either a spiral or Wye will perform this function – or to sink a float with suspended bait down to where fish are thought to be. This could be mid-water or just above the sea bed. Drilled bullets, barrels or even split shot can be used.

Sea anglers use far more "ironmongery" than their freshwater colleagues. Mind you, most of the metal is found in the boat fisher's tackle box! This metal work divides, roughly, into two categories:

Metal, plastic or combinations of both formed as booms and spreaders intended to make the hook link and bait stand away from the main line. The idea here is that fish may be wary of a bait if they feel a taut, though invisible, obstruction to their free passage through the water!

Metal devices that prevent twist in the line. Swivels are used to stop twist and to join various sections of the rig, in use, together. Metal booms, of a different type, which allow either a weight or another portion of the rig to slide easily on the reel line.

Some of these items do perform a vital job but many only serve to complicate an angler's tackle and add to the expense of angling when they are lost – hooked into the bottom. Wherever possible keep your end tackles and rigs as simple as the conditions allow. More "ironmongery" naturally means more knots to attach it by, which again tends to weaken the nylon for knots reduce the breaking strain of all lines.

When we think of presenting a bait to a fish consideration must first be given to where we expect that fish to be. If the species is bottom feeding we have two basic methods available. These are the running leger, which gives a fish the opportunity to pick a bait up, possibly to hold it firmly and then to swim off some

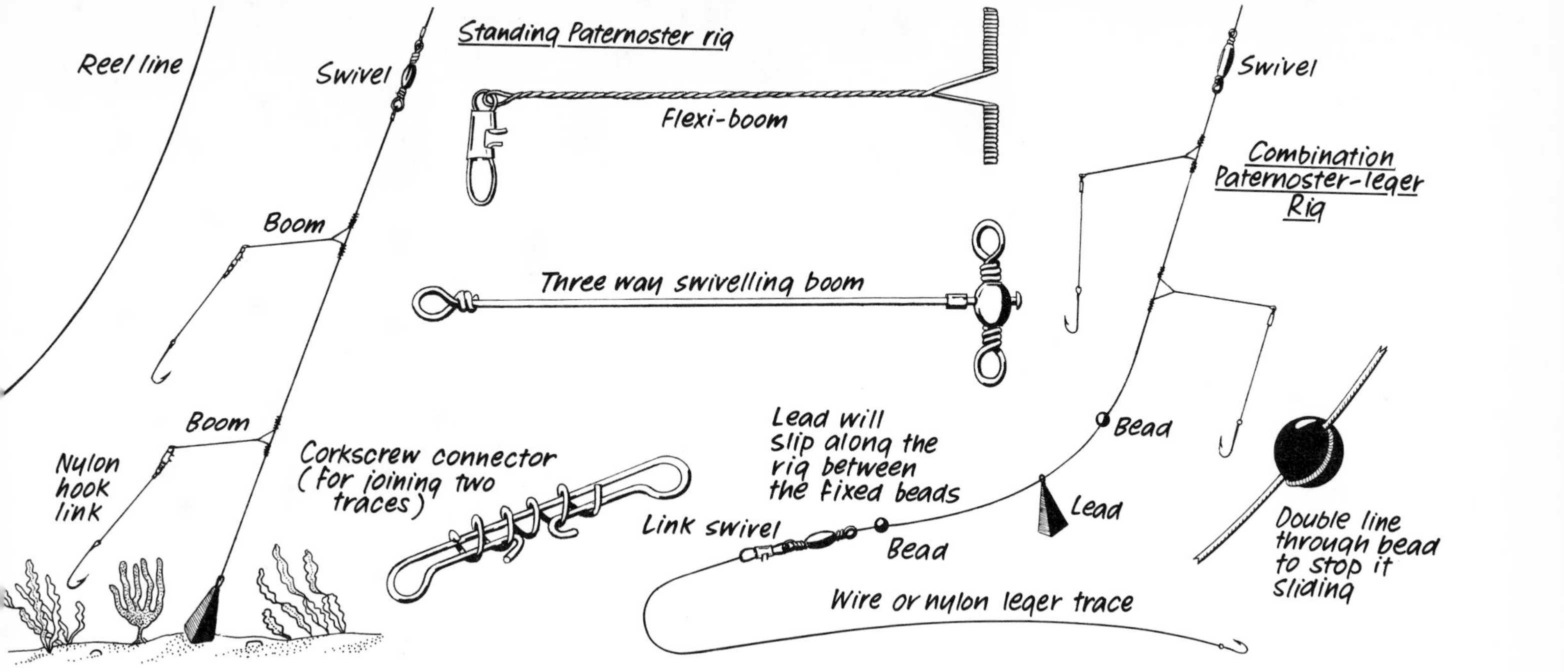

distance before feeling any resistance to its movement through the water. This rig is widely used for a variety of vastly different species.

The paternoster technique offers one or more baits close to, but above the sea bed. This rig gives a direct communication of a bite to the angler since the line is fished tight from rod tip to lead weight. Again, there are many variations and constructions.

Finally, there is a combination of both these basic rigs. This tackle is an attempt to bring together the best features of both paternoster and legering styles of fishing.

If one is aware that the available species are swimming at a determined level down through the depths then there are a further two other main ways of getting to grips with the fish. These are float fishing and tight line methods.

One good reason for ensuring that your rig is formed of quality components: a huge common skate can easily rip a weak trace apart during the fight.

Float fishing is used to catch small species like wrasse with worms or limpets fished a few inches off the bottom, but with modification, suitable for shark fishing where the fish may weigh many hundreds of pounds!

Tight line methods are for fishing at any depth, using a weight to take a bait down. This method is ideal when fishing with artificial lures that have no weight or the lure can have weight built-in, as in the case of a pirk or heavy spoon.

BOAT FISHING –THE FISH OF WINTER

Winter brings a strange quietness to the seashore and estuary. Gone are the dinghy sailors who speed, with wind-tousled hair and wet backsides, across the inshore waters or in the narrow channels that wind between high banks of glutinous mud towards the opening estuary. The fisherman who ventures out into the coastal seas or into the maze of creeks has little to disturb his concentration but the occasional cry of the curlew flashing, with quick wing beats, from the saltings. There are none of the bright, violent, colours of spring or summer; just the clear, pale sky and sombre browns of marsh and shore weed.

From a number of discreet hards and slipways small boats are launched every weekend. Only the bite of a gusting east wind will keep these boats and their anglers ashore. You will find the men, before launching, digging worms in the half-light of the morning. This breed of angler is very much a do-it-yourself man, gathering his own bait rather than buying worms at high winter prices. If the weather is kind the journey will be to favourite inshore marks for whiting or cod that follow the sprat and herring into the shallow water, but with any sort of a blow these boats will head for the shelter of headland, river mouth or creek to seek the winter flounder. It is a wise fisherman who ▶114

HERRING
Clupea harengus

Recognized by the dorsal fin placed halfway between the tip of the snout and the base of the caudal fin. The mouth of the herring extends to the middle of the eye. The belly is sharply keeled with a number of weak spines. The pelvic fins begin below the rear edge of the dorsal. The herring is a prolific species ranging throughout the Northern seas, feeding on minute fry of other fish and free-swimming organisms.

Bait: *Not specifically fished for but will take mackerel feathers and occasionally small strips of fish intended for other species.*

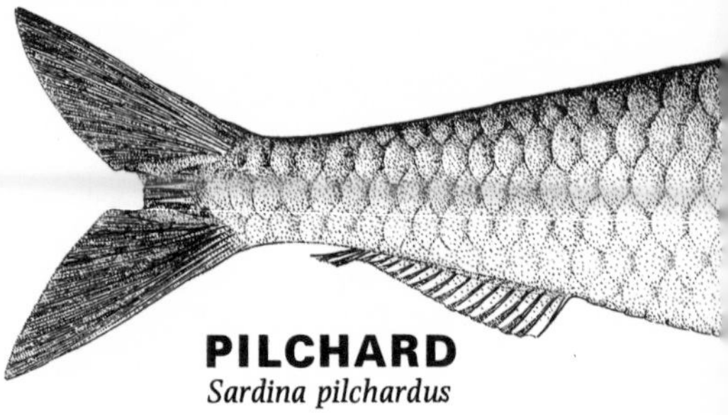

PILCHARD
Sardina pilchardus

Although a smaller species than the herring the scales of the pilchard are larger. The lower jaw is longer and the mouth extends to the beginning of the eye. The species possesses radiating lines on the gill covers and a well-rounded belly. The pilchard is a shoal fish that swims higher in the water than the herring and is frequently seen being harried by shark and other predators. Pilchards are the adult form of the sardine found in more southerly climes.

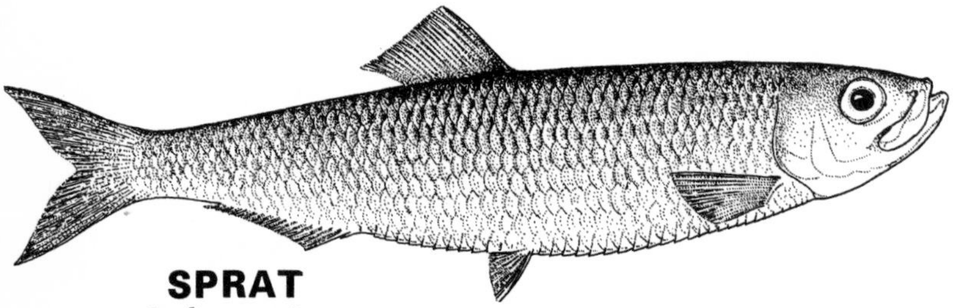

SPRAT
Sardina sprattus

An angler's baitfish, caught by commercial netters. The sprat is smaller than either the herring or pilchard but has a similarity to both of these fish. The dorsal fin is closer to the caudal fin than the head and the abdomen is sharply keeled with strong, stiff spines. A surface swimmer, it travels in huge shoals and feeds in a similar way to the other members of the Clupeidae.

SKIPPER OR SAURY PIKE
Scomberesox saurus

A long, streamlined fish bearing some resemblance to the garfish, it has jaws that are extended to form a beak. Behind both the dorsal and anal fins there are tiny finlets that reach back to the tail.

Bait: *Being a live fish feeder, the skipper will readily chase a small spoon or blade spinner near to the surface.*

ANCHOVY
Engraulis encrasicolus

The small fish has a snout which projects beyond its mouth, which in turn extends well beyond the fish's eye. The dorsal fin rises directly above the pelvic fins and the anal is midway between pelvics and the tail. The species averages between 5 to 8 ins in length and is not very common in our waters.

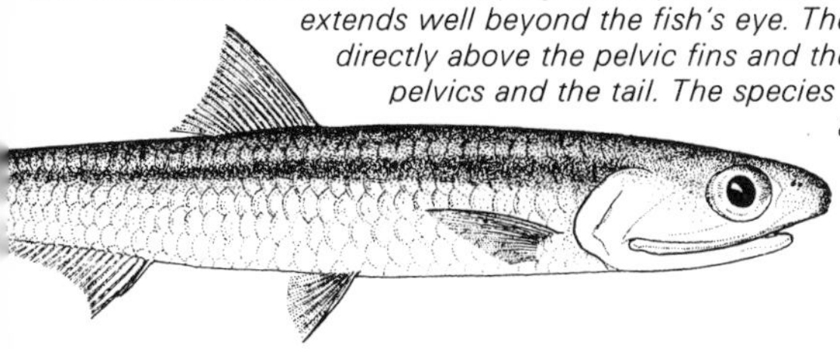

ARGENTINE
Argentina sphyraena

A tiny fish that can be found in the warm waters off the western coasts of the British Isles. Easily recognized by the size of its eyes, the argentine is a shoal fish taken commercially both for food and for the scales which are used in the cosmetics industry.

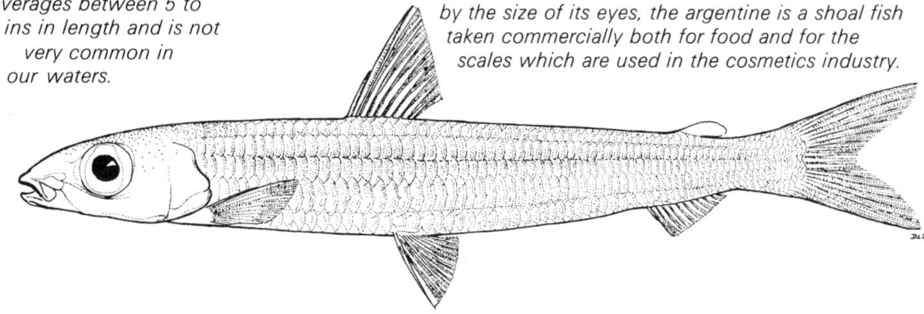

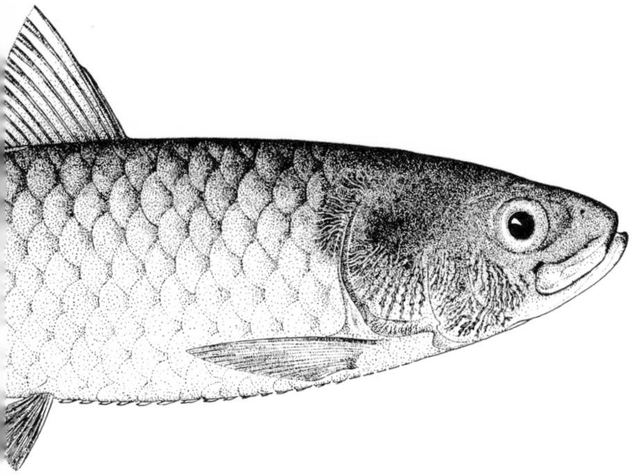

ALLIS SHAD
Alosa alosa

A sea species that enters freshwater to spawn, the allis shad has a deep body coming to a fairly sharp keel on the belly. There can be a dark blotch behind the gill cover. There are between 60 and 80 long and tightly-spaced gill rakers on the lower arch. Fish of 8 lbs are possible.

Bait: *Light tackle spinning with small blade spinners and fly fishing with little streamer or nymph flies. They will probably take small marine worms or tiny fish as well.*

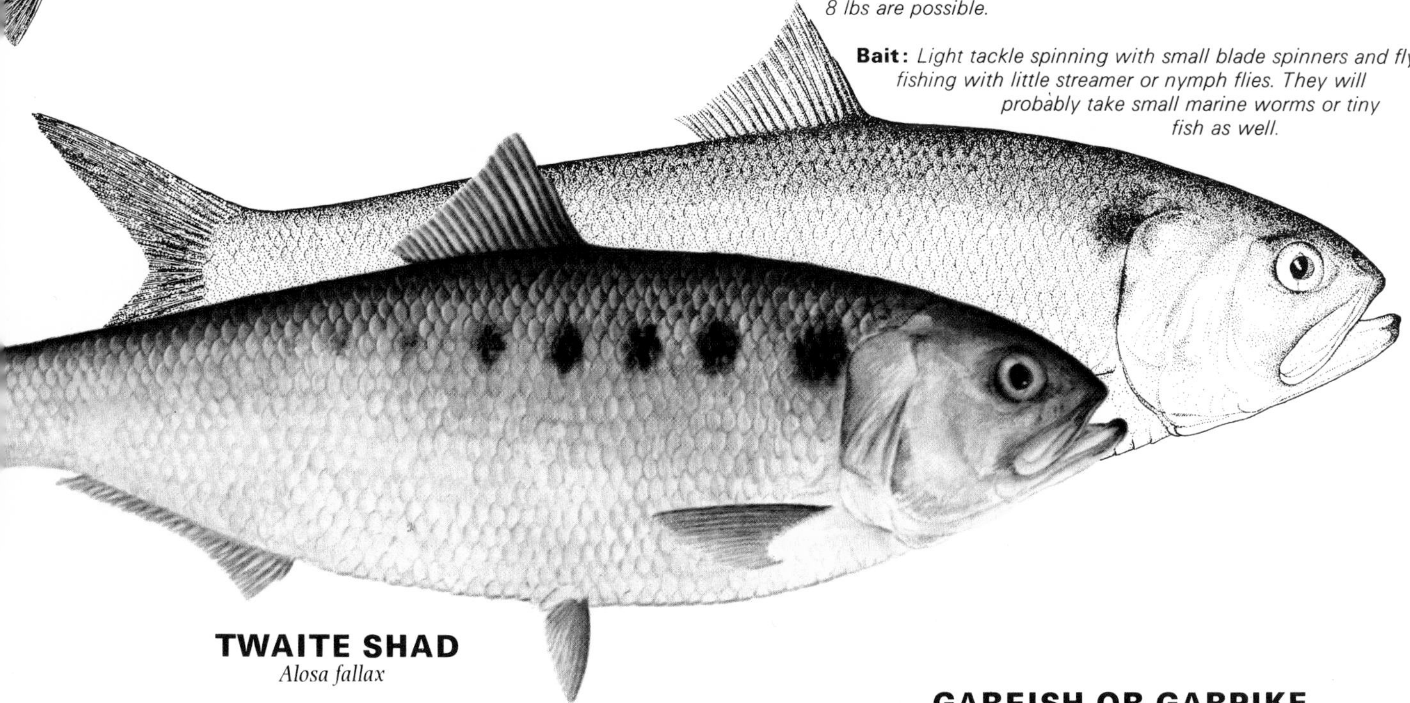

TWAITE SHAD
Alosa fallax

Like its relative, the allis shad, the species ascends into rivers to spawn but at a later period in the spring. May seems to be the usual time. The twaite shad is a smaller species, again with a sharp keel and stiff spines on the abdomen, and has far less gill rakers. In the adult fish these will number 25 to 29. There are a row of dark blotches running from behind the head to the dorsal fin. Fish average one to two and a half pounds for English rivers.

Bait: *Similar fishing methods, using artificial lures, as the allis shad.*

GARFISH OR GARPIKE
Belone belone

A more slender and longer fish than the skipper with no finlets behind the dorsal or anal fins. The upper jaw is sharp and finely pointed, no doubt as a weapon. The lower jaw is longer and has a softer end. The garfish is commonly found in company with shoals of mackerel skipping along on the surface or jumping across the wavetops. The bones are greenish coloured and the flesh does not seem useful as a bait for other species.

Bait: *Artificial lures, spoons, spinners and the inevitable mackerel feathers.*

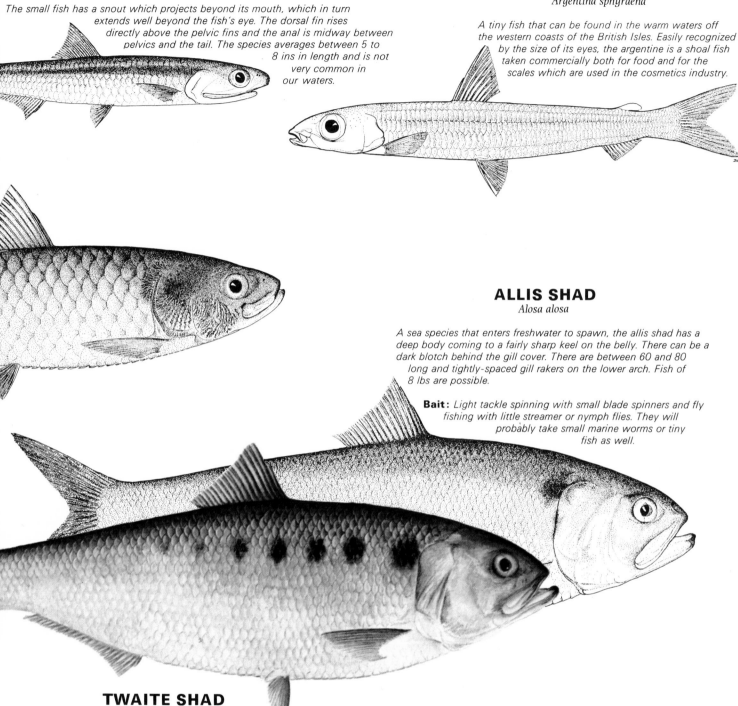

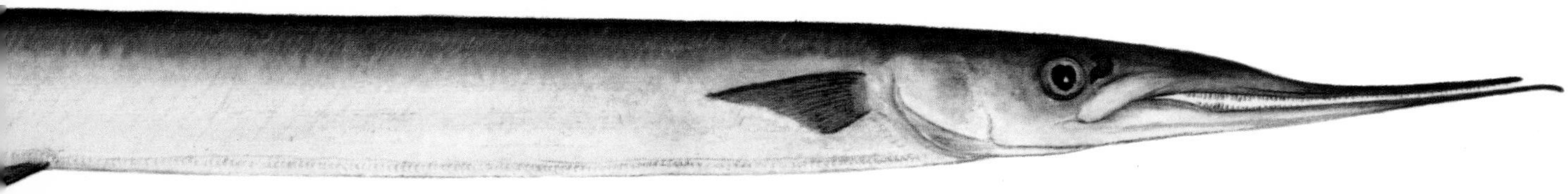

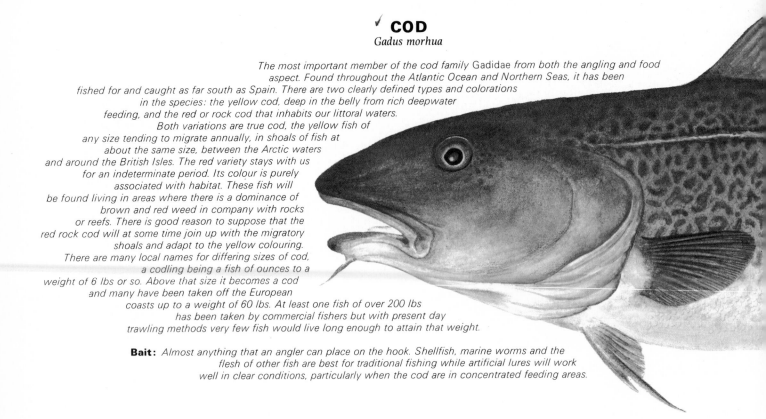

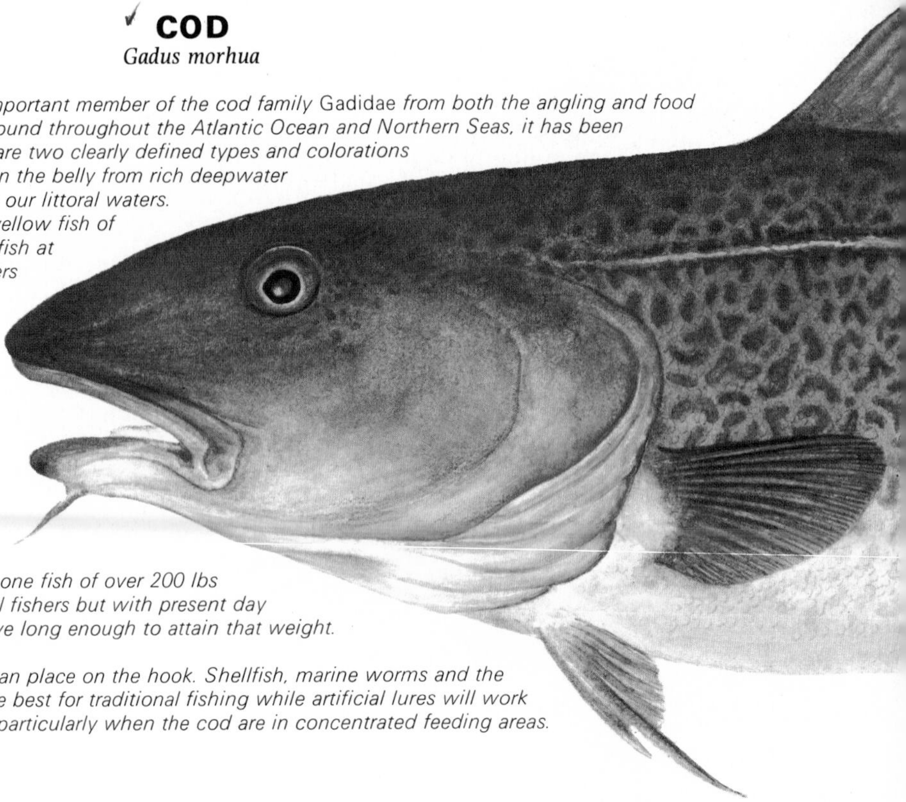

COD

Gadus morhua

The most important member of the cod family Gadidae *from both the angling and food aspect. Found throughout the Atlantic Ocean and Northern Seas, it has been fished for and caught as far south as Spain. There are two clearly defined types and colorations in the species: the yellow cod, deep in the belly from rich deepwater feeding, and the red or rock cod that inhabits our littoral waters. Both variations are true cod, the yellow fish of any size tending to migrate annually, in shoals of fish at about the same size, between the Arctic waters and around the British Isles. The red variety stays with us for an indeterminate period. Its colour is purely associated with habitat. These fish will be found living in areas where there is a dominance of brown and red weed in company with rocks or reefs. There is good reason to suppose that the red rock cod will at some time join up with the migratory shoals and adapt to the yellow colouring. There are many local names for differing sizes of cod, a codling being a fish of ounces to a weight of 6 lbs or so. Above that size it becomes a cod and many have been taken off the European coasts up to a weight of 60 lbs. At least one fish of over 200 lbs has been taken by commercial fishers but with present day trawling methods very few fish would live long enough to attain that weight.*

Bait: *Almost anything that an angler can place on the hook. Shellfish, marine worms and the flesh of other fish are best for traditional fishing while artificial lures will work well in clear conditions, particularly when the cod are in concentrated feeding areas.*

111◀ can resign himself to heeding the weather pattern that can make dinghy or small craft fishing a sport for the skilful.

I like to fish flounders in the cold months of the year. They are not great fighters but their presence is assured in the muddy creeks of my home coast. Most of the east coast estuaries and rivers can be fished from the sea walls but I prefer to take a dinghy up into the creeks that have no access to the land fisherman. The mudflats of the widening river are dangerous places to be, especially at low water. We have lost a number of anglers and wildfowlers in East Anglia, when the tide with a wind behind it came rushing in, filling the creeks and smothering the flats faster than the men could walk. Out among the channels fish get little, if any, disturbance from man or marine motors. And, although most of the dinghy fishers own an outboard motor, this will only be in use for the short time necessary to get among the creeks or out to off-shore channels and banks. Thereafter the oars, used silently and with care, will take the boat on to the fish. A noisy arrival, with accompanying splashing and thuds as the oars are brought into the boat, will kill all chance of getting quickly into fish. Although the silent approach matters most in the warm months, when after bass and mullet, even the winter flounders can be frightened off their feeding routine.

When flounder fishing, look for certain conditions of terrain and water before putting the anchor over the stem. Seek a fairly fast gradient to the sloping mudflats that lead down from the marsh vegetation. Evidence of worm casts on the mud and some patches of seaweed will indicate that there is relatively little pollution to worry about. Any sign of an oily film on the mud or lack of life, both small creatures and birds, is a sign that man has once more spoiled a habitat. I like to find a fast drop-off, from the mudflats, into a gully or sharply defined channel that has water in it at all stages of the tide. These conditions give good prospects for flounder fishing.

Sloping mudflats will enable a legered bait to be rolled across and into the channel when the tide is ebbing or flowing. A sign of worms means there is a life support system for fish, and a water-filled creek should mean that flounders can remain, during autumn and winter, moving up and down the gullies with the tide. A constant water level in gully and among the holes will keep the shore crabs and other small animals about. These are first-class feed for the fish, particularly when presented as peeler or softie hookbaits. The end tackles can be quite simple. A single-hook flowing trace with a drilled bullet lead will keep the bait rolling in any current. Sometimes the addition of a small spoon, baited with a small section of ragworm, fishes best. A form of rubby dubby can help greatly in concentrating flounders in one area. Most households

will have the odd polythene container or unwanted tin. Punch a few small holes around the sides, fix a stout cord to the handle and then it is only a matter of stuffing it with enough mashed fish, with a little pilchard oil or other smelly additive. Drop the container either on a rope or attached to the anchor warp. It is surprising how flounders and green eels will follow the scent of the rubby uptide to where the hook bait lies.

After settling the boat, give a thought to your own comfort. With a winter wind and little warmth from the sun it is sometimes difficult to fish a whole tide up and down. I've had days, mostly in November and February, when cold and damp ate right into my bones. Unfortunately in a small boat there is no place to jump up and down, to make the blood race. It is in these conditions that an angler's concentration goes, resulting in lost fish and a lack of attention to signs of change in the weather. Try to windproof yourself with good warm clothes. Oilskins and PVC jackets both help in this respect but thick woollen sweaters are necessary underneath. It is the layer of warmed air next to the body that insulates and keeps out the cold. A collapsible, canvas cuddy is both right and sensible in the dinghy. It will let you hide from sudden rain squalls and keep the wind off but can be lowered to give complete vision to the chap on the tiller when underway – an important consideration.

I have long since ceased to take tea and coffee in my lunchbox. I find soup kept in a wide-mouthed vacuum flask infinitely better both as food and drink. It gets the circulation going in all but the bitterest of weather. One word about your feet. Never wear thigh waders in the boat. Short rubber boots, perhaps, with insulated socks and PVC overtrousers are much safer. I have a halter-style lifejacket that does not restrict my movement and again serves to give an amount of protection from the wind. I realise that most dinghy fishers take great care when out at their sport but things can go wrong and one has a duty to ensure that the boat is fit to go to sea.

Now, let's get down to fishing. Bait your hook in an attractive manner and cast out to the side of the channel. As soon as the bait finds the bottom take the line between your fingers to feel the kind of ground the lead is traversing. Most of the rivers and creeks of my coast have a hard base to the channel. Cockle and oyster shells, from past fisheries, have settled and act as holdfasts for small clumps of bladderwrack and serrated weed. This is where the crabs live and where we can expect flatfish to be.

I use a spinning rod which is fast in the taper and ideal for flicking a bait away from the boat. It is essential to get the bait some distance off because any careless movement in the boat, of feet or tackle, will create a sound that is transmitted down to the fish

Three very famous angling characters. "The Trio", the late Doug Dinnie with Bill Freshwater and George Mann. They hit the headlines in the late Sixties with massive catches of cod from The Gantocks, a mark in the Firth of Clyde.

and that will put them off the feed for a time. I like an 8 ft rod since it gives that extra length and control to handle fish easily as the tide quickens and begins to flow hard. Fixed-spool reels are ideal for this work. Loaded with 6 lb nylon, they help in easily casting light leads and bait that a multiplier would find difficult.

When the bait has completed an arc of travel, one has to re-cast with a slight increase in the length of throw. This means we cover even more ground and possibly find a flounder that saw the bait swing round on the first cast. Suddenly the lead will stop rolling. It could be snagged on a patch of weed or be trapped against a stone. Give it a few seconds before lifting the rod tip to get the lead released. It could be a fish, so concentrate on the line between your fingers. If it twitches, a few trembles come back up the nylon but do not make the mistake of reacting too quickly. Flounders are notorious for playing around with the bait. Even though they have grabbed and tethered the bait, the lead is still free to move a small distance in the current. Wait for a definite pull from the fish. If it comes, lift the rod, feeling for the weight of the flounder, and strike the hook home. Should the bite not develop, lift the tip of the rod slowly, which will drag the bait towards you for a few inches. Many a flounder will then grab hard onto your offering, thinking that the food is getting away from it.

Hooking and playing flounders on this sort of gear will give far better sport than one can have when casting for them from the shore or sea wall. The fish has only to pull a bullet lead of an ounce or so, allowing it to make hasty progress toward the security of the deeper water in the channel. With the minimum of drag set on the spool, let the fish have its head and savour the vibrations up the line as it swims low over the mud. A finger jammed down onto the rim of the spool will increase pressure and turn your flounder when it tires. Floundering can be good sport. It comes nearest to the delicacy of coarse fishing, with the possible exception of mullet fishing on float tackle! They are easy to catch when they are around so don't kill more than are needed. Returned fish will give sport on another day because they are not hook shy and deserve to be given freedom after the fight!

On those bright, frosty, days in January, when the sea has a cold calmness with the slightest of winds that barely raise a lop to the wave pattern, it's time to seek the cod. They are the true winter fish of the British Isles. I suppose more sea anglers fish for this one species than any other. There are many migratory paths that the cod follow to our shores. Down from the Arctic Seas and Atlantic deeps they will move into the western waters of Britain and Ireland. Another group of fish come south from somewhere off the northern seas of Europe to cross the North Sea and arrive in the relatively shallow waters of the east coast. The temperature of the sea, presence of food, fish and places to spawn, will all determine where and when they hit our shores. Sometimes they will swim right on the beach, within easy reach of the shore angler but it is the boat angler who gets the first crack at them. Ever hungry, constantly moving, the shoals need huge amounts of food to satisfy the numbers of fish. Consequently the cod will take most kinds of bait offered on a hook. Natural feed, such as worms, squid, fish, molluscs and crustacea, and many kinds of artificial lures will and do attract the species.

The kind of tackle necessary to fish for cod is tremendously varied. More often than not it is determined by the sea conditions rather than by the weight of the fish that can be expected. Heavy rods and up to 2 lbs of lead might be the standard gear in the strong tides of the English Channel, whereas cod fishing in The Wash or Inner Hebrides might call for leads of no more than 6–8 ozs and a correspondingly lightish rod. Even in the areas of exceptionally strong tides it is possible to scale down the rod and lead weight by using wire, in a flexible form, as a reel line. It is rarely necessary to use a powerful rod and reel combination to subdue the fighting qualities of this species. One factor, above all others, matters when seeking the cod and this is the position of the bait. Cod feed right down on the sea bed and it follows that the bait must also be there if cod are to be attracted and hooked. It is no use having baits that lift up in the strong water. The cod will not come up to find them!

Not the greatest of fighters on rod and line but a fine addition to the family diet! The turbot, from deepwater marks, can put a steady strain on angler and tackle. This fish came to Leslie Moncrieff at Kinsale.

A general-purpose boat rod, in either solid or hollow glass with a multiplier or centre-pin reel capable of handling a 30–40 lb line will handle most cod fishing situations. Braided Terylene or monofilament nylon lines are equally suitable, although each has its pros and cons. Braided line will help in detecting the shy bite and provide better contact between fish and angler. It is more positive since it lacks stretch. Nylon stretches, sometimes up to a quarter of its length under stress. This can act as a buffer with large fish in heavy tide conditions but it can also cushion the shy bite. There are many rigs and each of them is subject to local variation, such is the number of cod fishermen and their patterns of local fishing and tradition. Both the simple running leger and the standing paternoster are good rigs – the leger for strong water where there is an advantage in having a bait that waves to and fro with a natural motion in a current. The standing paternoster is for slacker conditions and where the angler requires a more direct contact between hook and rod tip. I use both. I choose the leger for large single baits for times when the big fish are known to be around and the paternoster for smaller fish or when more than one bait is called for. One thing I would say. If you fish for cod with the paternoster rig make the hook droppers fairly long so that with any run of current the baits will fish right down on the bottom. In dead slack water, a straight up and down presentation will have the baits above the sea bed which can bring some species but rarely a cod!

In clear and moderately coloured water the addition of flashers (spoon blades), that twist and sparkle in the current, will often help to draw fish to the baited hooks. Feathers, tied on stronger line and hooks than the conventional mackerel trace, with the addition of hookbait, will also prove a deadly combination in conditions that allow the cod to see them. In murky water, like the stuff that runs off the East Anglian coast, some added attraction can be given to a bait either by dipping it in, or injecting it with, pilchard oil. In the water of the muddy estuaries fish are feeding and finding food by smell, grubbing along the sea bed turning over weeds and stones for their morsels. Anything that arouses their olfactory sense must be of benefit to the fisherman!

In the clear, clean waters of the north of Britain and the Atlantic, artificial lures come into consideration as baits. Cod in and from the deep water are conditioned to feeding on small live fish. Their eyesight plays a greater role in securing the daily food quota and so they will grab at the pirk lure that twists and jerks inches above the sea bed. "The Trio", those famous boat anglers of the Clyde, proved the value of the metal lure when they twice broke the cod record on the Gantocks. Natural baits are passed by in favour of the artificial lure on that mark. Not because the pirk tastes better . . . but because it has that action, imparted by the angler, that leads the cod to think that it is a living thing.

Since most of my cod fishing is done in southern waters I tend to use natural baits. I think that a large bait is best and preferably one formed as a "cocktail", with both lugworm and fish or squid strip on the hook together. Give the fish a choice and let them decide what they will take. When the first cod comes aboard, slit open its stomach and check the contents. More than once I have had a fish jammed full of hardback crabs. But I have learned not to try them as hookbaits ▶120

WHITING

Merlangius merlangus

A fish of the clean ground, the whiting figures largely in the catches of both shore and boat cod fishermen. The species arrives early in the autumn, preceding the cod by a month or so. October and November will find whiting in the shallow waters it searches for small fish of all varieties. The whiting feeds on the bottom in vast shoals until late winter, when the shoals depart for deeper water. They can be regarded as a sporting species but only when fished on light tackle that will allow them to fight. Fish average about a pound although the "channel whiting", as the larger fish are termed, could reach 6·lbs.

Bait: *Fish strips, such as herring and mackerel. Baited feathers and marine worms.*

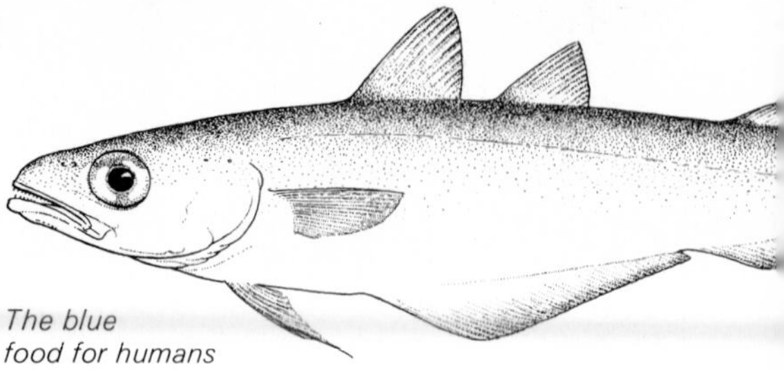

BLUE WHITING

Micromesistius poutassou

Not regarded as yet as an angler's quarry. The blue whiting will come into prominence as food for humans within the next decade. It is reported that this species alone is capable of providing a large part of the fish food requirement of our population. Found at much greater depths than its relatives in the cod family, it can be easily recognized and distinguished from the whiting by the unequal distances between the three dorsal fins. The first of the anal fins is long, close to the fish's body and straight.

Bait: *Small fry of other species and fish strip.*

√ POLLACK

Pollachius pollachius

The pollack is to be found in most of our coastal waters with the possible exception of the south-east corner of England. It can be said to be a fish of summer for it figures in angler's catches from April on to the late autumn. The species is by far the most sporting, in angling terms, of the Gadidae. The smaller fish haunt harbours and inshore rocky situations, whereas larger fish are found on offshore reefs and wrecks.

Bait: *Practically anything that can be put onto a hook. All kinds of fish bait, shellfish, marine worms and artificial lures. The pollack is one fish that can be sought with a man-made lure with confidence. Spinners, rubber eels, almost anything that flashes, glints or has a fish-like movement will be grabbed. Fly fishing will also take the smaller surface feeding fish.*

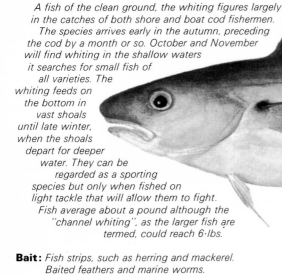

HADDOCK
Melanogrammus aeglefinus

A powerful fighting member of the cod family generally found in northern waters of the British Isles. The haddock favours a clean, mud or sand bottom with the availability of shellbeds.

Bait: *Crustaceans, scallops, mussels, cockles and razorfish. Marine worms and small strips of fishbait.*

✓COALFISH
Pollachius virens

Similar in appearance to the pollack, although there is much confusion in identifying the two species. The coalfish has a white, straight lateral line, whereas the pollack has a lateral line that is curved over the pectoral fin. The jaws of the coalfish are of equal length, whilst the pollack's underjaw is longer than the top jaw. The coalfish has a more northerly distribution and, although the small fish can be found right up to the shoreline, bigger fish inhabit deeper water than the pollack. Fish of over 20 lbs are taken from reefs in the north and some of our southern wrecks.

Bait: *Similar baits to the pollack, particularly artificial lures and feathers intended to take mackerel.*

POOR COD

Trisopterus minutus

Looking rather like a pouting, this species is often taken from similar fishing grounds. It is both smaller and less colourful, lacking the black spot at the base of the pectoral fins and vertical bars of the pouting. The poor cod is a small fish, hardly ever exceeding 9 ins in length.

Bait: *Similar baits as for the pouting.*

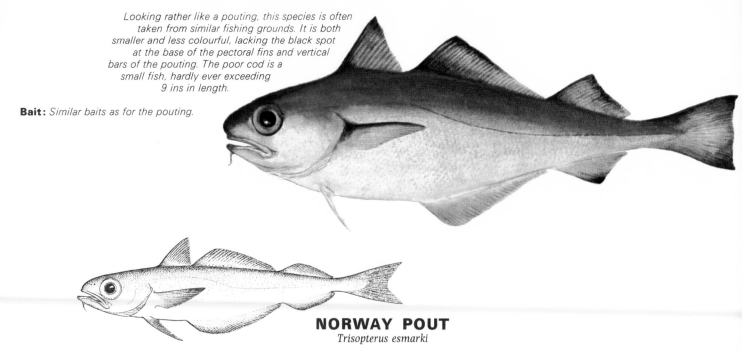

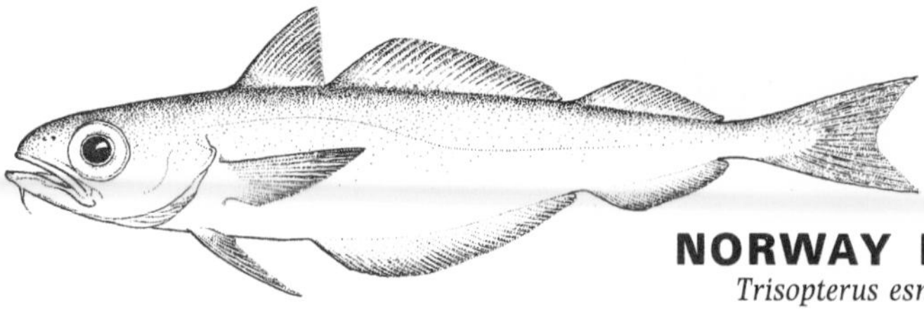

NORWAY POUT

Trisopterus esmarki

A small pouting-like species but less bulky. It has large eyes and a protruding lower jaw. The Norway pout has little angling significance.

117◀ because for some reason the cod will not take them from the hook. Whether it is because the hooked hardback lacks natural movement I cannot tell. If in shallow water I would be inclined to cast the bait, gently, to the side of the boat in an effort to get away from any angling noise and to cover more ground. When in a party boat or out over deep water the bait is lowered to find bottom and run back, downtide, to find fish. Don't use too heavy a lead, just enough to keep the bait hard down on the bottom but so balanced that you can lift the rod tip, run off a couple of yards of line and settle the lead once more. This procedure can be followed until the bait is too far away or the lead becomes difficult to feel. Then it is a matter of reeling in and inspecting the bait before fishing it down again.

Cod fishing is not just made up of baiting hooks and dropping them down to fish that are lying with their mouths open waiting. The successful angler is the fellow who works and who also asks himself intelligent questions about the conditions of the day. He reacts to his assessment of what he sees above the waves and what his muscles tell him is happening below them. Out in a charter boat, it is the paid skipper who makes the decision about where to fish. He has to earn a living and he can usually be relied upon to put anglers where fish are known to be. What he cannot do is hook the fish for each angler.

No one can be dogmatic about the way a cod bites. I have had the slightest of nibbles that resulted in 20-pounders coming aboard and wrenching takes that nearly took the rod clean out of my hands from codling of 3 or 4 lbs. Obviously, no two sea areas present the same set of conditions and this is the clue to types of bite. In deep water, where the tide run is usually the weakest, the fish have time to inspect a bait and take it in a leisurely way. You will get an initial knock, then the pull down of the solid take when the bait is in the mouth of the fish. In shallow water, with a fast rip of current, fish are feeding while swimming strongly against the tide. If they find a bait they grab at it, in the belief that it will either be swept from them or taken by another member of the shoal. Then you are liable to get a tremendous, thumping, bite out of all proportion to the size of the cod. One thing I have learned is not to hit the bite too early. Ease the rod up and feel the weight of the fish before striking. It is wise to select the right size of hook. Cod have enormous mouths. The head is almost a third of the body size and small hooks can be so easily pulled out of, rather than into, the mouth of this fish.

What a fight we would have if the cod could sustain its struggles of the first fathom off the bottom. All too quickly the change in pressure affects the fish and it becomes just a ponderous weight on the line. This is a more marked effect when fishing in deep water although cod soon tire in the shallows. With their mouths open, especially when hooked in the lower jaw, and the force of the water flowing into the mouth, the fight is soon knocked out of them. Nevertheless, the cod is predictable and visits us every year.

The turbot is not normally regarded as an angler's fish of winter. This species is associated with offshore

POUTING

Trisopterus luscus

Present all round the British Isles but particularly off the south and western shores. The species favours rough ground and is also fond of reefs and wreck situations. Like the young pollack, this fish is taken close in to the shore, in harbours and under piers. The pouting will figure largely in the catches of young anglers and competition sea anglers fishing with small hooks and baits. Though not generally regarded as a table fish, pouting can provide a tasty meal if cleaned and eaten soon after capture. They average two or three fish to the pound but run up to 3 lbs off the deepwater marks.

Bait: *Small strips of fish, mussels, cockles and small worms fished on or close to the bottom.*

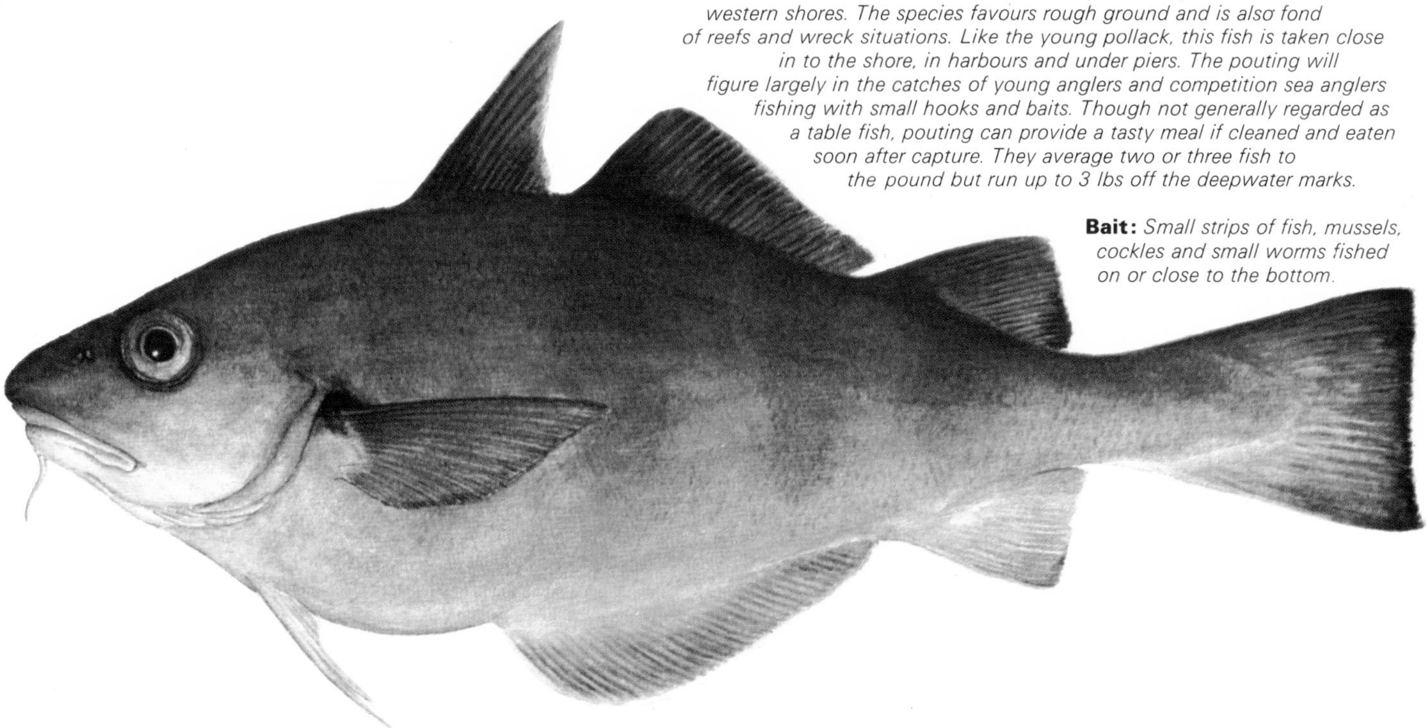

sandbanks that form in the shallow waters off coasts that have a fair run of tide. It is not always realised that there are banks farther out where the greater depths are not subject to the violent change in water temperature brought by the winter winds and changes in oceanic currents. Banks are good feeding ground for the cod, particularly for the big chaps that are able to withstand the strong tides. Anglers fishing for cod on the Varne Bank in the middle of the English Channel off Folkestone have often brought large turbot into harbour in the middle of winter. This proves two things – their baits must have been on the sand where both species feed and also that sand eels were still present in sufficient shoals to keep the turbot from leaving to find deeper water.

The turbot, our second largest British flatfish, is a fine table fish but does not give the battle of which its cousin the halibut is capable. When hooked, turbot will pull hard to keep the bait but they usually kite up in the tide when the power of the rod begins to apply lifting pressure. Nevertheless, they are a welcome addition to the basket and can always be fished for on standard cod rigs. Turbot strongly favour fish bait, such as herring, mackerel and sand eels. The method of fishing depends on an accurate positioning of the boat, which should be anchored on the side of the bank from which the tide is flowing, and the lines should be run out to fish just over the top of the bank. Any turbot on the sands will lie down the slope, out of the strongest flow, waiting for small fish to be swept over toward them. Some fishermen favour a multi-hook rig in the belief that where one fish lies there must be others. The danger in using more than a single hook is that the trace, unless joined with a number of quality swivels, will tend to twist as the baits move in the current. The twist can weaken the line and, of course, several swivels used will call for more knots to join the rig which again weakens the whole trace.

There are problems in attempting to boat two turbot in a strong tide flow and with the inevitable winter lop to the sea. Not only will the rod be fighting two weights, separated by a trace length, but each of the fish will be pulling in a different direction. I have seen two fish landed at one go but the risk is that one might lose either or both. Better to fish the single hookbait.

Two species figure strongly in the catches of sea match anglers – the whiting and the pout whiting. Neither of them is a huge or strong fighting fish but they can be found in vast shoals that bring sport throughout a tide. Most whiting caught will weigh about a pound and these fish move into the shore as early as October. Deepwater marks can produce channel whiting, as the larger fish are called, throughout the year. The tackle needed for both species is simple. The nylon paternoster with hooks of 1–1/0 size, will do. One thing to watch is the nylon snood when fishing for whiting since this species has fine sharp teeth and as it twists and turns the nylon can be weakened. Check out your hook lengths regularly. The whiting will generally be found swimming on the bottom over clean sand or mud ground. It is essentially ▶124

TORSK

Brosme brosme

Separated from the ling and hake, which it resembles, by the lack of a second dorsal fin, the torsk is a fish of northern waters, often taken by boats in the Shetland and Orkney Islands and off the Pentland Firth. There is one anal fin present and the pectorals and pelvic fins have roots at the same vertical line behind the gill-case. Fish of over 20 lbs have been taken in some areas of Arctic waters.

Bait: *Generally fishbaits are best, with pirks a possibility.*

LING

Molva molva

One of the hardest fighting members of the cod family, the species haunts rocky ground, either broken or as defined reefs as well as wrecks. The best of the inshore ling fishing is in the north of the British Isles although fine specimens have come, in recent years, from the deepwater wrecks of the West of England. There are two dorsal fins of roughly the same height, the first short and rounded with the secondary dorsal long and low to the body. Only one anal fin is present. The teeth are many and sharp but not as prominent as in the hake. Ling have oval eyes and are a nocturnal species that can grow to a length of 7 ft or more.

Bait: *Fish, squid and artificial lures.*

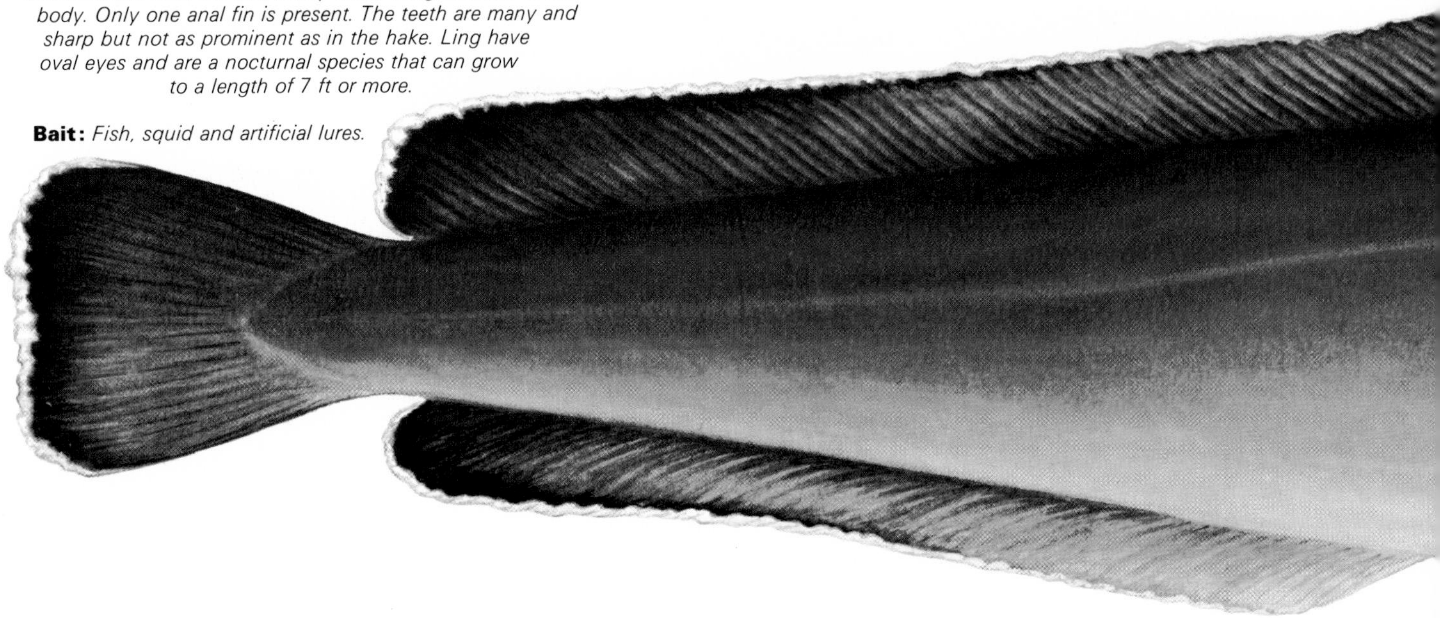

HAKE

Merluccius merluccius

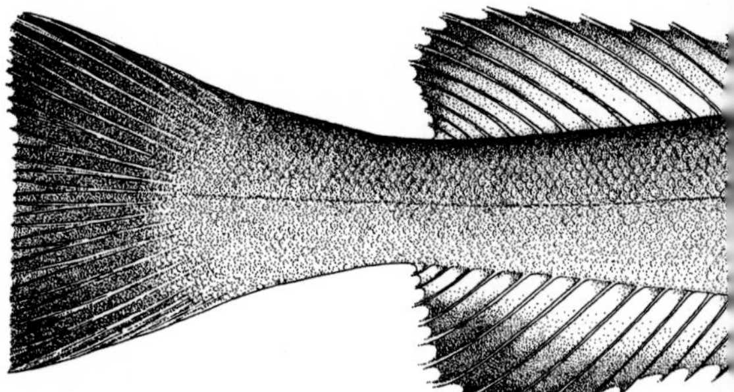

Another long, streamlined species with two dorsal fins, the first of which stands up in a rounded peak. There is one anal fin of the same length as the second dorsal fin. The teeth are thin and extremely sharp. Some of them are curved in toward the throat. There is no barbule under the chin. This fish was once fairly common but has suffered the attentions of severe commercial fishing. It is found off the north and west coasts of the British Isles where it could grow to 20 lbs or heavier.

Bait: *Fishbaits and lures that have flash, as this is a predatory species that will hunt out into open water, particularly at dusk.*

Ling Molva molva *juvenile.*

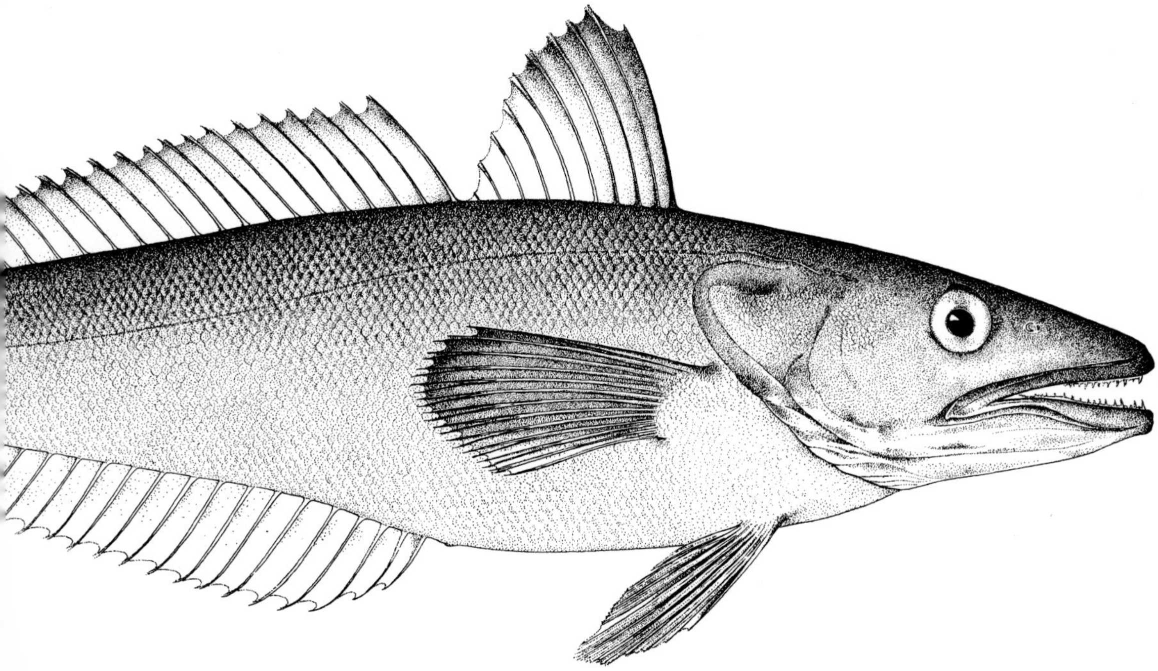

121◀ a fish feeder, preying on the fry of other species, but it will take worms and shellfish baits from the hook. Both species run to larger weights on the deep sea marks. The wrecks of the West Country produce fish throughout the seasons but it is noticeable that the northern waters of Britain contain much larger whiting than are found in the warmer waters of the south. The whiting is a major predator on smaller fish, even of its own kind, and is in turn preyed upon by the cod shoals that follow the inshore whiting during the winter months.

Pouting favour more broken ground in shallower water. Any outcrop of rock with weed cover will soon be populated by pouting. They are not the gamest of sea species although this fish gives great sport to youngsters fishing from piers and harbour walls in the winter months. They are catholic in taste and just about any form of bait will attract them.

If you hook small whiting or pout, send them back to the sea bed as a bait for the larger cod but do ensure that the hook is large enough to hold the bait and to hook and land the cod.

Much has been written about the disappearance of most sea-angling species from inshore waters during the colder months of the year. Certainly it is true that the cod, whiting and pouting are the mainstay of rod and line activity but we must not assume that all other fish species have left us completely. We frequently read of large dogfish, gurnards, coalfish, pollack and plaice that have been hooked in the middle of the winter. These and nearly all our sea fish have adjusted to the living requirements of their separate species by moving out into deeper water. The fishable areas around deepwater reefs and wrecks, together with the offshore channels, will harbour fish long after the open ground marks are denuded. More often than not it is the weather and condition of the sea that determines where fish are to be found and where we anglers can take a boat. A visit to the fish dock, as the trawlers bring in their catches, can be so revealing as to which species can be expected during the winter. With the exception of the warm water exotic fish, most of our traditional species will be represented in the trawled catches.

THE SPRING OF THE YEAR

Although there are no legislated seasons for the sea angler, nature imposes her own seasons upon us. Look at any sea angler's diary and it is clear that certain species are expected to arrive off our coasts at definite times. On my part of the East Anglian coast I expect to see the first sign of cod sometime around the end of October. Whiting are there already. Both species will have followed the shoals of sprat which move into the shallow coastal water in the autumn. A little later, toward the end of November, herrings will come down from northern seas. Both of these species provide food for the winter cod. Apart from certain deepwater marks, such as West Country wrecks which can provide a wide variety of species all the year round, most of our winter fishing is for cod or whiting with pouting making up the bags.

Although large cod and the lesser whiting come to the British Isles on an annual migratory path, some small codling will always be in residence. Even in the middle of summer there will always be a population of rich red-hued rock codling close into the shore among the kelp beds and reefs. They are so vastly different in coloration from the yellow-backed winter fish that there has always been a theory claiming they are a completely different breed of cod. I don't think this is so. It would appear that the smaller fish spawned in a particular year remain close into the shore, in shallow waters, both to escape the predatory attentions of bigger fish and to take advantage of the richer feeding to be found in the littoral waters. As they grow, so their feeding behaviour changes and they seek deeper water. There they form up into shoals of fish about the same size and begin a migratory mode of life that gradually develops a regular pattern of annual movement motivated by the urge to seek rich feeding grounds. This normally means that they begin to prey on other fish, such as the herring and the sprat, rather than feeding on bottom-dwelling crustaceans and worm

THE ROCKLINGS

There are five species of consequence among this group of fishes that are related to the cod family. The habits and habitat vary tremendously between species while there are only slight anatomical differences.

Bait: *They feed on minute crustaceans and molluscs and will take fishbaits of small sizes.*

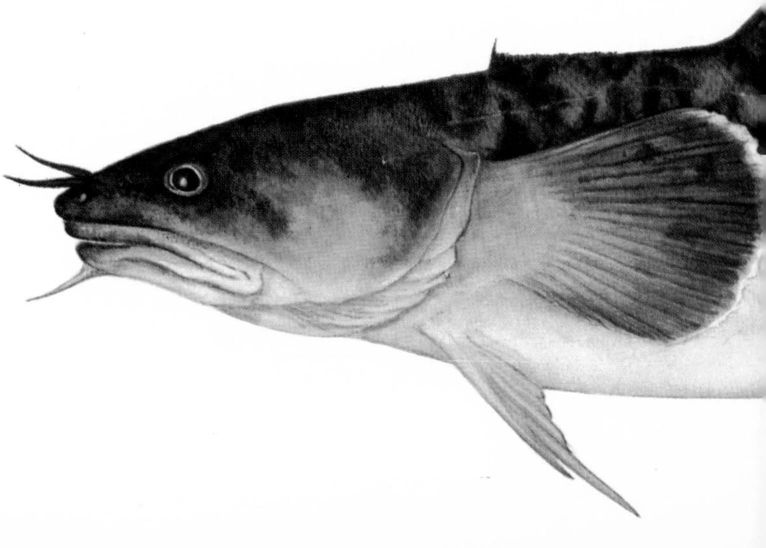

FIVE-BEARDED ROCKLING
Ciliata mustela

The leading dorsal fin is in the form of a spine followed by a low fringe, much of which lies neatly folded into a narrow cleft running along the fish's back. Only one anal fin is present. The fish has five beards or barbules, one in the centre of the lower jaw and four that protrude from the front of the upper jaw. The species favours inshore waters of moderate depth with a mixed ground of shingle, sand and rocky patches. As with the other species, they are small fish rarely exceeding a foot in length.

NORTHERN ROCKLING
Ciliata septentrionalis

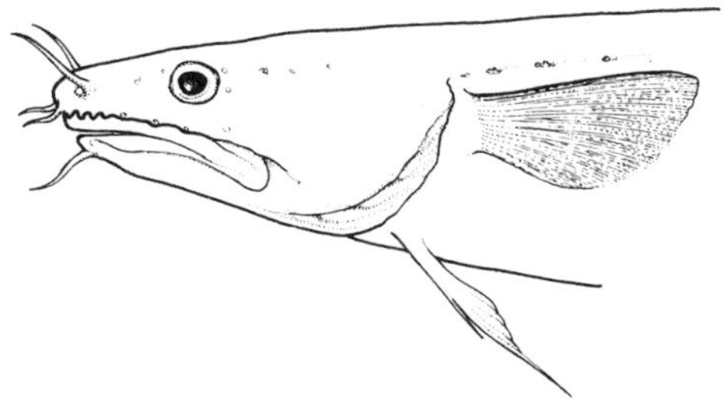

A small rockling with five barbules. Two of the barbules on the upper jaw are much smaller than those of the five-bearded rockling and the fish's pectoral fins are less rounded in shape. The main difference between the two species is the presence, in the Northern, of a series of further small barbules on the upper jaw, decreasing in size at the rear. A deepwater fish of much wider distribution than is thought because of confusion with the five-bearded species.

FOUR-BEARDED ROCKLING
Rhinonemus cimbrius

This species has a similar fin conformation to the five-bearded species although the anal fin starts at a position nearer to the caudal fin. There are three barbules on the upper jaw and one sprouting from the centre of the lower jaw. The species favours less rocky ground and has a more northerly distribution.

SHORE ROCKLING
Gaidropsarus mediterraneus

Similar to the three-bearded species although smaller when mature. The fish is a deep, chocolate brown with a light edging to the fins that is conspicuous. Colour in rockling depends on living surroundings. The fish has an indistinct lateral line and is essentially a shallow water species.

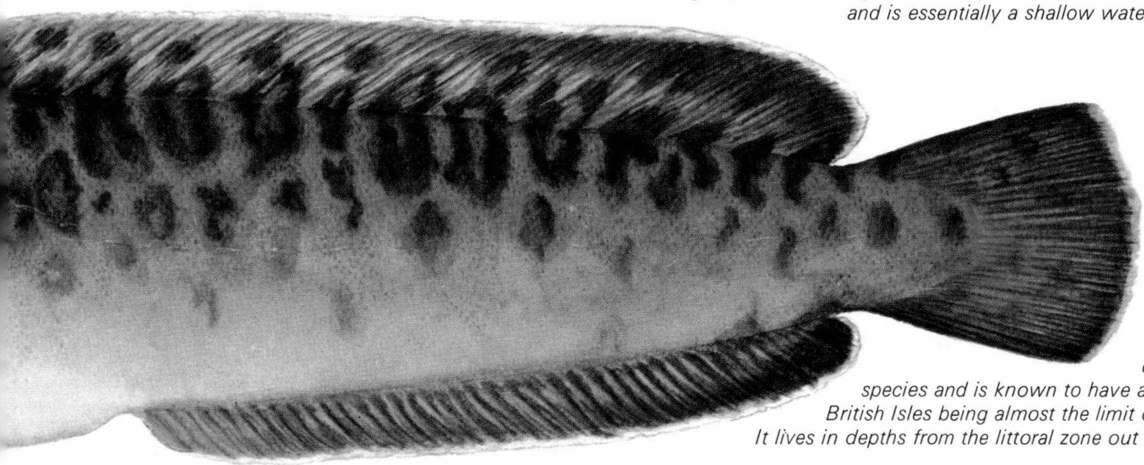

THREE-BEARDED ROCKLING
Gaidropsarus vulgaris

This rockling has two barbules on the upper jaw and one on the lower. It grows larger than either the four- or five-bearded species and is known to have a southerly distribution, the British Isles being almost the limit of its northward migration. It lives in depths from the littoral zone out to 100 fathoms.

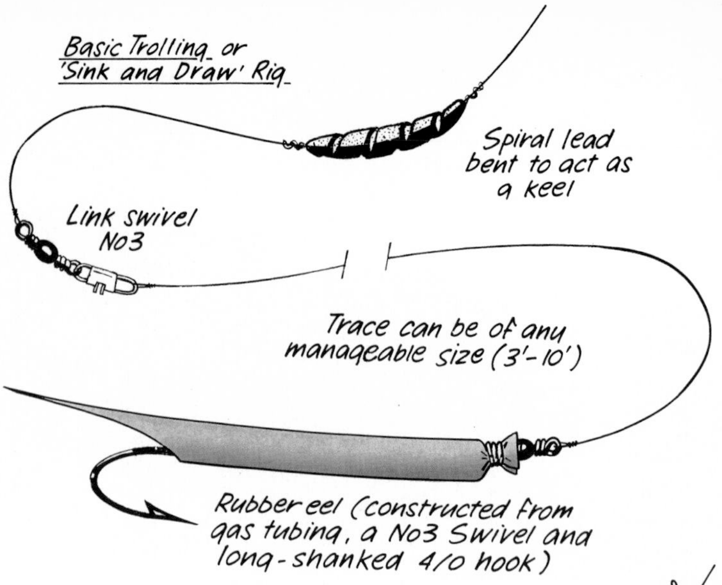

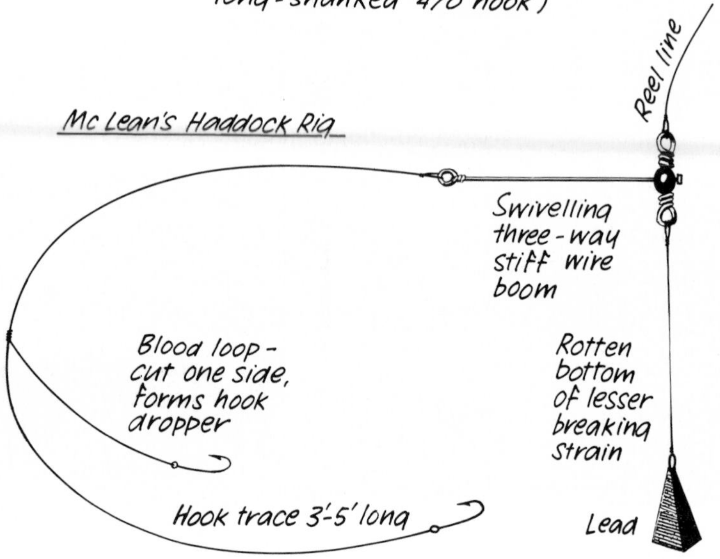

life. Of course, as they grow so they achieve sexual maturity which calls upon them to make further migrations to places that provide ideal spawning ground and where they can meet up in sufficient numbers to make the spawning successful.

After winter, as the cod leave our shores, there follows a slack period in the boat fisher's sport. We await the arrival of flatfish, plaice, dabs and turbot, from their winter quarters in the deeps. Thornbacks and other rays will come in the early spring but sport is quiet. The year is freshening, anglers begin to react to the lengthening days but there are few fish to be had. So for me it has become a ritual to travel to Scotland to catch the tail end of the winter sea angling and fish for a species that is rarely seen in large numbers in the south. The haddock is not a big fish. One of 10 lbs must be regarded as a rare catch on rod and line. I count myself lucky if I can hook half a dozen five pounders in the course of a year's sea fishing.

The haddock, although a member of the cod family, is a cold-water species. They can be found in southern areas of Britain and Ireland. I remember quite good catches being made off Canvey Island in the River Thames a few years ago. Similarly, there was a time in the late '60s when the sea off Kinsale, Co. Cork, produced a fantastic number of Irish specimen fish. But, gradually, the pattern of haddock fishing has re-established itself and one has to travel to the north to catch this species.

In my travelling to seek the haddock one place has never failed to produce the numbers, if not the "jumbo" size, of fish to the rod. The place is Arran, an island lying in the lower approaches to the Firth of Clyde. Washed by the warm waters of the North Atlantic Drift, its location off the western coastline of the mainland of Scotland ensures a remarkable ecology and a soft climate. Arran is said to be an island surrounded by fish. Nevertheless, amid this plenty there are clearly defined "hotspots". Lamlash Bay, the Corrie shore, Kilbrannan Sound near to the Mull of Kintyre and the lighthouse isle of Pladda are all established marks. One such spot where I have fished for haddock is off Pladda, at the south end of Arran. Here the tides meet with waters surging into a race that brings a variety of fish. Many factors contribute to making a successful mark. The availability of easy feeding, the type of ground and the conditions of water flow must be right. One factor, above all else, makes for Arran's superb "haddie" angling – the large beds of scallops all round the island.

The haddock and the scallop are synonymous in Arran and there must be many other areas of Britain where a similar situation exists – deepish water with shellbeds and sufficient broken ground to make the ground difficult for the commercial fishermen to drag. For a number of years the clam trawlers have consistently hauled heavy drags around the coast of Scotland, reaping a rich reward for their labours. True, they have to earn a living but the trailing gear they use tends to rake over the shellbeds in such a way as to disturb the spat, severely reducing the numbers of scallop that come to maturity in the succeeding years. Sea anglers also drag for the clams but they use lighter, smaller drags which do far less damage to the beds and only take enough bait to fish with!

I remember one Arran trip in particular, both for the fish taken and the weather endured. A sou'wester was gusting in short, sharp blasts as Neil McLean and I met on the old pier at Lamlash. Clouds were high in the sky, streaky and white as though winter were reluctant to give way to the spring. Not the best day to venture out to a tide race, I thought, as we paddled the pram dinghy out to where the boat *Katrina* rocked gracefully at her mooring. Although the wind was more than fresh, it was blowing from the west, which is a soft wind that rarely puts too great a difficulty on anchoring. We had to fish to the anchor swell as the amount of ground that held the feeding haddock would not allow drift fishing over the mark. Big haddock are slow to take a bait, requiring the offering to be held hard on the sea bed. McLean is a specialist in this kind of sea angling. He has definite methods,

Pladda, the lighthouse isle at the south end of Arran, a haddock mark of quality. In the distance, Ailsa Craig, haunt of huge pollack.

evolved over a long time, for fishing haddies so I took my time in tackling up to watch closely his rig and bait presentation. He uses a fixed paternoster with a long flowing double-hook trace. Neil says he has found little success in a leger rig because the haddock pick at a bait for a long time before taking it fully into their mouths. The direct contact between rod and hook given by the paternoster allows him to feel every movement of the fish, which is important when we consider the incredibly small mouth of the haddock trying to accommodate a bait of scallop size! I copied the rig and lowered the bait over the side.

The rig brought a pull from a fish almost immediately. The rod tip gave a number of fast trembles and went over hard. I hit the bite, tightened against the lead with a sharp lift of the rod and felt nothing. I'd lost it. I was told to take my time in striking, for the haddock was probably only inspecting the bait rather than taking it fully. McLean explained that when fishing for large specimens he puts the rod down to rest against the gunwhale and does not strike at anything until the rod pulls hard down and stays down. Then, and only then, should the rod be picked up to feel the weight of the fish and a positive strike made. I know this advice is contrary to general boat-fishing practice. Holding my rod all the fishing day has always been my idea of efficient angling. But I could see what McLean was getting at. His system depended not so much on holding the rod but on not striking prematurely. Haddock, in the conditions off Pladda, have to be given plenty of time to take so one must not react to the first tremble up the line. Fishing smaller haddock, say fish of 2 or 3 lbs in Ireland, required quite a different response as I found on an earlier trip to Achill Island. There the small fish hit a bait fast and I found it necessary to react with speed but with the larger specimens it pays to play it cool.

Later in this day's fishing, when some of the wind had gone out of the sky and the tide had slackened a little of its pull, I got the bite I had been waiting for. A sharp knock on the rod tip, just one and hardly noticeable, then a series of minute trembles transmitted up the nylon. The fish was obviously getting at the scallop, chomping it down to swallowing size. I waited for the solid take and struck. The pull came, down went the tip and stayed down and as I lifted the rod sharply I felt a jagging, boring motion. No doubt the fish was still trying to tear the scallop from the hook, unaware that it was itself tethered. I have taken many haddock and they all put up the same type of fight. Not the dour, steady, jerking of the cod or the headlong rush of the pollack but a series of quick, jagging, movements that take a line jerking from the reel. A haddock will fight every inch from the bottom up to the boat and even the pressure change that blows up most of the cod family seems to have less effect on the haddock. Many large fish of this species must be lost because of early striking or even too strong a pressure on the fish which can only result in the hook being torn away .

Like the cod, the haddock is very much a shoal fish. Where you take one you will often take several in succession. They also seem to swim in company with small codling as these fish favour a soft, muddy, ground which is also a suitable environment for the two main species of scallop found in northern waters. If we consider the difficulty these fish have in extracting a scallop from its shell we begin to see why the bite is slow to develop and why the strike has to be delayed. If a fish comes on an open shell, it must manoeuvre its head to prevent the shell from closing. Then, grasping the flesh of the scallop it has to tear it away from the shell. All this takes time for a fish to accomplish so when confronted with a scallop on a hook the fish will adopt a similar tearing and pulling feeding pattern.

Out from the Yorkshire coast, when baiting with slips of herring, lugworm and mussel, haddock bites were totally different. The ground had no positive holding features and I believe the fish were scavenging across the bottom in shoals. They grabbed at any bait presented on the hook. If food is scarce and there are a number of fish in a shoal there must be competition among them. No doubt the biggest and boldest members of the pack will get most of the available feed providing they move in fast and grab what there is!

Never give an inch of slack line to a big haddock, for they are masters of the art of throwing the hook. Also the small mouth is fairly soft and any sudden jerk from the angler will enlarge the hole made by the hook, possibly allowing the escape of a fish. Neil McLean had this happen to him in 1973. He was fishing alone, as he so often does, on the Pladda mark. He had hooked a really big fish in strong water and, while playing it, he realised that it was bigger than his average. His camera is always left hanging on the foc's'le door, within easy reach should he want to photograph anything. Neil's problem was this: should he try to net the fish and get a static picture of it lying on the floorboards or should he try to hold the haddock on a tight line, reach round for the camera and try for a picture as the fish lay beaten on the surface? He made the latter decision and it turned out to be the wrong one for, as he focused with one hand, grasping the rod tightly in the other, his fish gave a last despairing thrash with its tail and the hook-hold gave. Away went what looked like a new Scottish haddock record but at least he did get a photograph.

As spring progresses and warmth comes to the inshore waters it is time to look for the wrasse. They will be moving in to shallow areas from winter feeding grounds in the deeps. Long before they become available to the shore fisher, float fishing from the rock ledges, these fish will be around underwater reefs. Look for the fingers of jagged reef that extend out from the shore, sometimes continuing for miles on the seabed. Wrasse frequent the most atrocious ground, particularly where one finds a carpet of broken rock and kelp jungle between rock spurs. Pollack will also be around although they will tend to be the smaller

1

fish in the spring. It will be autumn before the large pollack return to haunt the reefs and the kelp jungles of the north and west coasts.

As the spring pollack are small so the tackle must be lightened to allow them to give the best sport. "Sink and draw" tactics will give both the element of sport and keep anglers busy, which is a necessary ploy when the weather can still have a sharp bite to the wind calling for all-action fishing to keep warm. With a sea spinning rod, fixed-spool or multiplying reel loaded with 10 or 12 lbs nylon line and artificial or natural baits, pollack can provide a lot of fun. The rig is simple, a spiral lead stopped by a barrel swivel and a long flowing trace intended to present a bait with a natural swimming motion. Either a strip of mackerel or squid on a size 1/0 hook or an artificial eel such as the Redgill completes the tackle. If one fishes over rock or reef, drop the lead until it taps the hard ground, then wind in a couple of turns of the reel. This will do two things. It will keep the lure out of the rock as the boat swings to anchor or drifts over the reef and it will ensure that, in the first rush of the pollack as it seeks to gain the security of the reef, it can take positively without immediately getting the angler into trouble.

Fish that live their lives on reefs know where to go

1 *Holy Island standing guard at the entrance to Lamlash Bay, Isle of Arran. The Firth of Clyde has much good fishing in this area for haddock, pollack, cod and plaice. The boat was anchored over the edge of the Pascoe Bank where ridges provide ideal habitat.*

2 *Taking a large landing net to a beaten fish is always a wise move.*

3 *Pat Auld, from Portpatrick, nets a plump haddie from an Arran mark. The fish take both razorfish and scallop baits with relish.*

2

3

4

4 *Neil McLean with a cod from the open ground in Whiting Bay, Arran. These are clean, well made-up fish from the Northern seas, firm-fleshed and rich in colour.*

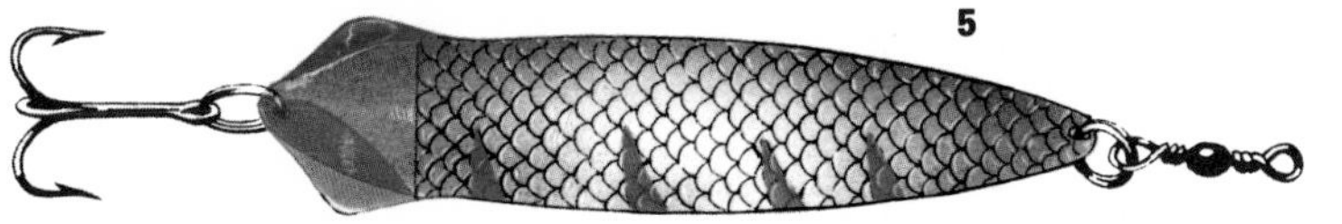

5

5 *A Winfield "Shanny" spoon, of the wobbling-actioned type.*

in time of stress. Their lives are a series of crises, one moment grabbing an unsuspecting smaller fish and the next moment rushing away to escape from something larger that is intent on eating them. Most pollack, once hooked, make this great attempt to plunge downward and, in my opinion, there are few fish that equal the pollack in the initial stages of a fight. If the reef or kelp-filled broken ground is in shallow water or reaches up to the surface we could well think of trolling a lure over the ground. Careful attention has to be paid to the speed of the boat over the holding ground and to the weight of lure being fished. Ideally, a natural or artificial bait should swim just under the surface, jinking and flashing in the light. Fish will come up from the darkness among the tangles, hit the bait and immediately nose-dive back into their lie.

If the lure is made of metal, a wobbling spoon of the Shanny or Toby type, the weight of the lure may be enough to sink just below the waves with small adjustment to the speed of the angling craft. With plastic or wooden lures or natural baits, a lead like the Wye or spiral type will be necessary, fixed ahead of the bait to get it to troll correctly.

Swivels are an important part of the trolling rig. If the lure presented twists in any way it will play havoc with the reel line unless sufficient swivels, that really do turn under pressure, are incorporated in the tackle set-up. One swivel near to the bait and another at the rear of the trolling lead should keep the tackle twist-free. Trolling leads may require a kink in them to act as a keel, thus preventing the lead from twisting as it cuts through the waves.

I remember fishing for pollack, using trolling methods, out from the little harbour of Kilmore Quay in the south-east corner of Ireland. Clive Gammon and I had been invited by Eamonn Doyle to spend a few days fishing for both pollack and bass. He had a small boat that was ideal for trolling baits across the mass of reef spurs that extend between the mainland and the Saltee Islands. We had all taken pollack trolling slowly over the mass of rock and weed fronds. I had a tremendous pull from a fish with the rubber eel bait way back from the stern at a distance of at least 50 yds. The rod yanked over and stayed bent in a half-circle. Repeatedly, the pollack tried to get its head down into the reef while I had one of the hardest fights from any fish of the species. Gradually I managed to get some line back onto the spool with the fish continuously plunging down and bursting up to the top of the water. I didn't see the fish, although Clive and Eamonn did.

According to Clive it could have been a new Irish record. The important thing about pollack fishing, particularly when employing sink and draw or trolling techniques, is to remember the first rush of this fish. Of all the sea species, the pollack pulls hardest on its first frantic movements to escape. Before fishing, the clutch must be adjusted to give the minimum of drag that will allow you to strike and set the hook yet yield line to the strong initial stage in the pollack's attempts to break free. Some other fish, notably the bass, can react in a similar fashion but not with the power of the pollack!

An odd thing happened to me when I was fishing a small reef known as the Deacon Rock. This lies in the middle of Lamlash Bay and I had always believed it to be a pinnacle reef, rising sharply from the sea floor. The Admiralty chart would certainly lead one to think that way. The mark has produced tremendous catches of haddock, codling and small pollack in a number of international sea angling festivals that have been held there. The reputation of the Deacon Rock grew fast and my idea of a pinnacle was shared by many anglers. Dennis Burgess, an angling friend of mine who also spends a great deal of time aqualung diving, exploded our view of the mark. He dived on the rock and found that the pinnacle, shown on the chart, does not exist as such. It is made up of a jumble of flat-topped rock slabs rising a few feet from the surrounding levels. So much for the accuracy of charts and the imagination of anglers. From Dennis's description of the reef there is little feed on it. It seems that this mark is more a haven of security into which fish that feed across the open ground retire to rest or hide. Moreover, it fishes best late in the evening and into the night when there seems to be an increase in the size of the fish using the rocks.

Springtime brings the ling to the inshore waters of the south of England. Places like Folkestone, that have a carpet of chalk boulders extending from the cliffs out into the deep water, provide an ideal habitat for the small fish of this species. There were many of them in the early months of 1975 but we do not expect to see the monsters that frequent off-shore reefs and wrecks. One has to travel to the West Country or up over the Border for the massive fish. They are rarely caught in shallow water although there are one or two cliff-angling marks, such as Neist Point, on the Isle of Skye, that have large ling close into the shore. I have had large specimens in a number of fishing areas but in each case the ling were living in association with a wreck or other underwater obstruction. Occasionally they are found out on open ground but they seem to require the close proximity of shelter. In Ireland, when fishing out in the middle of Dingle Bay, we came on a reef that showed as a cathedral of rock spires on the sounder. In Torbay the ling lurked among the wreckage of Second World War merchant ships and in Orkney the fish are to be found deep down among the mass of loose rock that annually falls from the towering Cliffs of Hoy. All three places have a common denominator: deep water and shelter from which to ambush smaller fish. It follows that this type of environment also provides the best possible conditions for smaller species to live and feed in, thereby creating a suitable habitat for the larger predatory ling.

When fishing this kind of mark I use a strong rod. Gear of 50 lb class is in no way too heavy because the species has tremendous strength, and they can beat any angler once they grab the bait and regain the hiding place in cracks and holes in the reef. Since the strong tides of deep water marks can often prevent anchoring the boat much of my ling fishing has been done on the drift, dropping simple, 50 lb, cable-laid wire traces with 6/0 hooks baited with large mackerel or herring lashes down to the waiting fish. Generally, the idea is to locate the uptide side of the mark and to begin the drift by letting the baits touch the bottom on the open ground. Then, with a watchful eye on the echo-sounder, the baits are fished back toward the start of the small rock at the base of the main reef. As soon as the trace on the chart begins to rise, the baits are wound up to draw the offerings up in front of the bulk of rock, taking great care not to let the lead or hook pull into the hard stuff to become fast. If you pay attention to the signals from the end tackle, expressed as tugs and hard knocks, it is possible to draw the bait up the rock-face then to swim it over the tips of the pinnacles, before lowering once again as both the sounder and the freedom from lead snags indicates the beginning of the fall-away to the reef. You will lose tackle when fishing for ling, for one moment's lack of attention sees the lead or baited hook go into one of the many crevices where it goes solid – and that is the end of that end-tackle!

I would not suggest that the spring is a time for big ling. There are much bigger fish in the early autumn. But of the ling marks that can fish early in the year the northern areas seem best. Not only do they have this species in the deepwater but they also contain Britain's largest flatfish, the halibut. The habitat is similar and the angling methods almost exactly the same.

Orkney and the northern tip of Caithness have gathered quite a reputation in recent years for the halibut. If you need to catch a halibut – and many sea anglers regard the fish as a must before hanging up the rod – then you must be prepared to travel. Halibut are thin on the ground. They have suffered from over fishing by commercial interests but each year the rod-and-line man gets his fish. Ted Simons, of the Caithness Tourist Board, regularly witnesses the capture of this species by anglers who travel to Dunnet Head and the

UPTIDE BOAT-FISHING TECHNIQUES

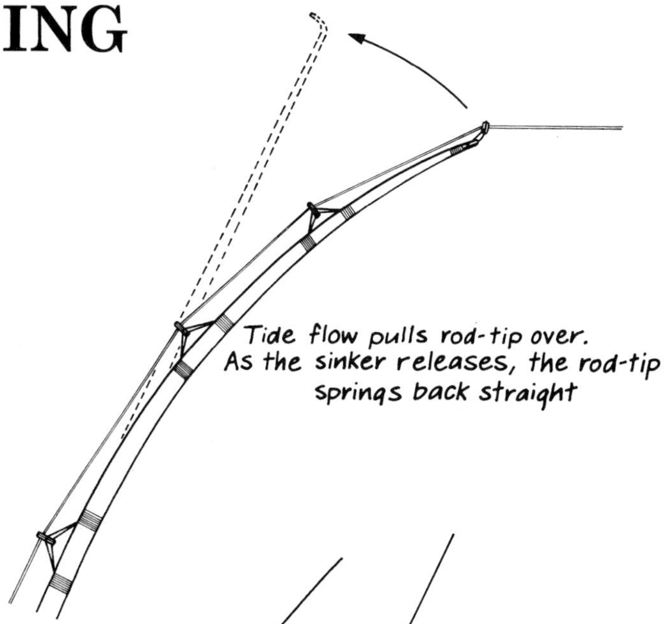

Tide flow pulls rod-tip over.
As the sinker releases, the rod-tip
springs back straight

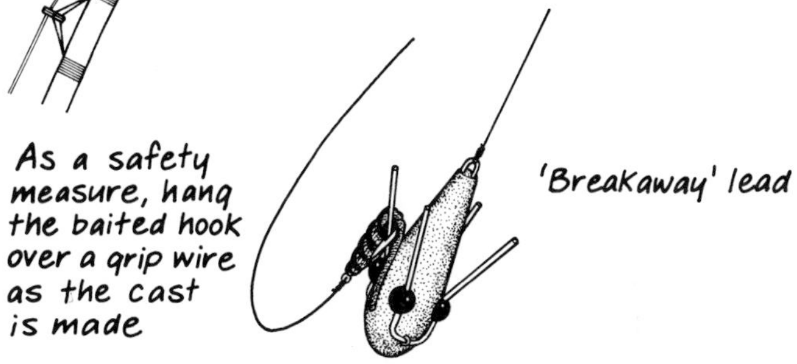

At first sight, uptide casting from a boat may seem a dangerous undertaking. It needn't be – if an essential rule is closely followed. There must be discipline from each of the boat's occupants, each waiting his turn to make a cast from as near the bows of the craft as possible. Uptide rods are lighter than conventional rods and slightly longer. I prefer a rod of about 9 ft long. This length is split into two unequal sections, a 3 ft 6 in butt spigotted into a tip of 5 ft 6 in so that the joint comes closer to the reel and does not get strained under vigorous casting. A fast-taper, medium-weight beachcaster blank is needed to cast a 6 oz weight.

I like to have more rings on uptide-casting rods than would be considered normal for traditional boat fishing. I have nine along the powerful tip with one one large ring on the butt section.

In turn, anglers cast toward the area (marked on the diagram as the killing ground) each side of the anchor. As it sinks through the water, the sinker will be carried back towards the boat. You can also expect a further movement of the weight back towards the boat as the lead tries to take hold in the seabed. The rod is rested against the gunwhale and the tip allowed to adopt a curve corresponding to the belly of line formed by the pressure of tide running past.

Bites are shown as a sudden straightening of the rod tip as the pressure on it is released. This movement comes as feeding fish take the bait, lifting the grip lead free of the bottom as they pull at the trace. Without doubt, such a bite indication is more positive than that given by the rod tip when fishing in the usual way downtide from the stern of an anchored boat.

Striking is not necessary. The taking fish is hooked as it drags the grip wires free of the sand. As the rod tip springs back from a curved to a straight line the rod is picked up and the slack loop of line recovered progressively until the weight of the fish is felt. Here, it is wise to give a sharp strike back, in case the fish has taken the bait without swallowing it. I have known fish to swim off some 30 yds before dropping the baited hook.

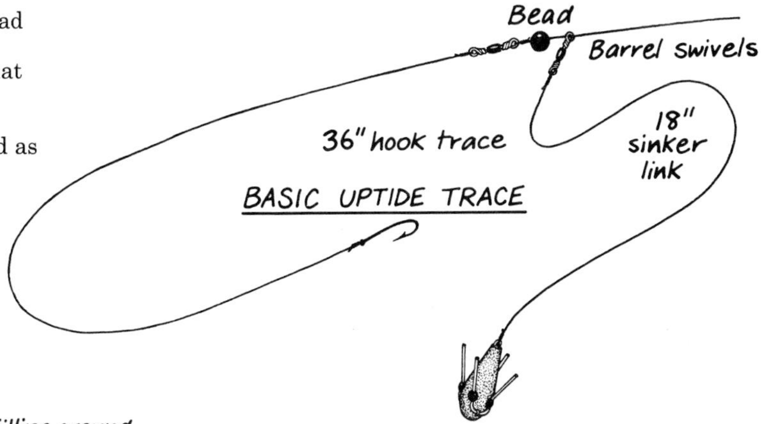

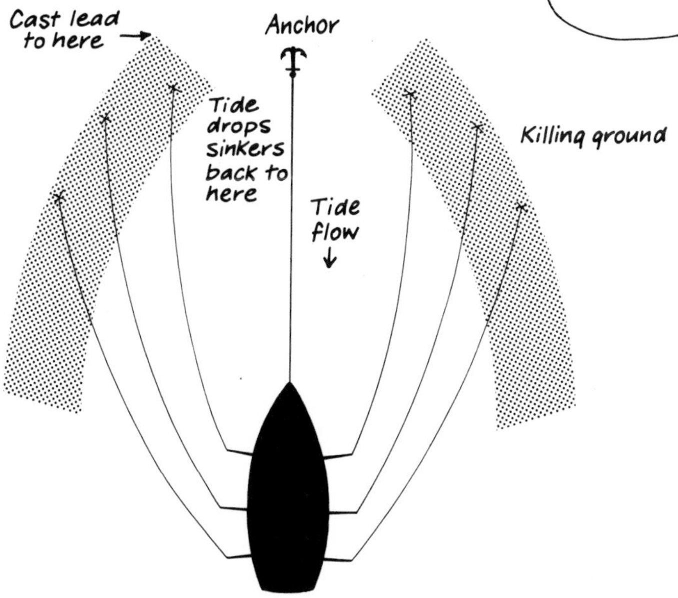

Lines of about 15 lb–20 lb b.s. are used when uptide fishing. Their diameters help to reduce the pull of a strong tide. As hooked fish feel the pressure of the line they will usually swim off uptide, fighting against the spring of the curved rod and the strength of the current flow. Keeping a bent rod, the angler need only recover line cautiously to bring the fish up to the surface. Try not to allow the fish to drift too far back on the tide. A fish that gets down-tide instead of being kept abeam becomes far more difficult to handle as its weight has the additional pull of the tide streaming past.

Apply safety and caution to your uptide casting. Never allow the baited hook trace to swing wildly about within the area of the boat. Hang it on one of the grip wires as the cast is made and it will stay out of harm's way until the rig hits the water.

Pentland Firth. I was fortunate to be aboard Frank and George Sinclair's boat when a fish was hooked in the Scapa Flow. The boat had been positioned alongside the vicious tide race that pours out from the Flow into the Atlantic. Fishing to anchor, the idea was that baits could be presented in the strong water where this species is known to search for the small pollack that make up its staple diet. Les Moncrieff, who has taken a halibut from similar conditions off Valencia Island, in County Kerry, swears that most of the halibut caught on rod and line have come from rough water around headlands where there are extremes of tide and current. Mike Shepley took this particular fish which grabbed, wildly, at his bait and swam down to the sea bed. Mike was using a tough rod with a 50 lb line but even with that gear the fish was able to sound, dragging the rod hard over the gunwhale. It put up a heavy fight. Something like 20 minutes was necessary to get it up through the inky blackness of the Flow before the fish was seen. As it broke the surface the gaff touched the fish and gave it a sharp jab which sent it tearing back down to the bottom.

Heavy fish must have the gaff drawn into the head, at the back of the eyes. If gaffed in the body, they will often tear themselves off the gaff-point, smashing their way to freedom because the unwary angler has tightened the drag up far too strongly. The halibut has tremendous power. With a thick-set, streamlined body and a huge tail-fluke they are nothing like their lesser relatives among the flatfish family. Their body suggests speed, while the sea conditions in which they live call for stamina to combat tide and enemies.

By late spring our coastal water will have warmed slightly and the gales of winter will have eased, encouraging our other large fish species to move closer in to the shore. The small rays, like the thornback, begin to show in the catches from the trawlers. This fish is one of the angler's earliest species to arrive on eastern and southern shores. Due to its popularity as a meal, the thornback has suffered from too many years of intensive inshore trawling.

Nevertheless, it is one fish that helps to bridge the gap between winter and summer boat fishing. Though not growing as large as the skates, most of the ray species can give a good account of themselves when hooked. All of them have the coarse, grinding teeth of the genus which demands that end tackles should be formed from wire. Not so stiff as to inhibit the movement of fish baits in tide, wire of around 30 lbs breaking strain will be sufficient. Hooks must be fairly strong in the wire and preferably forged to withstand the crushing power of the ray's jaws.

Look for the thornback in shallow water. It is fond of the channels that run between sandbanks and of those areas of clean, open ground that are periodically covered and bared by the tide. Many dinghy fishermen will find that this ray figures in their catches when working close into the shoreline and up into estuarine water. There is much confusion between the various species of ray and skate. From an angling point of view, we are interested in 10 species of ray and three of the larger, more powerful, skates. But of these fish one in particular holds a fascination for the boat angler. This is the common skate or *Raja batis* that can grow to weights of 500 lbs or more. The British rod-caught record stands at 226 lbs, taken in the Shetland Islands. That area, together with the Orkney Isles and the north-western waters of Scotland, holds most of our big skate. There are, of course, well-known skate marks across the Irish Sea that annually produce large commons and a number of specimens of other species, the white and long-nosed skate.

Skate like deep water, especially the white and long-nosed varieties, and, although they can be found at times in relatively shallow conditions that are not demanding upon angler's tackle, it is wise to choose gear that can be relied on. For the rays and small-sized

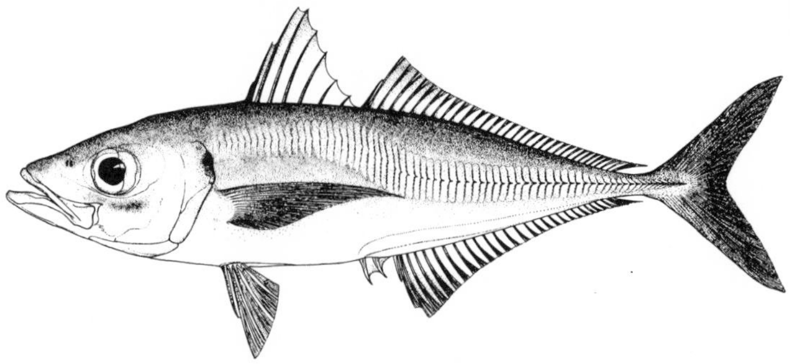

SCAD OR HORSE MACKEREL
Trachurus trachurus

The species has no relationship to the true mackerel. It has a wide distribution and is sometimes found in large shoals. The fish is of little value as an angling species or for the table. There are two separate dorsal fins, the first with spines and the second with one leading spine followed by soft rays. The anal also possesses spines at the leading edge. The lateral line is clearly marked with a number of keeled, bony plates more noticeable towards the tail.

Bait: *Small strips of fish, marine worms and feathered lures.*

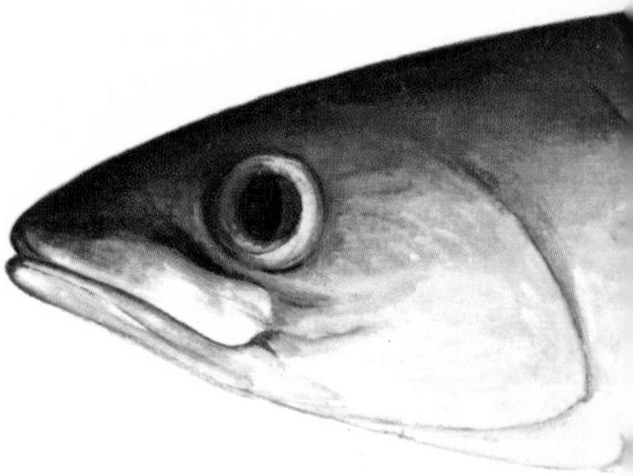

MACKEREL
Scomber (Scomber) scombrus

A fast-moving small fish related to the tunny. This species is probably the best known of our sea fishes. It is a prolific fish that moves into our littoral waters in the late spring in vast shoals providing both food and bait for sea anglers. Found in the pelagic layers, it feeds on plankton and the fry of other fish. No swim bladder is present and the tail is forked with two hardly noticeable keels on each side of the tail.

BOAR FISH
Capros aper

A similar shaped fish to the John Dory having spines in the first dorsal and anal fin with soft rays in the secondary dorsal and anal fins. The snout is pig-like, hence the name, with a large mouth and eyes. It is a small species rarely seen or taken by rod and line anglers.

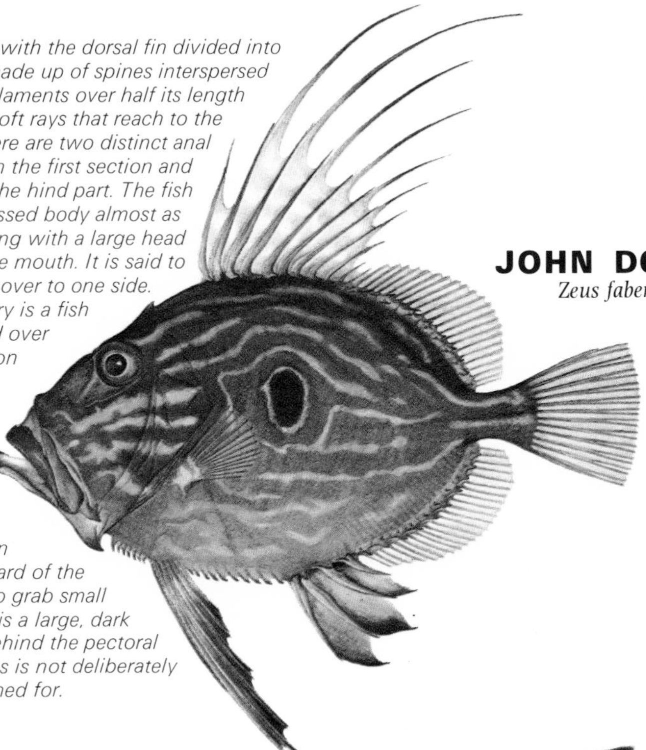

JOHN DORY
Zeus faber

A unique fish with the dorsal fin divided into two sections made up of spines interspersed with delicate filaments over half its length running into soft rays that reach to the caudal fin. There are two distinct anal fins, spined in the first section and soft-rayed in the hind part. The fish has a compressed body almost as high as it is long with a large head and protrusible mouth. It is said to swim leaning over to one side. The John Dory is a fish feeder found over rocky areas on southern and western shores. It relies on a deal of camouflage in its colouring and sudden shooting forward of the tube mouth to grab small fishes. There is a large, dark blotch just behind the pectoral fins. The species is not deliberately fished for.

The species moves to deeper water in the cold months of the year but here it is not safe from massive predation by man for commercial fishers have been taking vast quantities of mackerel deepwater trawling in the middle of winter in recent years. It is noticeable that the last few seasons have produced much smaller shoals, as though the numbers have been both depleted and dispersed by the trawling.

Bait: *A string of feathers are all that is needed when gathering the fish for use as bait but truly to experience a fight mackerel should be fished for with a light spinning rod and lure or fly rod complete with minute streamer fly.*

skates a medium strength boat rod will cope but one never knows when the huge fish will happen along. Certainly there are sea areas that regularly provide the large fish, such as the Shetland Voes, Scapa Flow, Ullapool, Lochinver, the Western Isles; also Galway Bay, Westport, Achill Bay, Valencia, Ballycotton and Kinsale, all in Ireland. If these marks are fished then tackle should be used that is capable of lifting and holding the great weight of the species during what can be a prolonged fight. I would suggest rods of at least 50 lbs class together with compatible line and reels. Braided Dacron is probably better than nylon line since its non-stretch properties can be of advantage in both detecting the bite and controlling a hooked fish. As with the rays, the trace material must be wire. About 150 lbs breaking strain is correct, not so much for the pulling qualities of the fish as for the tremendous crushing power of the fish's teeth, which are formidable. I use Mustad Seamaster hooks, size 8/0–10/0, crimped onto the wire to make a trace of 18 ins in length. It has been my experience that a short trace gives an immediate warning of the arrival of a fish at the bait. As the fish seeks and traps its food by gliding along the bottom and dropping, or rather flopping, down over its quarry we bait in a fashion that will help detect the taking behaviour. As the fish moves its body over the bait, to align the mouth which is way back from the snout on its underside, it strikes the reel line with its wings as it flops down. This warning results in the rod tip dipping accordingly. It then becomes a decision as to whether the fish has, in fact, got the bait so that the angler can hit the fish hard, setting the hook into the tough, gristly, jaw. If he is then able to lift the fish just a few feet, to get some water between skate and sea bed, the fish should begin to come.

If, however, a skate feels the pressure of the strike and subsequent pull of the line it will try to spread its wings, lying flat on the bottom. It then seems to create a vacuum, which is hard to break, by humping its back. I've seen anglers hooked into skate for twenty minutes before they could begin to retrieve any line. Many tricks are used to separate the fish from the bottom,

Brightlingsea Creek, starting place for many anglers who fish the Essex sandbanks. Skipper John Sait puts the boat neatly to the sandbanks where a ragworm can be drifted back to fish in the wild rush of water where the bass lurk. Occasionally a thornback will grab the bait as it passes over the top of the sand.

sliding leads down on the reel line in the hope that they will hit the fish on the snout, so annoying it and sometimes getting it to move off. Or even winding the reel line taught as a bowstring, plucking it hard, which sends twanging vibrations down to the fish's head and teeth. Sometimes these ruses work and sometimes they don't!

I like to use a large lash of fish bait for skate. I know that smaller baits are quickly taken by a fish which allows an earlier strike, but small baits are so often taken by fish of other species. At least a big bait takes time to whittle down, giving the old skate a chance to arrive on the scene. Tie your baits onto the hook with elasticated thread. This will also stop the fish from tearing it off the hook and will ensure a good presentation of the lash, in which the hook can be well hidden. There are not many big skate around and it would be foolish to make your bait too odd to be taken.

Because skate fishing can be a slow business, with a long wait before a fish finds a hookbait as it moves over the ground, some anglers put the rod down against the gunwhale and set up another rod to busy themselves with. The practice can be a good fishing method, since a lot of baits will produce activity from the smaller species that could excite the interest of a large skate in the vicinity. If you do this, make certain that the skate rod has its reel out of gear and that the ratchet is set in the on position. So many anglers have lost their gear over the side when a large fish has grabbed at the bait, dragging the tackle overboard.

I recall a skate that came to my bait in Westport which played the game according to the book. Things were slow in happening, with just a couple of lesser-spotted dogfish to the anglers. I'd set my gear up with the idea of waiting for a skate rather than building a progressive weight with smaller species. This is a decision one has to make in a competitive situation. From a comfortable seat in a corner at the stern I viewed the other boats tearing all over Clew Bay, a sure sign that there aren't many fish around and that anglers are harrying their skippers to move. I didn't get a pull down on the tip, just a tell-tale tick of the ratchet set me into motion. I picked up the rod, holding it almost horizontally but with the tip pointing in the direction in which the line would take off. A quick movement of the thumb and the ratchet was off, allowing the fish to take line without feeling any pressure – however minute – transmitted to its mouth. Whatever had given the smallest of bites was in no hurry to move away with the mackerel bait.

With the slight movement, from the boat and the occupants, a delicate nodding of the rod tip became noticeable. It then developed into a series of hard, thumping, movements. This was obviously a big fish. Slowly and ponderously it began to swim off. I knew straight away that I had a skate. I had had a number of

RAY'S BREAM

Brama brama

Found washed ashore in Yorkshire in 1681 by John Ray and named after him, the Ray's bream comes to Britain fairly regularly. The fish favours deep water and is said to range widely in the Atlantic from Arctic to Antarctic seas.

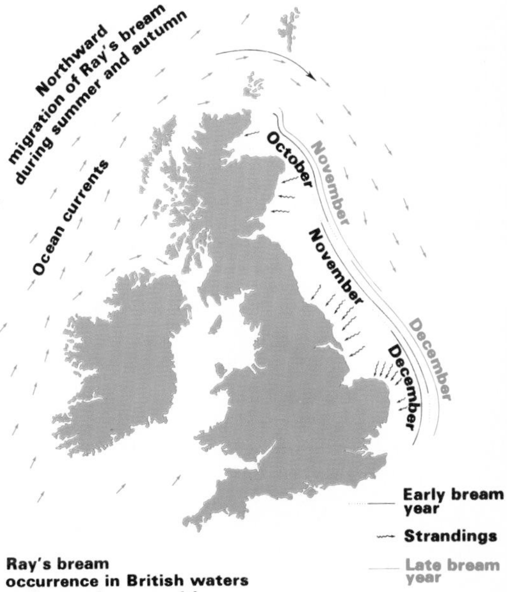

Ray's bream occurrence in British waters and coastal areas, with main times of strandings

Irish fish and they had all behaved in the same way. A backward glance and a grin to my compatriots and I struck once, reeled in to get the 50 lb line tight and hit the fish again to convince myself that my skate really was on the other end of the line.

A firm, solid, weight told me that I was in business. Looking back on the day, I feel just a trifle lucky with that Westport skate. It did not attempt to hold the bottom, but moved continuously across the tide with the rod dipping against the slip of the clutch – perhaps in time with the wing beats of the fish? It swam on for a few yards and turned and no doubt this movement caused the current to get under its wings for the line angle to the water lessened as the skate began to come up in the water. I find that when fish such as skates and congers keep swimming the angler has less of a problem than when the fish hang in the tide.

My rod had the right amount of backbone to absorb the occasional sudden change of direction and depth that the fish took. Too stiff a rod tends to pass on all the strain direct to the angler's back and shoulders without smoothing the jerking motions of a big-fish fight. Ten minutes' steady pumping of the rod with the occasional respite and slackening of the clutch, to give line when the skate made a short run, saw the first "barn door" slowly flapping its wings just under the surface. I had a couple of anxious moments as I exerted enough pressure to slide the fish back up against the tide. It was gaffed, expertly, at the stern by a member of the American Forces' Rod and Gun Club who were over for the Festival. There wasn't much time spent admiring the beast. My hook and those of the lads that had reeled in their gear to give me a clear field were soon re-baited. There is a saying that where there is one skate you will find another. Sure enough the adage was true, for my gaffing assistant was soon into another skate which demonstrated exactly the same type of bite and fight as mine had done. Our two fish turned out to be male and female, so it looked as though we might have broken up a happy relationship.

Two other fish occupy my time as spring draws to an end. These are the bass and the flounder, both of which come to our rods when dinghy fishing the sandbanks. Bass are moving up from sunnier climes into the southern British waters while the flounders have come down from winter quarters, right up into the estuary creeks, to spawn. They move down in February as a rule, seeking the slightly deeper water beyond the inshore sands. With warmer water and the flush of invertebrate life, bass start to work over the tops of the sand bars at both the last run-out of the ebb and the first of the flood. The fishing can be tricky from a boat-handling point of view. On my estuaries – the Crouch, Blackwater and Orwell – there is a fearsome run of water in and out of the rivers. As the ebb falls back it creates a mass of jumbled waves. The bed of the rivers

BOGUE
Boops boops

A Mediterranean species that comes on the warm drift to the western shores of the British Isles. The species is not at all bream-shaped, having an elongated, slender body. The species is not fished for specifically and fish of a pound weight would be a good specimen.

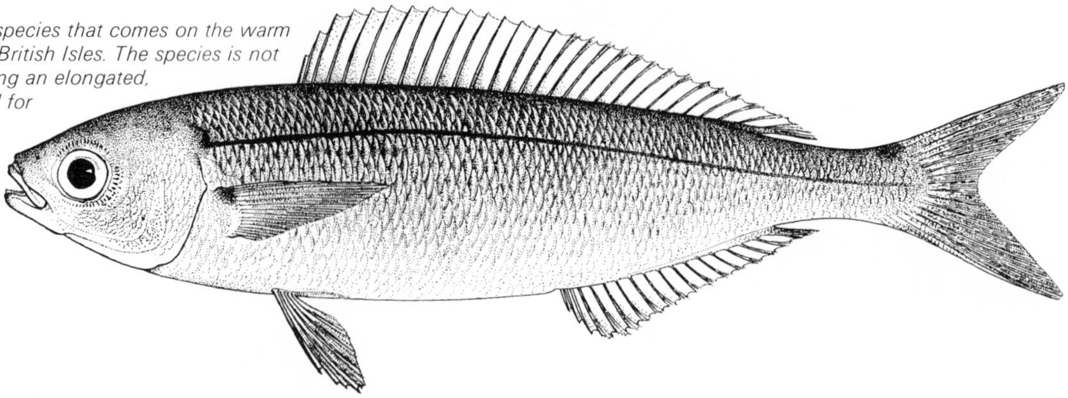

BLACK BREAM
Spondyliosoma cantharus

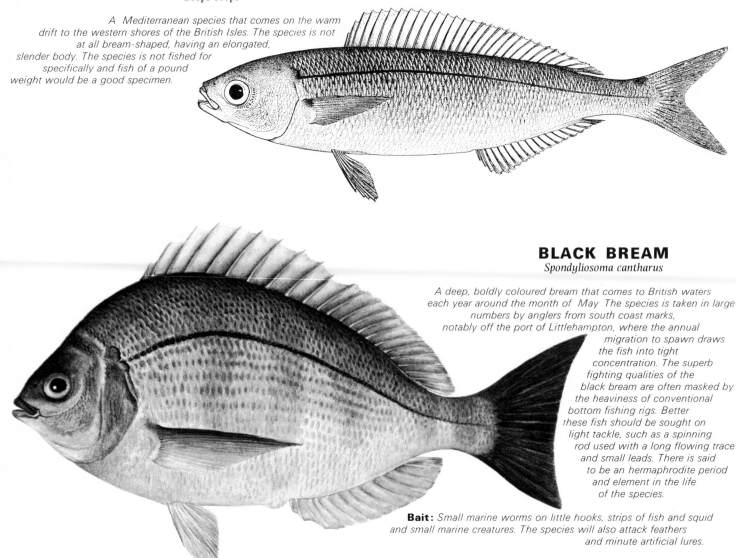

A deep, boldly coloured bream that comes to British waters each year around the month of May The species is taken in large numbers by anglers from south coast marks, notably off the port of Littlehampton, where the annual migration to spawn draws the fish into tight concentration. The superb fighting qualities of the black bream are often masked by the heaviness of conventional bottom fishing rigs. Better these fish should be sought on light tackle, such as a spinning rod used with a long flowing trace and small leads. There is said to be an hermaphrodite period and element in the life of the species.

Bait: *Small marine worms on little hooks, strips of fish and squid and small marine creatures. The species will also attack feathers and minute artificial lures.*

rise sharply, spewing the current across the top of the nearly uncovered sands. If the anchor fails to hold, the dinghy can be swept back through the rough water, probably throwing everything out into the sea as it goes. This terrifying run of tide has its advantages as well. The strength of the run forces sand eels and other minute feed out from the mass of the bank. Bass know this, so it is in the white water that they feed and it is in these that we should seek to fish our baits.

As with bass on the shorefisher's strands, this fish has become popular with anglers and has found a new reputation as a strong fighter – possibly as being the strongest thing in the surf. This is perhaps a slight exaggeration for there are many fish both on the beaches and out in deeper waters that can match and better the fight of the bass. On the sand bars it is the strength of the tidal flow that creates the illusion of the fantastic battles with bass. Most thornbacks, a heavy old monkfish or a sting ray will put up quite a resistance with the power of the ebb behind them. Nevertheless, bass over the bars is good sport, fished with a light beachcaster or medium spinning rod, a small lead which is just heavy enough to keep the bait down onto the bottom and a multiplier loaded with 12 lb line. I like ragworm baits, presented on a tandem-hook Pennell tackle although peeler crab, lugs and slivers of fish will also bring bites. Cast out the bait to one side of the boat. Let the flow carry the bait round in an arc behind the stern, covering all the ground as it rolls. Try to judge the bait position relative to the strongest area of spoil in the water. Fish this for a minute or so and then disengage the reel to let a few yards of line off. This will cause the lead and bait to trundle back through the broken water, over the lip of

RED BREAM

Pagellus bogaraveo

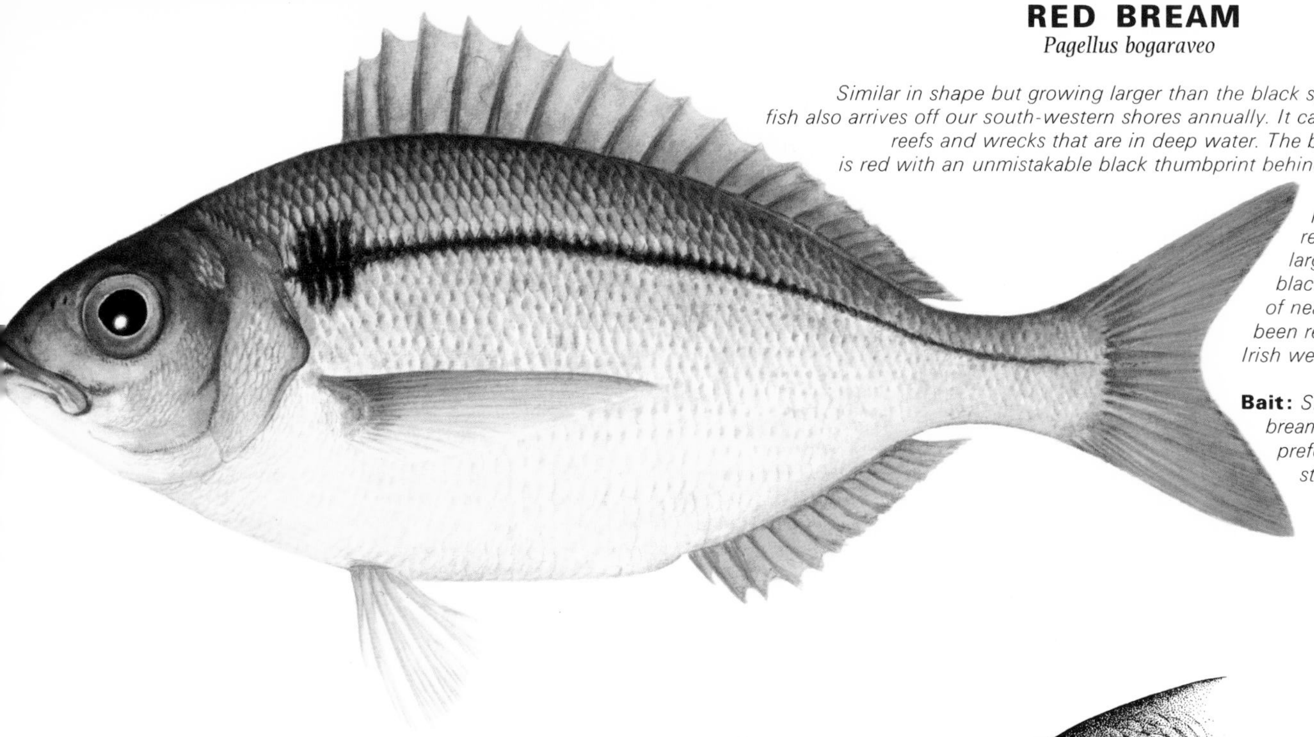

Similar in shape but growing larger than the black species, this fish also arrives off our south-western shores annually. It can be found over reefs and wrecks that are in deep water. The body colour is red with an unmistakable black thumbprint behind the gill-case, just above the pectoral fin. The red bream grows to larger sizes than the black species, a fish of nearly 10 lbs has been recorded off the Irish west coast.

Bait: *Similar to the other breams, with a preference for fish strip.*

GILTHEAD

Sparus aurata

The gilthead comes occasionally to British waters, more fish seemingly arriving each successive season. Probably as more anglers fish the reef and wreck marks the species will figure more in the catches of anglers. Similar in shape and colour to the black bream, this fish has a distinct golden bar across the head between the eyes. There are also patches of bright gold-orange on each gill-case. The young of the species will be found close inshore, on shallow ground over mud and sand.

Bait: *As for the other breams.*

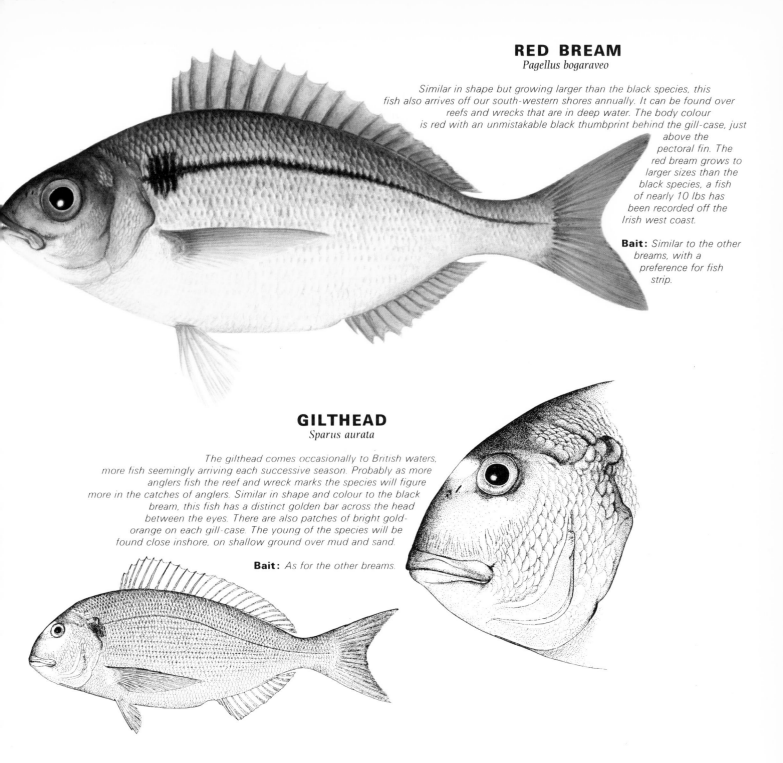

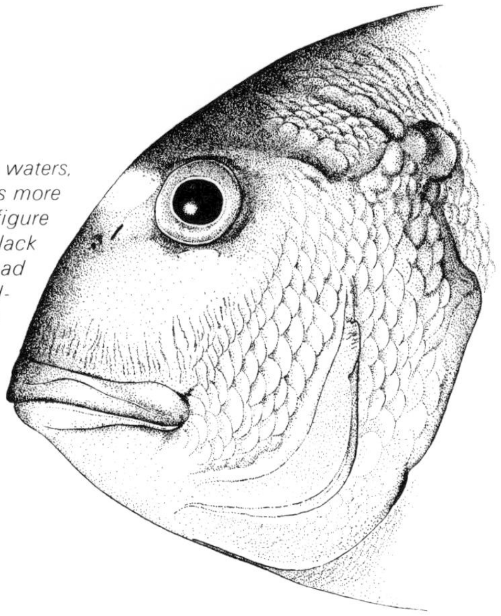

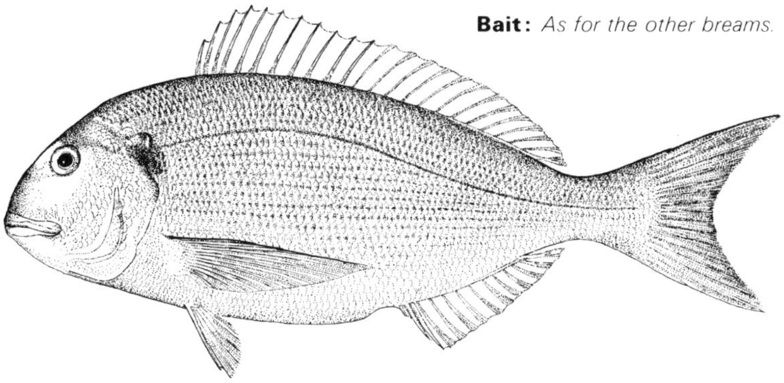

the sand and down to where the fish could be lying. They will be waiting to snap up any food that is swept to them. At least that is the theory! If you have an estuary without bars or with mudbanks at its mouth there may still be bass that enter the river with the flood tide to search out the food possibilities. The large, scavenging bass will move around gradually, dropping back to the river mouth as the tide slackens and starts to ebb. Areas of broken ground with weed-covered rocks, pilings and old harbour walls constructed with loose-fitting stones, will all provide a natural larder of food for this and other species.

At the top of the tide there will be an opportunity to fish in a similar fashion to the shore angler, with light float tackle set in sliding fashion if the channels are deep. Possibly the most productive method – certainly in the rivers and creeks of the western coast – will be to free-line a bait back down the stream without any lead at all. Baits such as live sand eel, soft crab and even prawns will be the most attractive food, since they can be given a natural presentation to the searching fish.

DEEP SEA IN THE SUMMER

In the middle of the year deep-sea boat fishing becomes a serious business. As the weather settles and daylight hours lengthen, our angling boats take advantage of fishing farther out to sea. Deep water extends the range of fishing marks and species available to the angler. Warmer waters, both at the surface and through the depths, bring the exotic species to our coasts. Black and red bream will come up from the Mediterranean. The sharks will arrive to harry the shoals of mackerel that are skimming through the surface layers chasing the fry or gorging themselves on the plankton. Best of all, and certainly to the fishermen of the west, is that calmer weather will let them steam out to the wrecks and deepwater reefs. The fish did not leave these marks. The gales and massive ocean swell kept the boats close to the shore.

The success of the wreck-fishing expeditions was brought about by the tremendous advances made in marine electronics associated with finding both fish and marks. Decca, the British navigational aid that is said to pin-point a ship's position to within a few yards, had arrived. Previous attempts to locate the far-flung reefs and wrecks depended on good eyesight and the ability of the skipper to pick up landmarks to establish an accurate cross-bearing. This meant that most of our deep-sea fishing had to be done within sight of the land. Now, with a Decca Navigator, any good skipper can put anglers over some of the finest fishing off our islands. The English Channel is full of wrecks. As the trawlers, equipped with Decca, fouled their nets on these underwater obstructions they noted the readings on the dials. Soon these commercial fishermen were able to tell anyone where to avoid hauling nets. It became apparent that the information was priceless to the angling charter skippers, for the trawlerman wanted to avoid precisely the places we rod and line brigade were seeking.

Away with a bang went the sport of wrecking. Within a couple of seasons big catches were being recorded, with conger eels measured in hundreds of pounds per angler. It took some time for the angling system to become established. Finding the wreck had become relatively simple but anchoring in order to fish it was something else. John Trust and Ernie Passmore, two Brixham skippers, developed an anchoring method based on using a number of floats strung out from a dan buoy, attached to a grapnel dropped over the wreck. The number of floats dragged under by the tide gave an indication of its strength and a pointer to how far uptide they had to anchor to ensure that the angler's baits would drop down to the side of the wreck. Wreck fishing is not a hit or miss affair. Due regard has to be given to the state of tide and its phase when planning a trip. Most West Country wrecking is done on slackish tides running down from spring to neaps and for a couple of days on the strengthening phase.

It can be a long trip out to some of the intact wrecks. I say "intact" because many of the inshore wrecks, marked on Admiralty charts, have been blown up so that they should not become a hazard to navigation. I have fished wrecks twelve miles out from Berry Head in Devon and some within a couple of miles off shore where they presented no danger to other shipping and so had been left whole on the sea bed. All of them, because of the availability of food, produce good quality fish. Generally, the larger the wreck and the deeper the water the more fish there are – and fish of a higher average size. The main reason why deep water wrecks produce better fish over longer periods of time during the year is because of the slow change in sea temperature when the depth, or volume, of water is greater. Violent changes, as would be expected in the shallow waters of estuaries and flat inshore areas, are brought about by a sudden change in wind direction. These cooling winds rapidly lower the prevailing temperature in the littoral waters, leading to an equally rapid departure of the fish population. With the wrecks the story is different. Most of our sea species are able to adapt to our summer-to-winter temperature range. Because of the depth of water off the West Country shores, the cooling process is a gradual one. Many of the wrecks provide a home for the conger eel, for instance, throughout the angling year. But in shallow grounds the conger will disappear to deep waters as soon as the first frosts of autumn are felt.

When setting out to fish a wreck efficiently, consideration must first be given to the conditions of tide and depth. The tackle used will to a great extent be determined by how one can fish rather than what one is fishing for. A few years ago I visited the almost entire hulk of a torpedoed merchantman, a virgin wreck in angling terms, with Leslie Moncrieff. We were looking for congers. This wreck lies about 14 miles south of the Devon Coast in just over 45 fathoms. The tides can be fierce and the depth is such that the wreck can only be fished for four or five days in each fortnightly cycle. Using the Decca Navigator to mark the position of the boat accurately, a grapnel and its associated conglomeration of floats and a dan buoy are dropped onto the wreck to give the skipper a visual indication of its whereabouts and of the strength of the tide. Then the angling craft is turned uptide and steamed for about a quarter of a mile. This distance will obviously vary according to the power in the tidal stream. When the skipper is satisfied that we are in the right position the anchor is lowered. Then the boat is dropped back, downtide, paying out the steel anchor warp as we go. Ideally, the anchor, angling boat and dan buoy ought to be in a straight line, although sometimes an adjustment has to be made to allow for any breeze or wind onto one or other side of the boat. With the anchor in and holding, the baits are prepared. There is no doubt that mackerel, preferably fresh, are the bait for conger. Sometimes a stop is made on the way out to the mark to let the anglers have ten minutes or so to feather for their own bait but more often than not it has been got by the crew before the start of the trip.

Most anglers make up the gear long before they arrive at the mark. Although from many manufacturing sources they vary little in type and performance. A rod, in hollow or solid glass, capable of balancing to a

1

2

1 *John Trust, co-skipper of* Our Unity, *swings a conger in on the gaff for Leslie Moncrieff. The angling party were fishing one of the many hundreds of merchant vessel wrecks that litter the area south of Torbay.*

2 *Ernie Passmore and John Trust, proud co-skippers of* Our Unity, *with a magnificent catch from a Torbay wreck: 2862 lbs of fish to 6 rods in 5 hours' fishing; congers from strap size to fish of over 70 lbs.*

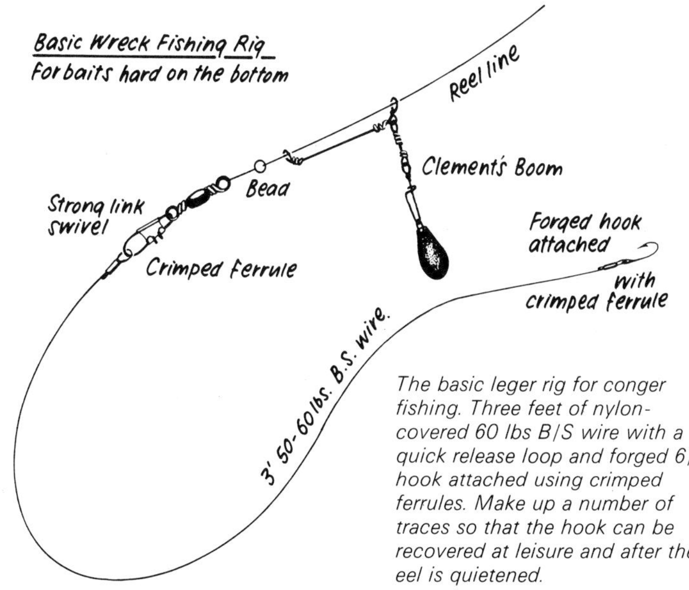

The basic leger rig for conger fishing. Three feet of nylon-covered 60 lbs B/S wire with a quick release loop and forged 6/0 hook attached using crimped ferrules. Make up a number of traces so that the hook can be recovered at leisure and after the eel is quietened.

50 lb line is usual. Again, reels are various but most people now use a quality multiplier or centre-pin. What *is* important is that the reel chosen is able to withstand the great pressures that are forced upon it by heavy fish and by the tortuous conditions. I prefer nylon line since this is less likely to fray on wreckage and gives that element of stretch which can be such a boon when attempting to control a powerful fish in mid-water. The end tackle is reasonably simple – a 3 ft length of 50 or 60 lb nylon-covered wire with a crimped-on hook and loop for attaching to the reel line. Make sure the hook is both strong and sharp. The Mustad Seamaster range are the hooks for me, but pay attention to both barbs and points before you use them. When they leave Norway the hooks are not really sharpened enough and sometimes the barb is too proud. Give your hook a touch with a hook hone. I like to use the whole fillet from a mackerel, tied onto the hook with the thick end nearest the bend of the hook. Elasticated cotton makes a neat job of fixing the lash which prevents the bait slipping down onto the hook bend. I won't suggest that a conger is so discerning as to forsake your bait in favour of a better presented one; it just makes the bait harder to tear off the hook and probably results in a more soundly-hooked fish.

The skipper will try to position the boat so that all the anglers' baits will drop down to an area alongside the wreck. Here the action of the tides will have cut away the sea bed material, gouging out a scour. It is in this scour or gully that conger are to be found. There is little point in dropping a baited hook into the heart of the wreck. A fish that took it would easily dive into the massed tangles of marine growth and metal from which it is virtually impossible to drag the conger. Far better to try to hook and beat them in the open, although not always clean, ground. Sometimes the baits will not reach the bottom since fish swimming above the wreck hit them hard. These offers will most likely come from pollack, coalfish and ling, particularly if the current is running with any strength. On a well-chosen day, 2 lbs of lead will get the bait to the scour, and once it is there you will not have to wait long for the first sign of interest. Take care dropping the bait, especially if the tide is slackish. If you are too fast in dropping down, this can cause the trace and bait to swing back up the line, beyond the lead, where it twists round. With a strong pull in the current the bait tends to stream away from the lead, giving less of a problem. Certainly a Clement's boom or similar wire boom will help to prevent this from happening.

The weight can take some time to hit the sea bed. Forty fathoms is some depth. As soon as the lead hits, give the tip a lift and let the lead settle once more. Try to get an indication of the composition of the ground. Whether you have the softness of sand below you or the hard, distinct knock of a lead on metal give

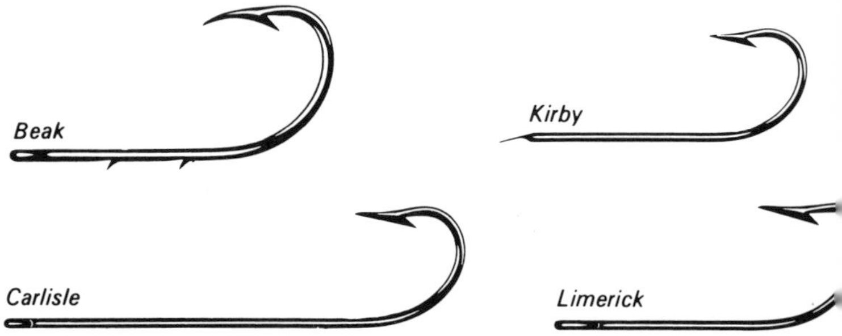

the bait a few minutes to work before deciding that the tackle is in the correct position relative to the wreck. Adjustment of the lead size will give some degree of control over where your bait fishes. Use a lighter lead to drop farther back toward the wreck hull or a heavier lead to come farther out onto the hard sand. When you are satisfied wait for the first nibblings at the last. Conger do not take with a bang, they tend to worry a bait. Sometimes they will mouth the last for quite a time if they are left to do so by other conger. When the scour is packed with fish – and it sometimes can be – there is competition among the eels for the bait. Then you will experience a fierce grab, followed by a series of arm-pulling tugs with the rod tip pulling over as the eel backs away with the hookbait.

When you have the bite, take up the direct pressure on the rod, feeling for the moment when you think that

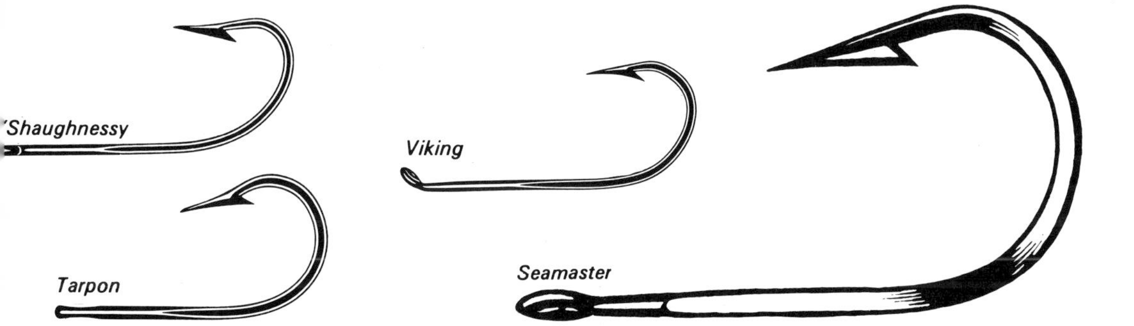

Conger fishing is a tough business.

Eight patterns of hook for the boat fisherman. Left to right: Beak hook with bait-holding nicks. Carlisle provides a grip when flat-fishing. Kirby is a hook for tying cod and mackerel flies. Limerick and O'Shaughnessy are general-purpose patterns. Seamaster is a big-game hook. Tarpon attaches easily to wire traces. Viking is the best all-round pattern.

the eel has got the bait securely. Then wind in a few turns of line to take the rod tip down toward the water. There is no need to strike with an exaggerated sweep over your shoulder. Make a positive strike and keep the rod up. This will let you feel whether the fish is definitely on and at the same time it will keep a tight line. Any slack given to a conger eel down in its own environment will give it the chance to wrap its tail around a convenient obstruction and then you will be engaged in a tug of war very few anglers win.

The first couple of fathoms are critical in the fight. Lift the fish up clear of any rough ground as quickly as you can, then begin to fight it out in clear water. An eel will often come easily for several fathoms, not realising that it is in trouble. But, when it does detect that something is wrong, it will make a crazed effort to regain the safety of the scour. In fishing the wreck I mentioned earlier several things became apparent as the fishing progressed. We had been told that the wreck had never been fished by rod and line although trawlers frequently fished the open ground around the hulk. Our first baits produced small congers, giving some truth to John Trust's theory that the scour around a wreck is full of conger of all sizes. The smaller fish are more mobile than the larger ones, grabbing any baits long before their larger brethren can get at them. In angling terms this means that the "strap" congers have to be removed before the angler can get access to the larger fish. Deep sea divers who have had occasion to work over these wrecks have stated that the area immediately around a wreck is often choked with smaller conger while the big fish appear to take up ambush stations either within the wreck or close to suitable cover, which gives them a position from which ▶144

CUCKOO WRASSE
Labrus bimaculatus

One of the few British marine species in which there is a colour difference between male and female fish. Male has white patch on forehead only during breeding season. The cuckoo wrasse is widely distributed and always found in association with rough ground. A fish of 2 lbs would be regarded as a fine specimen.

GOLDSINNY
Ctenolabrus rupestris

A small wrasse of brown overall colouring. It has a dark spot on the upper part of the fish's tail at a position between the junction of body and tail.

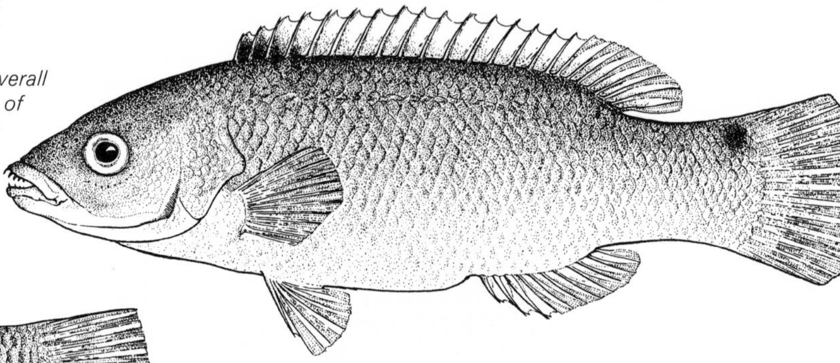

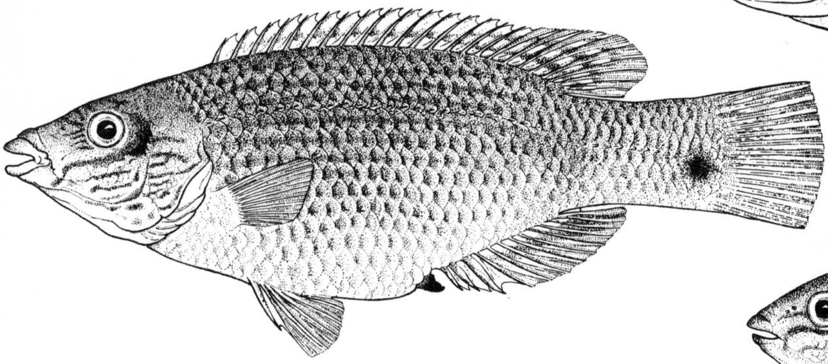

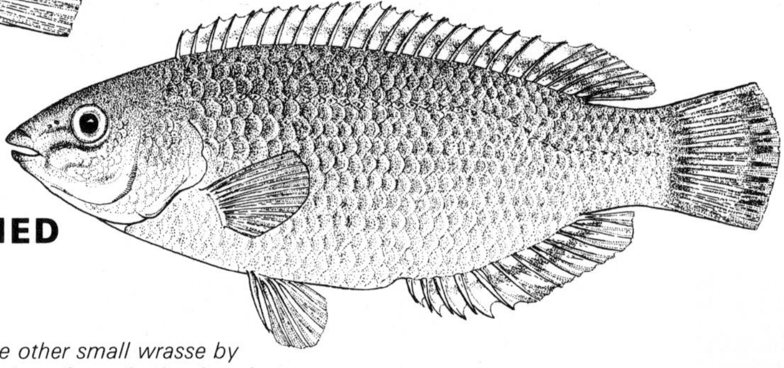

CORKWING WRASSE
Symphodus (Crenilabrus) melops

Has a similar body shape to the goldsinny wrasse but a dark spot will be positioned at the centre of the tail wrist. Both the fish's head and underjaw have variegated colour bands.

SMALL-MOUTHED WRASSE
Centrolabrus exoletus

This species differs from the other small wrasse by having a greater number of rays in the dorsal fin. It also possesses an extremely small mouth.

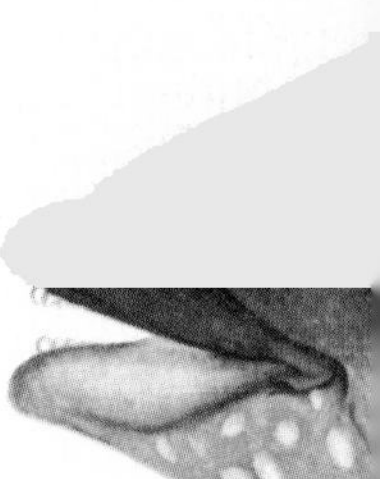

Pharyngeal teeth of the ballan wrasse.

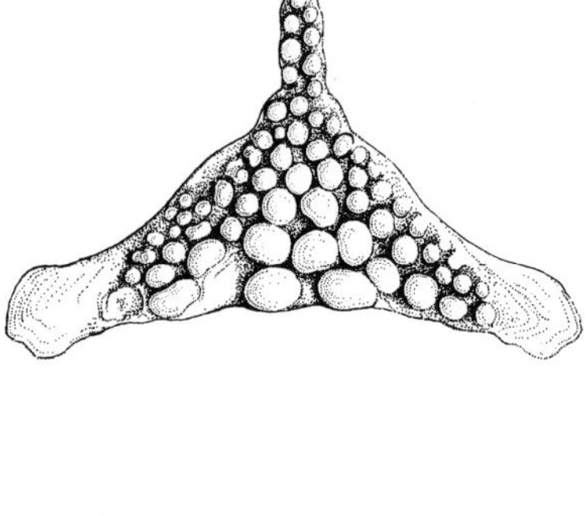

Upper and lower jaw of the ballan wrasse.

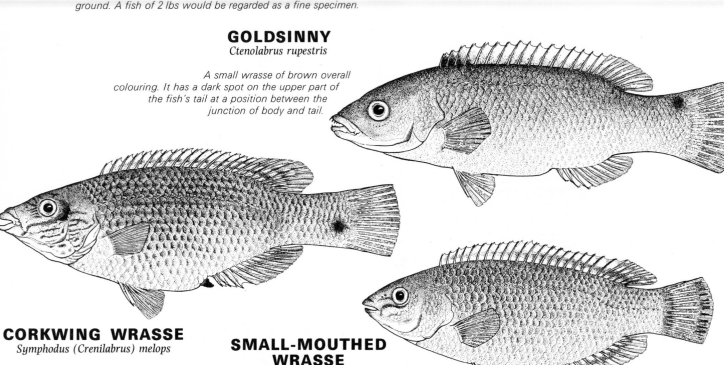

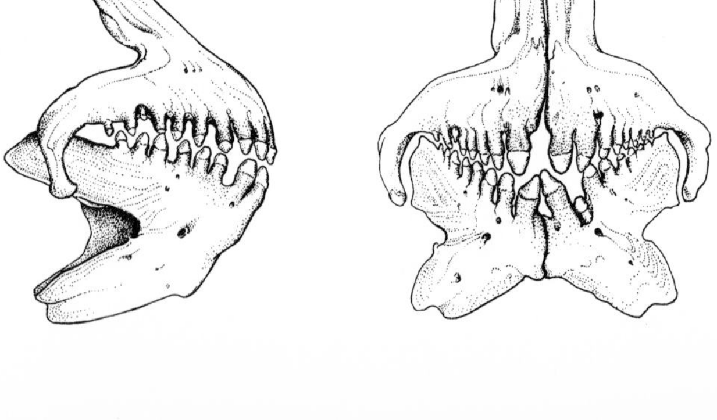

RAINBOW WRASSE
Coris julis

A small wrasse – a fish of 1 lb would be an exceptional specimen. Probably only found in south-western waters but still to be proven as an angling species in British waters. The rainbow is found on rocky ground in shallow water. The female is less brightly coloured than her mate.

GENERAL NOTE ON WRASSE

All members of the wrasse family are found on very rough ground that suits their feeding and breeding behaviour. They are adept at removing limpets and other molluscs from rocks in the inter-tidal zone, which means that wrasse are generally found in inshore waters. They like deepwater close into the rocks to establish some form of territory unaffected by the rise and fall of the tide The wrasses are nest builders.

Bait: *All marine worms, molluscs, crustaceans and even tiny slips of fish.*

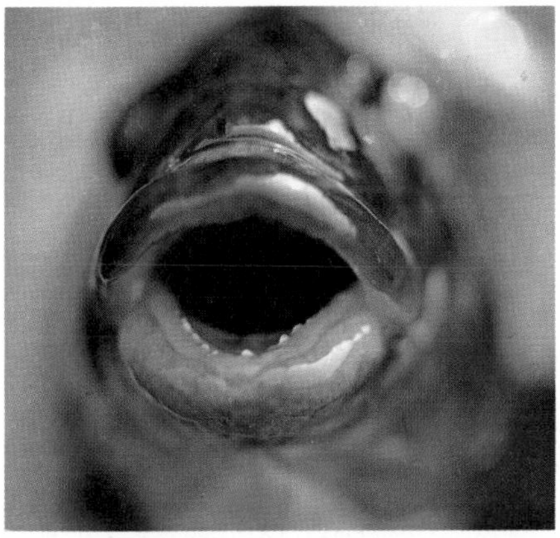

Dentition of the ballan wrasse.

BALLAN WRASSE
Labrus bergylta

Largest of the wrasse that are found in waters of the British Isles, this is the shore fisherman's species. Although it is thought of as a fish of summer, ballan wrasse can be taken throughout the angling year in south and western areas. The species is subject to a wide variation in colouring in both sexes, which can be allied to the habitat. Obviously these fish can adapt in pelage to suit both the mineral and vegetable colours in which they live and hide. A fish of 5 lbs would be a good-size specimen.

141 ◀ to ambush smaller, more easily caught, prey. I have found the theory to be true, for the initial fishing foray to any wreck has always been a slaughter of eels up to the 30 lbs class.

A second day's fishing tends to produce slower bites and larger fish. Sometimes one has almost to drop the bait into the scour hard against the hull of the boat before a conger is found. The time around dead slack water can be a trial. It is never a good time to fish for most species, but the conger seem to go right off feeding at this period.

A lot of big eels are lost on the surface and often the fault lies in the end tackle and with the angler. Congers twist on the gear. They are not a fish adapted to fast swimming or to an accurate aiming of the body. Like a snake they can twist their bodies very rapidly, rolling over and over if given any slack line or if allowed to lie on the surface before being brought to the gaff. As the fish comes up through the water, as soon as you get a glimpse of the flashing white of the belly, get ready with the gaff. Lower the gaff into the sea below your eel, then draw the point into the fish solidly. Don't let it hang on the bend, while you admire it. Get the eel into the boat, preferably dropped straight into a fish box. Never assume that the gaff point is sharp. Make certain that it is before your fishing commences. And, if there is a likelihood of massive fish, sharpen two gaffs. One to be used on the head and the other driven in behind the vent of the conger.

Leave the hook and trace in the fish. A quick-release swivel will enable you to get disconnected and to mount another trace long before you could hope to quieten a big fish sufficiently to retrieve the original end of the tackle. If you are forced to remove the hook, slow the fish down with a sharp blow behind the vent followed by another on the skull. Keep hands away from the mouth because the conger can cause fearful damage with those vicious teeth. It is far better to cut the hook out with a sharp knife or to spring the hook free with a king-sized disgorger. Conger eels are slow

VIVIPAROUS BLENNY
Zoarces viviparous

One dorsal fin extends from a position just above the gillcase back to the caudal fin. The soft rays, forming the dorsal fin, are split by a number (usually ten) of stiff spines at a point two-thirds of the length of the fin. The soft rays are equal in length while the spines are shorter. The fish is long and sinuous, living inshore among beds of weed and rock outcrops. It gives birth to many live young that are able immediately to fend for themselves. The species is not seriously fished for.

LESSER WEEVER
Trachinus vipera

A small fish that is widely found on our sandy beaches in shallow water. The fish is important in that it has poison glands that eject venom via the spines of the first dorsal fin and a large spine on each of the gillcases. The poison can kill if not treated, although generally a fit person will only suffer a painful wound. Not specifically fished for but could take a shore fisherman's bait.

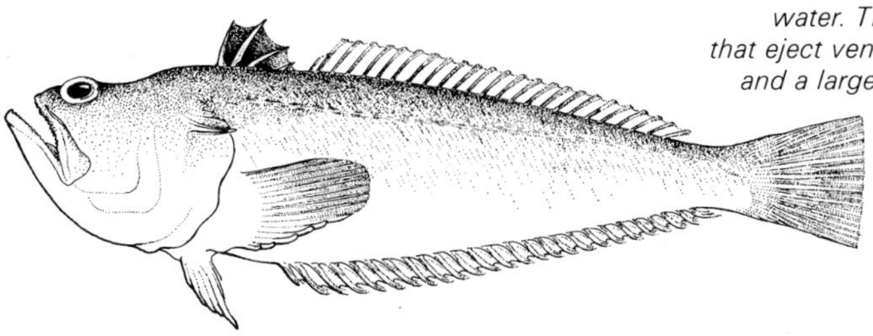

GREATER WEEVER
Trachinus draco

The species grows to a larger size and can be said to be the boat angler's version of the genus. It inhabits deeper water but is equally as venomous.

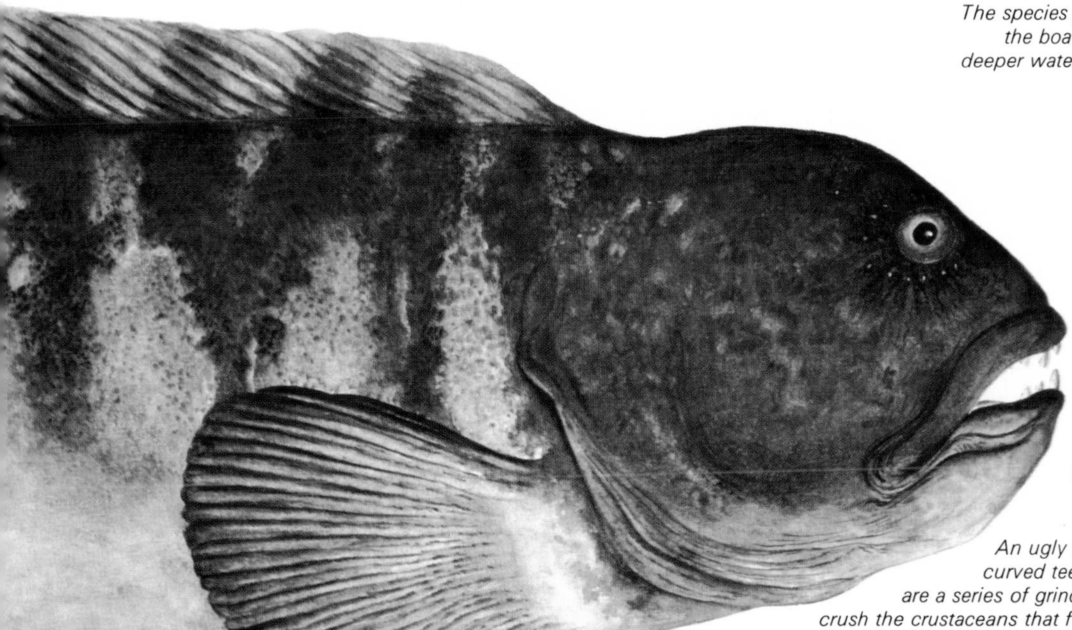

COMMON CATFISH
Anarhichas lupus

An ugly brute with enormous mouth and curved teeth in the jaws. Behind the canines there are a series of grinding molars that are used to crush the crustaceans that form the fish's diet. The catfish haunts the rocky ground in deepwater. Many tons of this species are landed from commercial boats each week where, from the dock, filleted and headless they become wholesome food for the public. Lupus grows to huge weights but does not figure largely in the catches of sea anglers.

Bait: *Possibly a mixture of worm, fish and shellfish baits.*

to die. They can be left in a fish box for many hours yet still possess the ability to inflict dire wounds on the unwary.

At slack water, especially when there is a breeze blowing, the angling boat will begin to drift off the wreck. The baits will drop onto the open sand, which forms a ridge at the edge of the scour. You may get the slow sucking bite, associated with conger, but it could be a bonus fish for the trip. Because the wreck forms an obstruction to the free flow of the tide, sandbanks are frequently formed around the vessel. They provide yet another habitat that is often perfect for the turbot. Many times, during slack water, I have been out over the wrecks knowing that my bait has drifted away from the eels. I have had the "sucking" bites that spelled conger but turned out to be turbot. Once you strike into the fish it gives itself away, fighting in a lethargic fashion but well worth having for the kitchen!

I choose to alternate my fishing methods during a conger trip, leaving the back-breaking work for a while to concentrate on light tackle and the superb fishing over the wreck. Here, above the superstructure, is a region where many species swim but one in which the pollack reigns supreme. Like the conger, the pollack is a fish that uses the mass of weed, tangles of metal plates and rigging to ambush from and to power-dive into when hooked. Standard tackle is a rubber eel or similar lure fished on a long flowing trace that carries the lead on the reel line. An extension of the sink-and-draw method is used to work the lure above and across the wreck searching out the depth and place in which the pollack shoal is feeding. A classical bite is felt as a sudden departure of all weight on the line, followed by a crash dive as the fish seeks to get away with its meal from other members of the shoal. I suppose the movement can be likened to the smash-and-grab antics of a starling that grabs bread from the unfortunate, suburban sparrow!

Changes in rod and reel, to get the most out of the above-wreck fish, are accompanied by different line. Braided Dacron comes into its own, giving that element of contact with the bite so necessary when seeking fish that swim in the middle layers of the sea. I choose a rod rather stronger than the average sea spinning rod, together with a multiplier carrying 20 lb line. I do not suggest that this gear will stop all pollack dead in their tracks but it will give the ultimate in action. Having got the take from the pollack and having previously set the drag to slip at about an 8 lb pull, you will have to let the first crash-down happen. There is little choice in this, for even a 50 lb line will break if any attempt is made to hold the fish. Let it go but steadily bring thumb pressure onto the spool to tire the fish. Very few pollack can keep the dive going. They have enormous power in the first rush but this weakens quite quickly. As soon as you detect a slowing down in the dive, jam on the thumbs to get the fish's head up. After a couple of fathoms rising in the stream, the pollack will be affected by the pressure change and the fish ought to be yours. Natural baits, fish or squid strip, will produce takes and so will many kinds of metal or feathered lures. The species is not fussy but it reacts best to a bait that is worked in the current, not just left hanging dormant.

Setting a known drag to a desired poundage is easily done. Buy an accurate spring balance, such as the Salter, attach a loop of line from the reel and twiddle the star drag until the strike drag needed is set. It is then fairly easy to arrive at a strong drag setting for playing a fish that you think is beginning to tire. On my 20 lb class reel, two movements of the star will take the drag setting from 8 to 14 lbs pressure.

As I stated earlier, pollack, coalies and cod can be found over a wreck or reef. All three species can be fished for on similar end tackles. Should the situation hold ling, especially the large fish, wire traces will have to be introduced to the gear. Ling have extremely sharp, fine-pointed teeth that can easily sever 50 lb nylon. The ling will not always be found swimming above an obstruction. They certainly do at times but I like to search the water down toward the wreck, as close to the top of the superstructure as possible. There is a similarity in the feeding behaviour of ling and conger in as much that they will both move out onto the open sand to feed. When hooked both species put up a terrific struggle and will endeavour to get back into the wreckage. You will find the first section of the fight is the same; though ling will be more noticeably affected by pressure change on the way up than the eel.

Sometimes the midwater bait will be met by gentle pulling bites that are difficult to hook. Scale down both hook and bait size and perhaps you'll get among the bream. Both black and red bream live in this kind of habitat although the red species prefer deep water. Bream are lively fighters, given the opportunity. Again, the spinning rod is best to use, offering tiny slips of fish bait on long-shanked hooks about size 1. The fish will do battle right up through the water. Being slab-sided, they are hardly affected by any change in pressure. They come from the Mediterranean area and are highly coloured, graceful little fish bringing a splash of brilliance to the fish box. Do not take more fish than you need. The two species have come into our seas to spawn and deserve the chance to build up in numbers.

Sooner or later you will hook a spurdog. One of the smaller members of the shark family, they hunt in a pack eating everything that comes their way. I can recall a shoal of spurdog moving into Dingle Bay as we were fishing off Slea Head. Having caught a number with the inevitable ruin of many traces, we decided to steam away for a couple of miles westward to get clear of them. Alas, down went the baits into more spur-

Peter Collins, Editor of *Sea Angler*, with a turbot hooked on the sandbanks that are formed around a wreck.

dog. There must have been thousands of the things moving like a plague of locusts up the coast of Ireland. Always hungry, spurdogs are not difficult to hook. If you set out to fish for them use both wire hook snoods and a wire paternoster trace. The incredibly tough skin of this and other dogfish will saw through even strong nylon. Their teeth are sharp, hence the wire. Take care bringing the fish into the boat. Each dorsal fin has a sharp spine at its leading edge which inflicts a painful wound. Like the other dogfishes, the spur has the nasty habit of twisting its body around the forearm of the unwary angler.

If I was asked to nominate a fish for the summer I think it might well be the mackerel. Much under-rated as a fighter, chiefly because the mackerel is our main bait fish and is so often sought with strings of feathers, it is capable of both speed and sustained power in the fight. Ideal tackle for good sport is a fly rod with a conventional floating fly line backed to a finely tapering nylon cast with a single fly that represents the fry of a marine fish. In fact, any sea trout wet fly, with a tinselled body, will do the trick. I know it is not easy to

PIRKING OVER WRECK AND REEF

Ask any wreck fisherman about pirking and he'll tell you that it is hard work. The constant action needed by arms and rod tip to impart life to the artificial lure, especially in a heavy sea, is a gruelling business. Some of that tough going can be reduced by using the correct rod. About 7 ft seems the right length, fast-tapered with a lot of strength right through to the butt section. As the fishing style covers a wide variety of situations it is difficult to settle on a particular rod/line combination, but the following combinations will be suitable:

Deepwater marks: 30 fathoms or more. Use 50 lb b.s. line. This combination will cope with the larger specimens expected, the tide that is ever-present and the weight of pirks needed – which can be as much as 3 lb.

Shallow-water wrecks and reefs: 20 fathoms. Use 30 lb b.s. line. Less tide, smaller fish and pirks allow the use of a lighter tackle approach even though there may be times when large fish will attack the artificial lure. A 30 lb class outfit will beat the fish and be far less tiring to use.

Inshore marks: 10 fathoms. Use 20 lb b.s. line. The dinghy angler has many fishing marks where a light but responsive rod will handle quite heavy fish. Fishing is normally done from the seated position, which does not allow a full expansion of the angler's shoulders, so the rod must have sufficient action to work the lure effectively.

Although braided line would help in transferring the angler's actions to the pirk, it cannot cope with the abrasive qualities of submerged, rusting wrecks or jagged reefs. Nylon lines have far more resistance to the rough and tumble of the underwater environment.

Pirks are expensive tackle items to lose. More often than not it is the hook that becomes tangled. Pulling to release it usually results in a lost lure. Losses can be less costly if a 'rotten bottom' connection of nylon is made between the hook and pirk body. Alternatively, one of the modern metal connectors, such as the Newark Positive Poundage Link, can be used. These links have a definite pull-out strain when a steady pressure is applied to the line.

The shape of pirks does not vary much. At one time they were made to represent small fish. Constant use and development has shown that action in the pirk is more important than appearance. Some of the pirk's attraction to fish is applied by the jerky movement that the fisherman gives it, but the shape and centre of gravity of the lure are equally important.

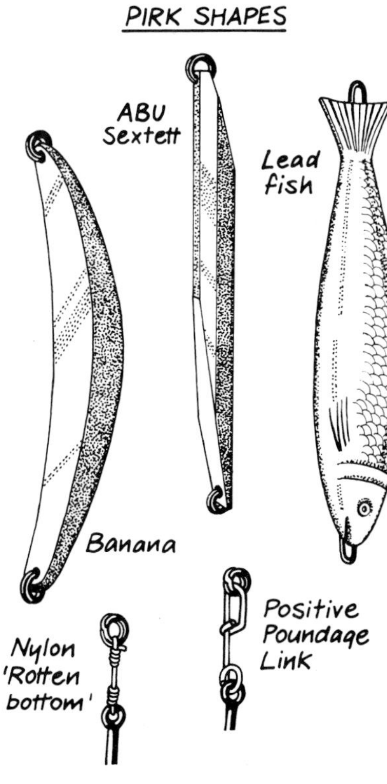

1 *Feathering for mackerel off the Isle of Wight. Strings of 6 hooks, to which are whipped bunches of chicken feathers, will rapidly fill the sea angler's bait box.*

2 *So often a shark will roll up in the wire trace, particularly if a small amount of slack line is given to the fish during the latter stages of a long and hard fight.*

cast a fly from the normal, crowded, sea angling boat but from a dinghy this is the best of fun. With the heat of summer and a show of fry or plankton in the sea, mackerel will spatter through the surface layers hounding the small fish. When hooked they tear line from a centre-pin, thrashing across the top of the water and then diving deep and hard in an effort to shed the hook. They can be likened to a wild trout for they can keep the action up for long periods. Mackerel will take a spinner. This must be small. Something like a fly spoon is suitable. Unfortunately most spinners need some lead weight to cast them effectively and it is the weight that can dampen the superb fighting qualities of the species. In many West Country ports holiday-makers are offered mackerel fishing trips that are neither sporting nor satisfying to the angler. They are handed a wooden frame on which is wrapped a length of strong Courlene line. The line carries a heavy weight and a traditional mackerel spinner. Lines are let out with the boat underway, trolling the spinners along below the surface. Very few people are aware that a fish has impaled itself on the spinner but at regular intervals they are required to haul in the line to take off the unfortunate fish that strike at the lure. This kind of fishing and the doubtful form of shark fishing offered as sport have done little to improve either the image of sea angling or to explain to the beginner what the angler seeks in his sport.

The late spring and summer will bring a flush of new growth to the undersea vegetation and to the shellbeds. What in winter was almost barren open ground becomes populated by many small creatures seeking minute scraps of feed from the sea bed. Worms, shrimps and prawns and other organisms have multiplied in the warm, plankton-filled sea. The small fish move into these areas and – as is nature's way – the predators follow. Smoothhounds and rays move over the bottom picking off the crabs that venture too far from cover. The monkfish and angler, slow in movement but with a canny patience, lie waiting for the juvenile bottom-feeding fish to venture close to the gaping maws. Both species can provide the angler with a heavy fight but these fish lack any ability to move with energy or cunning. Indeed they are credited with the fight of a wet sack. On the open ground it is the tope that most sea anglers seek: a fast, powerful and lean fish that can extend most anglers and their tackle. Pound for pound the tope can out-fight most blue sharks of the same weight, providing they are not hampered by over-heavy tackle and rods. Twenty pound class gear is correct for most tope, 30 lb rods and lines if you fish in a big tope area such as to the west of Wales. Attention must be given to the efficiency of tackle rather than its strength. Reels must be completely free-running for the species can rip well over 100 yds of line off the reel. A clutch must be easily adjusted, free from the jerky action that can lose a good fish with alarming ease.

Tope tackles vary from area to area. The simplest is a running leger, with a weight carried on the reel line. The line terminates in a quality swivel with a link attachment. The trace must be either all wire from swivel to hook, or be constructed from very strong nylon joined to a short length of wire at the hook to guard against the extremely sharp teeth of the tope. There is considerable difference of opinion regarding tope traces. Some anglers (and I subscribe to this theory) go for a short length of wire coupled to a rubbing length of strong nylon on the basis that tope may be able to detect something strange about a bait that is attached to a long piece of wiretrace. They pick the bait up, run with it but then drop the bait. It seems that the stiffness of a long wire trace is sufficient to cut down seriously the number of runs one can get from the species.

Not every run from a tope results in a hooked and landed fish, so every effort made to present a bait in an attractive fashion must help to increase the number of positive takes. The actual method of baiting calls for some attention from the discerning angler. Clive Gammon, when introducing me to the pleasures of tope fishing in south Wales, used plaice fillets from the supermarket. Buying them in a flat fillet allowed Clive to sandwich the hook between the fillets which he could then tie securely or, if time permitted, sew together to form an attractive and successful tope offering. The fish that he was after came in, on each tide, to a maze of gullies between sandbanks and were no doubt conditioned to feeding on flounders living in the estuary. The supermarket's plaice fillets went a long way to allaying the suspicion of the predatory tope.

2

When to strike is always a problem with tope in shallow water. Standard practice is to let them pick up the bait without feeling any tension on the line, the reel being out of gear and only left in check until the rattle of the ratchet indicates that a fish has arrived. The ratchet is then thumbed off and the fish is given line on its first run with only slight thumb pressure to guard against any over-runs. The fish will take perhaps 50 yds of line and will then stop. At this stage it turns the bait, preparing to swallow it, before moving off once more. Most tope anglers strike the fish after the second run has developed. This can be a mistake for the fish may have swallowed the bait down, and is then hooked in the stomach. That means it will have to be killed to retrieve the hook, or the hook removing operation becomes so difficult as seriously to reduce the chances of the fish living. I would always seek to strike the fish just after it stopped on the first run. With thumbs on the reel, an angler will receive those important trembles up the line that will let him know what the tope has done. If you strike and lose the fish through an inadequate hook hold, it is better for the fish to have escaped unharmed as well as giving the angler the experience of feeling the end-of-line activity resulting in an unsuccessful hooking. Tope from deepwater situations take a bait differently and both the tackle and the strike must be altered. As I go after tope from the deeps in autumn we will leave the methods until later in the book.

In the middle of the year, with its calm seas and clear water, plaice move into the shallow ground seeking to feed well after the rigours of spawning. They are particularly fond of shellfish, notably the mussel. It is not essential to find beds of shellfish although these areas will attract fish in numbers. Look for old pilings, with colonies of mussels attached to them. Sandy harbours that have chains stretched out on the bottom to moor buoys will often produce plaice. Weed grows on the chain to create a mini-ecology which is followed by a rapid colonization from different species of minute creatures and shellfish. Providing the water is clean the oasis of life will multiply, drawing fish species such as plaice, mullet, bass and wrasse into the immediate area to feed. With the arrival of bad weather the fish will move into deeper water to avoid the battering that disturbed inshore seas will bring. However, the shellfish and other minute organisms have attached themselves to solid support and are not swept away, so the colony is less likely to break down.

Although the plaice and other inshore summer species will feed on the natural animal life in an area, they will take baits not directly associated with the surroundings. Squid and fish catch a lot of these fish, but I much prefer to offer them a bait found in the locality such as ragworms dug from the soft harbour mud, slipper limpet gathered from pilings and breakwaters, mussels dragged from the shellbeds and cockles that can be raked out of the sands at low water. One thing I have found is that the plaice, in company with other flatfish, like a moving bait. Not something that is flashed across their vision but something just given the occasional twitch to give the offering life. The addition of a spoon when working a bait over clean sand will often encourage a positive take. Plaice are not hookshy, but give them a chance to display their fighting qualities by using fine tackle, something like 10 lb line to a legered rig with long-shanked No 2 hook will suffice, and you will get better sport.

▶152

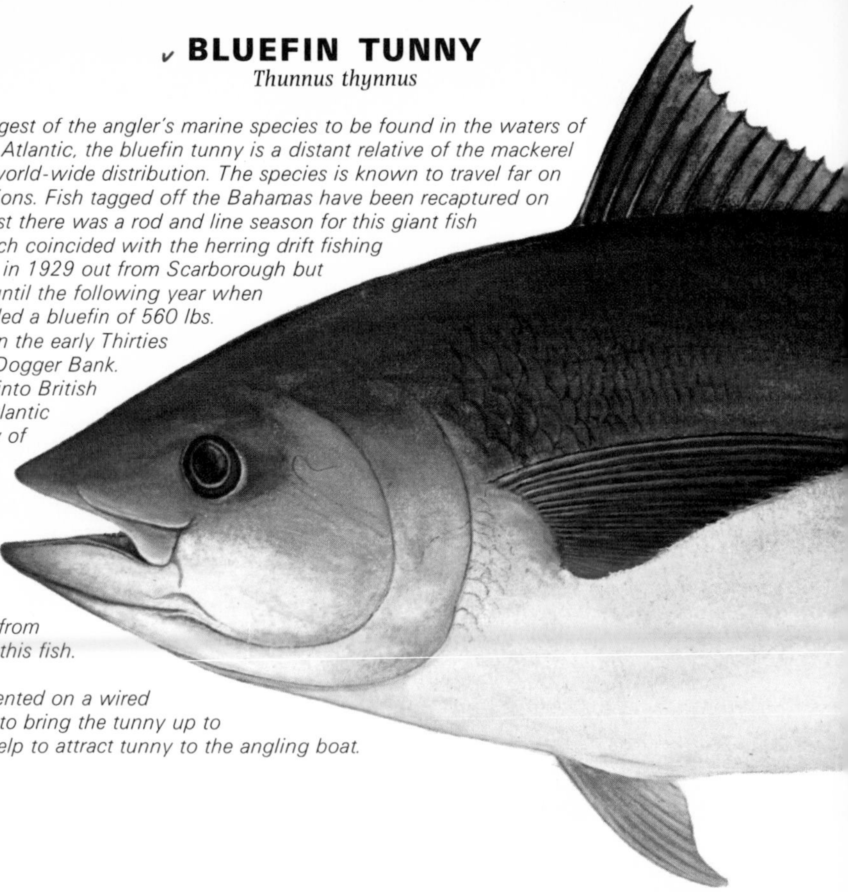

BLUEFIN TUNNY
Thunnus thynnus

The largest of the angler's marine species to be found in the waters of the British Isles and Eastern Atlantic, the bluefin tunny is a distant relative of the mackerel and, like its cousin, has a world-wide distribution. The species is known to travel far on both feeding and spawning migrations. Fish tagged off the Bahamas have been recaptured on the Norwegian tunny grounds. In the past there was a rod and line season for this giant fish off the coast of Yorkshire which coincided with the herring drift fishing activity. Rod and line fishing began in 1929 out from Scarborough but no fish were landed until the following year when Mr Mitchell-Henry landed a bluefin of 560 lbs. Mitchell-Henry went on fishing in the early Thirties finally to land a fish of 851 lbs off the Dogger Bank. Undoubtedly the tunny still comes into British waters after having first crossed the Atlantic to spawn off the shores of the Bay of Biscay, then travelling to the Coast of Norway to begin an orgy of feeding in the plankton-laden waters before following the herring shoals down into the North Sea. Only the necessary money to equip and use a boat capable of following the tunny in the dangerous seas of the Dogger Bank prevent sea anglers from once again getting to grips with this fish.

Bait: *Whole fish, herring or mackerel presented on a wired trace; chumming with whole fish seems to bring the tunny up to the surface. Possibly "rubby dubby" would help to attract tunny to the angling boat.*

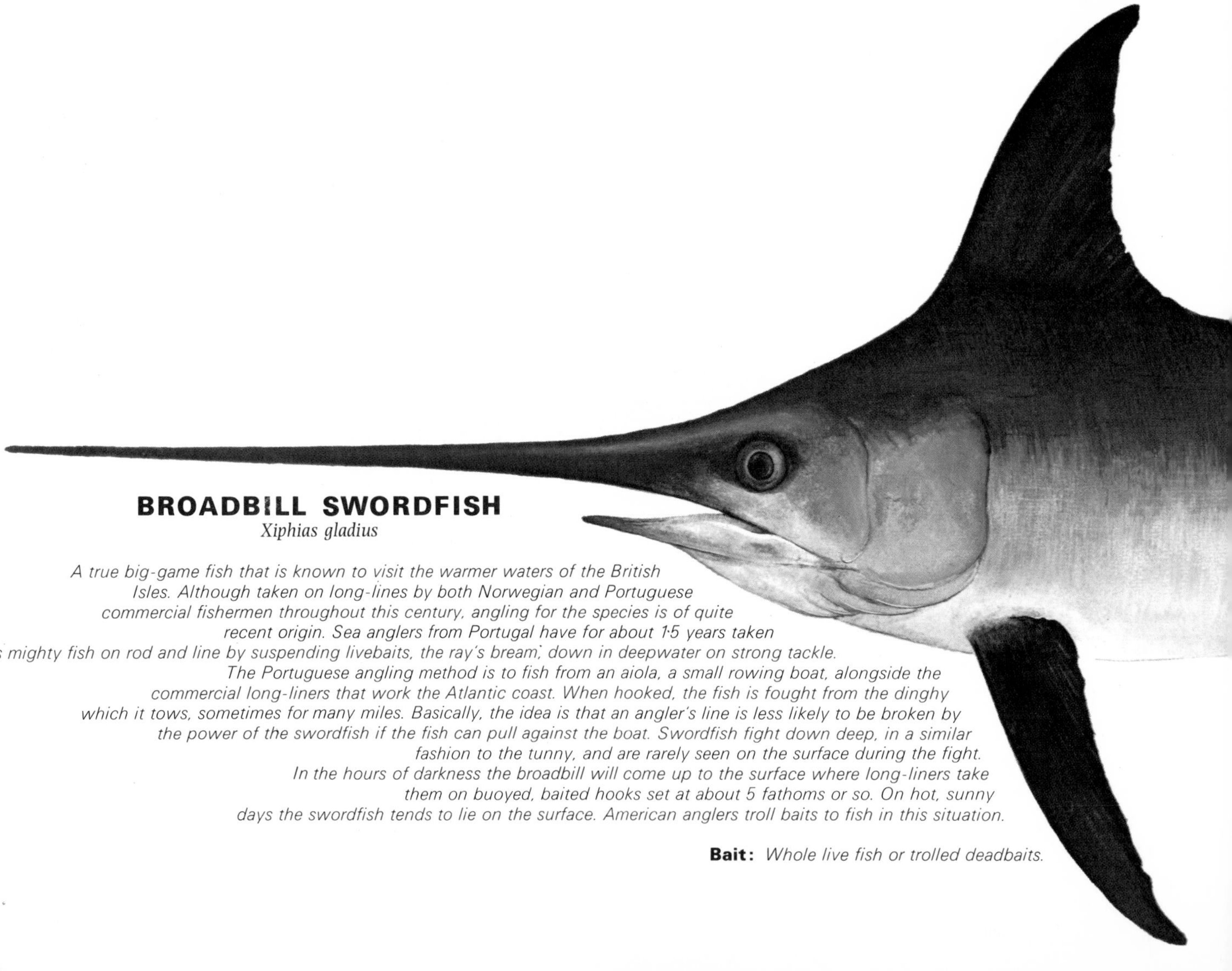

BROADBILL SWORDFISH
Xiphias gladius

A true big-game fish that is known to visit the warmer waters of the British Isles. Although taken on long-lines by both Norwegian and Portuguese commercial fishermen throughout this century, angling for the species is of quite recent origin. Sea anglers from Portugal have for about 1·5 years taken this mighty fish on rod and line by suspending livebaits, the ray's bream, down in deepwater on strong tackle. The Portuguese angling method is to fish from an aiola, a small rowing boat, alongside the commercial long-liners that work the Atlantic coast. When hooked, the fish is fought from the dinghy which it tows, sometimes for many miles. Basically, the idea is that an angler's line is less likely to be broken by the power of the swordfish if the fish can pull against the boat. Swordfish fight down deep, in a similar fashion to the tunny, and are rarely seen on the surface during the fight. In the hours of darkness the broadbill will come up to the surface where long-liners take them on buoyed, baited hooks set at about 5 fathoms or so. On hot, sunny days the swordfish tends to lie on the surface. American anglers troll baits to fish in this situation.

Bait: *Whole live fish or trolled deadbaits.*

1

1 *A sure indication that there are mackerel shoals moving up the rubby trail. Gannets hurtling down from over 100 ft to slice into the waves to seek the moving bait fish.*

2 *A male tope comes quietly to the surface. A tired fish will allow itself to be lead to the boat's side. Then the conservation-minded angler can boat the fish by grasping the dorsal fin and tail wrist.*

149◄ Shark fishing comes into fashion in the summer months. We are fortunate in the British Isles in that we sit in the path of the North Atlantic Drift. It breaks either side of the islands. The major stream goes up along the west coasts of Ireland, Wales and Scotland with a minor current coming up the English Channel. This stream peters out around the Isle of Wight, losing most of its warmth and rich saline water. Most of the shark fishing effort of British sea anglers would centre on fishing for the blue shark. The established Cornish fisheries have enjoyed the species for more than 20 years. For the last 10 years there has been increased interest in the porbeagle shark with the occasional capture of both mako and threshers. A system was developed by serious shark anglers in the West Country both to attract and hook these fish. Known as rubby dubby, this system was a means of pulling the sharks to the boat by streaming a trail of attractive material down the line of drift. Basically, the idea was this:

Fill a bag with mashed-up pieces of mackerel or other oily fish. Add a carrier which was usually bran or a similar cereal, although I believe that sawdust would do, to enable the oil and smell to be filtered down through the depths. The fish pieces must be small so as not to feed the shark but there must be enough of them to allow the sharks to see them. Sharks feed and hunt both by smell and sight. All shark fishing takes place while the boat is drifting before the wind. This means that the rubby dubby is constantly being deposited on and down through the water with the rubby trail growing longer as the boat drifts with the wind. Fish in a downtide area and upwind from the boat will pick up the trail, by sight or smell, and the theory is that the sharks will follow the trail until they find the angler's baits.

These baits are usually whole mackerel or similar oily fish presented on wired traces below a float. The float will do two things. It will establish a depth at which the bait will be set and it will give an indication of a bait being disturbed or taken by a shark. Ideally, one would want the sharks to swim up to the boat on the surface and nothing can give more excitement to the fishing than to see dorsal fins cutting through the waves. Unfortunately, sharks swim at the depth that their food fish are swimming at, so the best way to determine that depth is for anglers to set their baits at differing depths down through the water. Once a run has been had to a bait all the baits can then be adjusted to that particular setting.

I have found that blue sharks, coming from tropical regions, form the greater part of our catches during the summer, so let us establish a typical sharking day. The tackle would be 30 lb class rods and reels except where there is the possibility of picking up the odd mako or thresher shark. Since these fellows appear to be limited to the Cornish and possibly Isle of Wight waters we can assume they are pretty few and far between. The mako would need 80 lb gear to give an angler a real chance to subdue this powerful but rare shark. The line should be braided Dacron or Terylene since this has little stretch and gives an immediate response to the strike. Traces are made from flexible, cable-laid wire that can be nylon covered, although this is not an essential. A breaking strain of 150–250 lbs will do, for the wire has to be strong enough to withstand both the fearsome teeth and incredibly rough skin of the shark. Construct the trace with at least 15 ft of wire between the hook and the quality big-game swivel that joins it to the reel line. Most sharks tend to roll up in the trace if given slack line or the opportunity to do so, therefore the length of wire will keep the massive tail fluke away from the relatively delicate braided line. You must use a good hook. Ensure that it is sharp, big enough to accommodate the bait fish and with sufficient strength to withstand a powerful and sometimes prolonged fight.

Baits, which can be whole mackerel, herring or pilchards, are best presented by passing the hook through the fish from the tail and out at the gill case. This is easily done if the hook is fixed to the trace with a quick-release link. Take a baiting needle, insert the point at the wrist of the tail just below the backbone. Push the needle towards the fish's head, keeping the bait straight. With the needle point clear of the bait at the mouth, attach the quick-release link and draw the needle through the body of the fish. Connect the trace to the hook eye and pull the whole of the hook shank back into the body of the bait. It is important to hide as much of the shank as possible while keeping the business part, the point, clear of the body or bones of your hookbait. Sharks can sometimes be finicky feeders. They have seen many live fish in their time swimming naturally. A bait suspended by the tail and not moving must make them wary so all that the angler can do to present the bait with ironmongery hidden must increase the chance of a strike.

Feed the bait over the boat's side, measuring the

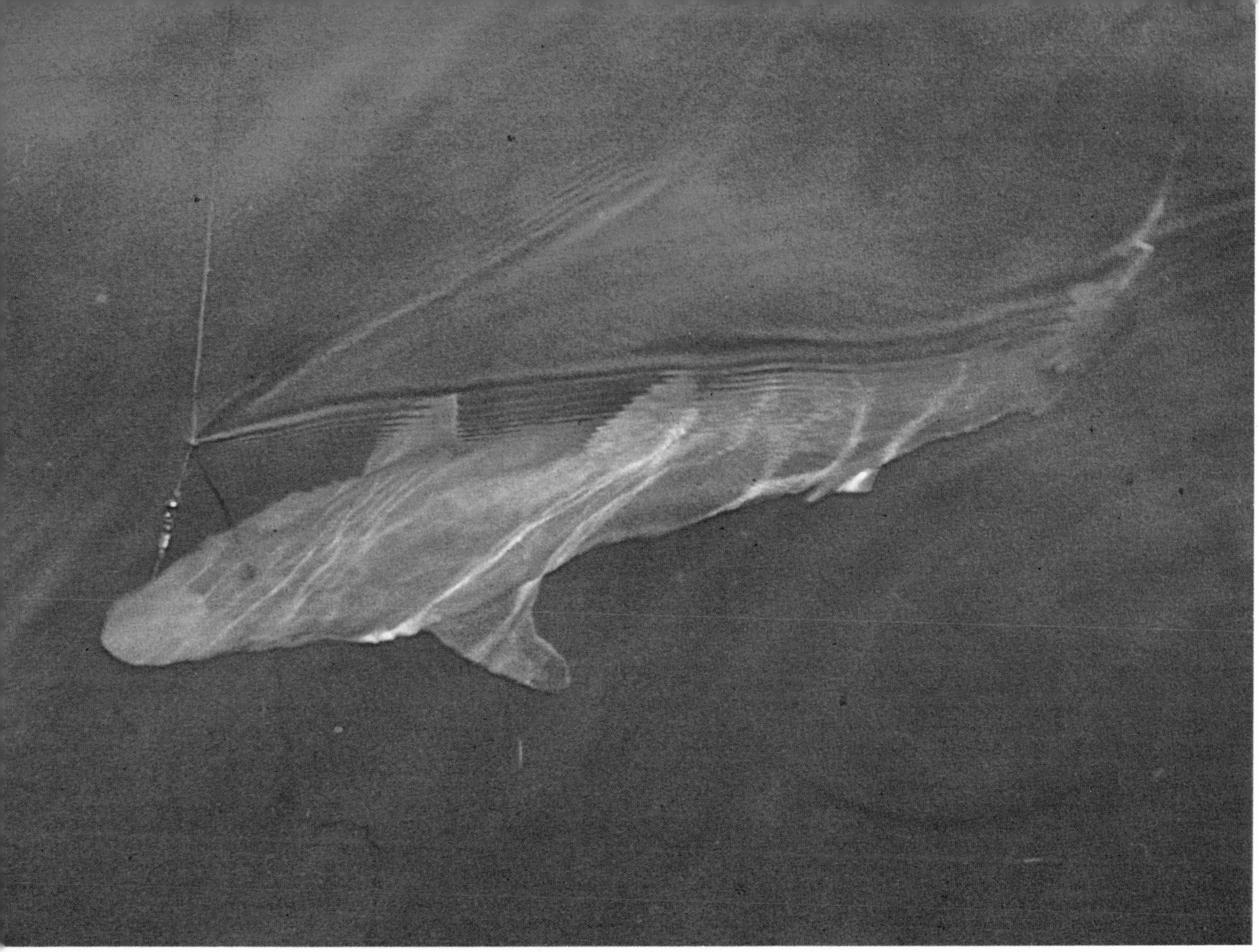

2

trace and line as it goes to establish the depth setting. I always go for 10 fathoms but for no particular reason except that it is part of my fishing ritual. Having measured the depth setting you will need a float. Anything that supports the bait and can be seen will do. Most anglers now use coloured party balloons. Use them if you must but don't over-inflate them – use just enough air to keep the bait supported and the float visible. There is a good reason for this. A full, huge, balloon will create a massive buoyancy and resistance to a fish that grabs the bait. The fish will attempt to pull the bait down in the water, will feel the unusual resistance to its attack and will probably let go. With the bait over the side and the float bobbing to your satisfaction, it must all be floated away from the boat. With say, 4 floats and baits out, 2 ought to be at least 40 yds from the boat and the remainder about 25 yds away. If they are all at the same distance the wind or drift can get them in a terrible tangle. Also, if one man gets a strike and a positive run from a fish his friends are duty bound to bring in their baits, giving him an unrestricted water in which to play his fish. Even with a fish running there is usually time to get the other tackle in board in order to avoid tangling the man with the fish. It is all a question of good fishing manners!

Not all blue sharks will come to a fixed pattern of attack. Sometimes a fin will be seen at a distance, moving lazily but purposefully up the rubby trail. The fish may veer off course, taking it out of the oil, but it will generally find its way back into the trail. As the blues get to the boat they often disappear below and beyond the fishing craft until realising that they are out of the stream of fishy particles dropping through the water. There seem to be two separate attack procedures. If the fish is a loner, it will tend to play with the suspended bait, often pulling it about with consequent visual signals to the anglers as the float bobs and jumps violently on the surface. The shark is in no hurry since it possibly suspects a mackerel that hangs in the stream. Often the fish can be induced to take the bait if the line is given a couple of sharp tugs which set the float and bait moving. Most predators will react to movement if they think that a potential meal is about to depart from them. Blue shark tend to hunt in a pack, driving bait fish into a frenzy of panic that causes them to ball up in the water, swimming round and round in an effort to escape. The sharks then tear into the mass of fish. I have seen this happen and it is a frightening sight. If a pack of blues come up a trail, with their appetites whetted by the smell and sight of blood, they will hit the anglers' baits hard. Because of the competition between fish to feed they appear to lose all sense of fear and suspicion. There can be situations where one fish will strike at a bait, then home in on another and take it before the first angler is aware that he has a run. When this activity happens shark fishing can mean a lot of action, curses, and lost tackle.

When you get the first indication of interest in your bait keep calm and do not attempt to throw the reel into gear. Keep the ratchet on check and the point of the rod tip in the direction of the run. This will prevent a possible over-run and keep the line pressure on the fish to the minimum. The shark will take off, holding the bait in its mouth. It may swim for 10 yds or a 100 yds. This distance depends on whether there is competition among the shark or on how large the shark is. I have found that the smaller sharks run the longest distances. When the initial run stops, throw the reel into gear and flip the ratchet off. Of course, you will have set the drag to a strike pressure that you are happy with. Raise the rod tip to about 45 degrees and wait for the fish to move again. Providing it has not dropped the bait, its second run will be slower now that the fish has the bait in its mouth. As the rod pulls over, strike firmly, taking the rod to an upright position. Two things happen on the strike. The angler takes the slack out of the line and the fish pulls against the tight trace, pulling the hook into the flesh of its mouth. If you delay striking you will possibly hook the fish way down in the gut, taking most of the fight out of the shark and ensuring its death. Far better to strike as soon as the second run begins, giving a hookhold, in the corner of the jaw, which is secure yet allows the removal of the hook and the fish to be set free.

BIG FISH IN THE AUTUMN

Autumn is a time of plenty both on the land and in the sea. As the sun warms the farmland earth, building body and substance into the crops, so the effect of the spring and summer sunshine produces its growth in the waters of the world. If anything, the cropping of the seas takes place a little later than on the land mass. Because of the gradual warming, over their expanse and through their depths, the seas take longer to warm and keep their temperature for a much longer period. Our seas are warmer in the months of September and October than at any other time of the year. These conditions are perfect for the quick growth that we find in most sea species.

Autumn is the time for big fish. They have moved in closer to the shore seeking rich feeding among the weeds and rocky areas of the littoral waters. A greater variety of fish, more than at any other time of the fishing year, becomes available to the angler. Traditional winter species, such as the cod and whiting, are approaching the coast while the sharks and other predators are still chasing the fish of summer that have yet to leave us. With the rich variety of species the angler has to bring the full choice of the angling armoury into play in order to take full advantage.

Let us go for the big fish first. Blue shark will still be with us providing the water stays warm and the mackerel shoals remain in good numbers. The porbeagle, a shark that inhabits our seas throughout the year, tends to be closer into the land. Both of these sharks can be fished for in the heat of summer but autumn brings something special to porbeagling. Most of the established fish areas for the species are over offshore reefs, particularly in association with holding ground for the pollack, which is a favourite bait. One known mark south of the Isle of Wight, over the St Catherine's Deeps, will have fish where there is no reef or heavily rocky ground, but this mark seems to be an exception to the rule. The porbeagle shark seems to favour the rich, saline waters of the south and west coasts of the British Isles. Some fish are regularly taken in the North Sea and off the northern islands of Scotland by professional boats so it may be that anglers ought to extend their activities to typical porbeagle ground that abounds in both areas. A number of halibut fishers, out from Caithness, have been badly smashed by huge fish and so have a number of people fishing in The Minch. By the descriptions of the angling method

1

and the way in which the fish fought, porbeagle have been hooked but not landed. One shark of the species was landed in Scotland by Dietrich Burkel fishing down the Mull of Galloway.

I have had the good fortune to fish for porbeagle in a lot of places over the past few years. Methods used varied widely and were an attempt to fix a pattern for catching this large shark. Off the Isle of Wight, fishing with Dave Adams – a great skipper from Hayling Island – traditional methods like using rubby dubby on the drift brought sharks to the boat, not the huge fish that Dick Downes has taken from these waters but fish up to 150 lbs and more. In such an open sea area one cannot pinpoint the fish easily. It becomes a matter of settling on a long drift and hoping that both sharks and mackerel shoals will come to the rubby stream. I much prefer fishing over a mark that is known to hold this shark in concentration. There are quite a few such marks. One or more in Galway Bay have produced a lot of fish for me and my fellow anglers. In that huge Bay, opening out to the Atlantic Ocean, there are substantial numbers of reef situations, especially around the Aran Islands that sit astride the entrance. It is argued by members of the Galway Bay Shark Angling Club that they are able to plot the path along which the sharks enter, swim around and leave the Bay. Certainly when Les Moncrieff and I fished with these chaps their theories proved correct and we caught large numbers of the species.

One sharking method we tried in Ireland for the first time has become standard practice along the Clare Coast. It is trolling. This involves choosing a path along which we troll deadbaits behind the boat. We found a place that was guaranteed to hold a number of sharks. There is a reef, rising from about 19 fathoms up to 9, below the Cliffs of Moher, which is south of Galway close to the little harbour of Liscannor. The reef cuts out sharp at right angles from the cliffs and the line of troll. After many fruitless hours searching and worrying we learned that the best method of fishing attack was to trail teasers, a dozen mackerel on a length of rope, behind the boat with hookbaits swimming either side and slightly ahead of the teaser fish. Of course, no rubby was used because the boat was continually moving up and down below the cliffs covering the available ground. At times we did put a little chum – cut up pieces of fish – over the side to interest any shark or other reef dwelling fish into a feeding behaviour. American anglers use chum regularly when attracting or seeking to hold predatory fish in a confined area.

The porbeagle, living on the reef or close to it, would be accustomed to rising from the base of the rocks up to the pinnacle tips to feed on the pollack and bream that we had found to be living there. Our idea was that the trolled baits, together with the teasers, would be motored across the reef tip at a couple of knots which would give predators sufficient time to see the baits and attack them but not so much of a clear view that they could interpret them as false fish with a doubtful swimming fashion. The tackle was reasonably simple – 50 lb class rods and reels with around 500 yds of line on each reel. There must always be enough line and

2

3

4

1 *John Holden into a porbeagle shark off St Catherine's Head. This Isle of Wight shark ground is producing good fish each season although the average size appears to be dropping.*

2 *Skipper, Dave Adams, and Holden have this shark neatly gaffed. Now comes the back-breaking task of getting it inboard.*

3 *A strong gaff is vitally necessary for this operation. Bigger fish demand the use of a tailing rope, used in conjunction with the gaff.*

4 *A good porbeagle of 110 lbs. It will be cut up and eaten. John kills very few of his sharks, preferring to tag and release them with the minimum of stress to the fish.*

the power and fighting qualities of this species must never be underestimated. Often the only insurance one has is the amount of line on the reel when a big porgy decides to go. The cable-laid, steel traces were slightly different from the normal shark end tackle: made in two sections from 150 lb wire, joined by quality big-game swivels and carrying a drilled-through 6 oz casting lead at the point where the hook mount joins. The reason for this is that a trolled bait must travel just below the surface and the speed of the angling boat will tend to skip an un-leaded bait across the waves. Both Les Moncrieff and I like to mount our baits on articulated, stiff-wire flights to avoid the risk of a really big fish biting clean through the flexible wire section. Also, a stiff-wire mount with hook at one end and quick release swivel at the other can be neatly sewn inside a bait fish to give a hidden hook presentation and a natural appearance. The articulated mount will give any fishbait a waving motion in the water, especially if the backbone is removed before sewing it around the mount. Copper wire is useful to fasten up the slit belly and remember to sew up the mouth of the bait neatly around the head of the mount. This will prevent water getting into the fish, causing pressure that will tear it from the wire or throw it off course.

Contrary to standard practice, after feeding out the baits, the reels are not put on the ratchet and out of gear. Trolling will mean that your shark will hit the bait hard, generally turning down as it takes the offering into its mouth. There is no need to wait for the usual shark run to develop – it has already developed! The set-up is to set a light strike drag, about 10 or 12 lbs, and hold the rod with the tip above head height. As a fish takes the bait you will get an immediate pull down on the tip which is generally enough to set the hook into the fish as both strike drag and the amount of line out in the water combine to put pressure on the fish which is diving against the pull angle of both. If the clutch setting is too strong the fish will easily break the line on its first rush and too slight a clutch drag could result in a massive over-run. Yes, you can get an over-run on a boat fishing multiplier!

Just a word about the line on the reel. It is best to use braided Dacron or other similar line that has little stretch so that subtle movements or a quick change in direction of the fight can be quickly recognised by the fisherman. When loading the braided line onto the reel, pack it on as hard and tightly as you can. A loosely filled reel will give terrible problems if the line is torn off, under great pressure and speed, for it will pull

NORWAY HADDOCK

Sebastes viviparus

A northern species of the rocky ground that does venture into fairly shallow waters. The Norway haddock is in no way related to the true haddock, which is a member of the cod family. The young are released alive as minute fry during the warm months of the year. A fish of $1\frac{1}{2}$ lbs is a good specimen.

Bait: *Fish strip and small shellfish.*

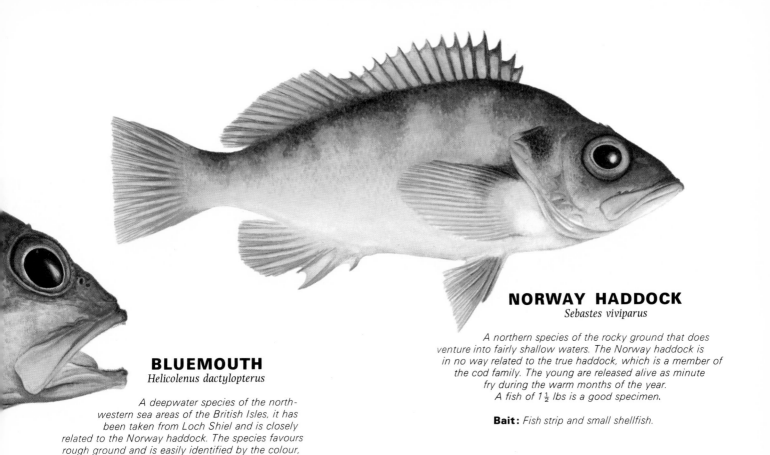

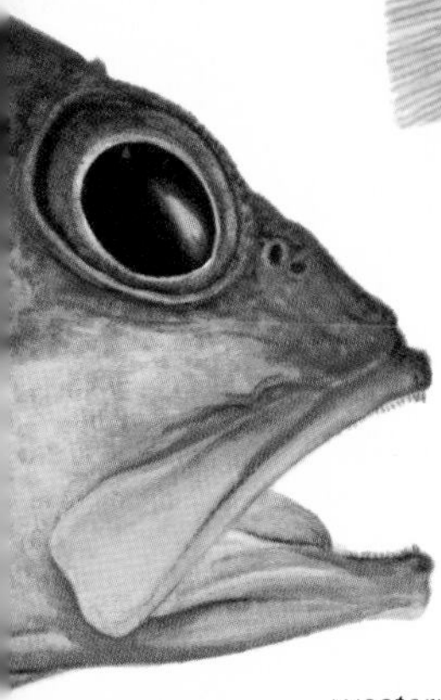

BLUEMOUTH

Helicolenus dactylopterus

A deepwater species of the north-western sea areas of the British Isles, it has been taken from Loch Shiel and is closely related to the Norway haddock. The species favours rough ground and is easily identified by the colour, a vivid blue, inside the fish's mouth. 2–3 lbs seems to be the average size of fish caught.

Bait: *Fishbaits.*

the line down through the loose coils where it gets buried and can jam the line, leading to a break. I often run the line out behind the boat as we steam from harbour to fishing mark, winding the line back onto the reel against the speed of the boat. This is enough to pack the line down hard.

To begin with, troll the baits at 50 yds behind the boat with the teasers fairly close to the hookbaits. If there is a sign of a fin, get the crew to wind the teasers into a position ahead of the hookbaits. This will mean that any shark following the boat will come on the noise and slap of your teaser fish as they splatter across the wake. There will be both a visual and a sound signal to a predator suggesting that a shoal of small fish are trying to escape from trouble. Shark will hear and see the baits and perhaps go for the hookbait. Don't leave the teasers out for the fish to get a hookless feed or to get them tangled in the angler's lines.

I said that you might see a fin cutting its way through the surface film. This has happened to me many times when fishing the Moher grounds. It is not normal to find porbeagle on the surface: this is more typical of the behaviour of the blue and thresher sharks, but the angling technique brings them up from the top of the reefs. I have never found that the sound and vibration of the screws and engine put the fish off striking a bait. Possibly predatory fish are tuned in to surface disturbance indicating a shoal of fleeing fish or perhaps their greed overcomes any natural suspicion of surface vibration. I well remember the first porbeagle shark that I saw caught by trolling methods. It came to Leslie's bait, showing as a black knife-like projection nosing through the water at least 50 yds behind our trailed mackerel. Kevin Linnane, who was skippering the craft, moved like lightning to haul the teasers ahead of the baited lines. The shark came up fast behind the bait, swerved off to the side, turned and cut into the mackerel at an acute angle and took it. Neither Les Moncrieff nor I were sure, at that time, how we ought to react so Les let the fish pull the rod over in a tight arc with the line running smoothly from the reel. When the shark slowed and stopped, Les struck back hard with the rod and everything went slack. I'll never forget the look on Leslie's face. He wound the bait in to find that it was almost shredded to nothing with deep gouges across the body of the mackerel. Something was wrong with the bait presentation – but what?

It seemed that the fish was struck too soon but we needed to strike early because the intention on this ▶160

RED GURNARD
Aspitrigla cuculus

A western waters species having a lateral line that is only really noticeable on partially dried out specimens as a series of fine vertical lines. The species grows to 3–4 lbs.

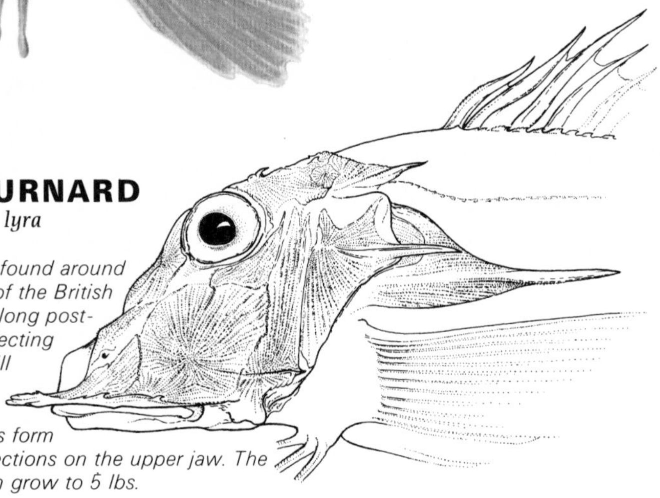

PIPER GURNARD
Trigla lyra

A deepwater species found around the western coasts of the British Isles. It has extremely long post-opercular spines projecting backwards from the gill cases above the pectoral fins. A series of connected spines form long forward projections on the upper jaw. The piper gurnard can grow to 5 lbs.

Bait: *All gurnards will take a wide variety of baits, including marine worms, crustaceans and shellfish. Fish bait will also lure the gurnard family.*

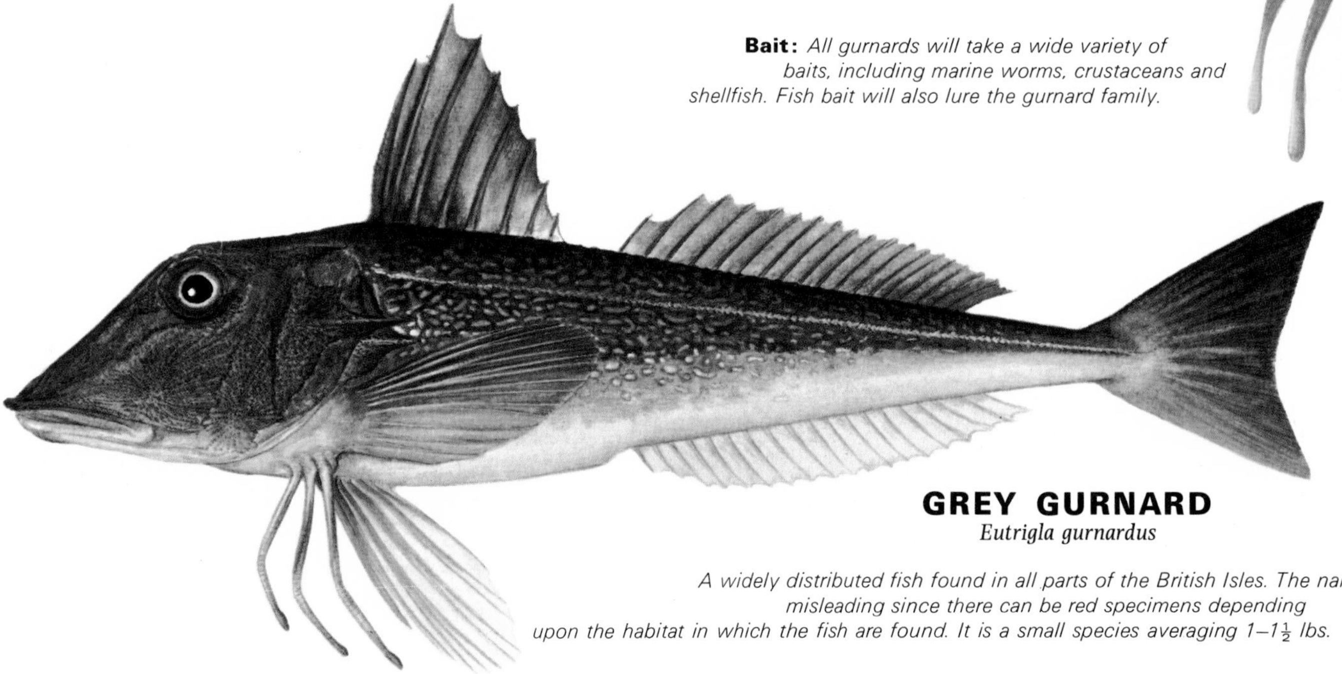

GREY GURNARD
Eutrigla gurnardus

A widely distributed fish found in all parts of the British Isles. The name is misleading since there can be red specimens depending upon the habitat in which the fish are found. It is a small species averaging 1–1½ lbs.

STREAKED GURNARD

Trigloporus lastoviza

Has a far wider distribution than angling accounts would suggest. The species is often confused with both the red and tub species but is unmistakable for it has a blunt head shape. The streaking is always described, for identification purposes, as yellow and blue lines on the pectoral fins. But the fish is more readily separated from other gurnards by the clearly defined streaks or vertical lines on the body of the fish. It grows to about 3–4 lbs in weight.

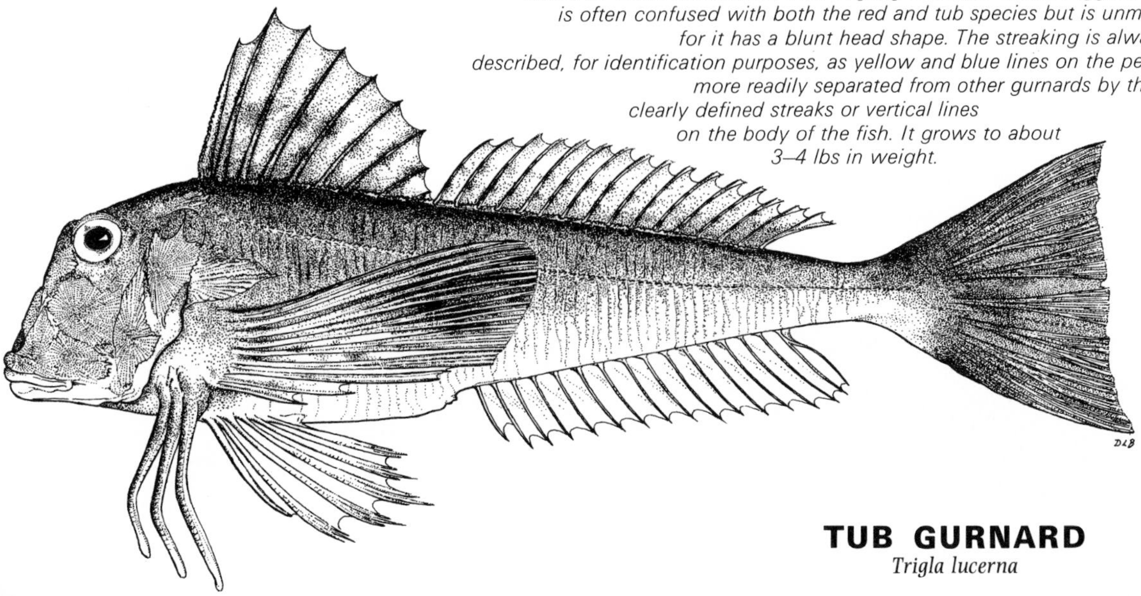

TUB GURNARD

Trigla lucerna

Distributed throughout the Eastern Atlantic and the Mediterranean Sea, this fish is the largest of the gurnards and is immediately recognized, from other species, by the weal-like lateral line.

LANTERN GURNARD

Aspitrigla obscura

A deepwater fish that can be regarded as an angling rarity in British waters. Usually red in colour, it can be distinguished by the lateral line which is made up of a series of large scales. The lantern gurnard grows to 2–3 lbs.

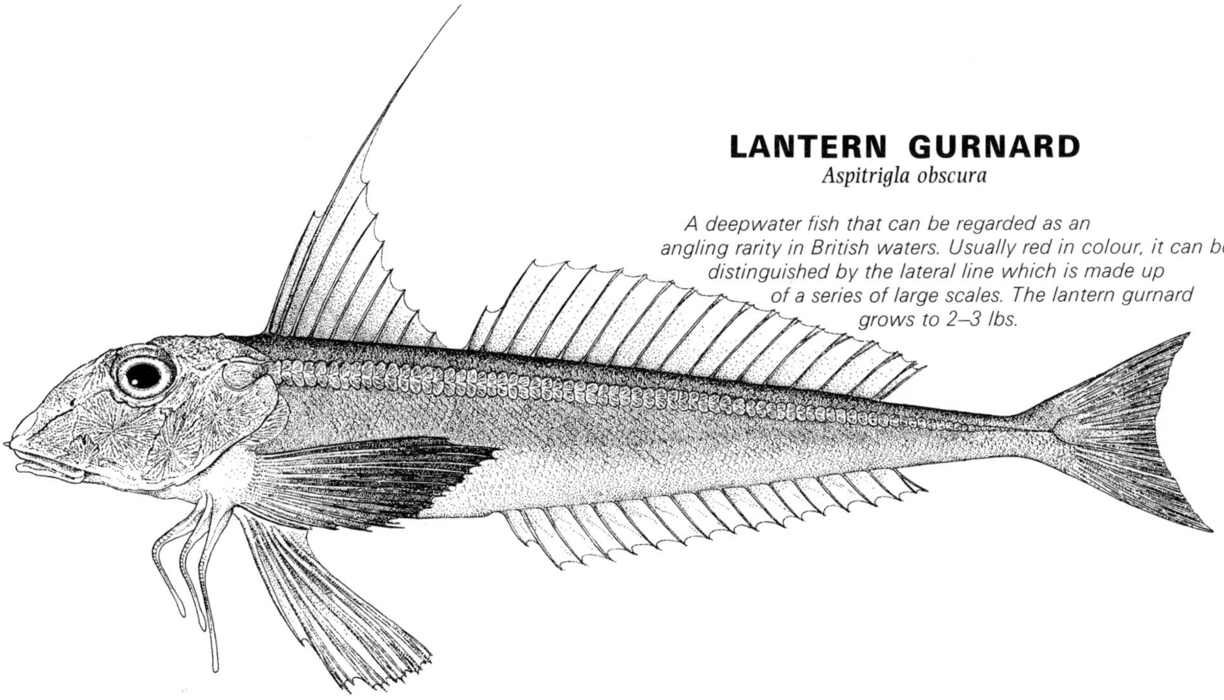

LONG-SPINED SEA SCORPION

Taurulus bubalis

A fairly common species found around Britain but favouring deeper water with a rocky, broken ground. Grows to a heavier weight than the short-spined species but rarely exceeds a foot in length.

Bait: *As for the near relative.*

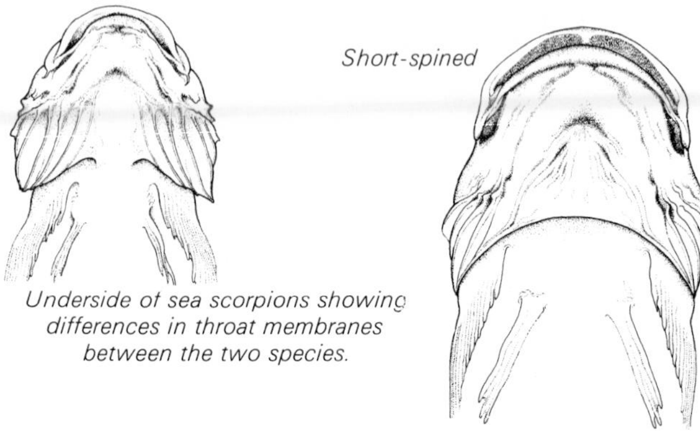

Underside of sea scorpions showing differences in throat membranes between the two species.

157◄ trip was to land the fish with the minimum of mouth damage, then tag the fish with a numbered disc and return it to the water. Kevin needed a lot of fish tagged for a population census and a study by the Irish Inland Fisheries Trust on the migratory habits of this superb shark. If we let the fish gorge the bait this would make the hook hard to recover and possibly cause the shark to suffer and die after release. Something was wrong with the hook mounting or its position within the bait. Then we realised the hook was sewn between the sides of flesh rather like a sandwich. If the fish grabbed the bait across the body any pull on the line would tend to jerk the hook out from the flat slippery halves of hookbait before it took an adequate hold within the shark's jaw. Somebody suggested a two-hook tandem rig but this tackle was discounted on the basis that it could still be pulled sideways from the fish. Then the answer came to us – a double hook in the bait, similar to the kind some sea trout fishers use when tying flies.

Now, Mustad Seamasters are darned good big-game hooks but they don't come as doubles. What we did was to have a garage braze two hooks together at right angles. When mounted into a bait they immediately improved the way in which the bait swam because the hooks, with the added weight, acted rather like a keel keeping the mackerel swimming perfectly upright. This system proved to be an infinite improvement when trolled out on my second try for the porbeagle. The bait was taken straight away. The shark hit the bait, stopped it hard and as the rod pulled over to the pressure the fish dived down toward the safety of the reef. I struck into the fish and had the satisfying heaviness of a good fish thumping on the line. We stopped the boat's forward travel as quickly as possible to take any unnecessary strain off the 50 lb line. The fight followed a pattern similar to preceding battles with porbeagle in Galway Bay and off the south coast of England.

The fish bore down, without pausing, from its attack on the hookbait. So often porbeagle dive, taking the bait and reel line straight to the bottom and this powerful run puts an immense strain on the reel line, for not only do we have to consider the amount of drag against the fish but also, and more importantly, the length of line between rod tip and fish that is being dragged in a curve that is cutting through the tide. It is this belly of line that is liable to break under stress if the least interference is made to clutch setting or to the even flow of the line off the reel. At such a time anything that smooths the passage of line off the reel, such as freely running roller rings and a clutch that lets the reel give line without releasing it in a wild series of jerks must help to defeat our large species on sensible breaking strains. It is not only the shark family that can put your tackle under stress, for the halibut, common skate, tope and big conger are all capable of powerful, speedy, movements that place critical strains on the angler's gear.

I fought that shark up to the boat where Leslie efficiently tailed it to allow Kevin and me to lift it into the boat. The hookhold was as we wanted it, right in the scissors as the trout fisher would say. The slightest

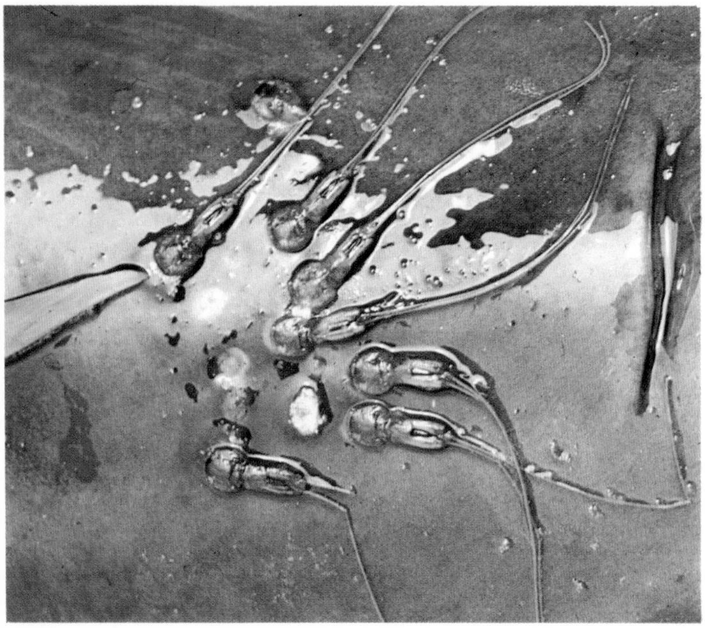

Most creatures, whether human or otherwise, have parasites that attach themselves to the host. These minute parasites are a form of sea louse that prey upon the porbeagle and other sharks. Called Lepeophtheirus sp. *they are found on the skin forward and at the base of the tail.*

SHORT-SPINED SEA SCORPION

Myoxocephalus scorpios

A fish of the northern waters common around the British Isles. Highly colourful with considerable variation between specimens. Often called Father Lasher, it can attain a length of 12 ins or more although a fish of 6–7 ins is an average size. When landed, the sea scorpion seems to blow up the area around its throat as if to emit a warning sound.

Bait: *Almost any of the conventional baits will be taken.*

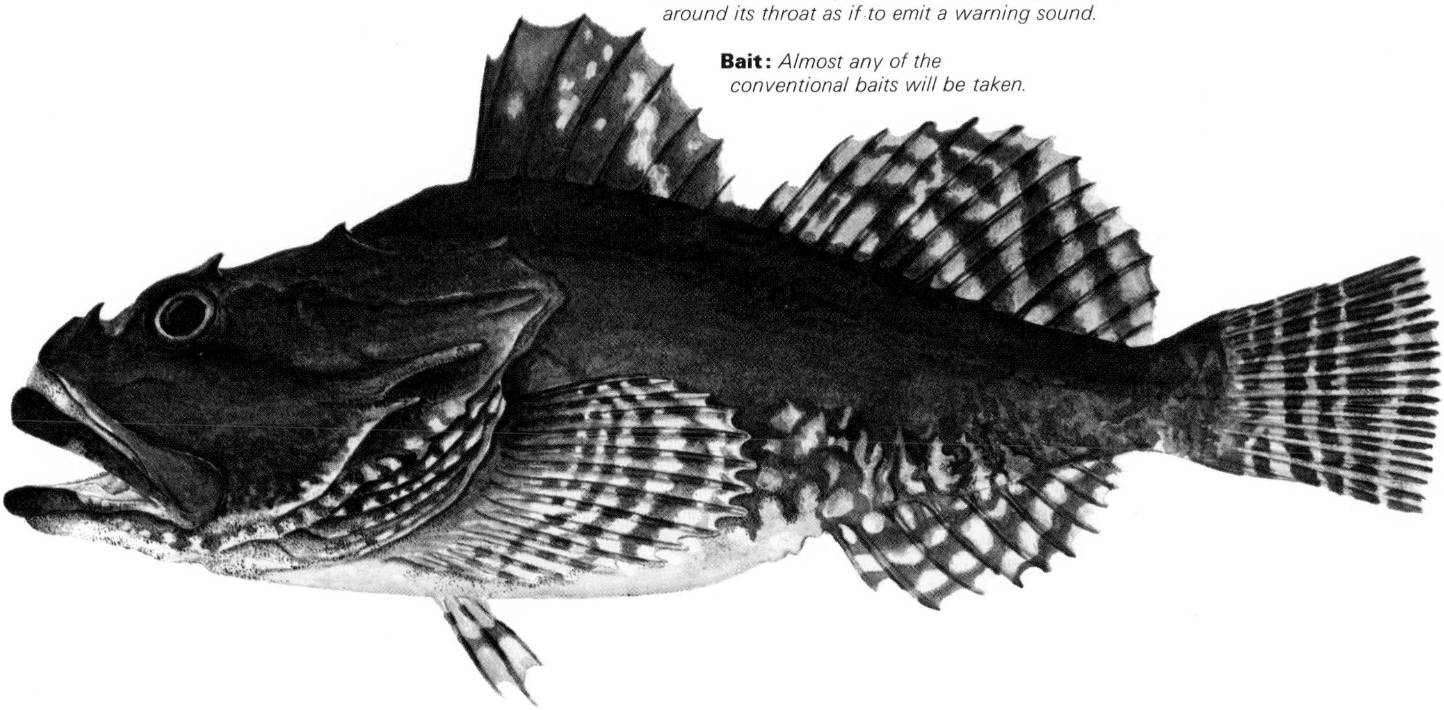

nick with a filleting knife and the hook came free. If you feel that your large fish, after providing fine sport, deserve to have their liberty it becomes vitally necessary that the boating and un-hooking procedure should cause the smallest degree of stress and injury. Obviously no gaff can be used to land the fish. It is far better to construct a tailing rope and to become proficient in the use of it. This gear is only a lassoo of 1 inch thick rope, with a free-running loop at one end. The idea is that during the latter stages of a battle with a fish, such as a shark, the loop is laid out on the deck around the angler's body. As the wire trace is brought to the surface and the fish is seen to be beaten the loop is taken up over the angler and along the rod. It is then dropped down around the trace, over the fish's head, to be drawn tight behind the dorsal fin. The loop will not slip down the body beyond the tail. As soon as the tail of a large shark is tethered the fish is immobilized. One precaution must be taken. Tie the end of the tailing rope, using a clove hitch, around a handy bollard. If a large fish does take off it could so very easily drag you over the side!

When we consider the vast quantities of sharks, skate and tope that are landed during a fishing year the question we must ask is are we, as supposed sportsmen, justified in bringing them ashore? We all like to photograph the fish with ourselves *in situ* but isn't this slightly selfish? The sea is not a horn of plenty, there are not never-ending supplies of fish for us to kill. I am aware that sharks, tope and dogfish are predators on the panfish and have to kill to live themselves. Personally, I feel it is much better to get your sport from fish and then return them to grow larger and perhaps provide sport for someone else on a future occasion.

Autumn is also a time for experimenting with both rigs and artificial lures. With the competition for food, fish are not as selective in their feeding habits as they become later on in the colder months. Some marine species follow the feeding pattern of the freshwater fish as the seas cool; that is, they eat less, are lethargic and have to be tempted into taking a bait. Pirks, baits in rubber and plastic, anything that can be made to work with a lifelike action will bring fish. A combination of both natural bait and the artificial, like the baited feather, is a grand lure. The feather simulates the small fry while the fish strip or worm will give that degree of taste and smell that makes your offering attractive. In shallow water, the baited spoon fluttered across the open sand is a killing system. Dabs and other flats fall to this method. Although a relatively small species, the dab can put up a tremendous struggle on tackle scaled down to their size. I remember finding a dab factory in the west of Ireland. It was in Keem Bay, Achill Island. Apparently one of the local industries was the harpooning of basking sharks. The livers were removed from these huge, plankton-feeding sharks to be rendered down for the fine quality oil they give. The problem then was what to do with the carcasses since they gave off a most noxious smell that could be detected miles away. Tourism is another industry for the Achill Islanders, so they got the idea of removing the smell by towing the carcasses out to the deep water off Keem Bay. This all happened in the month of May. When I arrived in Co. Mayo later in the year both immature turbot and huge dabs had found the heaps of flesh lying on the sea bed and were enjoying a magnificent meal. Fishing in the area with strips of mackerel or lugworm, locally dug, saw us catching vast quantities of both species. On one occasion I and two friends were able to feed everybody staying at the hotel with dabs that literally covered their dinner plates.

The coalfish, a close relative of the pollack, is a fish of the autumn months. It arrives well offshore around the end of May but moves into the reefs in September. Tackle for this species can be similar to the tackle we use for the pollack, reef cod, and ling. I like a single-hook paternoster fished with a rotten bottom, a weak link of nylon that will allow me to break the tackle out of the rock should the lead go foul. The species favours heavily-broken ground, so you can expect to lose some gear. The coalie is a big fish. Many huge specimens are taken each year from the wreck marks but, unlike the pollack, the coalie gives an initial smashing take and dive that can catch the angler unawares. Once it is fought up a few fathoms the pressure change takes effect and the fish becomes just a heavy weight on the line. To get the best out of the species the ideal fishing situation is to take them over the top of a reef that rises up out of deep water. The slight depth of water over the rock mass does not produce such a marked effect on their fighting performance and the fish will most often make frantic dashes into the security of the reef, which all adds up to increased sport for the fisher.

Large coalfish prefer fish baits or artificial lures that look like a fish. The smaller specimens – the ones that provide small boys with pierside angling – will take both worms and spinners. These fish, often called billet, are great fun when fishing with a spinning rod and they can be caught in most parts of our islands although they are of more northerly distribution than the pollack. There seems always to be confusion between these species. Identification is simple. The coalfish is almost black on the upper parts and possesses a straight, white lateral line along the flanks, whereas the pollack varies in colour from a rich, golden browny-green to red, with tinges of green. Its lateral line is curved over the pectoral fins and is dark in colouration. There is also a pronounced extension of the bottom jaw. Much is made of the barbule, seen on some coalfish, as an identifying feature but more often than not this barbule is so rudimentary that it is difficult to see.

Two other sea angler's species cause frequent problems in identification. The mistakes made are more of name than of actual fish because the monkfish and angler fish are totally dissimilar in appearance. Unfortunately, in many parts of the British Isles the monkfish is called angelfish, although nothing less like an angel could be imagined. The monk is a composite creature, half skate and half shark to look at. It belongs to that group of fish that have bodies with no real bones. Their skeletal structure is composed of gristle, whereas the angler fish, so named because it carries on the head its own fishing lure and line, is a true bony fish. Neither of them can be expected to put up much of a battle when hooked. The angler is not fished for deliberately but is taken when general fishing with a legered bait over sand or mud bottom. The monkfish is sought by some anglers but the fun is often in seeking the fish in shallow water where it can be seen lying on the sea bed. Westport, in Co. Mayo, has a particular mark where monks can be seen easily. The bait, usually a fish strip on a wired trace, is lowered down to a marked quarry, tempting the big

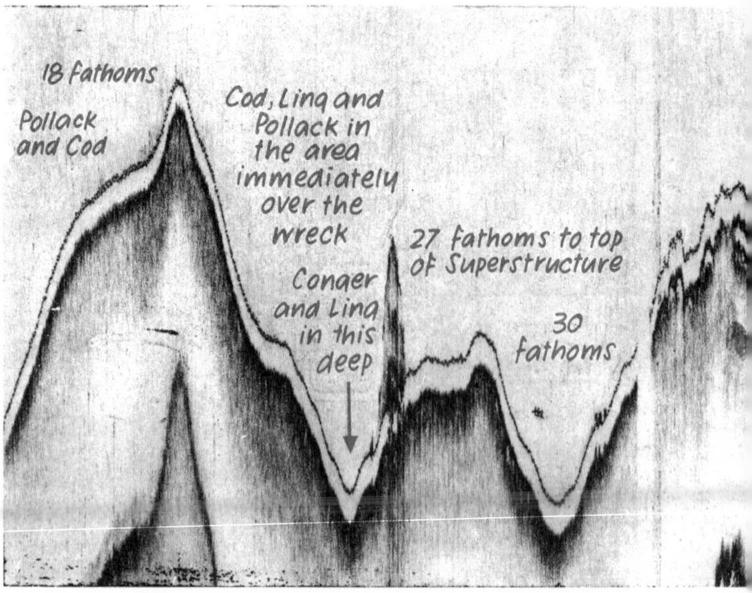

A portion of echo-sounder chart showing the position of a wreck in deepwater. The hulk lies between the peaks of fairly steep underwater hills. A softer image is produced from the weed and animals growing on the metal.

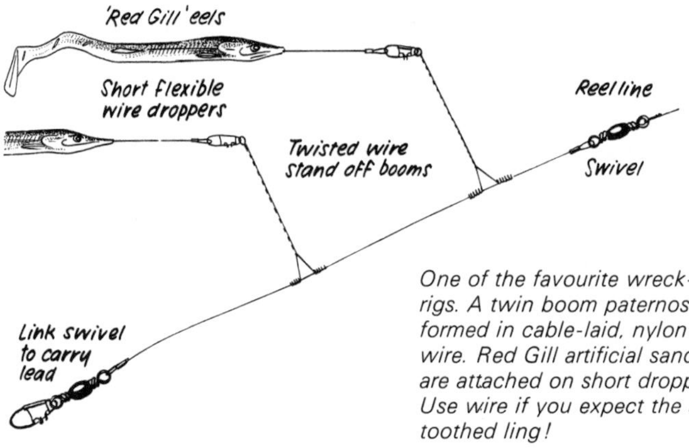

One of the favourite wreck-fishing rigs. A twin boom paternoster, formed in cable-laid, nylon coated wire. Red Gill artificial sandeels are attached on short droppers. Use wire if you expect the sharp-toothed ling!

LIGHT TACKLE TACTICS

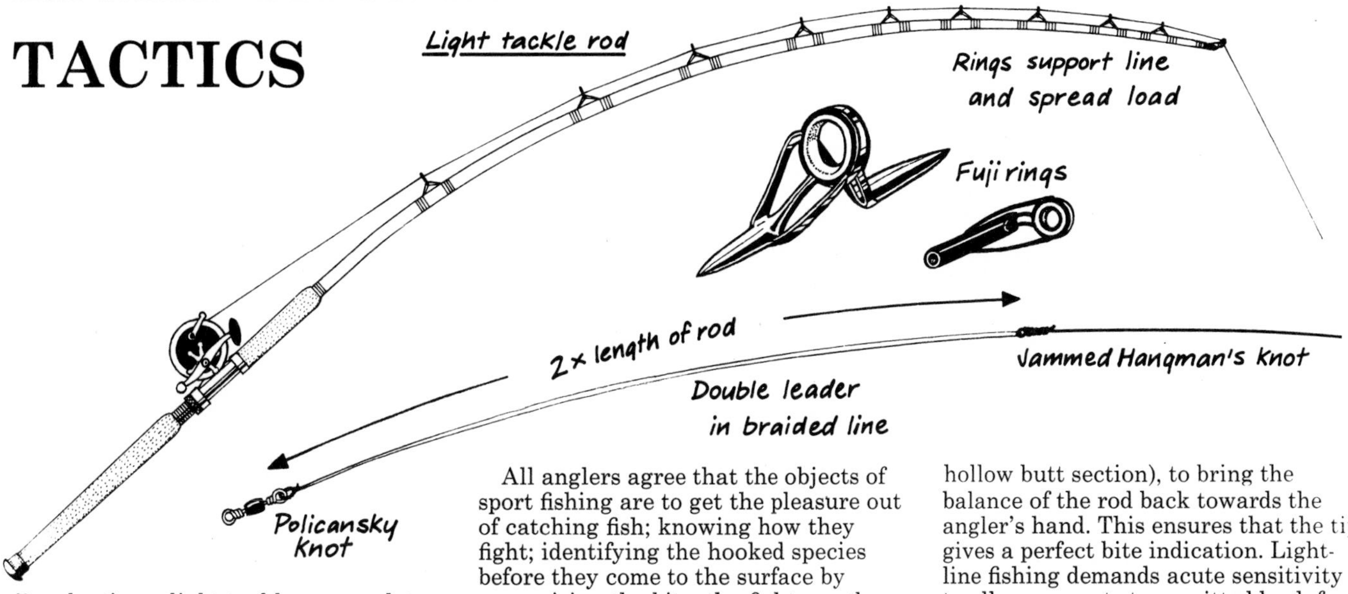

By adopting a light tackle approach to boat fishing the angler receives two distinct advantages: he will hook more fish and experience greater satisfaction from those that he does hook. Fining terminal rigs down, as well as adopting delicate baiting methods, will bring more fish to the baited hook. The seabed and the midwater areas can be searched with tackle that reacts to the slightest tweak from a fastidiously feeding fish.

The light-tackle style of sea angling has brought me back to braided lines, certainly for 12 and 20 lb class fishing. The almost total lack of stretch in braided line enables accurate detection of any movement of the lead or pluck at the hookbait. In these breaking strains, nylon has too much stretch to give such an indication and its spring absorbs the power of a strike. On the other hand, braided line transmits the strike positively.

All anglers agree that the objects of sport fishing are to get the pleasure out of catching fish; knowing how they fight; identifying the hooked species before they come to the surface by recognizing the bite; the fights on the initial hooking, and how the battle develops.

All these things are only really possible when the tackle allows fish to show their fighting ability. Light-tackle rods tend to be a little longer than the standard boat rod. The extra length, say a rod of about 7–8 ft, gives a greater safety margin when playing the really huge fish that at any time can come to us. This longer rod adds to the control of the fish thrashing around on the surface, enabling the angler to keep the fight farther away from the side of the boat, where a rough hull can quickly wear through a fine line.

Light-tackle rods of 7–8 ft should have at least eight rings. The line needs the support given as well as the even distribution of the playing pressure along the useful power section of the rod blank. It is a good idea to add weight (easly done with lead slugs in a hollow butt section), to bring the balance of the rod back towards the angler's hand. This ensures that the tip gives a perfect bite indication. Light-line fishing demands acute sensitivity to all movements transmitted back from the seabed, via the rod, to the angler's brain.

Knots must be perfectly tied. The correct knot is vital and a minimum number of them will ensure that the breaking strain of the reel line and terminal rig is kept close to the manufacturer's stated figure. Use booms and other sliding weight links that do not chafe the line. The hook is the most important connection between rod and fish. It must be fine in the wire, strong, and possess a low-cut barb that can be sunk into a bony jaw without excessive force. I like Aberdeen hooks for 12 lb class for they take a good hold and have a definite spring in the shank that gives a safety margin when the fishing is close to the line's breaking strain limit.

And remember that attention to fine detail must be the creed of the light tackle angler.

specimen into taking the bait. Once hooked there can be a ponderous weight on the line but no real excitement from the fight. Cynics have likened monk fishing to hauling up wet sacks of cement.

The same type of open but broken ground, in shallow or deep water, can produce yet another big but dull-fighting fish, the bull huss or greater-spotted dogfish. This dogfish, which grows much larger than the lesser-spotted variety, will accept almost any bait, with perhaps a slight preference for fish strips. Its size, nasal flap conformation and colouring will enable you to identify the species. Dogfish worry anglers' baits. They have the habit of tearing at a bait but not taking it in a positive manner and so are regarded as a nuisance fish. Another problem is that the bull huss has a rather hard mouth that is difficult to set a hook into. Many times I have hooked a huss then played it to the boat's side only to have the fish release its hold on the bait and disappear down into the murk. In fact, the fish had the slightest hold on the bait but would not let go, allowing itself to be brought up. Spurdogs, a reasonably close relative to the hounds, will also do this although they have such a voracious appetite that they normally hit the bait hard and hook themselves. Spurdog will often swim up through the water accompanying a hooked fish of their own species. Whether this is because they are inherently nosey or perhaps think that the hooked fish has some food they could share, I do not know. Tope, on the other hand, will follow hooked fish to the boat on the chance that they can steal the tethered species for themselves. Attracted by the angler's baits, they often lie in wait below the boat to strike at the fish as it nears the surface. It is wise to change to wired traces and slightly larger hook sizes if you suspect the presence of either species, to account for the sharp teeth and incredibly rough skins of these fish that can so easily cut through a normal rig made up of nylon.

At this time of our sea angling season fish will be shoaling up in preparation for moving out to winter feeding grounds. Because of the numbers of species that make up a group, their food intake requirements will keep them busy, constantly moving and searching the ground. Open ground can be covered effectively by fishing on the drift, stopping to anchor when concentrations of fish seem likely. The established reefs and wreck marks can be either anchored to or drifted over. If you anchor, use a grapnel of mild steel. These devices are a lot easier to break out from the rocks since the prongs will straighten and they are definitely a good deal cheaper to provide than an anchor. One system is to drop the grapnel with a buoy attached to it, on another light rope. If the direct pull out does not succeed in recovering the hook it can then be left for later recovery by a working boat that has stronger lifting gear.

On the open ground angling is a matter of fishing an expanse of sea bed both in length, along the coast, and breadth out from the shore. As you find fish, note your position by taking cross bearings from prominent features ashore. On the rocks and other holding marks you will fish in depth. Different species are found as the bait is progressively lowered but this can vary with the time of day and season. There is a vertical migration of many fish species, notably pollack and coalfish, during each 24-hour light cycle. As the sun leaves the water toward late evening, plankton animals rise toward the surface. They are followed by the small fish and fry of the year who feed on this ultra-rich harvest.

The larger species will follow both the minute creatures of the plankton and the small fry to get their meal. This vertical movement of fish has been recognised by anglers and commercial fishermen for centuries. Often termed suicide hour in the case of the pollack, it is a fact that the best of the fishing happens as the sun goes down and immediately after. During the early dawn the plankton will begin to sink and we can expect our angling species to follow the microscopic organisms in their behaviour. The conger eel is also said to exhibit this vertical rise, although I have never seen it happen with eels.

The only other big fish that comes to the surface regularly, and is caught because of doing so, must be the broadbill swordfish. In semi-tropical waters, around the entrance to the Mediterranean, commercial longliners always fish at night for the broadbill just below the surface. During the day it is caught at depths around 90 fathoms or so. Autumn brings the sea and weather conditions for safe night fishing so perhaps we followers of rod and line sport ought to extend our activities to this monster fish.

▶174

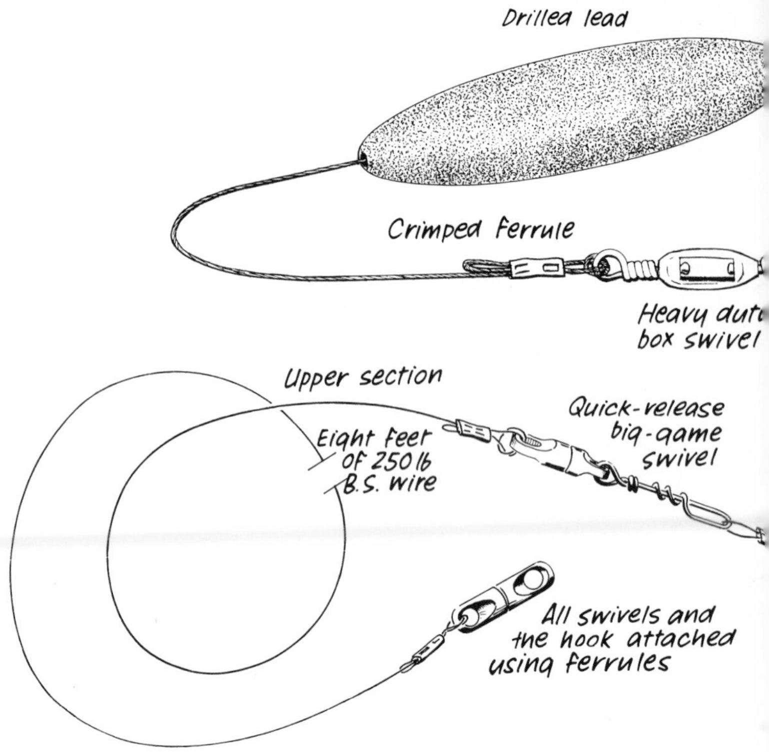

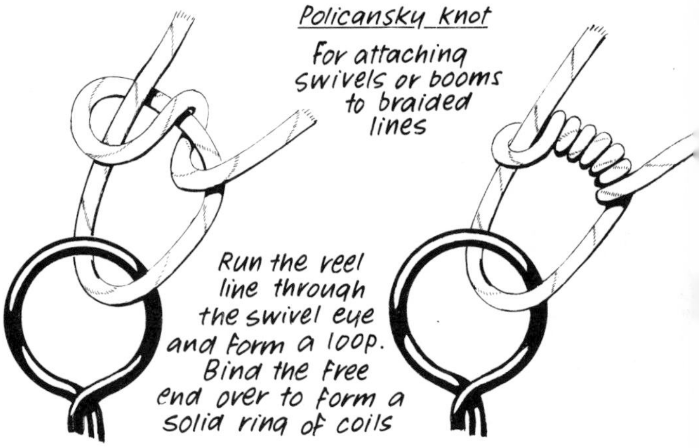

Policansky knot
For attaching swivels or booms to braided lines
Run the reel line through the swivel eye and form a loop. Bind the free end over to form a solid ring of coils

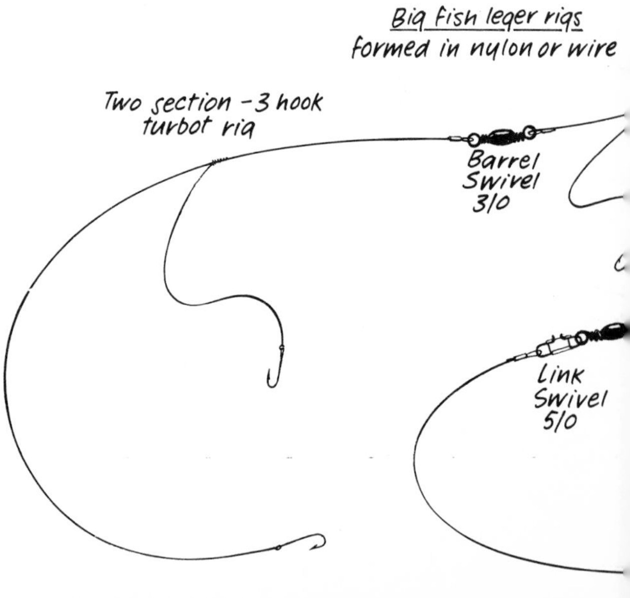

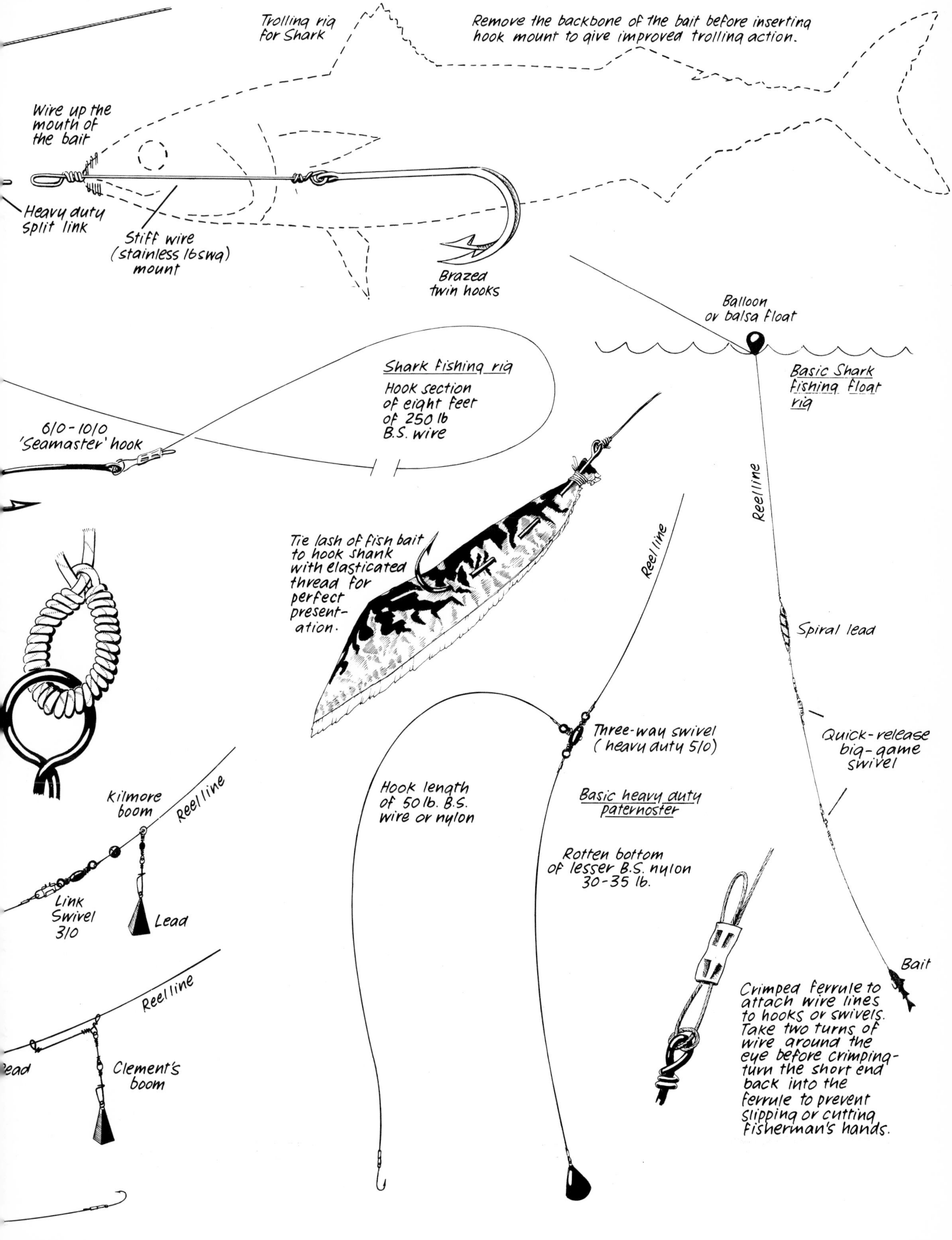

Trolling rig for Shark
Remove the backbone of the bait before inserting hook mount to give improved trolling action.
Wire up the mouth of the bait
Heavy duty split link
Stiff wire (stainless 16swg) mount
Brazed twin hooks
Balloon or balsa float
Shark fishing rig
Hook section of eight feet of 250 lb B.S. wire
Basic Shark fishing float rig
6/0 - 10/0 'Seamaster' hook
Reel line
Reel line
Tie lash of fish bait to hook shank with elasticated thread for perfect presentation.
Spiral lead
Three-way swivel (heavy duty 5/0)
Quick-release big-game swivel
Kilmore boom
Reel line
Hook length of 50 lb. B.S. wire or nylon
Basic heavy duty paternoster
Rotten bottom of lesser B.S. nylon 30-35 lb.
Link Swivel 3/0
Lead
Reel line
Bait
Crimped ferrule to attach wire lines to hooks or swivels. Take two turns of wire around the eye before crimping-turn the short end back into the ferrule to prevent slipping or cutting fisherman's hands.
ead
Clement's boom

John Holden / Sea angling from shingle, strand anc

Lead and baits whip into the sky. You concentrate on the reel: spray drifts from the spool as wet line tears off. A stray coil flickers up and your thumb dabs it smooth. Three, four seconds elapse before the lead splashes down. One hundred and fifty yards of nylon glisten in a high arch which sinks to the sea. Now the baits lie 120 yds offshore where the fish are bigger.

So much has been said about casting from the shore that we have probably forgotten the real issues. Casting is not the Black Art which some authorities imply. It is a skill, and like all skills is the product of knowledge, practice and natural flair.

Today, many anglers seem to consider 200 yds a practical beachfishing range. Ten years ago the magic figure was half that. But now, as then, the average standard of shorecasting is atrocious. Despite the new tackle and techniques, very few anglers cast 80 yds. Perhaps one in ten reaches 100 yds. Not one man in a thousand has seen a 150 yd cast, much less done one.

LONG CASTING

It is true that a 200 yd cast is nothing special on the tournament field, where the current British records exceed 220 yds. However, we cannot judge fishing distances by competition results. One hundred to 140 yds is still a realistically long distance beach cast.

Used without thought, long casting is as restrictive as dunking baits at your feet. How far to cast is the measure of your appreciation of a particular fishing situation; when the fish are close in, you lob the baits out and if they are running far out, you cast hard. Rarely, you will overcast, but winding in is easier than struggling for a few extra yards if the fish are just beyond reach.

Not being able to cast is tragic; it spoils your chances on nine beaches out of ten. For instance, most cod and whiting beaches demand very long casts especially in calm daylight seas. At night, in rough water, fish do venture close but it does not follow that the poor caster can then manage. If you cast 80 yds at best, an onshore gale might cut you down 40 yds. So if the fish are 60 yds from the beach you still drop short. By contrast, if you normally cast 120 yds you can sacrifice 60 and comfortably cast to where they shoal.

Good casting is no more than common sense. It is a simple physical exercise, not an athletic or intellectual performance. Most anglers cannot cast because they are too lazy to learn. If your lead falls short, the answer is literally in your own hands. It's not the rod; you do not need a new reel – *you are not casting properly.*

Now, criticism of an angler's casting is touching on a very sensitive area. But facts, no matter how bitter, have to be faced. If you want to cast well you must accept that knowledge and practice are vital.

Text and pictures are poor substitutes for personal

▶175

John Holden fishing into a wrasse cauldron off the West Coast of Ireland. Wit

off the rocks

depth of over 50 ft wrasse are unaffected by the tremendous surface surge as the Atlantic waves crash onto the Kerry cliffs.

DEVELOPMENT OF THE FLATFISH

All flatfish species are either left- or right-handed, ie. the eyes are both to the right of the mouth (left-handed) or to the left of the mouth (right-handed). Exceptions do occur, when a species shows the opposite condition to normalcy as in a right-handed turbot (very rare) or left-handed flounder (very common).

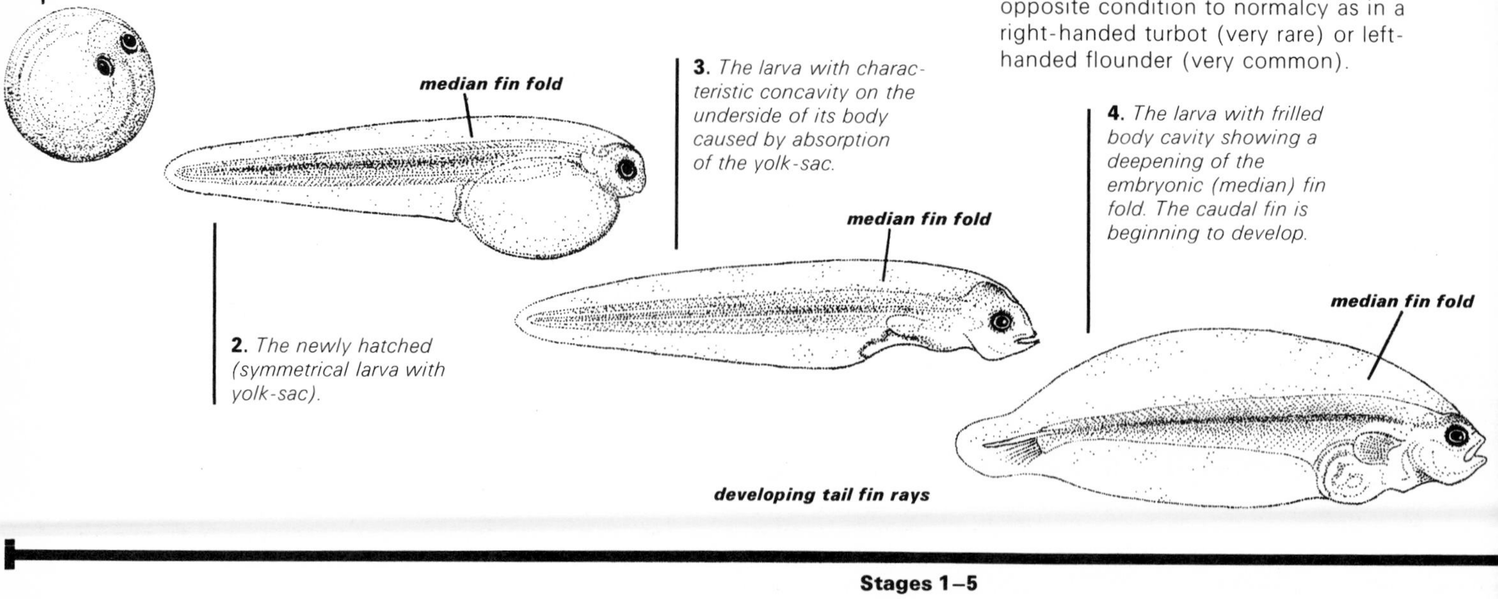

1. *The embryo within the egg.*

2. *The newly hatched (symmetrical larva with yolk-sac).*

3. *The larva with characteristic concavity on the underside of its body caused by absorption of the yolk-sac.*

4. *The larva with frilled body cavity showing a deepening of the embryonic (median) fin fold. The caudal fin is beginning to develop.*

Stages 1–5

The eggs and larvae are pelargic, living in the upper water layers.

Pigmentation in flatfish

Flatfish larvae, which are relatively transparent, show varying degrees of pigmentation during their development. Chromatophores, i.e. the cells which produce pigment, are variously developed and distributed over the body surface. Patches of coloration appear in later stages which reflect the deeper and larger colour patches exhibited in the adult fish.

With the assumption of a bottom-dwelling mode of life, and as the eye migrates from one side to join the other eye, just one side of the fish will become darkly coloured. The blind side of the flatfish, that side having no eyes, remains a drab white or grey (some species – Witch and Greenland halibut – have a distinct grey coloration to the blind side).

However, as with many things in nature, there are exceptions to the rules. Dark colouring does often show on the blind side, either as variously sized patches or over the whole body area with the head remaining white. This phenomenon happens most in those species in which reversal of body shape is most frequent. The commonest examples are to be found among flounders and has been termed ambi-coloration.

Reasons for ambi-coloration

1. Partial colouration of the blind side may be due to the light reaching it – as in individuals living on a hard bottom where they cannot bury themselves.
2. Piebald pigmentation of the blind side, found as a series of almost regularly arranged patches of colour, assumed to be remnants of striping from ancestral fish.

Totally ambi-coloured individuals showing a white patch on the head often have a "hooked head", a notch which runs along the top of the head and under the dorsal fin.

Reversal

Most species metamorphose over to the "correct" side; however, certain species exhibit individuals that are reversed. In waters of the British Isles, the most common species reversing its sides must be the flounder. Rarely, the plaice and halibut will also reverse. The phenomenon is common in some species of the world, to the extent of 50 per cent normal and reversed. The Californian Bastard halibut *Paralichthyis californicus* does this and fish of the genus *Psettodes*, in which the eye from the blind side lies on the side edge of the head as in the Greenland halibut *Rheindthartius*.

Albinism

Individuals with white "coloured" sides are also known but such fish will nearly always show a small patch of colour on the head, in front of their eyes.

Left-handed fish

Bothidae: Scaldfish
Scophthalmidae: Turbot, Brill, Megrim, Topknots

Right-handed fish

Pleuronectidae: Dab, Flounder, Plaice, Lemon sole, Halibuts, Witch and Long-rough dab.

Soles are not directly related to the other flatfish and divide as follows:

Left-handed fish

Cynoglossidae: No British Isles species (generally called tongue soles)

Right-handed fish

Soleidae: Dover sole, Solonette and Sand sole.
Many features describing the flatfish also apply to the soles although reversal is almost unknown.

1

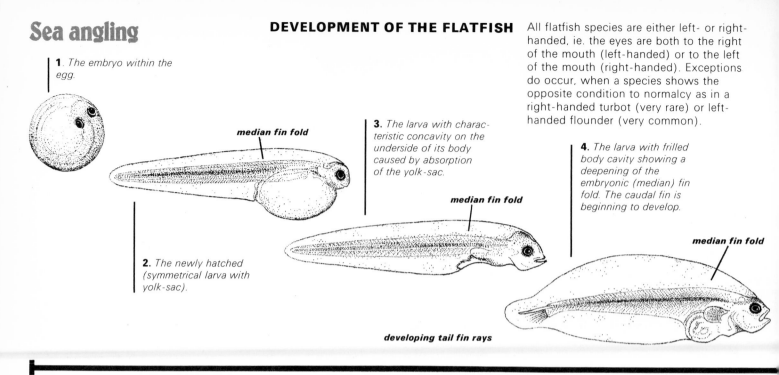

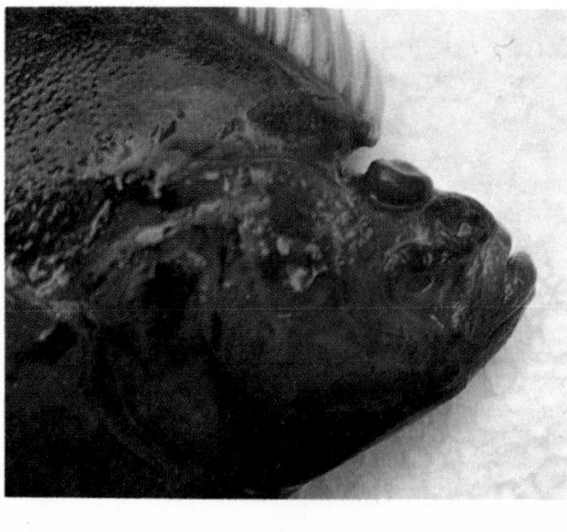

1. *A close-up view of the cephalic notch on the head of a correctly coloured flounder. In the ambi-coloured flatfish both eyes rarely migrate fully, the cephalic notch is more pronounced and the dorsal fin begins further back on the body of the fish.*

2. *A normally coloured flounder, with eyes placed to the left of the fish's mouth. Both eyes are on the coloured side of the body.*

3. *A completely ambi-coloured flounder with only one eye on the coloured side of the body, the other has failed to migrate around from the white side.*

5. *The body begins to deepen, traces of the dorsal and anal fin supporting rays appear. The caudal fin is more developed and now decidedly heterocercal with notocord upturned.*

6. *The fish's body continues to deepen. Fin-rays lengthen with the median fin fold. The eye has appeared on the side of the head in movement from one side to the other.*

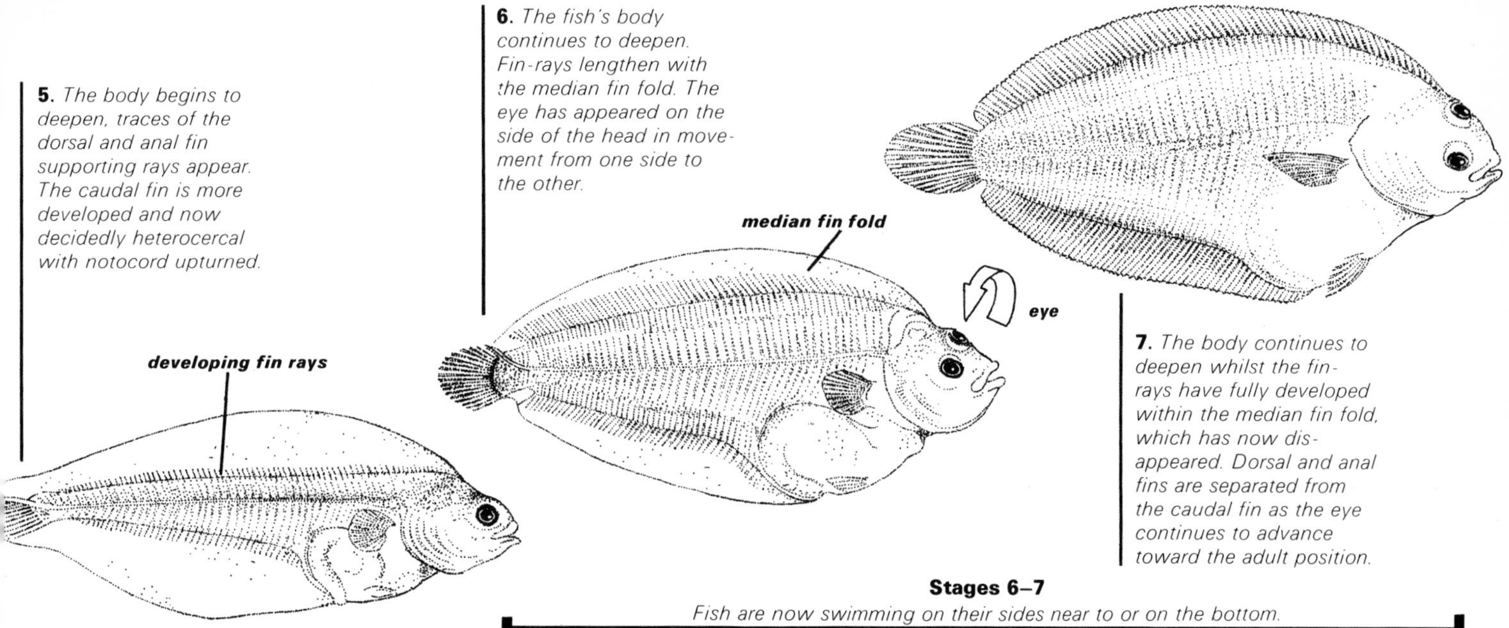

7. *The body continues to deepen whilst the fin-rays have fully developed within the median fin fold, which has now disappeared. Dorsal and anal fins are separated from the caudal fin as the eye continues to advance toward the adult position.*

Stages 6–7

Fish are now swimming on their sides near to or on the bottom.

Stages 5–6

Larvae begin to sink down from the top of the water.

Stage 7 onward

Fish now assume a totally bottom-dwelling life (benthic habit) as fully developed flatfish that swim on their sides.

2

3

MEGRIM

Lepidorhombus whiffiagonus

Another left-handed flatfish found in deeper water. It is a small species that rarely grows to more than a couple of pounds or so. More slender in shape than either the turbot or brill. The scales are rough and become easily detached from the body.

Bait: *Not specifically fished for but the species will accept small fish strips.*

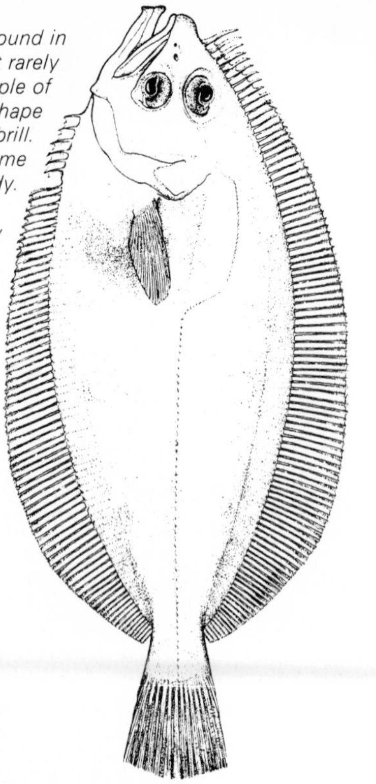

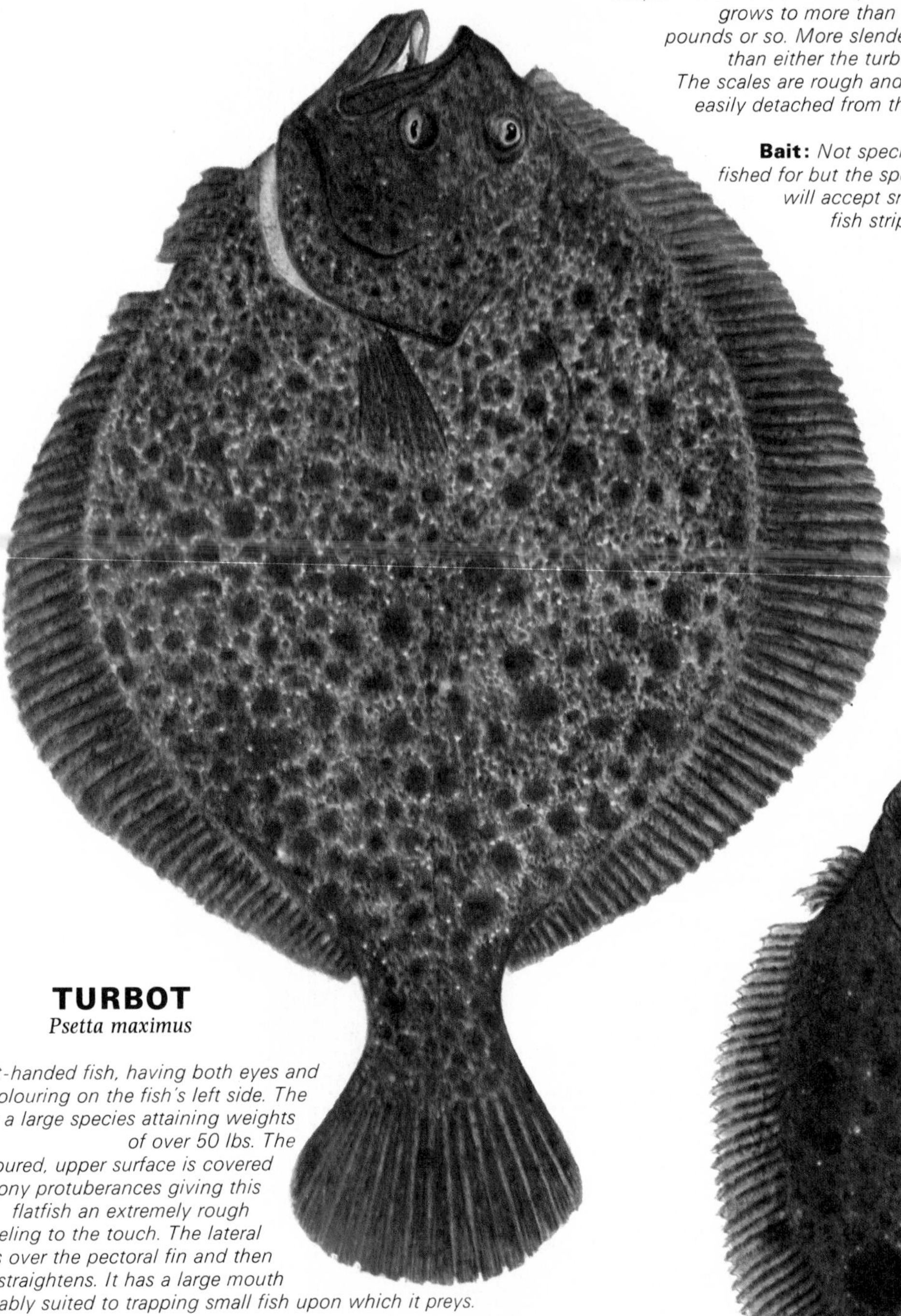

TURBOT

Psetta maximus

A left-handed fish, having both eyes and colouring on the fish's left side. The turbot is a large species attaining weights of over 50 lbs. The coloured, upper surface is covered in hard, bony protuberances giving this flatfish an extremely rough feeling to the touch. The lateral line curves over the pectoral fin and then straightens. It has a large mouth and teeth admirably suited to trapping small fish upon which it preys.

Bait: *Small, whole fish such as sandeels or thin slivers of fresh mackerel and herring.*

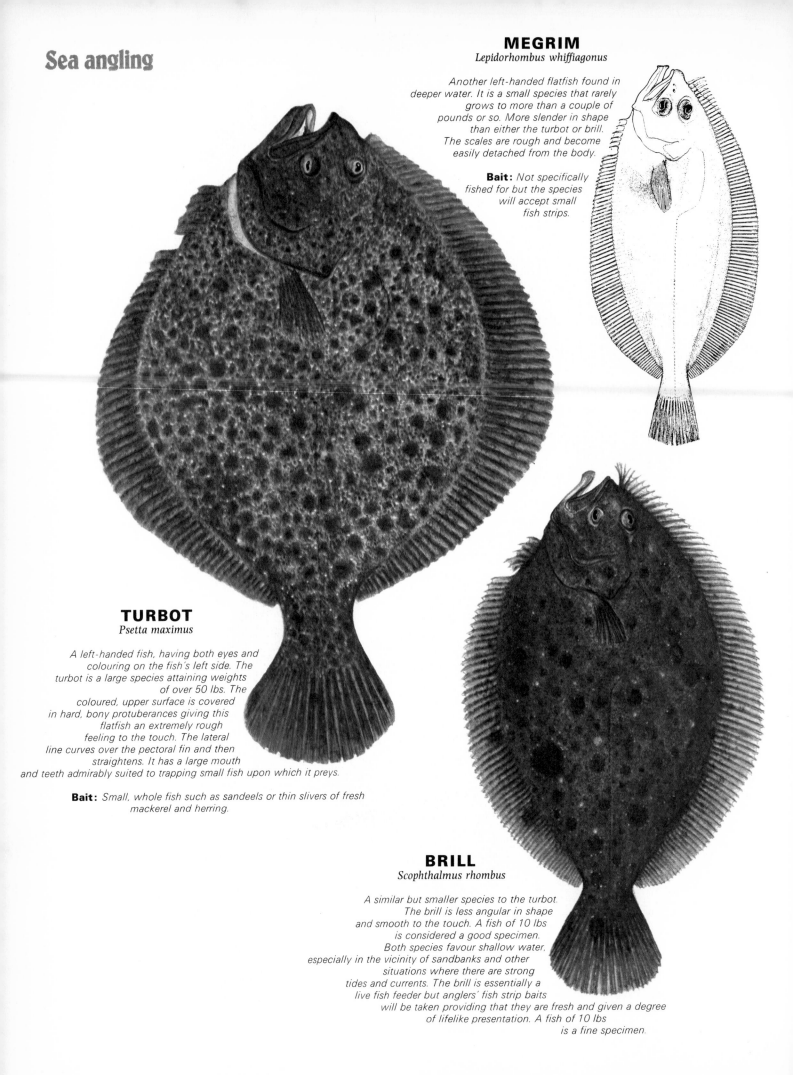

BRILL

Scophthalmus rhombus

A similar but smaller species to the turbot. The brill is less angular in shape and smooth to the touch. A fish of 10 lbs is considered a good specimen. Both species favour shallow water, especially in the vicinity of sandbanks and other situations where there are strong tides and currents. The brill is essentially a live fish feeder but anglers' fish strip baits will be taken providing that they are fresh and given a degree of lifelike presentation. A fish of 10 lbs is a fine specimen.

PLAICE
Pleuronectes platessa

The most widely sought-after fish among the flats. Has a powerful, oval body covered in bright orange spots. There are a number of bony tubercles on the fish's head behind the eyes. The body is smooth and the scales minute and embedded in the skin. The species is truly marine, rarely venturing into brackish water. It lives on sandy-muddy ground often in association with beds of mussels and other shellfish. The species can grow to over 10 lbs although inshore fish tend to be around 3 to 4 lbs in weight.

Bait: *Shellfish and worms; unlike the flounder the plaice rarely accepts fishbait.*

FLOUNDER
Platichthyes flesus

First of the right-handed fish with both mouth and eyes on the right, coloured side of the body. There is much confusion between the plaice and the flounder. Basic recognition points for the flounder are a line of small tubercles or raised scales along the bases of both dorsal and anal fins together with a similar line of tubercles behind the head and along the beginning of the lateral line. Both the dorsal and anal fin are widest at the hind section of the fins giving the flounder an angular appearance. The species can be spotted and sometimes these spots are as bright as those associated with the plaice. Many times flounders are taken that are left-handed or rather coloured on the wrong side, indeed there are specimens recorded that have been neatly coloured in two equal sections on the one side of the body

The flounder is a fish of the estuaries, mud creeks and brackish waters. Often the flounder is found far up into rivers where the water is entirely fresh.

Bait: *Almost anything that is animal will take flounders. Worms, crustaceans, molluscs, fish strip.*

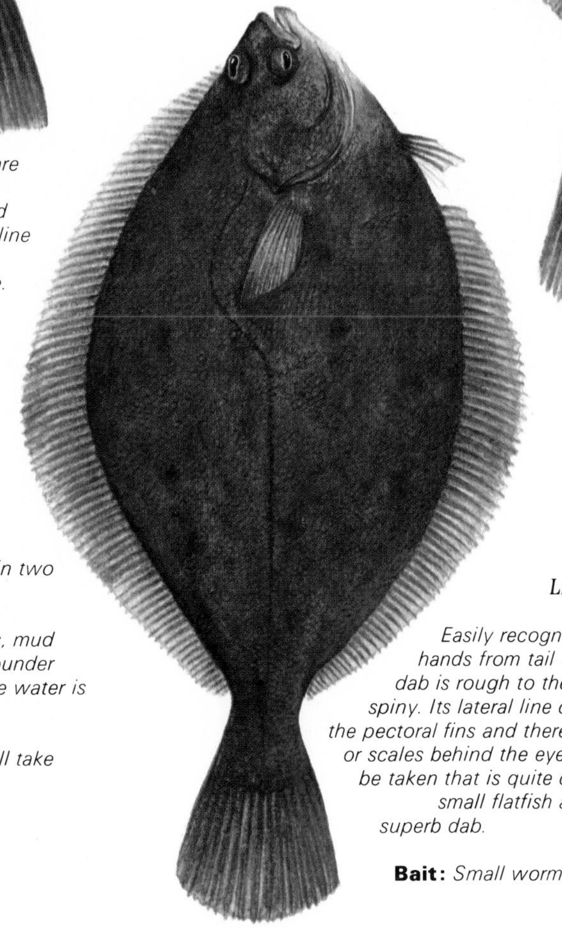

DAB
Limanda limanda

Easily recognized if rubbed with the hands from tail to head. The dab is rough to the touch because the scales are spiny. Its lateral line curves sharply over the pectoral fins and there are no rough tubercles or scales behind the eyes. Occasionally a specimen will be taken that is quite clearly spotted. The dab is a small flatfish and a weight of 2 lbs is a superb dab.

Bait: *Small worms and shellfish.*

Rocky Shore (sheltered)

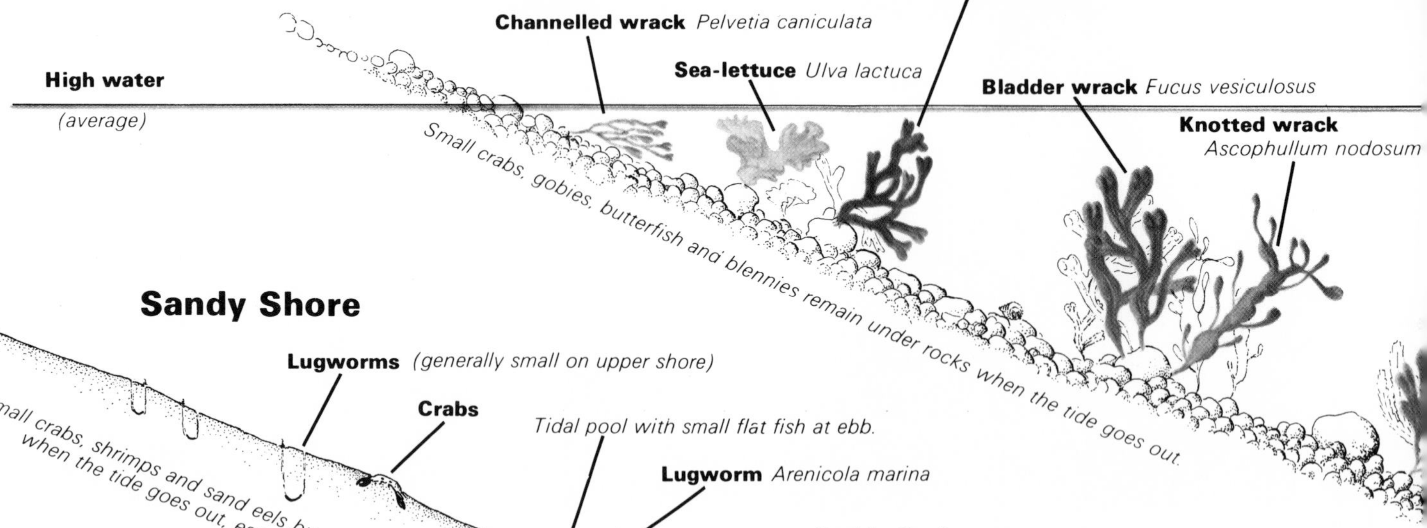

Sandy Shore

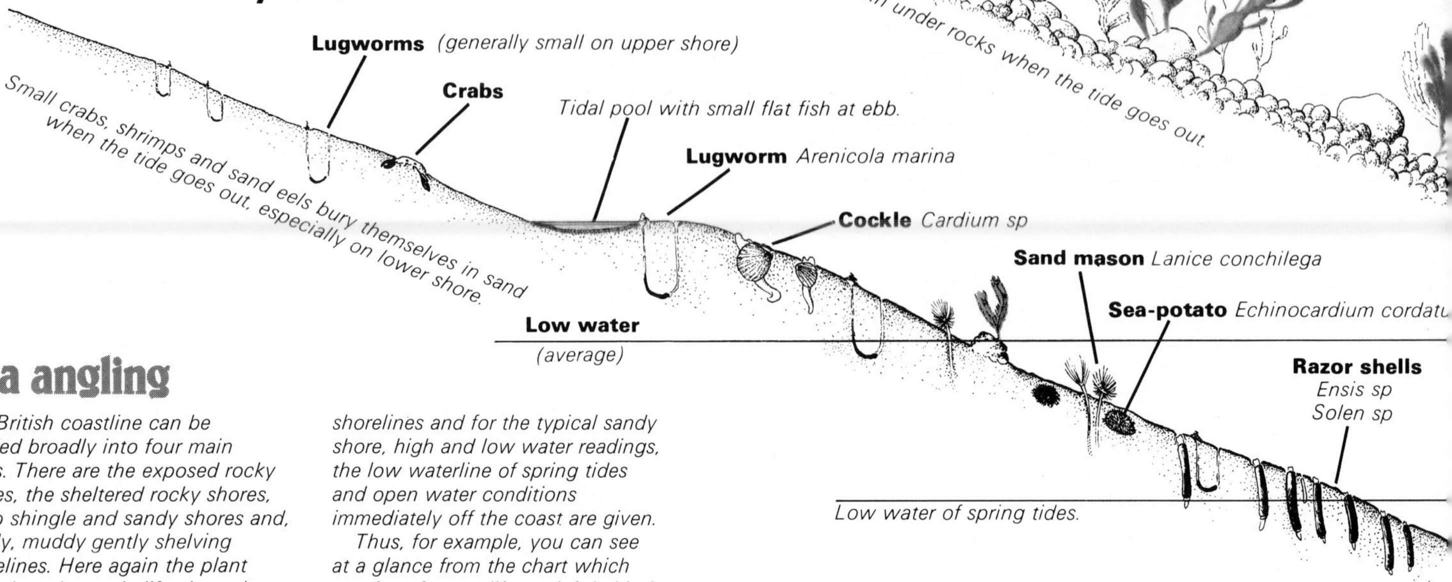

Sea angling

The British coastline can be divided broadly into four main types. There are the exposed rocky shores, the sheltered rocky shores, steep shingle and sandy shores and, finally, muddy gently shelving shorelines. Here again the plant growth and aquatic life along the shore and rocks varies from zone to zone. This shoreline chart helps you to identify the sort of life you can expect to find around the various shorelines and at different water depths.

To use the chart select the shoreline you require. For the exposed and sheltered rocky shorelines and for the typical sandy shore, high and low water readings, the low waterline of spring tides and open water conditions immediately off the coast are given.

Thus, for example, you can see at a glance from the chart which species of water life are left behind on the rocky shore by the retreating tide. You can also see the pools left on the shore at low water. Here special varieties of flora and fauna flourish because of the perpetually sheltered conditions. Muddy shorelines are dealt with separately since the flora and fauna are little affected by tidal action.

Muddy Shore

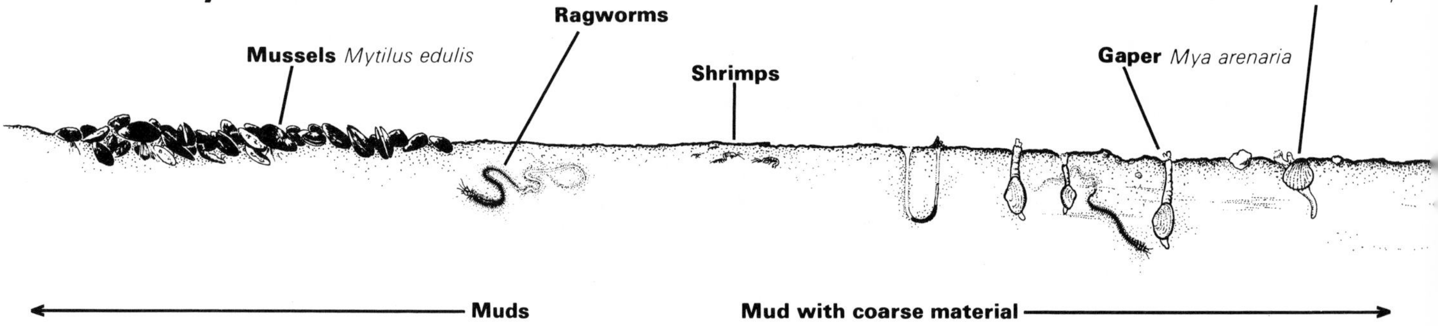

Rocky Shore (exposed)

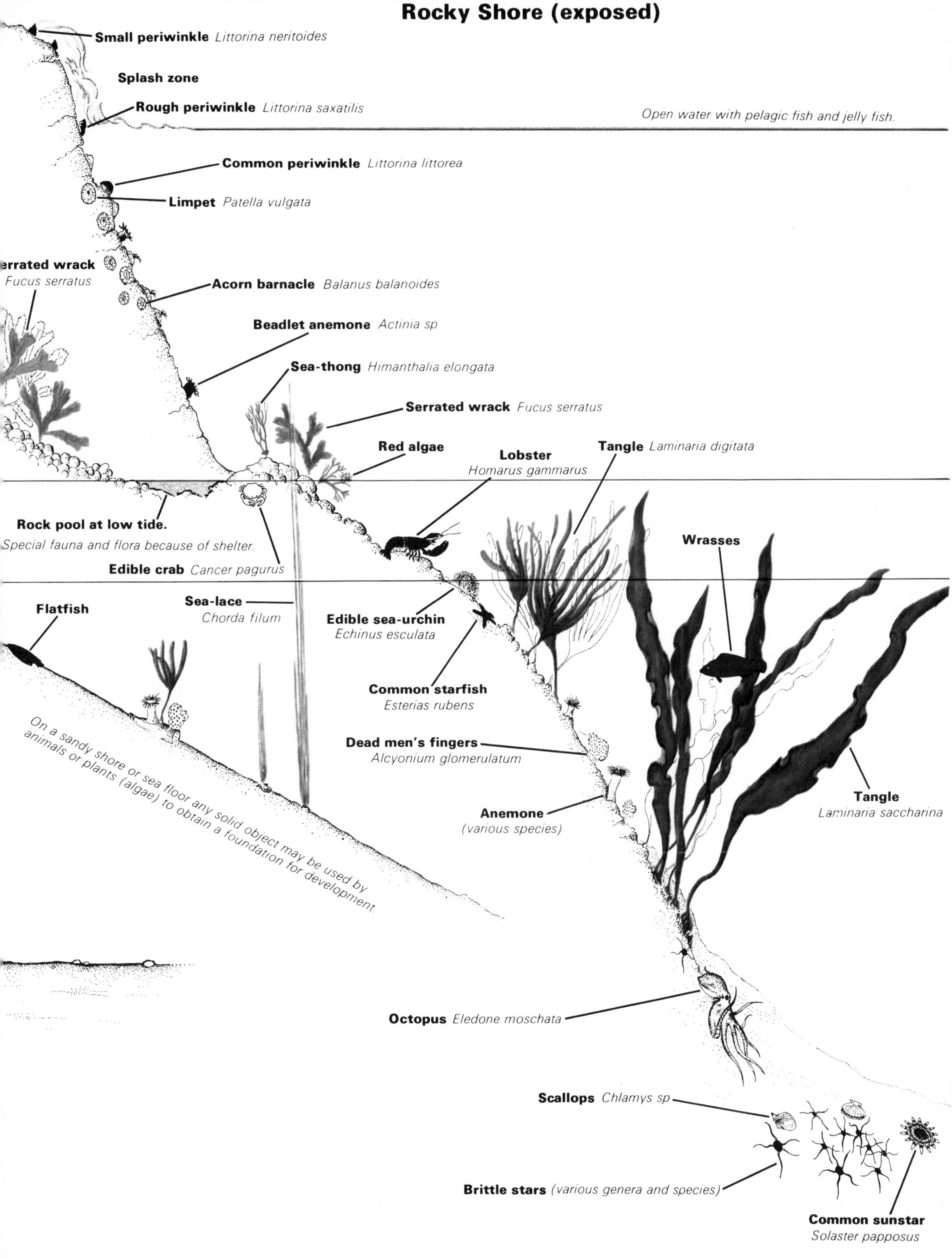

Small periwinkle *Littorina neritoides*
Splash zone
Rough periwinkle *Littorina saxatilis*
Open water with pelagic fish and jelly fish.
Common periwinkle *Littorina littorea*
Limpet *Patella vulgata*
errated wrack *Fucus serratus*
Acorn barnacle *Balanus balanoides*
Beadlet anemone *Actinia sp*
Sea-thong *Himanthalia elongata*
Serrated wrack *Fucus serratus*
Red algae
Lobster *Homarus gammarus*
Tangle *Laminaria digitata*
Rock pool at low tide.
Special fauna and flora because of shelter.
Edible crab *Cancer pagurus*
Wrasses
Flatfish
Sea-lace *Chorda filum*
Edible sea-urchin *Echinus esculata*
Common starfish *Esterias rubens*
Dead men's fingers *Alcyonium glomerulatum*
Anemone *(various species)*
Tangle *Laminaria saccharina*
On a sandy shore or sea floor any solid object may be used by animals or plants (algae) to obtain a foundation for development.
Octopus *Eledone moschata*
Scallops *Chlamys sp*
Brittle stars *(various genera and species)*
Common sunstar *Solaster papposus*

HALIBUT
Hippoglossus hippoglossus

The largest, slimmest and thickest of the flatfish of the British Isles. The lateral line curves sharply over the pectoral fins of this right-handed fish. Most of the halibut recorded as rod-caught fish have come from rocky ground or areas having a strong tidal race. The Pentland Firth, in Scotland, the Orkney Islands and the West of Ireland have all produced halibut to sea anglers. It is by no means a common species but each year more anglers are travelling to halibut grounds and producing fish. Specimens of 150 lbs are good fish though commercial fishing in the deepwater of the North Atlantic has brought halibut of 1000 lbs to the fish dock.

Bait: *Fish, either as large lashes or whole fish.*

GREENLAND HALIBUT
Reinhardtius hippoglossoides

A similar species to the halibut but with considerable colour variation. The dorsal side is a dark greenish-black, whilst the ventral side has a silvery-green sheen. The fish is found in the far north of the British Isles though it is essentially a fish of the Northern Atlantic. The lower jaw has sharp teeth and is more pronounced in this species.

Bait: *As for the halibut.*

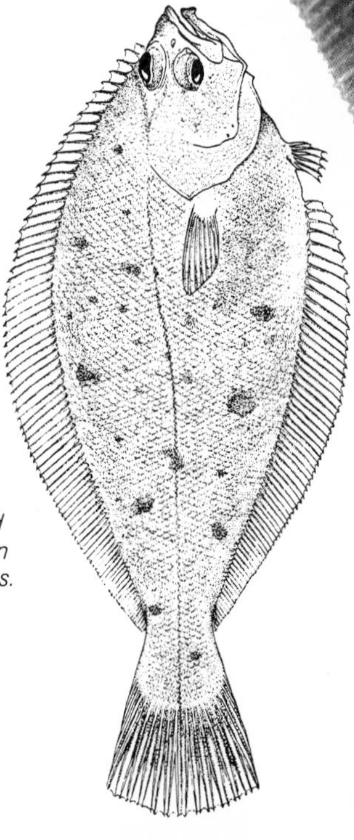

LONG-ROUGH DAB
Hippoglossoides platessoides

Rather similar in appearance to the halibut, though this species only attains a length of 15 ins or so. It has rough, spiny scales and the lateral line is almost straight. A fish of the deep water and found in the Northern seas where it feeds on minute crustaceans and molluscs.

WITCH
Glyptocephalus cynoglossus

A small bodied fish, thin and elongated in shape. It has large eyes and tends to be found in deep water. Not really an angling species. The lateral line is straight and there is a marked variation between the scales on the coloured and blind sides.

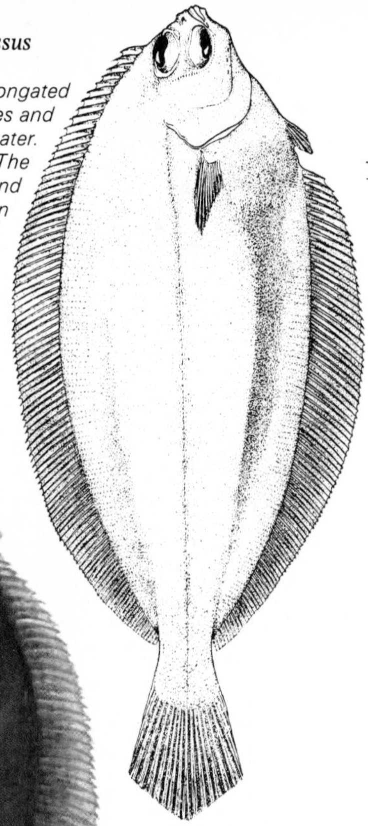

LEMON SOLE
Microstomus kitt

A brown flatfish with marled oval blotches. The head is small and the body slimy to the touch. The name, Lemon sole, is primarily a market name as it covers a number of the smaller flatfish species.

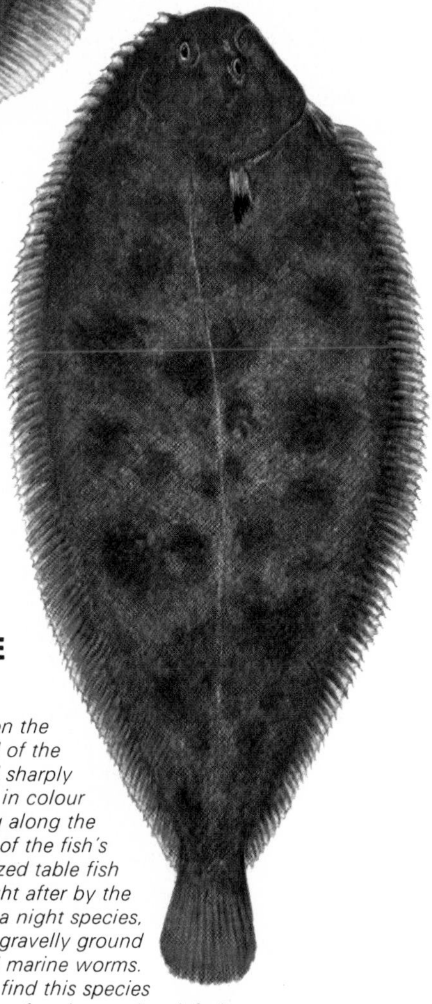

DOVER SOLE
Solea vulgaris

The dorsal fin begins on the snout of the sole just ahead of the eyes. The snout is blunt and sharply rounded. The species is brown in colour with marked blotching along the lateral line and at the junction of the fish's fins. The sole is a highly prized table fish and is much sought after by the commercial netsmen. It is a night species, feeding over sand and gravelly ground for crustaceans and small marine worms. Anglers will often find this species in extremely shallow water after the sun has left the water.

166◀ tuition. Helped by a professional caster, the average angler can learn to throw 100 yds or more in less than two hours. Fast results are almost guaranteed by having somebody at your side to guide and criticize.

Books and magazines are impersonal and remote. You cannot ask questions; they cannot watch you and point out the mistakes, so a blow-by-blow analysis of the actual cast is at best a guideline. In this chapter the basic casting styles are outlined in picture sequence. Far more important is to consider the mechanics of casting – why you need a certain weight of lead; how rods are made to suit various casting styles and which reels suit long range beach work.

LEADS AND TERMINAL TACKLE

Rods and reels are not the most important tackle. The things which count are those you throw into the water. There is no point in buying rods and reels without thought about leads, lines and terminal tackles. In beachfishing, we must first consider the weight, its capacity to tow baits through the air and, once in the water, how it holds in the current.

To carry a predetermined distance, a lead weight must expend a certain amount of energy. It derives that energy from its size and speed. For equivalent power, small leads must move faster than heavier ones. That is where practical fishing becomes involved: lead speed is directly proportional to casting speed. Casting too fast is a shortcut to over-runs and inconsistency. An easy, relaxed cast always pays off.

Slow leads are better for two more reasons. First, there is less tendency for baits to tear off; second, the considerable air resistance of even small baits will drastically slow a light lead. Big weights fly ponderously and tow big baits much more easily. Bait size is critical; it must never be cut to allow longer casting.

A 5 oz lead is sufficient for most medium and long range shorecasting. It combines adequate carrying power with comfortably light casting strains. Used with the right technique a 5 oz grip lead will hold in fast water.

However, being undergunned is a mistake. I personally prefer 6 oz leads for continuous long casting. The disadvantages of slightly heavier tackle are far outweighed by leisurely casting speed, firm anchorage and improved wind penetration. At night, when you cannot watch the flying baits, a big, slow lead is some insurance against losing the bait on the way out and thus fishing a bare hook. In really wild seas and gales, 8 ozs may be necessary. Naturally, tackle is heavy. But if the object of fishing is to catch fish you must select tackle to suit conditions, not personal whims.

On the other hand short range work in slack water allows a delicate approach. One to 4 ozs of lead matched

A B C D

1 2 3 4

to the appropriate rod and reel make for light and sporting fishing. Even so, don't overdo lightness, and never use it for its own sake. If in doubt, go heavier, and ignore the critics.

Over practical fishing distances lead shape is irrelevant. It doesn't matter whether you use a perfectly streamlined weight or an old nut and bolt. Bait drag more than cancels out any aerodynamic improvements in design. However, weights must be shaped to hold in the seabed and to allow the fitting of grip wires. On these criteria alone a bomb shape is ideal; that it

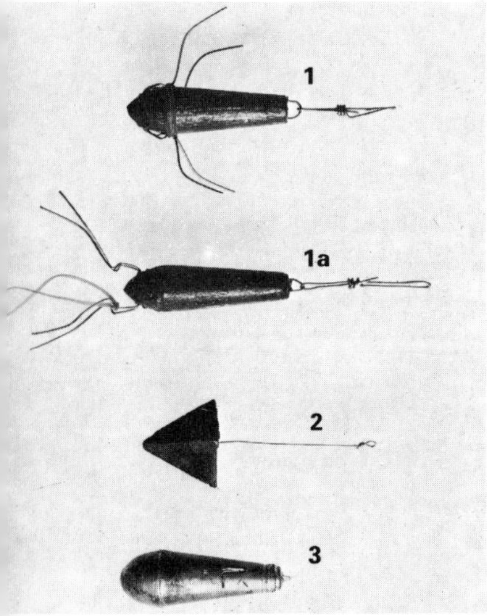

Leads for shorecasting:

1 *A simple breakout casting bomb with pivoting wire grips that are held in position with a rubber band.*
1a *A strong pull from the rod will slip the rubber band, allowing the grip to turn back and freeing the lead from the ground.*

2 *The conical Sandfast lead is ideal for taking a firm hold in sand and mud with gentle tidal pressures.*

3 *The plain casting bomb has its centre of gravity in the forward section of the lead, ensuring straight flight, without tumble, as it flies through the air.*

is thought to be a better casting shape is more of an aesthetic consideration than a ballistic one. A second type, called a Sandfast, is most useful over sand and other soft ground. It is basically a reversed pyramid with a long wire stalk which digs in like a ploughshare.

Bait on a hook always cuts distance, but there is no point in further aggravating the problem with unsuitable terminal rigs. Rigs for shorecasting must be a compromise between reasonable bait presentation and streamlining. As bait size must not be cut, the rest of the tackle should be as small and neat as possible. Most beaches and species can be tackled with two rigs, the paternoster and running leger. At long range it is better to use only one hook. Closer in, two or three hooks allow the angler to present a variety of baits – but at the cost of a few yards in casting distance!

LINES

Ideally, beachcasting lines would have a diameter of about 0·40 mm – equivalent to current 15 lb nylon – and a 35–40 lb breaking strain. Such material would combine minimal air resistance with sufficient strength for hard casting. Since a line possessing those properties does not exist, we compromise by knotting heavy line in front of the main line. The heavy line is called a casting piece, or shock leader, and is normally 6 to 10 yds of 30–40 lb nylon which absorbs casting strains. Sometimes it pays to lengthen the leader so that when fish come into the surf a few turns of heavy line are already on the spool – insurance against being smashed by a big fish in heavy water.

The main line should be between 15 and 20 lb breaking strain. There is no need to use anything stronger except for heavy work at short range – conger fishing from the rocks perhaps? Handling rods gives a false impression of their pulling power. At 100 yds range, the most powerful rods exert no more than a couple of pounds pressure. Heavy lines are thus completely wasted as they are impossible to exploit. Additionally, the heavier and thicker a line, the more it cuts range.

Unless you are fishing for fast running tope, 200 yds of line is adequate. Less line means a smaller reel, which makes for easier, longer casting.

Two casting methods for the beach angler, equally suitable for multiplying or fixed-spool reels. For the beginner the "Off the Ground" cast will give a smooth action, avoiding a stunted movement that causes over-runs. The "Layback" is a cast devised by Leslie Moncrieff that achieves a smooth action by extending the time taken and distance travelled by the lead before release. John Holden adds a pendulum swing to compress the rod tip at the beginning of the cast, so giving a more powerful action to the rod. At a point half way through the casting action the two methods come together producing a high release point and steady follow-through as the lead flies out to complete the cast.

E5

F6

The "Off the Ground" cast

A *The drop is measured by holding the lead against a known mark on the rod – a 7–8 ft drop is about right.*

B *The lead and bait are swung out to lie on the ground with the rod and trace fully extended. The lead will describe an arc of three quarters of a circle when cast.*

C *Point the rod tip at the lead, keeping a tight line to the lead. All the movement is imparted by a swing of the hips and slight pivoting of the feet.*

D *The angler's body position and angle of the rod, one third of the cast completed. The lead has been lifted and the rod is gradually rising to gain height in the cast.*

The "Layback" cast.

1 *A suitable drop to lead and bait for a fishing cast – John Holden favours between 4 and 5 ft of line between rod tip and casting lead.*

2 *With the body leaning into a layback position, the lead and bait are swung to the angler's rear.*

3 *The lead is allowed to swing back under and slightly out to the right of the rod. As it reaches the end of its swing the angler begins to pivot, compressing the rod.*

4 *Further into the cast the rod is under compression and the weight of the lead pulls the rod tip down as the power builds up in the cast. Cast continues as for* **E5**.

E5 *Almost at the maximum power and point of release for the lead. Height has been gained with the rod in order to give the best trajectory to the lead that will give distance.*

F6 *After release the rod tip is held high to follow the flight of the lead through the air. This will give that little more distance by reducing friction as the line pulls off.*

RODS AND REELS

Anglers choose tackle in two ways. Lines, hooks and weights are almost clinically selected: a 6 oz lead for long range cod fishing; size 4, long shanked hooks for flounders; 200 yds of 20 lb nylon for beachcasting.

But rods and reels are more subjective. Anglers buy them because *they feel right* or because *Fred's got one and he catches more than I do!* In other words they choose rods by appearance, price, the name on the rod bag, and so on. Very few anglers would ask for a medium tapered phenolic resin blank fitted with a spigot, stainless rings, and acrylic finish. They may indeed buy that rod, but as *that blue one with 25% discount!*

A modern beach rod is a hollow fibreglass tube and, to suit various casting styles, rods are of three basic actions: fast, slow and medium. The designs merge and overlap into medium-fast and medium-slow. A fast rod is steeply tapered. Butt and middle sections are so stiff they hardly flex; the flexible tip reacts very quickly to casting. It bends and straightens with a flick. Slow and medium rods curve more evenly, compress and unwind like a longbow. Medium rods have a fraction more butt stiffness, though.

It is a common misconception that fast rods cast significantly farther than the others. In fact power, not action, largely dictates distance. Each rod matches a particular type of cast. Used well, a slow rod will equal a fast tapered rod of equal power. Therefore, always look for sufficient strength to cope with your sort of fishing.

Many rods are marked with a recommended weight range. The majority of manufacturers underrate their tackle to incorporate a safety valve for abuse. Some makers go beyond that, though: many 4 oz rods will thrash 8 ozs of lead. A rod intended for long casting should always have a reserve of power, so it pays to select something just a little more than you really need.

Rod action is a personal preference. Slow rods are docile and put up a good performance with simple "off-the-ground" and "layback" styles. Fast rods are the racing models. If you can cast well enough, fine; if not, expect problems with timing. The medium action rod is the workhorse. It will cope with most sorts of casting, compensates to an extent for sloppy technique, but will show a clean pair of heels to many fast rods, especially mishandled fast rods.

I am sure that action and power are the overwhelming factors in rod design. Some anglers stress the importance of spigots, handles and rod rings. They don't consider the basic rod blank at all. True, ring numbers, types and position on the rod can affect casting to a minor degree. Except in rare cases they neither make nor ruin a rod. I gave up worrying about fittings years ago, and distance hasn't suffered. The length of rods seems to cause a great deal of argument. There is no practical difference between 10 and 13 ft.

Reels also require thought. It is no use assuming that expensive ones are better; or that if a manufacturer calls his reel a beachcaster it will necessarily do the job. Some designers are completely out of touch with modern casting and base their reels on traditional designs. It is paradoxical that one of the most successful surf-casting reels is a salmon spinner by design.

The choice is either a multiplier or fixed-spool. Since the invention of release gadgets, which prevent finger damage, there is nothing to choose between the two reels as far as distance casting is concerned. In deciding which to use you have to answer one question: do you want to cast easily but with some lack of control on retrieve, or would you prefer a smoother, more

1

efficient fishing reel which requires a great deal of mastering?

Fixed-spools are easy to use. A raw novice can be turned loose after a few minutes instruction, and should be able to cast far enough to catch fish. As he improves, the reel copes – 150 yds is straightforward with a fixed-spool. But there is a snag: most fixed-spools are badly geared, unbalanced, and tiring to use. However, these are all due to design faults – not to the principle of the reel. Given enough encouragement a reel maker could turn out excellent fixed-spools for shorecasting. If that happened, multiplier sales would halve overnight.

At present the multiplier is streets ahead in finesse. It won't cast any farther from the shore – it's not far in front on the tournament court – but it is more precise and satisfying to use. But (and it's a big but) it demands absolute attention to detail. You must pay attention to lubrication and spool winding patterns; it goes without saying that the angler has to be a competent caster. Competence results from practising and, unless you are prepared to do so, save a lot of heartache and stick with a fixed-spool reel.

When you are looking at reels for beach work ask questions on these lines:

FOR BOTH TYPES

1. Is it as small as possible? For shorecasting you seldom need more than 200 yds of 15 or 20 lb line. Big reels are harder to control, heavier, and cost more.

2. Is it easy to take apart; does it have a spare spool? Changing lines at night in the cold is difficult enough with a take-apart reel. Struggling with half a dozen

2

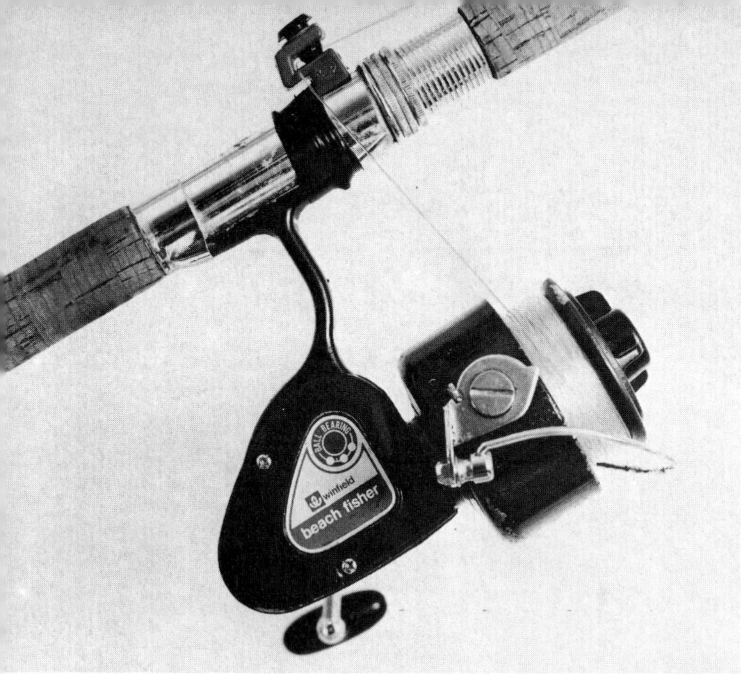

1 *Winter cod from an East Anglian shingle beach at Kessingland.*

2 *Fishing with a fixed-spool reel can sometimes give problems when casting in the cold of winter. A casting line release, operated by removing thumb pressure as the rod tip speeds the lead away, will aid distance and build confidence in putting muscle behind a big bait and lead.*

3 *Correct loading and even spreading of line reduces the risk of over-runs.*

3

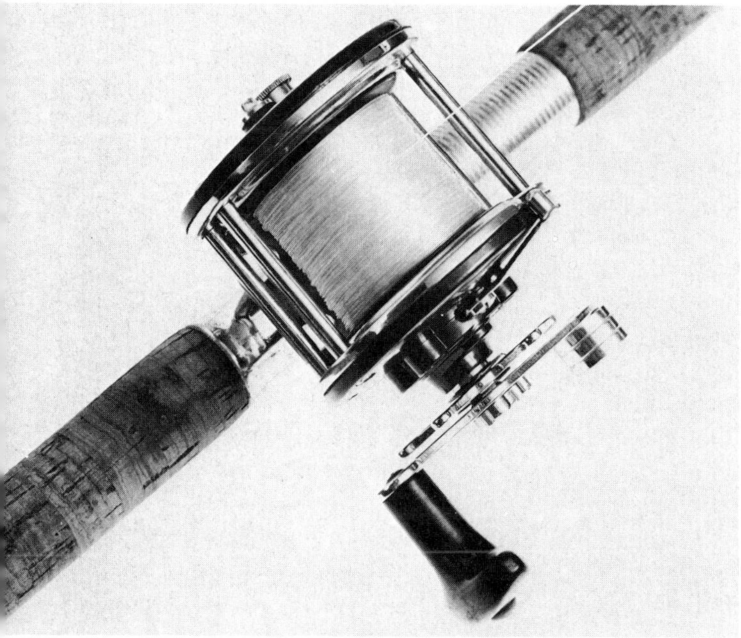

screws or reloading the only spool you have is a nightmare.

3. You will need spares and perhaps servicing. Are they available?

4. Is the clutch smooth and powerful? You don't often need the drag assembly, but when you do it is because a big fish is about to smash you. That's too late to find out that the reel is no good.

5. Will it fit your rod? Some winch fittings will not take certain makes of reel. Check before buying.

MULTIPLIERS

1. Is the spool right for casting? It must be small, light and made of plastic, glass-filled nylon, or lightweight metal. Heavy, brass boat reels are useless.

2. Are the bearings smooth and quiet, and can you lubricate without stripping down? Bearings often dry out when you are fishing. Oil porting requires only a quick squirt; otherwise you have to strip the reel.

3. Can you hold down the spool when it is filled with line? If the top of the line is too far above the rod, your thumb will slip during the cast.

4. There is no objection to a reel fitted with a brake. But can it be adjusted so that you attain a satisfactory minimum distance each cast?

5. Is there sufficient clearance between spool flanges and sideplates so that the spool doesn't rub; conversely, is the gap so big it traps line?

FIXED-SPOOLS

1. Does it sit close to the rod? Long reel stalks aggravate imbalance by allowing the reel to sway.

2. Can the spool be locked for hard casting? If the spool slips under pressure you lose distance.

3. Is the bale-arm of the anti-inertia type? If not, it could close in mid-cast! Nasty!

4. Is it really small? Most sea reels are too big. A freshwater reel might be better.

5. Is the gear ratio low enough? High retrieve rates will nearly break your arm off, especially with big weights.

WINTER COD FISHING FROM SOUTH AND EAST COAST BEACHES

The wind blew in from the sea and driving spray muted the roar of the water. Breaking waves splashed high up the beach into the Tilley lamp's glow where the foam reflected icy-white. Outside that circle of light there was only darkness, the wind, and shingle slithering in the backwash.

I lifted my rod from its rest and tightened the line. The lead weight broke free from the seabed; its anchor wires flipped from under the elastic band which had held them in place. It was easy to retrieve with the wires trailing uselessly behind the lead.

One hundred and fifty yards of line came back onto the reel before the leader knot tinkled down through the rod rings. I laid the knot to one side of the spool so that it would not cut into my thumb next cast. Because of the rough conditions my leader was extra long: 10 yds of 46 lb nylon blood-knotted to the 20 lb main line. Apart from absorbing casting shocks, the leader would help control a big fish in the surf.

As I wound in I combed the line between finger and thumb so that it spread neat and even on the spool. Lumps of weed had collected and I picked them off. Weed in a reel is always bad; on a multiplying reel tiny amounts will cause over-runs.

Big seas stir up weeds and all kinds of rubbish. ▶182

FIFTEEN-SPINED STICKLEBACK
Spinachia spinachia

An inshore species associated with kelp and weedbeds in which they build a nest similar to the three-spined stickleback.

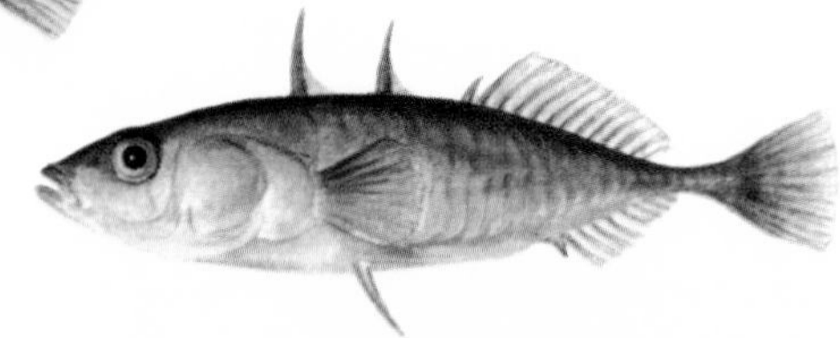

THREE-SPINED STICKLEBACK
Gasterosteus gasterosteus

Found in both fresh and salt water, the marine form is regarded as a "race" and is given the title "trachurus" because of the development of scad- and horse mackerel-like keeled scutes along the side of the tail. These are absent in the freshwater form.

COMMON DRAGONET
Callionymus lyra

The dragonet is a very common fish found on sandy ground in relatively shallow water. The male fish is brilliantly coloured with an elongated first dorsal fin. Not a big fish, it averages 6–10 ins in length.

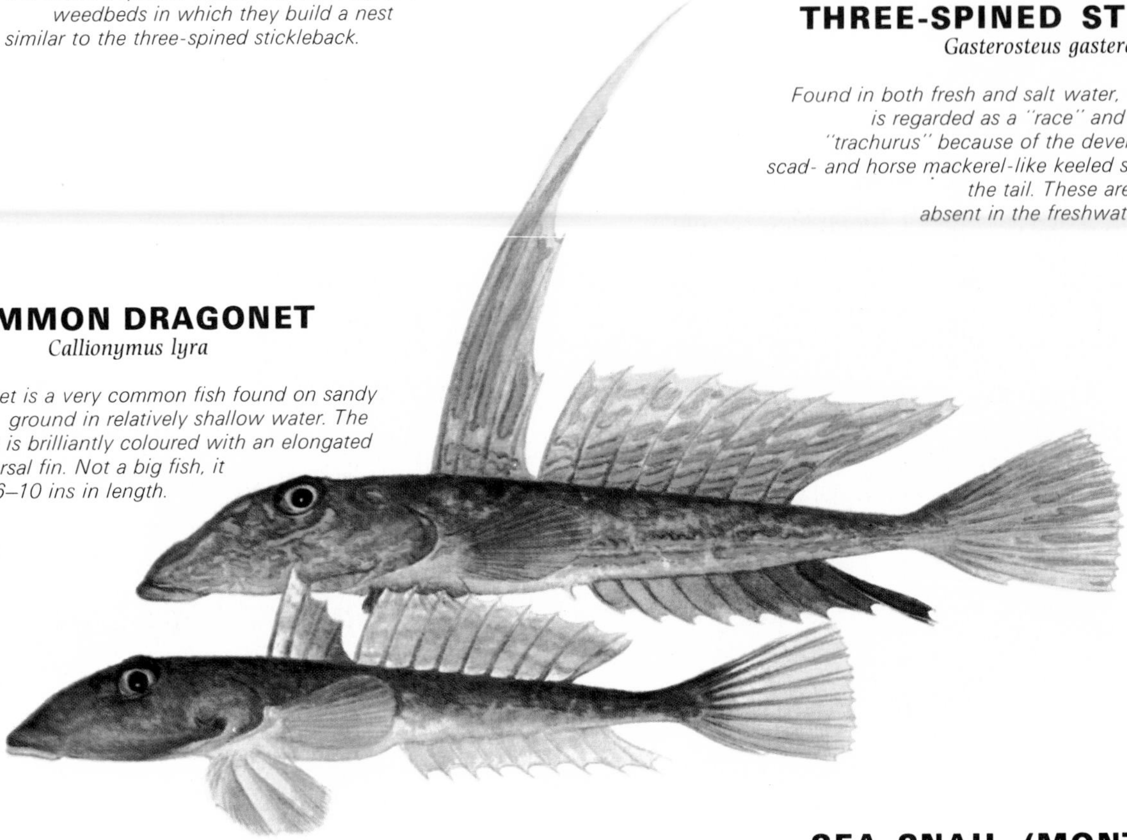

SEA SNAIL (MONTAGU'S)
Liparis montagui

An inshore fish fond of the patches of weed and rock in the inter-tidal zone. The sea snail will be found clinging to weed by means of a sucking disc formed by a fusing of the pelvic fins.

BLACK GOBY
Gobius niger

Found over both sand and rocky ground in the littoral zone. There are a great number of species, many of which are so similar in appearance that they call for expert knowledge in their separation. All gobies possess a strong, sucking disc used to attach themselves to weed or immovable objects during strong wave action.

COMMON GOBY
Pomataschistas minutus

A small and very common species of the goby family found in most rock pools. This goby exceeds 3 ins in length.

SANDEEL

Ammonddytidae

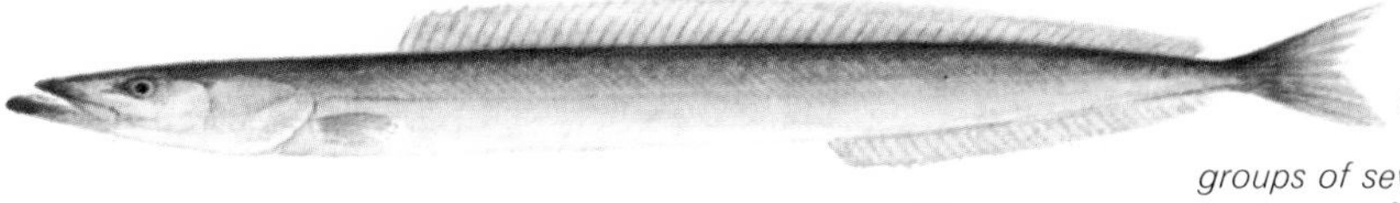

There are some five species, belonging to several genera, in British waters. All are similar in appearance. Sandeels are shoal fish, found in groups of several dozens up to shoals composed of thousands of slim, eel-like fish. Small individuals frequently remain on wet sand flats after the fall of the tide, where they bury themselves. Large specimens never do this, preferring to move out with the tide feeding on minute fry and marine organisms. The sandeel is an important angling bait and is gathered in fine-mesh nets.

Bait: *A string of small, lightly-dressed feathers or minute slivers of fish flesh.*

LUMPSUCKER

Cyclopterus lumpus

A bottom-dwelling species that moves inshore to spawn in the area around the extreme low water mark. Females spawn in shallow water where the males guard the clump of eggs and the nest. The female fish return to deeper water after spawning. The lumpsucker is a thick-bodied fish possessing pelvic fins that have fused to form a powerful sucking disc by which the fish can attach itself to rock strata. The male exhibits an orange colour to the belly during the breeding season. The species is not of angling importance, fish of 20 ins in length are a good size, with males slightly smaller than females.

POGGE

Agonus cataphractus

A fairly common visitor to inshore waters but ranging down into considerable depths throughout the year. The pogge is related to the sea scorpions and Miller's Thumb. It grows to 6 ins.

GUNNEL

Pholis gunnellus

A fish commonly found under stones in the inter-tidal zone. A distinctive line of dark spots marks the bottom of the dorsal fin. The female lays her eggs, produced from a single ovary, in a tight ball. Both sexes will fold their bodies around the egg mass to guard them. The gunnel grows to 12 ins.

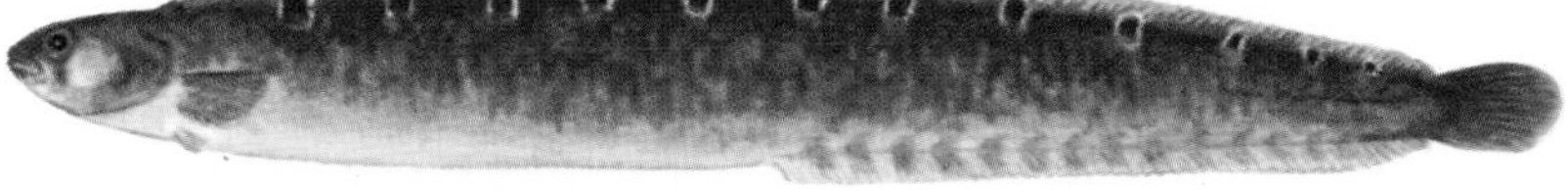

OPAH

Lampris guttatus

A brilliantly colourful fish that visits the western waters of the British Isles during the heat of summer, it moves along with the North Atlantic Drift as an occasional traveller. The body is deep and flattened with many colours. Blue, green, red and purple make up the ground hue, added to which there are a number of oval silver spots along the body sides.

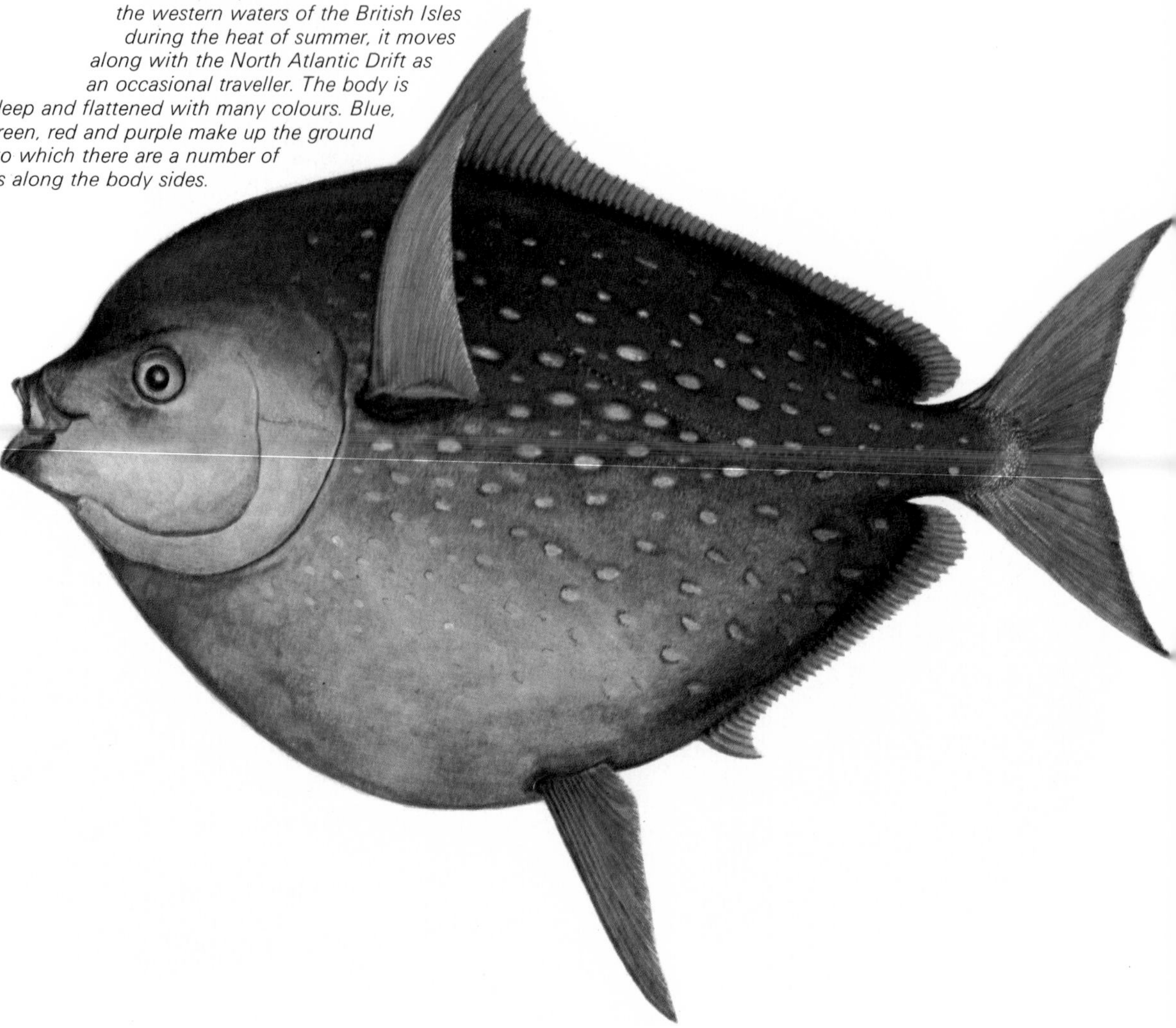

179◀ Obviously the farther the cast, the greater the problem of keeping it clean. A really long line might pick up several pounds of assorted flotsam from sea-wrack to plastic bags. Worst are fine strands of silky weed which bead the line and pass through the rings onto the spool. They must be removed before any significant build-up, or the line won't flow freely off the reel.

The trace, too, was weeded; lugworms on the hook were flecked with green slime. I untangled the paternoster and cleaned everything before re-baiting the 4/0 hook with four big lugworms. Finally, a couple of turns with the elastic band reset the anchor wires against the body of the lead weight.

With the wind in your face and the tide running hard, there is no room on a cod beach for finesse. You need a big lead to carry the bait into the wind and to hold against the water pressure. The rod must be strong enough to cast to where the cod lie. Sometimes the approach is crude, but you have to accept that codfishing in winter can be hard work. Without the right tackle, you catch nothing. That night there was no point using less than 6 ozs of lead. In a faster tide, 8 ozs might not have held bottom.

Two hours past high water, the ebb-tide lumped and churned as it pushed into the north-east gale. If I cast from my pitch by the Tilley lamp and immediately took in the slack line, the current would sweep the tackle back into the shallows. To avoid that, I trudged 20 yds uptide, climbing to the top of the shingle bank where casting space was not restricted, as it was on the steep slope nearer the water. By deliberately sacrificing 10 yds at this point, I could cast 30 yds farther.

My 12 ft heavy beachcaster flexed in a slow easy curve as a simple layback cast powered the lead away. I aimed low into the wind; throughout the cast my thumb hovered over the reel and braked the spool at the first sign of an over-run. Immediately the lead hit the water I thumbed the spool to a halt, then let it run free again. Perhaps 20 yds of nylon peeled off into the tide as I made my way back to the lamp. The slackness allowed the lead to fall to the seabed where the anchor wires dug into the mud. With the rod back in its rest

SUNFISH
Mola mola

This species, like the opah, makes sporadic visits to our waters. It drifts along in the warm currents, swimming in a lazy, swaying pattern whilst feeding on surface plankton. The fish has sharply pointed dorsal and anal fins and is without any ventral fins. The tail or caudal fin is hardly an addition to the fish's body, more a continuation of the lumpy, rounded body shape. Neither of these fish are considered as anglers' fish – more as oceanic oddities.

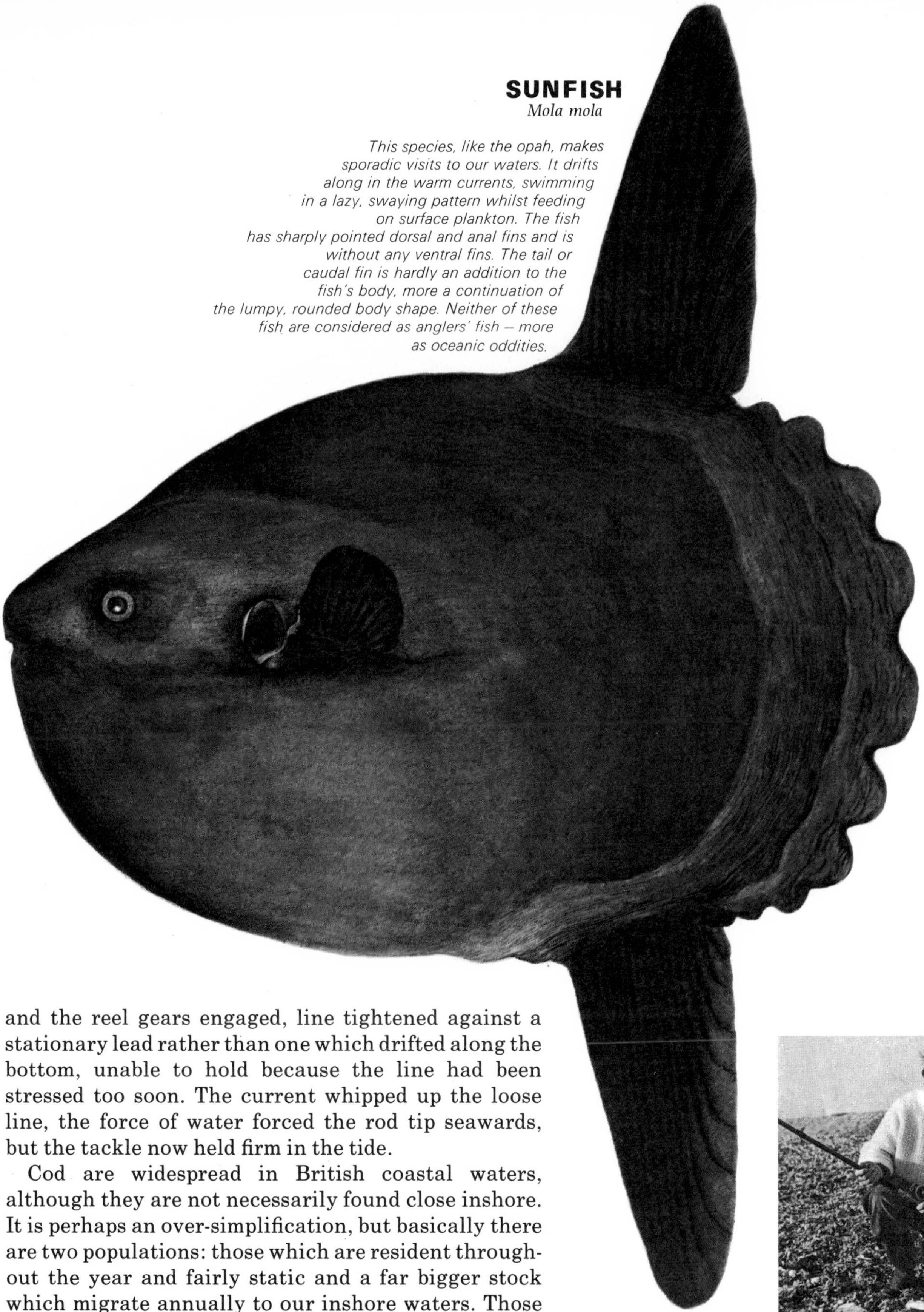

and the reel gears engaged, line tightened against a stationary lead rather than one which drifted along the bottom, unable to hold because the line had been stressed too soon. The current whipped up the loose line, the force of water forced the rod tip seawards, but the tackle now held firm in the tide.

Cod are widespread in British coastal waters, although they are not necessarily found close inshore. It is perhaps an over-simplification, but basically there are two populations: those which are resident throughout the year and fairly static and a far bigger stock which migrate annually to our inshore waters. Those are the fish which interest the south and east coast anglers. From Norfolk and Lincolnshire round to Sussex, shore and boat fishermen depend on cod for their winter sport. Sometimes they are the only worthwhile fish, the summer species being hardly worth the effort of fishing for.

Time of arrival and duration of stay depend on several factors. Among the most important of these are water temperatures, the herring shoal upon which the ▶186

Leslie Moncrieff, father of modern beach-fishing, with a catch of cod from the shingle at Dungeness. On the cold but bright days of January, cod will often harry the shoals of small fish close into the shoreline. Then a long cast, something in the order of over 100 yds, with bait on, will get out into the "Dustbin", a noted cod hole.

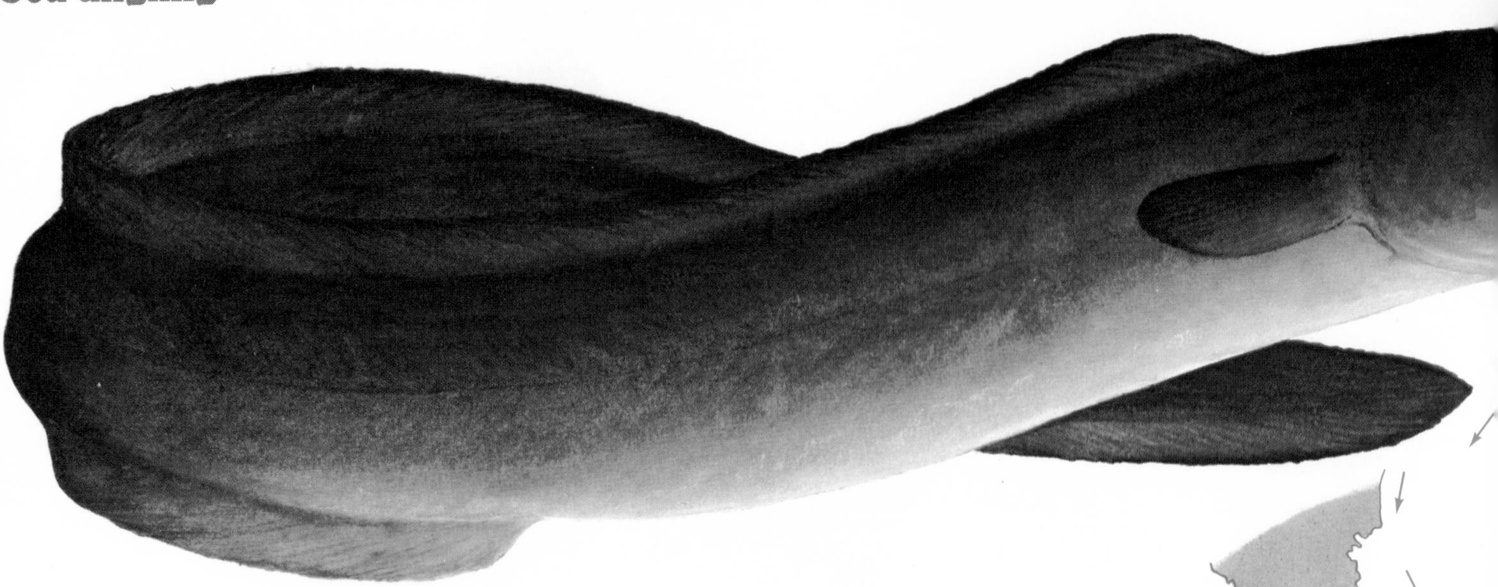

CONGER EEL

Conger conger

The conger eel appears to spawn in an area which stretches from the Sargasso Sea across the Atlantic to Gibraltar in water 6–9000 feet deep. Spawning, however, takes place in mid-water. The leptocephali are similar to those of the European freshwater eel although they are larger for each stage of growth. The conger eel grows to much greater sizes than its freshwater counterpart. Fish of over 100 lbs have been taken on rod and line in the West Country where there is now an established charter boat set-up for sea anglers based on fishing the many wrecks of two World Wars. Conger favour deepwater reefs, wrecks and broken ground from which they can ambush lesser species.

Bait: *Whole strips of fish, particularly mackerel, presented on wired traces.*

Eel larvae

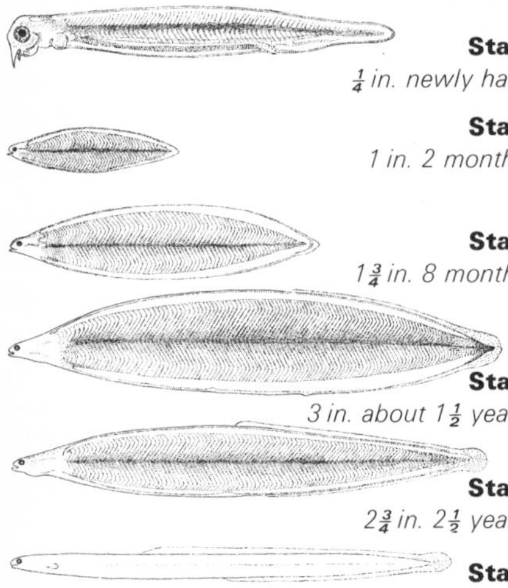

Stage 1.
$\frac{1}{4}$ in. newly hatched

Stage 2.
1 in. 2 months old

Stage 3.
$1\frac{3}{4}$ in. 8 months old

Stage 4.
3 in. about $1\frac{1}{2}$ years old

Stage 5.
$2\frac{3}{4}$ in. $2\frac{1}{2}$ years old

Stage 6.
$2\frac{1}{2}$ in. about 3 years old

Stage 4 was at one time thought to be a separate species, Leptocephalus brevirostris.

Stages 4–6 show a gradual reduction in width and a slight reduction in length as the larva becomes an elver.

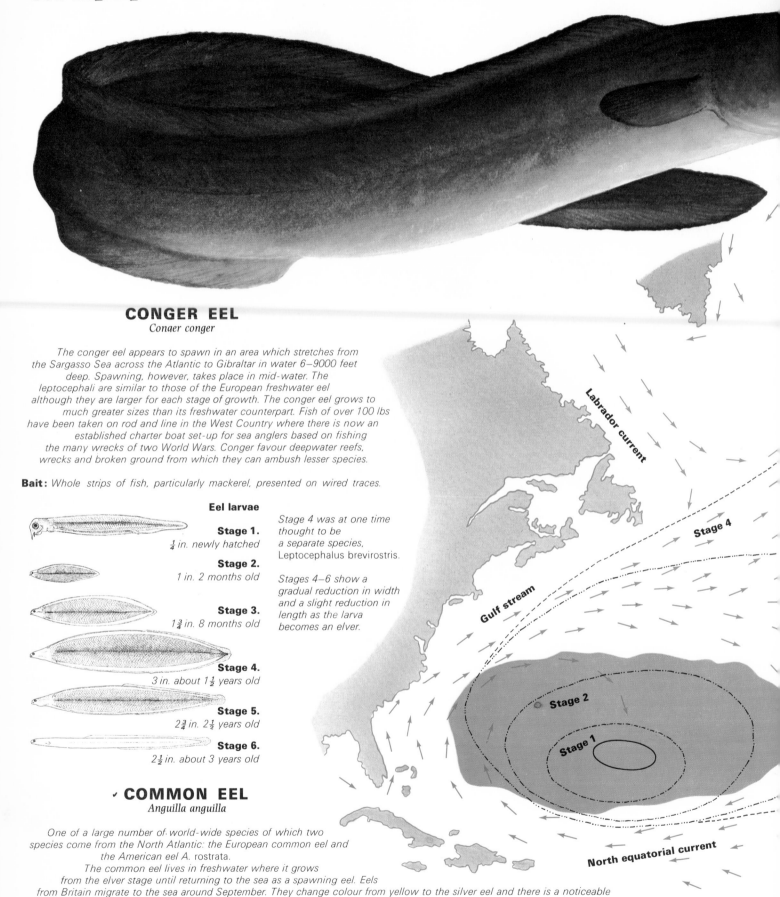

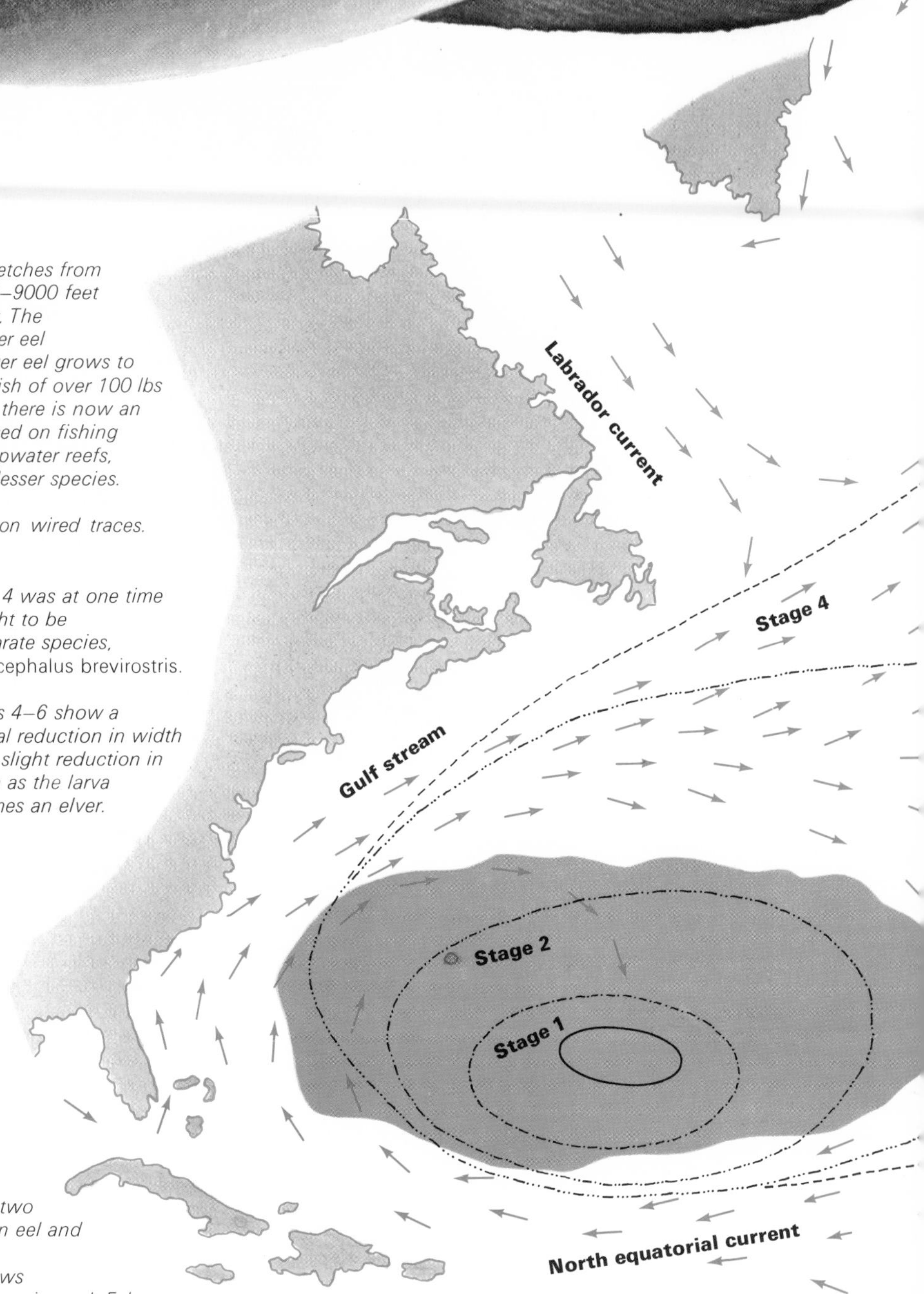

COMMON EEL

Anguilla anguilla

One of a large number of world-wide species of which two species come from the North Atlantic: the European common eel and the American eel A. rostrata.

The common eel lives in freshwater where it grows from the elver stage until returning to the sea as a spawning eel. Eels from Britain migrate to the sea around September. They change colour from yellow to the silver eel and there is a noticeable increase in the size of their eyes. Migrating eels have never been caught outside coastal waters so little is known of migratory spawning routes. Man learned of the species' reproduction by tracing the minute but developing larvae from a point of origin in the Sargasso Sea. Here minute larvae were found but no eggs. Though 3000 fathoms deep, the immediate sea locale produces eel larvae at depths of 300–900 feet during March.

Drifting on the warm currents the leaf-shaped Leptocephali *are moved toward Europe and North Africa by the North Atlantic Drift. Four years after leaving the Sargasso area they arrive as elvers, in fantastic numbers, wherever freshwater enters the sea. The yellowish colouring develops after entry into freshwater.*

Bait: *Dead fish and bunches of worms. Small eels will take grub baits intended for other angling species.*

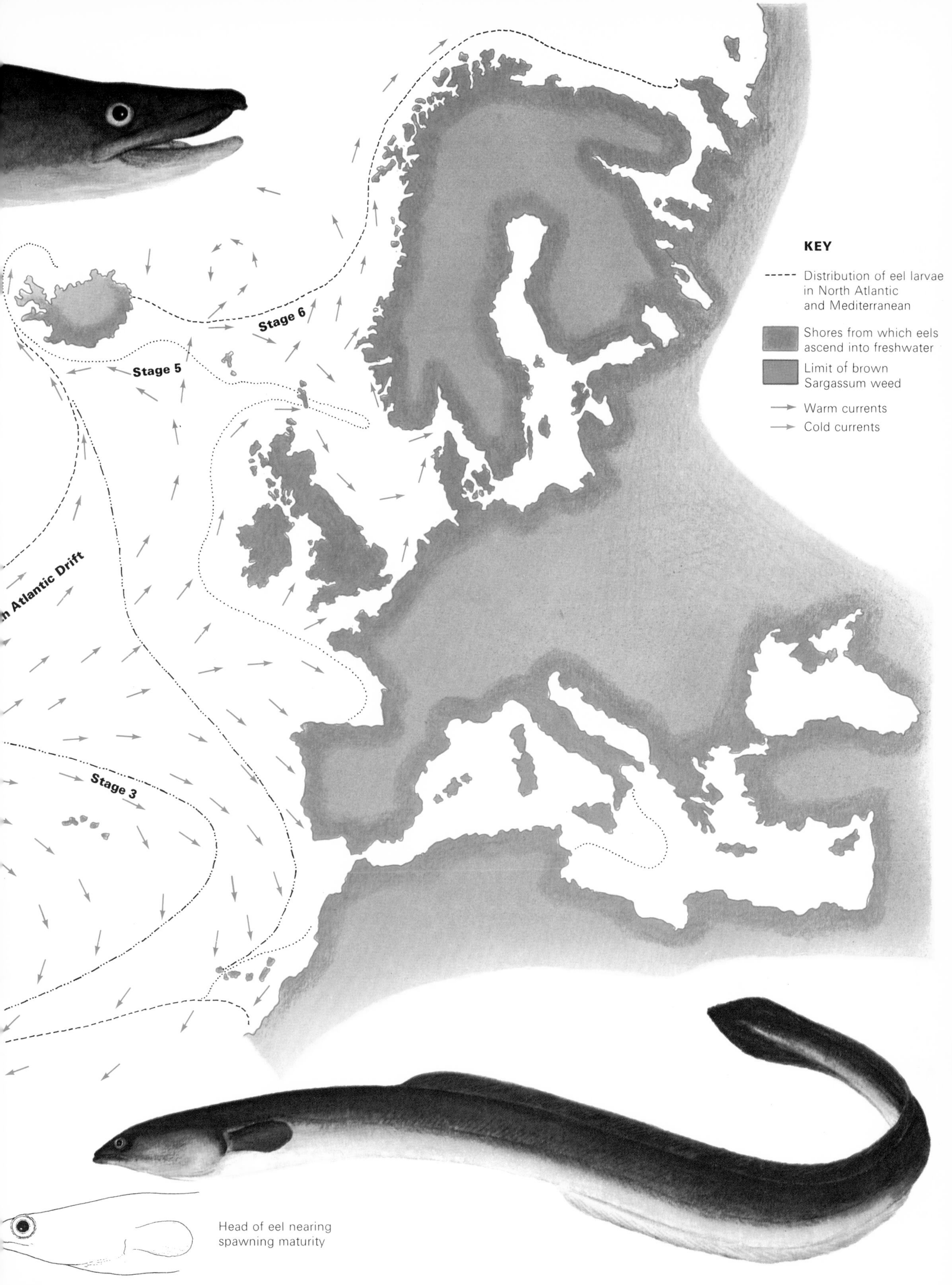

Head of eel nearing spawning maturity

183◀ cod feed, as well as the effects of commercial fishing on the amount of available cod.

Cod are normally preceded by shoals of whiting which arrive on the east coast in late September, often coming to coincide with the first autumn frosts. The cod move down from the north – first a few solitary fish out in the deep water, then a full-scale invasion of the inshore regions. By November there should be cod from the Humber to the Solent.

It is not unusual for codding to slacken around Christmas when spawning herring shoals tend often to preoccupy the cod's feeding pattern. Consequently, not many fall to the beach angler: first, herrings shoal well beyond casting range; also, cod don't look for food on the seabed while chasing herring in the surface layers. Baited hooks lying on the bottom are thus ignored. However, the boat angler often suffers this seasonal break in sport, so for once the shore angler is not the only one on the receiving end.

But in late January the fish return to bottom feeding with a vengeance. Under the right conditions they remain with us until late March or even April.

Left to their own devices, cod would probably be quite predictable in their movements and habits. Unfortunately, commercial fishing pressures no longer allow the once established patterns to continue. In the past few years, for economic and political reasons, our trawling of Icelandic and Arctic waters has been curtailed, and the North Sea is fished much harder. Cod, which previously had been allowed to spend summer in relative peace in areas such as the Dogger Bank, are now constantly harassed. As a result, fewer fish are left to depart on the autumn migration to British inshore waters. On the way, too, they are hammered by the fleets. After such relentless pressure it is no wonder that the yearly influx of the last decade has thinned to a small trickle of greatly depleted shoals. But, despite the lack of fish, you can still catch cod from most of the traditional cod beaches; what has changed is that you now have to fish harder for them.

When and where to catch cod are leading questions with, as far as I can see, few satisfactory answers. It all depends on which beach you fish, when you go there, on the wind, the temperature, whether it is daylight or after dark, on the roughness of the water, whether or not the fish are chasing herrings, where the local trawlers are working, on the colour of the water, its turbidity and the related light penetration.

The various factors which influence cods' whereabouts and willingness to feed are diverse and obscure. Much of the research already done into cod and their life cycle was specifically concerned with problems encountered in commercial fishing. What happens in deep water does not necessarily hold true in the shallows. As anglers, we must make our own observations. So much is conjecture and personal opinion that an in-depth discussion is pointless. To catch cod you have to get out with a rod and reel, and learn as you go along. Listen to those anglers who do catch cod, use your eyes, and – best of all – fish with someone who knows the game.

But as a rough guide, assuming you are fishing a known cod beach, the colder and rougher the sea the better. Night tides often produce most fish, especially when the water is clear, as it often is after an easterly. There are no inflexible rules about tides, but fast water generally fishes better than the slack at top and bottom waters (spring and neap tides). Some beaches are better on the flood, others on the ebb, some on both. Local knowledge is the only real guide though, because despite all the odds you can take good bags of cod on a few beaches when, in theory, there should be no fish within the vicinity.

By half tide, water pressure stretched my line until it whistled in the wind. Scraps of weed blew up from the sea, along the line, and bunched at the rod tip. They flapped and rattled in the beam of light reflected onto the rod by a shaving mirror wedged in the stones at the back of the Tilley lamp. Spray drifted onto the lamp glass and evaporated there into opaque grit.

The first tentative quivers on the rod tip seemed unreal in the flickering light. But the tip sank out of sight, then flipped back as the lead shifted in the mud. Out in the grey water a cod had located the worms and

1

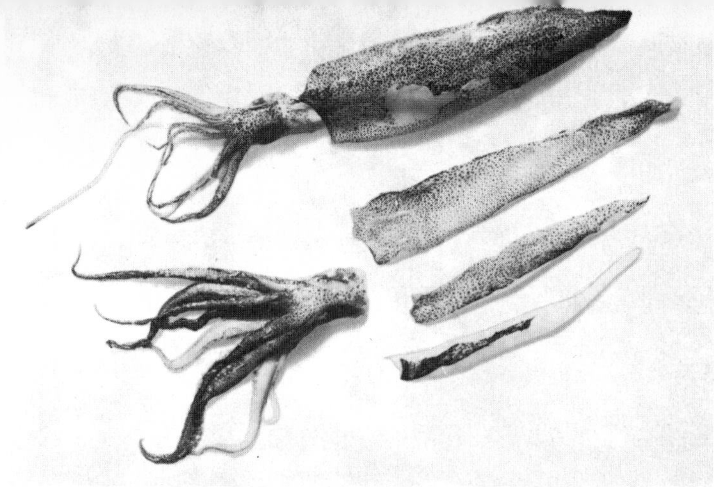

Squid, a favourite bait of the winter cod angler. Each of the small squids that sea fishermen buy from tackle and fish shops will provide four cod-sized mouthfuls of the right size to enable a long cast.

had snatched them with force enough to tear the lead from the seabed.

Fish and tackle drifted free in the tide. I took in the slack line, felt the fish's weight on the rod, and pulled the nylon tight. A smooth lift on the rod tip set the hook deep. The cod shook its head but the hook held. I pumped line back onto the spool . . . lift the rod, lower it, wind up the resultant slack line.

The fish swam uptide and I followed along the beach so that the line did not swing diagonal to the surf-line. The sea beats you more often than a cod. In fast water cod are like kites in the wind. Mere water pressure on their bulk can generate enough power to snap heavy lines. That more often happens if the line is picked up by the breakers and goes out of control. Cod, themselves, are not hard fighters – none of the dash and strength of tope, for instance. Take your time, give line if necessary, and they will finally beat themselves.

It came into the breakers and I loosened the drag so that, if the backwash swept it out again, the line would not break. Give it time, let the sea land it. I switched on my headlamp; its beam lit up the surf and shingle. The cod kicked and twisted in the shallows, then the line slackened as a big wave crashed down. Foam swirled around my feet and receded. White belly up, the cod lay stranded on the shingle. Careful of the next wave, I went down the slope to the water's edge, dug my fingers into the rubbery skin behind the cod's head, and lifted it clear of the sea.

It was a sleek fish weighing about 10 lbs. Not ugly like big cod with bulging bellies and overlarge heads. Its gill covers worked rhythmically; the dorsal and pelvic fins rippled against its body.

This fish was for eating, so I hit it on the back of the head with a big stone. It died instantly. If you intend to keep a fish, there is no excuse for letting it gasp and suffocate to death on the shore. Many photographs of cod show them open-mouthed – evidence of slow death inflicted by a careless or callous angler.

I twisted the hook from the cartilage at the back of its throat. Before rebaiting I lobbed the lead about 80 yds into the sea. As I fought the cod, line had bunched on the spool in an uneven heap and, as the retrieve pressure had varied from yard to yard, tension alternated from slack to taut. A badly loaded spool makes a

2

1 *Sea anglers stretched along the strand as far as the eye can see at Downhill on the Ulster Causeway Coast. They are competing in a heat of the Winfield-NFSA Shore Fishing Championship of Great Britain.*

2 *Another shore fishing contest, in Scotland, on the coast at Portencross. Cod figure largely in the winter catches off Scottish shores although flounders, pollack and small coalfish regularly appear in the catches.*

multiplying reel almost uncontrollable. Casting hard is the shortcut to an over-run at least and, perhaps, to loss of tackle. A short cast smooths out the tension; careful rewinding then prepares the spool for another long cast.

I rebaited the hook and reset the anchor wires on the lead weight. I cast again. The baits flew 120 yds; I propped the rod in its rest and as the tide took up the slack line the lead shifted in the bottom, then held. The baits were back in the cod run.

I turned the cod onto its back and slit its belly from between the pelvic fins to the vent, opened the gut cavity, and removed the viscera. Out of interest, I opened the stomach. In the grey sludge were the remains of a dab, a couple of hardback shorecrabs and the Christmas-tree skeleton of a herring.

Cod eat almost anything. According to their mood they will take crustacea, molluscs, fish, worms – even stones and rubbish. (English Channel fish seem partial to the disposable cups thrown overboard from British Rail ferries.) Research suggests that the cod's staple diet is Norway lobster, squid, cuttlefish and, in season, herrings and sprats. However, it does not follow that these make the best angling baits.

At times, squid is deadly. It is really a deepwater bait and so of more value to the boat angler. But squid in combination with worms, a "cocktail" bait, as it is called, can be an excellent bait from the shore. It has a two-fold advantage apart from its attraction: it helps make the worms go further and, being tough, squid will stand up to hard casting.

Herrings and sprats are much less attractive than their position on the cod's natural menu should suggest. In fact, shorecasting with sprats is singularly ineffective unless the fish are feeding on a sprat shoal right under the land. There are two reasons why this should be so: first, cod are used to chasing live fish, not picking them up dead from the bottom; and, secondly, most anglers never fish really fresh herrings and sprats. Those from the fishmonger are fit for human consumption, but are not necessarily fresh. Cod know the difference between a fresh herring and one which may have been kicking around in a deep freeze for months. The only baitfish worth using are those instantly frozen "stiff-alive" longshore herrings and sprats.

As hookbaits, crabs are an enigma. Just about every cod you gut contains shorecrabs. But you can fish all day with a hard crab on the hook and catch nothing. Changing baits might well produce a cod – a cod full to the gills with hard crabs. Why should that be? There are many theories; but as nobody has shown anglers how to fish hardbacks, we can assume that as yet nobody knows the answer. Soft and peeler crabs are another matter. They make good baits but often you cannot get them on the east coast in winter.

Generally, you cannot better worms. Both the big Dungeness worms and smaller East Anglian "blow-lugs" are excellent baits. It is interesting to note that each type of worm is best in its own area. For instance, the tough south coast worms are not always effective in Essex, and vice versa.

You must remember to load the hook with as many worms as it will take. The maxim "big baits for big fish" rings never so true as for cod. Worms are expensive. The tendency is to skimp on each hookful to make them last longer. Cod want a big mouthful. They don't know, or care, that worms cost £1 a score. If you want to catch cod you have to pander to their stomachs rather than to your pocket.

For cod, ragworms are not so good as lugworms but they are useful, especially when used in combination baits. Again, a big hookful will better attract fish. One advantage of ragworms is that they are tougher on the hook than lug.

Baits apart, there are, in my opinion, two major factors in codfishing which nine times out of ten separate success from failure. They are long distance casting and firm bait anchorage. Put simply, to catch fish you must cast as far as possible with a big bait and

1

make sure it holds flat against the bottom.

I have mentioned baits. Long distance casting has been given a section to itself. Perhaps now we should look briefly at bait anchorage in its relation to shore-fishing for cod.

Commercial longliners will tell you that the way to catch cod is with a heavy line anchored hard into the seabed. As well as having a heavy anchor at each end the line is further pegged with intermediate grips every few feet along its whole length. Any hook allowed to flap in the tide is less likely to take a fish.

The close-to-the-bottom idea is also exploited by many of the more successful anglers. Many of them standardize on a minimum 5 or 6 oz grip lead and use correspondingly powerful rods. The general theme is to get the baits well out from the beach and hard down. During the past 5 years there has been a trend towards lighter tackle. Its introduction coincided with, and was influenced by, the decline in codfishing. We reasoned that lighter tackle would probably help make the best of a bad job.

But despite its alleged virtues – which are subjective anyway – light tackle has yet to prove itself. Until cod return in their former numbers there will be no opportunity for objective comparisons. However, there are definite indications that light tackle misses fish. My own trials, admittedly on a scale so small as to have no real significance, show that, in the way I fish, heavy tackle beats light by two fish to one. For some reason the cod where I fish like their baits well tethered.

I suppose it all adds up to demonstrating that our knowledge of codfishing is less full than we imagine. Perhaps that's what makes codding such a challenge. Certainly, to take up codfishing is to take on more than a fish. There is the cold, the waiting, and the frustration.

But when the wind comes straight in, the waves churn and boil into the shingle, the spray soaks into tackle and clothing and the cod feed ravenously in the rushing tide, you'll understand what cod-fishing really means. Codfishing is shore angling without equal. And every Saturday night from November until March, a thousand twinkling Tilley lamps dot the East Anglian shoreline to emphasize its growing popularity.

SPRING – FLOUNDERS AND THORNBACK RAYS

Flounders live in the brackish ooze of salting and estuary creeks; among the rocks and weeds of the open sea; in the long, clean water-tables of surf beaches everywhere. They are humble fish: perhaps familiarity makes them so, for most sea fishermen catch flounders either by accident or design. The slimy, rather ugly flatfish are a cornerstone of sea fishing.

I fish for flounders as an alternative to cod. East Anglian cod and flounders complement each other. As one declines, the other comes into season. Cod shoals

2

3

4

1 *Not at first sight the place to seek flounders, a stormy steep-to beach but alive with flatfish searching out the worms that are forced out of the sand by the wave surge.*

2 *Mike Prichard into a flounder. The fight is out of all proportion to the weight of the fish because of the grip lead necessary to counteract the power of the undertow.*

3 *Although primarily a bass beach, this kind of shore will produce many species of fish. It has rich feeding and deepwater at all stages of the tidal phase.*

4 *A fat, fleshy flounder that will make somebody a good meal. With no pollution and plenty of marine life on which to feed, the flounder can be a fine meal.*

often move offshore in the early New Year and beachfishing becomes unproductive. At the same time, flounders begin their annual migration to the open-sea spawning grounds. Flounders are small, don't really fight and are easily caught. But there is something about floundering which gives it a special place in my angling calendar.

Flounders live happily in the upper reaches of a tidal system. Brackish and even fresh water attracts them, but they cannot breed there because the eggs and fry require specific saline conditions found in the deep sea. So, in January flounders begin their run downstream in preparation for the February–April breeding season.

Most rivers have traditional flounder marks: alongside wharves, in the channels, wherever there is deep water on the way to the sea. Finding the fish is the only problem because actually catching flounders is almost a foregone conclusion. The shoals are constantly moving, although they seem to hold back for a few days in good feeding places. To fish flounders, you may either follow individual shoals or ambush passing groups in the known hotspots.

My home waters, the Essex estuaries, offer two contrasting approaches. One is shorefishing in the accepted sense; the other owes more to freshwater fishing.

Near the river mouth the mud gives way to coarse sand and grit. The main channel is about 100 yds out from the sea wall where you stand to fish. Between the channel and the wall, the foreshore is clumped with bladderwrack and boulders – an obstacle course over which fish and tackle must be dragged.

Winter flounders stay in the channel, their highway to the sea. In summer they are resident and venture out of the deeper water into the shallows under the seawall. There they root under the stones for shorecrabs and shrimps, chase the fry and sand-eels. But cold weather keeps them far out, and you have to cast long distances.

The best way is casting out to the channel so that your bait lies in the path of the main shoals. Fishing closer in means that only the stragglers find your bait. Tackle must therefore be selected to cast rather than to extract the ultimate in sport from flounders. Standard codfishing tackle will do: 4 or 5 oz leads, shore rods and reels filled with 15 lb nylon. Sometimes, on flat calm days when there isn't a ripple, really light tackle can be used – an ounce or two of lead and rods to suit.

Regardless of the rod and reel, terminal tackle is invariable. Flounders need nothing more complicated than paternosters and running traces. Hooks should be small, but not so tiny that the fish swallow them right down. Size 4 up to 1/0 long-shanked hooks are small enough for the bait but too big to go down too far. One minor tackle point is trace abrasion. Flounders have tiny, razor sharp teeth which wear down the trace nylon just above the hook knot. A succession of fish will eventually file the line away; so always check the line after every fish.

A thornback ray from the mouth of a sandy estuary. Little freshwater enters the estuary, so the rays venture in to feed on the worms and mass of small shore crabs that live among the weed growths.

To fish the channel I cast a bunch of ragworms or a strip of herring as far as possible, then let the bait drift downstream in the current so it swings back to the shore in a big arc. That way the tackle covers far more ground; flounders are better attracted to moving baits anyway. In normal tides, a plain bomb or Sandfast lead drifts at just the right speed. But on spring ebbs, a grip lead with the wires bent slightly backwards helps slow the drift.

The secret is to be slow. Flounders nibble for ages, and too fast a strike pulls the hook away from them. If you hold the line between your fingers and thumb, the sucking and quivering is easily felt. Tighten the line when the fish moves off with the bait. There is no need to strike; just keep tension in the line. Playing and landing a flounder is a non-event with ordinary fishing tackle. Just let them trundle inshore in their own time.

Shorecasting for flounders is similar to other beachcasting. On the east coast there isn't much to choose between cod, bass and flatfish – as far as fishing technique is concerned, anyway. For that reason, flounder fishing soon pales. It can, in fact, become a boring slaughter. And slaughter is the right word, too: 50 and 60 fish on a tide is nothing special when the flounders are running. For that reason alone I prefer the inland creeks to open beach fishing.

A typical estuary to a small river in Kerry. There is a half mile of wide river mouth closing to a narrow channel and then opening into a saltwater lagoon. This environment suits flounders, mullet and the occasional bass that noses among the channels and weed for minute invertebrate life.

A hundred years ago the sailing barges drifted in through the estuary channels on the early flood tide. Ten miles from the sea, where the flat Essex farmland squeezes the river into a deep creek, the big, red-ochred sails came down. The crews poled the barges up to a quay fronting a mill. As the tide rose the barges took aboard a load of flour and grain. On the ebb the mooring lines were slipped, the sails unfurled and filled in the breeze, and the ships ploughed back downriver bound for London, perhaps.

The barges have gone now, except for the wrecks which sit bare-ribbed in the mud. The river is left to the swans and wildfowl, but the mill still stands. The dirty water swirls past the pilings; and in the deep channel February flounder mass for the spawning run. A sliver of herring drifts downtide. A dumpy grayling float buoys the bait so that it trips the bottom just clear of the snags. The line sinks and twists in the fast water, and I flick the Avon rod to bring it back in line. The float swings into the pilings, sidesteps, and slips. The 10 lb nylon tightens; the fish tugs with the characteristic humping motion of a flounder. It flaps for the bottom, and for a moment line slips off against the fixed-spool's drag. But it is a half-hearted gesture – now it is on the surface and splashing towards the net.

Floatfishing in the upper estuary is very similar to river fishing for perch. The tackle and methods are very similar; in fact, what goes for perch will do nicely for flounders. As well as floatfishing you may spin and leger. I prefer to use a float, simply because I like watching floats. Legering is probably more productive if you measure success by the number of fish caught. Spinning is also pleasant fishing but is really better restricted to boat fishing. Some deep water marks can be fished with a spinner, but muddy creeks are almost impossible from the shore – there is no depth of water in which to troll.

Flounder spinning relies on the baited spoon more than on traditional freshwater lures. However, small vibratory spoons baited with a sliver of fish or segments of ragworm sometimes fish as well as the conventional flounder spoon. It pays to experiment.

Flounders are not the most sporting species in the sea. They are an acquired taste in both senses. So why bother? The answer is that fishing is all things to all men; and some anglers like floundering. It doesn't worry me that flounders are ugly and messy, that I can't bear to eat them. I just like the fishing – some of the time anyway. Certainly the going of flounders would create an enormous vacuum in seafishing.

THORNBACK RAYS

June. Spring passes. The flounders arrive back inshore, spent and thin from spawning. Cod have disappeared. A few silver eels move into the estuaries.

The tide floods along the hot foreshore, fingering into the sand and over the pebbles. Out on the sandbanks which bar the river mouth the current humps and eddies over the rough ground. Terns flicker and dive in silhouette against the hazy sunset. Low cloud heaps on the horizon. Lightning backlights the coming storm, and thunder rumbles through the marshlands.

The tide swirls in the underwater sandhills; shadows lengthen between the valleys. The undersea wakes in the gloom: shorecrabs scuttle from under rocks; whelks and hermit crabs trundle their shells through tangles of flatwrack. Two golden-frilled eyeballs bulge out of the sand; spiracles wink open and shut behind them. The sand shifts and clouds the water as a big female thornback ray pushes out of the seabed and ghosts into the darkness. A smaller male fish slips from his hiding place to follow.

Uptide of the bar the shore slopes gently; 150 yds offshore there is no more than 10 ft of water. The current runs fast as the sea pushes into the estuary. On the bottom my griplead buries in the sand and shellgrit. A long, flowing trace unfolds from the leader to which it was attached for casting. The trace unravels and pulls straight in the tide. The chunk of frozen herring bait thaws in the warm sea. Oil and iridescent fragments drift downstream.

The rays hunt the foreshore, quartering the ground in search of crabs and small fish. They move furtively on pulsating wingtips. Scent from the herring reaches them, and although the oils are now diluted, thousands to one in sea water, their olfactory organs home in. They hover along the bottom, moving faster.

The female finds the herring and flops onto it. The lead shifts; back ashore the reel clicks off a few inches of line. She shuffles over the bait, guides it to her underslung jaws. The reel clicks again. She plays for 5 minutes, finally takes the bait and moves off. The lead rips out of the sand; the grip wires flip back. Line slackens, then retightens as she runs.

There is no reaction for 10 yds. Then the reel is in gear and the rod curved over. The hook drives into the scissors of her mouth and holds fast. At first, pressure leads her inshore, calmly. Uncertainty gives way to panic, and she is fighting back. Wings beat hard; she turns in the current like a kite. The clutch slips as a few yards of nylon tear off. Now she is on the bottom, the big flat body arched so that suction glues her down. But the tension is relentless; she tires, her body flattens, she is moving again. The ray kites once more in the shallows but the sea is still, with no undertow to help her. She glides onto the sand and I tow her clear of the water. She kicks and arches her back. The tail lashes. But I flip her onto her back and she lies still.

Thornback fishing time almost advertises itself. Often you look at the day knowing that in the evening rays will be close inshore. It is hot and still and June. Thundery. You know the rays have moved in because the dinghy men are catching them. And often, the rays came when the may blossomed. It seems so logical.

Thornbacks are easy to catch. There are two rules:

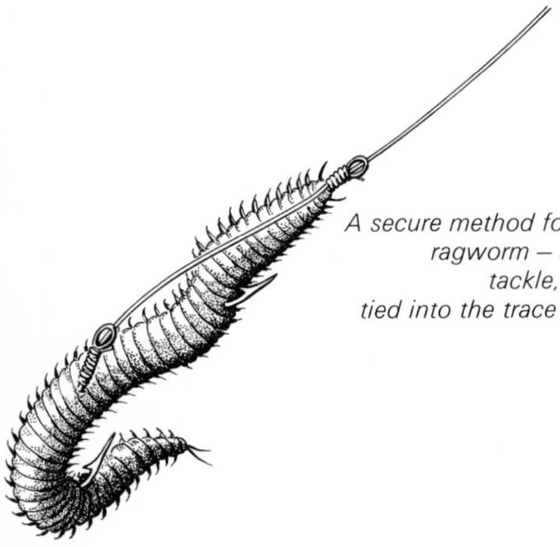

A secure method for hooking a large ragworm – a Pennell tackle, using two hooks tied into the trace in tandem.

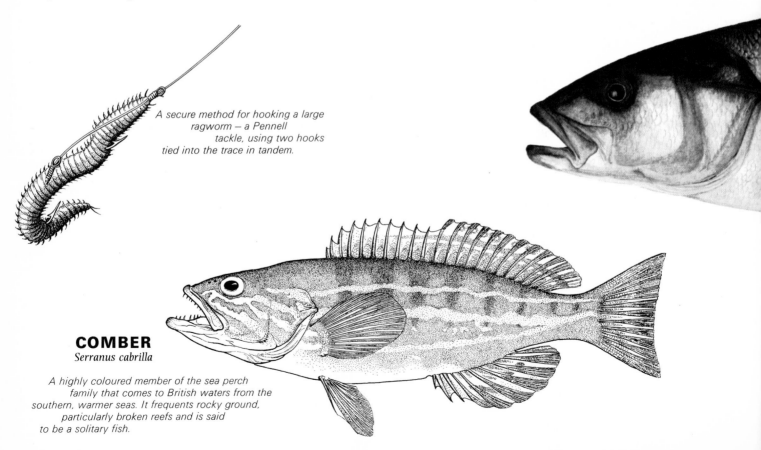

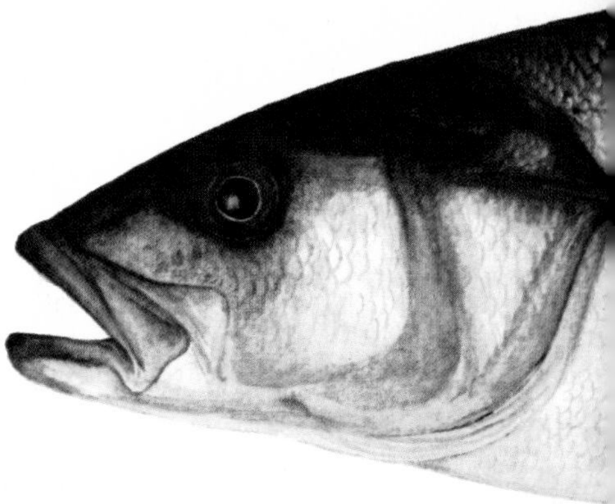

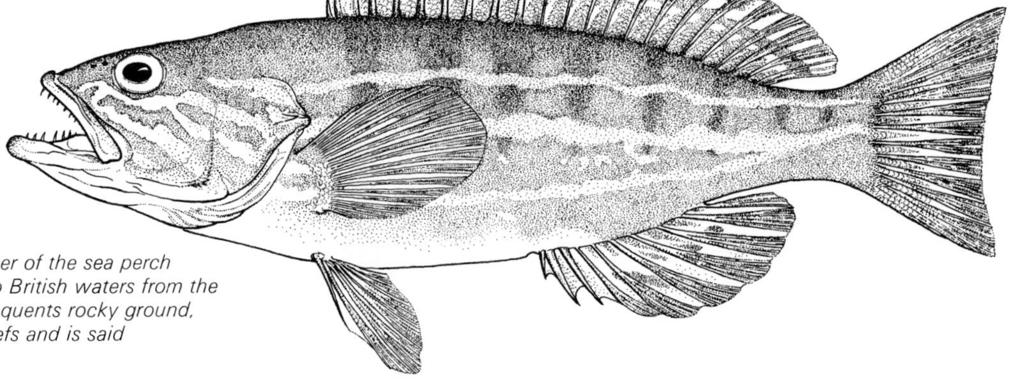

COMBER
Serranus cabrilla

A highly coloured member of the sea perch family that comes to British waters from the southern, warmer seas. It frequents rocky ground, particularly broken reefs and is said to be a solitary fish.

WRECKFISH

Polyprion americanus

A thick-bodied sea perch of the reefs and rocky ground. The dorsal fin has stiff spines joined with leathery webs, followed by a soft rayed section reaching from just above the gill case to a point above the tail wrist. There is a fairly prominent hard, bony ridge on the gill cover. The lower jaw protrudes markedly. The fish gets its name from its habit of shoaling up around wreckage and other undersea obstructions that harbour small fish and have a growth of shellfish.

Bait: *Fishbaits of large size.*

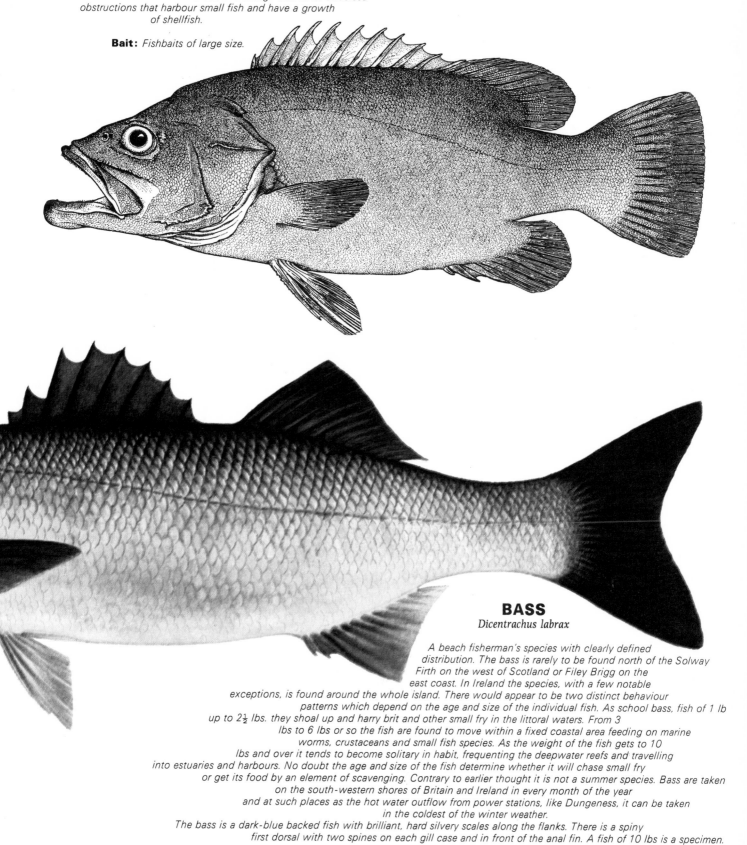

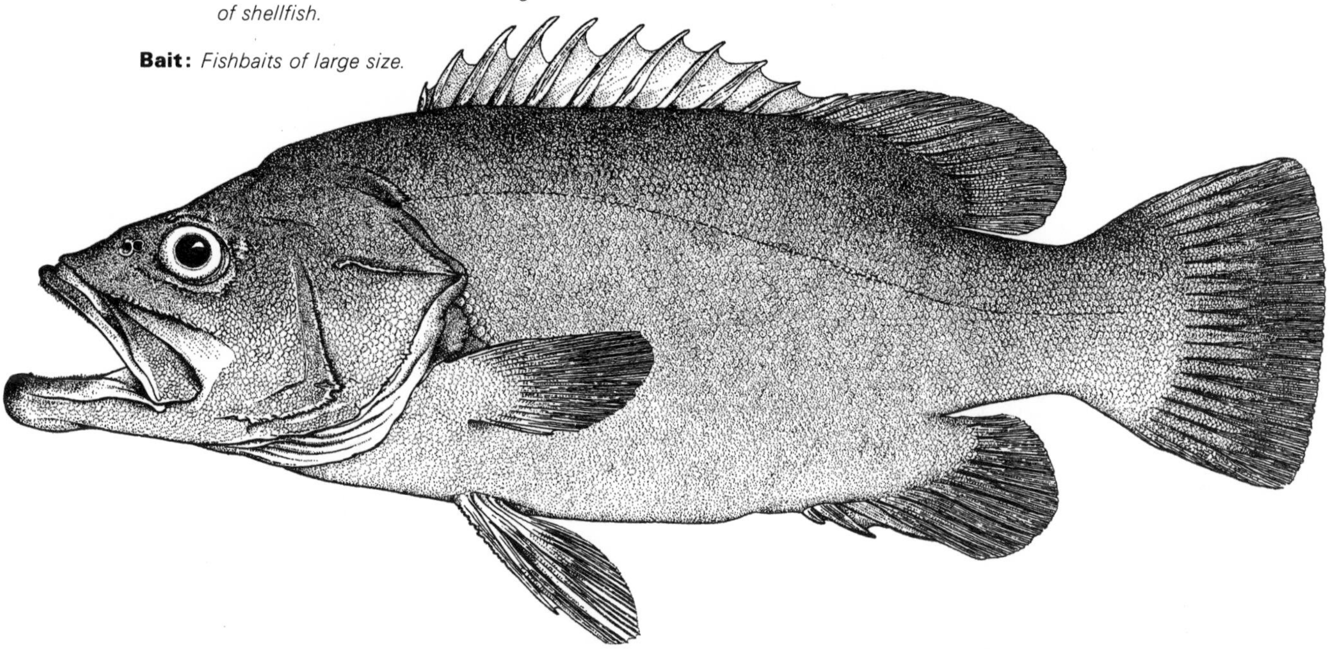

BASS

Dicentrachus labrax

A beach fisherman's species with clearly defined distribution. The bass is rarely to be found north of the Solway Firth on the west of Scotland or Filey Brigg on the east coast. In Ireland the species, with a few notable exceptions, is found around the whole island. There would appear to be two distinct behaviour patterns which depend on the age and size of the individual fish. As school bass, fish of 1 lb up to $2\frac{1}{2}$ lbs. they shoal up and harry brit and other small fry in the littoral waters. From 3 lbs to 6 lbs or so the fish are found to move within a fixed coastal area feeding on marine worms, crustaceans and small fish species. As the weight of the fish gets to 10 lbs and over it tends to become solitary in habit, frequenting the deepwater reefs and travelling into estuaries and harbours. No doubt the age and size of the fish determine whether it will chase small fry or get its food by an element of scavenging. Contrary to earlier thought it is not a summer species. Bass are taken on the south-western shores of Britain and Ireland in every month of the year and at such places as the hot water outflow from power stations, like Dungeness, it can be taken in the coldest of the winter weather.

The bass is a dark-blue backed fish with brilliant, hard silvery scales along the flanks. There is a spiny first dorsal with two spines on each gill case and in front of the anal fin. A fish of 10 lbs is a specimen.

Bait: *Lugworm, ragworm, squid strip and fishbaits. Artificial lures of all kinds.*

cast well out, and use really fresh baits. Casting and terminal tackles are the same as for other long distance work: 11–13 ft beach rod, fixed-spool or multiplier reel, 15 lb nylon, and 4 to 6 oz leads.

Thornbacks do require a slight modification to the terminal rigs. They are strong fish with tails like files. It is therefore essential to use line which withstands abrasion. The leader should be more than 30 lbs breaking strain with a hook length of the same material. Stainless steel hooks will load the dice in your favour too: rays will literally grind hooks to powder, and stainless steel stands up to the pressure better than most metals. Thin wire hooks are sharper, it is true, but they are absolutely useless for thornbacks.

The real key is bait. You may use ragworms, crabs and squid, but nothing beats fresh mackerel and herrings. And I mean fresh – you will not find anything suitable at the fishmonger's, I am afraid. Bait for rays has to come straight out of the sea and into the deep-freeze. No half measures here. On the east coast, longshore herrings are most easily obtained. I buy them from the quayside in winter when the commercial fishermen work the herring shoals in the Blackwater.

Fish baits are difficult to cast. They tear from the hook; sheer bulk slashes casting distance. To help overcome the problems I use a water soluble plastic to tie baits to the hook and the hook trace to the leader. In that packaged form, the bait flies farther. The plastic is called polyvinyl alcohol. It is just like polythene ribbon but melts in the sea. Many tackle shops sell it.

Cast the bait as far as possible, put the rod in a rest with the reel out of gear and ratchet on . . . and wait. Thornback fishing is a waiting game. Sometimes rays take hours to find the bait. On some beaches, two fish on a tide is good going. Actually, if you catch one fish, another is very much on the cards. Thornbacks travel in pairs, male and female together. Catch one, and the other is likely to be yours too. You can easily distinguish between sexes: males have long claspers hanging from the rear abdomen; females do not have claspers, and they are usually bigger fish.

Evening is the high spot of ray fishing. Rays feed all day in deep water, but tend to prefer dusk in the shallows. That could be for two reasons: light intensity deters fish from moving in close during the day; evening brings out more of the marine creatures upon which they feed. Dawn, too, sees activity among the food species, but is less satisfactory for rays perhaps because the water is cooler than at sunset.

Hooking and playing rays is uneventful provided you do not rush. It is ashore that most anglers start struggling. Rays are thorny, strong and slippery. You have two lines of attack: right and wrong. Do it wrong, and you risk chewed fingers and slimed-up clothing.

Once caught, few rays are returned to the sea. They are excellent eating – in fact, are the mainstay of the fish and chip industry, sold as skate or, in East Anglia, roker. So your first task is to kill the thing. There is a moral obligation to do that immediately and properly.

Face down – right way up – rays struggle and squirm. Turned over they lie still. So flip the fish on its back, then hit it very hard on the snout. Then hit it again. A couple of heavy blows will instantly kill it. Having done that, you must not leave it lying around on the beach. Thornbacks like other cartilaginous fish, contain much blood which stains the tissues after death. You must get rid of it.

Slit the gill clefts with a sharp knife, cutting right through to the other side of the body. Gut the fish by running a knife point around the abdominal cavity and afterwards shaking out the viscera. Cut down into the body to separate the wing roots from the back. That severs the other major blood collection area. Hang the fish for two days, then skin off the wings. If you want to freeze the meat, leave the skin on, or at least do not wash the flesh before wrapping.

It is easy to ruin thornbacks by avoiding this butchering process. For the best eating you must prepare them thoroughly – even if it is a gruesome procedure.

Thornback rays are a localized species. Though found all around the British Isles, they are by no means common from the shore. Even within their stamping grounds thornbacks tend to be choosy about their beaches. For instance, rays are widespread along the east coast, but only a handful of beaches are worth fishing. Shingle Street in Suffolk is a classic example.

Unfortunately, it seems that thornback rays are a threatened species. In the last five years, catches have fallen, dramatically in some areas. It is too early to say exactly why this should be; there are many diverse and inter-related reasons, all the way from pollution to commercial fishing pressures.

The sea is getting dirtier. Despite claims that our rivers and coastal waters are on the mend, any observant angler will see that in reality the situation is worsening. There are fewer crabs and shellfish; more sludge and greasy silt in the estuaries. Sometimes the sea stinks. Rays seem wary of polluted waters; so that is one valid reason why we might be catching less.

But it cannot be coincidence that catches dropped after the local fleets changed to beam trawling. Beam trawls scrape the bottom as the farmer's harrow smashes up fields. Nothing is left. For two years, ray hauls were fantastic; now they are pitiful. It is therefore reasonable to assume that, if not the sole cause, commercial fishing is at least a major factor. Economics will ensure that fishing stops before the species is exterminated – fishing costs will cease to justify sending trawlers to sea. But after being weakened by the trawler, rays could be more susceptible to natural hazards such as poor spawning years. Then they might

The smooth-hound, closely related to the tope and other small sharks, often comes into Essex waters in the spring. They are powerful fish that will give great sport on light tackle to the beach angler.

Superb rockfishing on the Atlantic coast of Ireland, but first there is a stiff climb that requires care before an angler can reach the flat rock shelves that form a perfect fishing situation.

disappear altogether in some areas. It seems such an injustice. Thornbacks are primitive fish, one of the lowest species on the evolutional scale. Nature has failed to alter or destroy them in millions of years. Man might well do it in ten.

SUMMER – SMOOTH-HOUNDS AND ROCKFISHING

Some fish are more popular than others. Bass are probably the most prized shore species, then come tope, the gadoids and all the way down to blennies and dabs. Smooth-hounds aren't on the list; most sea anglers don't even know what they are. As Kennedy, in *The Sea Angler's Fishes* observes: "It is of little angling interest."

Smooth-hounds are related to dogfish, tope and, distantly, to sharks. Their appearance is that of a dumpy, ungainly, tope with flat teeth similar to those of a ray. In fact a local name for smooth-hounds is "ray-toothed tope". There are several members of the smooth-hound group – family Triakidae – of which *Mustelus mustelus*, the smooth-hound, and *Mustelus asterias,* the starry smooth-hound, are most common in British waters. The two species are similar in superficial appearance, arguably in size (there is some confusion on that score) and habitat. The starry smooth-hound is covered with white flecks, hence the adjective starry but, unfortunately, the markings are not species-specific for the common fish may be spotted too. Sure differentiation is by dermal analysis and dental patterns; however, that becomes necessary only in record claims. For the purpose of everyday fishing, a smooth-hound is a smooth-hound – common, spotted, or paisley!

I began smooth-hound fishing by accident. At Bradwell, on the Essex Blackwater, the creek divides from the main channel and runs into the moorings on the waterfront. The creek is deep, full of crabs, shellfish and fish fry. A good place for bass and thornback rays.

A hot, sticky July evening. I had fished since dusk, casting for bass in the channel. The tide came full-bore into the creek and the lead began to drift across the muddy bottom. Eels and crabs patiently stripped the baits on every cast and, because the lead needs to be changed for one with grips, I thought it time to rebait. As the lead started to come back there was a nudge on the line. Just a bump – one of those things which make you stop and wait to see what happens. Not a bass, surely? Maybe a thornback ray. I slipped the reel out of gear. Line trickled from the spool in response to another bump. Ten yards slid out, then the reel accelerated so fast I had to thumb out an over-run. I flipped over the gear lever and held the rod high. The glass blank doubled over and the line snapped because I had forgotten to set the clutch . . . again.

The trace had been filed away. The leader was rough and abraded. Never a bass . . . no thornback . . . some stingray! I tied on a new trace and hook – much stronger tackle this time. A 5 oz grip lead replaced the 3 oz plain bomb; I rebaited with a big peeler crab.

The bait hit the water way out in the darkness, but in the still air you could hear it splash down. The line took up in the current. I wedged the rod between two loose stones on the seawall and set the reel in free spool with the check on.

The lead shifted in the current; the reel clicked in response. Or was it the lead? More clicks. Then a tearing, chattering rod-bucking wallop. This time I double-checked the clutch before slipping the reel into gear. This time the line held. The clutch throbbed as line came off the spool – not fast and wild but slow, determined and very powerful.

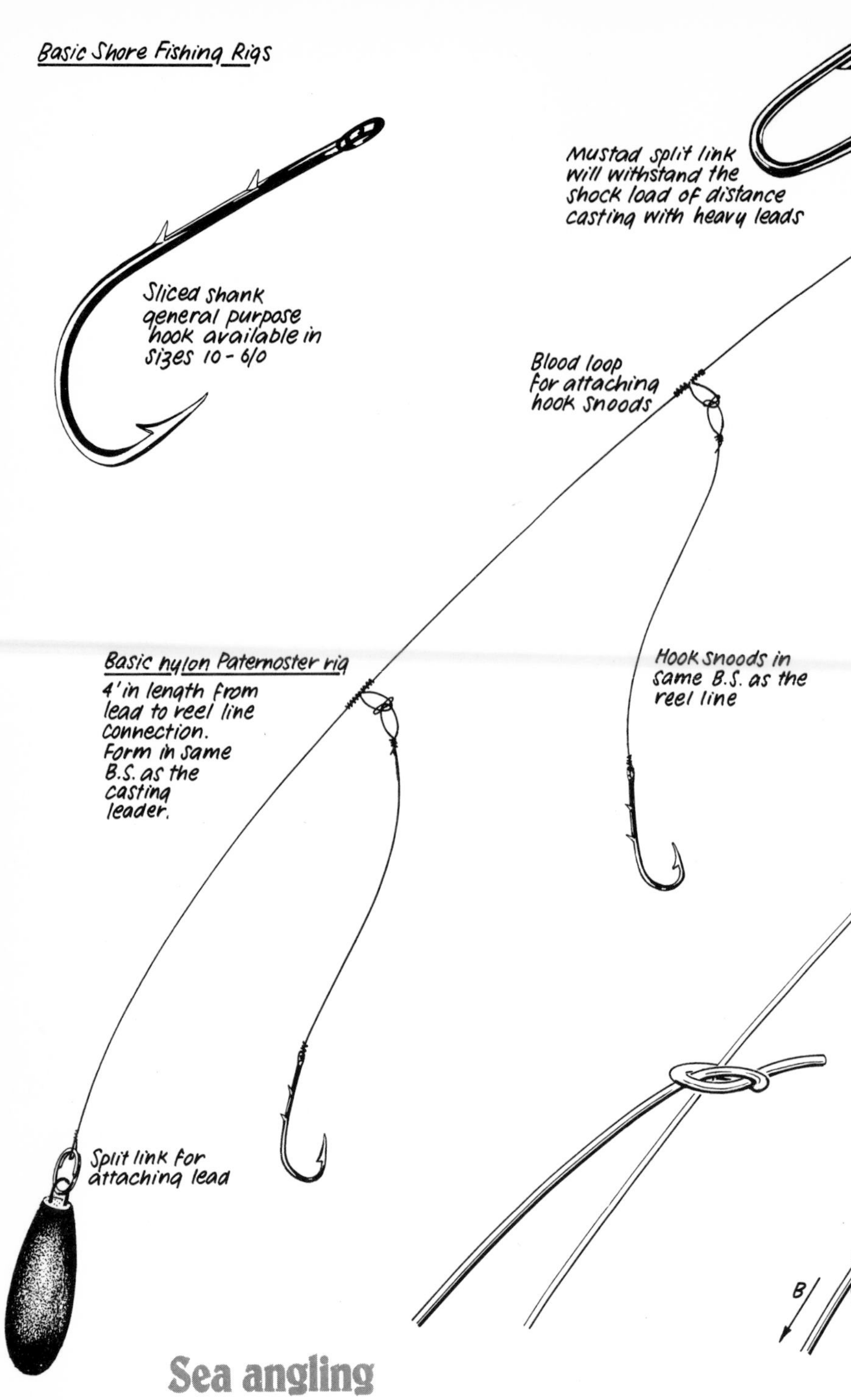

The Shorefisherman's Leader Knot

Used to attach a casting leader, of heavy gauge nylon, to the reel line.

Tie a half-hitch in the heavy nylon and pass the end of the reel line through the centre of the hitch. Pull the hitch tight, pulling at points A and B. Take five turns of the finer nylon around the casting leader material and then pass the loose end back through the first twist formed. Lick the nylon to lubricate the coils, this will allow the coils to slip up neatly to form the knot without scarfing the material. Pull the reel line at C and trim off the fine nylon. Trim the leader excess nylon leaving at least a $\frac{1}{8}$ inch stub. This knot will flow more easily through the rod rings because of the 'stepped section'.

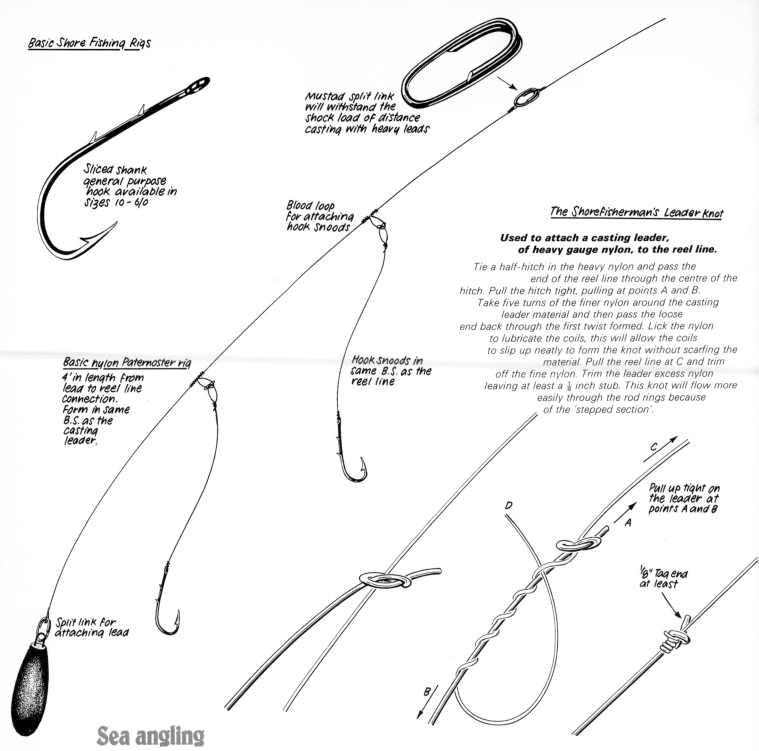

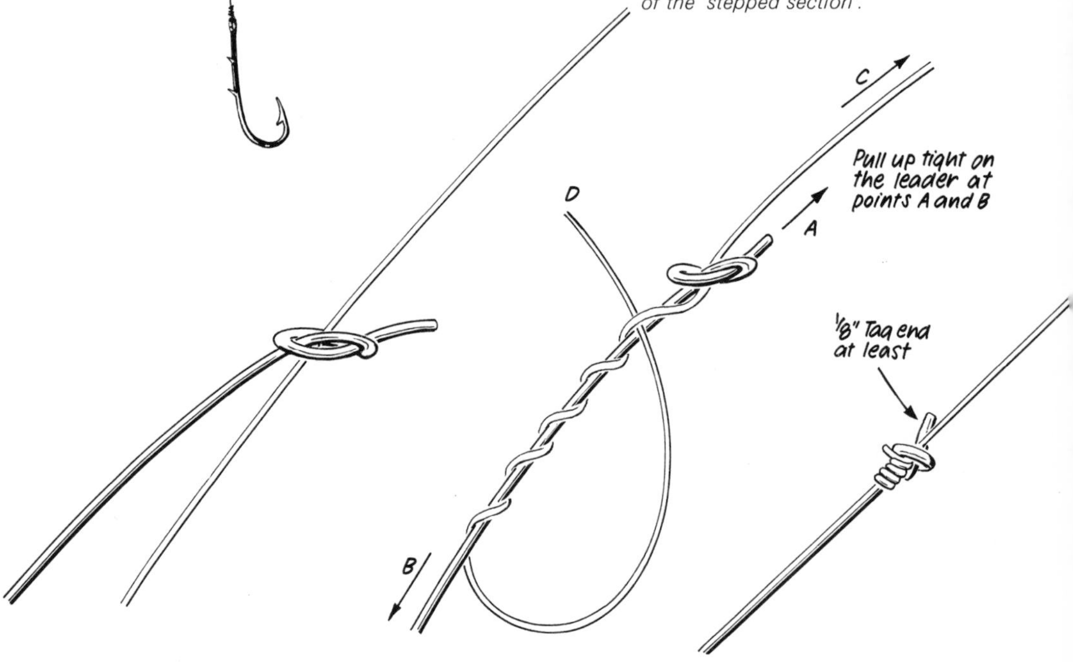

Fifty yards unwound before the fish stopped running. It turned and swam back upchannel towards the moorings. I took in the slack line; it drew parallel, continued past and line ran off again. The epithets of angling are many and stereotyped: diving, running, line stretching, rod bending . . . this fish did all that and then some more. I have never since hooked into a tougher fish and that includes conger and tope. After 20 minutes it ran in close to the wall, still far from beaten. I climbed down the wall to where the fish thrashed in the shallows. And at that moment, in the dark, on a slippery wall, and hooked into a big fish of unknown species, I was a bit worried. In fact, I was slightly scared.

The fish beat itself in the weeds. Disoriented for a second it plunged into a mass of bladderwrack fronds and became entangled. I grabbed the wrist of a tail so big my fingers would not go all the way round, dragged it up the wall and into the lamplight.

It looked like a tope with spots. Squat and clumsy perhaps, but a tope. No, the tail was wrong. And the teeth, too – tope have cutting fangs. This fish had jaws like a thornback ray. Of course, identification was easy with the right books. It was a smooth-hound and a big one at that. It weighed 25 lbs – possibly a record for that time. If the angling records had listed smooth-hounds I might have considered claiming. But the only references to smooth-hounds were in marine biology textbooks.

Since then I have often fished the creek in the long summer evenings of June until September. I have caught many smooth-hounds, too. The average fish weighs 15 lbs, although 20-pounders are common enough. Smooth-hounds are definitely shoal fish: when they move in on the tide fishing is non-stop for an hour.

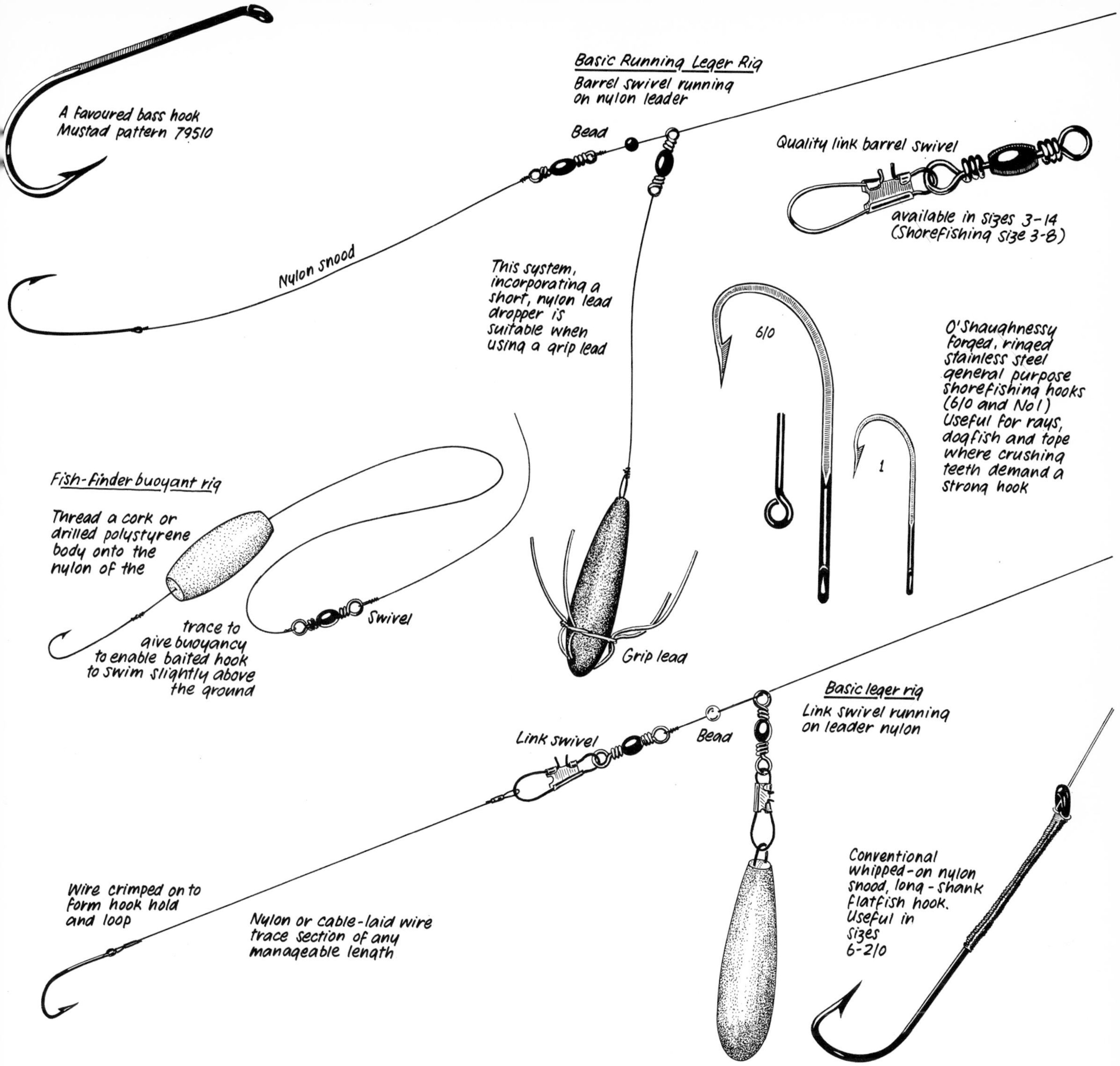
A favoured bass hook
Mustad pattern 79510
Basic Running Leger Rig
Barrel swivel running on nylon leader
Bead
Quality link barrel swivel
available in sizes 3-14
(Shorefishing size 3-8)
Nylon snood
This system, incorporating a short, nylon lead dropper is suitable when using a grip lead
6/0
1
O'Shaughnessy forged, ringed stainless steel general purpose shorefishing hooks (6/0 and No 1) Useful for rays, dogfish and tope where crushing teeth demand a strong hook
Fish-finder buoyant rig
Thread a cork or drilled polystyrene body onto the nylon of the
trace to give buoyancy to enable baited hook to swim slightly above the ground
Swivel
Grip lead
Basic leger rig
Link swivel running on leader nylon
Link swivel
Bead
Conventional whipped-on nylon snood, long-shank flatfish hook. Useful in sizes 6-2/0
Wire crimped on to form hook hold and loop
Nylon or cable-laid wire trace section of any manageable length

I am unsure of the smooth-hound's role. It appears to be a scavenger and bottom feeder, much the same as dogfish. There is a distinct similarity between smooth-hounds and spurdogs in that respect. Scavenging would certainly account for the fish being in Bradwell Creek, which is a very busy yachting centre. In summer, many of the sailing people use the creek as a rubbish dump and it may be that the fish are either attracted to the refuse or to the crabs that collect there.

The feeding and movement patterns of smooth-hounds are virtually uncharted. As fish with neither angling nor commercial value, they have never been closely studied. That means that anybody who wants to fish for smooth-hounds must work out the details for himself. My experience with them is limited to smooth-hounds in the Essex estuaries. What happens elsewhere, I cannot say. But we do know that smooth-hounds of both types are widespread around the coasts. The Solent, for example, is thought to have a reasonable head of the fish, some very big specimens among them.

It seems likely that many other areas have smooth-hound populations. In fact, many anglers probably catch them as either tope or dogfish. Indeed, the main problem with smooth-hounds is identification. After my first fish I began enquiring about them. Local anglers and trawlermen had never heard of smooth-hounds. Tope, yes; dogfish too. On closer questioning I discovered that some of the people described Essex tope as "fish like sharks but with skate's teeth". Some very big fish of this description have been taken from the trawls. Some were 5 ft long.

No tope has skate's teeth. Few tope I've caught have clearly outfought smooth-hounds, which these fish undoubtedly were. As I said in the beginning, most

THICK-LIPPED GREY MULLET
Chelon labrosus

A member of a large family of shoal fish, there are said to be more than one hundred species of mullet distributed around the world. The fish has two dorsal fins, the first with four sharp spines joined by tough webs. The second is composed of soft rays. The upper lip is swollen and prominent and the throat slit is much narrower than in either the thin-lipped or golden-grey species. The mullets are fish of the upper layers of the sea. They are plankton feeders, which means that they are conditioned to feeding upon minute organisms that anglers find hard to duplicate as a hookbait. Mullet can be conditioned to accept certain forms of feed. In the West Country fishermen have for years "browsed" the mullet in close to the shore by liberally feeding the tide with a mixture of pilchard oil, mashed fish scraps and bread. As the mullet become used to finding this food they lose their waryness and will accept small fish pieces and bread on a small hook. At Dungarvan, in Ireland, mullet are frequently taken on a hookbait composed of cheese paste used to simulate the curds that are discharged into the harbour from a creamery outfall pipe. The species grows to 10 lbs or more but a mullet of 3 lbs is a good fish.

Bait: *Minute fish pieces, bread paste or small ragworms.*

anglers have never heard of smooth-hounds. Perhaps it is time to start looking. "*It is of little angling interest*". I don't believe that.

ROCKFISHING

It is a rare shoreline which fishes well throughout the whole year. Some beaches, a typical example being the East Anglian cod beaches, are unequalled for autumn and winter fishing. The Irish strands provide superb bass fishing in spring and autumn. In other words as the seasons change the emphasis shifts from coast to coast and from species to species. It means, too, that the shore angler, wishing to avoid blank spells, must be prepared to travel.

In my part of the world, summer fishing is poor. There are the smooth-hounds, some bass and eels in the rivers; maybe a few soles on the beaches. But there is no single species which merits constant and intense work. So I travel to the West Country, Wales, Scotland and Ireland. Travel provides more than a change in scenery and species to fish for. Basically there are the rocks. At home, the nearest thing to rocks and cliffs is the sea wall. Cliffs, bouldery shores and coves are very attractive to the angler like me who lives most of his life where the highest thing on the coastline is the rod in his hand.

WRASSE

Wrasse are great fun. They are small, plentiful, and feed throughout the day. They haunt the inshore gulleys and kelp patches, so you don't have to cast very far either. Because wrasse are fairly easy to catch, and because they are not good to eat, most anglers underrate them. But wrasse are splendid fish, especially for the holiday angler. They feed anytime, even when the sea is flat-calm and the sun is shining. The bait you need is easy to find. And wrasse live where swimmers do not go, so there is no competition for water space.

Floatfishing is perhaps the most satisfying method. It is an economical technique too, because to cast leger gear into wrasse country is simply asking for trouble. A spinning rod, fixed-spool reel and 10 lb line are ideal.

Fixed-floats are useless on most rocks where the water is deep. Good wrasse water might be 30 or 40 ft deep right at the base of the rock from which you fish. Therefore a sliding float is essential. The float also needs to be fairly big so that it buoys up the $\frac{1}{2}$ oz or so of lead necessary to sink the bait. A pike bung will do. The most popular arrangement is a drilled bullet which slides on the line stopped by a split shot about 2 ft from the hook. Hooks should be small, size 4 up to 1/0.

Bait is no problem. Limpets scraped from the rocks are good, so are slivers of fish. Crabs are best of all. Peelers and soft crabs are the first choice, but penny-size hardbacks are satisfactory too. Wrasse are one of the few shore species to take hardback crabs from the hook.

To fish, set the hook a couple of feet from the bottom, then let the float wash the tackle along the rock borders. Sometimes wrasse feed hard on the bottom or even in mid-water. Experiment with the float setting until you locate them.

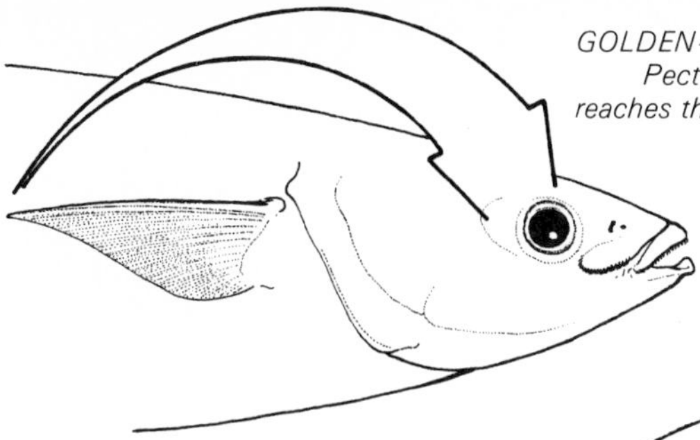

GOLDEN-GREY MULLET
Pectoral fin when folded forward reaches the middle of eye at least.

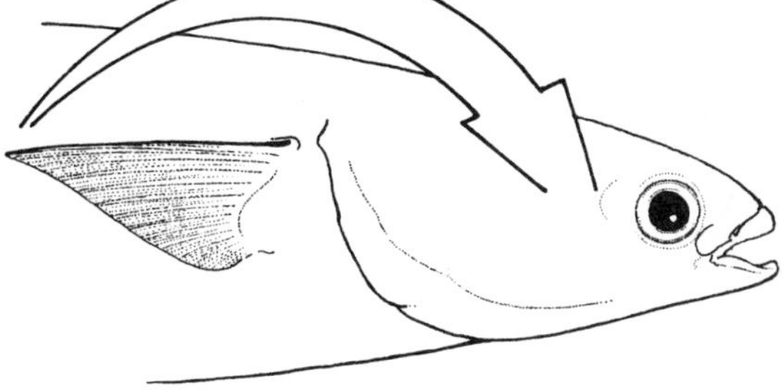

THIN-LIPPED GREY MULLET
Pectoral fin when folded forward does not reach eye, or only just so in young specimens.

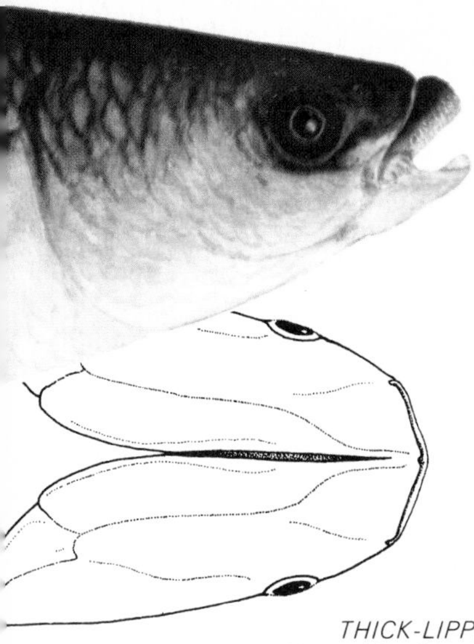

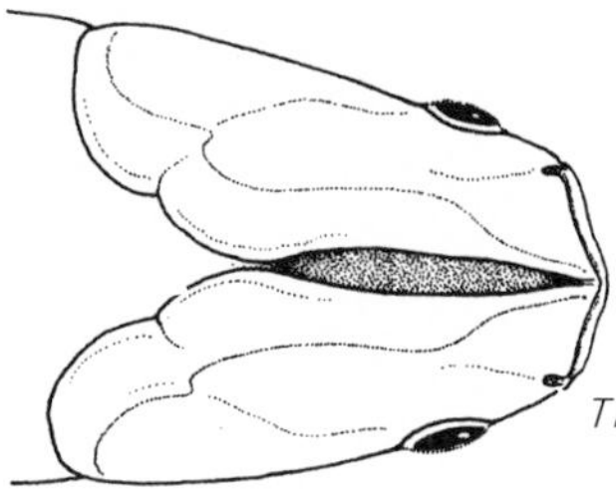

THIN-LIPPED GREY MULLET
Underside of head showing "wide throat"

THICK-LIPPED GREY MULLET
Underside of head showing "narrow throat".

THIN-LIPPED MULLET

Liza (Liza) ramada

A fish that grows larger than the thick-lipped variety and has a thin top lip and much broader throat slit. The pelvic fins are almost as long as the pectorals. All three true mullets are in evidence during the late spring to early autumn months. They migrate northward almost into the Arctic Circle.

Bait: *As for the thick-lipped species.*

GOLDEN-GREY MULLET

Liza (Liza) aurata

This species does not migrate quite as far north as the other two mullets. It is a smaller fish and much rarer in the British Isles. The fish has a golden sheen covering the head and forepart of the body, although this is not a reliable recognition feature on immature specimens. Often there is a golden patch on the gill cover.

Bait: *As for the thick-lipped species.*

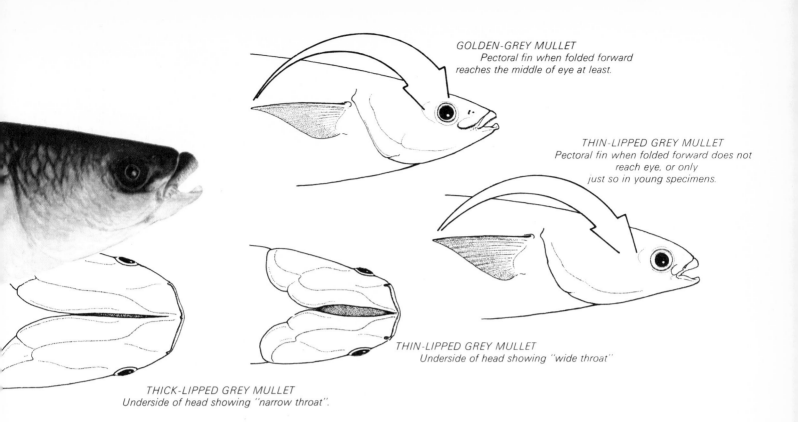

RED MULLET

Mullus surmuletus

An occasional visitor to the west and southern shores of Britain and Ireland. Unlike the true mullets this fish is a bottom dwelling species favouring ground which has a mixture of rocks and sand Two lengthy barbules, below the lower jaw, are used to detect small creatures in the sand. A 2 lb red mullet is a good size and wonderful eating. Not related to the grey mullets.

Bait: *Marine worms and crustaceans.*

Wrasse are positive feeders; the float dips down out of sight with few preliminary movements. You strike quickly, and wind hard to lift the fish before it can get its head under the rocks. All wrasse have bolt-holes – underwater crannies where they dash when hooked. If they get there, you will probably lose your hook. So hustle the fish into clear water before it realizes what is happening, then you can fight it on your terms. Landing nets are essential with this sort of tackle. Ten pound line will not drag fish out of the sea; it has only to scrape against the rock to snap. Additionally, nets do not harm the wrasse; that is important because you will want to return them to the sea after you have caught them. There is no point in killing wrasse.

CONGER EELS

Congers are rough, tough and an acquired taste. Something about eels upsets anglers. Many will not go near them; others commit atrocities on eels which they would never dream of inflicting on other fish. Perhaps there is a subconscious association with snakes, I do not know. But one thing is sure: a big shore-caught conger is a fish to be proud of, and a fish you have had to work for.

Eels are fishes of dark waters, of night tides. Small congers are as suicidal as most immature fish and you can hook them during the day. Big adults lurk in the rocks by day and come out to hunt when the sun leaves the water.

Fishing the rocks at night introduces a new set of problems. Unless the sea is calm, and this is usually the case with conger seas, rock fishing at night can be extremely dangerous. You must know your patch of shore for if you do not you could slip into the sea. Nobody but a fool fishes night-time rocks when there is a swell running. However, night fishing is only as black a picture as you wish to paint. Commonsense and sensible precautions are insurance enough to justify night eeling.

Conger fishing is a tug-of-war between you and the fish. There is little finesse in the sport – just brute strength. Obviously conger tackle has to be strong enough for you to heave on the fish; the terminal tackle must withstand the conger's teeth and sinuous body – and the rocks, too! To begin at the rod: conger rods should be shorter than the average beachcaster so that you can exert maximum leverage. Nine or 10 ft is an ample length. An adequate conger rod matches up to 30 lb line.

Because this is short range work (often you take congers at 20 yds) strong lines can be used to advantage. Thirty pound breaking strain will quell congers; beyond that most anglers cannot exploit the line's potential, anyway. Rough rocks suggest that nylon is used. However, nylon stretches far more than other lines.

1

Braided Terylene has no stretch and so feels more positive, but it does abrade. You have to balance the pros and cons here. I prefer Terylene even though a few yards of roughened line have to be discarded after each session.

Reels have to match the rod and line. In this case, the reel is like a winch. Fixed-spools are absolutely useless for serious congering. A big multiplier with a powerful clutch and low gear ratio is vital. Short-range congering is one instance where a boat reel can be used to good effect from the shore. But do not try long casting with one. The end tackle needs careful attention. There is no room for second-rate materials and poor knots. Thread a small Clements or Kilmore boom onto the line, slide on a stop-bead and attach a ballbearing swivel. On nylon line, use a tucked half-blood knot. Terylene requires the same Jammed Hangman's/Policansky Knot combination used in deep-sea fishing. Ballbearing swivels are essential because congers spin in the water and ordinary swivels, not properly rotating, will tangle the line. Attach the hook link to this basic rig. The trace is 2 ft of 100 lb multi-strand wire with a 4/0 Seamaster hook crimped to one end, and a link-swivel at the other. This is a quick release system so that you can change traces with each fish.

Fish for congers with a big oily chunk of fresh mackerel. Whole baby mackerel can be mounted with a baiting needle. If you use a whole fish, score its sides

2

3

1 *Bottom fishing for wrasse is a tough business on both angler and tackle. The most inaccessible rock platforms always seem to produce the best wrasse fishing locations. Strength is necessary in the tackle to haul fish out of the underwater rocks and lift them onto the shelf.*

2 *The ballan wrasse is a beautiful fish and so often underrated by sea anglers. To get the best from it one needs to use a pike or carp rod in conjunction with float fishing end tackle. Obviously a drop net is vital and adds to the excitement of landing the fish.*

3 *Small wonder that the wrasse can prise limpets and other marine animals from the rocks with these teeth. A great deal of the power in the mouth of the wrasse comes from the muscular folds in the fish's upper lips.*

with a knife so that blood and oil runs out. Throw the bait into the sea and leave the reel out of gear. Congers, for all their strength, are timid feeders which mouth the bait for minutes before running back to their lairs with it. Do not strike until they sneak off. But when you move, move fast. Strike hard and pump the rod to get the fish away from the bottom. Like wrasse, congers go straight into the rough ground. If they reach it, you can say goodbye to the fish and most of your tackle.

When you manage to land the thing – and that is something you must play by ear – the second round of the fight can begin. It is impossible and most unwise to attempt hook removal at this stage. If you wish to return the conger, snip the trace as near to the jaws as you can, then shove the animal into the sea. Leaving the hook in probably does no harm.

If you want the fish – and congers make very good eating – do not hit it on the head, which just spurs it into greater rage. Smack it over the vent; then cut the spine behind the head. Leave it alone afterwards. Do not try to dig out the hook. Many a "dead" eel has chewed his captor's fingers.

SPINNING

Most seafish are active predators which hunt by sight. Some, because of their nature and where they live, are unsuitable for artificial bait fishing. Even so, many species will grab at spinners and other lures. Some, like garfish and mackerel, live in the surface layers; others, cod and pollack, are more often deep down.

Spinning is a neglected sport. To throw artificial baits is alien to most anglers. They figure that bits of plastic and metal dragged through the water are pretty much a waste of time. That isn't true. The truth is that most anglers who spin do so because every other technique has failed. It is no more than a half-hearted gesture. Spinning, like all fishing, is something you have to work at.

A pike rod, fixed-spool reel and 10 lb line are sufficient for general spinning. The fixed-spool is ideal because it will throw light baits whereas the multiplier requires baits of at least $\frac{1}{2}$ oz to make it run. It is better to avoid extra weights as they always have some adverse effect on the lure's action. But if you must have one, spiral leads and drilled bullets work well enough. Of course, feathers must be used with a lead.

There are three common types of lures in seafishing: eels, spoons, and feathers. The rubber eel has been with us for decades. It is deceptively simple, perhaps no more than a piece of rubber tubing whipped to a hook. Or a length of electrical flex-covering. More sophisticated is the Redgill, a commercially produced replica of the sandeel which has a unique swimming action and is without doubt the most successful sea lure of all time.

Spoons come in all forms, from converted tablespoons to very expensive chromium-plated imitation fishes. It is impossible to say which are the more effective. Dragged along in the water, even the best lures are unattractive to fish; an old lump of copper pipe worked with skill and understanding takes fish by the dozen. I suppose the logical answer is a properly worked, purpose-made lure. That way, lure action and angling skill work towards the ultimate attraction.

Few sea-anglers realize that most freshwater lures are good in the sea. Small and medium vibratory lures are excellent for garfish and mackerel. A big spinner baited with an inch of ragworm or fish-strip is effective for flounders, cod and pollack. I can see no reason why we should not experiment with plugs. The majority of American anglers rely heavily on plugs and imitation squids for much of their sea fishing.

And then there are feathers: gaudy rainbows; bits of chicken feather whipped to 3 or 4 hooks; maybe not feathers at all – just slivers of coloured plastic on the hooks. There are hundreds of variations on the feathers theme. All represent a shoal of flickering baitfish. I suppose a survey of lure-caught seafish would show that 80 per cent fell to feathers of some sort. Feathers by themselves, baited feathers, deep-worked feathers, feathers skittered along the surface – there is just no end to it.

Practical lurefishing is best based on a search system. Chuck-and-chance methods will not do. Most anglers know the radial water-coverage procedure which pike anglers employ. But the sea is much too deep for that alone. Control over a lure is more or less limited to direction, speed and depth. Flicking the rod from side to side does no more than strain your wrist; the lure is unaffected by the jiggling. Basically all you can do is wind at various speeds, sink and draw, monitor depth, and cast to search all promising spots.

There is a very simple system of covering the full depth of the water. Cast as far as possible and let the lure sink to the bottom; count as it does so. Suppose it took 30 seconds. Next cast, start retrieving as soon as the bait hits the sea. Third cast, count to five before winding. Follow with casts at 10, 15, 20, and 25 seconds sinking time. If you wound at a set speed throughout, you will have covered the water from top to bottom. Variations are to fish another set of casts at different rates; fish each depth at various speeds, working progressively from surface to sea bed or vice versa. Or you can retrieve *sink and draw* fashion: wind for a yard, let the bait sink freely for one second, and so on. If you are sure the bottom is clean, or if losing lures is of no consequence, inch the bait along the seabed. It is surprising how many fish will pick it up.

Sea fish generally slash into lures, especially when they are moving fast. Striking is usually unnecessary. However, cod and pollack are sometimes shy of the artificial and peck at it. You feel a tap on the line. You might try striking at every hint of a bite, but it is better to bait the hook with fish or worms to encourage a more deliberate attack.

Many simple bar spoons used by the freshwater angler are good lures for saltwater species. Pollack, bass and rock codling will chase the metal bait.

Like wrasse and congers, lure-hooked species make for the bottom when they feel the hook. Mackerel and garfish, the mid-water species, are much easier to control as they fight it out on top – often with spectacular aerobatics. Cod, too, are no problem if you show them who is boss. They go down but are happy enough to fight in the clear water just above the rock faces. Pollack are the ones to watch. A hooked pollack is perhaps the most powerful diver in the sea. He thumps into the lure, then straight down. No hesitation; no means of getting him up a bit before he gathers his wits. You cannot stop pollack dead – not even the small fish. Slow them on the clutch, working the line to its maximum. In fact, big pollack are not light tackle fish – shorecasters and 15 lb line are necessary at times. After the first dive pollack give up without too much of a struggle. But that first crash-dive ... it is one of the high spots of seafishing, and ranks pollack among the most sporting of fishes. Any angler who has not hooked into a 10-pounder on light tackle has missed out on something special. And if he does hook one, and ultimately lands it, he can be very proud of himself.

AUTUMN – STRAND FISHING

According to the dictionary, surf is the foam created by wave action on a shore or reef. Therefore, to be absolutely accurate, fishing into breaking waves is surf fishing. But there are waves and there are waves. Some are more surfy than others. There are two

An Atlantic surf strand, facing the western blasts of autumn and winter winds. The breakers begin to form a couple of hundred yards out, then roll into the beach in regular lines. Theory has it that bass lurk behind the third breaker.

broad classifications of surf: wind surf and swell surf. As its name suggests, wind surf is associated with rough weather. It grows and dies in response to the wind. Swell surf is long distance water which travels miles across the open sea, perhaps reaching the shore when the local conditions are flat calm. It is not uncommon to see raging surf with a land breeze blowing into it. Of course, swell surf can be accompanied by a howling onshore gale.

Swell surf is more than a few lines of white water kicked up along the beach. You can find that sort of water on any reasonably exposed beach when the wind blows. Swell surf might begin with an Atlantic storm. Out in the ocean, hundreds of miles from land, the wind blows and the sea responds. The disturbance radiates. Days later swells reach land, travelling in smooth regimentation, regular as the lines ruled in an exercise book. In deep water they show as humped ridges slightly darker than the surrounding sea. They smash over rocks and into cliffs. On long, gently shelving sands they unroll into tables of surf.

Real swell surf is big and powerful. The crests begin to form over 400 yds from the shore perhaps. Because the necessary water force is generated over long distances, most surf beaches in this part of the world face between south and west – towards the Atlantic.

We find most surf beaches in the West Country, Wales, Eire and Scotland. The typical topography is a vast expanse of hardpacked sand. The beach slopes gently between high and low water marks, which may be up to half a mile apart.

Anglers do not class surf by its dictionary definition. If we did, a gale-swept Suffolk codbeach would compare with a Welsh bass shore. Both have surf on them at times but it is immediately obvious that the type of sea, the species and fishing techniques are quite separate. Perhaps "surf" is the wrong word, anyway. Sometimes we fish the "surf beaches" when there is no surf, yet we still say we are surfcasting. The Irish call their sandy beaches "strands" – Inch Strand, Stradbally Strand. To save confusion, therefore, let us call fishing a sandy, Atlantic facing beach "strand fishing". There might be surf; it could just as easily be still water. Either way, the fishing is good.

Strand fishing and bass have become almost synonymous. You will see magazine references to "white-water bassfishing . . . hunting the lordly bass in the wild water". Bass are indeed a common and interesting strand species, but they are neither the biggest nor the hardest fighters. In the same shallow waters might live tope, rays, flatfish and spurdog. No bass measures up to a tope. Big spurdogs run circles round bass, too.

However, the circumstances which favour bass work against most of the other fish. First, time of year: bass are more concentrated on Irish beaches, for instance, in the spring and autumn. Naturally, that does not mean you can guarantee bass in October; conversely, very big bass are caught in June. But you can say with reasonable confidence that winter will be poor for tope and rays. To classify strand fishing by season and species is difficult – the factors are too many and too interlinked. A more logical division is between surf conditions and relatively still waters. At certain times of the year both sorts of fishing are at a peak, either separately or together. September is excellent for both, especially in Eire, on the Kerry Peninsula.

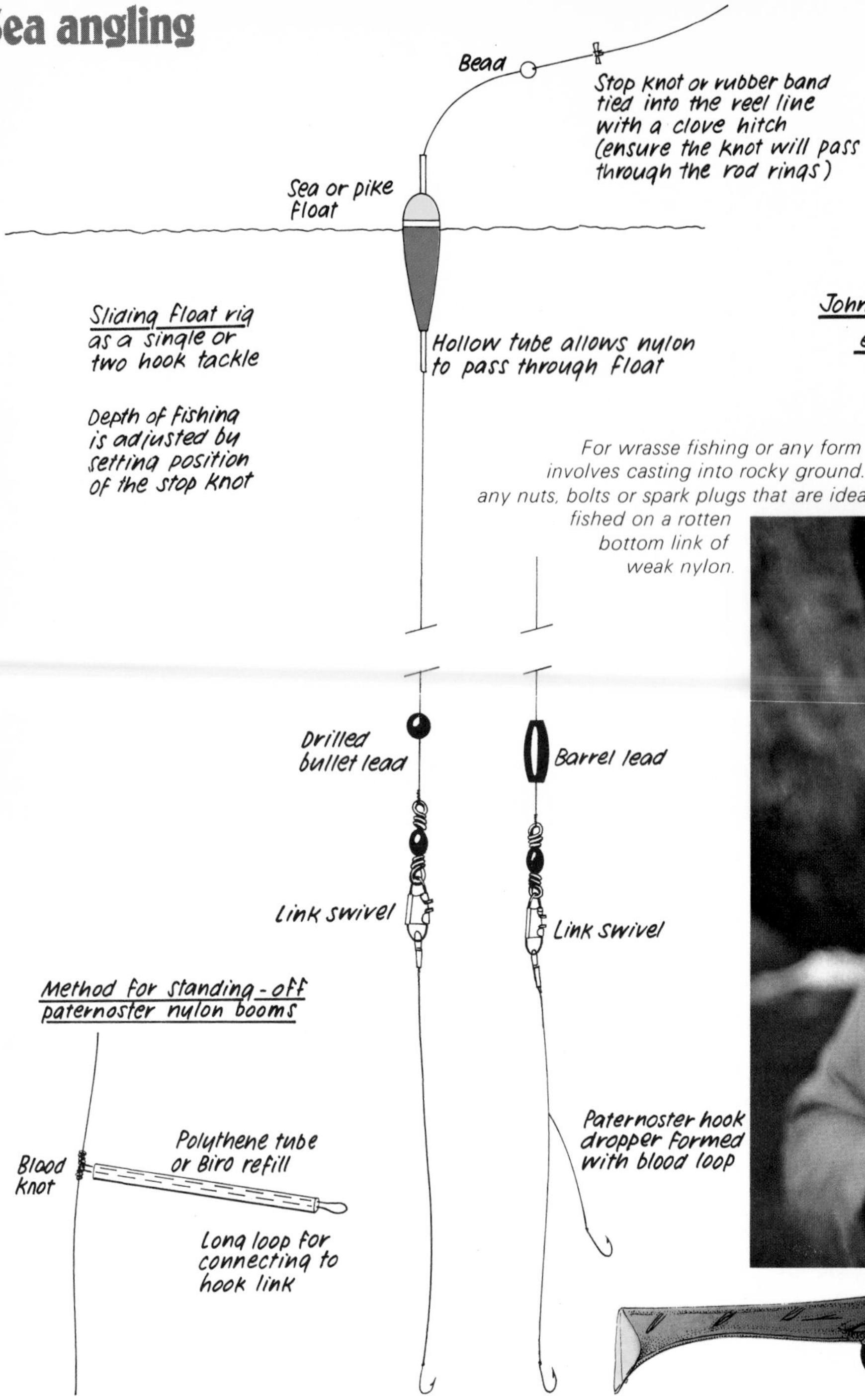

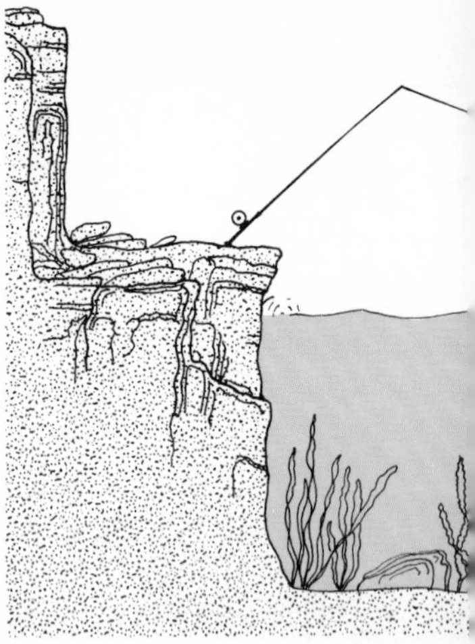

For wrasse fishing or any form of bottom fishing that involves casting into rocky ground. Save or scrounge any nuts, bolts or spark plugs that are ideal casting weights to be fished on a rotten bottom link of weak nylon.

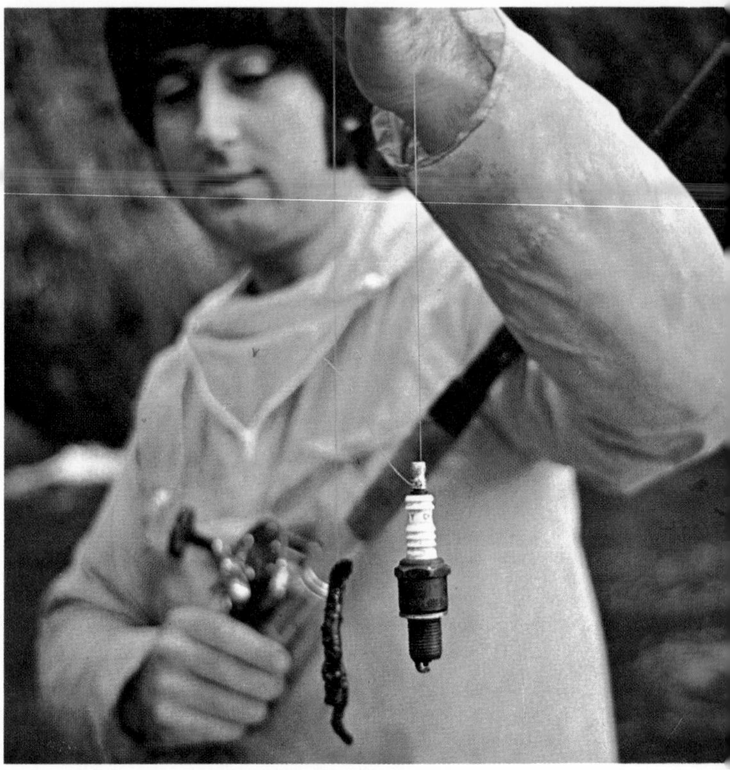

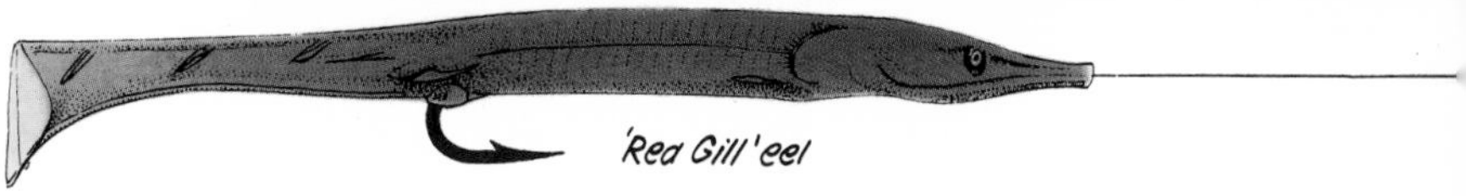

Before you think about tackle and fishing, it will pay seriously to consider one basic question: to wade or not to wade? If you walk down the strand towards the surf you come first to wet sand which is occasionally swilled by residual water from the high surfs. Farther on there might be a backwater of shallow sea no more than 2 or 3 ins deep. Past that are the first of the plateaux – the water-tables between the breakers. Here there might be a foot of water, rising by as much again as each wave slides in, afterwards falling back to the original level. This is the area of beach affected by the water's combing action – sand is picked up and stirred by the backwash. Occasionally the sea seems to take a rest – it falls right back – and there follows a powerful scouring of sand. If you stand in it, the water scoops the beach from under your feet. The farther out you go, the stronger the suction. Seawards from there, the water deepens progressively. The waves come in steps. One moment you stand in 3 ft, the next in 4 ft.

So, to wade or not to wade – and, if so, how far? Assuming you wish to remain dry, wading depth is dictated by your footwear.

In Wellington boots you have to be careful. Ordinary waders will take you out quite a long way, certainly far enough to fish. Chest waders allow more scope, but the farther you wade the greater the risk. You will wade to moderate depth and fish happily for a time. Then you think a few more yards might pay off, so you go deeper. Almost unconsciously you will go in to stomach height. Ninety-nine per cent of the time that is safe; but there could always be one big wave, or the backwash we have already mentioned might catch you unawares. You could slip over or be lifted up by the water. In rough water or at night that might be

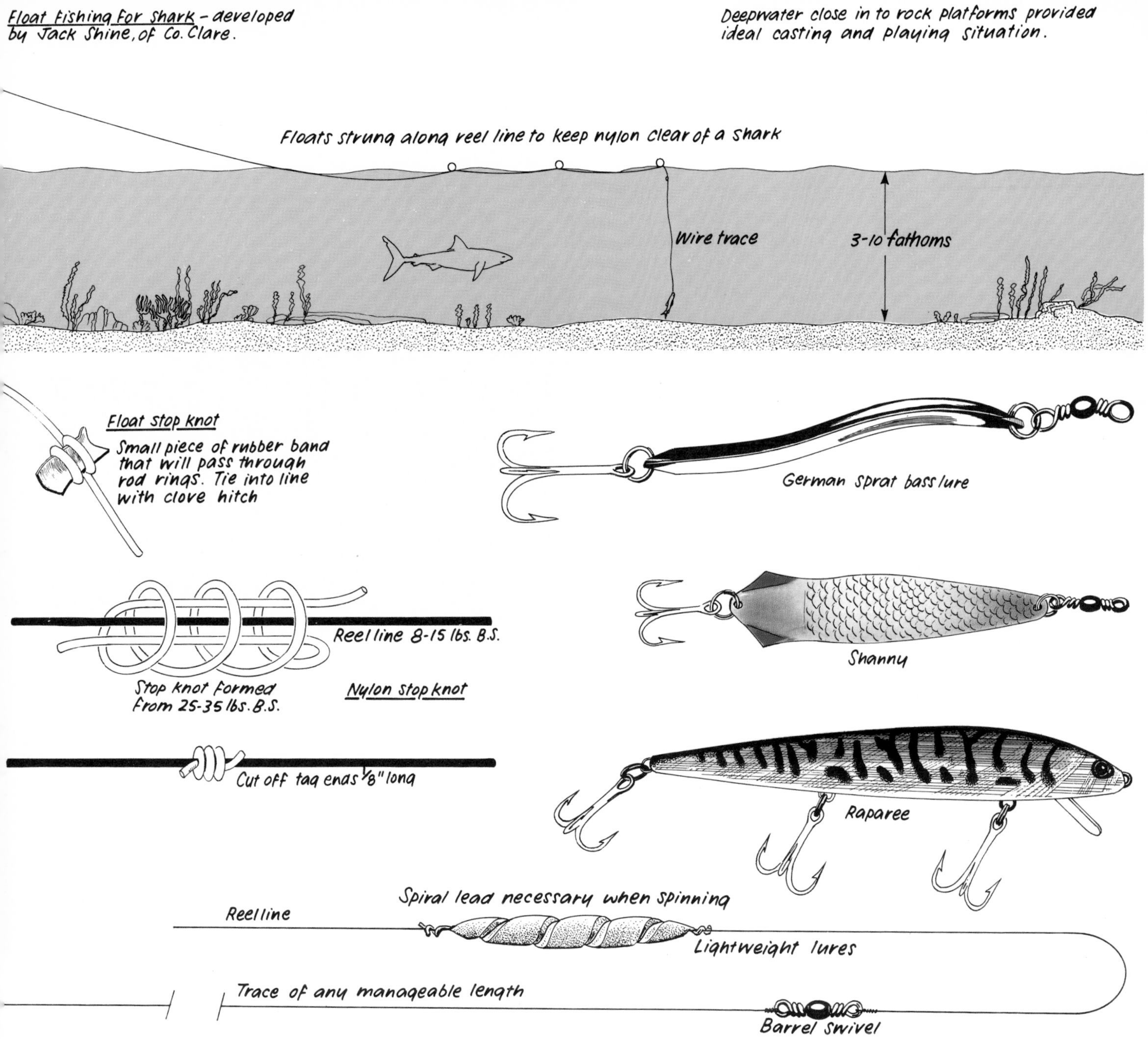

the last time you wade, or fish, or breathe. This may sound melodramatic but I can assure you it is not.

I will not use chest waders because I cannot trust myself in them. It is all very well to make promises on the shore, but out there in the surf reason goes to the wind. The case for ordinary hip length waders is overwhelming. A pair of waterproof overtrousers will prevent a wet backside; you will fish better and safer for staying within your depth. Neither will you lose distance: in deep water it is impossible to cast properly because your arms would have to start from underwater. By standing back you cast farther; the result is equivalent fishing range.

To fish strands in either surf or still conditions it is important to be mobile. With hundreds of yards between tide marks the water flows and ebbs very fast, so tackle and bait cannot be left to fend for themselves. Simplest of all, you must become a self-contained unit: spare tackle in your pocket, bait bag around your neck, and no rod rest.

Or you could use a rod rest to hold bags and bait above the water while you fish some distance away. Finally, there is the lazy man's way: dump everything, rod included, on the rod rest and stay with it, moving when necessary.

Tackle depends on what you intend to catch. Light rods and reels will do for bass and flatfish; tope and rays need something more substantial. Most strands and the species which live there can be tackled with normal beachcasting gear: 3 or 4 ozs of lead, matching line, and a medium rod and reel. Terminal rigs are little different from those you might use from shingle beaches. Since casting range is not as critical as, say, for cod, more attention can be paid to bait presentation than to aerodynamics. Two or three baits can be fished at once; traces can be long and free-flowing.

Strand tackle is a compromise between weight and power. You do not have to cast extreme distances; average bass and flatfish do not fight too hard and there is usually a clear sandy bottom with no snags. Everything points to light tackle, but never lightness for its own sake. Some anglers claim to use ultra-light tackle in the surf: 10 lb lines and an ounce of lead. Their motives are questionable: is it a genuine attempt to brighten fishing, or is it done for appearance's sake? I do not know what lies behind it. But I do know that if ever I hooked a very big fish only to lose it because of flimsy tackle, I would not be too happy.

It is fortunate for anglers that most fish do not care what you fish with. Given the right bait, enough of it, and assuming it is where they can find it, fish can be caught on just about any sort of tackle.

However, it pays to consider that you have to hold the rod most of the time and that you could hook into a very big fish, too. So the rod and reel must be light enough to carry all day, yet powerful enough to give confidence. Those considerations apart, the rod and reel are a purely personal matter. If you choose to fish bass with 30 lb line and 8 oz leads, fair enough. You will probably catch as many fish as if you had light tackle. What is more, if you hook a 20 lb bass, which I very much hope you will, you will then have a better than average chance of landing it.

THE STRAND IN CALM WATER

Unless there is some surf running, most strands fish poorly for bass. More precisely, still water generally rules out large numbers of bass; it certainly does not mean that you will not catch any. Indeed, some of the biggest bass ever caught came from calm, clear water. But a big bass (one over 10 lbs, in my book) is always more luck than judgment as there just are not that many big bass in the sea. When the strand is smooth try fishing for rays, tope and flatfish, but always bear in mind that a big old bass might turn up.

Few fish live out their lives on a strand. Most are visitors from the deep sea or from rocky waters. Rays are more common on rocky shores but they do move onto the strands when the sea is warm and calm. Tope move in from the deep water to hunt the shallows. Flatfish? Well, they are always where you find them – fishes of no fixed abode. Because most of the species are associated more with rocky ground, it is often better to fish the ends of the strand where the beach gives way to boulders and cliffs.

Flatfish – mostly flounders, dabs, plaice and the occasional turbot – are lazy fishing. Cast out and wait for the action. Slowly retrieving the baits along the sand helps attract some species, especially plaice and

1

flounders. Most flatfishes feed on crabs, worms and slices of mackerel. Turbot are fond of fish simply because that is their staple diet. However, they will take other baits.

The terminal rig is chosen to suit casting distance. I have already mentioned that strands do not necessarily demand long casting. A running leger with up to three hooks all baited differently is a good approach for short range work – say up to 100 yds. Over that you have to consider air drag in casting. A paternoster is far easier to cast extreme distances. Daylight and clear water have a major effect on undersea visibility. Even at night there is light down there. Such water is dangerous to small fish whose enemies hunt by sight. Therefore, in an effort aimed at self-preservation they lie well offshore in the relative safety of deep water. That is why you have to cast long distances.

Rays are the next step up from flatfish. If you regard them as big flatfish, which biologically they are not, you will not go far wrong. Ray tackle needs a few modifications from that which you would normally use for flatfish. Most rays are very strong and quite big. Millstone grinding teeth are a characteristic feature of the family. Some, like thornbacks, are spiky enough to snap a line with their tails.

A strong casting leader is essential for rayfishing. It acts as a buffer against them and is less affected by abrasion than ordinary reel lines. Hooks must be strong rather than large – 1/0–4/0 stainless steel Model Perfects are superb. Strictly, you do not need wire traces but since there is always the chance of a tope, a few inches of multi-strand wire does no harm. If you do use wire, crimp on the hook and swivel rather than rely on knots. Rays fish best with a running leger.

2

3

1 Inch Strand in calm weather. All plans for fishing bass have disappeared and thought of tope, monkfish, rays and dogfish take precedence. Often the fishing must be late into the evening and night for any success.

2 Easy does it! John Woods lands a spurdog and intends keeping well away from the spines. Often spurdog will come into shallow water in search of food when the surf has flattened away.

3 Cutting up fresh mackerel baits depends on the species sought and how eager they are to feed. The rays and dogfish will take large lashes but big baits are difficult to cast and are often torn rather than taken.

Rays are catholic feeders – anything fresh will do. However, nothing can beat really fresh mackerel. Half a fish is not too big; heads are good, too. If there are no fresh mackerel (and in places like Eire you have to be self-reliant for baits), crabs, squid and big bunches of ragworms will do. So will chunks of flatfish or even bass fillets. Nothing beats a hunk of blood-oozing, oily mackerel. Getting some is well worth the effort.

There are many species of rays. On westerly strands you can expect thornbacks, undulates, painted rays – just about any members of the tribe. Monkfish turn up now and again. They are a half-way stage between rays and sharks, which feed like rays and fight like wet sacks. Sometimes monkfish go mad and actually wriggle a bit, but usually the shark side of their nature stays well hidden.

Then there are tope. Tope are big, fast fish – brutal fighters. A shallow water tope is the nearest thing to big-game fishing for the British shore angler. Hooking tope is easy enough when they invade the strand waters. When a pack hunts the inshore waters fishing is non-stop until they move away. The average strand tope weighs about 30 lbs, although 40-pounders are nothing special.

Tope fishing is specialized enough to demand proper tackle. Normal 4 or 6 oz beachcasters are adequate. Main line does not need to be more than 20 lbs breaking strain because at long range you cannot use it to the full, and furthermore it creates excessive drag in the water. Hundred pound line will not hold the first run of a big tope. It must be allowed to run. Therefore, line quantity is vital. Four hundred yards is the minimum for safe fishing.

The reel will either make or break the angler. It must hold the necessary line; the clutch must be built to absorb tremendous friction without fading. Fixed-spool reels are useless for serious tope work unless you are absolutely sure what will happen. Tope fishing is one instance where multipliers are best for the beginner. The ideal reel holds 400 yds of line on a spool which is strong but light so that you can still cast a good distance. Nylon-filled fibreglass spools are resilient enough. Light alloy is better still. Always make sure the drag lever is smooth and easy to adjust. A tope reel must withstand a beating. Generally speaking, the more you spend on the reel, the better it will be for tope. This is a rare occasion where £30 reels are significantly more desirable than cheap ones. In most other shorefishing that is definitely not the case.

Traces must be strong and long because tope have bodies like sanding blocks. I suggest something like this: bloodknot 10 yds of 30 lb nylon to the main line. Follow with 10 yds of 50 lb line, again joined with a bloodknot. Slide on a link swivel for the lead, then tie on a swivel. You can add a bead to buffer the swivel and the link. The trace clips to the end swivel. Three feet of 50 lb multi-strand wire are sufficient. The hook must be big enough to hold the fish and bait, but small and sharp so that it sticks in at long range. A 4/0 Mustad Seamaster sets the standard by which other hooks must be judged. Always crimp the trace rather than rely on knots alone.

Tope eat fish: half a mackerel, a dab, a pouting. Cast the bait as far as possible, leave the reel out of gear – and wait for the explosion. If the incoming tide forces you back, let off the line rather than move the bait inshore. If your luck is in, the line will click off the spool as the tope examines the bait; then the spool speeds up so fast that the line blurs. Now it is up to you. Up with the rod, reel in gear, and hang on.

As soon as your first tope runs off with the bait you will forget everything you may have read. It is a unique experience for you. Tope are incomparable fighters; 200 yds of line will be stripped from the spool before you realize what is happening. Tope never give up. They go on and on and on. You will tire first – and half the time the fish will eventually win.

When the fish hits, hold the rod *high* to buffer any sudden shocks. Never point the rod along the line. Set the drag to a moderate pressure and leave it there. Adjust the braking power with your *thumb* – careful of friction burns here. Thumbs react faster than drag screws if you should suddenly need to slacken right off. Take your *time.* When the fish comes into shallow water grab it by the *tail.* Gaffs are more trouble than they are worth.

That makes just four key phrases to think about: rod high; brake with your thumb; time the fight; grab its tail. *And never in any circumstances wrap your hand round the trace.*

FISHING THE SURF

On most beaches you stand on the shingle or sand and cast out from there into the water. From rocks you fish perched above the sea. There is always a dividing line between fisherman and fish; two environments which remain separated. In the surf, fish and fisher are as close as they can be. Closer than out to sea in boats; almost total integration. You are in the water with the fish. Sometimes it will swim between you and the shore, or bump into your legs.

A man's reaction to surf fishing is pure escapism. The sea and the surf and the standing, with water churning all around, are reward enough for fishing. Fish are important, of course, but not vital to enjoyment. When the crests break and roll over the sand the bass follow. Surf and bass are aspects of a single picture. Perhaps that is why surf bass have been idolized by some writers.

Surf on a strand is majestic and beautiful. There is, on the strand, a clean freshness which no other shoreline quite matches. In such surroundings any fish would be highly regarded, not so much for itself as for the sights and sounds, and later on the memories, with which it is associated. The sparkling silver bass embodies all those factors by which we have come to judge the perfect fish. That, combined with the fishing conditions, probably distorts the realities of surf bassing. We subconsciously reason that such fish in such waters must be difficult to catch. Thinking otherwise shatters the illusions – destroys your gods!

Bass are no more difficult to catch than flounders. Unless you do something really stupid, you miss them

A bass from a typical surf. Jack Austin fished a lugworm out where the breakers were turning to produce a plump fish of 4 lbs. In the conditions, fish were running along the breakers only 50 yds out.

Bass fishing involves casting lead and bait out into the surf but just occasionally the fish are behind the angler, swimming and searching for their food in the flat tables of water running back to join the next breaker.

Bass fishing is often said to act rather like a drug. Certainly it refreshes the angler from the cares and problems of modern living. But is it the fishing or the regular sway of the water that is therapeutic?

A fine catch of rays from the beach by John Sait. This species is under severe pressure from the commercial fishermen, trying desperately to fulfil the demands of our fish and chip shops.

either because they are not there, or they do not want to feed. In both those cases, the best angler in the world would do no better. Are big bass so cunning and intelligent that they are almost impossible to hook? No, indeed; there are not many about, that is all. The odds against a 15-pounder are thousands to one simply because a 15 lb bass is a rare beast. Look through the angling papers to see who caught the big bass. Were they bass experts – or just ordinary anglers who happened to be in the right place at the right time?

The mechanics of rough water strand fishing are simple. Cast out a paternoster baited with lugworms, clam or fish strips. As bass move close in, you do not need to cast far. There is no powerful side-current on most strands so 3 or 4 oz leads will do the job. Grip wires or Sandfast leads anchor the bait into the sand, so biting fish hit against a tethered trace. Fish are pulled up with a jerk which drives in the hook and ensures a fast response so that you either hook the fish in its guts or miss altogether. Bass fight reasonably well, but it is a rare fish which takes line from the spool. You play it ashore, lead it into the shallows and wait for the receding water to strand it on the sand.

Techniques apart, it would be wrong and cynical to suggest that surf fishing is like other angling. Strands are special. I have only to think back to my last trip to Ireland and to one evening in September. Oyster-catchers dibbling in the freshwater stream which drains the mountain rainwater through the saltings and out over the hard sands. Tide begins to flood, shepherding the water onto Fermoyle Strand. The ground swell rolls in. White-flecked crests break in a long line; the dots of surf join up and the wave turns over in one long foaming line. A gull glides down the long tunnel of water as another wave arches up, breaks and rolls onto the sand. Behind comes another wave and another, and then the dark, heaving, humps of Atlantic swell. The deep bass roar of the surf rumbles through the saltspray haze. Water-tables swish in, swirl, turn and chuckle back over the sand. A mob of curlews pipe and chorus along the sandhills, over the marram grass tussocks and into the blue mountains. And from the mountains a mist of peat smoke and the earthy musk of the moorlands drift out to sea on the night wind. It is perfection, the surf strand. It must be experienced to be appreciated. Go there soon.

Reg Righyni /Game fishing for salmon, trout and

All the game fish of the British Isles are members of the salmon family and they can be identified as such by the presence of the adipose fin, a small, fleshy, rounded appendage situated between the dorsal fin and the tail. They comprise the Atlantic salmon, the trout (including both the migratory and non-migratory varieties), the grayling and an immigrant species from North America, the rainbow trout. All are bred in fine shingle in highly oxygenated water, which must be almost entirely free from pollution. No doubt this contributes to the fact that game fish make excellent eating, but of even greater importance to the angler are the influences of these environmental requirements of the fish on the methods of angling for them and the quality of the sport they provide.

The key factor is the type of food upon which they live from the time when the young fish must fend for themselves. This is almost certain to include – or, indeed, to consist entirely of – some type of aquatic fly-life, probably in the form of larvae or nymphs.

The protein value of this food is very high and promotes great strength. The result is that fly fishing is the basic method for all species and the hooked fish give splendid accounts of themselves before they can be subdued. There are also styles of bait fishing, more particularly those employing artificial lures, that are deemed to meet the sporting standards required in game fishing. Nevertheless, these are largely regarded as complementary methods to be resorted to only when circumstances are not favourable for fly fishing.

Our first thoughts of fly fishing may be restricted to sunny days in spring, but in fact there is not a single day in the year when, weather and water conditions permitting, it is not possible to have some exciting sport with the fly tackle and, on many occasions during all the seasons of the year, one is spoilt for choice –it is difficult to decide which of several promising and fascinating options should be followed. This, of course, calls for some versatility but, given that, there is no closed-season for the fly fisher.

The natural progression for the angler taking up fly fishing is to concentrate almost entirely on one style – probably dictated by the type of fishing most readily available to him – until he is reasonably proficient, and then to try his hand at other methods. This is very sound but at the same time there are great advantages to be gained in the way of appreciating more fully the principles governing the chosen method if these can be considered alongside those applicable to the other methods. Practical points to be mentioned later will show the truth of this better than abstract discussion, so for the present let us agree that the first vital step is to get a concise overall picture of all the basic styles of fly fishing.

Because the dry fly is fished on the surface and everything, including the mistakes made by the

Reg Righyni on his beloved Lune, a river that has both trout and salmon fishing

rayling

Rising in the stark, windswept hills of Westmorland, near Ravenstonedale, it flows down through Lancashire into the Irish Sea.

angler, can be observed relatively easily and clearly, this method provides the most simple introduction to the subject, although that does not necessarily mean that it is the easiest one in which to gain a good degree of proficiency. Indeed, the skills of the successful dry-fly fisher include a sound knowledge of the habits of the fish, of the water-bred flies upon which they feed, of the nature of river flows, of the various procedures collectively known as river craft, and the ability to cast and present the artificial fly with delicacy and accuracy. Armed with those capabilities it is really only a question of a small degree of adjustment for the individual to master any other form of fly fishing.

DRY-FLY FISHING

In the classic scenario of dry-fly fishing the plump brown trout of the chalk- or limestone-stream is seen to be "on the fin". This is the term used when the fish is fully alert and not lying dormant – the difference between the two postures is unmistakable. If the duns or spinners are drifting down and over the fish in quick succession, it will probably be stationed only a few inches beneath the surface so that it can put up its snout and intercept the food with the greatest efficiency. In such a position, close to the surface, its field of view of the approach of the flies is rather narrow but that is of no disadvantage when they are sufficiently plentiful to keep the fish busy without having to move very far sideways. When there are fewer flies, however, the feeding fish tends to lie a little deeper, thus giving itself visual command of a greater surface area ahead.

The problem could hardly be more simple in principle, but it is not always so simple in its practical solution. All the angler has to do is to cast a suitably deceptive artificial to a point a foot or so ahead of the lie and let it drift down over the fish in exactly the same manner as the naturals. This must be achieved without disturbing the fish, which usually means that it must be completely unaware of the presence of the angler.

When the fish takes the artificial, the angler allows sufficient time for it to close its mouth properly (of which more later) and then tightens smoothly and firmly to set the hook. Now the line must be kept tight onto the fish at all times, with the angle of pull as high as possible. Thus with the rod held near the vertical, the fish feels more or less the same degree of restraint in whichever direction it attempts to move, including downwards, and can be played and guided away from weeds and other obstacles until it is finally brought over the net and lifted from the water.

The first difficulty, having spotted the interested trout, is to get into a suitable casting position without putting the fish down, or scaring it away altogether. The most important thing is to keep off the sky-line and it may be necessary to creep and crawl to do this. There must be no quick or jerky movement, nor any heavy footsteps. The lateral line of the fish is highly sensitive to vibrations in the water and the dropping of the net onto the bank would be certain to send the trout scuttling away. Having the sun behind you must also be avoided so that the shadow from the rod when casting will not fall across the lie.

According to the location of weed beds and, perhaps, the branches of a tree in relation to the lie of the fish, the casting position selected will usually be in the area between a point more or less opposite to the fish and another as far downstream as will be permitted by the length of line that can be fished.

What is probably the most critical factor in dry-fly fishing now comes into play. The artificial must be placed on the water and made to drift over the trout without any unnatural movement caused by the leader or line restraining the free travel with the flow.

Any such check to the progress of the artificial is called drag and, even if it appears to be only very slight, it is almost certain to put the fish off. The tendency towards drag and the means of overcoming it vary a great deal in the different types of flow and, other factors permitting – such as the location of weed beds, branches of trees, etc. – this has to be taken into consideration when deciding which is likely to be the best position from which to cast.

The appearance of the surface of the water is very deceptive in respect of the extent to which it will cause drag. The extremely smooth surface of a fast, even-paced glide will probably look as if it will be easy to deal with but it is, in fact, most difficult. If the line thrown is straight, the only angle at which it is at all possible to avoid drag is in direct line with the flow and even then there is a big risk that the artificial will be pulled downstream at a faster rate than the flow, which is drag. (The reason is that the pace of the glide is likely to be faster at its lower extremity than it will be higher up.)

However, if the cast is made at a fairly narrow angle upstream and a lot of little wiggles are put into the line as it alights on the water, the fly will usually drift without any objectionable drag (while the curls in the line are straightening out) for the vital foot or so as it covers the fish.

Again, contrary to appearance, the type of water that presents the least problem concerning drag is the popply-looking stream. Providing the line or leader does not traverse a band of flow which is faster than that where the fly is required to be placed, a straight line will usually be satisfactory, and this may well be so with a fairly square cast. The result is that in this class of water the angler has a much wider range

A southern chalkstream, the Bourne at Winterbourne, Wiltshire.

of choice in the position he can select for casting. In view of the other variable factors such as the direction of the light, bank obstructions and the rest, the help this greater freedom can give may be quite invaluable.

Without any further delay it must be mentioned that when the cast is made at a narrow angle upstream and the flow is fairly fast, line must be retrieved in the free hand at a suitable rate to ensure that, when the rod is raised to hook the trout, there will be no undue amount of slack line to cause delay. With the squarish cast very little slack line is created while the fly is drifting over the lie – which can be an important consideration, especially when it is necessary to throw a long line in the first place simply to reach the fish.

Practice, of course, is essential in dealing with drag. Careful attention to the principles involved can save the almost endless frustration which becomes inevitable if too casual a view is taken of the importance of the different types of flow. Indeed, this question of drag remains permanently the great test of the dry-fly fisher and it is as if the trout recognize this fact, because the best fish always seems to occupy the lie where the drag problem is the greatest. Of course, it is easy to see why this is so. The check on the movement of the water caused by weeds and bank protrusions results in an acceleration in the flow in the adjacent, unobstructed area, and it is in speedier spots of this sort that the food drifts over the fish more quickly and hence in greater quantity. The fast water itself is not the difficulty with regard to drag. It is the fact that the line or leader is restrained by the steadier water close by. The feature of drag which ensures that it must always be considered apprehensively is that the permissible scope for trial and error is extremely small. Each time the artificial passes close to the trout incorrectly – that is, with easily visible drag – the less chance there is that the fish will be deceived when eventually an apparently suitable presentation is achieved.

No two lies are exactly alike and the flow at any one of them requires separate and detailed examination. Familiarity with the beat should, however, lead to the ability to deal quite satisfactorily with the majority of situations on the day. The inevitable failures here and there serve to make one suitably pleased with the better part of one's performance without any risk of becoming complacent about the problems of drag.

Coupled with the question of how the floating artificial behaves during the vital final approach to the feeding trout, there is always the complex problem of how it is seen by the eye of the fish, to what extent it succeeds in simulating the natural food and, indeed, whether or not effective imitation is important.

It must be said straight away that the way in which anglers cope with the subject in practice varies enormously. Some who enjoy a well above average amount of success get along with the minimum of knowledge ▶216

The illustrations show the gradual changes that are met with in the trout family coloration, starting at the top with a sea trout from the sea, going through to the bottom illustration showing a typical trout in breeding colour. The longer the sea trout spends in fresh water the greater his spots will grow until they join together and turn the trout completely brown.

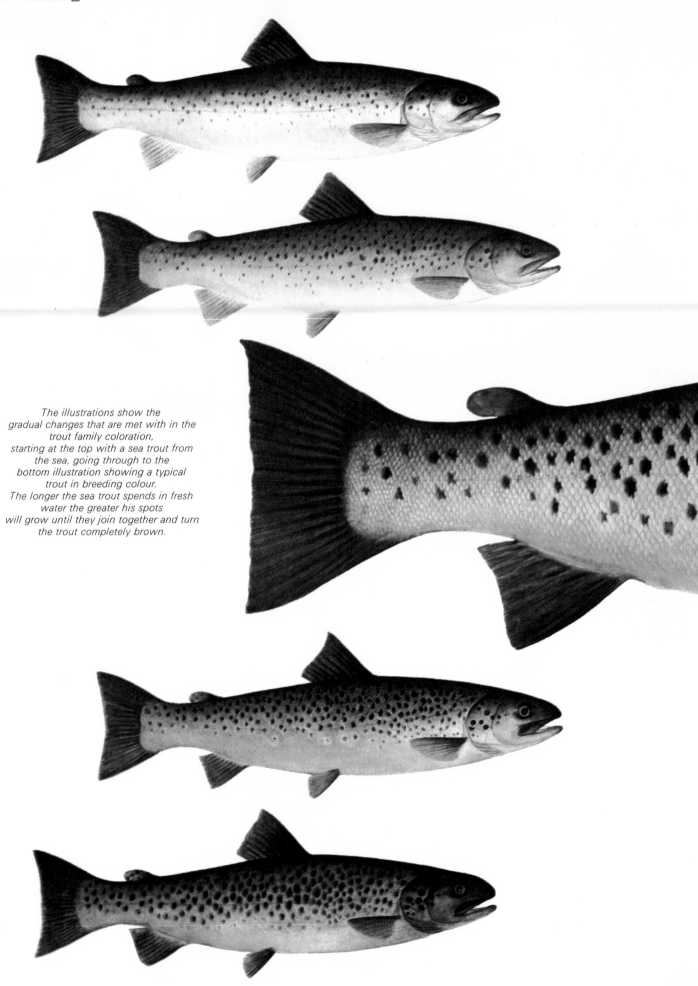

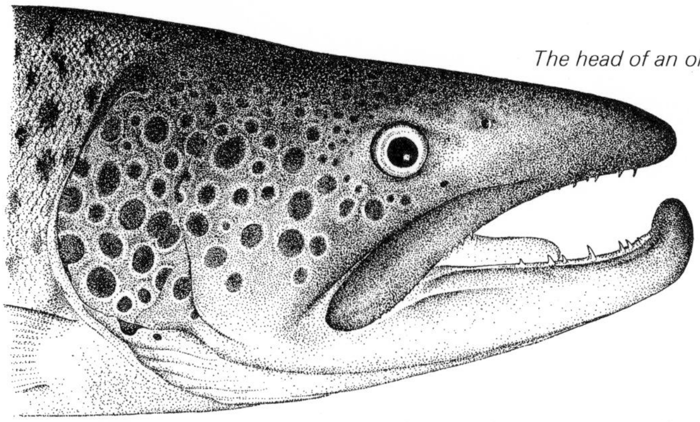

The head of an old or "Cannibal" male trout

Trout parr

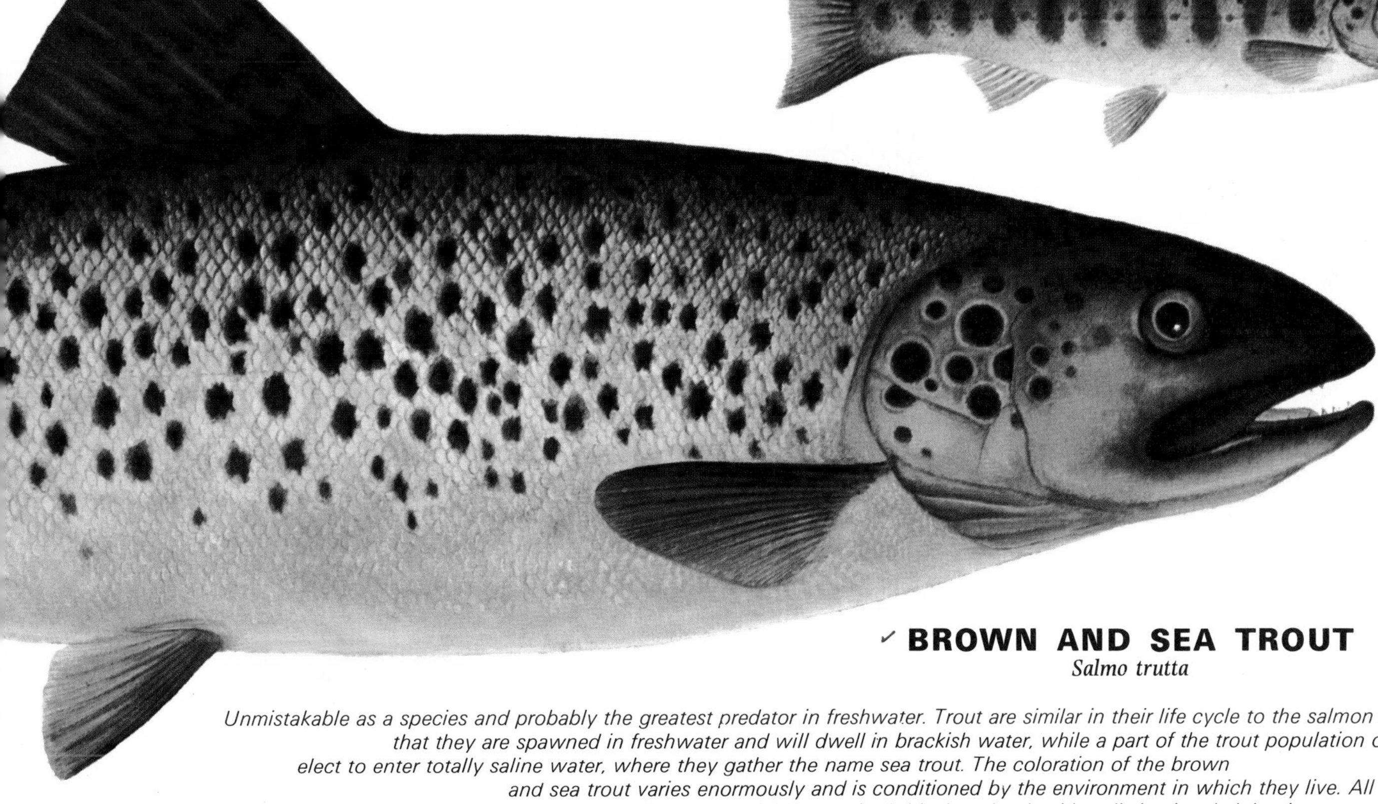

BROWN AND SEA TROUT

Salmo trutta

Unmistakable as a species and probably the greatest predator in freshwater. Trout are similar in their life cycle to the salmon in that they are spawned in freshwater and will dwell in brackish water, while a part of the trout population of a river will elect to enter totally saline water, where they gather the name sea trout. The coloration of the brown and sea trout varies enormously and is conditioned by the environment in which they live. All trout have a similar fry pelage, known as parr. They have vivid spots, both black and red, with a distinctive dark barring on the flanks. The adult brown trout will retain this vivid colouring although the bars will disappear in the smolt stage. Both the sea trout and lake trout will have a definite smolt stage in their lives, when they pass from the parr colours into a silvery pelage. As adults they exhibit black cross-shaped spots most clearly patterned above the fish's lateral line. Trout are strongly territorial. As juveniles a shoal will adopt a position within a river that depends on the needs of that shoal and on their ability to defend the chosen lie. As large fish they tend to be more solitary in behaviour. Both male and female trout undergo a marked change in coloration as the time for spawning nears. In late winter, at the time of the coldest weather, trout will move on to gravel stretches in the smallest of feeder streams. The males attempt to pair with several female fish, lying close alongside the hens as they dig into the gravel to create a depression in which to deposit the eggs. Depending on size, a female trout will spawn upwards of one hundred eggs which are then covered with gravel and left to hatch in the early spring. Many trout are artificially stripped of eggs and milt to be raised as both a food crop and as replacement stock for both still and running water. The trout is a fish that can tolerate a wide pH range (alkalinity-acidity values of the water) so man has been able to introduce them to a great variety of waters across the world as well as man-made situations in the British Isles.

Bait: *Live fish, natural and artificial insects, all types of spinning lures, worms and small crustaceans.*

213◄ of both entomology and the available artificials. They rely on a few favourite dressings and tend to assert that the standard of presentation is much more important than the actual pattern used.

There will be more on this point later, but for the moment let us say that such people use skills (almost amounting to a sixth sense) which are quite beyond the capability of the newcomer to the sport. The only safe course for the novice is to make a small study, which most will find enjoyable, of the life cycles of the main kinds of flies and details of the particular species most important in the diet of the fish. Then, as practical experience grows, the novice angler will become comfortably familiar with the naturals and their imitations and will make his selection of the pattern to be used with ever-growing and gratifying self-confidence.

By far the most important naturals so far as the dry-fly fisher is concerned are the upright-winged flies, including the famous mayfly, which belong to the family Ephemeridae. A nymph hatches from an egg at the bottom of the river and this small creature usually lives in the water for about a year, but in the case of the mayfly it will probably be two years. When the growth of the nymph has ceased and it stops feeding, it soon rises to the surface and the winged fly emerges from the nymphal case or, as the angler says, the dun hatches. After spells varying from a few minutes to a day or more according to the species, the dun undergoes a further metamorphosis and the fully mature fly, the spinner, emerges.

It is at this stage that mating takes place. This is the final act of the male but the female still has to deposit the eggs on or in the water. Soon afterwards there is what is called a "spinner fall". The dead spinners drift down the river and are obviously thoroughly enjoyed by the trout.

The species of duns which the trout seem to like best and which appear commonly enough and in sufficiently large numbers to be of serious interest to the angler are relatively few.

The principal ones are the large spring olive or large dark olive, which appears early in the season – March/April; the March brown and the false, or late March brown – March, April and early May; the medium olive – April and then on and off for the rest of the season; the iron blue – late April, May, and perhaps early June; the mayfly or green drake – late May/early June; the blue winged olive – June until the end of the season; and the pale watery – June onwards.

The times of appearance of the different species can vary considerably as a result of unseasonable weather and, of course, there are variations according to the character of the water and the general area of the surrounding country.

Some of the spinners have famous names. The March brown spinner is the Great Red Spinner. The male iron blue spinner is the Jenny Spinner. The medium olive spinner is the Red Spinner and the blue winged olive spinner is the Sherry Spinner.

No mention has yet been made of the beauty of the duns and spinners. In colouring, shape and movement most species are exceedingly attractive and this adds a great deal of charm and also of interest to the study of the flies.

The other interesting families are the Trichoptera, the caddis or sedge flies; the Perlidae, the stone flies; and the Diptera, the gnats, crane flies, ants and beetles. In all these cases the fly that emerges from the larva is the final, mature form of the species, there being no further change. The floating representations of some of these flies are very popular on a local basis in certain circumstances – for example, a dry sedge at dusk in summer – but, in the main, they are of more interest to the wet-fly fisher.

It is also necessary to become familiar with some of the dressings with very well-known names which do not necessarily indicate the species of flies which their inventors intended them to represent. Greenwell's Glory and the Gold-Ribbed Hare's Ear are both commonly used and mainly in the belief that they are taken for the medium olive dun. The Little Marryat was designed to imitate the pale watery dun. Then there are such highly popular patterns as the Grey Duster, the John Storey and the Sturdy's Fancy, each of which may represent more than one species reasonably well.

From this it will be clear that the dry-fly fisher must have a personal plan or scheme to ensure that he always has an adequate stock of flies at hand. At the same time this should not be too large for convenient use and, of course, not too expensive to acquire. Equally clearly this cannot be done on a rule of thumb basis without years of experience to produce the guide lines. If there is, indeed, a true short cut to success in mastering this question of dry fly patterns, it is to read some of the popular books on anglers' entomology. However, this can be quite rewarding in its own right apart from the practical usefulness to be gained and it should certainly not prove a chore to anyone who is naturally attracted to fly fishing.

A good understanding of the required behaviour of the floating artificial – drifting without drag and riding high on the hackle points to simulate the posture of the natural dun – is the best guide to the type of tackle that is most suitable. Obviously the point of the leader must be fine enough for it not to be seen too easily by the fish and it must be sufficiently supple because stiffness may contribute towards drag. In practice it is found that nylon of about 3 lb test is the best all round compromise. If one hooks a very heavy fish near dense growths of weed, one is inclined to wish

1 *A* Baetis *sp. nymph from the River Itchen, a Hampshire chalkstream.*

2 *The medium olive* Baetis vernus *female spinner.*

3 *The medium olive male dun.*

4 *An artificial medium olive fly tied by John Goddard.*

that this weakest link in the chain were a good bit stronger, but at the same time one recognizes that the offer from the fish would probably not have come had the nylon not been so fine. The compromise that has to be made between fineness and strength can often be a key factor and is common to all styles of fly fishing.

Knotless tapered leaders are available in all the various strengths that may be required. From 3 lb test at the point ranging up to about 10 lb at the loop is probably the most popular for trouting with small flies. Some anglers make up their leaders with short strands of different strengths joined by blood knots.

A regular steep taper will be found suitable in most situations, but there is a popular belief that a better turnover of the leader can be achieved by using a double taper – that is, having thicker nylon in the middle than at the loop. This is a subject the individual may find worth investigating.

Leaders with fine points require light fly lines to match them because the weight of the line imposes much strain that has to be borne by the leader at such crucial moments as when the fish is being hooked, or if it makes a violent jerk during the ensuing fight. Unfortunately, however, the novice usually finds that it is much easier to learn to cast with a line that is rather heavier than the size that makes the safest partner for the fine leader. And this position is further aggravated by the fact that the heavier the line, the more difficult it is to present the fly with delicacy and a minimum of disturbance. Consequently, if the effort is made in the first place to master the casting with a suitably fine fly line, a lot of other potential difficulties for the future are made much easier to deal with. In this context it should be mentioned that, weight for weight, the traditional oil-dressed silk line is easier to cast with than the plastic-coated floater because its smaller bulk causes less air resistance. But the silk line requires constant care and attention – drying, cleaning, greasing, etc. – to ensure that it does not fail to float well enough during spells of sustained fishing, whereas the plastic line should give a reliably satisfactory performance at all times without the need for treatment any more complicated than keeping it reasonably free from surplus water and dirt.

The range of sizes in both silk and plastic lines is both wide and detailed enough to suit every need. And when eventually the selection has been made there will be plenty of scope for a choice of rods to balance the line. But first one should consider the other duties – besides straight-out dry-fly fishing for river trout – for which the outfit will probably be wanted. If the secondary role is to be river fishing with wet fly and nymph, the emphasis should be in favour of the finest line that can be managed suitably well – a No 1 or 2 silk or an AFTM 4 or 5 floater. On the other hand, if some dry-fly work on stillwater or some sea-trouting is to have fairly high priority, it would probably be best to go for a No 3 or 4 silk or an AFTM 6 or 7 floater.

Probably the most popular length for a dry-fly rod at present is 8 ft 6 ins, but this is largely a hangover from the days before the appearance of modern glass rods when there were good practical reasons for keeping the rod down to this length. Today well-designed glass rods are so light in weight and so versatile in the line sizes they will carry that these factors need no longer be at all restrictive in considering the length of rod to be chosen. Generally speaking – and ignoring the question of possible personal preference – there is no reason why a dry-fly rod should be as short as 8 ft 6 ins or less except on water where casting space is badly restricted by thick foliage. Wherever there is enough space to use a longer rod it is almost invariably an advantage. Nine feet is probably as long as most anglers would care to see a dry-fly rod, but this extra 6 ins makes a remarkable difference to the performance in several important respects, including the casting range, ground clearance on the back cast, control of the line while fishing out the cast, taking up any unavoidable slack when striking and in the handling of a hard-fighting fish. The extra 6 ins can also be very helpful in all the secondary roles of the outfit whether it is for the more delicate work with nymphs and wet flies or the sturdier duties with the sea trout and on stillwater.

Sometimes it is said that the reel of the fly fisher is not important – nothing more than a receptacle to hold the line. The fallacy of this view cannot be appreciated to the full until you are playing a big fish that is powerfully taking line. Now, a nicely-made reel with an exposed rim for hand braking makes it possible to apply pressure very firmly but smoothly and to remain confidently in control of the fish. Additional braking pressure applied in any other way tends to be jerky and the increased strain that this puts on the fine leader, not to mention a possibly rather slender hook-hold, is most hazardous. Reels of about $3\frac{1}{4}$ ins diameter are the most suitable and the drum should be wide enough to accommodate 25 or 50 yds of backing in addition to the rather bulky fly line. And, needless to say, the lighter the reel, the better.

The most useful method of fastening the line to the backing is to whip a small loop at the end of the fly line and a large one – big enough for the reel to pass through – at the end of the backing. The loop in the backing is passed through the loop in the line and then the reel (containing the backing) is passed through this loop in the backing and the two loops are drawn together to make a neat knot.

The two can easily be separated again when a change of line is wanted. At the business end of the fly line the leader can be attached by a figure-of-eight knot. This is very convenient and serviceable but some anglers complain that it causes a small bow wave on the surface when the water is smooth if certain manoeuvres, such as working a nymph, are employed. Their answer to the problem is to attach a thick piece of nylon to the line by means of a pin knot, and then use a blood knot to join the leader to the now permanent piece of thick nylon.

The pin knot certainly does reduce the tendency to make a bow wave, but it does make the tip of the line more prone to sinking. This may not affect the way the fly and the leader float while the fish is being covered, but when the line is withdrawn in preparation for a

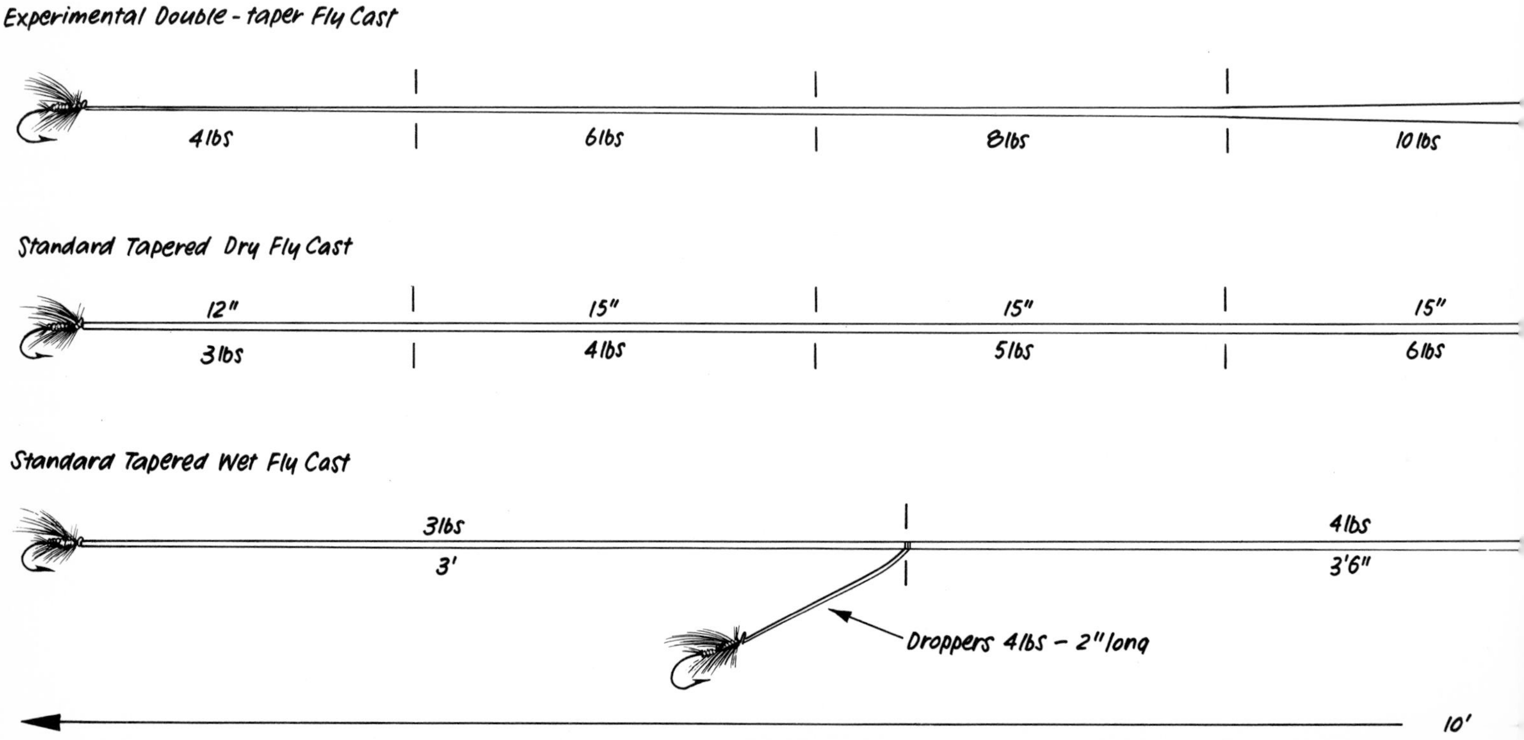

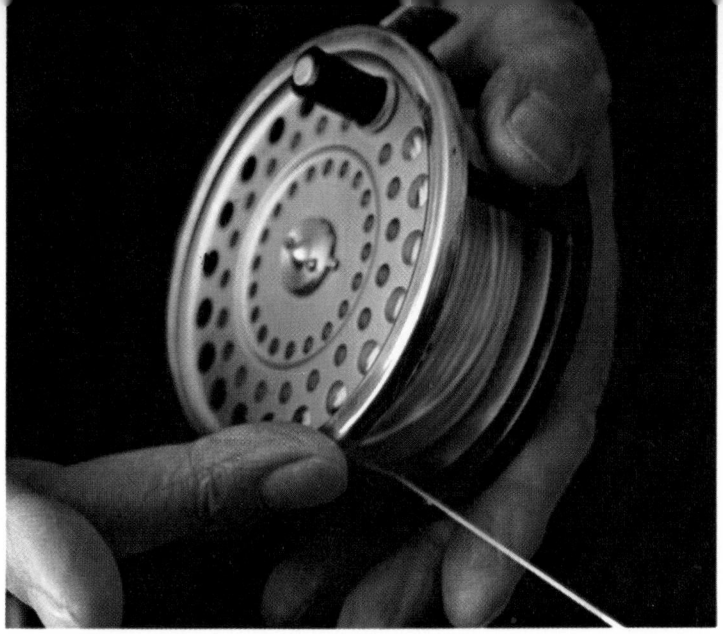

Fly reels with an exposed rim aid an angler in controlling the fight of a powerful fish. Pressure on the rim, acting as a smooth brake or drag, is more easily applied with the fingers than by attempting to restrict the flow of line by actual pressure applied to that line or on to the drum itself.

further cast the pin knot can cause the leader and the fly to be drawn beneath the surface, thus causing unwanted wetting of the artificial. This happens especially when one does not want to waste time drying and re-oiling the fly and, therefore, for the purpose of this primary role the figure-of-eight knot would seem to be best. For attaching the flies, the knots in common use are the double turle and the tucked half-blood. The latter is the easier to tie, but the double turle is the least obtrusive.

Armed with these basic ideas governing the outfit required, we can now look more fully into the different aspects of dry-fly fishing resulting from variations in the type of water and the species of fish to be sought. Only the brown trout of the chalk-stream has been mentioned more than casually so far, but the rainbow trout, the sea trout, the grayling, and the brown trout of the rain-fed river may each be the candidate to be offered the floating fly on the running water during the course of the year.

The broad principles to be observed remain the same for all species, but sometimes it is good policy to employ slight variations in tactics which are made necessary by the differences in the habits of the fish. As we have said, the feeding brown trout stations itself suitably close to the surface to intercept the maximum number of flies with the minimum of effort. The sea trout and the grayling never do this. They always lie very close indeed to the bottom and make a separate return journey for each fly they take from the surface. And – different again – the rainbow trout appears to observe no self-imposed rules which could be restrictive to its freedom of action. Its behaviour may be like any one of the others, but equally well it may be entirely different and may include some quite startling performances, such as making a surprise appearance at great speed from some unseen position, attacking the fly viciously and then charging off across the top of the water like a show-off that feels very pleased with how clever it has been. Indeed, to enjoy to the full the entertainment provided by the rainbow trout there are times when one must take a very light-hearted view and see the funny side of the fish having the upper hand.

The fact that brown trout feeding on the surface always do so from relatively close quarters is a matter of considerable influence in several respects. In the first place – which is apparently the intention – only a small, unhurried, movement is required to scoop in the fly and, in keeping with the action up to that point, the closing of the mouth is similarly unhurried.

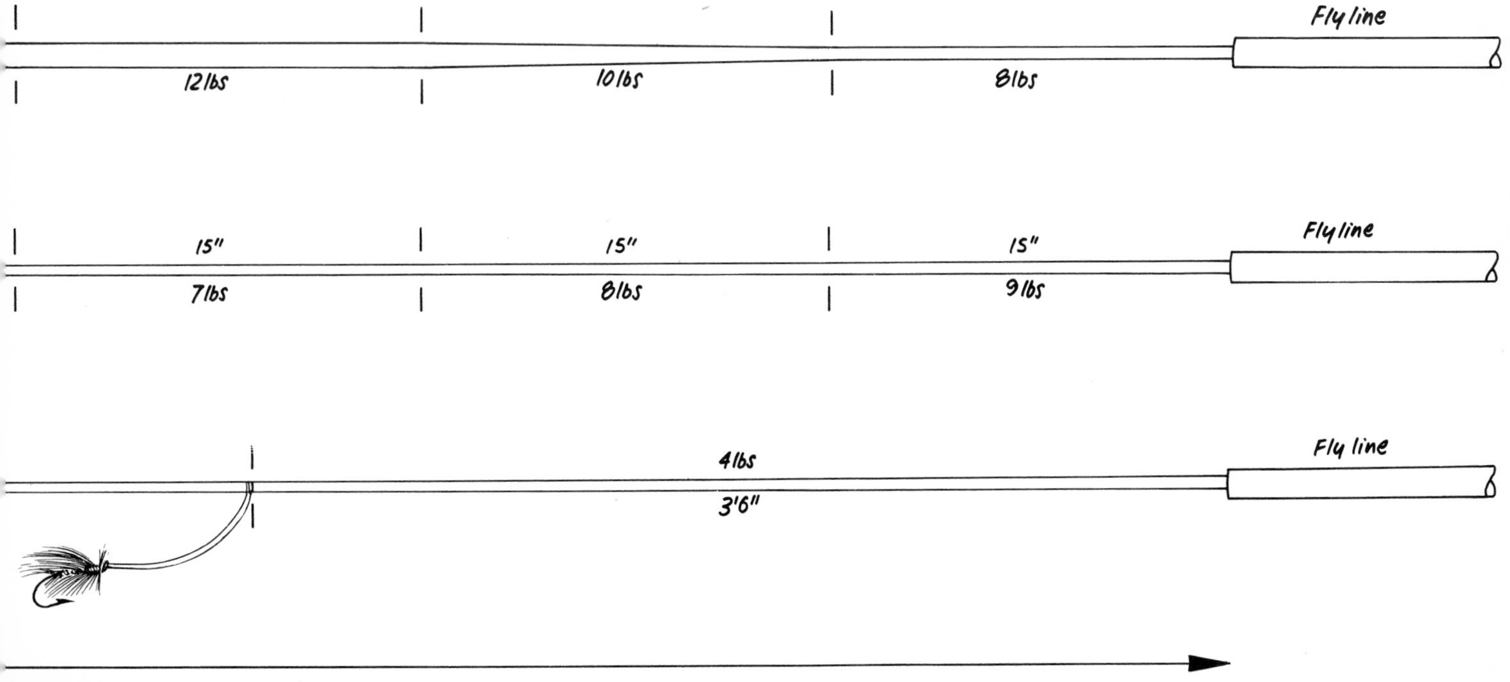

In a fast flow the whole sequence is naturally performed more quickly but in sluggish water the action can be remarkably slow. Of course, the rise of the fish is very exciting and it is not easy, particularly for the novice, to restrain himself from striking too quickly. But the attempt to set the hook must not be timed to occur before the mouth of the fish is properly closed and this involves what can seem to be a very lengthy delay. However, no standard timing can be prescribed and it is just as possible to be too slow as too quick, since the trout usually wastes no time in spitting the artificial out after his jaws have closed on it. Clearly, the correct drill is to watch the movements of the trout carefully and to react accordingly. This is fortunately not as difficult as it may sound after a bit of experience.

On the not-so-frequent occasions when sea trout or grayling can be caught on the dry fly in very shallow water, their movements are much the same as those of the brown trout and the striking policy should be the same. Much more commonly, however, the fish will rise through 2 or 3 ft of water or more to intercept the artificial. It is quite a speedy movement up to the surface and back again, even in a steady flow, and the turn that is made at the surface and the seizure of the fly are both executed quickly. Consequently the strike usually has to be made instantly if the fish is to be hooked successfully. This, of course, relates to the small dry flies we have so far been discussing. With large flies at dusk, or when a stiff breeze is ruffling the surface, the sea trout requires more time to get its mouth closed properly and then, of course, the strike must be suitably delayed. Rainbow trout are also capable of being extremely quick in ejecting the artificial and, as with grayling, there are times when there is little doubt that the rising fish has no intention of doing more than give the fly a very rapid nip, as opposed to taking it fully into the mouth. Then the only slight chance of hooking the fish depends on the strike being made extremely quickly. It so happens, though, that when the fish – both rainbow trout and grayling – are in the mood simply to challenge the fly, so to speak, they are usually inclined to repeat the action several times at close intervals and then sometimes take too clumsily to avoid getting hooked.

Normally if a brown trout fails to secure the artificial the first time it rises to it, it will not subsequently make more than one further effort to get it although the fish has not been otherwise disturbed. It seems that two abortive attempts are almost always enough to satisfy the trout that the artificial is not, in fact, a desirable item. However, after the lapse of a further quarter of an hour or so, the trout may possibly make another and more determined effort to seize the artificial, especially if it has consumed quite a few naturals in the meantime. But, generally speaking, it is the first encounter of the day that invariably offers the angler

THE RAINBOW TROUT

Salmo gairdneri

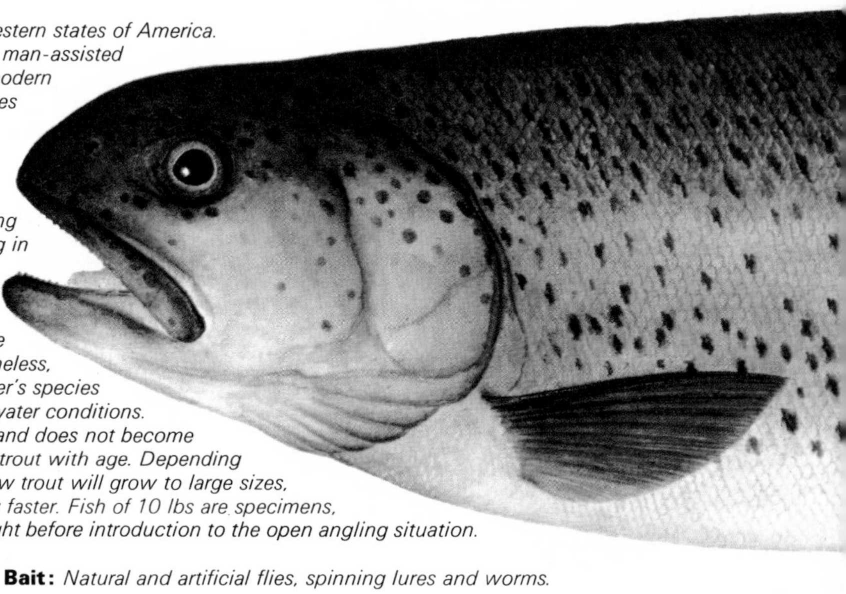

A species brought to the British Isles from the North-Western states of America. It thrives in stillwaters and has become the standard fish for man-assisted production of trout as food and as replacement stock for the modern stillwater trout fishery. Anatomically, the species resembles the brown trout in all but coloration. The rainbow has a vivid band of mauve-purple scales along the flanks roughly following the contours of the fish's lateral line. There are numerous black spots and blotches on the sides and back extending on to the caudal fin. The rainbow trout is not a successful spawning fish in our waters. Indeed, most of the fish swimming in lakes and reservoirs will have been bred and introduced by the fishery managements. There is some evidence to suggest that there are strains of rainbows that can exist as a free-living and breeding species but whether these fish are viable after a number of generations as wild fish is doubtful. Nevertheless, the rainbow trout is a useful addition to the angler's species as it seems to be more tolerant of pollution and otherwise doubtful water conditions. The fish appears to be more free-rising and does not become quite so predatory and bottom living as the brown trout with age. Depending on the type of water, the rainbow trout will grow to large sizes, often bigger than trutta *and certainly faster. Fish of 10 lbs are specimens, although trout farms can rear them to double this weight before introduction to the open angling situation.*

Bait: *Natural and artificial flies, spinning lures and worms.*

the best prospect of a really solid take on the line.

In steadily flowing water both brown trout and rainbow trout will sometimes approach to within a fraction of an inch of the floating artificial to examine it and then drift down alongside it with the current to maintain this very close scrutiny. This may well be repeated several times and after such inspections one would think that the fish could not possibly fall for the deception. On the contrary, however, it is not at all unusual for the trout eventually to open its mouth quite unhurriedly and to suck in the fly with utter deliberation. When grayling are smutting and are offered a sizeable fly, they will sometimes do a little bit of the close inspection routine but this is not really characteristic of them. What is quite typical of grayling performance, however, is to let the dry fly drift quite a long way past (as much as a yard or two downstream) and then, as if prompted by an afterthought, to make a quick turn, chase after the fly and take it very positively. Brown trout and rainbows will occasionally chase the fly in a similar manner, but this does not happen nearly so often as with the grayling.

These idiosyncrasies of the different species must always be considered both in respect of the point where one attempts to place the artificial relative to the position of the fish in the first place, and the distance it should be allowed to travel beyond the lie. Also it must be borne in mind that it is much easier to get the fly to drift nicely without drag for a short distance than for a longer one. Therefore, with a brown trout, and knowing that it does not take it long to move the short distance to make the interception, one does not normally attempt to place the fly more than about 1 ft ahead of the fish and then, if there is no rise, the artificial is lifted off the water when it is about 1 ft past the fish, hopefully before any drag has become at all pronounced and without any unnecessary wetting of the fly. If a bit of error results in the fly alighting closer to the trout, it should not put it off if it is well on the feed. Indeed, on those occasions when it proves exceedingly difficult to find a pattern that will deceive the trout when presented in the normal way, it may well be that the only chance of success will be to drop the artificial vertically above the nose of the fish. If this tactic succeeds, the trout usually takes the artificial immediately it touches the water and without it having had the chance to make any kind of real inspection. Occasionally rainbow trout can also be hooked by this means but, needless to say, it does not apply with sea trout or grayling during the daytime when they are lying in relatively deep water. Of course, if a sea trout is in very shallow water at dusk, a well-aimed dry sedge may be taken instantly. Indeed, this happens so quickly as to suggest that the impulse to seize the fly had occurred before it actually reached the surface of the water below which the trout was waiting.

In addition to the peculiarities mentioned so far, all species of game fish are subject to moods of selectivity, or the lack of it, ranging from being quite uncatchable on any artificial fly on some occasions to being seemingly quite indifferent to the details of the dressings they are willing to take at other times. There never seems to be any apparently logical explanation when either of the two extreme types of behaviour is met but, fortunately, they do not happen so frequently as to cause any more than a healthy amount of alternating doubt and confidence on the part of the angler. Much more commonly the fish are just moderately selective – willing to take a small variety of those patterns thought to be appropriate for the circumstances, but quite uninterested in anything out of keeping with the general appearance of the successful category.

This question is not, of course, confined to the floating fly and, although it is common in some degree to all the game fish, it cannot be dealt with more than casually in a general context. Furthermore, while it is related in some respects to that notorious old challenge of "Does the pattern matter?", some of the answers to the one do not necessarily apply to the other. Therefore, both these ever-recurring problems are dealt with under several of the different headings that follow. Meantime, the broad picture of dry-fly fishing needs to be completed.

Trout can be caught on the floating fly as early as the beginning of March in those areas where the season opens then. But in the main, dry-fly fishing does not get properly under way in reasonably seasonable times until about the middle of April. Then the most productive period is likely to be between about 11 o'clock in the morning until around 4 o'clock in the afternoon. The large spring olive dun and the darker variety of the medium olives will be the most interesting naturals and any of the popular patterns representing them should be worth a trial. When the warmer weather of May gets established sport may start earlier in the morning and continue throughout the evening, perhaps culminating in a hectic rise to a fall of spinners. But at this time of the year – and henceforth – there is likely to be a very quiet spell in the afternoon, say from about 1 o'clock until 4, or even 5, on a warm day. Now, the paler variety of the medium olive dun will generally be the chief fly, but on the warmer days there may be hatches around lunchtime of pale watery duns, while on cold, windy days the iron blue dun may make its most welcome appearance. There is no fly that the trout seem to relish more than the splendid little iron blue, and it is during hatches of this species that the newcomer to fly fishing is likely to have his most exciting and successful early experiences – encounters to remember for a lifetime.

On those rivers so favoured, the mayfly hatches

CHAR
Salvelinus alpinus

A minutely scaled member of the salmon family found in few waters of the British Isles. Our char population can be considered as land-locked, non-migratory fish that were left in a number of discrete locations by the last Ice Age.

Char are found in some parts of Scotland, the north-west of England, Wales and Ireland. They inhabit deep, cold glacial lakes where the lack of rich feeding does not allow the fish to grow to sizes attained by the char in other parts of Northern Europe where the species is often sea-dwelling for part of the year, only coming into freshwater to spawn. The species resembles the trout in shape, has a white fringing to the pectoral, ventral and anal fins. They adopt a vivid breeding colour, a brilliant red to both fins and belly, in the winter. A fish of 2 lbs would be regarded as a worthy specimen.

Bait: *Artificial flies and small spinners.*

NORTH AMERICAN BROOK TROUT
Salvelinus fontinalis

An introduction from the Eastern states of America at around the same time as the rainbow trout was brought to Europe. The brook trout is, in fact, a char and does not seem to have survived the initial introductions although there are a couple of fisheries that have a more recently introduced thriving population of this fine fighting species.

Bait: *Both artificial lures and worms.*

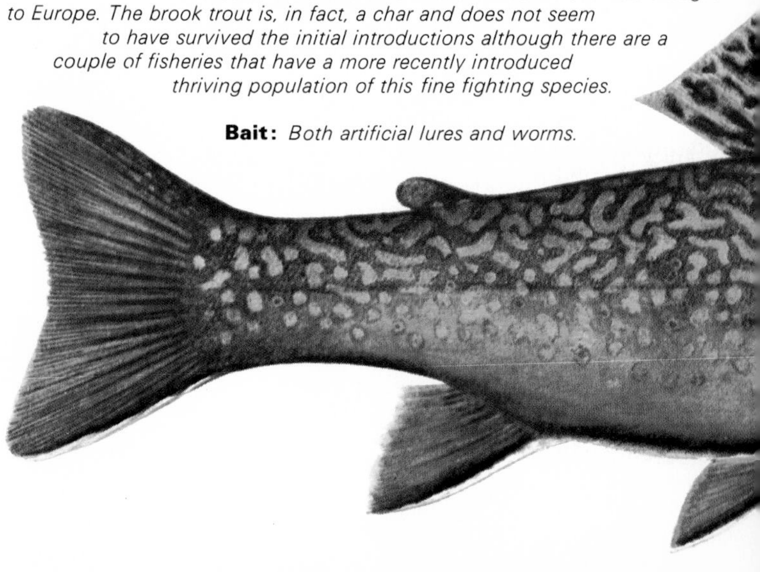

Map showing distribution of char (*Salvelinus alpinus*) in British Isles, both extant and extinct.

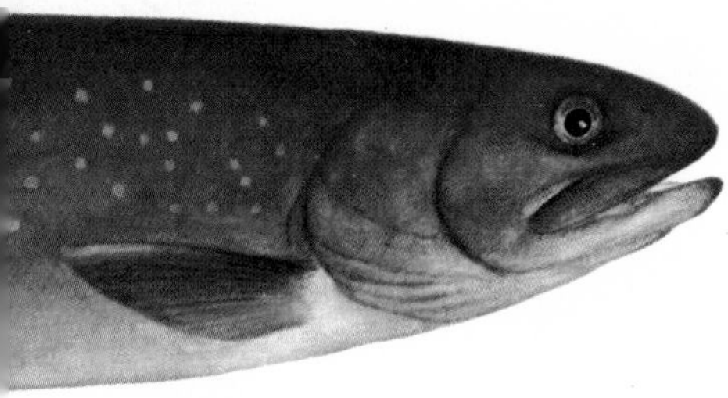

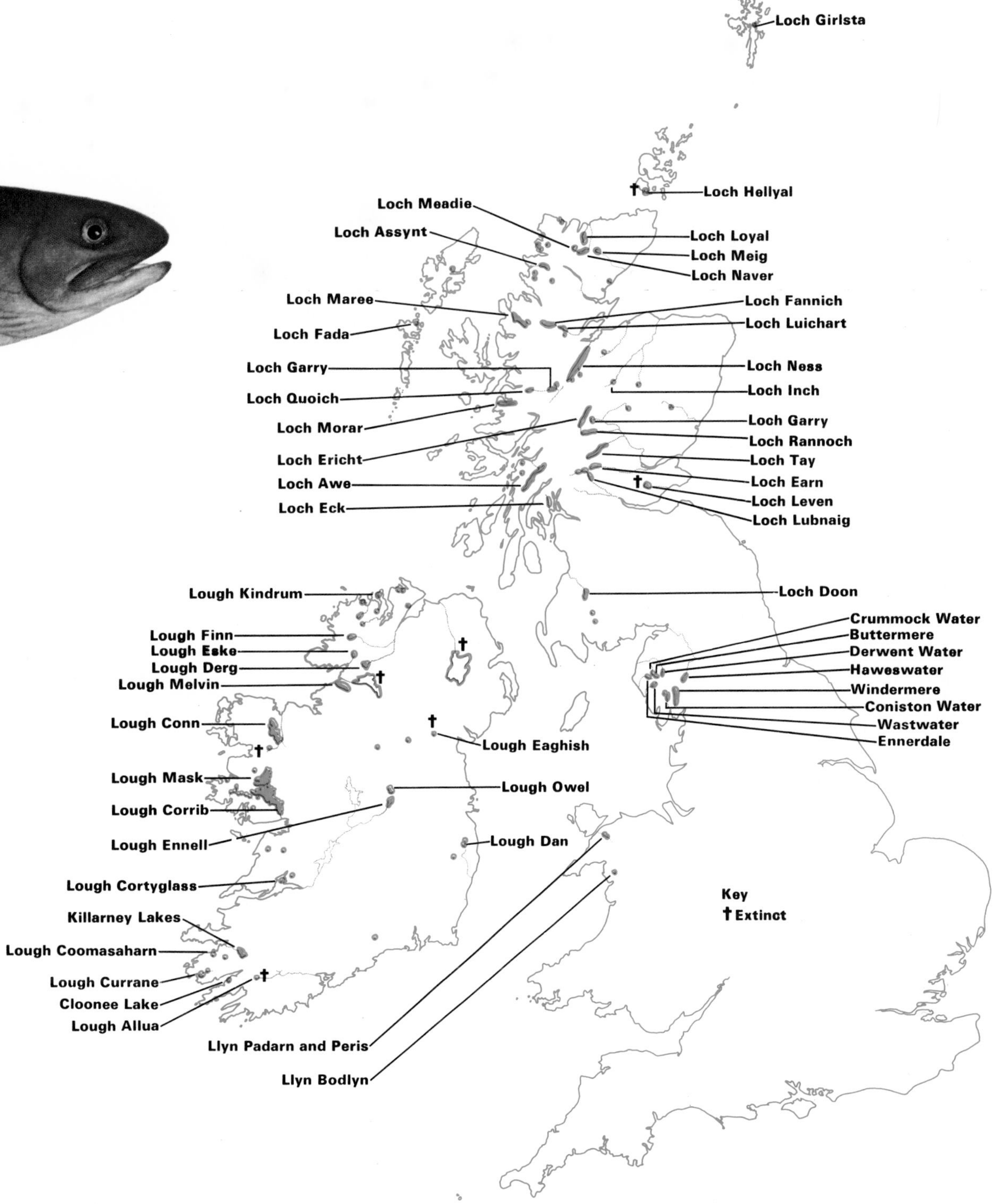

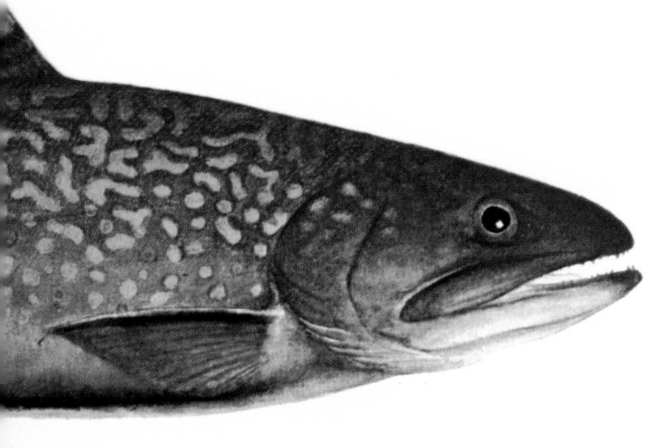

commence towards the end of May or early in June and last for about a fortnight. It takes a few days for the trout to become accustomed to these apparently huge flies but once the feasting starts in earnest it makes a fantastic scene, so much so that in some areas of the country it is the most celebrated event of the year, arousing the enthusiasm even of the non-angling sections of the community. This, of course, is an excellent time to match wits with any specially large trout known to frequent any particular area and, with the stronger leader that seems to be tolerated by the fish when they are taking the mayfly well, the chances of landing the big specimens are infinitely better than when the small fly and matching leader are being fished.

Although mayfly time assuredly means some very good baskets of trout, if not the best of the season, the fish are not always as easy to catch as some hackneyed versions of the "Duffer's Fortnight" suggest.

Indeed, a variety of frustrating difficulties can arise. It is not uncommon for there to be a spell of several hours during which just an occasional one of the many natural duns drifting down the river is taken by a fish and it seems quite impossible to get an offer to any pattern of artificial. But whatever the reason may be, this usually gives way eventually to a rather dramatic change – bold, solid takes in quick succession to just the same kind of offerings that had previously been ignored. Another common type of experience is to get a lot of irritable-looking nudges at the artificial and some seemingly complete takes, but find it is impossible to get a hook-hold of any sort. The mayfly being such a large object relatively, it is generally accepted policy that the fish should be given plenty of time – considerably more than with the small flies – before tightening. But no matter how long the strike is delayed when the trout are in this mood of apparent hesitation, the artificial comes away with seemingly no resistance. Once again, however, good sport is usually not very far away when the nudging game is in progress.

The artificial mayfly is the best subject for consideration of the matter of fly floatants. There are several kinds of liquid preparations on the market but not all of them are suitable for immediate application while actually fishing and few of the others are capable of keeping the popular Iceberg floating high on the water.

It should be remembered, of course, that most artificials are light enough to float of their own accord, but require to be reasonably waterproof to prevent moisture being soaked up. Some anglers prefer not to use any floatant and rely on drying the fly by means of false casting. One particularly good method is to melt a little solid silicone line grease on the end of the finger and to stroke this onto the hackles or hair of the fly. The same grease can be used on the leader but care should

THE COREGONIDS OR WHITEFISH

A group of fishes belonging to the salmonidae that can be divided into three species: Coregonus lavaretus: *powan, schelly and gwyniad;* Coregonus albula: *vendace and pollan;* Coregonus oxyrhinchus: *houting. All six fish are similar in appearance, looking like a finely scaled herring but all possessing an adipose fin. With the exception of the vendace, they have pointed snouts with protruding upper jaws. There is a similarity in feeding behaviour, all of the coregonids are plankton and small animal-life feeders. They inhabit stillwaters, mostly in the north and west of these islands. In European waters, these fish live in rivers and lakes and some of the species are known to have migratory instincts. The houting is partially sea-dwelling in Eastern Europe, only coming into freshwater to ascend rivers for spawning.*

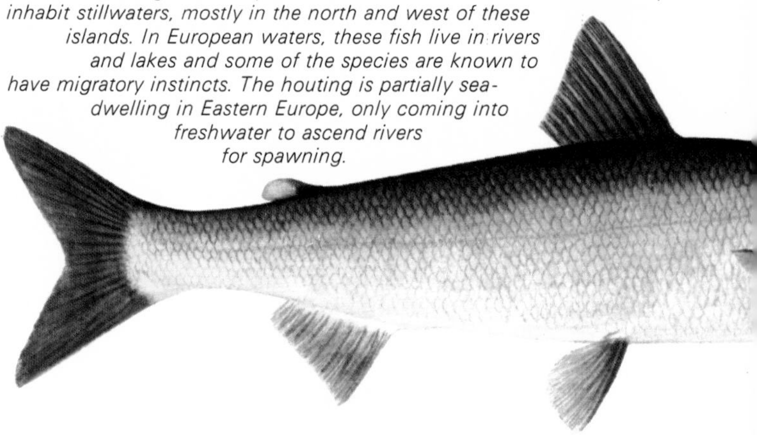

VENDACE AND POLLAN
Coregonus albula

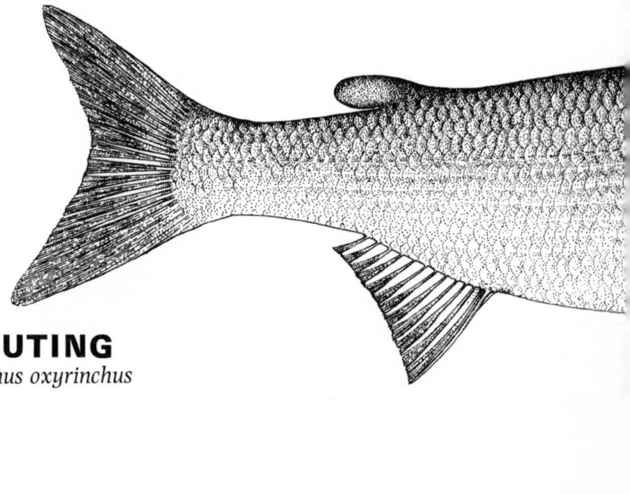

HOUTING
Coregonus oxyrinchus

POWAN, SCHELLY AND GWYNIAD

Coregonus lavaretus

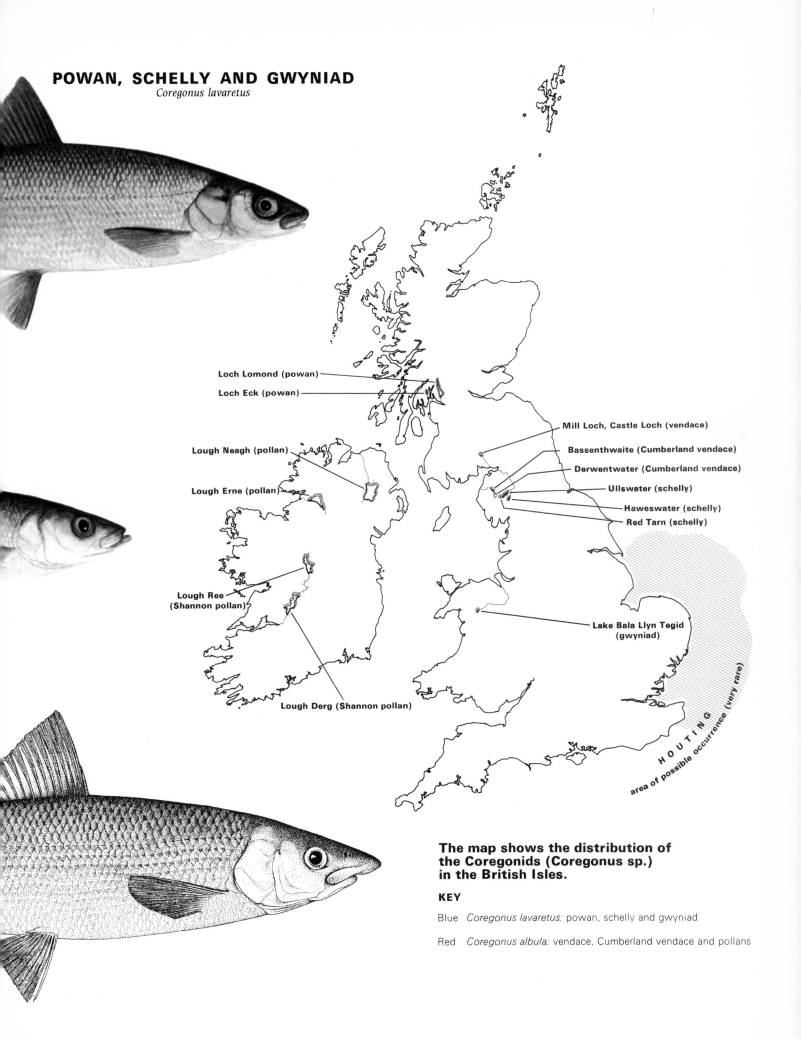

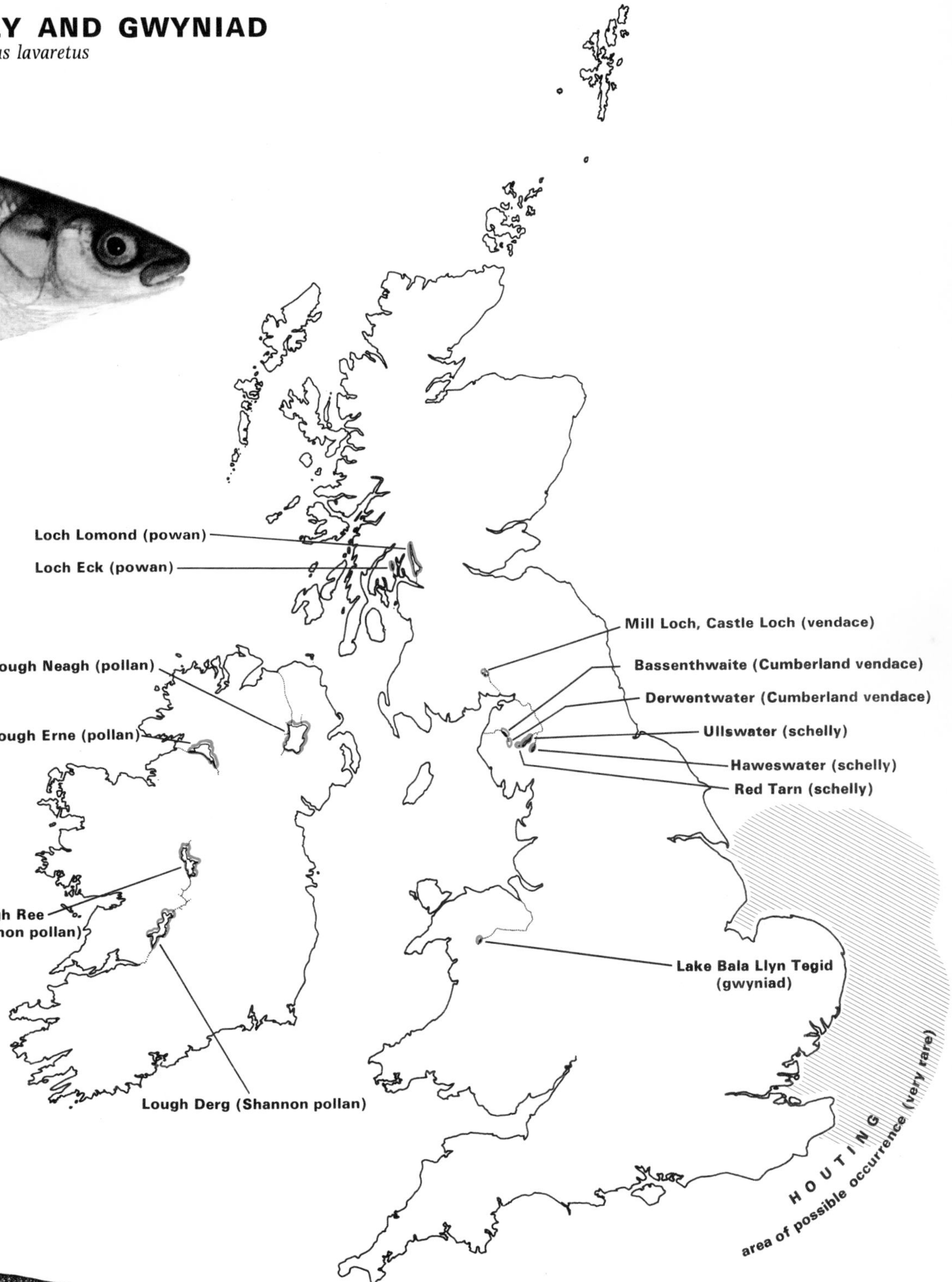

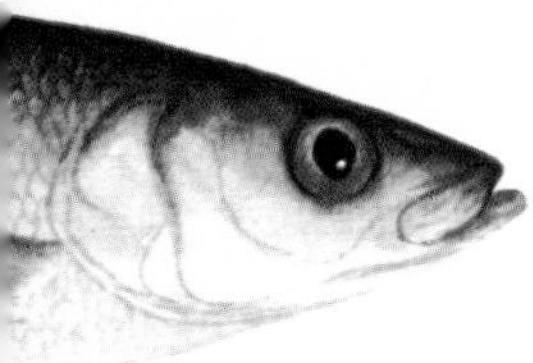

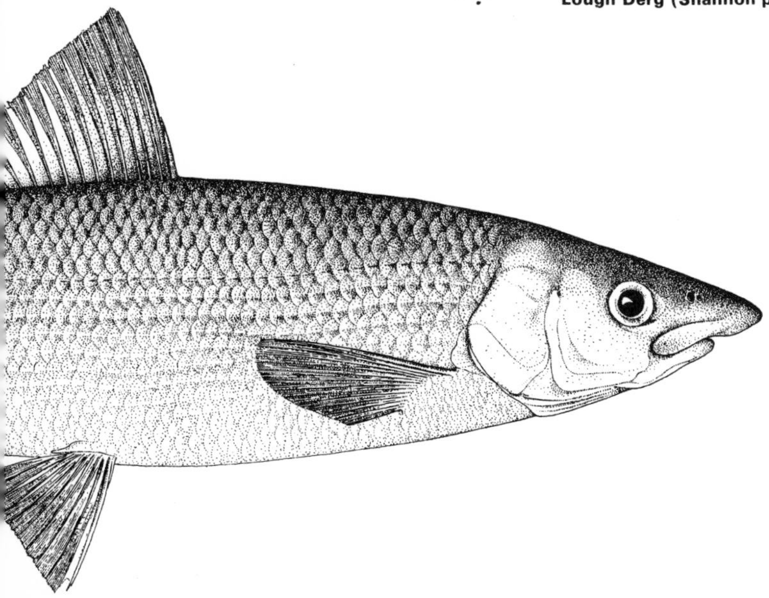

The map shows the distribution of the Coregonids (Coregonus sp.) in the British Isles.

KEY

Blue *Coregonus lavaretus:* powan, schelly and gwyniad

Red *Coregonus albula:* vendace, Cumberland vendace and pollans be taken to ensure that there is no more than the absolute minimum on the point section so that it does not make too obvious a trough in the skin of the water.

For some time after the end of the mayfly period the river tends to be very quiet indeed with the trout showing an almost complete lack of interest in food of any sort. It is sometimes said that this is because the fish have had such good feeding that they have to become quite hungry before recovering interest in the small flies. But a similar quiet period can happen at this time of the year on streams which lack hatches of mayfly, including many of the rain-fed rivers. In some such places it is believed that the fish are then gorging during the night on the large stonefly, which is a nocturnal creature. This may be so, but it seems equally possible that the middle days of June simply mark the time when, in seasonable conditions, the trout generally become more inclined to be nocturnal than diurnal in their habits. Certainly night fishing can be very good, particularly when the water is at a rather low level.

Now the blue-winged olive may be the most important of the duns that could be on the trout's menu. During flush hatches in the late evening, the fish feed very greedily indeed and the famous kidney-shaped rises can be seen all over the river. It is, however, a notorious fact that at such times when the trout appear to be guzzling up the naturals with complete abandon they are capable of being so utterly selective that the most skilful and experienced anglers cannot get a single offer. It is not easy to force oneself to depart from the scene of such activity, but when the great difficulty is met the best chance of finding a candidate for the basket is when a feeding fish can be spotted in an area where only a few straggling duns are passing over the lie. Such a trout can usually be interested in either an imitation of the dun or a Sherry Spinner.

It is also at this time of the year when opportunities to catch sea trout on the dry fly begin to appear. Even in the middle of the day, especially when there is a hatch of pale watery duns, fish lying in deep holes under steep banks or overhanging trees will sometimes rise and feed on the surface and, significantly, they will probably make no more disturbance than a tiny dimple. The whole event may pass unnoticed unless the angler knows just what he is looking for.

However, the sport then to be had with a lusty sea trout on a very small fly and a fine leader is something to be remembered. The period around dusk does, of course, offer the most reliable prospects and a variety of dun and sedge patterns may be successful, although one should not be surprised to find the sea trout behaving very selectively, especially when there are lots of blue-winged olives about.

Daytime sport with the brown trout usually remains quite difficult throughout July, and August can be a particularly poor month. A spell of wet weather may create some interesting opportunities, but usually if one has the alternative of some sea trout fishing it is by far the more attractive proposition.

September can be expected to bring a considerable improvement in the amount of fly to be seen during the daytime and the degree of interest shown by the brown trout and rainbows. Also the grayling should now be getting into sufficiently good trim to compete for the attention of the angler. Indeed, sport with the grayling on the same standard patterns of dry flies that would be used for the trout can be so good that many anglers find it to be the most attractive because a lot of the trout are then heavy in spawn. The rainbow, of course, will remain in the height of good condition for another month or so and provide most interesting fishing for as long as the law in the particular area allows.

For the rest of the autumn, on the days when there are good hatches of fly, dry patterns representing some form of the natural are to be recommended for the grayling. In the absence of naturals, however, it will probably be found that the fancy grayling patterns such as the Grayling Steel Blue, Red Tag, and the various bumbles, will attract more response than the more sober-looking trout flies.

Even in November and December there are days when the dry fly will do very well with the grayling, and the fight of the fish can be very exciting. Undoubtedly the wet fly is generally more reliable during the late autumn and winter but, particularly towards dusk, there is rarely a day when the water is in a reasonable condition that does not offer some promise of response to the floating fly. And by the time the grayling must be rested because of the approach of the spawning season the dry-fly fisher is again commencing his encounters with the brown trout.

WET-FLY FISHING FOR RIVER TROUT AND GRAYLING

There is a widespread tendency among anglers who have had no personal experience of wet-fly fishing to assume that because dry-fly fishing is such a superlative sport, it follows that wet-fly fishing must be of a less good standing, if not decidedly inferior. Indeed, it is not uncommon for wet-fly fishing to be described as a "chuck and chance it" method requiring little knowledge or skill.

This is most peculiar because a little research shows that the wet-fly method reached a high degree of efficiency and sophistication in both principle and practice long before any other style of game fishing. It is true to say that some of the very ancient patterns of wet flies of unrecorded origin, which are still used and unsurpassed today, reflect an understanding of entomology and the habits of the trout which is con-

A female dun of the mayfly Ephemera danica. *This large and important fisherman's fly spends up to three years below the water surface in clean rivers and lakes before emerging as the complete insect in late May or early June of the year, often providing hectic sport for two or three weeks for the trout fly angler.*

An artificial pattern named Nevamiss by the tier John Goddard.

siderably more involved than the level of knowledge required in modern dry-fly fishing. And the degree of manual skill needed in wet-fly fishing is such that the individual will probably find it more difficult to satisfy himself in that regard than when he is using the floating fly.

The wet-fly story starts on a rain-fed river when there is a flush hatch of fly, say large spring olive duns, on a damp, raw and breezy day towards the end of March or in early April. The location will probably be the streamy water towards the head of a pool and in the partial shelter of some trees. It can be seen that the trout are mainly concentrated in a dense group in the area where the duns are emerging the most profusely and each fish is clearly making sure that it gets its full share of the feast while it lasts. The observer cannot fail to notice that all the activity of the fish is very close to the surface and could be forgiven if he thought their interest was directed exclusively at the fully emerged duns riding on the skin of the water. Of course, a few duns are sure to be taken, but it is the hatching dun struggling to free itself from the nymphal shuck that is the big attraction because it is easier to catch than either the nymph, as it rises quickly through the fast shallow water on its journey from the bottom, or the dun which has succeeded in breaking through the surface skin of the water and is preparing to become airborne.

The famous Waterhen Bloa is a well-proved, old fly-pattern representing the emerging dun of the large spring olive, and it will be seen that the angler must attempt to make it drift unchecked with the flow at a level just beneath the surface so that it will simulate the general behaviour of the natural. Now, knowing how quickly drag sets in with the dry fly unless all sorts of precautions are taken, it can be judged that if a fairly straight floating line is dropped onto the water at any angle across the current, the slightly submerged artificial fly will be certain to be subjected to some small amount of drag. In the streamy water it can be assumed that this drag will not be steady and even, but varying in strength and intermittent. It is the slight, irregular drag of this sort that makes the hackles of the wet-fly dressing perform the opening and closing motion and thus complete the naturalistic appearance.

It is well documented that in the ancient days of plaited hair lines, which were too light to be thrown far, this desired performance of the wet fly was achieved by fishing more or less directly upstream with a short length of line and an extremely long rod – well into the teens of feet. After each cast, the rod point was continuously raised to keep the line reasonably tight as the team of flies drifted down towards the angler and trout could be hooked at very close quarters indeed. Silkworm gut was used for the cast as it was then called. This had to be soaked in water before use, otherwise it was too stiff and brittle, but having been thus treated it was heavy enough to penetrate the water slightly and fish the flies at the suitable level near the surface without any tendency for them to skim, although the light hair line did not sink at all. With the heavy rods then used this was, of course, very hard work, but nevertheless, as a method, it was excellent in principle and very effective in practice.

Eventually the oil-dressed silk line was introduced. This was quite revolutionary because of the very greatly increased casting potential and it resulted in rapid development in the design of rods to give the improved performance that had been made possible. The line would not float on its own accord, but the way in which it was kept tight onto the flies when used in the traditional upstream manner gave it the correct performance without there being any need for it to be greased. And it is quite wrong to interpret the legendary ungreased line for wet-fly fishing as indicating any intention that it should be a means of fishing the flies deeply. If the modern plastic-coated line is used, it should certainly be the floater, not the sinking variety.

In selecting the equipment, however, it is again necessary to start with the flies and leader. Standard practice is to use three artificials, the point fly and two droppers, but the top dropper is also known as the bob fly. The leader is usually about 9 ft long, this being the most manageable and trouble-free length, and the droppers are kept short, no more than about 1½ ins, so that there is less risk of their getting tangled round the main body of the leader. The flies are spaced at intervals of about 1 yd, and therefore the bob fly is about 1 yd from the top of the leader. And it can be seen that if the leader were tapered as steeply as the one for dry-fly fishing, the bob fly would be attached to very thick, unsightly nylon. Consequently the popular practice is to use fine nylon for the whole of the leader, say 4 lb test for big waters early in the season, and 3 lb test for more exacting conditions later on.

Needless to say, the finer the line the better from the point of view of balancing the leader, which is really quite delicate for the amount of strain it may have to cope with at times. But there is another factor of great importance which also makes the finest line that one can manage to be the most desirable. When fishing across the current one is often tempted to cast much farther than would be considered suitable for upstream work. Then it is absolutely certain that very soon after the trout has taken the fly, the strain of the pull of the water on the relatively thick line will be felt by the fish through the leader. And unless the angler is very quick indeed, the fly will be spat out before he has had the chance to secure a hook-hold. Of course, the occasional fish will hook itself, and some critics take this to be the basic principle upon which the wet-fly method functions. But the accomplished angler sees it as a failure on his part if a trout does, in fact, succeed in hooking itself. His objective is always to detect the offer and take action to set the hook before the suspicions of the fish have been aroused. Clearly, the thicker the line, the more quickly is the fish likely to become aware of it after intercepting the fly. And in practice, over a period of time, the angler usually finds that his efficiency in hooking the trout is largely governed by the line size. There is no doubt that an AFTM No 4 double-tapered floater (*AFTM* DT4F) offers great advantages over heavier lines and that a AFTM DT6F is the top limit of the range that can generally be considered to be suitable. In silk lines, a No 2 is the most generally useful and the No 3 the heaviest to be recommended. But the angler who can be at ease when fishing a No 1 in all favourable circumstances for sport has the highest degree of efficiency open to him.

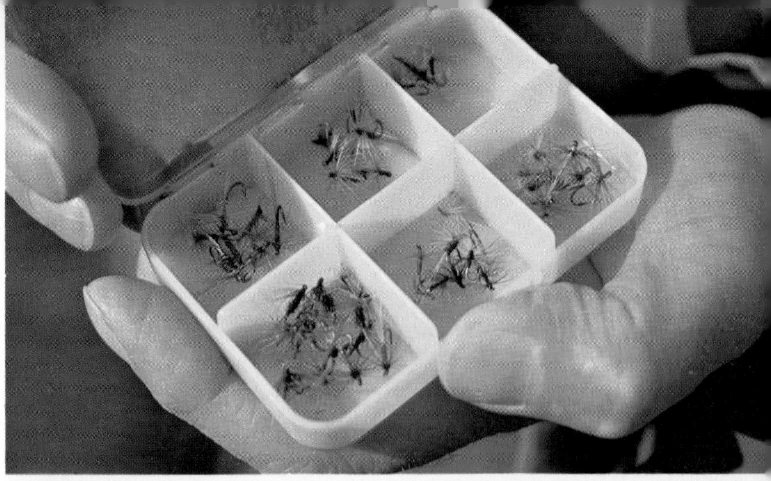

1

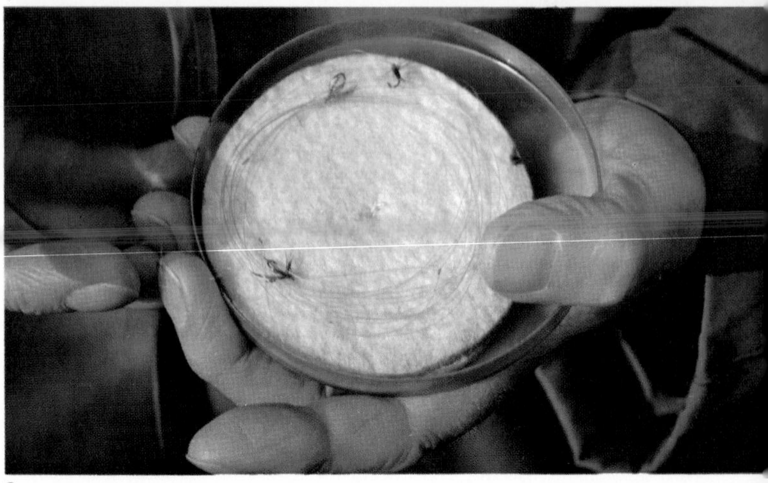

2

Normally the silk lines will require to be greased to ensure that the flies are fished at the most suitable level near the surface.

The selection of a truly suitable rod is of vital importance. To get the right performance out of the line, it must have an adequate amount of through action, yet it must have an element of steeliness in the tip to ensure that it is not necessary to strike very hard in order to hook the fish. Up to a length of about 10 ft 6 ins, the longer the rod, the better it handles and controls the line, and the faster is the movement transferred through the line to the fish when the strike is made. But, as with the selection of the dry-fly rod, one must take into consideration any other duties which it may be desired to perform. If the alternative role of the rod is to be dry-fly and nymph fishing, it is probably wise not to exceed about 9 ft, although then it must be recognized that a compromise is, indeed, being made and there will be some sacrifice in respect of the wet-fly performance. On the other hand, if the rod may be required to fish drifts from a boat for stillwater trout, the full length of 10 ft 6 ins will be an advantage. The problem of getting the best wet-fly rod is certainly very difficult. One should be very wary of any adviser who does not show a lot of concern for the very special requirements of such a rod.

The reel requires to be much the same as for the dry-fly work, about 3¼ ins, preferably with rim control, and as light as possible.

An essential item of the wet-fly fisher's outfit is some kind of preparation to apply to the leader to remove grease and prevent it from floating. A simple mixture of Fuller's-earth and water with the consistency of thick

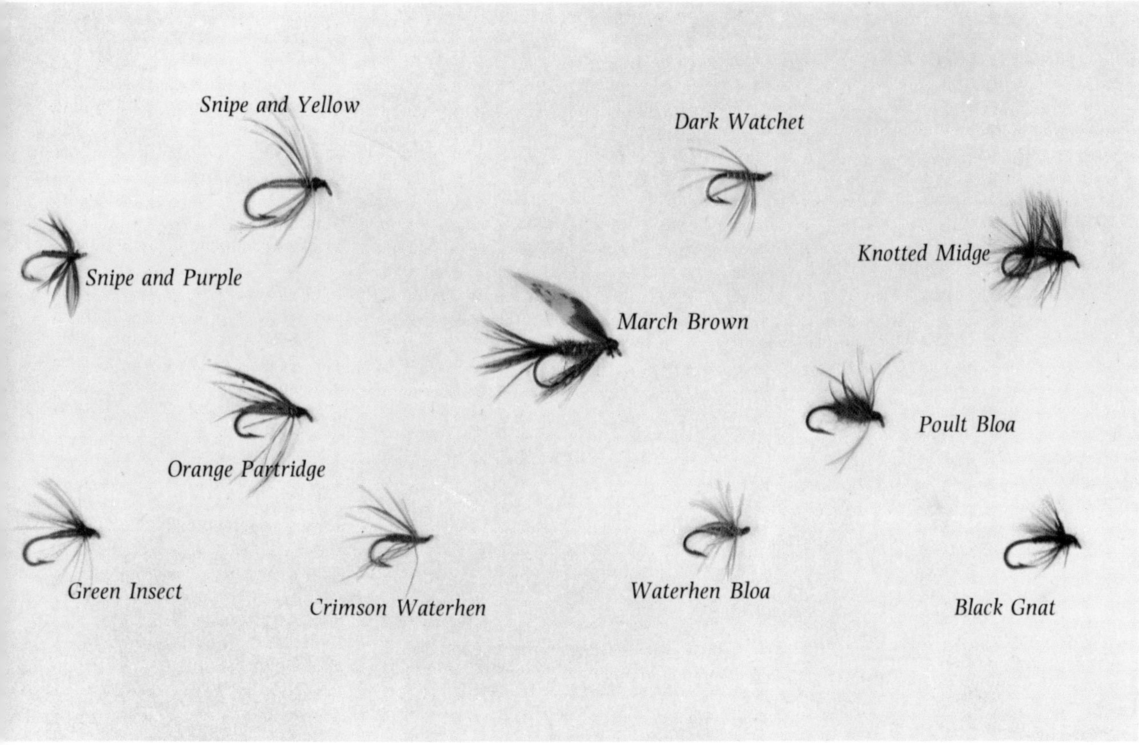

3

1 *A plastic wet fly box of a type that is both simple and giving good protection to its contents. Flies are less likely to lose their points.*

2 *A simple, circular cast case, made in plastic with a piece of soft felt giving protection to the contents and separating wet from dry casts.*

3 *A selection of small wet fly patterns that will serve most fishing needs throughout the trout season. They have been photographed to a magnification of X2 to show the minute differences between patterns and dressing. Some patterns simulate a number of different natural insects.*

cream is very effective and quite harmless in all respects. The powder can be obtained from any chemist and, of course, there is nothing more sinister in the word Fuller than that he was an old craftsman engaged in finishing cloth.

Although it is rare to see a wet-fly box that does not contain a big variety of patterns covering all the main types of aquatic flies, the probability is that just a small selection accounts for the big bulk of the season's catch of trout. And while the principal ones may be known by different names in various parts of the country, they are just the same dressings that are the most successful everywhere. This is also basically true of the second line of patterns, but here there is sometimes an added complication.

In some districts certain ones of these well-known supporting flies enjoy a specially good reputation and, as a result, they get used so much that they are given an exceptionally good chance to be successful, often at the expense of other, potentially more suitable patterns for certain occasions. Therefore it is not surprising that the records appear to justify the faith placed in those constant favourites. This should be seen by the novice as a warning to avoid becoming unduly prejudiced and to make his trials on a properly planned basis.

Another rather confusing matter with which the novice has to contend is that there appears to be a lot of disagreement among the authors as to the naturals which some of the most popular patterns are supposed to represent. And there are cases where two apparently opposing views may both be correct because the pattern in question is a reasonably good simulation of more than one species of natural. Therefore, it should be understood that, while recommendations of certain patterns for certain conditions and times of the year can be extremely reliable, statements concerning the purpose for which any particular dressing was originally designed may be no more than arbitrary.

As already indicated, the dressings representing the emergent duns are the principal patterns, but much more use is made of the various species of the other families of water-bred flies than is generally the case in dry-fly fishing. No list of recommendations can be expected to be free from omissions thought to be serious in one quarter or another and the short one that follows is simply a useful selection covering the whole of the season:

Pattern	*Size*	*Natural*	*Period*
Waterhen Bloa	14	large spring olive	Mar./April & Sept.
Waterhen Bloa	16	small dark olive	Mar./May & Sept.
Orange Partridge	14	March brown and some stone flies	Mar./May & Sept.
Snipe & Purple Dark Snipe	16 & 18	spring black (gnat) & iron blue dun	Mar./June & Sept.
February Red	14	small stone fly	Mar./April
March Browns (various)	12 & 14	March brown	Mar. & early April
Snipe & Yellow Dark Snipe	16	Medium olive	April to June & Sept.
Dark Watchet	16 & 18	iron blue dun	late April/June & Sept.
Dark Needle	16	small stone fly	April/June & Sept.
Brown Owl	16	small sedge or stone fly	April/June.
Black Gnat	16	small gnat	May to end of season.
Poult Bloa	16	pale watery dun	May to end of season.
Crimson Waterhen	16	small red spinner	May to end of season.
Knotted Midge	16	black midges mating	May to July.
Rough Bodied Poult	16	blue winged olive dun	late May to end of season.
Green Insect	16 & 18	aphid	June to end of season.

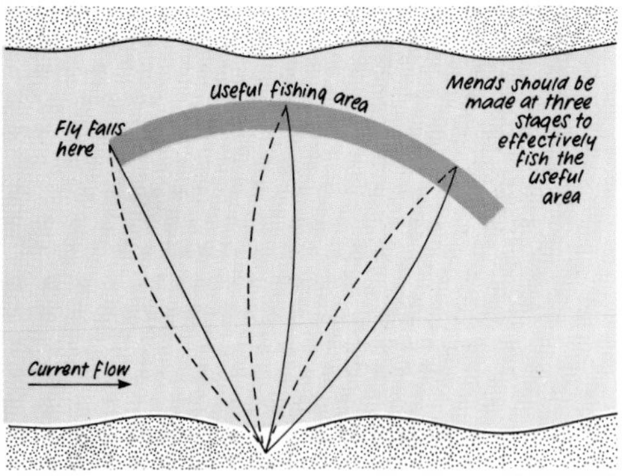

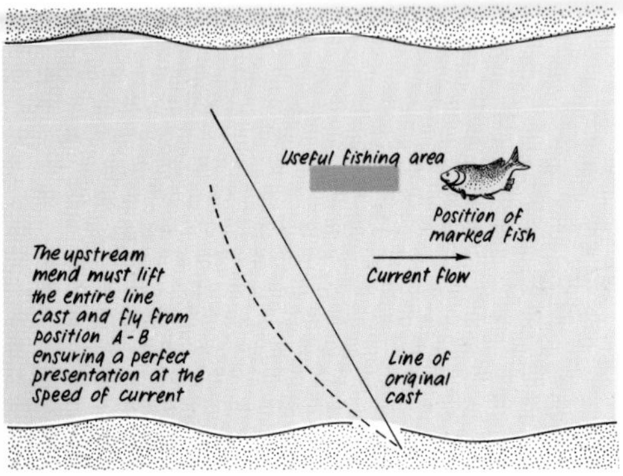

GRAYLING
Thymallus thymallus

A sleek, beautifully scaled fish with a large dorsal fin, found in clean rivers and streams that have a fairly fast-flowing current. The fish is a salmonid although not enjoying quite the same protection, both seasonally and in reputation terms, that the brown trout enjoys. Both species live together but the trout almost always comes first in the minds of anglers. The grayling is not only a fighter. It is also good eating and brings an additional period of sport for the game fisherman after the trout is denied to him.

Grayling are not a large-growing species, a fish of 4 lbs is a good one. They spawn in the spring, usually March to late April, so tend to be thought of as a coarse fish. They fight well on artificial flies and are famous for the way in which they use the power of the current and the large dorsal fin to cut across the stream in an effort to shed a hook.

Bait: *Flies and trotted worms. The grayling will also grab baits, notably maggots, intended for coarse fish.*

The best guide to the amount of dressing that should be used in the tying of the standard patterns is to take a drowned natural, say a medium olive dun or a dark needle, place it on the thumb nail, and do likewise with a well wetted artificial. The comparison will show how light the dressing requires to be to simulate the natural.

In practical fishing the various factors affecting the decision as to whether one should fish definitely upstream, or across and down, must be given careful and constant consideration. When a lot of trout are feeding close together during a flush hatch of flies and they are, in fact, in such a position that they can be covered adequately by casting more or less straight upstream, there are several good reasons why that is by far the best tactic. Firstly, as the old masters were quick to realise, the presence of the angler below the fish is the least disturbing to them. Secondly, since the strike draws the hook towards the corner of the mouth of the fish, there is much less risk of failing to get a good hookhold. Thirdly, it is usually possible to draw the hooked trout downstream away from the rest of the feeding fish quite quickly and then play it out where the disturbance will do the least harm.

At this point it should be mentioned that since appearances would suggest to the novice that this could be a glorious opportunity, with the trout feeding so eagerly, to do some dry-fly fishing, the wet fly is by far the most efficient in these circumstances. In the first place, it is extremely difficult in the popply water that is further disturbed by the activity of the trout to keep one's eye on the floating artificial, which, of course, is a basic essential in dry-fly fishing. But if, for the sake of experiment, one perseveres and succeeds in keeping track of the floater, the number of offers that come to it compared with the amount of feverish activity all around is usually very disappointing. With the wet fly, the end of the line, which hopefully is floating, is watched carefully and any stoppage or unnatural movement of any sort is the signal to tighten on the fish smoothly but firmly. And usually, at times like these, one soon learns how eminently suitable for the job are the famous old patterns. Indeed, it often happens that offers come so readily that one spends most of the time during the hatch in playing trout and hence gets far less practice at actually fishing the fly than one would expect.

The other circumstances in which it is really essential to fish very much upstream are when there are exposed rocks dotted about which would make it almost

SMELT
Osmerus eperlanus

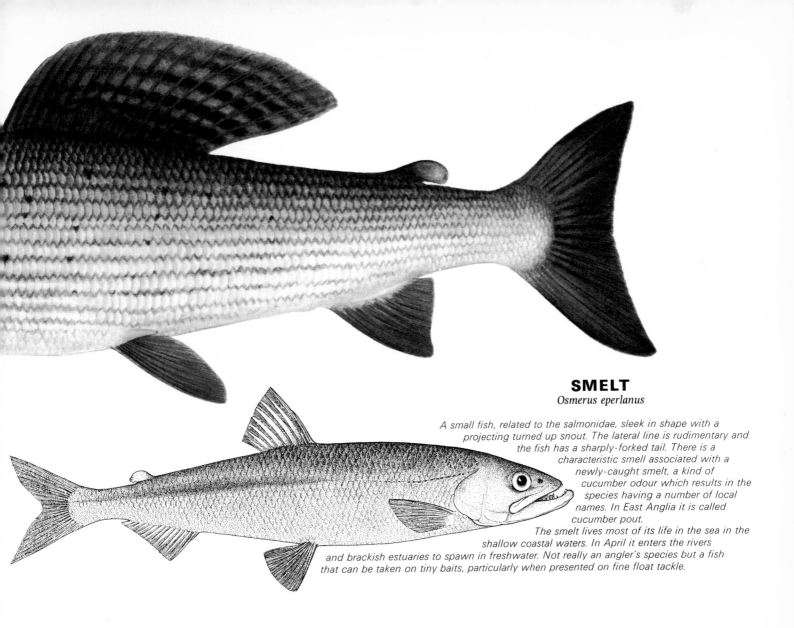

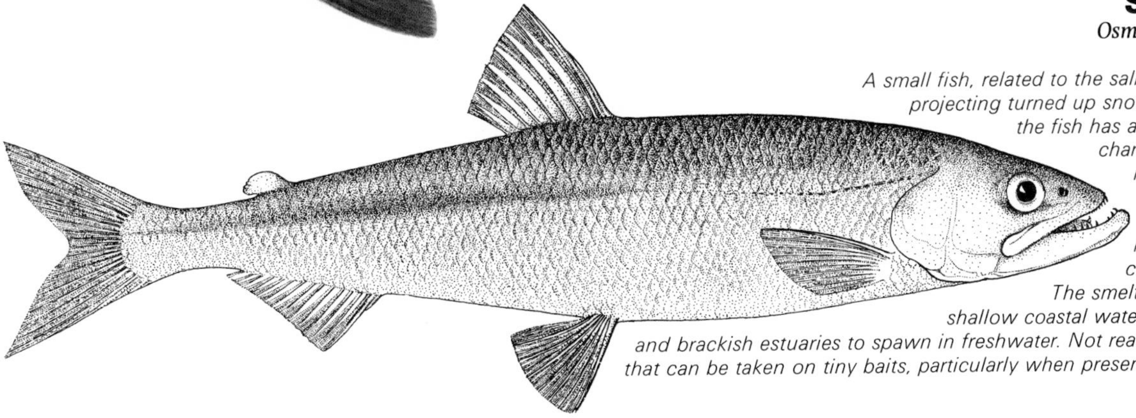

A small fish, related to the salmonidae, sleek in shape with a projecting turned up snout. The lateral line is rudimentary and the fish has a sharply-forked tail. There is a characteristic smell associated with a newly-caught smelt, a kind of cucumber odour which results in the species having a number of local names. In East Anglia it is called cucumber pout.

The smelt lives most of its life in the sea in the shallow coastal waters. In April it enters the rivers and brackish estuaries to spawn in freshwater. Not really an angler's species but a fish that can be taken on tiny baits, particularly when presented on fine float tackle.

impossible to cover the lies with casts made across the stream, and when the fish are feeding in a glide. As we have said earlier, during flush hatches on rain-fed rivers, the trout seem to be able to read the signs well enough always to be concentrated in the areas where the duns are emerging the most profusely and then the glides are very much neglected. During spinner falls, however, narrowing fast glides can be expected to provide both the greatest quantity of food and the easiest to intercept. And, as usual, the best trout in the area will be in the most lucrative feeding spot. But unless the cast is made very much upstream the force of the gliding water sweeps the leader round so quickly that at the best the artificials perform rather unnaturally and will be subject to skimming round uselessly on the surface.

On days when there is a very sparse hatch over a prolonged period, the trout tend to be well spread out in all the potentially suitable areas. Then it is very hard work to persevere for a long time with upstream casting and, furthermore, one cannot cover a satisfactorily large area of water quickly enough. The most promising and least fatiguing tactic is to cast across and slightly upstream, say 30° above the square, and allow the flies to drift with the flow until they reach an angle of between 30° and 40° downstream, then make a fresh cast. In a stream with a very favourable flow the flies will perhaps fish correctly throughout their travel, but more often there will be irregularities here and there in the speed of the current and these will necessitate action to ensure that the flies do not get dragged round too quickly. This takes the form of what is called "mending the line" – an invaluable manoeuvre in many styles of fly fishing. It is simply a matter of lifting part of the line off the water, without disturbing the flies, and replacing it in a position where it will be relieved of the pressure that was causing the drag. A gentle bowling action with the rod gives the most effective and controllable results.

In practice it is usually quite easy to see how the mend should be made. The most frequent need is to make a small upstream mend, and this tends to apply particularly to the period just after the cast has been made, when the line does seem to have the habit of getting ahead of the leader and thus causing drag on the flies. The positive indication of this is the formation of a downstream belly in the line, and the upstream mend makes the correction needed. The rod tip should follow round, pointing at the same angle as the line while it moves downstream. And as it approaches the lower limits at which it will fish correctly – usually short of about 45° downstream – the most common tendency is for the leader to start to swing round too quickly. The effective remedy then is to make a small downstream mend. But after travelling a little more, there is no possible further action that would prevent the line from ultimately reaching the angle at which it would be "at the dangle". This is undesirable because any offers that might come would almost certainly be missed, the fish being practically straight downstream of the leader and direction of the strike. Therefore, nicely before such a position arises, the line is smoothly withdrawn and a fresh cast made.

It is no secret that competence in this matter of controlling the line so that the flies fish correctly and at an angle, offering a good chance of a secure hookhold, is the vital factor in the practical side of wet-fly fishing. It is, of course, the equivalent of the avoidance of drag in dry-fly fishing and, although faults in presentation with the floater are undoubtedly easier to detect, the tell-tale behaviour of the line in wet-fly fishing is a thoroughly reliable guide when it is needed soon enough.

As the season progresses it becomes more difficult to deceive the trout with the wet fly during the daytime and, particularly when the water is on the low side and tending to lack a good enough flow, it is often a much better proposition to resort to the dry fly. A little experience of situations of this kind is all that is necessary to convince one that it is much easier for the trout to detect the falsity of the artificial fully immersed in the water than the floater that has to be viewed through the skin of the water. The refraction and distortion that take place can often make the image of the artificial that is riding high on the hackle points perfectly acceptable to trout that show complete indifference to the wet fly.

When the trout are feeding greedily on spent spinners in the evenings, however, the wet fly comes into its own again. This is very fortunate because during this hectic spell, which may be very short, one does not want to waste time drying and re-oiling dry flies. The trout will undoubtedly take the floater, but the waterlogged artificial fished just slightly beneath the surface is effective and ideally suited to this fishing under pressure, as the late evening rise could be described.

NYMPH FISHING

In waters that are sufficiently alkaline for liberal amounts of aquatic vegetation to thrive, the brown trout, rainbows and grayling do not have to wait for the activity that occurs during hatches of fly if they feel the urge to feed; they can rummage among the weeds and flush out nymphs and shrimps. And it could be said that they become "nymph-minded". But on the more acid, pebbly, rivers where a bit of thick moss on some of the larger boulders permanently situated in the fast water is the lushest vegetable growth to be found, the fish get very little chance to see nymphs except during hatches. Then, of course, as the wet-fly fisherman knows so well, much more interest is shown in the emerging dun than in the nymph. And no doubt it is for this reason that the modern style of fishing the leaded nymph which can be so effective on the chalkstreams and similar waters, rarely has any real success on the weed-free streams.

The technique popularly employed in the chalk streams requires either the dry or wet-fly rod, reel and line, and the same type of steeply tapered leader as used with the dry fly. The weighted artificial nymph (a pheasant tail with copper wire dressing is used almost universally) is mounted and the lower part of the leader is left free from grease so that it will sink readily, but the upper section is well greased. The ungreased length should be a little longer than the estimated depth of the water, which will not often be more than 3 or 4 ft.

Ideally one should be able to see every detail of the nymph's descent through the water to the point intended just a few inches ahead of the fish and then, after a well-timed twitch with the rod point, its life-like movement as it rises again and passes over the head of the trout. Of course it is very exciting to watch the reactions of the fish and to see the speed with which it can intercept the nymph.

Where practicable it is best to cast as nearly straight upstream as possible because the nymph then sinks the most quickly and in line with the flow, which makes it very much easier to achieve accuracy in the positioning of the nymph than when the cast is made at an angle to the flow. And so long as all the details can be observed without too much difficulty, no attention need be paid to the leader. But if for any reason the underwater view is obscured one watches the floating end of the leader and, as a matter of fact, some anglers tie a bit of flue from a white feather to the leader at this point so that it can be seen more easily. Any quick little movement seen at the greased end of the leader on the surface must be assumed to be an offer from a fish and the strike must be made immediately. If nothing has happened by the time that it is judged that the nymph has reached the target area on the bottom, the quick little movement is made with the rod tip to produce the simulation of life-like movement in the nymph. When fishing "blind", this often proves to be the vital factor, no doubt because the rising of the nymph from the bottom attracts the attention of fish from a greater distance than when it is simply trundling along on the gravel or sand on the bottom.

There is no doubt that nymph fishing is a very valuable subsidiary method on the chalkstreams. During

An American nymph, the Dark Montana, closely resembling a wasp, that has a great following in the States. Could it have a dapping use here?

much of the fishing season the amount of food that is available to the fish is so great that inevitably there are long spells on many seemingly favourable days when the angler observing strict dry-fly rules – casting only upstream and only to fish that are seen to be rising – would have no chance of sport at all with sizeable fish. But when upstream nymphing is allowed, one can be most enjoyably occupied for the long hours that would otherwise be rather frustrating, and there can be no criticism of the degree of skill required to catch good fish in this way.

In the circumstances it is not surprising that attempts have been made over the years at fairly frequent intervals to apply nymph-fishing techniques to the less alkaline rivers. Some well-meaning anglers have even gone so far as to design special patterns of nymphs for the rain-fed rivers and success has been claimed for some of the efforts. But the fact that nymph fishing as such has never achieved any popular following on the weed-free rivers is proof enough that it cannot be regarded either as a good substitute for, or alternative to, the conventional wet-fly method. This does not mean to say that nymph patterns will not catch fish: they certainly will when employed in the same way as the standard wet-flies but, in general, they have not done well enough to encourage their regular use and have certainly never threatened to usurp the position of the old-established wet-fly dressings in the esteem of experienced anglers.

In recent times there has been a tendency for wet-fly fishing and nymph fishing to be regarded as nothing more than slight variations of the same method – that is, by the non-participants. But it will be seen that, as emphasized earlier, the really effective area to be fished with the wet fly is the upper level, very near to the surface, while the true zone for the nymph is close to the bottom. And the peculiar fact is that in the type of water where the nymph can be really successful, it fills the gap when fish cannot be caught on the dry fly, but it is the dry fly itself that performs this redeeming role on the rain-fed rivers when the wet fly proves to have lost its charm.

A trout angler fishing the streamy water below a low rocky sill on the River Barrow in County Kilkenny. Although a salmon river of repute, the Barrow has both sea and brown trout fishing with wide glides containing many coarse fish. The feed is lush and trout can grow to good sizes.

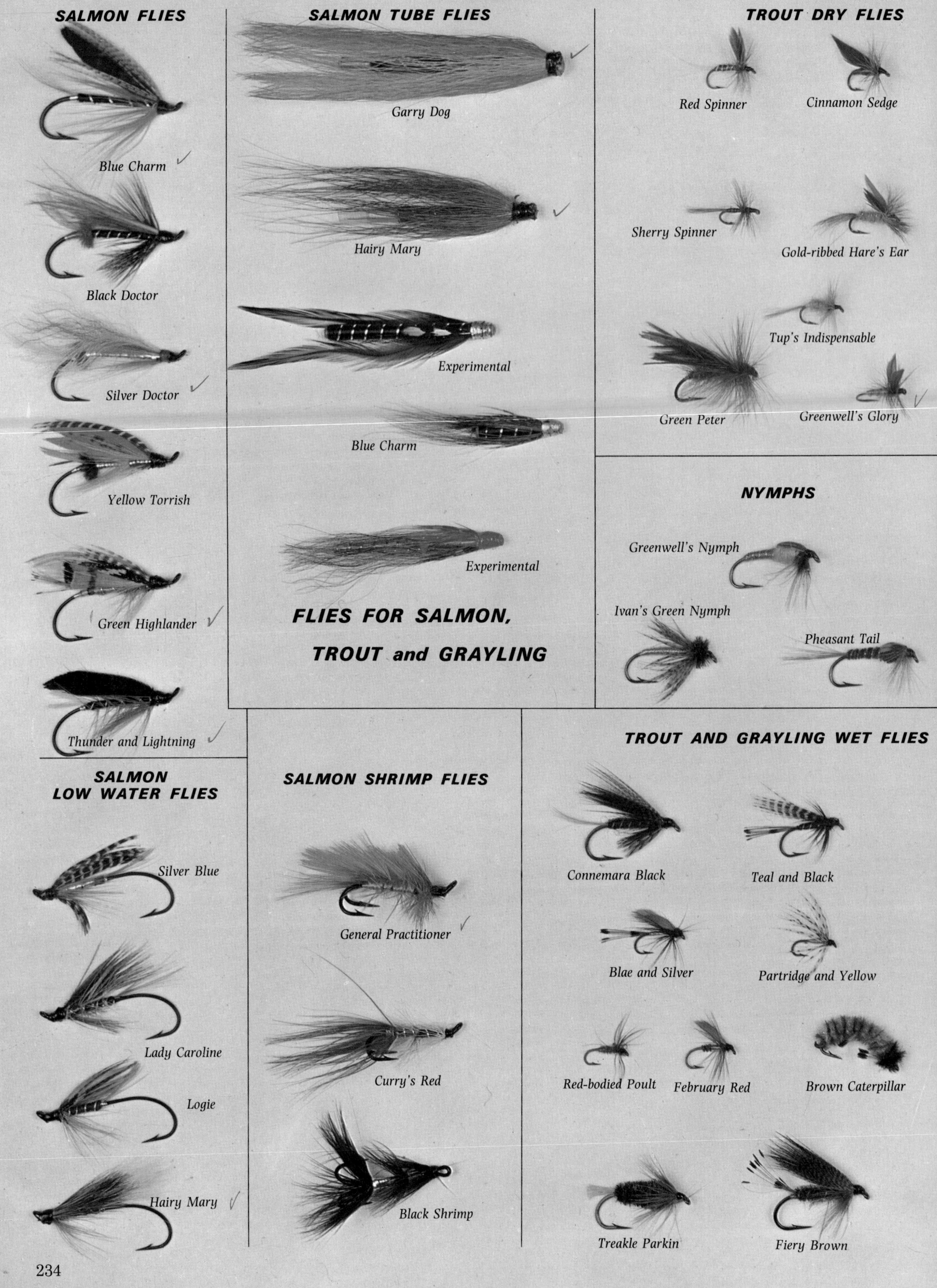

SALMON FLIES

Blue Charm ✓

Black Doctor

Silver Doctor ✓

Yellow Torrish

Green Highlander ✓

Thunder and Lightning ✓

SALMON LOW WATER FLIES

Silver Blue

Lady Caroline

Logie

Hairy Mary ✓

SALMON TUBE FLIES

Garry Dog ✓

Hairy Mary ✓

Experimental

Blue Charm

Experimental

FLIES FOR SALMON, TROUT and GRAYLING

SALMON SHRIMP FLIES

General Practitioner ✓

Curry's Red

Black Shrimp

TROUT DRY FLIES

Red Spinner

Cinnamon Sedge

Sherry Spinner

Gold-ribbed Hare's Ear

Tup's Indispensable

Green Peter

Greenwell's Glory ✓

NYMPHS

Greenwell's Nymph

Ivan's Green Nymph

Pheasant Tail

TROUT AND GRAYLING WET FLIES

Connemara Black

Teal and Black

Blae and Silver

Partridge and Yellow

Red-bodied Poult

February Red

Brown Caterpillar

Treakle Parkin

Fiery Brown

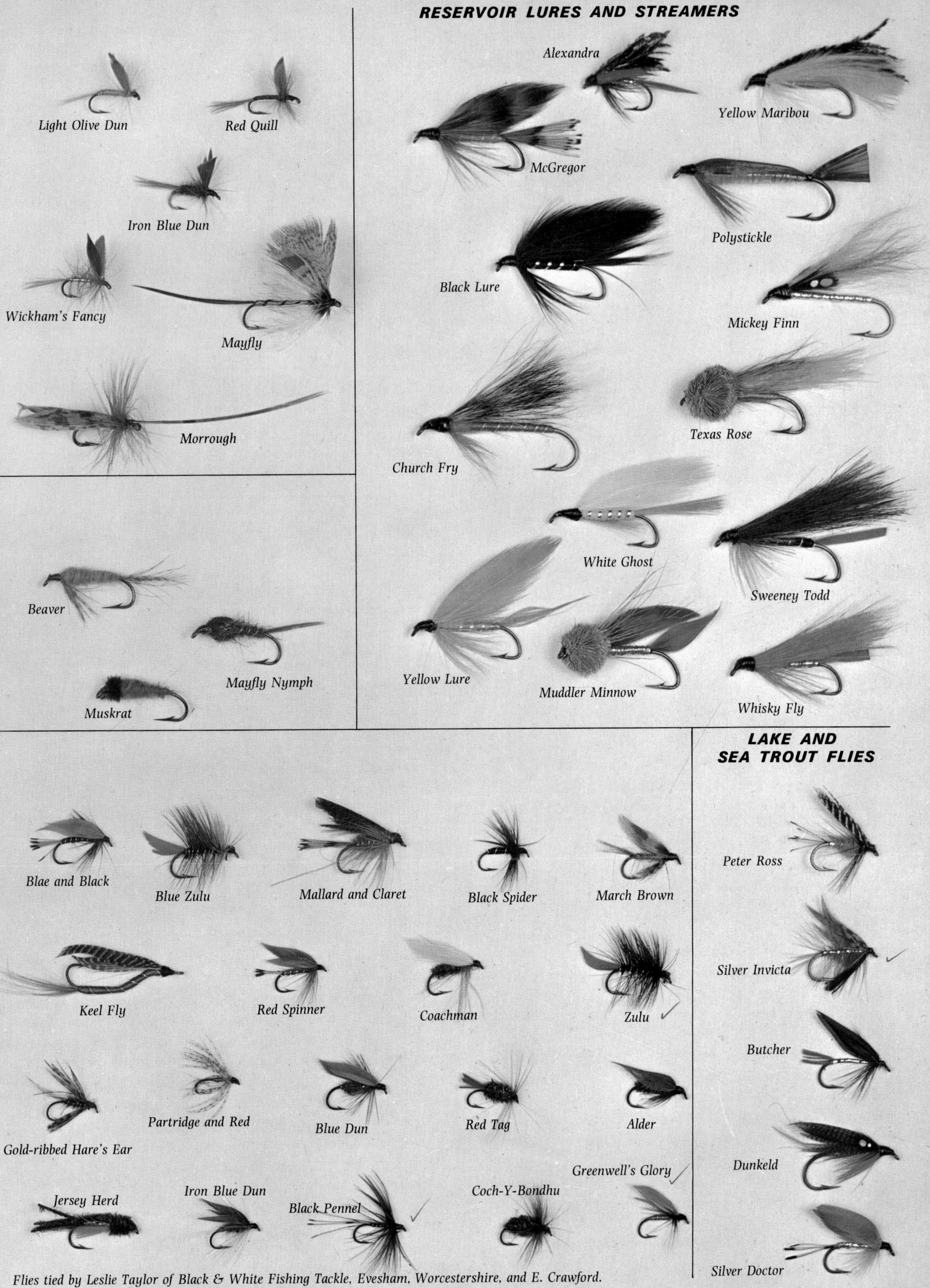

Flies tied by Leslie Taylor of Black & White Fishing Tackle, Evesham, Worcestershire, and E. Crawford.

STILLWATER FLY-FISHING

The developments that have taken place in stillwater fly-fishing since World War II tend to overshadow the traditional styles of loch and lake fishing, but it is a serious mistake to think that the old methods are in any way outdated. Indeed, they still provide what many experienced anglers consider to be the most pleasing sport and it behoves the newcomer to become sufficiently conversant with the subject to avoid a purely prejudiced approach.

In the old days the basic tenet was that the angler did his fishing when the trout were feeding, or at least thought to be on the lookout for food. The result was that over the years a comprehensive coverage was made of the ways to deal with all such opportunities. It is well to recognize today that our predecessors, despite their less good equipment, made a thorough assessment of the problem and saw the principles that are involved correctly. The fact that they ignored the question of the periods when the trout were dormant is no reflection whatever on their positive accomplishments. In those times, of course, the restocking policy was also very different. Anglers really only thought in terms of wild trout or fish that had a fair chance to become acclimatized to the particular environment before they were fished for. There were a few waters where a very modest amount of stocking with rainbows was done, but in the main, lake and loch fishing was for brown trout, and rainbows were a rarity.

To assess the relative merits of the old and new approaches, it is first necessary to get a general view of the feeding habits of the fish in stillwater. The times when flies appear and arouse the response of the fish are not much different from those for the rivers. In the early spring the trout can be expected to be moving for a few hours in the middle of the day. Gradually this gives way to greater activity in the morning and early evening and eventually, in the summer, real evidence of serious feeding may be restricted to the period of dusk, the night-time and a very short spell at dawn. There are, of course, considerable variations according to the kind of weather that characterizes any particular fishing season, but even in the most favourable circumstances, there are certain to be many occasions when the new techniques of attracting response from basically disinterested fish have to be employed if there is to be any chance of sport.

Lochs and lakes differ more noticeably from rivers in the matter of the variety and sizes of flies that may be successful. Quite a few of the naturals that inhabit the running water have their counterparts in the stillwater and appropriate patterns covering lake olives, sedges and gnats are popular. But such species as water boatman, water cricket, etc., are much more important on stillwater than on rivers, and the same can be said of land-bred flies, such as daddy long-legs, heather moths, cowdung flies and so on. Additionally the fry of the stickleback, minnow and a variety of coarse fish can form an important part of the diet at times of the trout and rainbows. The ever-popular old-established lake and loch patterns include dressings to represent all the types of trout food mentioned.

Comparatively new arrivals on the trout fishing scene, the Midlands reservoirs provide fantastic sport to the fly fisherman. More public water properties will be opened to anglers in the next few years.

SELECTING THE PATTERN

It will now be appreciated that in much of the stillwater fishing there is little option but to take a fairly open-minded view of what the fish are likely to be feeding on and therefore attempt to cater for as many alternatives as possible in the selection of the patterns and the way they are used. The most popular of the traditional styles, fishing drifts from a boat, is very well suited to this approach. Take a mild day in April with a good breeze. As the boat drifts, the cast is always made downwind with quite a short line, not more than about twice the length of the rod. Then, without delay, the rod point is raised steadily and perhaps also some line is gathered in the free hand so that the flies will move towards the boat. At the same time, of course, the boat is drifting towards the flies. Therefore the speed at which they move through the water is not quite as great as is suggested by the movement of the rod and the gathering of line. In other words, some of the retrieving of the flies is neutralized by the movement of the boat. Trout often take flies very close indeed to the drifting boat and the attempt should always be made to keep them fishing nicely right up to the last moment when they must be withdrawn to make the next cast, which, in these circumstances, should be a roll cast. A typical trio would be a size 14 Greenwell's Glory (wet) or Woodcock Yellow on the point; a size 12 Butcher as dropper, and a size 12 Grouse Claret as the bob fly. Most anglers are careful to keep the bob fly "bobbing" on the surface as it is worked towards the boat. Thus the coverage given, in the same order, is thought to be the drowned dun of the lake olive, a small fish, and some kind of fly in the process of hatching in the surface film of the water. Similar results can be achieved when fishing from the bank or wading. Then it is much easier to judge exactly the speed at which the flies are being fished. On lochs and lakes with gravelly shallows at the edges that are almost free from weeds, the normal drill is for the angler to keep on the move so that he covers fresh water with each cast, but this is not possible where there is too much vegetation, or where the verges are boggy.

If the amount of ripple on the water is rather less than would be wished for conventional wet-fly fishing, a floating fly may be very effective, especially if a few rises to naturals are to be seen. When the circuit of a feeding trout can be worked out, the fly may be left in the track that it is thought the fish will shortly be taking, but it can be quite rewarding simply to make reasonably long casts and retrieve the floater with alternating little movements along the surface and short rests. A dry Greenwell's Glory or a Black Gnat on size 14s are good standbys. In calm conditions with trout seen to be moving, nymph patterns can also be very successful. The artificial is dropped more or less as close to the fish as possible, allowed to sink for a few moments and then drawn away in little jerks. If it is a particularly good fish that has been marked down, it may be helpful to rest it for a few minutes after each unsuccessful cast has been made. In this style of fishing, the surprise element can sometimes be more important than the pattern or the precise way in which it is fished and leaving the trout undisturbed for short spells can be very useful in this respect.

A little later in the year, in the evenings, there are often large hatches of long-legged gnats. The dressing representing the pupa, often called the "buzzer", is fished in very much the same way as the nymph, but now it is unlikely that feeding fish will be isolated and the policy should be to keep the artificial in the water rather than resting the fish. At the same time, a medium sedge fished dry can be very successful. Because of opportunities of this sort, stillwater anglers often fish both a dry and a wet fly on the same leader. Most frequently the wet fly will be seen on the point and the floater on the dropper, but there is not the slightest doubt that this is not the best way, the trouble being that very soon the floater is dragged under. If the dry fly is mounted on the point and the whole of the leader is greased except for the short dropper carrying the wet fly, both artificials will fish exactly as they are intended to do and keep on doing so for long periods. A dry sedge and a wet buzzer make a very good pair. As in all the traditional style fishing on stillwater that we have written about so far, the strike should never be hurried. The fish do not close their mouths on food as quickly as in running water. A smooth tightening of the line after the fish has had fully enough time to get its head down again is the most reliable drill.

The new methods mostly require the casting of very long lines and the use of various techniques, from retrieving large lures very rapidly by means of stripping line with the free hand, to fishing nymph-like patterns slowly and close to the bottom, sometimes in very deep water. But although there is ample evidence of the good potential of the new styles, they have not yet been standardized, so to speak, and many anglers are cur-

RESERVOIR TROUTING

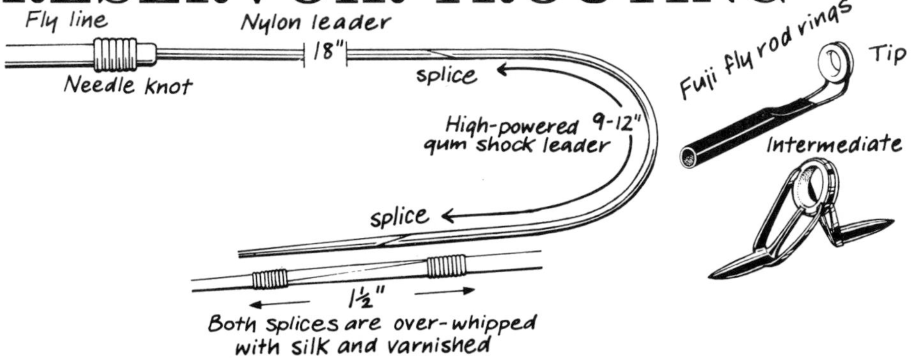

The creation of so many reservoirs and trout fisheries has introduced a new element into game fishing. On these stillwaters, many of which cover vast acreages, distance casting has become vitally necessary, coupled with continuous retrieval of the line. Here, fly casting has become an arduous activity that has resulted in a different approach to rod construction and materials. To get the distance, reservoir rods have to be powerful, yet their weight must not be such that they tire the caster. Carbon fibre, now rapidly becoming the major rod-building material, gives lightness combined with strength. Added to this is a decrease in the blank diameter which helps greatly in that it reduces the air resistance as the rod is passed through the compression arc under the weight of the fly line. The lighter weight of the carbon rod allows the designer to make it longer, which gives a higher clearance of the fly line from the angler's head – always a problem with heavy lure casting.

Modern rings, such as the centred Fuji guides, cut down line wear and the friction associated with older-style rod rings. A recent and exciting development in fly fishing has been the introduction of a sprung nylon, called *high-powered gum*, used when splicing a shock leader into the cast. Placed below the permanent thick nylon leader and the tapered cast, the 'gum' can be spliced, over-whipped and varnish finished, or tied at both ends to minute barrel swivels. This novel product gives a measure of controlled elasticity, so useful when fishing small lines and fine points. The nymph fisherman will find the new material a boon when trout make that sudden, slashing take which tests the cast and often ends in a break.

rently engaged in developing their own programmes of modification and innovation. This process will probably have to go on for many more years before a really sound, fully comprehensive evaluation can be made. In the meantime, the fact that most of the new style of fishing puts a big premium on good casting and the really purposeful selection of equipment must be beneficial generally to the development of technique.

It is possible to make one rod serve for all stillwater fishing styles, but the angler who takes the trouble to learn to cast well can get so much extra pleasure and improvement in performance from rods designed for specific purposes that it is unlikely that he will settle for fewer than 2 rods, while 3 or even 4 (including 1 or 2 chosen primarily for river fishing), would not be thought too many by the enthusiast.

For fishing drifts from boats and for bank fishing in which you will wish to make fairly long casts as well as quite short casts with delicacy, the rod must have enough through action for it to be developed satisfactorily when a moderate length of medium-sized line, say an AFTM DT6F, is aerialized. This facilitates roll casting and the smooth, accurate and delicate use of a short length of line, which is regularly necessary, particularly in the evenings. It also involves some limitation in the potential regarding the distance that it will cast, but a well designed modern rod of this kind will handle around 20 yds of line very nicely and this is about as long as is normally desirable in the traditional styles of fishing. Good length, up to about 10 ft 6 ins, in this class of rod has decided advantages over shorter ones. It makes roll casting more effective, and is very helpful when it is wished to keep the bob fly fishing on the surface. Also when casting overhead, it gives better ground clearance behind. When it comes to the playing of the fish, the behaviour of the longer rod with through action makes it more pleasant and is a good safety measure if fairly fine tackle is used, since much of the strain is absorbed by the rod.

Probably the most popular line size for the traditional methods is an AFTM DT7F. Sometimes in rather calm conditions a little lighter line, a 6 or possibly a 5, may be better, but as a compromise between ease in use and acceptability as far as the fish are concerned, the No 7 is very suitable. The 3¼ ins reel favoured for the rivers can be used, but if the primary purpose is the stillwater fishing, a slightly larger size has advantages, particularly in retrieving line more quickly. The 3½ ins size, or 3¾ ins if the rod is 10 ft 6 ins, are very suitable, but they should be as light as possible.

Leaders any heavier than really necessary should be avoided, but they must be strong enough to stand up to the rather rough treatment that is unavoidable Hooking a fish on a size 12 fly and a No 7 line at say 18 yds range puts much more strain on the leader than is likely to be the case in most river trouting. Therefore 4 lb test nylon at the point is the finest that should be used in the most trying of conditions when a nymph or dry fly is being used and usually 5 lb test will be found suitable for those purposes. The wet-fly leader with droppers should be 5 lb at the most delicate, 6 lb for general use in unobstructed water, and 7 lb minimum where there is the weed hazard. After fishing for river trout and getting the feeling that finer and finer nylon is needed, the stillwater leaders tend to look very clumsy indeed, but for reasons which would appear to be fairly obvious the fish in big lakes and lochs do not seem to be so shy in this respect. Providing that there is a reasonable balance so that the nylon is not too stiff for the size of fly being used, the strengths quoted can usually be relied upon.

As very long casting, 30 yds and more, or the use of a fast-sinking line at a big depth may be required in the new methods, the rod must naturally be considerably more powerful than those mentioned so far. It follows, too, that the lines must be heavier and the leaders stronger. Both for distance and reaching big depths with sinking lines, the shooting-head line with monofilament backing is popular because when the maximum performance is required, it can be achieved with the least effort. At the same time many anglers dislike bringing monofilament backing into play when casting and they prefer either the forward taper (or weight forward) lines of various designs, or even the double taper line. However, for this long range casting the rod must have quite a fast action and that being so, about 9 ft 6 ins is the longest that most anglers can use for long periods without too much fatigue. It is not only a question of the weight of the rod. Good modern rods are so light that while it is nevertheless desirable to keep the weight down as much as possible, it is the greater amount of leverage that comes into play with the longer rod that is the limiting factor. Between 9 ft and 9 ft 6 ins is certainly the most popular length. The fact that the fast action rod of this type will cast a double-taper line long distances does not mean that it can be made to serve as a completely satisfactory all-purpose rod, as it is too powerful for use with light lines and/or fine leaders. Therefore, as mentioned earlier, at least two rods are required if one is to be equipped to cope pleasurably with both the traditional and the new methods.

SEA-TROUT FISHING SPECIALITIES

The timing of the runs of sea trout into rivers varies considerably according either to the general area or the class of river in question. It is not uncommon for the larger fish to make their appearance in the early spring, but the smaller ones – fish of less than 2 lbs which are variously called herling, finnock, peal or sprods – rarely begin to run before July. And basically

Playing a sea trout on the River Spey at Castle Grant.

The "Figure of Eight" knot used to attach the fly cast.

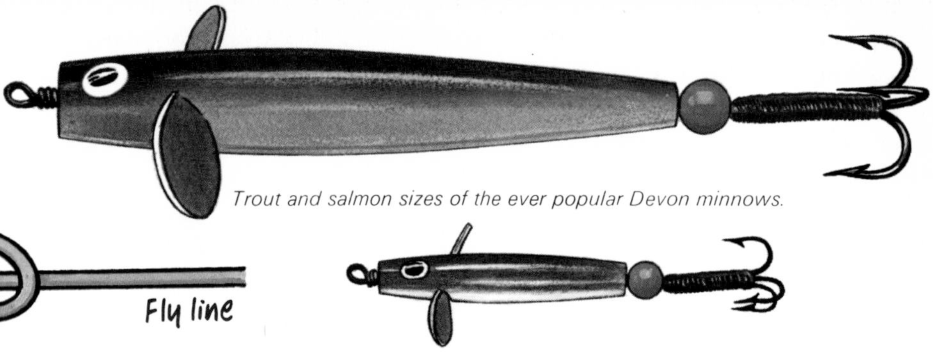

Trout and salmon sizes of the ever popular Devon minnows.

the sea trout is a fish of the long summer months.

If necessary, sea trout have the capability of entering the rivers and moving upstream to deep, suitably sheltered lies when the water is quite low. But the big runs usually occur when the river is falling after a good spate. Then very fine sport can be enjoyed with the floating or sink-tip lines and fairly large, gaudy sea-trout patterns. In recent years tube-flies about 1 inch in length have become popular, but if ordinary hooks are used, size 8s and 6s are favoured. Worm fishing and spinning will also catch fish in these circumstances, but when conditions are right for sea trout to be in a really responsive mood in a coloured water, it is the fly that produces the really hectic sport.

On those occasions when the sea trout are to be caught during the daytime in clear water on brown-trout patterns, the flies should be allowed to drift with the current in the same way as for brown trout and grayling. But with the large artificials in a big coloured water the effective method is to cast at a fairly big angle downstream, 45° or more, and then fish the flies across the current quite slowly, mending the line when necessary in order to do this. This amounts to giving the fish a longer time to see the flies and an easier opportunity to intercept. Coloured waters sometimes tempt novices to try to fish as deeply as possible with the idea that they will be getting the lure closer to the fish. But when moving upstream they remain very close to the surface and if they take a rest it is nearly certain to be in quite a shallow place. And since it is required that the fly should be at a higher level than the fish, so that it will be the most easily seen against the brightest background in the generally dull surroundings, it is the most effective to have the fly no deeper than a few inches.

Some difficulty is often experienced in hooking sea trout and when they are fresh-run their mouths are inclined to be so soft that many are lost in the fight. Care must be taken to ensure that the first indication of an offer is not simply a vicious tug which, to the surprise of the novice, usually results in nothing more than a pricked fish at the best. If the rod is held high so that the line hangs in a big arc down to the water, the angler can expect either to see the line beginning to tighten or feel some smooth tension building up against the rod. Then he has the necessary warning to apply pressure to hook the fish before it has felt enough resistance to cause it to eject the fly.

The sea trout is most famed, of course, for the splendid night fishing it can provide. But for this the river requires to be clear and low rather than high. When there is a good flow, even though the water is clear, the fish tend to move upstream during the hours of darkness. And although this may not prevent sport altogether, the prospects are not nearly so good as when the fish remain settled in the pools.

Many of the really dedicated night-fishers believe that the water must be left completely undisturbed until darkness has fallen and they refrain entirely from fishing during the most promising period of all at dusk when the sea trout nearly always show an active interest, particularly in any flies there may be on the surface. They claim that hooking and playing fish at this time can put the shoal in the vicinity down for the rest of the night! The opposing argument is that, in any case, there is never any guarantee that the fish will continue to feed after darkness has fallen and therefore it is foolish not to take advantage of the remarkably consistent opportunity of good sport there is during the short period while the light is fading. In support, they quote occasions when they did, in fact, start catching fish at the commencement of dusk and continued to have good sport well into the night.

Fishing with the floater at dusk has already been mentioned under the general heading of dry-fly fishing. Small sea-trout patterns, say size 12s, fished wet can also be successful, but with the current now steadier, it often pays to fish the flies considerably faster than in the coloured water. This can be done either by casting fairly square and letting the flies swing round as quickly as the stream will take them unaided, or, if the flow is rather too slack, by retrieving line with the free hand.

Fast, shallowing glides at the tails of pools are greatly favoured by the sea trout from dusk onwards. Here, of course, owing to the extremely smooth surface, you must be extremely cautious in every way to avoid upsetting the fish, but this is by no means as difficult as some would have us believe and really wonderful sport can often be had before night has fallen. However, when the sea trout do eventually come out of their sheltered daytime lies, when the sun is going down, and the natural flies come into more plentiful evidence, they may equally well be attracted by the more aerated water in the fast streams. There it is not nearly so difficult to fish hard without disturbing the sea trout too much.

The floating line and standard sea-trout patterns in sizes from say 12s down to 8s can be very effective at any hour of the night when the fish are moving. Some night fishers consider this to be the most interesting and pleasant method, beside being the easiest in practice. But others, especially those who are particularly keen on catching extremely large specimens, insist that sunk-line fishing is by far the best. Usually they prefer large flies, about size 6, or 2- and 3-hook lures up to about 2½ ins long. And they fish their artificials very slowly and down among the stones on the bottom. This is undoubtedly a very effective method of catching good sea trout, but quite a bit of practice is required before the angler can feel that he has mastered the inherent difficulties. The trouble is that everything has to be done purely by judgment, employing a kind of sixth sense. One has to judge the angle at which the line must be thrown so that it will, in fact, go down to the right level and then fish at the right speed. Some of the offers, even from big fish, are barely detectable (more of a suspicion than anything really concrete) but you must tighten firmly and smoothly to be on the safe side, although it may be nothing. Also, of course, there are a lot of false alarms caused by the fly knocking or grazing against a stone. Then comes the danger of assuming that the touch felt will be a stone and only realizing that it was, in fact, a fish, when it is too late. All the scraping about on the bottom also means that hooks quickly lose their sharpness and this problem must have constant attention. Nevertheless, as already stated, it is a very good method for big fish and it has one very special advantage over all other ways of fishing for sea trout with fly: if the fish are not in a willing, taking mood and will not rise from the bottom for a fly, there is nevertheless a good chance that the large artificial dangled in front of their noses will annoy them into taking.

Wake-fly fishing with a floater is another fascinating method for sea trout. Some anglers build their own artificials with cork bodies, but any densely-dressed pattern, such as a Zulu, on about a size 8 hook and well greased, will serve the purpose. A squarish cast is made and the fly is retrieved at about the same speed as the natural great red sedge travels on the surface of the water to the shore. On smooth glides the V-shaped wake that the fly makes is very obvious and to a lesser degree it even appears on popply water. It is thought that the wake helps to attract the attention of the fish to the fly and it is often effective in deep water which lacks sufficient flow for other methods to be very suitable. A common mode of attack is for the sea trout to circle round and head the fly off. Then the take is very rough and the rod must be held high to avoid the line being too tight, otherwise there is little chance that the fish will be hooked. A point should be made of always keeping the fly fishing properly right up to the edge because the final stage of the journey to the shore appears to be the most irresistible to the larger sea trout and should not be missed.

The late Paddy Avery with a fresh-run fish from the River Tweed, near Norham. Some of the Tweed's finest fish come at the back end of the salmon fishing year when the nets are off and a spate provides plenty of water.

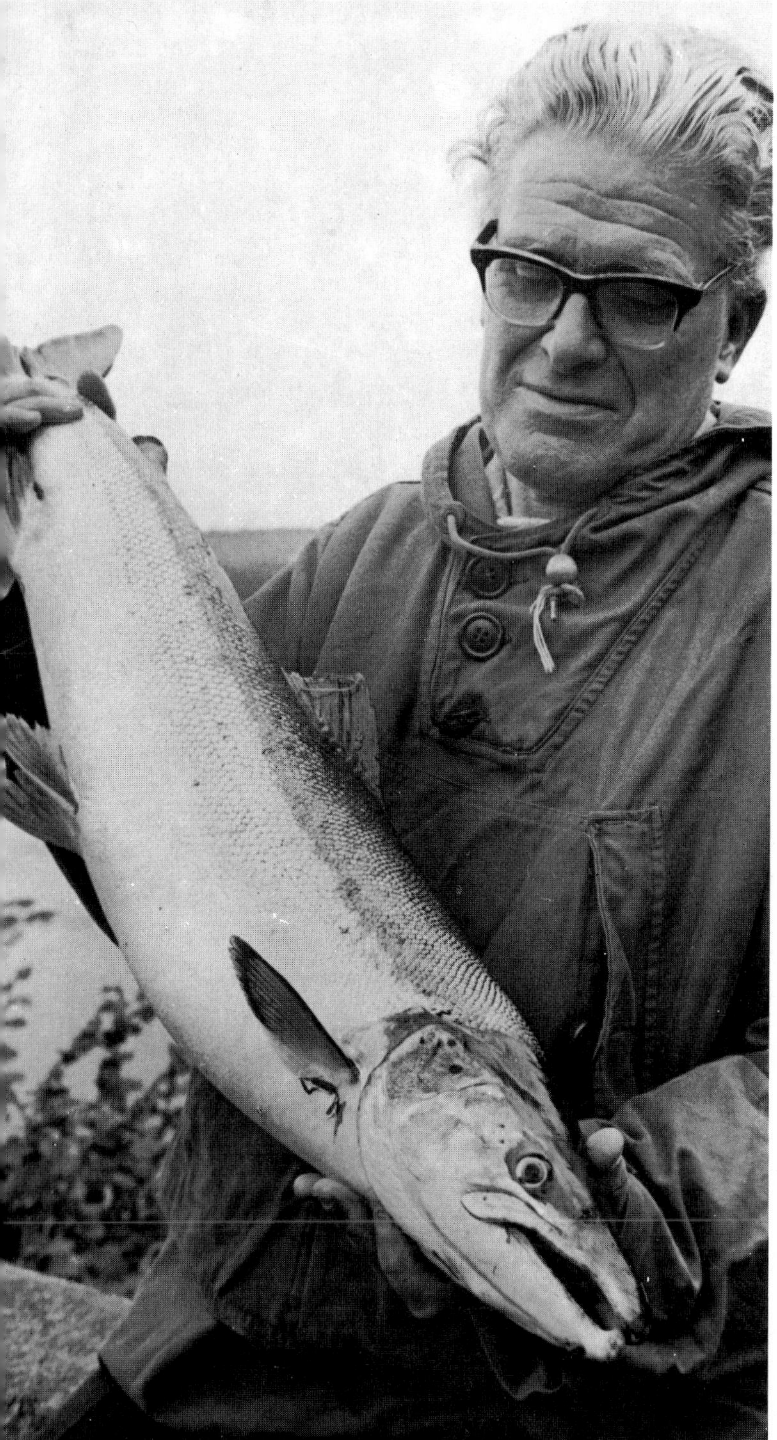

On some of the lochs, sea-trout fishing is very good indeed. All the traditional methods of fishing still-water are practised with success, but fishing drifts from boats is undoubtedly the most popular. Standard lake and sea trout patterns are used, the sizes being determined chiefly to suit the strength of the wind and the resulting amount of wave. The size 12s used in a gentle breeze may be replaced with as large as size 6s when the wind gets up. Dapping with a floss silk blow-line and densely dressed bumble-type flies is still very popular on certain lochs. The artificial is kept bobbing on the surface and the great thrill of this famous old method is to be able to watch the take by a big sea trout.

To be suitable for both the floating and the sunk line, the sea-trout rod requires to be quite powerful and for several reasons it is best to have it as long as really practicable for a single-handed rod, that is about 10 ft 6 ins. A short rod that has sufficient power to handle a sunk line well tends to be too pokerish to be pleasant to cast with and is not very suitable for use with the floating line when a certain amount of delicacy may be required. The good length is also helpful in the way of giving good ground clearance behind, which is most important in the dark; and for the more efficient handling of large fish. For such a rod an AFTM No 7 or 8 line will be required, and for the leader it is too risky to use anything less than about 10 lb test for the sunk line, but 7 lb test should be quite suitable for the floating line.

For other methods than sunk-line fishing, various of the rods mentioned for river trouting and stillwater fishing are very suitable. On the lochs, however, some sea-trout fishers prefer light double-handed rods. The modern versions of the 12-footers are extremely light and are considered by some anglers to be easier to use for long periods than any length of single-handed rod. The light double-handed rod is also very useful for sea trouting in estuaries and elsewhere, particularly when there are grilse about. With a little care, the individual should be able to choose a rod that will serve well for quite a few different purposes without sacrificing any of the very desirable features for its primary role.

Anglers wishing to spin for sea trout will find that the optimum speed at which to fish the lure is largely controlled by the amount of colour in the water. During the early stages of the subsidence of the spate before the water has cleared much, the spinner should move only very slowly and usually a small bar spoon can most easily be made to behave as wished. Even so, it is still necessary where the flow is fast to cast well downstream and be satisfied with a rather short traverse across the current. As the water clears and the pace of the flow slackens, small metal devons fished rather faster than spoons begin to be quite attractive to the fish. Then, just before the last of the colour finally goes, leaded quill minnows fished at quite a fast speed can be expected to do very well. In all sea-trout fishing it is difficult to judge in advance exactly the speed that will be best and some trial and error is often necessary. If fish are seen to follow but not touch the lure at all, it is usually an indication that greater speed is required. On the other hand, if they snap at the bait and fail to get hold properly, it may be because it is travelling too quickly.

The spinning rod requires to be light and supple enough to throw light baits, down to about ¼ oz. Eight foot is a good length and with a fixed-spool reel and 6 to 8 lb test line, the angler is also equipped for worm fishing if he so desires.

Worm can be a very useful bait for sea trout. When the water is high and coloured, a small drilled bullet is placed above the swivel at the top of the trace and, with this as the anchor, the worm is tried in a stationary position for a short spell in any very steady area which can be found that is preferably not very deep. As the water lowers, the bait can be trundled downstream on the stretches of smooth gravel, to good effect. When the river is back again to normal level, casting upstream into the likely lies and retrieving the worm sink-and-draw fashion may take a sea trout when all other methods are at a discount.

GRAYLING-FISHING SPECIALITIES

After about the middle of November, when the trout-fishing methods already described may not be very successful with the grayling, leaded flies in the famous old fancy patterns may provide some excellent sport.

The idea is to get the flies part way down towards the fish but not necessarily at their eye level. Hence in water around 4 ft deep, the aim would be to fish the flies at a depth of about 2 ft 6 ins. With the floating line, the cast is made quite square in order to give the flies the chance to sink to the right level by the time the line reaches an angle of about 45° downstream: then they will fish round as wished. There is certain to be quite a bit more drag than is wanted when attempting to simulate the emergent dun, but with fancy patterns such as the Red Tag, Grayling Witch, etc., this bit of added movement appears to increase the attraction. And this is an excellent, expeditious way in which to search longish stretches of suitable water in which a shoal of grayling may be lying.

When a shoal has been located, the best policy is to fish over the productive area with a space of a yard or so between each cast, and then, after a short rest, to start at the top again and repeat the process. The grayling are put off very soon if the water is fished down too slowly with wet or leaded flies, or, in other words, if they are allowed to see too much of the flies at any one time.

It may be thought that a sinking line would be more efficient for fishing at a greater depth than the surface area with the fancy flies, but this involves a serious disadvantage. Fish taking the artificials feel the resistance of the submerged line and eject the flies so quickly that the big bulk of the offers are missed. With the floating line there are the usual warnings of an offer that make it possible to hook the fish before it has felt the weight of the line.

Long-trotting with small red worms – gilt-tails or brandlings – is a popular and effective method for grayling, and is particularly useful for the times when conditions are not favourable for fly fishing. In cold weather when there is very little fly life about and the water is rather high, trotting is a very speedy and efficient means of locating a shoal. And having caught one grayling, it is often possible to have quite a spell of sport from the one spot.

A modern 12 ft match rod is ideal for trotting. Either a centre-pin or fixed-spool reel can be used and the line should be very fine, $1\frac{1}{2}$ or 2 lb test. If it can be obtained, braided Terylene may be preferred because it is easier to see. This helps when mending the line. Also it lifts off the water without delay when the strike is made to hook a fish. Nylon monofilament handles very nicely in many respects but it can be difficult to see and it does tend to suck onto the water. Bob floats of various designs are very suitable for the popply water that is often the most productive and, with stems treated with bright fluorescent paint, they can be seen well for the long distances necessary.

The depth below the float should be fixed so that the bait will be a few inches clear of the bottom. One or two medium shot are required at about 1 ft above the hook, which should be a 16 or 14, and the worm should be hooked near the head with the tiniest bit of skin so that it will wriggle well for a long time. Some anglers like to check the float almost continuously so that the bait does not trail behind. But others think it better not to check because then, with suitable mending of the line when necessary, it is much easier to prevent the float from being dragged to the side before it has travelled as far as wished. Those who do not check the float catch plenty of grayling, therefore it cannot be said that checking is essential.

SALMON FISHING

Salmon do not feed in freshwater. They may go so far as to swallow worms, but they do not digest them. The scientists assure us that they do not even absorb the juices out of the worms. Nevertheless they do respond to the lures of the angler – artificial flies and spinning baits; metal spoons; and natural baits both fresh and preserved, including sprats, prawns and worms.

The popular belief is that while salmon may sometimes take lures because of aggressive impulses, the bulk of the response is due to reflex action.

Although it is not uncommon for salmon to take natural flies such as March browns and mayflies, again no doubt due to reflex action, few anglers today think that artificial salmon flies owe their success to any imagined similarity to natural flies. Fly fishing is seen to be effective because it is a very suitable means of physically presenting acceptable lures to the fish in typical salmon rivers.

Not big grayling but a fine catch of late autumn fish from Yorkshire's River Ure by Reg Righyni. The fish average three quarters of a pound and can be had on a Red Tag or a float-fished gilt tail worm.

Many anglers say that they prefer to fish fly and, in particular, to play salmon on fly tackle, but the decision whether to fish fly or to spin should be based on the state of the water and the type of lure that is judged will behave the most suitably. No method purely in its own right can be claimed to be the best – each can do better than the others if circumstances are at all tilted in its favour. This, of course, assumes equal proficiency in all methods and it must be said that, as will be shown later, appearances in this respect are inclined to be very deceptive.

The runs of fish that form the stocks in the rivers in January, February and March (the so-called "spring salmon" or "springers") are of a very good average size in most areas, up to as much as 20 lbs. It is remarkable, however, that on the Tweed, reputedly the most productive of the early rivers, the average size is no more than about 8 lbs. In April many rivers get very good runs of salmon – in some cases the best of the season – ranging from about 8 to 12 lbs. Then May and June tend to be rather quiet as far as the appearance of newly-run fish is concerned, no doubt because this tends to be a dry period, but July usually makes up for it. Now on many rivers a good spate can bring large numbers of summer salmon and grilse, besides, of course, the sea trout. August tends to be another poor month in a normal season when the fish have not been held back at sea until then due to the lack of water in the rivers, and September may not be a lot better. October may see the beginning of the runs of true autumn fish – salmon fresh from the sea that will spawn during the approaching late autumn or winter. But November is the prime month for the autumn fish to come and probably the chance of the heaviest salmon of the season. And at the same time, some springers (fish that will not spawn until the autumn of the following year) may begin to appear. By December, when no salmon fishing is allowed anywhere in the British Isles, the spring fish may be arriving in large numbers.

SPINNING FOR SALMON

In the early part of the season, when the water temperature is low (below 42°F/6°C), the salmon are relatively very sluggish. They tend to remain in the very big pools with plenty of depth in the lower reaches of the rivers. The most successful lures are large and must be fished very slowly, close to the bottom.

Particularly when the river is carrying extra water and the current is rather heavy, spinning is by far the most efficient method of presenting suitable lures correctly.

Devon minnows, spoons and sprats up to about $3\frac{1}{2}$ ins in length are used together with leads at the top of the trace up to about 1 oz. In view of this, the heavy current, and the prospective size of the fish, the line requires to be about 20 lb test and, accordingly, the rod must have plenty of power. Fixed-spool reels can be used, but with the relatively thick line, the distance that can be cast tends to be more limited than with the multiplier. And

SALMON

Salmo salar

The Atlantic salmon has a most interesting life cycle, from the moment it is spawned on the redds to the time it incautiously grabs at the angler's fly the species is constantly under attack from the world's major predator . . . man! As a parr, or juvenile fish, it is so easily taken by the tiny flies of the trout fishermen wading the hill becks. Having fed well it changes its coloration, becoming a bright silver and called a smolt, to begin the long journey to the sea. There it grows fast on the rich feeding, among the shrimps and krill and then on to small fish of the herring and other shoal types. With rapid growth comes sexual maturity and the desire to return to freshwater to spawn. Nearly always the salmon will return to the river of its birth, there are many theories as to how the fish finds its way back to that river but nobody really knows which mechanism operates in the brain of the fish to enable it to return. Arriving in the estuarine water it has to undergo a metabolic change that will allow the salmon to live in the water of the river. On the oceanic feeding grounds the species had been constantly harried by the activities of the deepwater trawlers but as it nears the land so the activity becomes greater. Offshore boats and then estuary nets lie in wait for the fish. As the salmon begins its ascent of the river it will still have to pass the river netsman and then comes the rod and line angler and more than the odd poacher. Small wonder that the species has been severely reduced in numbers or that man has artificially to spawn the salmon in an attempt to increase the viability of stocks. Spawning takes place in the middle of winter and though the fish may have returned to the river in any month of the spawning year it will not feed at all. Living on its accumulated fat the fish will change its colouring, adopting a nuptial dress before gathering on the gravels to produce the eggs and milt. Spawning is a rigorous time and the fish lose condition rapidly. At this time they are referred to as kelts, not many of which ever succeed in returning to the sea to recover their strength and body weight.

Bait: *Artificial flies, metal spinning lures, plugs, worms, prawns and a trailed fish will all take salmon.*

in view of the probable use of the multiplier particularly, the rod requires to have sufficient through-action for smooth casting.

The cast is made at, say, 50° to 60° downstream. The line is checked when the bait hits the water, but is then allowed to run again long enough to let the bait sink towards the bottom unrestrained. (If the check is not made when the bait hits the water, an over-run or an unwanted big belly of line in the air is almost unavoidable.) When the bait has been felt to touch the bottom the line is again checked, and with the rod point held high so that a minimum of line is submerged thus avoiding unnecessary side-pull, the bait is allowed to drift round without any winding of the reel. If the correct judgment has been made of the total amount of weight required in the bait and lead and also of the angle of the cast, the prospective lies of the fish will be searched very effectively in this way.

The layman and possibly the novice may think that spinning is the easy method of fishing for salmon, but even anglers with a lot of experience will acknowledge that they have to pay careful attention at all times to ensure that their assessment of the way the pool should be fished is reasonably correct. However, rather than detracting from it, this makes spinning most interesting and it is not the monotonous mechanical grinding away that the over-prejudiced opponents declare it to be. On the contrary, it is very gratifying when one can fish down a big pool on a powerful river and feel happily confident that it is being done well.

The array of baits and items of tackle on offer to the salmon spinner can be quite overwhelming, but the true needs are not very complicated. In Devons, Yellow Bellies are wanted for dull conditions, and Black or Brown and Golds when it is bright and the water clear. Sizes from $2\frac{1}{2}$ ins to $3\frac{1}{2}$ ins are popular, but $2\frac{3}{4}$ ins will nearly always be found to be satisfactory. Wobbling spoons are very successful indeed on occasions, although they can undoubtedly put the fish down in clear water conditions. Their great asset is that their particular action makes them cross the current relatively very slowly, which is extremely helpful when the flow is on the strong side for Devons. Three and a half inches wobbling spoons weighing $\frac{5}{8}$ oz and 1 oz are the most useful sizes, while Black and Gold and All

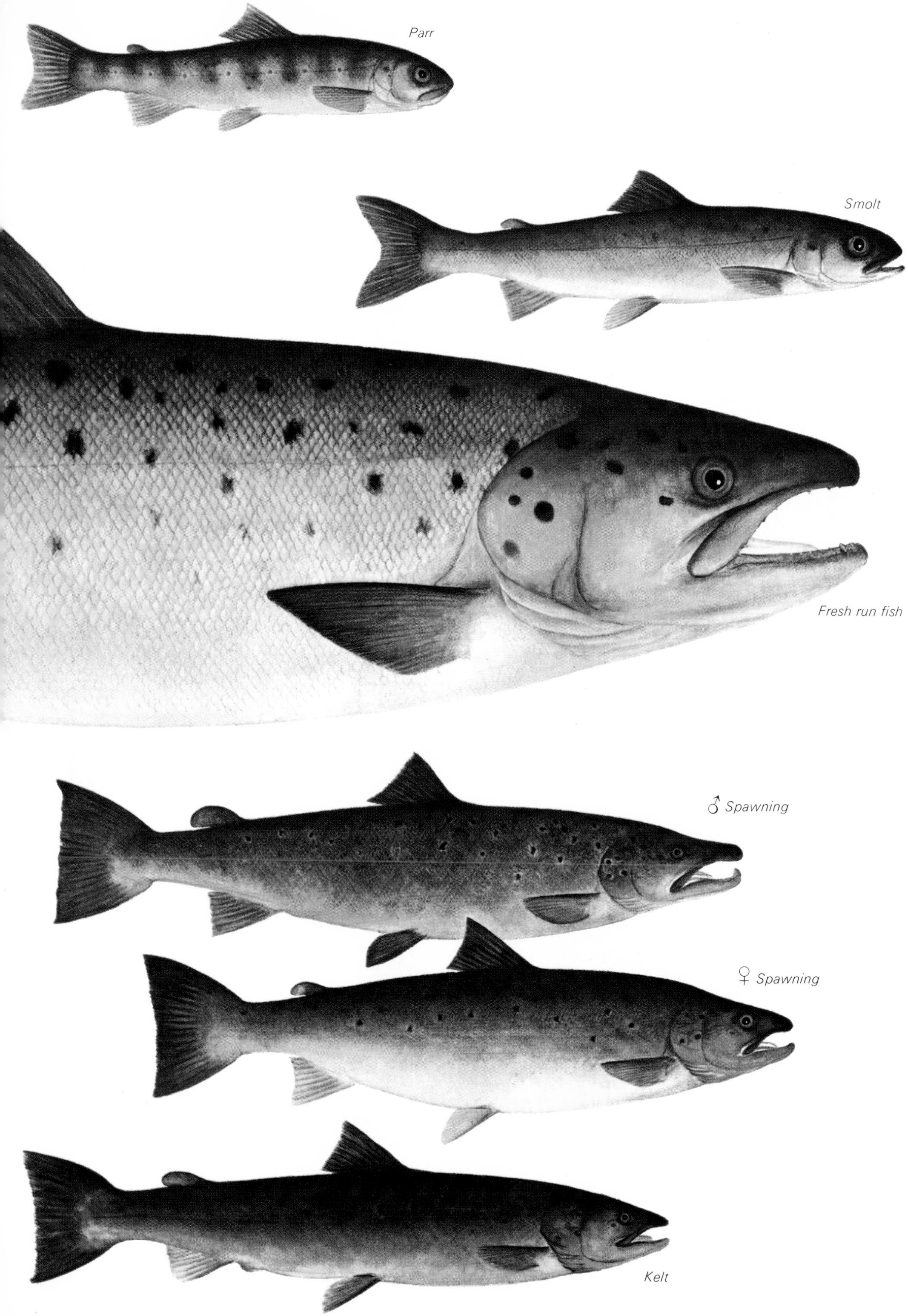
Parr
Smolt
Fresh run fish
♂ Spawning
♀ Spawning
Kelt

Silver are perhaps the most popular of the colours.

In swivels the ball-bearing type are the most favoured. Leads that can be attached to the top ring of the swivel are the most convenient because small variations in the total weight can be made by adding or removing little individual leads. The leader should not be too short because that means that the lead would be too close to the bait to allow it to fish at its best, free from jerkiness, but too much length causes a lot of difficulty in casting. About 1 yd is the most suitable length.

A little later in the season when the water temperature is ranging above 42°F/6°C, salmon that are in the responsive mood are much more alert than at low temperatures. They take interested notice of lures at greater distances and are prepared to rise some way or move sideways for a few yards in order to intercept. Now slightly smaller baits (2 ins to 2½ ins) make sufficient impact and should be fished farther from the bottom and a little faster. After the water has become a little warmer again – say in the mid-50s – it may be better to cast upstream and reel in moderately fast so that the bait does a big U-turn in front of the lie of the fish. This tactic reduces the length of time during which the salmon can see the bait while it is approaching taking range, thus increasing the degree of surprise and the chance of inducing reflex action.

Lighter lines are necessary for smaller baits if they are to be thrown adequate distances. About 8 lb test gives both sufficient range and confidence to deal with heavy fish. Most anglers find the fixed-spool reel to be the most versatile with the light tackle, and to make the most of it, a lighter rod suitable for single-handed casting is helpful.

SUNK-LINE FISHING FOR SALMON

When the "fly only" rule applies on early rivers and the water is at a high level, the only chance of getting the fly down to the right depth and fishing it suitably slowly is to have it weighted and also to put a spiral or anti-kink lead at the end of the fly line, in which case the leader should not be longer than about 4 ft. Suitable flies (a tube or a treble with an articulate body, of about 3 ins in length) are difficult enough to cast without the addition of a lead, but with the extra weight it becomes too ungainly and too dangerous unless an extremely powerful rod is used. Then it is classed as super-heavy sunk-line fishing.

The outfit comprises a rod of about 15 ft that is powerful enough to keep the heavy fly and lead aerialized at a safe distance above the head when casting; a fast-sinking double or forward taper or shooting-head line in AFTM size 12 with 100 yds of backing: and 20 lb test nylon for leaders. Most anglers think that the best and only pattern really required is the yellow bucktail with strips of brown and perhaps orange.

With this equipment the policy should be to try to

1

1 *The River Nith, a salmon river of the Scottish Borders that enjoys a run of late autumn fish. Because of the overhanging trees many parts of the river are best wormed through the many deep pools that hold fish.*

2 *Both a salmon and trout river, the Clydagh in the West of Ireland can provide excellent sport in the spring and autumn.*

get the fly to behave in exactly the same way as the large spinner in the same conditions. Immediately after the cast has been made, a large upstream mend should be put in the line to assist it to sink without being dragged across the current too much. But after this has been done, no further helpful action can be taken, except perhaps the feeding of some slack line in very deep water, and the fly must then fish across the lies as it will, correctly or incorrectly. However, the method does catch a lot of fish. It will be found that some spots are much more favourable for it than others and it pays not to waste too much time in places that pose more than the normal amount of difficulty.

If a boat and gillie are available, the same outfit can be used for harling. Although tough on the oarsman, this is much easier for the angler. A suitable amount of line, say 15 to 20 yds, is extended below the boat. The gillie rows as squarely as possible and slowly across the current so that the fly covers the lie suitably. This is a very popular and successful method on the lower and middle reaches of the large rivers.

With the river at normal level and the pools not excessively deep, conventional sunk-line fishing can be very effective and is much more enjoyable for the angler. Rods from 12 to 15 ft are suitable, 14 ft probably being the most popular length. An AFTM No 9 or 10 line is required and this should be a double taper so that Spey casting can be done when necessary. Unweighted or slightly weighted flies of the yellow bucktail type and similar are fairly standard. The leader may be a little finer, say 14 to 16 lb test.

Once again the policy should be to fish the fly slowly and near to the bottom, but after the temperature of the water has risen above 42°F/6°C, it is necessary, as with spinners, to reduce the size of the fly a little and fish it both a little faster and slightly higher in the water. According to the height and colour of the water and the state of the light, a variety of other fly patterns may now be used to advantage, such as Thunder and Lightning, Logie, Jock Scott, Dunkeld, etc. and sizes down to 1 in. in length may be required.

The need to be able to fish at different depths with the conventional sunk-line outfit makes the type of line used quite a critical subject. Many anglers have a very strong preference for the oil-dressed silk line because it does not cut down through the water as quickly and positively as the synthetic sinkers. If one of the latter is used, however, it should be the slow sinking variety for general purposes. For particularly heavy currents, of course, the fast sinker is best.

THE FLOATING LINE FOR SALMON

In spring when the water begins to warm up, much smaller flies fished just beneath the surface become the most attractive to the salmon. The crucial temperature is said to be 48°F/9°C. Once this reading has been established as the minimum for several days the major-

ity of anglers turn to the floating line, not only as the prospectively best method, but because they consider it to be the most interesting, pleasant and easy way to fish for salmon. Furthermore, the sub-surface fly is recognized to be effective on a wider range of rivers for a longer part of the season than any other method.

The basic equipment is a rod of 12–15 ft carrying an AFTM No 8 to 10 line. With the very light modern rods, the same one that was used for conventional sunk-line fishing should be quite suitable for the floating line. The double taper line is the most generally useful because it is essential for the Spey casting which is so often required. In the warm weather in summer when the river is low and the fish more easily put down, a very fine leader, say 7 lb, and the finest line possible are helpful: a single-handed rod may be most suitable.

The range of suitable flies is large, including many famous patterns, but a small selection that covers all the variations in tone from dense to very light will cover all requirements. On very bright days black-looking flies such as the Stoat's Tail and Blue Charm are generally the most useful, but when the angle of the sun is not very high, a very bright fly such as the Silver Blue may be best. On dull days, or when there is a little colour in the water, the Logie and similar medium toned dressings are the most popular. With more colour in the water or the combination of a little colour and very poor light, the Thunder and Lightning with both black and bright colours is the favourite on most rivers.

As for sizes, it is generally thought that the water temperature is often the most reliable guide and many anglers believe in a scale that is after the style of the following:—

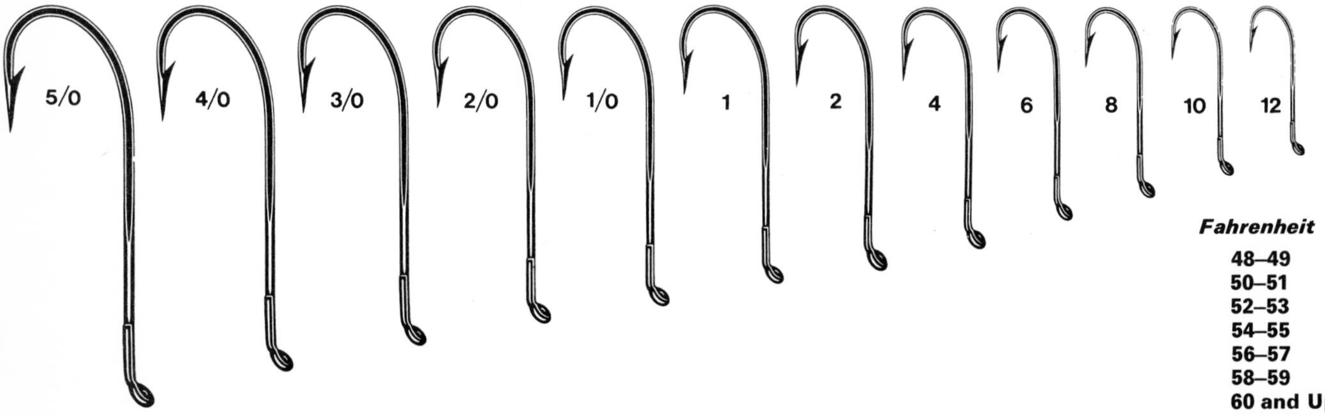

Fahrenheit	Low water Hook Size
48–49	4
50–51	5
52–53	6
54–55	7
56–57	8
58–59	9
60 and Up	10

The leader should be about 12 ft and the strength should match the size of the fly. About 11 lb test is suitable for sizes 4 and 5: 9 lb for sizes 6 and 7: and 7 lb for sizes 8 and smaller.

At the lower end of the temperature bracket for the floating line, the usual policy is to fish across the flow rather slowly so that the fish gets plenty of time in which to spot the fly and then rise to intercept it. This probably requires the cast to be made at an angle of about 60° downstream. If a noticeable belly forms in the line, it will probably cause the fly to be drawn across the flow more quickly than wished, and it should therefore be corrected by means of an upstream mend. As the water gets warmer, the cast should be made progressively squarer so that the fly will travel more with the flow as it also swings round, thus reducing the length of time available for the reflex action to become effective. If the salmon can lie watching the fly for a long time as it approaches, it may in these circumstances be bored with it before it reaches taking range. In hot weather a tiny fly (Low Water No 10 and smaller) travelling almost at the speed of the flow and practically in the skin of the water is often the only means of getting response from the small summer salmon and grilse.

HOOKING SALMON ON FLY

Early in the season the fish are very slow to get their mouths properly closed on the large flies. It is essential to try to give them enough time to do this and also for the leader to drift downstream of the fish so that, when the line tightens, the hook will be drawn towards the corner of the mouth, and not to the front. The easiest way of ensuring that all this will occur as wished is to hold the rod high – at an angle of 45° minimum – so that the line drops to the water in a big arc. Then, when the offer comes, either the line will be seen to be straightening or a gentle build up of tension will be felt. That is the signal to lower the rod, thus producing some slack line, and also, if wished, to allow a coil of line to go free from the left hand. Then there should be no danger of the salmon feeling so much resistance from the tackle that it will eject the fly before there is an opportunity to get a secure hook-hold.

As the water temperature rises and the fish become more alert, the delay required before attempting to secure the hook-hold tends to become less. By the early summer it may simply be a matter of holding the rod still as the curve of the line down to the water straightens and then allowing the fish to hook itself. When the small salmon and grilse are taking tiny flies cast almost

With a high water temperature and low water height, autumn fish will often rise in the stream to a comparatively small, lightly dressed, fly fished on a floating line and single-handed lake rod.

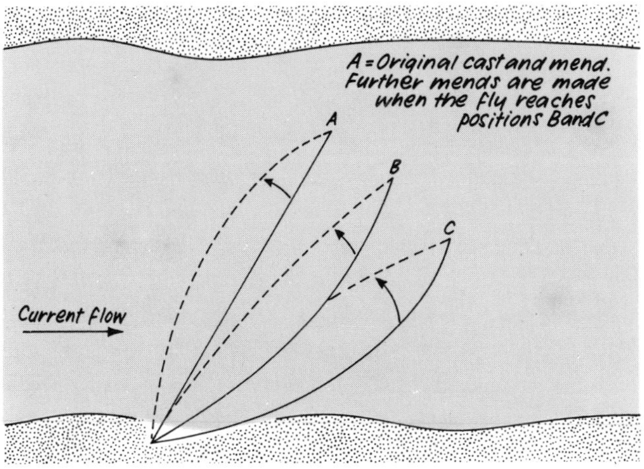
A = Original cast and mend. Further mends are made when the fly reaches positions B and C
A
B
C
Current flow

Mending when fishing the floating line to salmon.

Playing an autumn fish on the Tweed. Hooked in a fast run under the far bank, the fish stayed deep before coming into the angler through the weed still growing in the river. It weighed 15 lbs fresh run.

square, however, it is necessary to tighten quite positively as soon as the rise is seen, otherwise the fly will probably be spat out.

FISHING NATURAL BAITS FOR SALMON

In the old days, the fly rod and line were used for worm fishing. A spiral lead was put at the end of the fly line and a large, single fly hook was used on a leader of about 6 ft. The tackle was lobbed out and the bait was allowed to trundle downstream on the gravel. In those days, of course, it was largely a matter of resorting to worm because the river was out of order for fly.

Today, with modern spinning tackle, worm fishing can be just about anything the angler cares to make of it, from a lazy legering type of fishing, to a highly skilled stalking method. Allowing the worm to proceed down the pool in short drifts by lifting the lead at intervals is probably the most commonly used method. But no matter how the worm is fished, there is inevitably a lot of time when it is not in a position to be seen by a salmon and there is no means of the angler knowing this. And for this reason alone, if not for several others, worm fishing cannot be compared with fly fishing and spinning as a satisfactory and efficient method of fishing in typical salmon rivers.

Prawn can be very effective bait, but also many anglers assert that on occasions it will scare fish right out of the pool. Consequently it is not allowed on many waters.

The normal method is to fish it on spinning tackle in much the same way as a spoon or artificial minnow. On some rivers, however, the pools lend themselves to the use of a type of float fishing. The fascination of watching a large float move away jerkily as a salmon plays with the prawn (or shrimp as some anglers prefer to call it) cannot be denied, but this method is not applicable to the fast-running popply water that most salmon anglers like best to fish.

BASIC KNOTS FOR THE FISHERMAN

Many knots are used in fishing but here are the basic ones which will preserve the breaking strain of both nylon and Terylene materials. These knots are simple and they have proved to be the most effective. All the ones shown here are tied in nylon, with one special knot for Terylene braided material – the Jammed Hangman's knot.

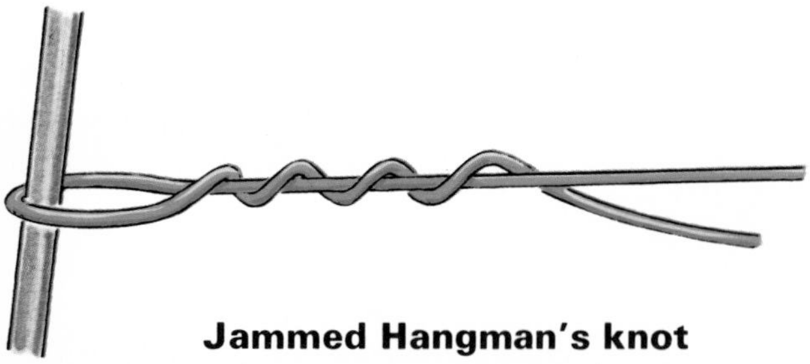

Jammed Hangman's knot

Used to form a loop in a braided Terylene or Dacron line making a leader.

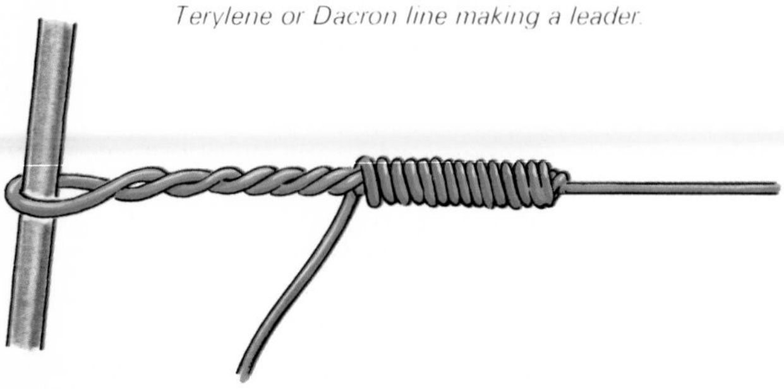

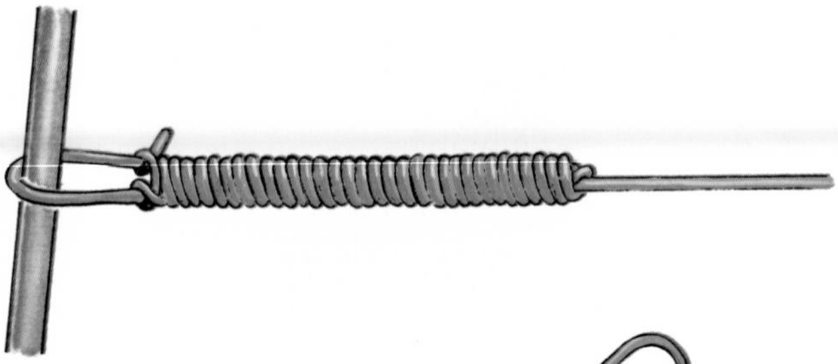

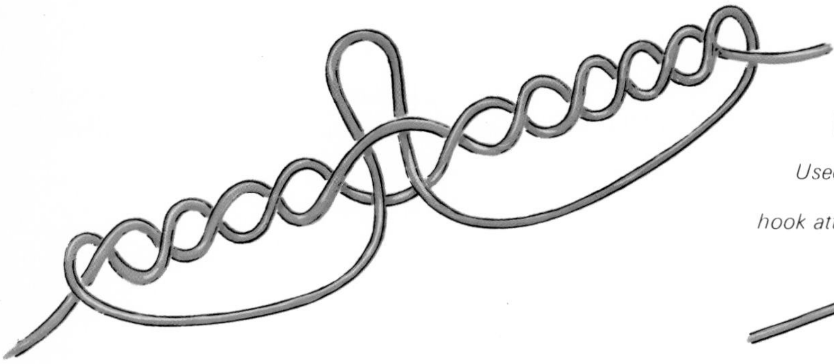

Blood loop

Used to form a snood or dropper for hook attachment.

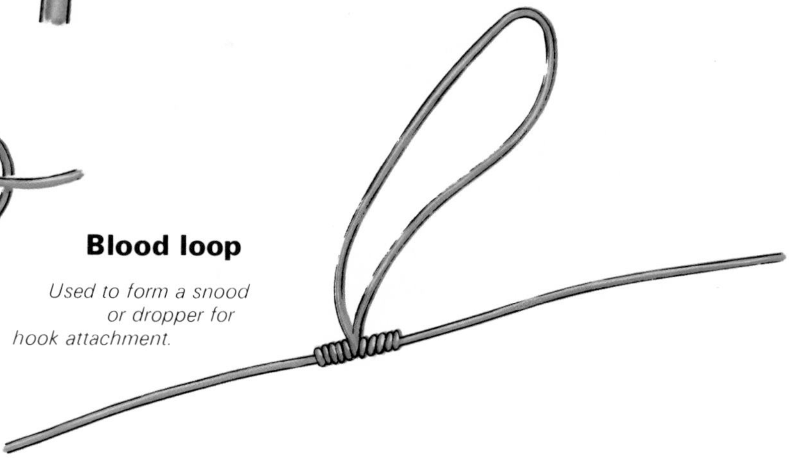

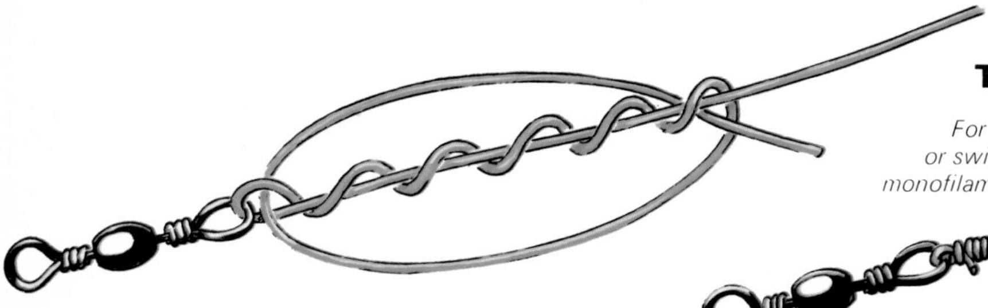

Tucked half-blood knot

For attaching booms, hooks or swivels to a monofilament nylon line.

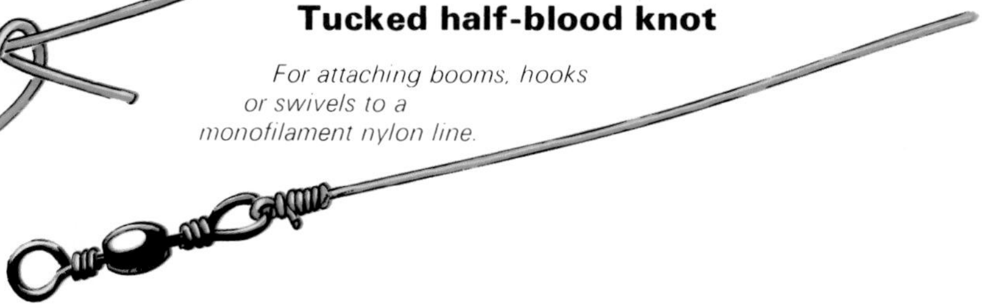

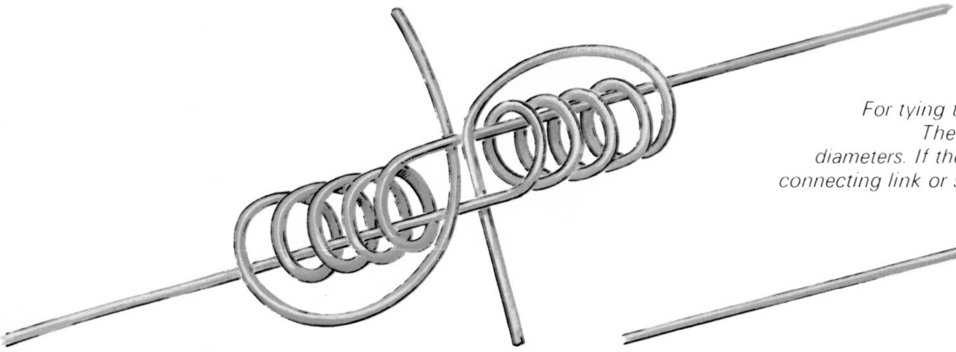

Blood knot

For tying two pieces of nylon line together. The lines must not have vastly different diameters. If they do, use a connecting link or swivel.

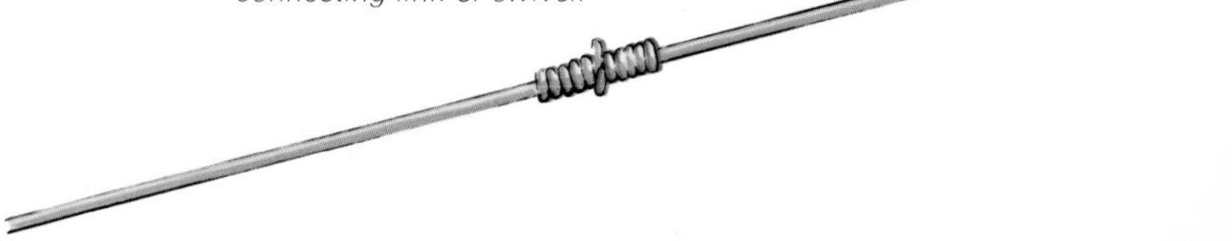

Grafham pin knot

Joins a fly line to a permanent nylon leader. Casts are then tied to the nylon leader which preserves the fly line taper.

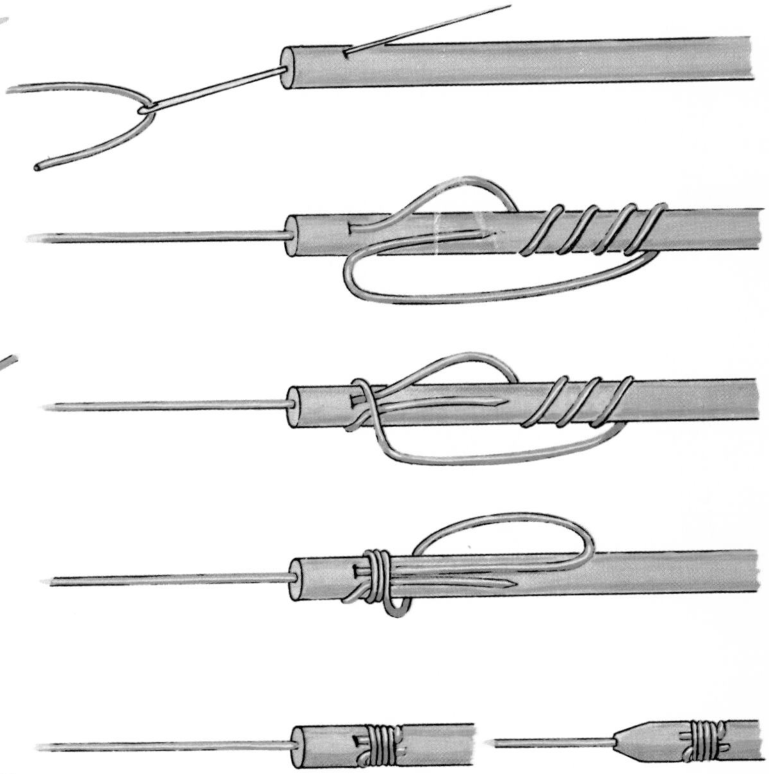

Single turl

A useful knot for attaching flies to the cast. The turl knot keeps the head of the fly in line with the nylon cast.

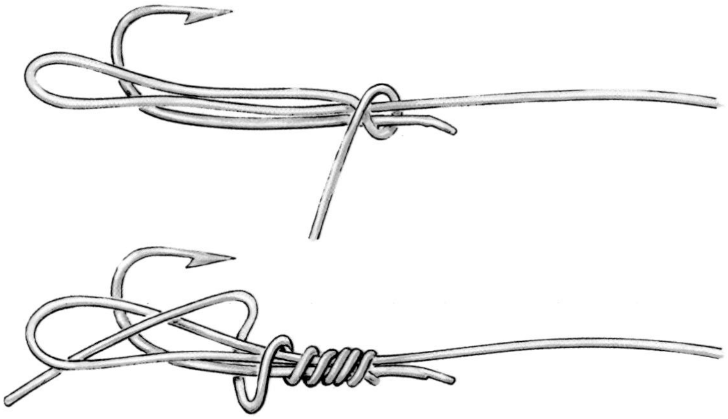

Spade end whipping knot

Used to attach a nylon link or dropper to a spade end hook which does not possess an eye.

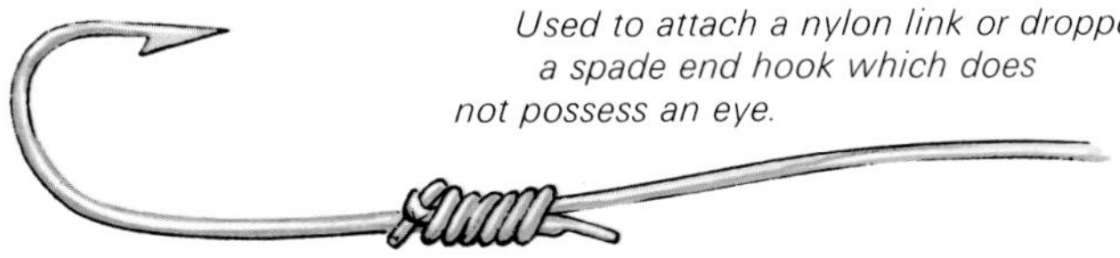

Overhand or Figure of Eight knot

Forms loop in a hook snood or dropper.

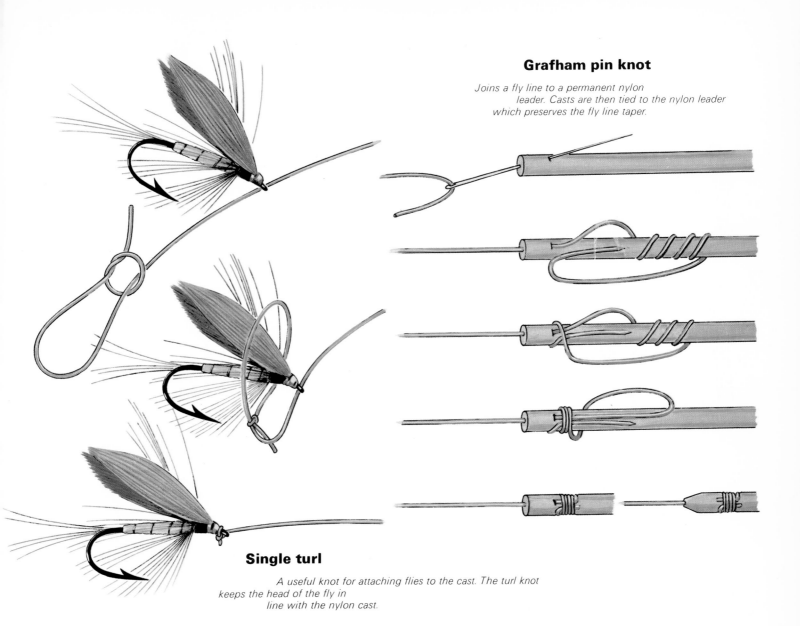

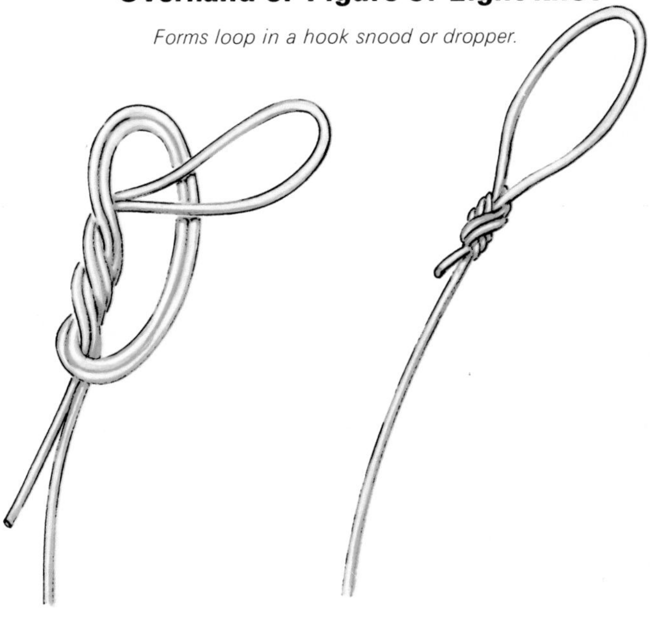

GLOSSARY OF FISHING TERMS

ADIPOSE FIN
A fleshy appendage between dorsal and caudal fin on members of the salmon family.

AFTM
Association of Fishing Tackle Manufacturers.

ALASTICUM
Single strand, stiffish wire used to form short traces. Withstands the cutting action of sharp teeth and resists rust.

ANNATO (MAGGOTS)
Artificial colouring mixed into feed that is eaten by the maggots, resulting in a golden-yellow stained grub said to be a more attractive bait.

ANTENNA
A float that has most of the body, supporting shot and bait below the surface of the water. The fine tip is relatively unaffected by strong breezes.

ANTI-INERTIA
A stiffening up of the bale arm release mechanism to prevent the bale closing in mid-cast.

ANTI-KINK
A lead used in spinning that adds weight and acts as a keel, preventing line twist.

BACKING
Braided or monofilament line attached to a fly line to extend the amount of line that a strong fish can pull from the reel.

BACK SHOT
Split shot placed between float and rod tip to sink the reel line in a wind.

BAG
A number of fish forming an angler's catch.

BALE-ARM
A hinged metal arm that picks up the reel line and wraps it around the drum of a fixed spool reel.

BARBULE
A fleshy appendage situated near to the mouth of a fish.

BEAT
A length of water and bankside allocated to one or more game fishermen for exclusive fishing use.

BELLY
A curve in a fly or other fishing line caused by a current moving the line downstream faster than the fly or bait, resulting in drag.

BITE
Indication from a fish, either visual or felt, that a bait has or is being taken into the mouth.

BLADDERWRACK *Fucus vesiculosus*:
A brown seaweed with wavy-edged fronds and a number of swollen air bladders along the central rib of each frond or branch.

BLANCHED MAGGOTS
Maggots dipped into heated water to stretch them for use as loose feed that cannot wriggle down into mud or silt.

BLANK
A hollow or solid glass tube from which a finished rod is made.

BLOODWORMS
The larvae of midges found in the mud and detritus of small ponds.

BLOW-LINE
A light fly line with which a natural or artificial fly is "dapped" upon the surface of a lake. The technique relies on a breeze to carry the line and fly out.

BOB FLY
In a team of flies, the fly nearest the rod tip or fly line. Intended to bob or dance on the water surface.

BOMB
An aerodynamically shaped casting lead.

BOOMS
Metal, plastic or nylon accessories used to make hook droppers stand away from the main reel line. Also a metal device intended to slide freely on a line.

BREAD FLAKE
Bread bait pinched out from the soft inside texture of a new loaf.

BREAD PUNCH
A cutting tube used to form small pellets of bread of equal shape and size.

BREAKING STRAIN or B.S.
The pounds test pull at which a line will break in a dry state.

BUNG
A thick-bodied, onion-like float.

BUTT INDICATORS
A form of bite indicator located near the butt section of a rod. Used in legering (see below).

BUZZER
The *Chironomid* flies, midges and gnats that hover close to the surface on all waters.

CARBON FIBRE
Introduced from the US and originally used in light spinning rods, carbon fibre is now used for all kinds of equipment including reel casings and rod blanks.

CASTER
The chrysalis stage of a maggot.

CASTING
The act of compressing a rod to throw out a bait or lure.

CENTRE-PIN REEL
A revolving drum reel with a fixed spindle with a 1 : 1 gear ratio. The handles are fixed to the side of the drum.

CHECK THE FLOAT
To halt the passage of a float downstream to ensure that the bait precedes the float.

CHUM
Small pieces of baitfish fed into the water to attract predatory species.

CLOUD BAIT
Fine groundbait intended to sink slowly down through the water, producing a clouding effect attractive to the feeding instincts of fish.

CLUTCH
A mechanical device allowing a reel to be put in or out of gear. Also a slipping system of washers which allows strong fish to pull off line from a reel before reaching the breaking strain of the line.

COCKTAIL
A mixture of several types of hookbait.

CONTROLLER
Form of float used to provide the weight to cast an ultra-light bait without resort to leads.

CRIMPED
A method of securing accessories to wire lines by squeezing metal ferrules around the wire.

CUDDY
A collapsible hood or shelter in the forward section of a small boat.

DT4F
Denotes a Double Tapered size 4 floating line. (About 120 grains weight for the first 30 feet of line).

DAN BUOY
A buoy, usually topped by a flag or marker, at the end of a long-line or drifting net.

DAPPING
The art of presenting a natural or artificial lure by skilfully placing the bait through obstacles, such as bankside trees, as though it had fallen naturally from the branches.

DEAD BAITING
Presentation of a bought or newly-killed fish as a bait to scavenging species.

DEVONS
Wooden or metal spinning lures that revolve around a wire mount carrying a treble hook. The Devon is fitted with plastic fins, twisted, to impart spin.

DINGHY
A small boat, made from wood or glass fibre.

DORSAL
Fin or fins placed on the top of a fish's body.

DOUGH BOBBIN
A simple method of bite indication made by fixing a piece of paste onto the line to register the pull of a biting fish.

DOUBLE TAPER
A line having a tapering section at either end of a swollen middle.

DRAG
An unnatural movement of a fishing lure caused by the line and lure travelling at different speeds or the slipping clutch found on most multiplying and fixed spool reels.

DRAINS
Man-made, canal-like, waterways draining huge areas of agricultural land, as in the Fens and East Anglia.

DRESSINGS
The combination of different materials – fur, feather, silk and other items – used to form an artificial fly

DROPPER
A hook link of nylon or wire attached to the main line

DRUM
A spool around which line is wrapped. Usually refers to a centre-pin reel.

DRY FLY
An artificial fly intended to float on the surface of the water.

DUN
The emergent fly after it leaves its nymphal case.

ECHO SOUNDER
An electronic device that transmits a signal to the seabed from where it rebounds and is picked up as a returned, but delayed, signal. The amount of time taken for the return journey by the signal indicates the depth below the keel.

ELASTICATED THREAD
Used by dressmakers to "gather" pleats etc. in material but perfect for tying on fishbait to a hook in such a way as to ensure good presentation.

FALSE CASTING
A method of casting the line backwards and forwards several times to remove water from the fly and line to ensure they continue to float.

FATHOM
Six feet. A nautical depth measurement.

FIXED SPOOL REEL
A reel on which the line is wrapped around a spool, set at right angles to the axis of the rod, by a rotating bale arm. The spool or bobbin does not turn to recover line, although it can turn to provide a slipping drag facility.

FLASHERS
Spoon blades or metal strips used to attract predatory species, normally used in conjunction with natural baits.

FLOATANTS
Grease or silicone aerosol sprays, applied to lines or flies to float them on the surface of the water.

FLOAT FISHING
Using a float of buoyant material to suspend bait and lead weights at a given depth. The float is also used to register a bite.

FLY
A rather loose term describing most lures presented on a fly line and rod. The lures may simulate flies, fish or invertebrate creatures.

FLY LINE
A line having weight to sink it, or buoyant material to enable it to float, coated onto the line.

FLY SPOON
A tiny metal lure that can be cast using fly fishing tackle.

FOLD OVER LEAD
A washer-like sliver of lead that is folded over a line to add weight and perform an anti-kink function.

FORWARD TAPER
A fly line that has a tapered section in only one direction – toward the fly.

FREELINE
A fishing method dispensing with any form of float or lead to carry bait to fish.

FRY
The very young fish of most species.

GAFF
A metal hook fixed to a shaft used to lift a fish from the water by impaling it upon the hook.

GEAR RATIO
The difference between one turn of a reel handle and the number of turns produced on the reel. (Usually defined as 1 : 3.5, indicating that one turn of the handle gives three and a half turns of the spool.)

GORGE FISHING
An illegal method of fishing that depends on giving a fish time to get the baited hook or hooks down into the stomach.

GOZZER
A maggot produced by the species *Calliphora eryphrocephala*, a favourite bait for home production. The fly blows in the dark, producing a large, white, succulent grub ideal for warm weather use.

GRAPNEL
An instrument used to anchor a boat over rocky ground. Made of mild steel, it resembles a treble hook without the barbs and is more likely to be retrieved than an anchor because a strong pull will straighten the prongs.

GRILSE
A small salmon thought to have spent only one year feeding at sea.

GRIP LEAD
A sea lead with either grip wires or cast protrusions that tend to hold into sand, mud and shingle in strong tidal conditions.

GROUND BAITING
Feeding a predetermined area with cereal or hookbait to attract and hold fish near to the angler's hook-bait.

HACKLE POINTS
Two stiff hackles from a cockerel cape used to represent wings.

HATCHES
A time when the nymphal form of water-living flies rise to the surface and emerge as fully-winged insects, often producing frantic feeding activity among the trout.

HOLT
The place in which a pike lies up after feeding. A resting place.

HOOK LENGTH
The length of nylon to which hooks are whipped. They are tied commercially to various lengths. The hook lengths are looped for quick attachment to the reel line.

ICEBERG
A pattern of artificial mayfly.

KEEP NET
A tube of netting, sealed at one end, used by coarse fishermen to contain their catch alive in the water.

KELP
A term used loosely to describe a number of strong, lengthy, thong-like brown seaweeds that have holdfasts (root systems) permanently covered by water.

KELT
A salmon in its weakened state after spawning. Many kelts die in their efforts to return to the sea. It is illegal to take fish in this condition.

KNOTLESS TAPERED LEADERS
A cast of nylon in which there is a continuous taper from butt to point, drawn in one piece.

LARVAE
A grub that has hatched from the egg and has mobility. Not yet in the chrysalis or pupa stage.

LASH or LASK
A thick slice of flesh cut from the side of a baitfish, usually from head to tail to resemble a fish and to exude strong smell.

LATERAL LINE
The canal of connected cells running down the side of fish that feel vibration, waterborne sounds and pressure changes.

LAYBACK
A method of casting from the shore devised by Leslie Moncrieff.

LAYING ON
A float fishing technique where the bait is fished hard on the bottom. An amount of the lead is also lying on the bottom with the float virtually tight-lined.

LEAD
Various forms of weight used to assist casting or to sink baits and floats.

LEADER
A piece of nylon line preceding the main line. It can be of lesser or greater breaking strain.

LEADER KNOT
A knot for joining a shorefisher's reel line to the shock leader that will pass easily through the rod rings.

LEGERING
Uses a lead to tether the bait firmly on the bottom.

LIE
A known resting place of fish. Something that anglers never tell!

LINE-BITE
A false indication of a true bite brought about by fish striking the line or cast with part of their bodies.

LINK
Metal accessory used to join two other tackle items or lines.

LINK SWIVEL
Useful swivel for quick attachment of traces and casts.

LOADED-FLOAT
A float carrying an in-built weight to assist casting or to overcome part of the float's buoyancy.

LOCK SHOT
Split shots placed either side of the float to fix its position relative to the depth of fishing.

LURE
Any artificial bait, spinner, plug, pirk or fly.

MAGGOT
Larval form of a fly (*Diptera*).

MAGGOT DROPPER
A case that is filled with maggots, dropped into the swim and then opened from above the surface to place bait accurately into position to lure fish.

MARK
An area or navigational position known to produce fish.

MENDING THE LINE
Throwing a loop of line upstream to avoid drag and sink a fly down in the water.

MULTIPLYING REEL
A drum reel that rotates for more turns of the spool than are applied at the handle.

NYMPH
A larva of the *Ephemeridae* family of flies or an angler's artificial representation.

OPERCULAR BONES
The several bones that form the gill case or cover that protect the gill filaments.

OVER-RUN
A bunch of intertwined nylon on the drum of a multiplying or centre-pin reel caused by inefficient casting or control of the line.

PARTY BOAT
A boat manned by professional boatmen taking angling parties to fish on a cost per head basis.

PASTE
Hookbait made by soaking bread, squeezing out the water and kneading into a stiff dough.

PATERNOSTER
A terminal tackle having the lead at the bottom and fished with a tight line to the rod. Booms are used to carry the hook links and baits.

PATTERN
A fixed design of material and position of parts that form an artificial fly.

PECTORALS
Paired fins behind the gillcase of a fish.

PEELER or SOFTIE
Stages in the growth of crabs. They shed their shell, when mature, in an annual moult. Anglers use them in the softie stage before the new shell has hardened and in the peeler form when the shell can be easily removed from the body.

PEG
A numbered position, drawn by a match angler on a stretch of competition water.

PELVICS
Paired fins placed low down on the fish's body, usually behind the pectoral fins and sometimes called ventrals.

PENNEL TACKLE
A two-hook rig with the hooks in tandem.

PICK UP
The bale arm of a fixed spool reel.

PINKIE
The grub of the greenbottle fly (*Diptera*)

PIRK
An artificial bait, madè in metal, having enough weight to act as both a sinker and fish lure.

PITCHES
Places from which anglers fish.

PLANKTON (ZOO and PHYTO)
Minute animal and vegetable life, free-floating and moving in both salt and freshwater.

PLUGS
Artificial lures intended to simulate the movements of fish and other creatures. Generally made of wood or plastic.

PLUMBING
Assessment of the depth of water by lowering a lead attached to the hook; the float is raised or lowered accordingly.

POINT
The finely tapered end section of a fly cast or the fly at the tip of the fly cast.

PRICKED
To pull lightly the point of the hook into a fish in such a way as to feel the fish momentarily but not to hook and land it.

PUT-AND-TAKE
A fishery where trout are placed into the water, having been reared elsewhere, for anglers to catch and remove for food.

QUILL MINNOWS
An "old-timer's" light bait for use in spinning in fast, streamy water for trout.

QUIVER TIPS
A bite indicator that trembles because of the springiness of the material from which it is made.

RATCHET
A checking device that prevents line running too freely off the reel and gives an audible warning of a pull on the bait.

RAY
A group of fishes, comprising skates and rays, that are flattened when seen from above and have the pectoral fins elongated into wings. These fish have a gristly structure without bones.

REDGILL
Probably the most attractive and efficient fish lure of its kind. Made in soft plastic to represent and simulate the movements of a swimming sandeel.

RIG
A number of items of tackle joined by a length of trace form a rig.

RIM CONTROL
An exposed rim on a fly reel allows an angler to control the running out of line to a hooked fish by applying light finger pressure on the reel rim.

RINGS
Circular guides, whipped or sleeved onto a rod blank, that spread the stress of playing a fish along the entire length of the rod and allow the free passage of line off the reel and out to the end tackle.

RISE
Surface indication of a fish.

ROACH POLE
A multi-sectioned pole or rod to which a float rig is fished on a fixed length of line.

ROD REST
A metal stand for holding a beach rod vertically to keep the line above the waves breaking inshore, also used to carry the weight of rods while anglers wait for a bite.

ROLL CAST
A method of fly casting in places where the angler is unable to back cast.

RUBBY DUBBY
A mixture of fish offal and oil that is mashed up and hung over the gunwhale in a bag. It spreads in a trail attracting predatory species, drawing them to the angler's hookbaits.

SAND BARS
Barriers of sand and silt swept down estuaries by the ebbing tide to be deposited where the current loses its power as it is met by the counter-force of the incoming tide. A hazard to deep-keeled boats but often a place to find fish.

SANDFAST
A lead, shaped like an upside down pyramid, that pulls into sand and soft ground, holding a bait securely.

SEA-WRACK
A general term for the brown and red seaweeds. Often applied to the weed thrown up onto the shore after a storm.

SEDGES
Waterside plants or flies belonging to the *Trichoptera* order.

SHOCK LEADER
Stronger nylon than the reel line, intended to absorb the shock of casting.

SHOT LOAD
The amount of lead weight that a float will carry before sinking under the surface.

SINKING LINE
A fly line with in-built weight that sinks below the surface.

SLIDER
A float used to fish a greater depth than the length of the rod. The float is stopped by a stop knot that can be any distance from the hook, yet will pass easily through the rod rings.

SMUTTING
Fish that are feeding on minute flies, midges and other small insects.

SNAP TACKLE
Two treble hooks joined by a wire trace on which a live or dead fish is mounted when fishing for pike.

SNOODS
Short pieces of nylon attached to hooks and looped to join to split links or link swivels making a rig.

SPECIMEN
A good fish in relationship to the average size known to be in the water.

SPIGOT
A modern method for joining two sections of hollow glass blank together.

SPINNERS
A general term for metal, artificial lures although the term should mean that they spin around the axis of the bait rather than wobble.

SPIRAL
A form of lead with grooves cut into the material in a spiral pattern around which the line is wrapped. The position of the lead along the trace can be easily adjusted.

SPLIT CANE
Material used to produce rods by glueing together a number of pieces to form a circular section with longitudinal flats. Strength and a sweet action are produced by the method.

SPOONS
Metal fishing lures that wobble or move erratically but do not spin.

SPRING TIPS
A form of quiver tip that relies on the tension of a spring to indicate the bite of a fish. Can be more sensitive than glass fibre tips.

SQUATT
The grub of the common housefly (*Diptera*).

STOP BEAD
A bead placed between a sliding float and stop knot or between a running boom and swivel to prevent jamming of the knots.

STOP KNOT
Used to stop or fix the depth of a sliding float.

STRAND
A term applied to an Irish beach.

STREAMER FLIES
Large artificial flies that generally represent fish.

STRET-PEGGING
Float fishing down a river in stages. The bait is settled and left to fish for a short time. If no bites come it is progressively moved down the river in a series of static fishing movements.

STRIKE
The sharp movement of the rod tip that sets the hook in a fish's jaw.

STRIPPING LINE
A term applied both to pulling off a fly line from the reel and to playing in a fish by pulling line back through the rod rings by hand rather than recovering line by reeling in.

S.W.G.
Standard wire gauge.

SWIM
An area, in a coarse fishing situation, known to hold fish.

SWIM BLADDER
An organ present in most bony fishes, filled with air, that assists in buoying the fish's body weight and enabling it to combat pressure change at varying depths.

SWIM-FEEDER
A container, attached to the terminal tackle, from which maggots or other forms of feed trickle in close proximity to the hookbait.

SWING TIPS
A swinging arm, through which the line runs, that is lifted by the pull of a biting fish. Like quivertips, it is screwed into the rod tip ring.

SWIVEL
A metal device for joining lines and preventing line twist that could be transmitted back along the line by a spinning lure.

TACKLE
A common term describing an angler's fishing gear or a definite fishing rig.

TAKES
Bites from fish but more often applied to game fishing.

TAKING SHORT
Any bite from a fish where the bait or lure is nipped at the extreme end of the lure but the fish does not take the hook.

TAPER
The amount of decrease in diameter of a rod from butt to tip.

TARES
A type of pea used to feed pigeons.

TEAM OF FLIES
Three wet flies fished on a cast.

TEASER
A bait presented to predatory fish in a lifelike fashion to make them strike at a hookbait.

TERMINAL TACKLE
The trace, rig or combination of parts that form the business end of the angler's gear. Make-up of items nearest the hook.

TEST CURVE
The amount of pull on a line that will put a curve into any rod so that the tip and butt section are at right angles. Often used as a way of expressing the line strength that a rod will accommodate.

TILLEY LAMP
Paraffin pressure lamp that gives off a strong light. Used by beach fishermen when night fishing.

TINSEL
Metal foil in a thin strand used to wind around the body of an artificial fly to give it flash or to break up shape.

TRACE
A length of nylon or wire used to form a particular rig or terminal tackle.

TRAIL
Hook length between leger weight and hookbait.

TREBLE HOOK
Three hooks joined together onto a common eye, mostly used on spinning lures, tube flies and pirks.

TROLLED
A lure or bait that is towed behind a boat.

TROTTED
Allowed to run downstream at the speed of the current.

TUBE FLIES
Salmon and trout flies where the dressing is applied to a tube made of plastic, aluminium or brass, depending on the weight of fly needed. The line or cast runs through the tube to a treble hook.

WARP
A cable-laid steel rope often used to anchor a large boat.

WATER-LICKING
A day or time when one does not catch fish, although every method has been tried.

WET FLY
An artificial fly intended to fish below the surface of the water. The hackles sweep backwards.

WINGS
The slip of joined fibres, taken from the wing of various birds to form the wings of an artificial fly or the pectoral fins of skates and rays.

WORM CASTS
The spiral of sand forced out of the beach by the passage of a worm through the medium and of the sand through the worm, for this is how it feeds.

WRIST
That section of a fish's body between the body bulge and the fanning-out of the tail.

ZOOMER
An antenna type float with an in-built weight to ensure long and accurate casting distances.

INDEX

Page numbers in *italics* refer to illustrations and captions

INDEX

Page numbers in *italics* refer to illustrations and captions